International Environmental Law and Policy
for the 21st Century

International Environmental Law

VOLUME 9

The titles published in this series are listed at brill.com/IEL

International Environmental Law and Policy for the 21st Century

2nd Revised Edition

By

Ved P. Nanda
George (Rock) Pring

Chapter Seven: Energy and the Environment
by Don C. Smith

MARTINUS
NIJHOFF
PUBLISHERS

LEIDEN • BOSTON
2013

Library of Congress Cataloging-in-Publication Data

Nanda, Ved P.
    International environmental law and policy for the 21st century / by Ved Nanda,
George (Rock) Pring ; with a new chapter on 'Energy and the environment : an international
perspective' by Don C. Smith.—2nd revised edition.
        p. cm. — (International environmental law ; volume 9)
    Includes bibliographical references and index.
    ISBN 978-90-04-24286-9 (hardback)
1. Environmental law, International. 2. Environmental policy. I. Pring, George W.
(George William), 1942– II. Title.

    K3585.N36 2013
    344.04'6—dc23

                                                                    2012031419

ISSN 1873-6599
ISBN 978-90-04-24286-9 (hardback)
ISBN 978-90-04-25023-9 (e-book)

Contents

PART TWO: LAWMAKING

PART THREE: THE KEY ISSUES

Acknowledgements

We owe a great debt to many of our colleagues and students at the University of Denver Sturm College of Law and elsewhere for their contributions to this extensively revised 2nd edition of our treatise on *International Environmental Law and Policy for the 21st Century*. This undertaking to capture the developments in the field over the past decade since our 2003 edition would not have been possible without them.

The law student research assistants, now almost all graduates and lawyers, who labored so long and well on this edition are (in alphabetical order) Nadav Aschner, Jonathan Bellish, Anne Bingert, Chris Conrad, Kristi Disney, Lara Griffith, Alexandra Haas, William Kent, Caitlin May, Teresa (Tessa) Mendez, Jonathan Murley, Julie Nichols, Megan Sheffer, Eric Subin, and Sandy Teixeira.

Deserving very special thanks are our Dean, Martin (Marty) Katz, Senior Associate Dean for Academic Affairs Federico (Fred) Cheever, and Associate Dean for Faculty Scholarship Alan Chen for so generously encouraging and supporting our scholarship. We are truly fortunate to have had the assistance of the dedicated and skilled professional staff of the Sturm College of Law, including Joan Policastri, Foreign, Comparative, and International Law Librarian for DU Law's Westminster Law Library; Diane Burkhardt, Faculty Research Liaison for the Library; Keri Grundstein, former Administrator of the International Legal Studies Program; and McKenzie Gaby, former Faculty Support Team Leader.

Over the years, our students in International Law and International Environmental Law have added immensely to our understanding of this relatively new frontier in the International Law field. We indeed are grateful to them for their interest and concern for the health and well-being of the planet and for the inspiration they have given us.

We are indebted to our colleagues Professor Don C. Smith, Lecturer and Director of DU Law's Environmental and Natural Resources Program and an expert in EU, Natural Resources, and Energy Law, for contributing Chapter 7 on "Energy and the Environment: An International Perspective," and Professor Robert Hardaway for his thoughtful suggestions on the population crisis, as covered by the authors in section 14.8. We owe a special debt of gratitude to Professor Lakshman Guruswamy at the University of Colorado School of Law for his advice and counsel to add these chapters as he graciously reviewed the prior edition of the book.

We are honored to have had the American Bar Association's Environmental Issues Working Group use Chapter 2 of our book to present the "fundamental substantive and procedural principles" of international environmental law in its adopted 2007 "Environmental Issues and the Rule of Law White Paper" (copy at http://apps.americanbar.org/intlaw/committees/division_chair/section/ Environmental_Issues_White_Paper.pdf). Our special regards to Howard Kenison of Lindquist & Vennum, Denver, Chair of the ABA effort.

We are grateful to our *Brill*-iant publisher team for their encouragement, patience, and outstanding skill. Special thanks to Marie Sheldon, Senior Acquisitions Editor at Brill / Martinus Nijhoff Publishers, and Lisa Hanson and Lauren Danahy, Assistant Editors.

Our most special tributes go to three beautiful people without whom there would be no book. To our wonderful partners, Katharine Nanda and Catherine Pring, who reviewed endless drafts, argued, critiqued, counseled, revised, cajoled, and added immeasurably to the final product. And to Tessa Mendez – JD University of Denver Sturm College of Law 2011, MA University of Denver Korbel School of International Studies 2011, Editor-in-Chief of the *Denver Journal of International Law and Policy* 2010–2011, and now a member of the California Bar – who reviewed every chapter and footnote for publication and who personally authored Section 5.5.3 on "Corporate Social Responsibility."

Acknowledgements to the 1st Edition (2003)

Above all, we wish to express our gratitude and affection to Heike Fenton, our publisher, for her vision, support, and friendship. So many friends, colleagues, and former students have helped us with the work that resulted in this book. For all it has been a labor of love for the environment. We wish to acknowledge the substantial research contributions to this book made by Martha Keister, International and Comparative Law Librarian, Diane Burkhardt, Faculty Services Liaison, and the Staff of the Westminster Law Library at the University of Denver College of Law. Former students, now graduates of the College of Law, Bruce Baizel, Laura Childs, David Demaray, Tamar Fitzgerald, Nicolle Fleury, Jennifer Lee, Marco Madriz, Katharine Nanda, Caroline Payne, Tanya Poth, Lainie Resnick, Linda Siegele, Shana Smilovits, Elle Tauer, and David Whiting all deserve great commendation for their substantive contributions to various chapters. We are deeply indebted to our dedicated College of Law professional staff who keep us honest and on track, Camilla Adams and Nancy Nones, for their hard work and loyalty. And we send fondest thanks to our friends Duane and Jean Gall and Robinson and Reese Goldman for their love of the Earth and their inspiration of us in our efforts.

Part One: Introduction

Chapter One

International Environmental Law: The Nature and Scope of the Challenge

1.0 *Introduction*

Earth is our ultimate shared resource.

Reflect for a moment on the miracle – the extraordinarily rare combination of factors that together makes life on earth possible. Our planet's ideal position in the right kind of galaxy, the right distance from a perfect star, the right tilt for seasons, exactly enough of a protective stratospheric radiation shield, a thin layer of breathable atmosphere, ample water resources, a moderate temperature range, sunlight, moderate terrain, energy and minerals, photosynthesis, the hydrologic cycle, the carbon cycle, living soils, flora, and fauna.[1] Contemplate its magnificence – from outer space, the "piercingly beautiful" blue globe our astronauts see hanging in the void, or from a down-to-earth panorama of its incredible landforms, mountains, canyons, plains, oceans, sea beds, rivers, lakes, wetlands, forests, jungles, archipelagos, deserts, fjords, glaciers, and ice fields. Then think of the incredibly rich life forms, species, and ecosystems that exist at this brief point in the billions of years the earth has been evolving.

For evolution – change – is the one constant on earth. Incredibly durable and resilient in the face of natural change, our planet is also shockingly vulnerable and defenseless to human-induced change. As the pioneering ecologist Aldo Leopold observed over a half century ago, natural evolution itself is change – a process "to elaborate and diversify the biota" (which we now call "biodiversity") – but "[m]an's invention of tools has enabled him to make

---

[1] *See* Peter D. Ward & Donald Brownlee, Rare Earth: Why Complex Life is Uncommon in the Universe xxvii–xxviii (2000). The authors would like to credit Daniel Ritchie, former Chancellor of the University of Denver, for inspiring this "Rare Earth" vision of the environment in his welcoming address to the Symposium on Environmental Education at the University of Denver, Apr. 23, 2002.

changes of unprecedented violence, rapidity, and scope," and the more violent the human changes, the greater the likelihood the affected individuals, species, or ecosystems will never recover.[2]

Now, in the 21st century, we can see around us the truth of Leopold's warning. Lord Byron's "Man marks the earth with ruin"[3] may be an overstatement, but anthropogenic (human-caused) environmental change is now widespread and serious on all three levels – global, regional/transboundary, and local.[4] Earth faces "global" environmental problems including anthropogenic climate change, stratospheric ozone depletion, nitrogen loading, species extinction, biodiversity loss, ocean pollution, natural areas destruction, deforestation, desertification, topsoil loss, declining food production, depleted fish stocks, grinding poverty, spiraling population, and grave human health problems (such as the AIDS pandemic, international tobacco sales, and lack of safe drinking water and sanitation for billions of people). At a "transboundary" or multiple-nation level, we face human-caused environmental problems like acid deposition, other forms of border-crossing air pollution, diminished freshwater quality and quantity, nuclear accidents, environmental warfare, sprawling urbanization, resource extraction impacts, spread of disease vectors, and a booming international trade in hazardous wastes, toxic chemicals, and dangerous technologies. Natural catastrophes can multiply human impacts, as with Japan's disastrous March 2011 earthquake that damaged a nuclear power plant, causing extensive sea and air release of radioactivity. We face all of the above and more as "local" environmental problems within individual countries.

The UN-sponsored Millennium Ecosystem Assessment, the largest body of natural and social scientists ever assembled to assess the state of the environment, ominously concludes:

> [A]pproximately 60%... of the ecosystem services examined during the Millennium Ecosystem Assessment are being degraded or used unsustainably, including fresh water, capture fisheries, air and water purification, and the regulation of regional and local climate, natural hazards, and pests. The full costs of the loss and degradation... are substantial and growing.

---

[2] ALDO LEOPOLD, A SAND COUNTY ALMANAC 214–20 (1948). With regard to older quoted sources like this that appear gender-insensitive, we simply ask the reader to construe them in the generic sense, to include all human beings.

[3] George Gordon, Lord Byron, *Childe Harold's Pilgrimage*, Canto IV, Stanza 179 (1818), *in* PROJECT GUTENBERG, http://www.gutenberg.org/dirs/etext04/chpl10h.htm.

[4] For more details on these global, regional, and local environmental problems and crises, *see e.g.*, UN Environment Programme (UNEP), *Disasters and Conflicts*, http://www.unep.org/conflictsanddisasters/; WORLDWATCH INSTITUTE, STATE OF THE WORLD 2009: INTO A WARMING WORLD (2009).

Over the past 50 years, humans have changed ecosystems more rapidly and extensively than in any comparable period of time in human history, largely to meet rapidly growing demands for food, fresh water, timber, fiber, and fuel. This has resulted in a substantial and largely irreversible loss in the diversity of life on Earth.[5]

How are we to address what some see as "abstract" or "secondary" environmental issues, given the almost overwhelming social and institutional problems that plague the world's populations? How do we justify spending money on the environment when some of the poorest countries in Africa spend more annually on servicing their massive Western-loan debts than on health and education combined?[6] How are we to stop deforestation, when it may be the only way out of a hideous Rio de Janeiro slum or the only way to keep from freezing in a village in Afghanistan? How are we to protect land and water resources from indiscriminate mining, logging, overfishing, and wildlife poaching when exploitation of those resources provides the only source of cash income in some developing countries and when demand for those resources is so high in developed countries? How are we to protect our air, when our way of life is integrally linked to pollution producing activities?

The Millennium Development Goals (MDGs), adopted by world leaders in 2000, seek to answer this by attacking poverty in its many dimensions including: hunger, education, gender equality, child mortality, maternal health, HIV/AIDS and other diseases, environment, and partnerships.[7] The eight MDGs, form a blueprint of concrete, numerical benchmarks to be achieved by 2015. MDGs 7 – Ensure Environmental Sustainability – targets sustainable development, deforestation, climate change, biodiversity loss, safe drinking water, sanitation, and urban slums.[8] While the MDGs set ambitious objectives, the world continues to struggle to find the right balance between environmental protection and poverty alleviation.

To return to the heart of the matter, what is this thing called "environment" that so many international and domestic laws, policies, and programs seek to protect? "Environment" has been described as "a term that everyone understands and no one is able to define."[9] There is no one consistent definition of the term in the legal authorities. In international environmental

---

[5] Millennium Ecosystem Assessment, Ecosystems and Human Well-Being: Synthesis 1 (2005), http://www.maweb.org/documents/document.356.aspx.pdf.

[6] *See* Ved P. Nanda, *Global Aid Debate*, Denver Post, Aug. 30, 2000, at 11B.

[7] *Millennium Development Goals*, United Nations, http://www.un.org/millenniumgoals/index.shtml.

[8] *Goal 7: Ensure Environmental Sustainability*, United Nations, http://www.un.org/millenniumgoals/environ.shtml.

[9] Ronald B. Mitchell, et al., The International Environmental Agreement Database Project (2010), http://iea.uoregon.edu/page.php?query=static&file=definitions.htm.

law, it can mean any system from a microscopic wetland to the cosmos of outer space, from a wilderness area to an urban ghetto, from the Himalayas to the deep seabed, from a mine mouth to the human mouth.[10] Perhaps one of the most comprehensive definitions appears in the 1991 Convention on Environmental Impact Assessment in a Transboundary Context; there "environment" includes: "human health and safety, flora, fauna, soil, air, water, climate, landscape and historical monuments or other physical structures or the interaction among these factors...[and] cultural heritage or socioeconomic conditions resulting from alterations to those factors."[11]

The subject covered by this field of law is enormous and enormously flexible, challenging international environmental lawyers to be enormously creative,[12] as can be seen from the following overview of the legal sources protecting it.

1.1   *The Sources or Bases of International Environmental Law*

It was not until the late 20th century that serious scientific, public, and political attention focused on the world's environmental problems. From this has emerged one of the newest and most vigorously evolving branches of international law – international environmental law – the law dealing with environmental issues affecting more states or countries than one. A "growth industry," today international environmental law already consists of over 1,000 multilateral agreements and 1,500 bilateral agreements,[13] as well as declarations, resolutions, judicial decisions, and other legal authorities, most since 1970.[14] Of course, we can trace international environmental law back much further in time, as governments, like people, have been struggling to

---

[10] Even smoking has becoming a focus of international treaty law. World Health Organization (WHO), *Global Tobacco Treaty Enters Into Force with 57 Countries Already Committed*, Feb. 24, 2005, http://www.who.int/mediacentre/news/releases/2005/pr09/en/index.html.

[11] Convention on Environmental Impact Assessment in a Transboundary Context (Espoo Convention), art. 1(vii), Feb. 25, 1991, 30 I.L.M. 800 (1991), http://www.unece.org/env/eia/.

[12] Ved P. Nanda, *Trends in International Environmental Law*, 20 CAL. W. INT'L L.J. 187, 193 (1990).

[13] MITCHELL, *supra* note 9.

[14] George (Rock) Pring, James Otto & Koh Naito, *Trends in International Environmental Law Affecting the Minerals Industry*, 17 J. ENERGY & NAT. RES. L. 39, 49 (1999) http://heinonline.org/HOL/LandingPage?collection=journals&handle=hein.journals/jenrl17&div=10&id=&page=(Part 1) and http://heinonline.org/HOL/LandingPage?collection=journals&handle=hein.journals/jenrl17&div=21&id=&page=(Part 2); George W. Pring & David Joeris, *Various International Environmental Law Collections*, 4 COLO. J. INT'L ENV'TL L. & POL'Y 422 (1993); PATRICIA W. BIRNIE & ALAN E. BOYLE, INTERNATIONAL LAW & THE ENVIRONMENT 10–18 (2002).

define the relationship between humans and nature since the dawn of time. The earliest known treaty of all – the very beginning of the "Law of Nations" – was an environmental one, a 3100 BC treaty settling a literal "water war" between two Mesopotamian city-states in what is now Iraq.[15] In 1609, Hugo Grotius, the "father" of modern international law, established the doctrine of freedom of the seas in his monumental treatise *Mare Liberum*, even before the emergence of the modern "state" later in that century.[16] International watercourse-use treaties began in earnest in the 18th century,[17] and early in the 20th century, treaties began to take account of environmental values other than human consumption, but only sporadically.[18]

Prior to 1970, international law largely left the environment alone, on the theory that individual countries have "sovereignty" (complete, supreme, and independent political and legal control) over their natural resources,[19] just as they do over persons, businesses and other entities, and activities within their territory. The most prominent statement of this nationalistic or "statist" view is found in one of the best known international environmental legal authorities, Principle 21 of the Stockholm Declaration: "States have, in accordance with the Charter of the United Nations and the principles of international law, the sovereign right to exploit their own resources pursuant to their own environmental policies...."[20] Or, as Professor Edith Brown Weiss puts it more bluntly, "states have traditionally asserted the right to pollute at self-determined levels."[21]

This claim that a state has a "sovereign right" to use and abuse its "own" environment – without reference to the impact on other countries – flies in the very face of the extreme *interconnectedness* of life, environmental media,

---

[15] Stephen C. McCaffrey, The Law of International Watercourses 59–60 (2d ed. 2007).

[16] *See* Arthur Nussbaum, A Concise History of the Law of Nations 111 (1954).

[17] *See infra* Chapter 9, International Freshwater Resources.

[18] Pollution and preservation concerns can be found, for example, in such landmarks as the 1909 US-Canada Boundary Waters Treaty, the 1940 Convention on Nature Protection and Wildlife Preservation in the Western Hemisphere, the 1958 Convention on the High Seas, and the 1959 Antarctic Treaty. Texts in Supplement of Basic Documents to International Environmental Law and World Order (Lakshman D. Guruswamy *et al.*, eds., 2d ed. 1999).

[19] *See, e.g.*, UN Economic and Social Council [ECOSOC], Report of the Secretary-General, *Permanent Sovereignty over Minerals and Water Resources* (Feb. 18, 1993), UN Doc. E/C.7/1993/2.

[20] *See* Report of the UN Conference on the Human Environment, Stockholm, June 5–16, 1972, UN Doc. A/CONF.48/14/Rev. 1 at 3 (1973), 11 I.L.M. 1416 (1972) http://www.un.org/documents/ga/conf151/aconf15126-1annex1.htm.

[21] Edith Brown Weiss, *International Environmental Law: Contemporary Issues and the Emergence of a New World Order*, 81 Geo. L.J. 675, 704 (1993).

and ecosystems on this planet. Environmental degradation challenges traditional notions of national sovereignty, since the environment does not
stop at political borders. Also, much of the global environment falls outside
the jurisdiction and sovereignty of individual states, such as the high seas,
Antarctica, and outer space.[22] Today, to paraphrase John Donne, no state is
an island,[23] and the pollution, resource utilization, or environmental damage done in one country now is routinely seen to have impacts in other
countries, in areas outside any country's jurisdiction, and even globally. This
realization – that a doctrine of absolute sovereignty over the environment
means a given nation could be a loser as easily as a winner – has led states to
cooperate to protect the environment, if only out of enlightened self-interest.
From this has emerged international environmental law.

Fortunately, an equally fundamental premise of international law is that
states can "surrender" portions of their sovereignty through the creation and
acceptance of international laws. International law can arise from several
sources: (1) long-term practice of legal customs (customary international
law); (2) binding treaties and other formal written agreements (conventional
international law); (3) general principles widely adopted in national laws; and
to a lesser extent (4) judicial decisions and experts' writings.[24] Each of these
sources will be analyzed in depth in the sections to follow. Collectively, all of
these rules make up what we call "international law." However, in the more
modern view there is another category to watch, and a particularly fertile one
in international environmental law. This is the category somewhat oxymo-
ronically called "soft law" – initially nonbinding and aspirational authorities,
such as most United Nations General Assembly (UNGA) "resolutions," the
"declarations," "principles," "rules," "articles," and "guidelines" of international governmental organizations (IGOs) and even some nongovernmental organizations (NGOs), the "policies," "guidance," and "conditions" of

---

[22] *See* A. E. Boyle, *State Responsibility for Breach of Obligations to Protect the Global Environment, in* CONTROL OVER COMPLIANCE WITH INTERNATIONAL LAW 69, 72–73 (W. E. Butler
ed., 1991).

[23] John Donne, *Devotions Upon Emergent Occasions, Meditation XVII* (1623), *in* M. H.
ABRAMS ET AL., 1 THE NORTON ANTHOLOGY OF ENGLISH LITERATURE 795, (1962) ("No
man is an island, entire of itself; every man is a piece of the continent, a part of the main.
If a clod be washed away by the sea, Europe is the less.... [T]herefore never send to know
for whom the bell tolls; it tolls for thee").

[24] Pring, *et al., supra* note 14, at 47. Article 38 of the Statute of the International Court of
Justice (ICJ) is commonly cited for codifying these five categories, June 26, 1945, 1976
U.N.Y.B. 1052, 59 Stat. 1031, T.S. No. 993, http://www.icj-cij.org/documents/index
.php?p1=4&p2=2&p3=0. Two good short treatments of these categories can be found in
THOMAS BUERGENTHAL & HAROLD G. MAIER, PUBLIC INTERNATIONAL LAW IN A NUT-
SHELL 18–34 (4th ed. 2007); LAKSHMAN GURUSWAMY, INTERNATIONAL ENVIRONMENTAL
LAW IN A NUTSHELL 1–33 (3d ed. 2007).

international financial organizations (IFOs), such as multilateral development banks (MDBs), development assistance agencies (DAAs), and national
export-promotion agencies (Ex-Ims), and even private-sector companies',
industry associations', standards organizations', financial institutions', insurance underwriters', and trade groups' codes of conduct, operating rules, and
other "green conditionalities."[25] While not initially intended to have the force
of law, some of these "soft laws" receive such acceptance and practice over
time that, like wet concrete, they gradually solidify into "hard law."[26]

A word of caution: It is tempting to dismiss all international law as "vague,"
"unenforceable," or "irrelevant." The "Law of Nations" does operate very differently from the national laws we are used to. Because it regulates sovereign nations, the international legal system lacks conventional law-making
bodies, lacks normal enforcement agencies, relies on governments' political
will more than command-control regulation, and consists of rules of varying
specificity and enforceability.[27] However, the temptation to ignore international law should be avoided. In the famous observation of Professor Louis
Henkin: "[A]lmost all nations observe almost all principles of international
law and almost all of their obligations almost all of the time."[28] The world's
environment would be in much more serious disrepair were this not also
true of nations' overall level of observance of their international environmental law rights and obligations.

1.1.1   *International Conventional Law*

Bilateral (two-states) and multilateral (three-or-more-states) treaties –
whether called treaties, conventions, charters, covenants, codes, protocols,
or agreements – have become the primary means for developing new rules of
international environmental law, with over 2,500 now extant. Treaties, being
voluntary undertakings between sovereigns, are in part like legislation and
in part like contracts. They are attractive for states because, of all the sources
of international law, they are the most controlled and controllable way states
can create new binding obligations upon themselves. Another way to view
treaties is to recognize that they surrender some portion of "absolute sovereignty," being concessions of some portion of a state's claimed sovereign
rights to do as it alone wishes with "its" environment, in return for a cooperative *quid pro quo* from other states. Initially, these treaties were more concerned with division and exploitation of a resource shared by several states

---

[25] Pring *et al., supra* note 14, at 49, 162–76.
[26] *Id.*
[27] Guruswamy, *supra* note 24, at 52.
[28] Louis Henkin, How Nations Behave – Law and Foreign Policy 47 (2d ed. 1979).

than with the conservation of the resource or prevention of adverse impacts from its exploitation. Today, treaties address all of those values and cover problems of atmospheric and stratospheric air pollution, climate change, water and land pollution, the oceans, international freshwater resources, Antarctica, outer space, historical and cultural preservation, endangered species, biological diversity, marine mammals and fish stocks, energy, hazardous waste and dangerous chemicals, human health, human rights and the environment, international trade, even the military use of environmental modification (ENMOD) in warfare.

The emergence of treaties as the primary source of international environmental law has had profound ramifications. It has enabled the development of more systematic environmental obligations of states, codified and clarified customary international law and declarations, highlighted the existence of collective international interests and not simply the national interests of individual states, provided a foundation for the development of more detailed standards, created international supervisory entities, and expanded the role of civil society in international environmental law, particularly NGOs and multinational enterprises (MNEs). Treaties follow fairly standard approaches:

> The main features [environmental treaties] share are: (1) an emphasis on national implementing measures being taken by the states parties; (2) the creation of international supervisory mechanisms to review compliance by states parties; (3) simplified procedures to enable rapid modification of the treaties; (4) the use of action plans for further measures; (5) the creation of new institutions or the utilization of already existing ones to promote continuous cooperation; (6) the use of framework agreements; and (7) interrelated or cross-referenced provisions from other environmental instruments.[29]

However, relying on treaties to build a new field of law presents several downsides. First, treaties are negotiated on a case-by-case basis so that most treat relatively narrow, site-specific or problem-specific issues. This piecemeal approach may focus only on a particular river (without covering its entire ecosystem or even all of its tributaries), or only on certain "listed" wildlife species, or a limited list of chemical pollutants. Second, treaty negotiation and ratification is a slow and cumbersome process (a notable exception being the world's quick response to stratospheric ozone depletion).[30] Third, negotiations often tend to produce least-common-denominator solutions in order to maximize the number of states that will sign and ratify; this frequently means either weak provisions or a "framework" treaty (really little more than a skeletal "agreement to agree," with the hard decisions postponed for later protocol negotiations, as with the 1990s global climate change efforts).

---

[29] Alexandre Kiss & Dinah Shelton, International Environmental Law 33 (2000).
[30] *See infra* Chapter 10.2.

Fourth, treaty implementation is always a significant and uncertain concern; compliance can easily falter if the treaty lacks (1) widespread ratification, (2) support of both developed and developing states, (3) a respected supervisory or overseeing institutional structure, (4) an effective incentive and coercive system, and (5) a compulsory and effective dispute-resolution mechanism.[31] Fifth, treaties generally bind only the parties, making it very difficult to achieve global solutions given the unwillingness of some states to participate in treaty regimes.

1.1.2   *International Customary Law*

The primary method of international law formation prior to the 20th century, customary international law still plays an important role in international environmental law, but a much lesser one today than treaties.[32] Custom is "largely unwritten law inferred from the conduct of states undertaken in the belief that they were bound to do so by law (*opinio juris*)."[33] Thus, it has two required elements: (1) the "objective" element of state practice and (2) the "subjective" or "psychological" element of *opinio juris*, that is, the states' conviction that the conduct is required as a *legal* obligation, not simply as a matter of comity, convenience, discretion, or diplomacy. State practice must be relatively consistent, uniform, widespread, and representative. State practice can be evidenced through legislation, governmental documents and statements, treaty ratifications, scholarly analyses, and judicial opinions.[34] *Opinio juris* can be evidenced by these same proof sources. The chief arbiters of what is or is not customary law are court opinions (of international or national courts) and scholarly books and articles.

Customary lawmaking is chiefly attractive because, unlike treaties, it does not require a state's affirmative endorsement to become binding on that state, simply its lack of timely and persistent objection. Thus, "the inactive are carried along by the active,"[35] a particular advantage in developing environmental law, where acquiescence may be more easy to achieve than express agreement.[36] Custom is also advantageous in that it avoids the delays, procedural requirements, and least-common-denominator "horse trading" of treaties and because there exist institutions focused on codifying or crystallizing custom, such as courts, arbitration panels, Restatements of the Law, and international "think tanks" like the UN International Law Commission

---

[31] *See* Nanda, *supra* note 12, at 193.
[32] BIRNIE & BOYLE, *supra* note 14, at 16–18.
[33] GURUSWAMY, *supra* note 24, at 15.
[34] *See* DAVID H. OTT, PUBLIC INTERNATIONAL LAW IN THE MODERN WORLD 13–16 (1987).
[35] Meijers, quoted in BIRNIE & BOYLE, *supra* note 14, at 15.
[36] *Id.*

(ILC), the International Law Association (ILA), and the Institute of International Law (IIL). (*See*, for a good example of this think-tank development, Chapter 10 on International Freshwater Resources.)

However, on the whole, custom has more disadvantages than advantages in environmental law. First, its form – generally unwritten and uncodified – creates enormous uncertainties and openings for disputation. Second, its requirement of widespread practice is extremely difficult to meet, with nearly 200 nations in the world. The economic, religious, cultural, and other gulfs between, for example, developed and developing nations or common law, civil law, and Islamic law nations are often sufficient to prevent the formation of any common custom. Third, while "instant" custom creation is not impossible,[37] lengthy duration of state practice is the norm, hardly responsive to today's urgent environmental problems. Fourth, custom does not create international institutional structures to systematically and coherently address the problems it solves.[38] Fifth, custom approaches problems in a piecemeal fashion, inadequately given the complex, interconnected nature of most environmental problems and the comprehensive, integrated solutions required.

Not surprisingly, only a few environmental rules have been accepted as customary international law. Some – like the principles of good neighborliness or cooperation, the prohibition against transboundary harms, and the requirements of prior notice and consultation for projects and activities with potential transboundary impacts – seem to have become binding legal custom.[39] Others are "emerging" (a euphemism for still in dispute), like the polluter-pays, preventive, and precautionary principles and sustainable development.[40] These principles are discussed in Chapter 2. Not all rules are created equal; some are deemed so important that they pass into the peremptory category of *jus cogens* – norms viewed as so basic, fundamental, and morally necessitated that they invalidate, override, or preempt national and international laws to the contrary, even agreed treaties (analogous to the national law principle of "void as against public policy"). While controversy often surrounds the question of what principles arise to the level of *jus cogens*, there is general agreement that they include the prohibitions against force or the threat of force, genocide, slavery, piracy, and racial discrimination, among others.[41] It is unsettled to what extent environmental norms can

---

[37] *See* North Sea Continental Shelf Cases (Ger./Den., Ger./Neth.) (Judgment), 1969 I.C.J. 3, ¶ 74 (Feb. 20), http://www.icj-cij.org/docket/files/51/5535.pdf.

[38] *See generally* Geoffrey Palmer, *New Ways to Make International Environmental Law*, 86 Am. J. Int'l L. 259 (1992).

[39] Birnie & Boyle, *supra* note 14, at 109–11.

[40] Guruswamy, *supra* note 24, at 19.

[41] Barcelona Traction, Light & Power Co., Ltd. (Belg. v. Spain) (Second Phase), 1970 I.C.J. 3, ¶ 33 (Feb. 5), http://www.icj-cij.org/docket/files/50/5387.pdf. *See* sources in Guruswamy,

be included in the *jus cogens* category and cannot be "negotiated away," but leading contenders could well be protection of the stratospheric ozone layer and endangered species.

Interestingly, custom can become codified in treaties, and the reverse, treaty negotiations can crystallize custom. The negotiations from 1973–1982 that led to one of today's most important environmental treaties, the UN Convention on the Law of the Sea (*see* Chapter 11), exemplify both. First, a number of long-standing customary international rules were codified, such as "freedom of the seas," coastal state jurisdiction over the territorial sea, and right of innocent passage. However, there also emerged agreement that several new norms had become "custom" and were therefore worthy of codi-fication, including the existence of an "exclusive economic zone" between the territorial sea and the high seas and the obligation of states to preserve the marine environment and prevent marine pollution. Then too, "soft law" pronouncements – IGO resolutions, declarations, action plans, and the like – have a positive role in the creation of custom; often enough repeated, states' soft law declarations can become supportive evidence of both the practice and *opinio juris* elements of customary law.

1.1.3 *General Principles of Law*

"[G]eneral principles of law recognized by civilized nations" (in the some-what patronizing colonial-era phrasing of the 1945 Charter of the Inter-national Court of Justice (ICJ))[42] have also proved to be a contributor to international environmental law and may have considerable potential to do so in the future.[43] This is the category of international law consisting of legal principles that are so fundamental that they are found in most of the world's major *national* legal systems. In this fashion, national or "municipal" law becomes both the birthplace and the testing ground for new international legal rules, and international law grows by adopting those rules that emerge and find widespread adoption by national, state, and local legal systems. Standard examples include such general principles as "legal obligations must be fulfilled" (*pacta sunt servanda*), "no one can be judge in his own cause," "breach of a legal duty entails the obligation of restitution," and "rights must be exercised in good faith."[44] The troublesome customary law element of actual practice is not required, just widespread acceptance in most national legal regimes (*in foro domestico*).

ET AL., INTERNATIONAL ENVIRONMENTAL LAW AND WORLD ORDER 132–37 (2d ed. 1999).

[42] I.C.J. Statute, *supra* note 24, art. 38(1)(c).

[43] BIRNIE & BOYLE, *supra* note 14, at 20–22.

[44] HERSCH LAUTERPACHT, 1 INTERNATIONAL LAW 68–74 (Elihu Lauterpacht ed. 1970).

Professors Kiss and Shelton note two good examples of this method of growth in international environmental law.[45] First, in the famous *Trail Smelter Arbitration* of the 1940s (for details, see both Chapters 9 and 10), no clear international law was found to apply to the dispute over a private smelter in Canada causing transboundary air pollution of the US. In the absence of an international legal norm, the arbitral panel turned to national judicial decisions – of the US and Switzerland in particular – to establish the now-fundamental principle that states have an obligation not to cause significant harm to the environment of other states and areas. Second, the procedure of environmental impact assessment (*see* Chapter 6) was pioneered in national legislation of the US in 1969, was quickly picked up over the next decade in the laws of other countries, then began appearing in multilateral regional treaties and finally in global treaties such as the Law of the Sea Treaty and the Transboundary EIA or Espoo Treaty. This merger of law also works in the other direction: international law rules can have the "trickle down" effect of inspiring the adoption of new national laws, as the international treaties protecting wildlife have done and as the new international Biodiversity Treaty likely will do.

1.1.4   *Judicial Decisions*

Interestingly, international law relegates judicial decisions to a lower rung on the ladder, viewing them, along with scholarly writings, as only "subsidiary means for the determination of rules of [international] law."[46] This is always a surprise to common-law-trained lawyers of the US and UK/Commonwealth states, programmed as they are to look to courts as highly authoritative interpreters, indeed pronouncers, of "what the law is."[47] However, this view is counterbalanced by the reluctance of the civil law and other legal traditions to give their courts so much power. Nevertheless, while limited in number, international judicial and arbitral decisions and even the decisions of some national courts that are highly respected internationally for their objectivity and independence, like the US Supreme Court, have contributed substantially to international environmental law.

The basic building block of international environmental law – the rule against significant transboundary harms – emerged in the 1941 *Trail Smelter Arbitration* decision (*see* Chapters 9 and 10). Other significant international judicial decisions about the environment include a quintet of water cases

---

[45] Kiss & Shelton, *supra* note 29, at 86–88.

[46] ICJ Statute, *supra* note 24, art. 38(1)(d).

[47] The extreme being the United States, since the pronouncement of judicial supremacy in *Marbury v. Madison*, from which this quote comes, 5 U.S. 137, 177 (1803), http://www.law.cornell.edu/supct/html/historics/USSC_CR_0005_0137_ZO.html.

(broadly applicable to other environmental media and issues): the 1929 *River Oder* Case, the 1937 *River Meuse* Case, the 1949 *Corfu Channel* Case, the 1957 *Lac Lanoux Arbitration*, and the 1997 *Gabcikovo-Nagymoros Dam* Case. (For a full discussion *see* Chapter 9.) Also, a series of ICJ decisions in the Nuclear Test Cases[48] plow new, if indecisive, ground in the area of nuclear-radiation pollution.

1.1.5   *Scholarly Writings*

The other "subsidiary" source of international law is the written work of respected legal scholars and commentators in the field. This too comes as something of a surprise to US lawyers, whose view of the role of law review articles and law professors' books can scarcely be called flattering. While less authoritative today than judicial decisions, in past centuries, scholars were a major source for expanding international law, as the great 17th century Dutch jurist Hugo Grotius' treatises on Freedom of the Seas and the Law of War and Peace exemplify. Since the Stockholm Conference in 1972, scholarly treatises and articles on international environmental law have become a "growth industry" and, in some instances, have clearly influenced the development of the law.

The clearest example of this power of scholars and experts to "make" international law is the work of the ILC, the permanent UN organ of international law experts created in 1947 to encourage "the progressive development of international law and its codification," mentioned above. The ILC has done just that, producing highly regarded "draft articles" with extensive commentaries that have become or are in the process of being adopted as treaties or stand alone as authoritative codifications and progressive development of the law. The ILC has done this in such areas as state responsibility, state liability, and international watercourses (*see* Chapter 9). Two similar NGO think tanks, the ILA and IIL, have also made very substantial contributions to international law through their writing, drafting, and publications.

1.1.6   *New Sources of International Law*

A growing source of international environmental law – not even recognized in the 1940s at the time the ICJ Charter list of sources – now comes from intergovernmental organizations (IGOs) and other entities. The resolutions, declarations, statements of principles, guidelines, action plans, etc., produced

---

[48] Nuclear Test Cases (Aust. v. France), 1974 I.C.J. 253; Legality of the Use by a State of Nuclear Weapons in Armed Conflict, Request for Advisory Opinion, 1993 I.C.J. 467; Legality of the Threat or Use of Nuclear Weapons, 1995 I.C.J. 3; 1995 I.C.J. 288, 1995 I.C.J. 288, 1996 I.C.J. 93.

by the UN General Assembly (UNGA), UN agencies, and other multilateral groups, IFOs, and conferences (such as the 1972 UN Stockholm Conference, the 1983–87 World Commission on Environment and Development (WCED), and the 1992 Rio Conference) are making a profound contribution to international environmental law. Few of these are initially adopted as "binding" international law, as IGOs rarely have more than recommendatory power.[49] Virtually all are adopted as "nonbinding" aspirational statements or "soft law," but, as mentioned before, these can have enormous force and significance over time.

The influence of soft law is a very controversial concept. While lawyers used to firm, binding, governmental "command-control" laws and regulations at the domestic level may express contempt for nonbinding, soft law pronouncements ("moralizing without consequences" is one of the kinder epithets one will hear), such pronouncements nevertheless have numerous advantages when it is recalled that we are dealing with sovereigns, not subjects. They are (1) much faster to negotiate, (2) have no immediate negative political costs (not needing ratification), (3) draw in states that would otherwise refuse to agree to such norms and goals at their present state of ability to comply, (4) provide flexibility where there is scientific or other uncertainty about the problem and/or the solution, (5) leave room for development of other approaches, (6) create a climate of cooperation and agreement that can be built on in the future, and (7) can "harden" over time into agreed treaties or customary law.[50] Soft laws are admittedly "halfway stages in the lawmaking process,"[51] or, in Professor Lakshman Guruswamy's graphic phrase, "a grey zone between gestation and labor."[52]

How does soft law harden? If one looks only at the direct route – a soft law declaration is made and years later it becomes a part of a binding treaty or accepted customary international law – one will be missing significant parts of the process. Soft law is not necessarily hardened by its creators; courts or IFOs can set it in stone. "Nature abhors a vacuum," as philosophers from Parmenides in the 5th century BCE have argued,[53] and so do judges. In the absence of clearcut legal standards to decide an international case, the trend is for *national courts* to step in and apply international soft law, provided it has sufficient state backing.[54] Also IFOs, stung by environmental disasters

---

[49] KISS & SHELTON, *supra* note 29, at 91–94.

[50] *Id.*

[51] BIRNIE & BOYLE, *supra* note 14, at 25.

[52] GURUSWAMY, *supra* note 24, at 27.

[53] *Nature Abhors a Vacuum*, ENCYCLOPEDIA OF HUMAN THERMODYNAMICS, http://www.eoht.info/page/Nature+abhors+a+vacuum.

[54] Pring *et al., supra* note 14, at 163.

they have financed in developing countries, are currently undergoing "a greening" and creating new environmental guidelines and conditions for their loans, aid, insurance underwriting, and other involvement in states' and private companies' projects and actions; to do so, they turn to soft law and incorporate it as their binding rules of engagement.[55]

Given this proliferation of sources – treaties, custom, general principles, judicial decisions, scholars, and soft law – what international environmental law principles have emerged? The next chapter details the key principles that underlie our international legal system for the environment.

---

[55] *Id.* at 163–67.

Chapter Two

The Fundamental Principles of International Environmental Law

2.0 *Introduction*

In its short history, international environmental law has already developed (and developed around) a core of fundamental, guiding legal principles. Because these principles are embodied in the issue-specific chapters that follow this one, this chapter acts a guide for topics and concepts to come. While some of the principles discussed here apply generally in international law, many others apply specifically to international environmental law. Unlike some other fields of international law, international environmental law has no single treaty or declaration setting out the basic rules and principles.[1] Its fundamental principles range from the clearly accepted "hard law" ones, to those said to be "emerging" or "in progressive development" (accepted by many but still lacking thorough consensus), to the merely "aspirational" or futuristic values.

Some of the principles address substantive issues, focused on ends or outcomes – such as sovereignty, the no-harm rule, sustainable development, common heritage, etc. Others can be seen as more procedural in nature, focused on means or process – prior notification, consultation, negotiation, equal access to justice, etc. Still others are hard to classify as one or the other, partaking of both – such as good neighborliness/cooperation, *erga omnes*, and the right of access to information. While the following sections use the substance-procedure categories, this is simply for ease of organization and should not be taken as a limitation on the principles.

---

[1] Patricia W. Birnie, Alan E. Boyle, & Catherine Redgwell, International Law and the Environment 108 (3d ed. 2009).

2.1   Fundamental Substantive Principles

2.1.1   State Sovereignty

The state-centered nature of the modern world exacerbates environmental problems and is the main reason for the inadequacy of international environmental law and institutions.[2] As discussed in Chapter 1, international law must work around the doctrine of state sovereignty – the doctrine holding that, within its territory, each nation-state has complete, supreme, and independent political and legal control over persons, businesses, entities, and activities, and over "its" environment and natural resources. There is a "fundamental tension between a State's interest in protecting its independence (i.e. its sovereignty) and the recognition that...regional and global environmental problems, require international cooperation."[3] No state is a sealed-off "island" with impenetrable boundaries, given the interconnectedness of the environment and globalization today.

While the modern nation-state is a relative newcomer historically, dating only from the 17th century,[4] its doctrine of sovereignty is firmly fixed, and international law is, in one sense, a body of state-created exceptions to that sovereignty. National sovereignty over natural resources and the environment has been affirmed in numerous international agreements and declarations (*see* Chapter 1). The tension between sovereignty and the environment is captured perfectly in the "First Commandment" of international environmental law, Stockholm Principal 21:

> States have, in accordance with the Charter of the United Nations and the principles of international law, the sovereign right to exploit their own resources pursuant to their own environmental policies, and the responsibility to ensure that activities within their jurisdiction or control do not cause damage to the environment of other States or of areas beyond the limits of national jurisdiction.[5]

---

[2] *See* Ved P. Nanda, *International Environmental Challenges: "Sustainable Development" and "Environmental Terrorism,"* 3 Touro J. Transnat'l L. 1, 17 (1992); George (Rock) Pring, James Otto & Koh Naito, *Trends in International Environmental Law Affecting the Minerals Industry*, 17 J. Energy & Nat. Resources L. 39, 47 (1999).

[3] David Hunter, James Salzman & Durwood Zaelke, International Environmental Law and Policy 442 (4th ed. 2011).

[4] Starke's International Law 11 (I. A. Shearer 11th ed. 1994).

[5] United Nations Conference on the Human Environment, Stockholm, Swed., June 5–16, 1972, *Stockholm Declaration of the UN Conference on the Human Environment*, Principle 21, UN Doc. A/CONF.48/14/Rev. 1 at 3, UN Doc. A/CONF.48/14 at 2–65 and Corr. 1 (June 16, 1972) (hereinafter Stockholm Declaration), http://www.unep.org/Documents.Multilingual/ Default.asp?documentid=97&articleid=1503.

Typical of international environmental law's general approach, the first clause pays deference to the state sovereignty doctrine, while the second clause creates a large exception to that doctrine, proclaiming that sovereignty does not shield states from responsibility for the adverse effects of their actions on environments outside their territory. International environmental law thus professes not to interfere with entirely internal domestic actions affecting the environment, purporting to leave those to the sovereign control of the state, but does claim to control from a state's borders out. In fact, international environmental law also has substantial in-state effects as well, since many treaties and other agreements oblige states to take "appropriate measures" domestically to implement and enforce their international commitments.[6]

Still, sovereignty is a huge impediment to the success of international environmental law. In a system where sovereignty is paramount, state compliance is seen as voluntary. Few incentives pressure compliance, no centralized enforcement authority exists, national self-restraint is the primary means of enforcement, and negotiation/diplomacy is the norm for dealing with violations, rather than penalties, litigation, economic sanctions, or unilateral action.

2.1.2   *"Good Neighborliness" – The Duty to Cooperate*

All of international environmental law flows from the duty to cooperate. Enshrined among the Article I peacekeeping "purposes" of the UN Charter is the purpose "to achieve international co-operation in solving international problems of an economic, social, cultural, or humanitarian character."[7] The reason for this duty to cooperate is really enlightened self-interest and self-preservation, as the UN General Assembly (UNGA) candidly recognized in a 1970 declaration:

> States have the duty to co-operate with one another, irrespective of the differences in their political, economic and social systems…in order to maintain international peace and security and to promote international economic stability and progress, the general welfare of nations and international co-operation free from discrimination based on such differences.[8]

---

[6] A typical example of "appropriate measures" treaty language can be found in Article VIII(1) of the Convention on International Trade in Endangered Species of Wild Fauna and Flora (CITES), Mar. 3, 1973, 993 UNTS 243, 27 U.S.T. 1087, T.I.A.S. No. 8249, 12 I.L.M. 1085 (1973), http://www.cites.org/eng/disc/text.php.

[7] UN Charter art. 1, para 3, http://www.un.org/en/documents/charter/.

[8] Declaration of Principles of International Law Concerning Friendly Relations and Cooperation Among States in Accordance with the Charter of the United Nations, G.A. Res. 2625 (XXV), UN Doc. A/RES/2625(XXV) (Oct. 24, 1970), http://www.unhcr.org/refworld/topic, 459d17822,459d17a82,3dda1f104,0.html.

This duty of cooperation is also known as "the general principle of good-neighborliness," as recognized in the UN Charter, where it is defined as "due account being taken of the interests and well-being of the rest of the world, in social, economic, and commercial matters."[9]

This "good neighborliness" or cooperation duty was seized on as a principle of international environmental law from the outset. Stockholm Principle 24 states:

> International matters concerning the protection and improvement of the environment should be handled in a co-operative spirit by all countries, big or small, on an equal footing. Co-operation through multilateral or bilateral arrangements or other appropriate means is essential to effectively control, prevent, reduce and eliminate adverse environmental effects resulting from activities conducted in all spheres, in such a way that due account is taken of the sovereignty and interests of all States.[10]

Note that the duty is not only "essential" but also specifically made compatible with sovereignty. Cooperation is even more imbedded throughout the Rio Declaration of 1992,[11] and its concluding Principle 27 is devoted to it: "States and people shall cooperate in good faith and in a spirit of partnership in the fulfillment of the principles embodied in this Declaration...."[12] In creating the UN Environment Programme (UNEP), the UN General Assembly made its first duty "to promote international co-operation in the field of the environment and to recommend, as appropriate, policies to this end."[13]

Because environmental problems are frequently transnational in scope, cooperative action is often the only way to successfully solve them. Numerous success stories exemplify international environmental cooperation, as the issue-specific chapters will explore. Two good examples are the international cooperation leading to swift action on stratospheric ozone depletion (*see* § 10.2) and the cooperation among Mediterranean Sea coastal states which has

---

[9] UN Charter, *supra* note 7, art. 74.

[10] Stockholm Declaration, *supra* note 5.

[11] United Nations Conference on Environment and Development, Rio de Janiero, Braz., June 3–14, 1992, *Rio Declaration on Environment and Development*, Principles 5, 7, 9, 12, 14, 26, 27, UN Doc. A/CONF.151/26/Rev. 1 (Vol. I) (Aug. 12, 1992) (hereinafter Rio Declaration), http://www.unep.org/Documents.Multilingual/Default.asp?documentid=78&article id=1163.

[12] *Id.* at Principle 27.

[13] Resolution on the Institutional and Financial Arrangement for International Environment Cooperation (Establishing the United Nations Environment Program, UNEP), G.A. Res. 2997 (XXVII), UN Doc. A/RES/2997 (Dec. 15, 1972). Likewise, The first principle of UNEP's Draft Principles of Conduct in the Field of the Environment for Guidance of States in the Conservation and Harmonious Utilization of Natural Resources Shared by Two or More States is "[i]t is necessary for States to co-operate...." Mar. 10, 1978, principle 1, UN Doc. UNEP/GC.6/17 (1978).

led to some success in protecting that shared marine environment.[14] Countless international legal authorities as well as state practice support this general principle. As the following sections will illustrate, the duty of cooperation is a basic building block of international environmental law because environmental damage is often too big a problem for one state to handle unilaterally.

2.1.3   *The No-Harm Rule*

The most basic prescriptive rule and the backbone of international environmental law is the principle that states have an obligation not to cause or allow environmental harm outside their borders. The no-harm rule is based on the time-honored common law principle of *sic utere tuo ut alienum non laedas* (that is, "One should use one's own property so as not to injure another"). This concept is deeply rooted in the world's cultures, from the Christian "Golden Rule" ("Do unto others what you would have others do unto you")[15] to the Confucian principle of *shu* ("Do not impose upon others what you do not want for yourself").[16] Obviously, the no-harm rule is a specific manifestation of the "good neighborliness" principle, and enlightened state self-interest and self-preservation can be seen as the stimulus for states to accept such a *quid pro quo* limitation on their sovereignty.

However logical, the no-harm rule is a relatively recent international customary law principle. Its first major recognition came in the famous 1941 *Trail Smelter Arbitration* (*see* § 10.1.2 for details), in which the panel concluded, on the basis of national law, that there was an international law general principle that:

> [N]o state has the right to use or permit the use of its territory in such a manner as to cause injury…in or to the territory of another or the properties or persons therein, when the case is of serious consequence and the injury established by clear and convincing evidence.[17]

Several things should be noted about this famous early statement of the rule. In its favor, it: (1) implicitly denies the existence of a sovereign "right" to engage in or allow activities having harmful transboundary effects, (2) applies both to government action and inaction (that is, it also applies to private sector activities that are not adequately controlled by the government

---

[14] *See* A. E. Chircop, *The Mediterranean Sea and the Quest for Sustainable Development*, 23 Ocean Dev. & Int'l L. 17 (1992).

[15] *Matthew* 7:12; *Luke* 6:31, The Bible.

[16] T. R. Reid, Confucius Lives Next Door: What Living in the East Teaches Us About Living in the West 112 (1999).

[17] Trail Smelter Arbitration, (US v. Can.), 3 R.I.A.A. 1911, ¶ 157 (1941), http://untreaty.un.org/cod/riaa/cases/vol_III/1905-1982.pdf.

to prevent transboundary harm), and (3) creates a duty running not only to the victim state but to private persons and properties therein. On the other hand, it is limited in that it: (1) applies only to harms outside the perpetrator state, not within, (2) requires that the injury be "serious" (thus setting a threshold for allowable transboundary pollution or other injury), (3) appears to place the burden of proof of serious consequences on the victim, and (4) elevates that burden of proof to the very demanding "clear and convincing evidence" level (in contrast to the precautionary principle, below).

Numerous international environmental declarations and treaties have adopted variations on this concept,[18] notably Stockholm Principle 21 and its twin Rio Principle 2, which specifically limit states' sovereignty with "the responsibility to ensure that activities within their jurisdiction and control do not cause damage to the environment of other States or of areas beyond the limits of national jurisdiction."[19] The last phrase expands the prohibition to protect the oceans, Antarctica, stratosphere, and outer space. Note also that the Stockholm and Rio no-harm rule does not specify that the injury must be "appreciable," "serious," or "significant" as other statements of the rule do, thus suggesting it is an absolute. This is clearly not consistent with its acceptance in customary international law, where sensibly a threshold level of harm is required before the rule is operative.

After its incorporation in both the Stockholm and Rio declarations, most commentators believed the no-harm rule had become accepted as international law, but it was not until 1996 that the International Court of Justice (ICJ) confirmed its status, in the *Nuclear Weapons Advisory Opinion*, stating:

> The Court also recognizes that the environment is not an abstraction but represents the living space, the quality of life and the very health of human beings, including generations unborn. The existence of the general obligation of States to ensure that activities within their jurisdiction and control respect the environment of other States or of areas beyond national control is now a part of the corpus of international law relating to the environment.[20]

A year later, in the *Gabčíkovo-Nagymaros Dam Case*, the Court reaffirmed this ruling and further stated, "It is primarily in the last two decades that safeguarding the ecological balance has come to be considered an 'essential interest' of all States."[21]

---

[18] Collected in HUNTER ET AL., *supra* note 3, at 472.

[19] Stockholm Declaration, *supra* note 5; Rio Declaration, *supra* note 11.

[20] The Legality of the Threat or Use of Nuclear Weapons, Advisory Opinion, 1996 I.C.J. 226, ¶ 29 (July 8, 1996), http://www.icj-cij.org/docket/files/95/7495.pdf.

[21] The Gabcikovo-Nagymaros Project (Hung. v. Slo.), 1997 I.C.J. 7, ¶ 53 (Sept. 25, 1997), http://www.icj-cij.org/docket/files/92/7375.pdf (*see* details in Chapter 9).

Thus, we have an international rule prohibiting transboundary environmental harms, but there are still many unanswered questions about its application in real cases. What degree, amount, or level of harm is required – is it an absolute no-harm rule or is there a *de minimus* harm threshold that is acceptable? If so, what is the harm threshold – "appreciable," "significant," or "serious"? Is there a standard of care which, if the offending state meets it, absolves it of the harm? If so, is it a standard of "due diligence," "reasonable care," "best efforts under the circumstances," or "international best practice"? Should there be a "differentiated" (i.e., lower) standard for developing states (*see* § 2.1.12)? How much private sector activity should be considered under a state's "jurisdiction and control"? What remedies are provided and to whom? These and related questions will be developed in the discussions of other principles and the issue-specific chapters to come.

2.1.4   *Sustainable Development*

The most significant change in international law in recent years is the emergence of "sustainable development" as the new international paradigm for balancing society's often-conflicting environmental, economic, and social aspirations.[22] Proponents of sustainable development seek to integrate peacefully the separate (if not warring) disciplines of ecology, economic development, and human rights. We now have "sustainable development" commissions, treaty provisions, IGOs, NGOs, IFO conditions, restructurings, studies, action

---

[22] Detailed analyses of "sustainable development" include UN WORLD COMMISSION ON ENVIRONMENT AND DEVELOPMENT, OUR COMMON FUTURE (1987); INTERNATIONAL UNION FOR THE CONSERVATION OF NATURE AND NATURAL RESOURCES (IUCN), ET AL., CARING FOR THE EARTH: A STRATEGY FOR SUSTAINABLE LIVING (David A. Munro & Martin W. Holdgate eds., 1991); Philippe Sands, *International Law in the Field of Sustainable Development*, in 1994 BRIT. Y.B. INT'L L. 303 (1995); George (Rock) Pring, *Sustainable Development: Historical Perspectives and Challenges for the 21st Century*, in UN DEVELOPMENT PROGRAM & UN REVOLVING FUND FOR NATURAL RESOURCES EXPLORATION, PROCEEDINGS OF THE WORKSHOP ON THE SUSTAINABLE DEVELOPMENT OF NON-RENEWABLE RESOURCES TOWARDS THE 21ST CENTURY (1998); M. C. W. Pinto, *The Legal Context: Concepts, Principles, Standards and Institutions*, in INTERNATIONAL ECONOMIC LAW WITH A HUMAN FACE 13 (Friedl Weiss *et al.* eds., 1998); AGENDA 21 & THE UNCED PROCEEDINGS (Nicholas A. Robinson *et al.* eds., 1993); Ben Boer, *Institutionalising Ecologically Sustainable Development: The Roles of National, State, and Local Governments in Translating Grand Strategy into Action*, 31 WILLAMETTE L. REV. 307 (1995); JEREMY CAREW-REID ET AL., STRATEGIES FOR NATIONAL SUSTAINABLE DEVELOPMENT: A HANDBOOK FOR THEIR PLANNING AND IMPLEMENTATION (IUCN *et al.* 1994); UN DEVELOPMENT PROGRAMME, IMPLEMENTING THE RIO AGREEMENTS: A GUIDE TO UNDP'S SUSTAINABLE ENERGY & ENVIRONMENT DIVISION (1997); and Madeline Cohen, *A New Menu for the Hard-Rock Cafe: International Mining Ventures and Environmental Cooperation in Developing Countries*, 15 STAN. ENVTL. L.J. 130 (1996).

plans, guidelines, learned publications, and conferences spreading over the landscape like some new exotic species. Everything, it seems, can and must be made "sustainable." According to the UN, we now have "sustainable consumption," "sustainable livelihoods," "sustainable planning," "sustainable technologies," "sustainable agriculture," "sustainable construction industry activities," "sustainable social development," even "sustainable development of non-renewable resources."[23]

Surprisingly, given this massive conversion, what "sustainability" actually means is still very uncertain and controversial. Its best known formulation – the Brundtland Commission's "*development that meets the needs of the present without compromising the ability of future generations to meet their own needs*"[24] – is descriptive at best, hardly a bright-line standard. "Is it an objective, or a process, or a principle, or all of those things?" international environmental law expert Philippe Sands asks (clearly believing the latter).[25] Answering this question – giving sustainability definition, content, and limits – will be a major preoccupation of international law, lawmakers, and institutions throughout the 21st century.

Sustainable development did not, as some believe, leap full blown onto the world stage in the 1990s, like Athena from the brow of Zeus. The concept draws on a rich history of legal, political, scientific, social, and economic thought.[26] The very first UN "environmental" conference, the 1949 UN Conference on the Conservation and Utilization of Resources (UNCCUR), focused on this interrelationship between conservation and development, producing little agreement but legitimizing the UN's competence in both areas. By the 1970s, perceptions of a conflict between the twin aspirations of environmental protection and economic development were already emerging. The first "Earth Summit," the 1972 UN Stockholm Conference, "gave birth" to international environmental law, but it almost fell apart as developing countries (the "South") made it clear that the environmental standards of developed countries (the "North") could not be imposed so as to block the South's economic betterment. The influential Stockholm Declaration that emerged, while still heavily weighted toward environmental protection, moved toward compromise by validating both environment and development simultaneously, as in its famous Principle 21 (above), as well as Principle 11,

---

[23] *See* Pring, *supra* note 22, at 20–26.

[24] OUR COMMON FUTURE, *supra* note 22, at 43.

[25] Sands, *supra* note 22, at 305, 379.

[26] For the early history of the concept, *see* authorities in note 18. For a precedent-setting effort to define the emerging "science" of sustainability, co-authored by 23 of the world's most eminent experts, *see* Kates, *et al.*, *Sustainability Science*, 292 SCIENCE 641 (Apr. 27, 2001), http://www.sciencemag.org/content/292/5517/641.summary.

which states: "environmental policies of all States should enhance and not adversely affect the present or future development potential of developing countries...."[27] Credit for first actually putting the two words "sustainable" and "development" together goes to the respected International Union for the Conservation of Nature and Natural Resources (IUCN or World Conservation Union) in a 1980 report.[28]

To find solutions to the "North-South" dilemma, in 1983 UNGA established an independent body of experts from 21 developed and developing nations, creating the World Commission on Environment and Development (WCED or Brundtland Commission).[29] In 1987, after four years of work, it published its influential report, *Our Common Future*,[30] adopting "sustainable development" as its centerpiece and recommending its application worldwide. "The message of the Brundtland Report was that it is *possible* to achieve a path of economic development for the global economy which meets the needs of the present generation *without* compromising the chances of future generations to meet their needs."[31] Significantly, the WCED Report "failed, as have all subsequent documents using the phrase, to define its legal content."[32] It was, in the words of one expert observer, "a concept whose time had come, without anyone really knowing what it meant."[33]

---

[27] Stockholm Declaration, *supra* note 5.

[28] INTERNATIONAL UNION FOR THE CONSERVATION OF NATURE AND NATURAL RESOURCES (IUCN) ET AL., WORLD CONSERVATION STRATEGY: LIVING RESOURCE CONSERVATION FOR SUSTAINABLE DEVELOPMENT (1980). The first international treaty to use the phrase "sustainable development" was the 1985 ASEAN Agreement on the Conservation of Nature and Natural Resources, art. 1(1), July 9, 1985, 15 E.P.L., http://www.ecolex.org/server2.php/libcat/docs/TRE/Multilateral/En/TRE000820.txt.

[29] Process of Preparation of the Environmental Perspective to the Year 2000 and Beyond, G.A. Res. 38/161 UN Doc. No. A/RES/38/161 (Dec. 19, 1983), http://daccess-dds-ny.un.org/doc/RESOLUTION/GEN/NR0/445/53/IMG/NR044553.pdf?OpenElement. The name is in honor of its chair, Dr. Gro Harlem Brundtland, then Norway's Prime Minister, from January 1998 to January 2003, Director General of the World Health Organization.

[30] OUR COMMON FUTURE, *supra* note 22; the Report was endorsed by UNGA later that year. The WCED also created another influential entity, the Experts Group on Environmental Law, which adopted a definitive set of international environmental law principles. Experts Group on Environmental Law of the World Commission on Environment and Development, Legal Principles for Environmental Protection and Sustainable Development, June 18–20, 1986, UN Doc. WCED/86/23/Add. 1 (1986), http://habitat.igc.org/open-gates/ocf-a1.htm.

[31] D. PEARCE ET AL., BLUEPRINT FOR A GREEN ECONOMY xiii (1989) (emphasis in original).

[32] Pinto, *supra* note 22, at 16.

[33] M. Redclift, *Reflections on the "Sustainable Development" Debate, in* INTERNATIONAL SUSTAINABLE DEVELOPMENT AND WORLD ECOLOGY, *supra* note 22, at 3. Other pre-Rio uses of the sustainable development concept include the 1986 Single European Act, which injected a chapter on environmental protection into the European Community's economic treaty,

That has certainly not stopped people from trying to state a simple, generic definition. The WCED description of meeting-present-needs-without-compromising-future-needs seems excessively development-focused, without explicit concern for protecting environmental systems. To seek a better balance, the IUCN defines it as "improving the quality of human life while living within the carrying capacity of supporting ecosystems";[34] however, even this seems a bit "anthropocentric and utilitarian" to some.[35] To avoid this, the Australian government goes to the other extreme and uses the altered phrase "ecologically sustainable development" (ESD), defining it as "development that improves the total quality of life, both now and in the future, in a way that maintains the ecological processes on which life depends."[36] There are also those who reject the concept entirely:

> [S]ustainable development...ideas reflect ignorance of the history of resource exploitation and misunderstanding of the possibility of achieving scientific consensus concerning resources and the environment....[R]esources are inevitably overexploited, often to the point of collapse or extinction....[E]ven well-meaning attempts to exploit responsibly may lead to disastrous consequences....Distrust claims of sustainability.[37]

Nevertheless, the sustainability concept caught on and became the focus of the Second Earth Summit in 1992. The UN Rio Conference was the largest international undertaking on any subject in history, attended by 176 states, dozens of IGOs, thousands of NGOs, and hoards of media. Having enthusiastically endorsed the WCED Report,[38] UNGA charged the Rio Conference to "elaborate strategies...to promote sustainable and environmentally sound development in all countries."[39] This Rio did in the form of five important new developments in international environmental law: two binding treaties, the Convention on Biological Diversity[40] and the Framework Convention on

---

25 I.L.M. 503 (1986), and the 1990 Agreement establishing the European Bank for Reconstruction and Development, Article 2(1)(vii) of which requires the EBRD to "promote in the full range of its activities environmentally sound and sustainable development," 29 I.L.M. 1077 (1990).

[34] CARING FOR THE EARTH, *supra* note 22, at 10.

[35] Boer, *supra* note 22, at 318.

[36] *Id.; see also* Nanda, *supra* note 2.

[37] Donald Ludwig *et al., Uncertainty, Resource Exploitation, and Conservation: Lessons from History,* SCIENCE, Apr. 2, 1993, at 17, 36, http://www.sciencemag.org/site/feature/data/sust/pdf/260-5104-17.pdf.

[38] G.A. Res. 42/187, UN Doc. A/RES/42/187 (Feb. 29, 1988), http://www.un.org/documents/ga/res/42/ares42-187.htm.

[39] G.A. Res. 44/228, ¶ 3, UN Doc. A/RES/44/228 (Mar. 22, 1990), http://www.un.org/documents/ga/res/44/ares44-228.htm.

[40] Convention on Biological Diversity, June 5, 1992, 1760 U.N.T.S. 79, 143, 31 I.L.M. 818 (1992) (entered into force Dec. 29, 1993), http://www.cbd.int/.

Climate Change[41] and three nonbinding instruments, the Rio Declaration on Environment and Development,[42] Agenda 21,[43] and the Statement of Forest Principles.[44] All five use sustainable development as their central tenet.[45]

The Rio Declaration contains 27 principles, which reaffirm and build on the Stockholm Declaration, but are even more specific, and nearly half contain the phrase "sustainable development." Agenda 21 is a unanimously adopted, 470 page "action plan" providing numerous policies, plans, programs, processes, and other guidance for IGOs and national governments for actually implementing sustainable development in the 21st century.[46] Realistically, much of this "agenda" will never happen because of the immense multi-billion dollar per year price tag.

Both the Rio Declaration and Agenda 21 and subsequent treaties using the term "sustainable development" avoid defining it in any simple, direct way. Instead, embedded in all those pages, are at least a dozen clear principles that are the framework for the concept: (1) human needs are paramount, (2) environment and development must be integrated, (3) there must be intergenerational equity, (4) likewise intragenerational equity, (5) states have sovereignty over resources, (6) natural resources should be conserved and not be exhausted, (7) international cooperation is essential, (8) the precautionary principle should be applied, (9) the polluter-pays principle should control, (10) environmental impact assessment should become standard, (11) public participation in governance must be increased, and (12) all of this will require increased regulation at the national, local, and international levels.[47]

---

[41] United Nations Framework Convention on Climate Change, May 9, 1982, 1771 U.N.T.S. 107, 31 I.L.M. 849 (1992) (entered into force Mar. 21, 1994), http://unfccc.int/key_documents/the_convention/items/2853.php.

[42] Rio Declaration, *supra* note 11; the Rio Declaration has been "endorsed" by the UN General Assembly, G.A. Res. 47/190, ¶ 2, UN Doc. A/RES/47/190, ¶ 2 (Dec. 1992), http://www1.umn.edu/humanrts/resolutions/47/190GA1992.html.

[43] Agenda 21, at Annex 1, http://www.un.org/esa/dsd/agenda21/. A copy with excellent historical and critical commentary can be found in AGENDA 21 & THE UNCED PROCEEDINGS, *supra* note 22.

[44] Statement of Principles for a Global Consensus on the Management, Conservation, and Sustainable Development of All Types of Forests, at Annex III, http://www.un.org/documents/ga/conf151/aconf15126-3annex3.htm.

[45] For further discussion of the "sustainability" elements of all five instruments, *see* AGENDA 21 & THE UNCED PROCEEDINGS, *supra* note 22, at I, *et seq.*; Sands, *supra* note 22, at 319, 324–26 and 335 *et seq.*

[46] Agenda 21, *supra* note 43.

[47] For detailed citations to the Rio and Agenda 21 provisions supporting each of the 12 principles, *see* Pring, *supra* note 22, at 17–20.

Some of these principles have already emerged as "law" and others are in gestation, as discussed earlier in this chapter. Perhaps the single most important feature of "sustainable development" is its requirement that environmental, social, and cultural factors must be linked to, considered with, and integrated into all economic development planning and implementation.[48] Neither development which fails to take environmental protection into account, nor environmental protection which interferes with fundamental human development needs can be considered sustainable. Quite clearly international environmental law has a new standard, weighty and complex, but what exactly it means in specific contexts could take another century to work out.

2.1.5   *Right to Development*

The controversial claim that countries should recognize a "right to development" should not to be confused with the concept of "sustainable development." The right to development is a major plank in the political agenda of many developing countries,[49] and actually represents two rights in one. First, it is the relatively accepted, sovereignty-based notion that individual states have the right to control their own economies and their own path of development, even if that development exploits and damages the state's environments and resources. Second, and much more controversially, it is the view that states and individual people have a right to expect a *minimum* level of economic development or wealth, a view that the US and other rich nations have steadfastly rejected.

The first aspect, state economic self-determination with regard to natural resources, has been recognized by a majority of UN members since at least 1952.[50] The second had emerged at least by 1966 in the International Covenant on Economic, Social and Cultural Rights.[51] The dual concept flowered at the 1992 Rio Conference, Rio Principle 3 announcing: "The right to development must be fulfilled so as to equitably meet developmental and environmental needs of present and future generations."[52] This position is juxtaposed with Principle 4, which states: "In order to achieve sustainable development, environmental protection shall constitute an integral part of

---

[48] *Id.* at 17–18; Sands calls this Rio's "most important contribution," *supra* note 22, at 338.

[49] *See generally* IAN BROWNLIE, THE HUMAN RIGHT TO DEVELOPMENT (1989).

[50] G.A. Res. 626 (VII), UN GAOR, 7th Sess., Supp. No. 20, UN Doc. A/2361 (1952) (Dec. 21, 1952), http://www.un.org/depts/dhl/resguide/r7.htm.

[51] International Covenant on Economic, Social and Cultural Rights, arts. 1, 2, 10, Dec. 10, 1966, 993 U.N.T.S. 3 [hereinafter ICESCR], http://www2.ohchr.org/english/law/cescr.htm.

[52] Rio Declaration, *supra* note 11.

the development process and cannot be considered in isolation from it."[53] The developing countries fought to ensure this Principle 3 right to development would not be turned into a more limited right to "sustainable development."[54] The US and many other developed countries opposed Principle 3, denying such a right existed (calling it only a "goal") or arguing that, if it did exist, it was constrained by the Principle 4 requirement that the development be "sustainable."[55] Each side put its own "spin" on Principles 3 and 4 in their Rio interpretive statements, but, as Professor Ileana Porras points out, the right to development in Principle 3 is "unconditional," giving developing nations the better argument that their right to develop need not be accomplished only "sustainably."[56]

2.1.6 Right to a Clean, Healthful Environment

Do humans have a right to live in an environment that is clean, healthy, and not likely to hasten their deaths? It appeared the US Congress thought so in 1969 when it adopted Section 101(c) of the National Environmental Policy Act, which states in part: "The Congress recognizes that each person should enjoy a healthful environment…";[57] however, subsequent court decisions treated this as only an observation, not the creation of a legal (let alone litigatable) right. There is no right to a healthful environment in the US Constitution or other constitutions drafted before the modern-era; however, over 100 nations with modern-era constitutions have such a provision. For example, Chile's Constitution provides persons the "right to live in an environment free from contamination" which is even buttressed by a person's right to sue violators.[58]

The origins of such a human right at the international level (see further Chapter 15) can be traced to Article 3 of the 1948 UN Declaration of Human Rights, which states simply: "Everyone has the right to life.…"[59] This became binding treaty law with Article 6(1) of the International Covenant on Civil and Political Rights: "Every human being has the inherent right to life."[60]

---

[53] *Id.*

[54] Ileana Porras, The Rio Declaration: A New Basis for International Cooperation, in PHILIPPE SANDS, GREENING INTERNATIONAL LAW 20, 25 (1994).

[55] *Id.* at 25.

[56] *Id.*

[57] National Environmental Policy Act, 42 USC § 4331(c).

[58] SVITLANA KRAVCHENKO & JOHN E. BONINE, HUMAN RIGHTS AND THE ENVIRONMENT: CASES, LAW, AND POLICY 67 (2008).

[59] Universal Declaration of Human Rights, G.A. Res. 217 (III) A, UN Doc. A/RES/217(III) (Dec. 10, 1948), http://www.un.org/en/documents/udhr/.

[60] International Covenant on Civil and Political Rights, art. 6, ¶ 1, Dec. 16, 1966, 999 U.N.T.S. 171, International Covenant on Civil and Political Rights.

Stockholm Principle 1 also declares that "Man has the fundamental right to…adequate conditions of life, in an environment of a quality that permits a life of dignity and well-being…,"[61] and Rio Principle 1 pushes this to a homocentric extreme with "Human beings are at the centre of concerns about sustainable development. They are entitled to a healthy and productive life in harmony with nature."[62] Recognition of the right is finding its way into environmental treaty law, as well. Article 1 of the 1998 Aarhus Convention on Access to Information, Public Participation in Decision-making and Access to Justice in Environmental Matters (*see* § 2.2.1 for details) specifically makes the treaty's prime objective "the protection of the right of every person of present and future generations to live in an environment adequate to his or her health and well-being."[63]

Given these and other supportive legal texts, some experts take the position that the right to a healthful environment is becoming an international human right.[64] Some even argue that it is more than that – a broader "universal" right of survival for the whole human race.[65] However, the present very unequal distribution of health and wealth around the world denotes state practice does not support this. In a world where over one billion people do not have clean disease-free water to drink, where millions live in urban centers breathing uncontrolled industrial and vehicular pollution, where further millions live crushed in slums and barrios with no sanitation, where at least a billion people have less than US$ 1 a day to live on, the sad truth is that there is no apparent practice or *opinio juris*, and a legal right to a clean, healthful environment for human beings remains a dim, distant, aspirational goal.

2.1.7   *Environmental Justice: Intergenerational and Intragenerational Equity*

Sustainable development requires both a long and a broad view. The long view requires consideration of the environmental, social, cultural, and economic needs of future generations – in other words, the principle of "intergenerational equity" or equitable treatment between the generations. The

---

[61] Stockholm Declaration, *supra* note 5.

[62] Rio Declaration, *supra* note 11.

[63] UN Economic Commission for Europe (UNECE) Convention on Access to Information, Public Participation in Decision-making and Access to Justice in Environmental Matters, preamble, June 25, 1998, UN Doc. ECE/CEP/43 (1998) (entered into force Oct. 30, 2001) [hereinafter Aarhus Convention], http://www.unece.org/fileadmin/DAM/env/pp/documents/cep43e.pdf.

[64] *E.g.*, Philippe Sands, *The Environment, Community and International Law*, 30 Harv. Int'l L.J. 393 (1989).

[65] Noralee Gibson, *The Right to a Clean Environment*, 54 Saskatchewan L. Rev. 5 (1990).

broad view requires consideration of how equitably we are meeting the needs of all people in all countries in the present generation – known as the principle of "intra-generational equity" or equitable treatment within this one generation. Collectively, these values are often called "Environmental Justice," and some nations already have adopted national laws and created agency programs to advance some of these goals.[66]

The leading authority on intergenerational equity, Professor Edith Brown Weiss, explains it as follows:

> To derive the principles of intergenerational equity, it is necessary to return to the underlying purpose of our stewardship of the planet: to sustain the welfare and well-being of all generations....Four criteria should guide the development of principles of intergenerational equity. First, the principles should encourage equality among generations, neither authorizing the present generation to exploit resources to the exclusion of future generations, nor imposing unreasonable burdens on the present generation to meet indeterminate future needs. Second, they should not require one generation to predict the values of future generations. They must give future generations flexibility to achieve their goals according to their own values. Third, they should be reasonably clear in application to foreseeable situations. Fourth, they must be generally shared by different cultural traditions and be generally acceptable to different economic and political systems.
>
> We propose three basic principles of intergenerational equity. First, each generation should be required to conserve the diversity of the natural and cultural resource base....Second, each generation should be required to maintain the quality of the planet so that it is passed on in no worse condition than the present generation received it. Third, each generation should provide its members with equitable rights of access to the legacy from past generations and should conserve this access for future generations.[67]

A review of global poverty statistics demonstrates the reason for the lack of intragenerational environmental equity. Perhaps it provides sufficient perspective to recall the late Indian Prime Minister Indira Gandhi's famous saying, "The major environmental problem is poverty." It is hard to see a pattern and practice of intragenerational equity when, for example, three-fourths of the devastating deforestation occurring in the world is attributable to rural poverty which forces people to destroy their environment to attain subsistence food and fuel.[68]

---

[66] *See, e.g.*, US Environmental Protection Agency, *Environmental Justice*, http://www.epa.gov/compliance/environmentaljustice/index.html.

[67] EDITH BROWN WEISS, IN FAIRNESS TO FUTURE GENERATIONS: INTERNATIONAL LAW, COMMON PATRIMONY, AND INTERGENERATIONAL EQUITY 37–39 (1989).

[68] *See* Ved P. Nanda, *Trends in International Environmental Law*, 20 CAL. W. INT'L L.J. 187, 205 (1990).

Of course, some view these two equitable principles as being in conflict, and some even reject them as nonsense. For example, when he was the World Bank's chief economist, Lawrence Summers stated:

> The argument that a moral obligation to future generations demands special treatment of environmental investments is fatuous. We can help our descendants as much by improving infrastructure as by preserving rain forests, as much by educating children as by leaving oil in the ground, as much by enlarging our scientific knowledge as by reducing carbon dioxide in the air. However much, or little, current generations wish to weigh the interests of future generations, there is every reason to undertake investments that yield the highest returns....Once costs and benefits are properly measured, it cannot be in posterity's interest for us to undertake investments that yield less than the best return....I, for one, feel the tug of the billion people who subsist on less than $1 a day [today] more acutely than the tug of future generations.[69]

However, this point of view assumes the inevitability of ever-increasing living standards, assumes that depletion of resources is "income" rather than a loss of wealth, and assumes the infallibility of this generation's foresight in choosing the right environmental tradeoffs and investments to benefit both itself and the unborn future.

The Rio Declaration heartily endorses both intergenerational and intragenerational equity values in Principle 3, which calls on states to "equitably meet developmental and environmental needs of present and future generations."[70] It specifically endorsed intragenerational equity further in:

- Principle 5 calling for "eradicating poverty...to decrease disparities in standards of living."
- Principle 6 giving "special priority" to "[t]he special situation and needs of developing countries."
- Principle 7 noting "States have common but differentiated responsibilities" and that "developed countries" have a particularly strong responsibility both because of their past and present contribution to environmental "pressures" and because of their wealth and technology.
- Principle 11 observing that environmental standards of some countries (i.e., developed) "may be inappropriate" for others (i.e., developing).

---

[69] Lawrence Summers, *Summers on Sustainable Growth*, ECONOMIST, May 30, 1992, at 65; Dr. Summers also served as the Clinton Administration Secretary of the Treasury. A marvelously ruthless book title that sums up this perspective is economist Robert L. Heilbroner, AN INQUIRY INTO THE HUMAN PROSPECT: WITH SECOND THOUGHTS – WHAT HAS POSTERITY EVER DONE FOR ME? (3d ed. 1991).

[70] Rio Declaration, *supra* note 11.

- Principle 14 discouraging states from relocating or transferring to other states activities and substances dangerous to the environment or human health.
- Principles 20–22 emphasizing the need to advance traditionally disadvantaged or underrepresented groups, such as women, youth, and indigenous peoples.[71]

However, is this vision of equity realistic? Can we be equitable both to this generation and succeeding ones simultaneously? Garrett Hardin's "Tragedy of the Commons" counsels otherwise, telling us that "[i]t is not mathematically possible to maximize for two (or more) variables at the same time."[72] If "double maximization" is a logical impossibility, how can we fulfill our ethical obligations to the billions currently living in poverty and future generations, and the Earth itself?

2.1.8   *Equitable Utilization of Shared Resources*

Many of the earth's resources are physically shared by one or more states, including international watercourses, the oceans, migrating wildlife, transboundary ecosystems, the atmosphere, stratosphere, etc. Are these resources to be shared, and if so how? The absolute-sovereignty answer would lead to a "first-in-time-first-in-right" rule, advantageous to the earliest-developed states and disadvantageous to later-developing states, the environment, and principles of conservation. Rather than the absolute-sovereignty answer, however, the doctrine of "equitable and reasonable use" has evolved – led historically by developments in the law of international water rights and ocean fishing rights. (For a full discussion of this principle, see Chapter 9.) The doctrine of equitable and reasonable use is a sharing principle based on the balancing of a number of equitable factors in addition to historic use.

Early in the 20th century, the Permanent Court of International Justice (PCIJ) faced this issue in the *River Oder Case*, a multi-state European dispute over navigation rights on a shared river, and ruled that the riparian states had "a common legal right, the essential features of which are the perfect equality of all riparian States in the user of the whole course of the river."[73] This principle has evolved into a 1997 UN treaty which provides that states shall utilize shared international waters in "an equitable and reasonable manner,"

---

[71] *Id.*

[72] Garrett Hardin, *Tragedy of the Commons*, 162 Science 1243, text at fn. 3 (Dec. 13, 1968), http://www.sciencemag.org/content/162/3859/1243.full#xref-ref-8-1.

[73] Relating to the Territorial Jurisdiction of the International Commission of the River Oder (Czech., Den., Fr., Ger., Swed., U.K., Pol.), 1929 P.C.I.J. (ser. A) No. 23, at 5, ¶ 74 (Aug. 15), http://www.worldcourts.com/pcij/eng/decisions/1929.09.10_river_oder.htm.

balancing factors such as physical and ecological characteristics, social and economic needs, population needs, conservation, availability of alternatives, and so forth (*see* Chapter 9). The same principle has been upheld with regard to ocean fishstocks in the 1974 *Iceland Fisheries Case.*[74]

Equitable utilization has become an accepted rule of international environmental law with respect to freshwater and ocean resources. However, it is only in "progressive development," moving toward acceptance, with regard to other resources (wildlife, atmosphere, etc.) which have considerably less history of being viewed as a "shared resource."[75] Nevertheless, because the notion of equitable utilization permits a certain level of flexibility, its application can be adapted to other resources. This flexibility stems from the fact that the principle emphasizes the "reasonable" allocation of resources, based on what are deemed to be relevant factors, such as need, prior use, and other relevant interests.

2.1.9   *Conservation*

One need only look around to see that there is no consistent state practice supporting a general principle requiring conservation of natural resources. While conservation could be deemed a core legal principle of international environmental law, states have been reluctant to adopt it in any binding generalized form, preferring instead to adopt it in binding form only in treaties with discrete focus and limited application.

A great body of international environmental treaty law requires the conservation and preservation of natural areas, spectacular scenic wonders, paleontological-cultural-historic sites, endangered wildlife and plant species, biodiversity, global commons like Antarctica, even outer space (*see* Chapter 8 for details). The UN Convention on Law of the Sea (UNCLOS), while acknowledging ocean resources will be developed and exploited, imposes on states in Article 192 "the obligation to protect and preserve the marine

---

[74] Fisheries Jurisdiction (U.K. v. Ice.), 1974 I.C.J. 3 ¶ 70 (Jul. 25), http://www.icj-cij.org/docket/files/55/5977.pdf. The case, however, also transferred jurisdiction of many former "common species" to the coastal states of the world, which now share jurisdiction as the resource moves across marine boundaries. The equitable sharing concept is also proffered by UNEP as Principle 1 in its 1978 Draft Principles of Conduct in the Field of the Environment for Guidance of States in the Conservation and Harmonious Utilization of Natural Resources Shared by Two or More States, *supra* note 13.

[75] *But see* 1978 UNEP Draft Principles of Shared Natural Resources, *supra* note 13, which would apply the principle to all natural resources shared by two or more states; it need only be noted that these are an IGO pronouncement and still a "draft" after nearly a quarter century.

environment"[76] (*see* Chapter 11). Numerous other treaties create issue-specific conservation requirements.

However, no binding international legal authorities transcend the issue-specific and mandate generic, across-the-board conservation with regard to all aspects of the environment. Those that do, like the Rio Declaration and Agenda 21, are clearly aspirational. Rio broadly calls upon states to cooperate "to conserve, protect and restore the health and integrity of the Earth's ecosystem,"[77] forgo "unsustainable patterns of production and consumption,"[78] and otherwise engage in "sustainable development," one of whose central tenants is of course conservation (*see* § 2.1.4). Agenda 21 has detailed provisions on conservation of resources in Chapters 10–18.

2.1.10   *Common Heritage of Humankind – The "Global Commons"*

International law faces a unique challenge in addressing the "global commons," those areas of the environment *outside the boundaries of any state*, areas such as the high seas, deep sea bed, Antarctica, outer space, and, some authorities would add, the ozone layer, certain world-class cultural landmarks, endangered species, rainforests, coral reefs, and some genetic resources.[79] Traditional legal notions of sovereignty, capture, conquest, police power, and property rights do not fit these regions or resources comfortably in the modern world's eyes. Some kind of legal controls are needed, however, because otherwise, as Garrett Hardin warned in his seminal article, the international community will face a situation tailor-made for uncontrolled exploitation and a "Tragedy of the Commons."[80]

The international community has responded to this challenge with a new concept, "the common heritage of humankind" (CHH; occasionally one still sees the older, politically uncorrected phrase "common heritage of mankind" or CHM). CHH is generally defined as areas and/or resources: (1) "beyond the jurisdiction and sovereignty of any State,"[81] (2) that "exist for the common benefit of all,"[82] and (3) whose existence and use "affects human beings around the world."[83] One of the earliest appearances of the CHH concept

---

[76] United Nations Convention on the Law of the Sea, Dec. 10, 1982, 1833 U.N.T.S. 3, 397, http://www.un.org/depts/los/convention_agreements/texts/unclos/UNCLOS-TOC.htm.

[77] Rio Declaration, *supra* note 11 at Principle 7.

[78] *Id.* at Principle 8.

[79] *See* HUNTER ET AL., *supra* note 3, at 452.

[80] Hardin, *supra* note 72.

[81] A. E. Boyle, *State Responsibility for Breach of Obligations to Protect the Global Environment*, *in* CONTROL OVER COMPLIANCE WITH INTERNATIONAL LAW 69 (W. E. Butler ed., 1991).

[82] *Id.*

[83] Harvey J. Levin, *Regulating the Global Commons: A Case Study*, 12 RES. IN L. & ECON. 247, 252 (1989).

is in the 1972 UNESCO World Heritage Convention, which speaks of the loss of any single cultural and natural heritage site as a loss of "the heritage of all the nations of the world."[84] CHH regimes have been created by treaty, including the 1967 Outer Space Treaty ("province of all mankind"), the 1979 Moon Treaty ("common heritage of mankind"), and the 1982 Law of the Sea Treaty (the deep sea bed is "the common heritage of mankind"), all as more fully described in Chapter 8.

The idea of a "commons" system of land and resource management is not new. Time out of mind, a diverse array of resources have been managed as commons, including pastures in Switzerland, Iceland, Syria, India, medieval England, and colonial America, farmlands in Japan, fisheries in Turkey and Brazil, and irrigation systems in India, Spain, and the Philippines.[85] In modern times, the legal consequences of designating something as a "common heritage" resource are: (1) it is free from sovereignty claims of individual nations, (2) it should be under global governance and management, (3) its use must be solely for peaceful purposes, (4) information about it should be shared, (5) its access and utilization is open, provided there is no ecological harm, and (6) any economic benefit derived from it should be shared equitably by all states, not just the exploiter.[86]

The chief proponents of the CHH principle usually (but not always) are the developing nations, the "have nots." Also, the usual opponents of the concept are the "haves." For example, the US and other developed countries active in Antarctica opposed application of the concept there fearing it would wrest control from the treaty parties (*see* Chapter 8). The US and other high-tech nations also vigorously opposed applying the concept to the deep sea bed in UNCLOS for years, because of factor (6) – having to share the profits of one's exploitation with other nations – and only signed after the "shared benefits" provisions were eliminated (*see* Chapter 11). In the case of the Biodiversity Convention, making genetic stock a CHH was opposed by the biologically rich developing countries, like Brazil and Colombia, which feared losing control and income from possibly patentable genetic resources in their own rainforests.[87]

---

[84] Convention Concerning the Protection of World Cultural and Natural Heritage, Dec. 17, 1975, 2d Preamble, 27 UST 37, UN Doc. ST/LEG/SER.C/10US, http://whc.unesco.org/en/convention/.

[85] *See* E. Ostrom, Governing the Commons: The Evolution of Institutions for Collective Action 48–102 (1990); T. Eggertsson, *Analyzing Institutional Successes and Failures: A Millenium of Common Mountain Pastures in Iceland*, 12 Int'l Rev. L. & Econ. 423 (1992); Making the Commons Work (D. W. Bromley ed., 1992).

[86] Christopher C. Joyner, Comment, *Legal Implications of the Concept of the Common Heritage of Mankind*, 35 Int'l & Comp. L.Q. 190, 192–95 (1986).

[87] Christopher Stone, The Gnat Is Older Than Man 35 (1993).

While the CHH concept has received very favorable support from many expert commentators, concededly there are those who deride it as a mere "label [that] simply divides the same amount of resources among an increasing number of people."[88] When nations cannot agree to designate something a CHH – they may default to another important, but more limited principle: "common concern of humankind," as discussed next.

2.1.11 *Common Concern of Humankind* – Erga Omnes

International law is gradually turning its eyes toward things long considered "wholly domestic." For example, international human rights, humanitarian, and labor laws predominantly look at treatment of people within national borders. The "common heritage of humankind" principle may work on global commons, but it encounters strong sovereignty-based resistance when attempts are made to apply that international-control/benefits-sharing concept to environments, resources, or actions within individual nations' jurisdictions. Nevertheless, "a growing consensus has emerged that the planet is ecologically interdependent and that humanity may have a collective interest (based on environmental concerns) in certain activities that take place or resources that are located wholly within state boundaries."[89] The compromise that has emerged in these cases is to designate the matter a "common *concern* of humankind" (CCH).

CCH means the international community should have both the right and the duty to take joint or separate action to prevent environmental harm which can adversely affect all or large segments of humanity.[90] Examples include ozone layer depletion, global climate change, loss of biological diversity, extinction of endangered species, etc. Thus, CCH can be considered an application of the doctrine of *erga omnes* ("towards all"), recognized by the ICJ in the *Barcelona Traction Light and Power Co. Ltd. Case*:

> [A]n essential distinction should be drawn between the obligations of a State towards the international community as a whole, and those arising *vis-à-vis* another State.... By their very nature the former are the concern of all States. In view of the importance of the rights involved, all States can be held to have a legal interest in their protection; they are obligations *erga omnes*.[91]

---

[88] Erin A. Clancy, *The Tragedy of the Global Commons*, 5 IND. J. GLOBAL LEGAL STUD. 601, 603 (1998).

[89] HUNTER ET AL., *supra* note 3, at 459.

[90] Commentary to Article 3 of the International Union for the Conservation of Nature (IUCN), Draft Covenant on Environment and Development 36 (2004) http://www.i-c-e-l .org/english/EPLP31EN_rev2.pdf.

[91] Barcelona Traction, Light and Power Co., Ltd. (Bel. v. Sp.) ¶ 33, 1970 I.C.J. 3 (Feb. 5), http://www.icj-cij.org/docket/files/50/5387.pdf.

The ICJ has made it clear that this principle applies in the environmental context, ruling in the 1997 *Gabčíkovo-Nagymaros Dam Case* that "safeguarding the ecological balance has come to be considered an 'essential interest' of all States."[92] Viewed another way, the CCH or *erga omnes* interest is a doctrine of standing, authorizing states to bring *actio popularis* (legal action on behalf of the people).

Thus far, several treaties have designated their specific subject matters as "common concerns of humankind" in their preambles, including the 1992 UN Framework Convention on Climate Change[93] and the 1992 Biodiversity Convention.[94] Perhaps more significantly, without using the CCH phrase, two of the newer treaty regimes – the Montreal Ozone Protocol and the Basel Hazardous Waste Convention – permit parties to challenge other parties' noncompliance without requiring that they demonstrate actual injury.[95] A somewhat related treaty approach is to insert a "take-appropriate-measures" provision, which expressly gives all parties both the right and the obligation to "take appropriate measures to enforce the provisions" of the treaty.[96]

Aside from express recognition in these specific-subject treaties, there is insufficient state practice to claim that customary international law recognizes a broad CCH or *erga omnes* right exists to protect the environment generally, other than possibly in recognized global commons like the high seas, Antarctica, or outer space. No doubt part of this is the international community's general reluctance to accord states "unilateral" law enforcement powers (*see* Rio Principle 12). While support for the CCH concept is growing, there are still glaring instances of contrary state practice, such as the complete failure of states to take action against the former Soviet Union for the 1986 Chernobyl nuclear plant disaster, the US resistance to CHH applying to the deep sea bed, and the failure to date of the World Trade Organization (WTO) adjudication bodies to recognize a state right of unilateral or "extraterritorial" action to protect the environment if such actions interfere with free trade.[97]

---

[92] The Gabcikovo-Nagymaros Project, *supra* note 21, ¶ 53.

[93] Framework Convention on Climate Change, *supra* note 41, 1st Preamble ("change in the Earth's climate and its adverse effects are a common concern of humankind").

[94] Convention on Biological Diversity *supra* note 40, 3d Preamble ("the conservation of Biological Diversity is a common concern of humankind").

[95] The Basel Convention on the Control of Transboundary Movements of Hazardous Wastes and Their Disposal, art. 9, Mar. 22, 1989, 28 I.L.M. 649, http://www.basel.int/. The Montreal Protocol on Substances that Deplete the Ozone Layer, Sept. 16, 1987, S. Treaty Doc. No. 100–10, 1522 UNTS 29, http://ozone.unep.org/new_site/en/index.php.

[96] *E.g.*, CITES, *supra* note 6, art. VIII(1).

[97] *See* collected authorities excerpted in LAKSHMAN GURUSWAMY ET AL., INTERNATIONAL ENVIRONMENTAL LAW AND WORLD ORDER 924–51 (1999).

2.1.12   *Common but Differentiated Responsibilities*

Successful national programs of environmental protection such as those adopted by the North American or European countries are enormously expensive undertakings. The US Environmental Protection Agency (USEPA), in FY 2011 had over 17,000 employees and a budget of nearly US $8.7 billion a year.[98] The costs of the environmental, social, and economic programs necessary to achieve sustainable development worldwide will total hundreds of billions of dollars a year, according to Agenda 21.[99]

Not only do many developing nations feel their economies cannot afford this, many feel that they should not have to bear this expense because they "did not cause the problem." Therefore, they view attempts by developed nations to "export" their environmental standards as a cynical subterfuge to suppress the South's economic development ("environmental colonialism"). Part of the developing countries' argument is that the US and Western European nations became rich because they exploited their environments to build their economies in the 19th century, and therefore are "hypocrites" for now trying to prevent other countries from doing the same.

A sad, but frequently heard slogan in these debates is that environmental degradation is "rich man's problem, rich man's solution."[100] What are the "rich" countries doing to help solve the problem? Developed countries' environmental foreign aid to developing countries is low. The US, for example, spends less than 0.5 percent of the federal budget on all foreign economic and humanitarian assistance, and only about $493 million annually funds environmental programs in other countries.[101] While the largest donor in dollars, in terms of gross national product (GNP), the US provides the least foreign assistance of any major industrialized nation.[102] Japan has a larger foreign assistance program than the US, and Germany and Denmark both spend a much higher percentage of their foreign aid on the environment than does the US.[103]

On the other hand, some developing countries are already, or on track to become, the world's biggest polluters (think of the giants – China, Brazil,

---

[98] US Environmental Protection Agency, *EPA's Budget & Spending*, http://www.epa.gov/planandbudget/budget.html.

[99] *See* Robinson, *supra* note 22 at xxxvii–xciv.

[100] E. P. Barratt-Brown, *Building a Monitoring and Compliance Regime Under the Montreal Protocol*, 16 YALE J. INT'L L. 519, 534 (1991).

[101] US Agency for International Development (USAID), *About USAID*, http://www.usaid.gov/about_usaid/; USAID, *Frequently Asked Questions*, http://www.usaid.gov/faqs.html#q7; USAID, *Where Does USAID's Money Go?*, http://www.usaid.gov/policy/budget/money/.

[102] *Id.*

[103] *Id.*

and India).[104] Thus, any environmental treaty regime must secure the support and participation of the developing nations to avoid pollution havens and economic free riders if it is to have any hope of success.[105]

The 1992 Rio Conference recognized this "North-South" dichotomy and made significant strides to solve the controversy. Specifically, the Rio Conference adopted the principle that all states have a "common" obligation to protect the environment but, depending upon their wealth and technology, they have "differentiated" levels of duty to act. Rio Principle 7 states:

> States shall cooperate in a spirit of global partnership to conserve, protect and restore the health and integrity of the Earth's ecosystem. In view of the different contributions to global environmental degradation, States have common but differentiated responsibilities. The developed countries acknowledge the responsibility that they bear in the international pursuit of sustainable development in view of the pressure their societies place on the global environment and of the technologies and financial resources they command.[106]

Thus, Rio recognizes that states have "common but differentiated responsibilities" (CBDR) for two distinct reasons: first, because the developed industrialized nations have contributed more to today's environmental problems; second, because they have vastly more technological and financial resources to contribute to the solution.[107] Principle 7 furthers Principle 6, the latter calling for a "special priority" to be given to "the special situation and needs of developing countries, particularly the least developed and those most environmentally vulnerable...."[108]

A leading authority on CBDR, Dr. Anita Halvorssen, points out that it is both an ethical principle (an extension of the intragenerational equity principle discussed in § 2.1.7 above) as well as a very pragmatic participation-maximizing device:

---

[104] China has surpassed the US as the world's largest carbon emitter. *See, e.g.*, Elisabeth Rosenthal, *China Increases Lead as Biggest Carbon Emitter*, New York Times, June 14, 2008, http://www.nytimes.com/2008/06/14/world/asia/14china.html; UN, *Millennium Development Goal Indicators: Carbon Dioxide Emissions*, http://mdgs.un.org/unsd/mdg/SeriesDetail.aspx?srid=749&crid=. China, Brazil, and India emit more greenhouse gases than the US and EU combined. *See* George W. (Rock) Pring, *The United States Perspective, in* Kyoto: From Principles to Practice 189 at n. 16 (Peter Cameron & Donald Zillman eds., 2001); Edith Brown Weiss, *International Environmental Law: Contemporary Issues and the Emergence of a New World Order*, 81 Geo. L. J. 675, 706 (1993).

[105] Anita Halvorssen, Equality Among Unequals in International Environmental Law: Differential Treatment for Developing Countries 3 (1999).

[106] Rio Declaration, *supra* note 11 at Principle 7.

[107] *See* Porras, *supra* note 54, at 29.

[108] Rio Declaration, *supra* note 11 at Principle 7.

This principle [of CBDR] emanated from the application of the broader principle of equity in international law, and from the acknowledgement that the differing situations of the developing countries need to be considered if they are to be encouraged to take part in international environmental agreements. The application of this principle likely requires all states to participate in…adopting environmental standards, yet there should be different obligations for specific states, taking into account their contributions to a particular environmental problem, and ability to respond, prevent, reduce, or control the identified threat. This method allows for greater flexibility…thereby increasing the likelihood of their participation in the treaties.[109]

While some decry CBDR as inequitable, asymmetrical, or wealth redistribution,[110] it has become an established principle of international environmental law. The Kyoto Protocol on Climate Change provides specific greenhouse-gas-reduction requirements for developed countries only, and it establishes different reporting requirements for developed, developing, and least developed countries. However, this asymmetry became one of the major arguments against ratification in the US (*see* § 10.3).[111] Similarly, the Montreal Protocol in Article 5 sets up a delayed compliance schedule for developing countries (*see* § 10.2). One of the strongest arguments against CBDR is that when international agreements are watered down to secure participation by developing and least developed countries (LDCs), the results may become more symbolic than effective.[112]

CBDR is a principle we can expect to see utilized more in international environmental treaties. While it is unlikely to emerge anytime soon as acknowledged international customary law, its growing acceptance in treaties can be attributed to ethical and pragmatic benefits. For now, its application is limited as countries seek to avoid true wealth redistribution, which would require developed countries to provide developing countries financial assistance, capacity building, technology transfer, and trade advantages (since deferred compliance schedules can be viewed as a competitive cost advantage).

2.1.13   *The Polluter-Pays Principle*

A core principle of mainstream economics is that prices for goods and services should reflect or "internalize" the *full* costs of their production, including the total costs of their human health, environmental, natural resource,

---

[109] HALVORSSEN, *supra* note 105, at 3–4 (footnotes omitted).
[110] Time Magazine's pithy description of the Rio Conference was, "It comes down to a matter of cash. The North has it. The South needs it." Philip Elmer-Dewitt, *Rich v. Poor (Earth Summit)*, TIME, June 1, 1992, at 43.
[111] Pring, *The United States Perspective, supra* note 104.
[112] *See* Nanda, *supra* note 2, at 17.

social, and cultural impacts. However, economists recognize that the market system often fails to make producers or their customers accountable for paying their full costs, so that many of these costs become "externalities," falling outside that market system.[113] For example, when a factory discharges untreated wastes and injures the lives and properties of others, it is not paying the "total social costs" of its product and is in fact shifting some of those costs so that innocent persons are made to bear them involuntarily. This begins a chain of diseconomic events: the externalized costs will not be taken into account by the polluter; the polluter will have no (dis)incentive to reduce the pollution; costs will then shift to victims not benefiting from the economic activity; this amounts to a subsidy to the polluter and a tax on the victims; as a result the polluter's conduct will be economically inefficient; and total social wealth will not be maximized or properly distributed.[114]

This polluter-pays principle has a fairly long history of acceptance in US and EU environmental law. It has been a central tenet of US common law and statute at least since the 1970s,[115] and it was endorsed by the OECD and EC in 1972 and 1973 respectively.[116] However, it is very controversial with developing countries, where the burden of internalizing pollution control and other presently externalized environmental costs is viewed as a luxury their economies cannot afford. An opposite rule would be "make the victim pay," and, while this seems outrageous at first blush, "bribing polluters not to pollute" is a market approach advanced by economist and Nobel Laureate Ronald Coase among others.[117] It can also be seen in some of today's environmental transactions, for example when an affluent Germany pays for the pollution control equipment on a near-bankrupt Polish factory to stop its transboundary pollution, or when the US sends millions of dollars in foreign aid to the Russian Federation to assist it in its cleanup of its North Sea nuclear submarines, or when the NGO Nature Conservancy subsidizes Brazil to protect its rainforests in "debt-for-nature swaps."

---

[113] *See* GURUSWAMY ET AL., *supra* note 97, at 277; ALEXANDRE KISS & DINAH SHELTON, INTERNATIONAL ENVIRONMENTAL LAW 95 (2000).

[114] *See* ROGER W. FINDLEY & DANIEL A. FARBER, ENVIRONMENTAL LAW IN A NUTSHELL 81–82 (2000).

[115] *See generally id.* at 133 *et seq.* Perhaps the most notable recent US manifestation can be seen in the "Findings and Policy" section of the Pollution Prevention Act of 1990, 42 U.S.C. § 13101.

[116] OECD, Council Recommendation on Guiding Principles Concerning International Economic Aspects of Environmental Policies, C(72)128 (May 26, 1972); *Sources and Nature of EU Environmental Law and Policy*, 3 EU L. REP. (CCH) 3347-1 (1995).

[117] Ronald Coase, *The Problem of Social Cost*, 3 J. LAW & ECON. 1 (1960).

The 1972 Stockholm Declaration does not mention the polluter-pays principle, so that even its qualified acceptance in Rio Principle 16 is a significant
step forward: "National authorities should endeavor to promote...internal-
ization of environmental costs" so that "the polluter should, in principle,
bear the cost of pollution, with due regard to the public interest and without distorting international trade and investment."[118] Agenda 21 echoes this
allocation of responsibility (*see* ¶ 8.28);[119] however, this was a highly divisive
issue in Rio and the resulting compromise language can best be called very
"soft" law that is not yet a universally accepted rule.

2.1.14   *State Responsibility and Liability*

International law cannot deal with violations of law by sovereigns in quite
the simple way national tort or contract law deals with violations by individuals. Instead, under international law states are "responsible" for violations
or breaches of their duties or obligations.[120] Thus, a state that violates international environmental law – the no-harm rule, the prior notice rule, and
other "hard" laws described in this chapter – will, in theory, be held responsible for that violation.[121] Put another way, every internationally wrongful
act of a state subjects it to responsibility.[122] The remedies for responsibility
include both cessation of the conduct threatening or causing the violation
and reparations. Reparations are actions which "must 'as far as possible' wipe
out all of the consequences of the illegal act."[123] This can include restitution
in kind, monetary compensation, or satisfaction (an apology, disciplinary
action against individuals responsible, and the like).[124]

---

[118] Rio Declaration, *supra* note 11.

[119] Agenda 21, *supra* note 43, ¶ 8.28.

[120] The Factory at Chorzow, (Ger. v. Pol) 1928 P.C.I.J. (ser. A) No. 17, 29 (July 26), http://
www.worldcourts.com/pcij/eng/decisions/1927.07.26_chorzow.htm; The Corfu Channel,
(U.K. v. Alb.) 1949 I.C.J. 4, ¶¶ 65 and 70 (Apr. 9), http://www.icj-cij.org/docket/files/1/1645.
pdf.

[121] *See* Restatement (Third) of the Law of Foreign Relations Law of The United
States § 601 (1987).

[122] International Law Commission, Draft Articles on Responsibility of States for Intentionally
Wrongful Acts, July 12, 1996, art. 1, Report of the ILC on the Work of Its Forty-Eighth
Session, UN Doc. A/51/10 and Corr. 1, at 125, 37 I.L.M. 440 (1998), http://untreaty.un.org/
ilc/texts/instruments/english/commentaries/9_6_2001.pdf.

[123] The Gabcikovo-Nagymaros Project, *supra* note 21, ¶ 150.

[124] *See* Restatement, *supra* note 121, § 602.

There is a great theoretical debate among scholars whether responsibility requires "fault" or can be assigned in circumstances where there is "no fault."[125] The highly respected UN International Law Commission (ILC) in its Draft Articles on State Responsibility takes the position that responsibility requires fault (wrongful intentionality or negligence). That assessment, however, leaves uncovered much environmental harm that is caused by states without fault (unintentionally, non-negligently, or despite due diligence), so the ILC has created a parallel basis for remedies if the state is not at fault, calling it state "liability."[126] These articles bear the self-defining title of Draft Articles on International Liability for Injurious Consequences Arising Out of Acts Not Prohibited by International Law.[127] Thus, the ILC conceives two alternative jurisprudential bases for rectifying harms to the environment or environmental principles: fault-based "responsibility" and no-fault (strict or absolute) "liability," meaning essentially that a state act which does not violate international environmental law might well give rise to liability if its damaging consequences are sufficiently severe.

In practical fact, both principles remain underutilized and theoretical in the real world. Few treaties incorporate either concept explicitly (the way national legislation would have an "Enforcement" section). Indicatively, both Stockholm Principle 22 and Rio Principle 13 contain the identical aspiration that states must cooperate to "develop further" rules of liability and compensation, which suggests not much progress is being made.[128] Few countries bring judicial or arbitral challenges against other countries on either theory, as the paucity of international environmental cases attests, preferring to use diplomatic channels and more collegial forms of dispute resolution (although in these, concededly, responsibility is the stated or assumed basis of the diplomatic claims). While responsibility is a firmly fixed principle in theory, as compared to liability which is not, experts lament that there is very little overt state practice of either.[129]

---

[125] For an overview of the conflicting authorities and arguments, *see* GURUSWAMY ET AL., *supra* note 97, at 348–70.

[126] *Id.*; LAKSHMAN GURUSWAMY, INTERNATIONAL ENVIRONMENTAL LAW IN A NUTSHELL 95 (3d ed. 2007).

[127] International Law Commission, Draft Articles on International Liability for Injurious Consequences Arising Out of Acts Not Prohibited by International Law, Report of the ILC on the Work of Its Forty-First Session, UN GAOR, 44th Sess., Supp. No. 10, at 222, UN Doc. A/44/10 (1989).

[128] Rio Declaration, *supra* note 11, at Principle 13; Stockholm Declaration, *supra* note 5, at Principle 22.

[129] *See* GURUSWAMY ET AL., *supra* note 97, at 336.

2.2 Fundamental Procedural Principles

2.2.1 Public Participation

A public participation explosion has been occurring throughout the world in the last four decades, particularly in the environmental arena.[130] "Public participation," "citizen involvement," or "stakeholder engagement" in government decision-making has been a defining feature of democracies and communal societies since the dawn of time. Today a number of nations' laws, institutions, and political styles encourage citizens to speak out, petition, lobby, debate, campaign, testify, demonstrate, litigate, and otherwise attempt to encourage or discourage government action.[131] The 1948 Universal Declaration of Human Rights recognized that "Everyone has the right to take part in the government of his country, directly or through freely chosen representatives."[132] The right to participate politically is viewed as an essential component of sustainable development by Agenda 21, ¶ 23.2:

> One of the fundamental prerequisites for the achievement of sustainable development is broad public participation in decision-making.... This includes the need of individuals, groups and organizations to...participate in decisions, particularly those that potentially affect the communities in which they live and work [and to]...have access to information relevant to environment and development...[and] environmental protection measures.[133]

The concept that the governed should engage in their own governance is "explosive" not only in the way it is expanding in law and practice, but also in its types, which can range from the mildest of spoken or written comments to obstreperous public hearings to mass protest demonstrations, even to violent rebellion. Its pragmatic rationale is captured in the classic observation of US Supreme Court Justice Louis Brandeis:

> Those who won our independence believed...that public discussion is a political duty.... [T]hey knew that...it is hazardous to discourage thought, hope and imagination; that fear breeds repression; that repression breeds hate; that hate

---

[130] These public participation sections are drawn from the detailed treatment of this topic in George (Rock) Pring & Susan Y. Noé, *The Emerging International Law of Public Participation Affecting Global Mining, Energy, and Resources Development, in* Human Rights in Natural Resource Development: Public Participation in the Sustainable Development of Mining and Energy Resources (Donald Zillman, Alastair Lucas & George (Rock) Pring eds., 2002). That chapter and book can be referred to for more in-depth discussion and citation to sources.

[131] George W. Pring & Penelope Canan, SLAPPs: Getting Sued for Speaking Out 15 (1996).

[132] Universal Declaration of Human Rights, *supra* note 59, at 71.

[133] Agenda 21, *supra* note 43.

menaces stable government; that the path of safety lies in the opportunity to discuss freely supposed grievances and proposed remedies; and that the fitting remedy for evil counsels is good ones. Believing in the power of reason as applied through public discussion, they eschewed silence coerced by law – the argument of force in its worst form.[134]

The spread of public participation is certainly uneven. While some countries (notably in the "North") have incorporated the concept in their laws and political ethos, other countries are only beginning to experiment with it, and still others are opposing it as a threat to established public and private interests.

> Of course, not all states are democratically constituted in such a way as to even maintain the pretense of vesting ultimate authority in the citizenry. What is more, as in many countries where the real power lies with the military rather than with elected representatives of the people, authoritarian structures often persist behind the façade of constitutionalism. In other countries, like the United States, moneyed interests vastly distort the representative process, as do national security doctrine and practice, which lend credence to broad claims of secrecy and even public deception.[135]

Nevertheless, a number of modern factors are accelerating the spread of public participation, including in (1) the independence-democratization trends in the Arab world, some of the former Soviet bloc countries, and Africa, Asia, and Latin America; (2) adoption of the "sustainable development" principle in international environmental law; (3) the international NGO environmental movement and its insistence on political participation; (4) incorporation of public participation requirements by major IFOs like the World Bank; (5) international human rights law recognition of political participation as a human right; (6) increasing recognition of rights of indigenous peoples, local communities, and other previously marginalized groups; and (7) the internet and social media, which has so vastly increased the public's ability to obtain, analyze, and spread information and views.

What does "public participation" mean? One of the best (and broadest) definitions is that of the Organization of American States (OAS): "[A]ll interaction between government and civil society...includ[ing] the process by which government and civil society open dialogue, establish partnerships, share information, and otherwise interact to design, implement, and evaluate development policies, projects, and programs."[136] It further defines the key

---

[134] Whitney v. California, 274 US 357, 375–76 (1927) (Brandeis, J., concurring).

[135] Richard Falk & Andrew Strauss, *On the Creation of Global Peoples Assembly: Legitimacy and the Power of Popular Sovereignty*, 36 STAN. J. INT'L L. 191, 192 (2000).

[136] Organization of American States Inter-American Council for Integral Development (OAS CIDI), *Inter-American Strategy for the Promotion of Public Participation in Decision Making for Sustainable Development*, at "Introduction," para. 2, CIDI/RES. 98 (V-o/00), OEA/Ser.W/II.5, CIDI/doc.25/00 (Apr. 20, 2000), http://www.oas.org/dsd/PDF_files/ispenglish.pdf.

term "civil society" as including "individuals, the private sector, the labor sector, political parties, academics, and other non-governmental actors and organizations."[137]

The benefits of public participation arguably include public awareness and education, expression, empowerment, strengthening, conflict-reduction, acceptance of decisions, government accountability, political legitimacy, and decisions that are better, more equitable, more environmentally protective, and more reflective of local needs and public values. Arguments against it include the perceptions that the general public is ill-equipped to deal with technical issues, the substantial time and resource demands, its tendency toward lowest-common-denominator decisions, control by special-interest groups, elitism (upper classes participate more), and citizen frustration if goals are not achieved.

While the United States is frequently held up as a "democratic model," the truth is no comprehensive right or practice of public participation existed even in the US until the 1960s.[138] In that decade, three legal developments occurred that empowered the then-fledgling environmental, peace, civil rights, women's rights, consumer rights, and other movements and actually gave rise to today's extensive public participation in the US:

> 1. In 1966, Congress adopted the Freedom of Information Act,[139] requiring every agency of the federal government to make available for public inspection and copying all of the agencies' "records," with only limited exceptions and with substantial monetary penalties for failure to produce;
>
> 2. Also in 1966, Congress amended the Administrative Procedure Act to require advance public notice of government agency plans and actions and extensive opportunities for the public to make input through written comments, public meetings, hearings, and the like;[140] and
>
> 3. In 1971, US tax laws and regulations were administratively interpreted to recognize "public interest law firms" (PILFs) as tax-exempt charitable organizations,[141] qualifying them to receive millions of dollars in tax-deductible funding from individuals and foundations, effectively subsidizing the proliferation of such "law reform" litigation groups in the US.[142]

The international law of public participation began in the 1970s, expanded in the 1980s, and really began to take hold in a number of "hard" law treaties

---

[137] *Id.*

[138] For further discussion of this, *see* Pring & Noé, *supra* note 130.

[139] Freedom of Information Act, 5 USC § 552. State and local governments followed suit with "Public Records Acts," adding immeasurably to citizen access to information.

[140] 5 USC § 553 *et seq.*

[141] US Internal Revenue Service, Rev. Proc. 71–39, 1971–2 C.B. 574 (July 1971); 1971 IRB LEXIS 340.

[142] *See* Oliver Houck, *With Charity for All*, 93 YALE L.J. 1415 (1984).

in the 1990s. Foremost among these is the 1998 UNECE Convention on Access to Information, Public Participation in Decision-making and Access to Justice in Environmental Matters (Aarhus Convention).[143] It would be hard to overstate the significance of this treaty. The Aarhus Convention is the first international treaty devoted entirely to public participation, the first to cover comprehensively all aspects of the subject, and the first to link it with government accountability, transparency, and responsiveness. Then-UN Secretary-General Kofi Annan praised this extraordinary international law development as "the most ambitious venture in environmental democracy undertaken under the auspices of the United Nations... [and] a remarkable step forward in the development of international law.[144]

Aarhus' sponsor and promoter, the UNECE, is by no means limited to Europe – its 56 member states span virtually the entire "North" or developed industrial world, including Western, Central, and Eastern Europe, the Newly Independent States (former USSR), Israel, Canada, and the US. The Aarhus Convention entered into force in 2001,[145] and as time goes on it is expected to have a "trickle-down" effect among many other countries as well.

Today public participation has moved beyond mere public relations and political sloganeering and is emerging in a growing body of legal requirements nationally and internationally. In becoming "law," public participation promises to define and redefine the major economic development projects and the major environmental protection efforts of the 21st century. Public participation is typically divided into three distinct forms, as seen in the title to the Aarhus Convention: (1) access to information, (2) access to public participation in decision-making, and (3) access to justice. Each of these three "pillars" of public participation is treated differently in the law, but they are closely interrelated in practice, because none can succeed without the support of the other two. Since so many issues today have multistate or transboundary aspects, a fourth key factor in public participation law is how it applies to citizens or interests of countries other than the decision-making country. This fourth factor is variously called "nondiscrimination," "equal treatment," or "national treatment."

The following four subsections take up each of these factors in turn.

2.2.1.1 *Access to Information*
Access to information is the most basic of political rights, as no meaningful public participation can occur without relevant knowledge. How is the

---

[143] Aarhus Convention, *supra* note 63.

[144] UNEP, *UNEP welcomes entry into force of Aarhus Convention,* http://www.unep.org/ Documents.Multilingual/default.asp?DocumentID=224&ArticleID=2950&l=en.

[145] *Aarhus Convention,* UNECE, http://www.unece.org/env/pp/welcome.html.

public to participate in environmental decision-making or access to justice if it lacks necessary information about the nature of a project, the timing and scope of planning, resources affected, impacts expected, risks involved, or alternative approaches?

This right of access to information is a recognized human right,[146] an element of the domestic legislation of many states,[147] and a central concept of EIA systems (*see* Chapter 6). Access to information imposes two different duties on government: first, a reactive duty to produce information in response to requests; second, a proactive duty to compile, prepare, and distribute certain information to the public without being asked. This latter duty appears in "right to know" laws, such as those requiring governments to warn of certain environmental dangers.[148]

Since the 1970s, access to information provisions have found their way into a number of international environmental law authorities. The first steps were faltering at best: The very statist 1972 Stockholm Declaration does not expressly mention public information access or participation at all, although its Principle 19 does term environmental education "essential," and its preambles recognize that "citizens and communities and…enterprises and institutions at every level" need to share in defending and improving the environment.[149] However, in an apparent first, that same year the 1972 World Heritage Convention included a proactive access to information requirement, stipulating that states "shall undertake to keep the public broadly informed of the dangers threatening this heritage and of activities carried on in pursuance of this Convention."[150]

The 1980s saw a number of new information access provisions, including the 1982 World Charter for Nature (adopted by the UN General Assembly by a vote of 111-1, with only the US voting against),[151] the 1985 EC Directive

---

[146] Universal Declaration of Human Rights, *supra* note 59, art. 19; ICCPR, *supra* note 60, art. 19(2).

[147] Maria Gavouneli, *Access to Environmental Information: Delimitation of a Right*, 13 Tul. Envtl. L.J. 303, 306 (2000) ("a fundamental right of access to administrative information is contained in the domestic legislation of all EC Member States"). Comparably, the US has its statutory Freedom of Information Act (FOIA), 5 USC. § 552 (1994).

[148] *E.g.*, the US Emergency Planning & Community Right-to-Know Act of 1986 (EPCRA), 42 U.S.C. § 11001 *et seq.*

[149] Stockholm Declaration, *supra* note 5.

[150] World Heritage Convention, *supra* note 84, art. 27(2).

[151] World Charter for Nature, G.A. Res. 37/7 (Annex), UN GAOR, 37th Sess., Supp. No. 51, at 17, UN Doc. A/37/51, art. 16, (Oct. 28, 1982) (all planning affecting nature "shall be disclosed to the public by appropriate means in time to permit effective consultation and participation") http://www.un.org/documents/ga/res/37/a37r007.htm.

on Environmental Impact Assessment,[152] the 1985 ASEAN Conservation Agreement,[153] the 1986 WCED Experts Group on Environmental Law Legal Principles,[154] and the 1989 Basel Hazardous Waste Convention.[155]

The 1990s moved the right to know into high gear. In a pioneering step, the European Community in 1990 adopted a complete directive "On Access to Environmental Information,"[156] which served as the inspiration for the 1998 Aarhus Convention. There followed the 1992 Rio Declaration Principle 10 which states that "[a]t the national level, each individual shall have appropriate access to information concerning the environment that is held by public authorities, including information on hazardous materials and activities in their communities."[157] The 1992 Agenda 21, the detailed "blueprint" for sustainable development approved at Rio, expands on this by extending the right to "groups and organizations" in addition to individuals.[158] A number of 1990s treaties put access to information into "hard" law, including some with extremely detailed provisions and sanctions for violations of the public right to know.[159]

---

[152] Council Directive of 27 June 1985 On the Assessment of the Effects of Certain Public and Private Projects on the Environment, Council Directive 85/337/EEC, art. 6(2), 1985 O.J. (L 175) 40, http://ec.europa.eu/environment/eia/full-legal-text/85337.htm. The directive has since been amended.

[153] ASEAN Agreement on the Conservation of Nature and Natural Resources, *supra* note 28.

[154] WCED, *Legal Principles for Environmental Protection and Sustainable Development, supra* note 30, Principle 4(b) (states "shall establish systems for the collection and dissemination of data"); *id.* art. 6 (states "shall inform all persons in a timely manner of activities which may significantly affect their use of a natural resource or their environment").

[155] *Supra* note 95, at art. 4(2)(h) (states "shall take the appropriate measures to…co-operate in…the dissemination of information on the transboundary movement of hazardous wastes and other wastes").

[156] Council Directive 90/313/EEC of 7 June 1990 on the freedom of access to information on the environment, 1990 O.J. (L 158), at 56, http://eur-lex.europa.eu/LexUriServ/LexUriServ .do?uri=CELEX:31990L0313:EN:HTML. In 2003 this directive was repealed and replaced by a more comprehensive directive.

[157] Rio Declaration, *supra* note 11.

[158] Agenda 21, *supra* note 43 ¶ 23.2.

[159] *E.g.*, United Nations Framework Convention on Climate Change, *supra* note 41, arts. 6(a) (ii), 12(9), 12(10); Convention for the Protection of the Marine Environment of the North-East Atlantic arts. 9(1)–(4), Sept. 22, 1992, 1999 U.N.T.S. No. 14, http://www.ospar.org/ html_documents/ospar/html/ospar_convention_e_updated_text_2007.pdf; Convention on the Transboundary Effects of Industrial Accidents art. 9(1) and Annex VIII, Mar. 17, 1992, 31 I.L.M. 1330, http://ec.europa.eu/environment/seveso/pdf/98685ec_conv.pdf; Convention on the Protection and Use of Transboundary Watercourses and International Lakes arts. 16(1)-(2), Mar. 17, 1992, C.E.T.S. 150, 31 I.L.M. 1312 (1992), http://www.unece.org/ env/water; Convention on Civil Liability for Damage Resulting From Activities Dangerous to the Environment arts. 14(1)–(6), 15, 16, 32, June 21, 1993, I.L.M. 1228, http:// conventions.coe.int/treaty/Commun/QueVoulezVous.asp?NT=150&CL=ENG; North

The apotheosis of this principle occurred in 1998 with the adoption of the Aarhus Convention.[160] Article 1 of the Aarhus Convention makes it clear that the right of access to information is not an end in itself but is a means to the greater goal of assuring "the right of every person of present and future generations to live in an environment adequate to his or her health and well-being."[161] "Environmental information" is also extensively defined to include all aspects of information about the state of the environment, activities and administrative measures affecting it, economic analyses and assumptions, and human health and safety.[162] Article 4 outlines in considerable detail requirements for states' reactive release and dissemination, without requiring requesters to state their interest, within a reasonable time, and only for a reasonable charge.[163] Like the 1966 US Freedom of Information Act (FOIA)[164] on which it is modeled, Article 4 also contains a number of standard exceptions (for some types of confidential information, national defense, criminal information, intellectual property, etc.). Article 5 contains proactive requirements for public authorities to possess and update environmental information, make it accessible, utilize electronic databases, and encourage those whose activities have a significant impact on the environment to provide regular public information on their activities and products.[165] A very important Article 5.9 calls for parties to "take steps" to implement a centralized, computerized national pollution inventory or registry, a provision modeled on the very effective US Toxics Release Inventory (TRI) system.[166]

The Aarhus Convention is a giant step in transparency and in the effectiveness individuals and NGOs can expect to have in discovering, participating in, and influencing development and other activities affecting their health and environments. Naturally, full disclosure will not become a global policy of governments overnight, as government resistance to the US FOIA illustrates. FOIA was one of the major building blocks of the US environmental movement, but government agencies have responded to it unevenly –

American Agreement on Environmental Cooperation (NAFTA's "Environmental Side Agreement") arts. 1(h), 2(1)(a) and numerous other articles, Sept. 14, 1993, US-Can.-Mex., 32 I.L.M. 1480 [hereinafter NAAEC], http://www.cec.org/Page.asp?PageID=1226&SiteNo deID=567.

[160] Aarhus Convention, *supra* note 63.
[161] *Id.* art. 1.
[162] *Id.* art. 2.
[163] *Id.* art. 4.
[164] Freedom of Information Act, 5 USC § 552.
[165] Aarhus Convention, *supra* note 63, art. 5.
[166] The TRI is required by § 313 of the US's 1986 Emergency Planning and Community Right-to-Know Act (EPCRA) 42 USC § 11001 *et seq.*' Rolf R. von Oppenfeld, *Emergency Planning and Community Right-to-Know Act*, in ENVIRONMENTAL LAW HANDBOOK 801 (Gov't Institutes ed., 20th ed. 2009).

some creating smooth systems for compliance, while others take an extremely uncooperative and secretive approach to their "public" records, as an annual review of the numerous FOIA lawsuits still filed against US government agencies discloses. It can be expected that political cultures lacking a tradition of public participation will struggle against the Aarhus approach. Nevertheless, given globalization, the Internet, the power of NGOs, IFOs' "green conditions," and other pressures, the trend toward greater public access to environmental information seems inexorable.

2.2.1.2   *Public Participation in Decision-Making*

The central pillar of public participation is the right of the public to utilize information to express support, objections, conditions, or alternatives to government officials and other decision-makers. The expanding public participation laws introduce new "players" – citizens, NGOs, indigenous peoples' interests, local community representatives, and other previously marginalized stakeholders – and therefore introduce new challenges to environment-development decision-making, that may previously have been the exclusive province of government officials, project developers, and financing entities.

Two different strands of public participation laws have developed. First are the environmental impact assessment (EIA) laws which typically require public review and comment as an integral procedural step in drafting the EIA documents (*see* Chapter 6). Second are the more recent laws which inject public participation into decision-making processes other than EIAs, such as general environment-conservation planning, use of multistate shared natural resources, sustainable development, government decision-making in general, and IFO requirements.

Public participation law grew little until the 1980s. The government-focused 1972 Stockholm Declaration, as mentioned in the section above, only alludes to public participation in a vague reference. The 1980s, however, was a watershed decade for public participation. The 1982 World Charter for Nature, adopted overwhelmingly by the UN General Assembly, contains a clarion call for conservation of nature and "disclos[ure]" of all planning "to the public by appropriate means in time to permit effective consultation and participation."[167] The first international EIA law, the 1985 EC Directive on Environmental Impact Assessment, threw the weight of Europe behind the issue, requiring that the public have the opportunity to express an opinion before development consent is granted, that such views be taken into consideration by the government decision-makers, and that the public be

---

[167] World Charter for Nature, *supra* note 151, art. 16.

provided with information on the decision outcome.[168] Subsequent international agreements then began routinely incorporating public participation elements, including the 1985 ASEAN Nature Conservation Agreement,[169] the 1991 Antarctica Environmental Protocol,[170] and the 1991 UNECE Transboundary EIA Convention (Espoo Convention).[171]

As with the information-access right, the 1990s moved public participation into high gear. The 1992 Rio Declaration included the broadest and perhaps most influential endorsement to that time in Principle 10, which states:

> Environmental issues are best handled with the participation of all concerned citizens, at the relevant level. At the national level, each individual shall have…the opportunity to participate in decision-making processes. States shall facilitate and encourage public awareness and participation….[172]

Rio further encourages the participation of women, youth, and indigenous peoples, in Principles 20–22. Agenda 21 likewise contains numerous references to public participation.[173] The 1993 NAFTA "Environmental Side Agreement"[174] contains the most detailed public participation processes of any free-trade treaty. The 1994 Desertification Convention also contains numerous articles calling for "participation" of "populations," "local communities," "women and youth," "non-governmental organizations," "resource users," etc.[175]

The full flowering of public participation came with the 1998 UNECE Aarhus Convention,[176] which contains the broadest and most detailed provisions for public participation to date, including requirements for states to:

---

[168] Directive on Environmental Impact Assessment, *supra* note 152, arts. 6(2), 8–9.

[169] ASEAN Agreement on the Conservation of Nature and Natural Resources, *supra* note 28, art. 16(2).

[170] Protocol on Environmental Protection to the Antarctic Treaty art.7 and Annex I art. 3, Oct. 4, 1991, 40 C.F.R. 8. XI ATSCM/2; 30 I.L.M. 1461 (1991), http://www.antarctica .ac.uk/about_antarctica/geopolitical/treaty/update_1991.php.

[171] Convention on Environmental Impact Assessment in a Transboundary Context arts. 2(6), 3, 4(2), 6(1),, Feb. 25, 1991, 30 I.L.M. 800 (1991), http://www.unece.org/env/eia/.

[172] Rio Declaration, *supra* note 11.

[173] Agenda 21, *supra* note 43 ¶¶ 7.41(b), 8.1, 23.2.

[174] NAAEC, *supra* note 159, arts. 4, 9, 10, 12, 13, 17.

[175] Convention to Combat Desertification in Those Countries Experiencing Serious Drought and/or Desertification, Particularly in Africa arts. 3(a), 5(d), 10(2)(f), 19(1)(a), June 17, 1994, UN Doc. No. A/AC.241/15/Rev. 7, 33 I.L.M. 1328 (1994) http://www.unccd.int/en/ about-the-convention/Pages/Text-overview.aspx.

[176] Aarhus Convention, *supra* note 63.

- Implement national procedures for public participation on a host of specified developments (such as mining, energy, chemical, waste disposal, incineration, water, pipeline, and road projects as well as the release of genetically modified organisms);
- Inform the public concerned early in the decisional process and in an adequate, timely, and effective manner;
- Specifically include environmental NGOs;
- Encourage private sector permit applicants to engage in dialog with the public;
- Provide opportunities for public input;
- Take "due account" of the public input in making the decision;
- Publicly announce the decision and the reasons therefor; and
- Include the public in legislative and administrative rule-making adoption.[177]

As stated before, Aarhus is a giant step forward in public participation. Paralleling as it does the US Freedom of Information Act and Administrative Procedure Act amendments, which so enabled and empowered the US environmental and other movements,[178] Aarhus can be expected to do the same globally.

2.2.1.3   *Access to Justice*

The reason the United States government had to institute the famous *Trail Smelter Arbitration*[179] against Canada in the 1930s was that US citizens and companies injured by the transboundary air pollution coming from the private smelter in Canada had no effective recourse. Government-to-government arbitration was necessary because, given the law at that time, US citizens could not bring actions in the Canadian courts. This famous example raises the question: What rights do citizens, businesses, or NGOs of Country X have if they suffer harm from pollution or other activities situated in Country Y? Historically, most states have not provided non-citizens the same access to their judicial and administrative bodies as they provide their own citizens, an injustice that becomes increasingly apparent as the world recognizes the transboundary nature of environmental harms.

Access to justice in international environmental law concerns three different adjudication procedures: (1) to challenge the refusal of access to information; (2) to seek prevention of and/or damages for environmentally harmful activities; and (3) to enforce environmental laws directly. A cross-cutting theme with access to justice is the principle of "nondiscrimination" (also

---

[177] *Id.* arts. 6–8.
[178] *See* text, *supra* notes 120–24.
[179] Trail Smelter Arbitration, *supra* note 17.

called "equal access" or "national treatment"), the requirement that a state permit noncitizens to have the same access to administrative and judicial proceedings as its own citizens do (the subject of the next section).

Ironically, international law in the early 1970s – like Principle 22 of the 1972 Stockholm Declaration and the 1974 Nordic Convention,[180] – focused on providing nondiscriminatory access to justice for noncitizens, while neglecting citizens' rights to sue in their own countries. However, Europe's geopolitically close-knit nature soon made it a natural incubator for developing international access to justice. In a famous 1976 case, *Bier v. Mines de Potasse d'Alsace*,[181] the European Court of Justice ruled that one injured by transboundary pollution could sue in either country, and either country's judgment was executable in the other. The Organization for Economic Cooperation and Development (the OECD, whose 34 – largely developed-country members – make it somewhat synonymous with "the North") has been a leader in promoting this principle (and the related principle of nondiscrimination discussed in the next section). The OECD's 1977 Recommendation on Implementation of a Regime of Equal Right of Access and Non-Discrimination in Relation to Transfrontier Pollution,[182] while not binding, moved the issue onto the front-burner for its members. By the 1980s, both citizens' and noncitizens' justice-access rights were receiving attention in instruments like the 1982 World Charter for Nature[183] and the 1986 WCED Experts Group Environmental Legal Principles.[184]

Like the other public participation principles mentioned previously, the access to justice principle strengthened during the 1990s. The 1992 Rio Declaration contains a typical modern directive in Principle 10: "Effective access to judicial and administrative proceedings, including redress and remedy,

---

[180] Convention on the Protection of the Environment Between Denmark, Finland, Norway and Sweden, art. 3, Feb. 9, 1974, 1092 UNTS 279, 13 I.L.M. 591 (1974) (hereinafter Nordic Convention), http://sedac.ciesin.org/entri/texts/acrc/Nordic.txt.html.

[181] Case 21/76, Bier v. Mines de Potasse d'Alsace, 1976 E.C.R. 1749, http://eur-lex.europa.eu/LexUriServ/LexUriServ.do?uri=CELEX:61976CJ0021:EN:PDF.

[182] OECD, Recommendation of the Council for the Implementation of a Regime of Equal Right of Access and Non-Discrimination in Relation to Transfrontier Pollution, May 17, 1977, O.E.C.D. Doc. C(77)28, 16 ILM 977, http://webnet.oecd.org/oecdacts/Instruments/ShowInstrumentView.aspx?InstrumentID=17&Lang=en&Book=False.

[183] World Charter for Nature *supra* note 151, Principle 23 ("All persons, in accordance with their national legislation...shall have access to means of redress when their environment has suffered damage or degradation").

[184] WCED, *Legal Principles for Environmental Protection and Sustainable Development*, *supra* note 30, art. 6.

shall be provided."[185] Other examples include the 1993 Environmental Civil Liability Convention[186] and the NAFTA "Environmental Side Agreement."[187]

The 1998 Aarhus Convention, the first treaty wholly devoted to public participation, not surprisingly contains elaborate access to justice coverage in Article 9. Article 9 requires, *inter alia*, that states permit legal challenges to the substantive or procedural legality of any decision, act, or omission subject to the convention, as well as over enforcement of national environmental laws (including acts and omissions on the part of both private persons and public authorities).[188] This last is truly a groundbreaking provision internationally, akin to the "citizen suit" or "citizen standing" provisions in some US pollution laws.[189] As with the other pillars, the Aarhus Convention can be expected to have a profound influence on the spread of access to justice in the coming decades.

Access to environmental justice is also increasing dramatically around the world – through the development of specialized environmental courts and tribunals at the national and subnational level. The Environmental Courts and Tribunals (ECT) Study at the University of Denver Sturm College of Law has identified over 465 ECTs in 46 different countries, over 70 percent of which have been created since 2005.[190]

2.2.1.4   *Nondiscrimination*

An important concept that cuts across all aspects of public participation is the principle of nondiscrimination (or "equal treatment" or "national treatment"). Nondiscrimination is both a substantive and a procedural principle that, simply put, means states should treat other states' people and environments as well as they treat their own.

On the substantive level, nondiscrimination seeks to prevent one state from discarding problems on another state's environment or people. To

---

[185] Rio Declaration, *supra* note 11. *See* also *id.* at Principle 13 ("States shall develop national law regarding liability and compensation for the victims of pollution and other environmental damage").

[186] Convention on Civil Liability for Damage Resulting from Activities Dangerous to the Environment, *supra* note 159, arts. 1, 6–11, 19.

[187] NAAEC *supra* note 159, arts. 5(2), 6, 7.

[188] Aarhus Convention, *supra* note 63, arts. 9(1)–(3).

[189] Upheld decisively (7 votes to 2) by the US Supreme Court in Friends of the Earth, Inc. v. Laidlaw Environmental Services (TOC), Inc., 528 US 167 (2000).

[190] George (Rock) Pring & Catherine (Kitty) Pring, Greening Justice: Creating and Improving Environmental Courts and Tribunals (World Resources Institute/ The Access Initiative 2009), free copy downloadable at http://www.law.du.edu/ect-study; George (Rock) Pring & Catherine (Kitty) Pring, *The Future of Environmental Dispute Resolution, in Perspectives on International Law in an Era of Change* (ed. Den. J. of Int'l L. & Pol'y, 2012); (most recent statistics), http://www.law.du.edu/ect-study.

this end, it requires states to treat environmental harms they cause to other states just as seriously as they would if the harms occurred to their own state and citizens. As Rio Principle 14 puts it: "States should effectively cooperate to discourage or prevent the relocation and transfer to other States of any activities and substances that cause severe environmental degradation or are found to be harmful to human health."[191] Again, this is an issue on which the OECD took the lead with its 1974 Principles Concerning Transfrontier Pollution.[192] The 1978 UNEP Draft Principles on Shared Natural Resources[193] and the 1986 WCED Experts Environmental Law Principles[194] concurred that this had become a legal principle. While part of the rationale behind the nondiscrimination concept is simple good neighborliness, equity, or fairness, another part of its rationale is that equal access to justice is yet imperfectly available, so that a state's environmental harms in other states may leave those victims without a practical remedy.

The procedural or public participation components of nondiscrimination have received far more attention in recent years, however. The procedural component requires a state whose activities have transboundary environmental effects to provide the same public information, participation, and justice-access rights to the affected citizens and interests in other states as it provides its own people. This procedural nondiscrimination principle has received most of its development in public participation and access to justice provisions, but it is obviously equally applicable to other aspects of multistate environmental law, such as access to information.[195] Some feel nondiscrimination's acceptance is sufficiently widespread to have attained the status of "general international law,"[196] but this categorization may be premature.

Nondiscrimination began receiving serious attention in the 1970s. The 1972 Stockholm Declaration in Principle 22 urged states "to co-operate to develop further the international law regarding liability and compensation for the victims of pollution and other environmental damage caused by activities within the jurisdiction or control of such States to areas beyond their jurisdiction."[197] The first nondiscrimination treaty was the 1974 Nordic

---

[191] Rio Declaration, *supra* note 11.

[192] Principles Concerning Transfrontier Pollution, Nov. 14, 1974, C(74)224, 14 I.L.M. 242, http://webnet.oecd.org/oecdacts/Instruments/ShowInstrumentView.aspx?InstrumentID= 12&Lang=en&Book=False.

[193] UNEP Draft Principles on Shared Natural Resources *supra* note 13, Principle 13.

[194] WCED, *Legal Principles for Environmental Protection and Sustainable Development*, *supra* note 30, art. 13.

[195] *See* Jonas Ebbesson, *The Notion of Public Participation in International Environmental Law*, 1997 Y.B. INT'L ENVTL. L. 51, 82 (1998).

[196] *Id.* at 81–83.

[197] Stockholm Declaration, *supra* note 5 (emphasis added).

Convention, which provides that persons affected by environmentally harmful activities originating in another state shall be entitled to sue in the originating state under rules not less favorable than those accorded that state's own citizens.[198] Other developments in the late 20th century furthered nondiscrimination in access to justice contexts,[199] including Rio Principle 13. These have been capped by the extensive nondiscrimination provisions in the 1998 Aarhus Convention.[200]

While the US Restatement recognizes that countries where pollution originates are "obligated to accord...access to the same judicial or administrative remedies as are available in similar circumstances to persons within the [country],"[201] US court practice has not been quite so generous with foreign claimants,[202] and it can be hoped that the on-going development of the North American Free Trade Agreement (NAFTA) and Aarhus will help cure this discrepancy. The US is just one example of the states not yet according equal access to justice in practice, thus relegating this right for now to treaty law. Interstate lawsuits are now being filed that should slowly develop an international common law as their decisions come down.[203]

2.2.2   *Prior Notification, Consultation, and Negotiation Duties*

As noted in at the beginning of this chapter, the duty of "good neighborliness" or cooperation (*see* § 2.1.2) has many offshoots. Three of its most important sub-principles arise when activities have the potential to damage the environment outside a state's borders. In such circumstances, the acting state may be obliged to (1) give potentially affected states *prior notification* of the plans, then (2) engage in *consultation* or discussions of the plans with them, and possibly even to (3) *negotiate* in good faith about alternatives to the plans.

Prior notification is the most firmly established of these three principles in both international customary and conventional law. As early as the 1949 *Corfu Channel Case*, when Albania failed to warn British ships of explosive mines in its waters, the ICJ ruled that Albania had an "obligation" of

---

[198] Nordic Convention, *supra* note 180, arts. 3–4.

[199] *See* § 2.2.1.3.

[200] Aarhus Convention, *supra* note 63.

[201] *See* RESTATEMENT, *supra* note 121, § 602(2).

[202] The doctrine of *forum non conveniens* is frequently used by US courts to dismiss foreign claimants. US Dept. of State, *The Doctrine of Forum Non Conveniens in the United States*, http://www.state.gov/www/global/legal_affairs/us_annex-c.html; Stephanie A. Scharf & Traci M. Braun, *Foreign Plaintiffs Battle to Keep Class Claims in U.S. Courts*, FOOD & DRUG LAW INSTITUTE UPDATE, Jan./Feb. 2007, at 32, http://www.schoeman.com/publications/documents/ForeignPlaintiffsBattle.pdf.

[203] *See* Pring *et al.*, *supra* note 2, at 162–63.

"notifying" and "warning" of the danger "based...on certain general and well-recognized principles, namely: elementary considerations of humanity, even more exacting in peace than in war...and every State's obligation not to allow knowingly its territory to be used for acts contrary to the rights of other States."[204] The prior notification duty began to appear by the 1960s in treaties and nonbinding authorities, and now appears in many more.[205] The duty is enshrined in Rio Principle 19: "States shall provide prior and timely notification and relevant information to potentially affected States on activities that may have a significant adverse transboundary environmental effect...." The principle is most firmly established in the water arena, where the 1982 UN Convention on the Law of the Sea (*see* Chapter 11), and the 1997 UN Convention on International Watercourses (*see* Chapter 9) require it.[206]

Under the second principle – the duty to enter into consultation – the notifying state must be prepared to: (1) discuss in more detail the information it has provided, (2) listen to comments the notified state may have, and (3) take the comments into consideration in a reasonable manner. However, the consultation principle does not, in itself, require the notifying state either to enter into compromise negotiations, to agree, or to obtain the other states' prior consent. The principle is illustrated by the famous 1957 *Lac Lanoux Arbitration* in which upstream France's plans to reroute a river it shared with downstream Spain required prior notification and consultation but did not give Spain a "right of veto" (a ruling then softened by the further statement "provided that [France] takes into consideration in a reasonable manner the interests of the downstream state").[207] This judicially announced norm now appears in treaties and other authorities, including Rio Principle 19.[208]

The third principle – requiring the notifying state to engage in actual negotiations, including consideration of alternatives and possible compromises in the substance of the plan or activity – remains aspirational, and is not yet an agreed norm, even with regard to shared resources. The notable

---

[204] Corfu Channel, *supra* note 120, ¶ 65.

[205] For lists, *see* HUNTER ET AL., *supra* note 3, at 493.

[206] Of course, a notable exception to the state practice is the former Soviet Union's failure to provide timely notice and information about its 1986 Chernobyl nuclear reactor disaster and the affected European states' failure in turn to make any claims based on state responsibility; however, as there are diplomatic reasons why this may have occurred (other nuclear states not wishing to create a precedent that could haunt them), it is not sufficient to deny the general practice and *opinio juris* on this principle. See GURUSWAMY ET AL., *supra* note 97, at 337.

[207] Summary of Lac Lanoux Arbitration (Spain v. Fr.) 12 R.I.A.A. 281 (1957), http://www .ecolex.org/server2.php/libcat/docs/COU/Full/En/COU-143747E.pdf.

[208] For examples, *see* HUNTER ET AL., *supra* note 3, at 493.

exception is the water field (which has been the leading area for extending all these principles). The 1997 UN Convention on International Watercourses has codified detailed negotiation requirements (beyond notification and consultation) in Articles 11, 17, 18, and 19 (*see* Chapter 9).

2.2.3   *The Prevention Principle*

The old adage, "An ounce of prevention is worth a pound of cure" is a central truth of all environmental protection because the ecological and economic costs of environmental damage are so steep. Environmental damage is often irreparable, as in the case of species extinction, waste of nonrenewable resources, ocean pollution, and nuclear releases, to name a few examples. Even if the environmental harms are reparable, waiting to cure is almost always uneconomic compared to the costs of advance prevention. Yet, the US and other countries' pollution control systems have focused heavily on "cure" – end-of-the-pipe pollution treatment approaches – instead of focusing on preventing the occurrence of pollution in the first place. Quite simply, prevention requires anticipatory investigation, planning, and action before undertaking activities which can cause environmental harm. It stems logically from other principles, such as good neighborliness, and branches into others like the no-harm rule and the obligation to do environmental impact assessment.

"Pollution prevention" or "P2" is the principle's most obvious manifestation. The US Pollution Prevention Act of 1990[209] legislates a logical "hierarchy" of methods for pollution control: pollution prevention or "source control" – keeping pollution from happening in the first place – is the top priority; if that is infeasible, recycling/reuse/reduce is second, followed by treatment, with disposal "only as a last resort."[210] Other national laws, such as the US Resource Conservation and Recovery Act (hazardous waste law) now mandate P2 management strategies with considerable effectiveness.[211]

The prevention principle is thus well-grounded in some national laws, well-represented in international soft law, but only beginning to become a standard states will expressly commit themselves to in binding treaties. On the soft law side, the prevention concept can be found in Stockholm Principles 6 and 21 and Rio Principle 2, but even more expressly in the 1982 ILA Rules on Transfrontier Pollution,[212] the 1986 WCED Experts' Legal

---

[209] 42 U.S.C. §§ 13102–13109. *See further* John M. Scagnelli, *Pollution Prevention Act, in* Environmental Law Handbook 577–92, *supra* note 166.

[210] Section 6602(b), 42 USC § 13101(b).

[211] *See* Scagnelli, *supra* note 209, at 102, 126.

[212] ILA Rules on International Law Applicable to Transfrontier Pollution, Sept. 4, 1982, arts. 34, 60 I.L.A. 158 (1983).

Principles for Environmental Protection and Sustainable Development,[213] the Restatement,[214] and the 1989 ILC Draft Liability Articles,[215] among others. Nations have committed to "prevent" environmental harms in a number of specific treaties, including Article 194 of the 1982 UN Convention on the Law of the Sea (*see* Chapter 11), Article 2(1) of the 1991 Transboundary EIA Convention (*see* Chapter 6), Article 4(3)(f) of the 1991 Bamako Convention on Hazardous Waste in Africa (*see* Chapter 12), and in several other modern treaties.[216]

The standard of care for prevention is the flexible one of "due diligence," rather than an absolute prevention standard.[217] Due diligence in customary international law requires effective national legislative, administrative controls, and the conduct "expected of a good government" – an admittedly vague and situational standard.[218] This is putting affirmative pressure on treaties to come up with more specific definitions of due diligence, and these can range from the simple "best available technology (BAT)," "best practicable means (BPM)," and "best management practices (BMP)" to more elaborate definitions, as in the Basel Hazardous Waste Convention (*see* Chapter 12).

2.2.4   *The Precautionary Principle*

Legislators are often hesitant to adopt costly environmental regulations when there is little scientific evidence to suggest that the proposed regulations will have the intended effects. Thus, lack of scientific certainty represents one of the biggest impediments for environmental regulation. How should governments regulate in the face of ever-present scientific uncertainty? It is generally impossible to determine beforehand with certainty whether a given level of water pollution will or will not affect a particular fish population, or whether stricter automobile emission standards will reduce hospitalizations, or whether a proposed new drug will have longterm adverse side effects.

If scientists are not absolutely sure a particular substance, project, or activity will cause human health or environmental harm or that a tougher law will produce human health or environmental benefits, should the government regulate or wait? The quandary is made especially difficult, because

---

[213] WCED, *Legal Principles for Environmental Protection and Sustainable Development supra* note 30, arts. 10–12.

[214] RESTATEMENT, *supra* note 121, § 601(1)(a).

[215] ILC, Draft Articles on State Responsibility, *supra* note 122, art. 8.

[216] Further examples of "prevention" treaties and declarations are listed in KISS & SHELTON, *supra* note 113, at 263.

[217] *See* PATRICIA W. BIRNIE, ALAN E. BOYLE, CATHERINE REDGWELL, INTERNATIONAL LAW AND THE ENVIRONMENT 91–95 (1992).

[218] *See id.* at 92–93.

scientists and scientific data "speak in terms of probabilities, not [the] certainties" public policy and regulation require.[219] As a practical matter, laws and regulators have only two choices: (1) postpone response/regulation until further knowledge clarifies the uncertainty or (2) regulate as soon as possible to avoid uncertain but possible harm. Put another way, should policies and regulations "permit-until-proved-harmful" or "prevent-until-proved-safe"?

One of the "most far-reaching"[220] agreements attempted at Rio was advancement of the later principle – "the precautionary approach." Principle 15 states: "Where there are threats of serious or irreversible damage, lack of full scientific certainty shall not be used as a reason for postponing cost-effective measures to prevent environmental degradation."[221] The approach is central to Agenda 21, most notably in scientifically uncertain areas like climate change and oceans.[222] This position reflects a 180-degree shift of the traditional burden of proof. No longer should opponents of a risky action or potential victims have the burden of proving harm; now the burden is on the proponents of the action to prove it safe. Thus, the Rio 15 precautionary principle is a reversal in the evidentiary presumption toward a presumption of harm.

The principle is of course an extension of the general "prevention" principle (see section above). It is also a surprisingly recent one, first appearing in the 1982 World Charter for Nature.[223] Prior to Rio, authorities could confidently state that there was insufficient international consensus to establish the principle as international customary law;[224] however, it has now appeared in virtually all of the key international treaties and declarations adopted since 1992.[225] It would appear that the Trail Smelter Arbitration standard of proof for transboundary harms of "clear and convincing evidence,"[226] is being replaced (at least in this anticipatory context of significant harms) by the precautionary principle.

Certainly, difficult questions about the precautionary principle remain. What actions are required other than those that are "cost effective"? And what does cost effective mean if human life or great environmental values are at risk? When or how early does it apply (what is meant by "threats")?

---

[219] Daniel Bodansky, *Scientific Uncertainty and the Precautionary Principle*, 33 Env't 4 (Sept. 1991).

[220] Sands, *supra* note 22, at 346.

[221] Rio Declaration, *supra* note 11.

[222] Agenda 21, *supra* note 43 ¶ 9.6–9.8 and ¶ 17.5(d) respectively.

[223] World Charter for Nature, *supra* note 151, Principle 11(b).

[224] *See* Birnie & Boyle, *supra* note 1, at 98.

[225] Kiss & Shelton, *supra* note 113, at 94. For lists of the treaties and other authorities, Birnie & Boyle, *supra* note 1, at 95–99.

[226] Trail Smelter Arbitration, *supra* note 17.

What level of harm is required to trigger the rule (what does "serious or irreversible" mean, and which side has the burden of proof of that)? What does it require when it applies: total prohibition, balancing, or mitigation-abatement? The two certainties at this point are (1) a very strong new factor has entered the environmental decisional dialog and (2) its detailed ramifications will have to be worked out in concrete treaties and court cases in the years ahead.

2.2.5 Duty to Do Environmental Impact Assessment

The term environmental impact assessment (EIA) describes the process of investigation and analysis of proposed projects, plans, permits, policies, programs, and other actions. This EIA process is designed to fully inform decisionmakers and the public of the potential environmental impacts, alternatives for achieving similar goals, and mitigation measures for reducing negative impacts of proposed projects (for a full discussion *see* Chapter 6). EIA is one of the oldest and most widely accepted methodologies in environmental protection. Pioneered with the US National Environmental Policy Act of 1969,[227] EIA has become a fixture of many international treaties, IFO rules, and over 60 states' national laws.

The 1986 UN Convention on the Law of the Sea, the 1991 Espoo Convention on EIA in a Transboundary Context, the 1992 Biodiversity Convention, and the World Bank's Operational Directive on Environmental Assessment are just a few of the international legal authorities requiring EIA. Rio Principle 17 specifically states that there is an international obligation to adopt and implement EIA laws and programs at the national level; moreover, EIA seems necessarily implied in the affirmations in Rio Principles 4 and 25 of the need to link and integrate environmental protection into the development process, as EIAs are far and away the major mechanism to accomplish that.[228] The extent of the practice by states and international organizations suggests to some authorities that EIA "may already be obligatory as a matter of customary law," as an integral part or extension or combination of the good neighborliness/cooperation, prior notification and consultation, and/or the prevention rules.[229] That assessment is probably overly optimistic, however, given the number of countries which still find EIA a much-too-expensive luxury or a much-too-revealing obstacle to business-as-usual development or government. Despite resistance by some states and development interests, we can expect the EIA duty to spread internationally through

---

[227] 42 U.S.C. § 4321 *et seq.*
[228] Rio Declaration, *supra* note 11.
[229] BIRNIE & BOYLE, *supra* note 1, at 97.

the proliferation of requirements in specific treaties and IGO/IFO financing "conditions."

2.2.6   *Duty to Adopt Effective National Law – The Duty to Enforce*

Ultimately, international environmental laws can only be truly effective if states adopt, fund, and implement appropriate national laws, regulations, and enforcement programs to make these grand pronouncements work "on the ground." The international community can adopt all of the CITES, bio-diversity, and other wildlife protection laws it wishes, but, if the states where the wildlife live and the states where their body parts are sold as merchandise do not adopt and enforce supportive legal regimes, the death toll and extinctions will go on. The international community can adopt massive legal edifices around transboundary air pollution, climate change, or ozone depletion, but, if individual states do not adopt complementary internal controls, there will inevitably be "rogue states," "pollution havens," and "free riders" reaping profit at the expense of human health and the environment, and the protective scheme will fail. Internationally, we can draw up the most protective possible Forest Principles, but, if individual nations allow roads to be built into their rainforests, old-growth timber, and wilderness areas, destructive development will follow. Ultimately, international law and national law must mirror each other if environmental protection is to be successful.

The duty to adopt effective national legislation and enforcement to carry out international legal obligations is a well-recognized principle, but hardly one that can yet claim uniform state practice. Rio Principle 11 encapsulates it: "States shall enact effective environmental legislation," but then goes on to qualify that with the "common but differentiated responsibilities" doctrine (*see* § 2.1.12), stating that standards applied by developed countries may be inappropriate and too expensive for developing countries.[230]

"National capacity building" – legislation, administration, institution-building, management and enforcement systems, training, technology transfer, and above all funding – is widely recognized as a necessary component of effective national legislation.[231] Capacity building is now being factored into the modern treaty systems. CITES Article IX requires parties to establish a "Management Authority" to enforce the treaty's detailed undertakings domestically (*see* Chapter 8). UNCLOS Article 207 obliges parties to "adopt laws and regulations" to control land-based pollution (*see* Chapter 12). The Basel Hazardous Waste Convention Article 4(4) specifies that parties "shall take appropriate legal, administrative and other measures to implement and

---

[230] Rio Declaration, *supra* note 11.
[231] *See* Chapter 37 of Agenda 21, *supra* note 43, which is devoted to this subject.

enforce the provisions of this Convention" (*see* Chapter 12). The 1998 Aar-hus Treaty states it most comprehensively in Article 3: "Each Party shall take the necessary legislative, regulatory and other measures... as well as proper enforcement measures, to establish and maintain a clear, transparent and consistent framework to implement the provisions of this Convention."[232]

The duty to adopt effective national laws and enforcement is a corollary of the most fundamental treaty rule of all, *pacta sunt servanda*, defined in the Vienna Convention on Treaties as meaning "Every treaty in force is binding upon the parties to it and must be performed by them in good faith."[233] The Vienna "Treaty on Treaties" further provides that: "A party may not invoke the provisions of its internal law as justification for its failure to perform a treaty."[234] However logical a rule requiring treaty-implementing national laws and systems may be, not all states comply. Many states enter into treaties, then fail to take the next logical step for economic reasons, lack of capacity, or domestic political resistance. CBDR can be both a negative force, pro-viding an excuse for inaction, or it can be a positive call for international aid – technical assistance, technology transfer, training, and funding – to assist those countries with the necessary capacity building.

2.2.7   *The Integration Principle*

For environmental protection to work, environmental considerations must be made an integral part of government and development decision-making. This was recognized at least as early as the US National Environmental Policy Act of 1969, which requires all US government agencies to

> utilize a systematic, interdisciplinary approach which will insure the integrated use of the natural and social sciences and the environmental design arts in planning and in decision-making which may have an impact on man's envi-ronment.[235]

In 1972, Stockholm Declaration Principle 13 called on states to "adopt an integrated and coordinated approach to their development planning" to ensure it was compatible with environmental protection.[236] The 1992 Rio Declaration is even more forceful, stating that "environmental protection shall constitute an integral part of the development process and cannot be

---

[232] Aarhus Convention, *supra* note 63.
[233] Vienna Convention on Treaties art. 26, May 23, 1969, 1155 U.N.T.S. 331, http://untreaty .un.org/ilc/texts/instruments/english/conventions/1_1_1969.pdf.
[234] *Id.* art. 27.
[235] 42 USC § 4332(2)(A).
[236] Stockholm Declaration, *supra* note 5.

considered in isolation from it."[237] The EU and other countries have adopted the integration principle in their laws. Even private sector business codes, like the International Chamber of Commerce "Business Charter for Sustainable Development"[238] and ISO 14000,[239] support and reinforce this precept of "integrated environmental management."

These 24 fundamental principles will serve as our guide in the following subject-specific chapters, as they describe how far we have come and how far we still have to go in creating a workable and effective body of international environmental law.

---

[237] Rio Declaration, *supra* note 11 at Principle 4.

[238] International Chamber of Commerce, International Business Charter for Sustainable Development http://www.iisd.org/business/tools/principles_icc.aspx. Principle 2 calls for integrated environmental management.

[239] International Organization for Standardization, *ISO 14000 – Environmental Management*, http://www.iso.org/iso/iso_catalogue/management_and_leadership_standards/environmental_management.htm.

Part Two: Lawmaking

Chapter Three

The Early Years

3.0 *Introduction*

Humanity's concern with the environment goes back in history, as ancient civilizations and religious traditions practiced, as well as promoted, environmental protection and preservation.[1] Records show that as early as 1273, a statute was enacted in England to address air pollution.[2] A Royal Proclamation banned the use of coal in village furnaces in 1307.[3] While nations have long endeavored to address environmental challenges, it has been well recognized that environmental degradation respects no political boundaries. And early efforts toward international environmental management were sporadic and ineffectual.[4] The cause of this ineffectiveness lies in the horizontal structure of the international community and its resultant emphasis on state sovereignty.

Despite the need for international cooperative measures to control transboundary environmental damage caused by state activities in the course of industrialization and exploitation of natural resources, the concept of "global management" of the environment developed only during the second half of

---

[1] *See generally* C. G. Weeramantry, *Islam, Buddhism, Hinduism and the Environment*, Asian Tribune, Jul. 7, 2007, http://www.energybulletin.net/print/32153; J. R. Thorngren, Religion and Environment, http://daphne.palomar.edu/calenvironment/religion.htm; R. Renugadevi, *Environmental ethics in the Hindu Vedas and Puranas in India*, 4 Afr. J. Hist. & Culture 1, 1–3 (2012) http://www.academicjournals.org/AJHC/PDF/pdf2012/Jan/Renugadevi.pdf:

> The messages of environmental conservation contained in the Vedic and Puranic literatures [and in other Hindu scriptures] are all based on Hindu religious philosophy. "Non-violence," that is, non-injury to both the living as well as the non-living creations of nature, such as plants, animals, air, water, land (earth), hill and forest is the core of Hindu religious philosophy which extended up to Jainism and Buddhism.

[2] *See* UNEP, *Environmental Law: An In-Depth Review*, 5 UNEP Rep. No. 2 (1981) [hereinafter UNEP Rep. No. 2].

[3] *See id.*

[4] *See id.* at 5–6.

the 20th century.[5] Until the 1950s, transnational environmental efforts found expression in either a limited group of diplomatic arbitral cases[6] or a number of weak international treaties in selected areas of conservation, such as the protection of whales or of migratory birds.[7] International environmental law as we know it today had its origins in the concept of enforcement of these agreements, primarily through damages for harm caused.

3.1   *International Agreements*

3.1.1   *Early 20th Century Agreements*

The first examples of international environmental law in the early 20th century are found in specific agreements,[8] such as the 1902 Convention to protect birds useful to agriculture[9] and the 1911 Treaty between the United States and Great Britain to protect fur seals.[10] Although these agreements were aimed at protecting the environment, it must be acknowledged that the parties tended to view the environment from a utilitarian perspective, and hence the resulting agreements were designed for their short-term benefits to the parties.

3.1.2   *The 1909 Boundary Waters Treaty*

In 1909, the United States and Great Britain entered into a treaty regarding transboundary waters between the United States and Canada which has been recognized as one of the major landmarks of the early development of modern international environmental law.[11] The Boundary Waters Treaty of 1909

---

[5] *See* Chapter 4, *infra.*

[6] *See* UNEP Rep. No. 2, *supra* note 2, at 5–6.

[7] *See id.* at 5.

[8] *See* A. Kiss & D. Shelton, International Environmental Law 33–34 (1991) [hereinafter Kiss & Shelton].

[9] International Convention for the Protection of Birds Useful to Agriculture (Paris, Mar. 19, 1902), 30 Martens (2d) 686, 102 B.F.S.P. 969.

[10] Treaty for the Preservation and Protection of Fur Seals (Washington, D.C., Feb. 7, 1911), 104 B.F.S.P. 175.

[11] Treaty Relating to Boundary Waters and Boundary Questions (Jan. 11, 1909), U.S.-Great Britain, 36 Stat. 2448, T.S. No. 5481 [hereinafter Boundary Waters Treaty]. *See generally* D. Piper, The International Law Of The Great Lakes (1967); 3 M. Whiteman, Digest of International Law 826–71 (1964); R. Bilder, *Controlling Great Lakes Pollution: A Study in United States-Canadian Environmental Cooperation*, 70 Mich. L. Rev. 469 (1972); J. P. Erichsen-Brown, *Legal Implications of Boundary Water Pollution*, 17 Buff. L. Rev. 65 (1967); F. Jordan, *Great Lakes Pollution: A Framework for Action*, 5 Ottawa L. Rev. 65 (1971) [hereinafter Jordan I]; F. Jordan, *Recent Developments in International*

was meant primarily to protect the water levels and navigability of the Great Lakes and other boundary waters between the two countries. However, the Treaty was then and remains a useful instrument of cooperation between the United States and Canada for controlling transboundary water pollution.

Although the treaty contains a prohibition against pollution on "either side to the injury of health or property on the other,"[12] it includes no definition of "pollution" or "injury," nor does it contain enforcement procedures.[13] Article IX does provide, however, that "any other questions or matters of differences arising between them involving the rights, obligations, or interests of either in relation to the other or to the inhabitants of the other, along the common frontier"[14] shall be referred to a body established and administered under the treaty, the International Joint Commission of the United States and Canada (IJC). A synopsis of its history aptly illustrates the effective employment of an international agreement over a specific area of international environmental concern.

The Commission – an independent and impartial body – initially comprised six members, three each from the governments of the United States and the United Kingdom (appointed by His Majesty on recommendation of Canada's Governor). The IJC's establishment was a visionary step, as it constituted a major advancement toward the protection and management of the environment.[15] Article IX of the Treaty entitled the two governments to refer transboundary water pollution problems to the IJC for investigation. Upon examination of questions referred to it, the Commission could make appropriate recommendations and supervise compliance with water quality standards.[16] The Treaty also has a provision for the governments' referral

---

Environmental Pollution Control, 15 McGILL L.J. 279, 289–301 (1969) [Jordan II]; H. Landis, *Legal Controls of Pollution in the Great Lakes Basin*, 48 CAN. BAR. REV. 66 (1970); G. Rempe III, *International Air Pollution-United States and Canada-A Joint Approach*, 10 ARIZ. L. REV. 138 (1968); M. Welsh *et al.*, *The Work of the International Joint Commission*, 59 Dept. State Bull. 311 (1968); M. Welsh *et al.*, *International Joint Commission-United States and Canada*, in 5 INTERNATIONAL CONFERENCE ON WATER FOR PEACE 104–09 (1967); Comment, *Pollution of the Great Lakes: A Joint Approach by Canada and the United States*, 2 CA. W. INT'L L.J. 109 (1971); Note, *Pollution of the Great Lakes: A Study of International Environmental Control Efforts*, 19 WAYNE L. REV. 165 (1972). *See also* K. Wardroper, *Canada's Interests as Regards Protection and Regulation of the Great Lakes*, 1 SYRACUSE J. INT'L L. & COMM. 205 (1973).

[12] Boundary Waters Treaty, *supra* note 11, art. IV, para. (2). It is noteworthy that this treaty is one of the earliest bilateral agreements to address transboundary pollution.

[13] *See* Bilder, *supra* note 11, at 483.

[14] Boundary Waters Treaty, *supra* note 11, art. IX, first para.

[15] *Id.*, art. VII.

[16] For a discussion of the limitations on the workings of the IJC which make it extremely hard for the Commission to supervise compliance with the water quality standards it has

to the Commission of questions for binding arbitral decisions or findings,[17] although this has not been implemented.[18]

Since the Second World War, the IJC has been utilized increasingly by the two governments, as evidenced by their references to the Commission.[19] Of particular significance are the 1964 request to inquire into the extent, causes, and location of pollution of Lake Erie, Lake Ontario, and the international section of the St. Lawrence River,[20] and the various investigations and reports of the Commission.[21]

In his detailed 1972 analysis of the work of the IJC, Professor Bilder concluded that:

> [T]he United States-Canadian experience demonstrates that international envi-
> ronmental cooperation can yield useful dividends at relatively low costs and
> with limited political risks. While Great Lakes problems are still a long way
> from solution, the IJC has performed a valuable function in developing gov-
> ernment and public awareness of Great Lakes pollution problems, providing
> scientific and technical information relevant to rational policy choice, suggest-
> ing the nature of the remedies required, and furnishing a means through which
> national programs can be better coordinated.[22]

3.1.2.1   *The 1909 Boundary Waters Treaty – Selected Developments Since the 1970s*

In 1972 Canada and the United States entered into an agreement on Great Lakes water quality,[23] which was a direct response to a 1970 Commission report that detailed the critical state of water pollution in the Lower Great Lakes Basin and outlined the Commission's recommendations for preventive

---

recommended, *see* Jordan II, *supra* note 11, at 299–301. For a more detailed account of the constraints under which the IJC works on matters concerning water quality and for recommendations to improve the situation *see* Jordan I, *supra* note 11, at 67–83. *See also* Note, *supra* note 11, at 173–79. For a highly critical article concluding that the International Joint Commission has proved to be an ineffective means of conflict resolution "with respect to the use and development of trans-boundary waters," *see* I. A. McDougall, *The Develop-ment of International Law with Respect to Trans-Boundary Water Resources: Cooperation for Mutual Advantage or Continentalism's Thin Edge of the Wedge*, 9 Osgoode Hall L.J. 261 (1971).

[17] Boundary Waters Treaty, *supra* note 11, art. X.

[18] *See* 3 M. Whiteman, *supra* note 11, at 816.

[19] *See id.* at 852–71 (1964); Bilder, *supra* note 11, at 489–501.

[20] For a succinct summary of the reference and the Commission action, *see* Jordan I, *supra* note 11, at 72–77.

[21] *See id.* at 68–81; 3 M. Whiteman, *supra* note 11, at 826–71; Bilder, *supra* note 11, at 489–501.

[22] Bilder, *supra* note 11, at 555.

[23] Agreement with Canada on Great Lakes Water Quality, Apr. 15, 1972, 23 U.S.T. 301, T.I.A.S. No. 7312.

and remedial action.[24] Under this agreement, the IJC was granted additional responsibilities and enhanced authority and competence.[25]

The agreement was revised in 1978[26] in order to reflect the parties' concern about toxic pollutants and their preference for an ecosystem approach.[27] It was further amended in 1983 and 1987.[28] In its 1990 biennial report[29] the IJC noted that, while the parties had made considerable progress in eliminating the discharge of nutrients, the zero-discharge goal was still distant.[30] Thus, the IJC recommended that Lake Superior be designated "a demonstration area where no point source discharge of any persistent toxic substance will be permitted."[31] The following year, the parties accepted the IJC recommendation by establishing a bi-national program for restoration and protection of the Lake Superior Basin.[32]

A 1993 report by the IJC, entitled Great Lakes-St. Lawrence Basin Study,[33] made 42 recommendations to the parties for methods of controlling water levels, including the establishment of a $10–$20 million annual fund for land use and shoreline management projects.[34] Although there is no specific provision in the 1909 Treaty that addresses the regulation and control of air pollution, the IJC was asked to investigate the question of atmospheric pollution in the Detroit-Windsor area as early as 1949.[35] Subsequently, in 1966, the governments broadened their earlier reference, requesting that the IJC determine whether transboundary air pollution was detrimental to the public health, safety, or general welfare of citizens or property on either side of the boundary and, if so, recommend preventive and remedial measures.[36] While

---

[24] *See id.*, preamble, third para. *See generally* Jordan I, *supra* note 11, at 73–77.

[25] *See* Agreement with Canada on Great Lakes Water Quality, *supra* note 23, arts. VI–VIII.

[26] Revised Great Lakes Water Agreement of 1978 (Nov. 22, 1978), U.S.-Can. 30 U.S.T. 1383.

[27] *Id.* art. 11. 26 Phosphorous Land Reduction Supplement (Oct. 16, 1983), T.I.A.S. No. 10798, amended by Protocol (Nov. 18, 1987).

[28] Phosphorous Land Reduction Supplement (Oct. 16, 1983), T.I.A.S. No. 10798, amended by Protocol (Nov. 18, 1987). *See* generally Lee Botts & Paul Muldoon, Evolution of the Great Lakes Water Quality Agreement 11–13 (2006).

[29] *See* IJC, Fifth Biennial Report on Great Lakes Water Quality (1990).

[30] *See id.* at 10–12.

[31] *Id.* at 24.

[32] A Bi-National Program to Restore and Protect the Lake Superior Basin, Sept. 1991, U.S.-Can. For a comment, *see* L. Satterfield, *The Bi-National Program to Restore and Protect the Lake Superior Basin: Talk or Substance?* 4 Colo. J. Int'l Envtl. L. & Pol'y 251 (1993).

[33] IJC, *Great Lakes-St. Lawrence Basin Study* (July 1993). For a summary report, *see* 16 Int'l Env't Rep. (BNA), Curr. Rep. 596 (Aug. 11, 1993).

[34] *See id.*

[35] 3 Whiteman, *supra* note 11, at 855–56.

[36] *See* Rempe, *supra* note 11, at 143 and n. 33.

the primary focus of the IJC is with water rights disputes, it has played an important role in the transboundary air pollution control regime, as well.[37]

Efforts to devise regional management mechanisms to ensure that waters and natural resources of the Great Lakes Basin which are water-dependent are protected, conserved, restored, improved and effectively managed include the creation of the Great Lakes Charter in 1985, which was created on behalf of the Council of Great Lakes Governors (acknowledging the Great Lakes Basin as one hydrologic system and recognizing the dangers of diversion and consumptive uses and the need to act with a "continuing spirit of comity and mutual cooperation"),[38] the 1996 Water Resources Development Act (Congress federally mandating that no water could be diverted outside the Great Lakes system without unanimous approval of every Great Lakes state),[39] the 2001 Great Lakes Charter Annex (introducing concepts such as conservation, ecological impacts and return flow to the basin-management framework and acknowledging groundwater as an important part of the watershed),[40] and eventually the 2008 Great Lakes – St. Lawrence River Basin Water Resources Compact (establishing a comprehensive framework for the sustainable management of the Great Lakes water resources).[41]

To commemorate the centennial of the Boundary Waters Treaty the Wayne Law Review held a symposium in Detroit, Michigan, on February 5, 2009, at which a dozen of the leading experts in the field participated, including all the six Commissioners and the secretaries of the International Joint Commission.[42] In his keynote address, the Canadian chair of the IJC, Rt. Hon. Herb Gray, stated that "the Commission has been developing ways to encourage a better integrated, more participatory, ecosystem-based

---

[37] *See generally* Jason Buhi & Lin Feng, *The International Joint Commission's Role in the United States – Canada Transboundary Air Pollution Regime: A Century of Experience to Guide the Future*, 11 Vt. J. Envtl. L. 108 (2009).

[38] Council of Great Lakes Governors, *The Great Lakes Charter: Principles for the Management of Great Lakes Water Resources* (Feb. 11, 1985) http://www.cglg.org/pub/charter/index.html.

[39] Pub. L. No. 99–662, § 1109, 100 Stat. 4082, 4230 (1986) (codified as amended at 42 U.S.C. § 1962d-20 (2000)).

[40] Council of Great Lakes Governors, *The Great Lakes Charter Annex: A Supplementary Agreement to the Great Lakes Charter* 2–3 (June 18, 2001) http://www.cglg.org/projects/water/docs/GreatLakesCharterAnnex.pdf.

[41] Great Lakes-St. Lawrence River Basin Compact, Pub. L. No. 110–342, 122 Stat. 3739. *See generally* Nicholas T. Stack, *Note: The Great Lakes Compact and an Ohio Constitutional Amendment: Local Protectionism and Regional Cooperation*, 37 B.C. Envtl. Aff. L. Rev. 493 (2010).

[42] *Boundary Waters Treaty Centennial Symposium*, 54 Wayne L. Rev. 1451–1706 (2008).

approach to issues in transboundary water basins under its 'International Watersheds Initiative.'"[43]

Marking the 100th anniversary date of the actual signing of the treaty, then-Secretary of State Condoleezza Rice said on January 11, 2009: "The Boundary Waters Treaty remains vibrant as it enters its second century.... The Treaty continues to be a model for managing shared resources and a tribute to the enduring friendship between the United States and Canada."[44] Also marking the occasion, incoming Secretary of State Hillary Clinton stated she was pleased to announce that the US and Canada will initiate negotiations to update the Great Lakes Water Quality Agreement, as the Great Lakes Agreement in its current form "does not sufficiently address the needs of our shared ecosystem."[45]

3.1.3   *Other Agreements*

In the 1930s the attention of states turned to a broader range of ecological concerns, as reflected in several interstate agreements. To illustrate, in 1933, colonial powers signed a convention aimed at the creation of national parks and the preservation of animals and plant life in then-colonized Africa (*see* Chapter 8).[46] This was followed in 1940 by the Convention on Nature Protection and Wildlife Preservation in the Western Hemisphere,[47] which created animal reserves and provided for the protection of migratory birds, plants, and animals.

---

[43] Rt. Hon. Herb Gray, Boundary Waters Treaty Centennial Symposium: Keynote Opening Address, 54 WAYNE L. REV. 1451, 1457 (2008). *See also* INTERNATIONAL JOINT COMMISSION, *International Watersheds Initiative: Implementing a New Paradigm for Transboundary Basins, Third Report to Governments on the Intenrational Watersheds Initiative* (Jan. 2009) http://www.IJC.org/php/publications/pdf/ID1627.pdf; INTERNATIONAL JOINT COMMISSION, *The IJC and the 21st Century: Response of the IJC to a Request by the Governments of Canada and the United States for Proposals on How to Best Assist Them to Meet the Environmental Challenges of the 21st Century*, http://www.ijc.org/php/publications/html/21ste.htm.

[44] U.S. Dept. of State, Statement by Secretary of State Condoleezza Rice (Jan. 9, 2009) http://bwt.ijc.org/index.php?page=statement-by-secretary-of-state-condoleezza-rice&hl=eng.

[45] U.S. Dept. of State, Press Release No. 2009/T9/1, Remarks at the 100th Anniversary of the Boundary Waters Treaty, June 13, 2009), http://www.state.gov/secretary/rm/2009a/06/124716 .htm; John R. Crook, ed., United States and Canada Announce Negotiations to Update Great Lakes Water Quality Agreement, 103 Am. J. Int'l L. 604, 604–605 (2009).

[46] Convention Relative to the Preservation of Fauna and Flora in Their Natural State (London, Nov. 8, 1933), 172 I.N.T.S. 241; U.K.T.S. 27, Cmd. 5280 (entered into force Jan. 14, 1936).

[47] Convention on Nature Protection and Wildlife Preservation in the Western Hemisphere (Washington D.C., Oct. 12, 1940), 161 U.N.T.S. 193; 56 Stat. 1354, T.S. No. 981; 3 Bevans 630.

The heightening awareness of the global environment and concern for global management of the environment during this period can be attributed to several factors, including: (1) the accelerated exploitation of natural resources in much of the world; (2) the devastation that the "second industrial revolution" had brought about on the environment; (3) the recognition and understanding that national environmental protection remedies alone were insufficient to cope with transnational pollution, confirmed by a number of well-publicized disasters such as the wrecks of the Torrey Canyon and the Argo Merchant;[48] and (4) the availability of several international organizations – such as the United Nations and the European Economic Community – as suitable fora in which to address crucial international environmental concerns.

By the late 1960s, these factors catalyzed a proliferation of bilateral, regional, and multilateral conventions on such diverse issues as oil pollution on the high seas, nuclear transportation and waste disposal, river pollution, protection of endangered species, acid rain, weather modification, and transboundary air pollution.[49] By the early 1970s, over 20 institutional arrangements and over 300 bilateral and multilateral conventions existed related to rivers (*see* Chapter 9).[50] Although the largest percentage of these river basins are found in Europe, basins in Asia, Africa, and South America are increasingly becoming subject to international control.[51] Another subject of frequent international agreements is the management of oil pollution on the high seas.[52] By 1974, there were over 30 multilateral conventions and numerous protocols governing the transport of oil.[53] Despite these advances, it was clear by the early 1970s that environmental efforts were scattered, redundant, and insufficient to meet the global environmental challenge.

3.2   Case Law

A few selected decisions rendered to resolve international environmental disputes will be discussed here. The following cases, including diplomatic correspondence and arbitral decisions, helped define the responsibility of

---

[48] *See generally* V. Nanda, *The 'Torrey Canyon' Disaster: Some Legal Aspects*, 44 Denv. L.J. 400 (1967); P. Dempsey & L. Helling, *Oil Pollution by Ocean Vessels – An Environmental Tragedy*, 10 Denv. J. Int'l L. & Pol'y 37 (1980).

[49] *See generally* U.N. Doc. UNEP/GC/Information/5 & Corr. 1 (1977).

[50] *See* Developments in the Field of Natural Resources – Water, Energy and Minerals – Technical Aspects of International River Basin Development, U.N. Doc. E/C.7/35, at 13 (1972).

[51] *See id.*, Annex VI, at 21.

[52] *See generally* T. Mensah, *International Environmental Law: International Conventions Concerning Oil Pollution at Sea*, 8 Case W. Res. J. Int'l L. 110 (1976).

[53] *Id.*

states toward one another regarding the use of the environment. Although many of these decisions have been criticized in retrospect as narrow and ineffective,[54] they provided a theoretical framework and enunciated norms on state responsibility – such as *sic utere* and the duty to forewarn – which influenced the subsequent development of international environmental law. It is possible to be critical of some of these cases in light of present standards, yet the decisions were rendered at a time when a notion of nearly absolute state sovereignty was the norm in international law and international environmental law was in its embryonic stage.

3.2.1   *Bering Sea Fur Seals Arbitration*[55]

Pursuant to the US legislation designed to protect populations of fur-bearing animals, including fur seals, from overexploitation, the US seized British vessels engaged in the hunting and killing of seals at a distance of at least 60 miles from the nearest US land. The US owned the breeding grounds to which seals resorted, although they were being hunted on the high seas. The issue for arbitration was couched in property terms and it was held that British ships were exercising freedom of the sea when they hunted fur seals more than three miles off the US coast. It was determined that the US had no right of protection or property in the fur seals outside the three mile limit.

3.2.2   *The Trail Smelter Arbitration*[56]

This arbitral proceeding between the United States and Canada involved the operation of a smelter plant located in British Columbia. Sulphur dioxide emissions from the smelter were causing substantial damage to a number of farms in the State of Washington. In 1935, the United States and Canadian governments signed a convention under which a tribunal was established in order to resolve questions concerning the nature and extent of the damage caused by the Canadian facility, provide remedies including indemnity and injunction, and prescribe measures or regimes to be "adopted or maintained by the Trail Smelter."[57] Under the *compromis* the arbitrators were to apply the "law and practice followed…in the United States of America as well as international law and practice."[58]

---

[54] *See, e.g.*, P. Waxler, Protecting the Global Atmosphere: Beyond the Montreal Protocol, 14 MD. J. INT'L L. & TRADE 1, 5 (1990).
[55] Bering Sea Fur Seals Arbitration (GB v US), 1 J. Moore's Int'l Arb. Awards 755 (1893).
[56] Trail Smelter (US. v. Can.), 3 R.I.A.A. 1905 (1938 and 1941).
[57] *Id.* at 1905.
[58] Convention for Settlement of Difficulties Arising from Operations of Smelter at Trail, B.C., Apr. 15, 1935, *id.* at 1907, 1908 (1938).

After examining available precedents under the principles of both international law and United States law, the Tribunal, in its final decision of March 11, 1941, concluded that

> under the principles of international law, as well as of the law of the United States, no State has the right to use or permit the use of its territory in such a manner as to cause injury by fumes in or to the territory of another or the properties or persons therein, when the case is of serious consequence and the injury is established by clear and convincing evidence.

∗   ∗   ∗

> Considering the circumstances of the case, the Tribunal holds that the Dominion of Canada is responsible in international law for the conduct of the Trail Smelter. Apart from the undertakings in the Convention, it is, therefore, the duty of the Government of the Dominion of Canada to see to it that this conduct should be in conformity with the obligation of the Dominion under international law....[59]

The Tribunal implemented its decision by imposing a detailed regime of controls on the emission of sulfur dioxide fumes from the smelter.[60]

The United States claimed indemnity for injury that was primarily economic in nature, in regard to: (1) cleared land and improvements on it, (2) uncleared land and improvements on it, (3) livestock, (4) property in the town of Northport, and (5) business enterprises.[61] The Tribunal found that damage had occurred through reduction in crop yield due to fumigation and awarded indemnity.[62] It also awarded indemnity for damage to timberland[63] and for special damage by the reduction in use or rental value of some 40 farms.[64] However, it denied indemnity on other US claims on the ground that either the United States had failed to prove the alleged damage, or that the damage, "even if proved, too indirect and remote to become the basis, in law, for an award of indemnity."[65] Although the existence of damage to the health of the inhabitants was asserted by the United States, no indemnity was claimed for such damage.[66]

Furthermore, although the United States had alleged that the disposal of slag from the Trail Smelter injuriously affected the waters of the Columbia River, no evidence was adduced before the Tribunal to support this claim.[67]

---

[59] Trail Smelter, *supra* note 56, at 1965–66, pp. 157, 158 (1941).
[60] *Id.* at 1974–78.
[61] *Id.* at 1920 (1938).
[62] *Id.* at 1925.
[63] *Id.* at 1926–31.
[64] *Id.* at 1926.
[65] *Id.* at 1931.
[66] *Id.* at 1961 (1941).
[67] *Id.* at 1931–32 (1938).

It should, however, be mentioned that Canada argued that this item of damages was not within the meaning of the words "damages caused by the Trail Smelter," as used in Article 3 of the 1935 Convention between the United States and Canada, under which the Tribunal was constituted. Because of the lack of evidence on the question, the Tribunal did not feel obliged to pass on the Canadian contentions.[68]

The value of the case as a precedent has been questioned primarily on two grounds: (1) the Tribunal granted the injunction based on a dictum[69] in a United States case, Georgia v. Tennessee Copper Co.;[70] and (2) it ignored the restrictive language of the compromis under which it was instructed to look to United States law, thus expanding "its own powers to decide the issues in accordance with the less easily ascertainable international law."[71] The Tribunal, however, found it reasonable "to follow by analogy, in international cases," precedents established by the United States Supreme Court which addressed controversies concerning the "quasi-sovereign rights" of states of the union, as there was "no contrary rule [of] international law" and no reason to reject such precedents due to the "limitations of sovereignty inherent in the Constitution of the United States."[72]

The Tribunal found that it did not have to decide whether international law or United States law governed the dispute, for it made a determination that "the law followed in the United States in dealing with the quasi-sovereign rights of the States of the Union, in the matter of air pollution, whilst more definite, is in conformity with the general rules of international law."[73]

In considering the implications of the Trail Smelter decision it should be noted that under the Convention, Canada specifically had assumed international responsibility for damage caused to the United States from activities within Canada.[74] However, the importance of this arbitral decision lies in one of its most often cited pronouncements on international environmental law and state responsibility: "No State has the right to use or permit the use of its territory in such a manner as to cause injury by fumes in or to the territory of another or the properties or persons therein" (*sic utere tuo, ut alienum non laedas*). This affirmation of the principle of good neighborliness set the stage for the international community to eventually develop norms

---

[68] *Id.* at 1932.
[69] *See* A. P. Lester, River Pollution in International Law, 57 AM. J. INT'L L. 828, 837–38 (1963); A. Rubin, *Pollution by Analogy: The Trail Smelter Arbitration*, 50 ORE. L. REV. 259, 270–71 (1971).
[70] 206 U.S. 230 (1906).
[71] A. Rubin, *supra* note 69, at 262.
[72] 3 R.I.A.A. 1964 (1941).
[73] *Id.* at 1963.
[74] *Id.* at 1912 (1938).

of state responsibility regarding transboundary pollution; it remains one of the guiding principles of international environmental law, as evidenced by its crystallization as Principle 2 in the 1992 Rio Declaration:

> States have, in accordance with the Charter of the United Nations and the principles of international law, the sovereign right to exploit their own resources pursuant to their environmental and developmental policies, and the responsibility to ensure that activities within their jurisdiction or control do not cause damage to the environment of other States or of areas beyond the limits of national jurisdiction.[75]

It is worth noting that the Rio Declaration rejects the Trail Smelter's "clear and convincing evidence" standard of injury as well as "serious consequence" requirement to meet the threshold standard of harm. However, the "damage" requirement in the Rio Declaration does connote a "significant" level of harm that is actionable.

3.2.3   *The Corfu Channel Case*

In 1949, the International Court of Justice reaffirmed the *sic utere* principle in the Corfu Channel case,[76] expanding the rule to obligate a state to warn others of imminent danger and imposing liability if it fails to disclose information that might have a harmful effect on other states. This case arose after two British warships passing through the Corfu Channel, in Albanian territorial waters, struck mines. The vessels were damaged and there was loss of lives among the crews. The Court determined that since Albania had allowed its waters to be mined it had breached its international obligation to ensure that actions on its territory did not cause harm to others. As Albania had failed to take steps necessary to warn ships approaching the danger zone or to avoid the harm caused by mines, the Court concluded that under international law Albania was responsible for the explosions and was required to pay compensation for the loss of human life and property. This rule has been expanded by analogy to include transboundary environmental dangers or risks.[77] This principle also finds expression in a number of subsequent cases which are discussed in the following sections.

---

[75] UNCED, Rio Declaration on Environment and Development, U.N. Doc. A/CONF.151/26/ Rev.1 (Vol. 1), Annex 1, Principle 2 (1992), *reprinted in* 31 I.L.M. 874 (1992). The 1972 U.N. Conference on the Human Environment (U.N. Doc. A/CONF.48/14/and corr. 1 (1972) enshrined this concept in Principle 21.

[76] Corfu Channel Case (Uk. v. Alb.), 1949 I.C.J. 4.

[77] *See, e.g.,* Comment (e) to Section 601, *ALI Restatement (Third) Foreign Relations Law of the United States* 103 (1967).

3.2.4   *The Lac Lanoux Arbitration*

This Spanish-French controversy, decided in November 1957, concerned the claim of the lower riparian, Spain, that France could not unilaterally decide to divert the waters of a shared watercourse flowing from Lake Lanoux as part of a hydroelectric project.[78] The arbitral decision appeared to support the principle that a state has an affirmative duty to notify other states that may experience environmental damage due to its proposed activities.[79] Yet the Arbitral Tribunal rejected Spain's claim for want of demonstration that

> the works would bring about a definitive pollution of waters [of the river Carol which flowed from Lake Lanoux into Spain and to which the diverted water would be returned] or that returned waters would have a chemical composition or a temperature or some other characteristic which could injure Spanish interests.[80]

In the absence of proof of actual damage caused by alteration in either the quantity or quality of water, Spain could not assert her territorial integrity as the basis for vetoing any change proposed by another riparian state.[81]

3.2.5   *The Japanese Fishermen Case*

This case arose out of the 1954 United States hydrogen bomb tests conducted in the Marshall Island Trust Territories.[82] The hydrogen bomb tests were regarded as a violation of the United States Trusteeship Agreement, a violation of the UN Charter and therefore an illegal action under international law and a cause of pollution of international waters and air space.[83] Although no tribunal was established in order to determine the extent of damages or the issue of liability, the United States paid $2 million through diplomatic channels as compensation to Japan for subjecting the crew of a Japanese fishing vessel to excessive levels of radiation and for contaminating the catch of a number of other Japanese fishing boats during the course of the tests.[84]

---

[78] *See* Lac Lanoux (Spain v. Fr.), 12 U.N.R.I.A.A. 281 (1957). *See generally* 53 Am. J. Int'l L. 156, 158–61 (1959).

[79] *See* G. Palmer, *New Ways to Make International Law*, 86 Am. J. Int'l L. 259, 265 (1992).

[80] 53 Am. J. Int'l L *supra* note 78, at 160.

[81] *See id.* at 160–71.

[82] For background information *see Lewis Straus's Complete Statement After Bravo and the Japanese Government's Response*, American Experience, http://www.pbs.org/wgbh/amex/bomb/filmmore/reference/primary/straussbravo.html.

[83] *See* E. Margolis, *The Hydrogen Bomb Experiments and International Law*, 64 Yale L.J. 629, 637–39 (1955).

[84] For a report on the payment, *see* N.Y. Times, Jan. 5, 1955, at 6, col. 1. The United States note specified that the payment was made as an "expression of its concern and regret," and that it was tendered "without reference to the question of legal liability." *Id.* at col. 2.

Even staunch defenders of the United States position conceded that in international controversies over air and water pollution, the standard of reasonableness should apply, to be "determined by the familiar process of balancing 'the utility of the conduct' causing damage, and 'the gravity of the harm' to the injured party."[85] Whether the United States conduct was legal or illegal is beside the point; for the present discussion, it is pertinent that the US action created the expectation that a state be responsible for conduct that results in injury or damage.

3.2.6   *The 1958 US Pacific Nuclear Tests*

A 1958 Japanese-United States diplomatic exchange sheds further light on the then-emerging norm of state responsibility for environmental damage or injury. In February 1958 the United States Atomic Energy Commission issued notice of the establishment of a danger zone of approximately 390,000 square miles in connection with the Marshall Islands nuclear tests.[86] In a diplomatic note, the Japanese government expressed its concern "in view of the fact that said zone is near to routes of the Japanese merchant marine and to fishing grounds of Japanese fishing boats,"[87] and notified the United States of the Japanese government's position that

> the United States Government has the responsibility of compensating for economic losses that may be caused by the establishment of a danger zone and for all losses and damages that may be inflicted on Japan and the Japanese people as a result of the nuclear tests.[88]

In its response the United States government said that, due to precautions to be observed during the tests, it anticipated "no economic losses from radioactive contamination of marine life."[89] However, the reply went on to state that

> if, after the test series has ended, any evidence is officially presented that substantial economic losses for Japan or Japanese nationals have been incurred as a result of establishment of the danger area and the tests, the United States is prepared...to give consideration to the question of compensation in the light of such evidence.[90]

---

[85] M. McDougal & N. Schlei, *The Hydrogen Bomb Test in Perspective: Lawful Measures for Security*, 64 YALE L.J. 648, 691 (1955) (footnote omitted). *See also* M. McDougal, *The Hydrogen Bomb Tests and the International Law of the Sea*, 49 AM. J. INT'L L. 356, 361 (1955).

[86] 4 WHITEMAN, *supra* note 11, at 578–79.

[87] *Id.* at 585.

[88] *Id.* at 585–86.

[89] *Id.* at 587.

[90] *Id.*

Although the American Pacific nuclear tests continued until September 1958, no claim for damages was made by the Japanese government. On the other hand, efforts were made to secure an early suspension of all such tests.[91] To illustrate, in 1957 the Federation of Japan Tuna Fishermen's Cooperative Association requested suspension of the forthcoming British nuclear tests in the Pacific Ocean.[92] In reply, the British government reiterated its position that "if any claim is received for damage or loss said to have been incurred as a result of these tests, it will be carefully examined and Her Majesty's Government's attitude will depend on the facts in each particular case."[93]

3.2.7   Nuclear Tests Cases (Australia v. France and New Zealand v. France)[94]

In 1973, the governments of Australia and New Zealand instituted proceedings before the International Court of Justice challenging the legality of French atmospheric nuclear testing in the South Pacific at France's Mururoa Atoll in French Polynesia, claiming that it violated their territorial sovereignty and their right "to be free from atmospheric nuclear weapon tests";[95] they sought a declaratory judgment from the Court that the "carrying out of further atmospheric nuclear weapon tests in the South Pacific Ocean [was] not consistent with applicable rules of international law."[96] The applicants contended in particular that the conduct of French nuclear tests in the atmosphere created anxiety, apprehension, and concern among the people of Australia and New Zealand; further, that any radioactive material deposited on the territories of these states would be potentially dangerous and "any injury caused thereby would be irreparable."[97]

The French argued that, "in the absence of ascertained damage" attributable to their nuclear tests, they did not violate any international law rule.[98] While the court ordered interim measures, asking France to "avoid nuclear tests causing the deposit of radio-active fallout" on the territories of Australia and New Zealand,[99] it did not pass upon the validity of the applicants' claims.

---

[91] *Id.* at 593.

[92] *Id.* at 598.

[93] *Id.* at 599.

[94] Nuclear Tests Cases (Australia v. France), 1973 I.C.J. 99 (June 22); 1973 I.C.J. 320 (July 12); 1973 I.C.J. 338 (Aug. 28); New Zealand v. France, 1973 I.C.J. 135 (June 22); 1973 I.C.J. 324 (July 12); 1973 I.C.J. 341 (Sept. 6).

[95] Nuclear Tests, (Australia v. France; New Zealand v. France), Interim Protection, 1973 I.C.J. 103, 139–40. The New Zealand and Australian claims were quite similar.

[96] *Id.* at 99 and 135.

[97] *Id.* at 104, 140–41.

[98] *Id.* at 105.

[99] *Id.* at 106, 142.

Subsequently, in its judgment of December 20, 1974, the Court found no reason to address the merits of the case.[100] It concluded that, since France had ceased conducting these tests, the applicants' objective was presumably met and the dispute had ceased to exist.[101] Therefore, the Court declared the cases moot and dismissed them both without reaching the merits.[102]

The Australian and New Zealand claims to enjoin the French nuclear testing on the basis of territorial sovereignty were contested by Judge Ignacio-Pinto, who felt that the injunctive relief granted by the Court was not provided for between states under international environmental law. He said, to the contrary, that "each State is free to act as it thinks fit within the limits of its sovereignty, and in the event of genuine damage or injury, if the said damage is clearly established, it owes reparation to the date having suffered that damage."[103] In Judge Ignacio-Pinto's opinion, however, there were

> no existing legal means in the present state of the law which would authorize a State to come before the Court asking it to prohibit another State from carrying out on its own territory such activities, which involve risks to its neighbors.[104]

It is worth noting that although the ICJ did not base its decision on the merits of the applicants' claims, its granting of interim measures endorsed the emerging international environmental norm that no state may cause transboundary environmental harm to another. It should also be noted that in their Joint Dissenting Opinion four judges contended that there was a valid legal basis for Australia's and New Zealand's claims to warrant judgment on the merits.[105]

3.2.8   *Pollution of Ciudad Juarez*

On April 6, 1961, the Chargé d'affaires ad interim of Mexico addressed a note to the United States Secretary of State concerning alleged offensive odors caused by two American companies which were said to be "polluting the air with gaseous fumes [and] throwing fetid offal in the Rio Grande," thus causing "serious physical and economic damage" to the residents and businesses of Ciudad Juarez.[106] The government of Mexico hoped that the United States government would take the steps necessary to have the companies "cease to

---

[100] *See* Nuclear Tests (Australia v. France), 1974 I.C.J. 253; (New Zealand v. France), 1974 I.C.J. 457 (Judgment of Dec. 20). *See generally* 12 UN MONTHLY CHRON., Jan. 1975, at 99.

[101] 1974 I.C.J. 253, 271; 1974 I.C.J. 457, 475; UN MONTHLY CHRON., *supra* note 100, at 103.

[102] 1973 I.C.J. 131.

[103] *Id. See generally* Don MacKay, *Nuclear Testing: New Zealand and France in the International Court of Justice*, 19 FORDHAM INT'L L.J. 1857 (1996).

[104] 1973 I.C.J. 131.

[105] 1974 I.C.J. 253, pp. 110 *et seq.*

[106] 6 WHITEMAN, *supra* note 11, at 256–57.

cause odors to be emitted from their plants, to pollute international waters illegally by throwing offal into the Rio Grande, and to discharge gaseous fumes in preparing their products, all of which is causing serious injury to the people of Ciudad Juarez, Chihuahua, Mexico."[107]

In his reply, the Secretary of State noted that the companies had in the meantime taken measures "at considerable costs" to control the odors.[108] He enumerated the measures taken and observed that residents who had previously complained had subsequently stated that the objectionable odors had been removed. He concluded: "The Department is gratified that it can make so favorable a report in a matter of concern to the Government of Mexico."[109] It is worth noting that in this case the term "damage" was not interpreted in the narrow sense as done in the Trail Smelter arbitration. Thus, it could be argued that the case effectively extended the doctrine of state responsibility as set forth in the Trail Smelter arbitration.[110]

3.2.9   *The 1969 Gut Dam Case*[111]

This case involved the arbitration of a prospective agreement between the United States and Canada, under which the United States consented to the Canadian construction of the Gut Dam on the two nations' border, while Canada agreed to indemnify for any damage caused by the dam. The tribunal's arbitration of damages was based on the agreement between the parties.[112]

3.2.10   *Legality of the Threat or Use of Nuclear Weapons, Advisory Opinion*[113]

In response to the UN General Assembly's request to the Court to render its advisory opinion on the following question: "Is the threat or use of nuclear weapons in any circumstances permitted under international law?",[114] an evenly divided International Court of Justice, with the President's casting vote, decided that "the threat or use of nuclear weapons would generally be

---

[107] *Id.* at 258.

[108] *Id.* at 259.

[109] *Id.*

[110] *See generally* Rubin, *supra* note 69, at 276–82.

[111] Gut Dam Claims (Can. v. U.S.), 8 I.L.M. 114 (1969).

[112] *Id.* at 121.

[113] Legality of the Threat or Use of Nuclear Weapons, Advisory Opinion, I.C.J. Rep. 1996 ICJ Rept. 226, *reprinted in* 35 I.L.M. 809 (1996). *See generally* VED P. NANDA & DAVID KRIEGER, NUCLEAR WEAPONS AND THE WORLD COURT (1992).

[114] Resolution 49/75 K adopted by the U.N. General Assembly on December 15, 1994, *cited in* Legality of the Threat or Use of Nuclear Weapons, July 8, 1996, *supra* note 113, at para. 1.

contrary to the rules of international law applicable in armed conflict," but that "the Court cannot conclude definitively whether the threat or use of nuclear weapons would be lawful or unlawful in an extreme circumstance of self-defense, in which the very survival of a State would be at stake."[115] The Court made a few significant observations related to the environment, including the following:

> The Court recognizes that the environment is under daily threat and that the use of nuclear weapons could constitute a catastrophe for the environment. The Court also recognizes that the environment is not an abstraction but represents the living space, the quality of life and the very health of human beings, including generations unborn. The existence of the general obligation of States to ensure that activities within their jurisdiction and control respect the environment of other States or of areas beyond national control is now part of the corpus of international law relating to the environment.[116]
>
> …States must take environmental considerations into account when assessing what is necessary and proportionate in the pursuit of legitimate military objectives. Respect for the environment is one of the elements that go to assessing whether an action is in conformity with the principles of necessity and proportionality.[117]

3.2.11   *Case Concerning the Gabcikovo – Nagymaros Project*[118]

Hungary and then-Czechoslovakia brought for resolution before the International Court of Justice a dispute which raised issues related to pertaining to transboundary environmental law as well as transboundary water law. These countries had entered into a treaty in 1997 to build dams on the Danube River.[119] With the political transformation in these countries in 1989 Hungary suspended construction of the Nagymaros Dam and subsequently in 1992 unilaterally terminated the agreement, purportedly on environmental grounds, contending that if the project were concluded as planned, it would inflict serious environmental harm. Slovakia rejected Hungary's environmental claim and after changing the design continued its part of the project, the Gabcikovo Project, so that the dam was to be built totally on Slovak

---

[115] *Id.* at para. 105(2)E.

[116] *Id.* at para. 29.

[117] *Id.* at para. 30, citing as support Principle 24 of the Rio Declaration, which provides that: "Warfare is inherently destructive of sustainable development. States shall therefore respect international law providing protection for the environment in times of armed conflict and cooperate in its further development, as necessary."

[118] Case Concerning the Gabcikovo – Nagymaros Project (Hung. v. Slov.), Judgment of 25 Sept. 1997, 1997 I.C.J. 7.

[119] Czechoslovakia-Hungary Treaty Concerning the Construction and Operation of the Gabcikovo-Nagymaros System of Locks, 1109 U.N.T.S. 235, *reprinted in* 32 I.L.M. 1247 (1993).

territory. It completed the project in 1992, unilaterally diverting a substantial part of the Danube River away from the Hungary-Slovakia border.

The Court acknowledged that Hungary's concerns "for its natural environment in the region affected by the Gabcikovo-Nagymaros Project related to an 'essential interest' of that State." It cited the Court's 1996 Advisory Opinion on the Legality of the Threat or Use of Nuclear Weapons, in which it had stressed "the great significance that it attaches to respect for the environment, not only for States but also for the whole of mankind."[120]

The then-Vice President of the Court, Judge Christopher Weeramantry, wrote in a separate opinion that "sustainable development" should be considered as more than a mere concept" and "as a principle with normative value which is crucial to the determination of this case."[121]

As a "key issue" the Court recognized "the Project's impact upon, and its implications for, the environment."[122] It added that it "is mindful that, in the field of environmental protection, vigilance and prevention are required on account of the often irreversible character of damage to the environment and of the limitations inherent in the very mechanism of reparation of this type of damage."[123] It referred to "new norms and standards" that have been developed during the prior two decades, which must be considered "not only when States contemplate new activities but also when continuing with activities begun in the past."[124] It stressed the "need to reconcile economic development with protection of the environment [which] is aptly expressed in the concept of sustainable development."[125] Thus it called upon the parties to "look afresh at the effects on the environment of the operation of the Gabcikovo power plant. In particular they must find a satisfactory solution for the volume of water to be released into the old bed of the Danube and into the side-arms on both sides of the river."[126]

Notwithstanding the importance given by the International Court of Justice to environmental considerations in this case, environmentalists were disappointed that the Court did not apply the Precautionary Principle to decide the case.[127]

---

[120] *Id.* at para. 53, citing I.C.J. Reports 1996, para. 29, already noted above.

[121] *Id.* (Separate Opinion of Vice President Weeramantry).

[122] *Id.* at para. 140.

[123] *Id.*

[124] *Id.*

[125] *Id.*

[126] *Id.*

[127] *See* Chapter 9, *infra*, for further discussion of the case.

3.2.12   *The MOX Plant Case (Ireland v. UK)*[128]

The dispute raised transboundary environmental issues. At Sellafield in Northwest England on the coast of the Irish Sea, the United Kingdom authorized British Nuclear Fuels (BNFL), a government-owned company, to start operating a plant for the manufacture of mixed oxide (MOX) fuel from uranium and plutonium oxides. Ireland had been unsuccessful through diplomatic means in obtaining environmental and safety information and resorted to arbitration under the United Nations Convention on the Law of the Sea (UNCLOS)[129] and the Convention for the Protection of the Marine Environment of the North-East Atlantic (OSPAR Convention).[130] The Irish claim before the International Tribunal for the Law of the Sea (ITLOS) was that operation of the MOX Plant would result in an increased level of radioactive discharges into the marine environment, thus the United Kingdom had violated basic procedural and substantive obligations in the UNCLOS Convention, including assessment of environmental impacts. The OSPAR Convention claim concerned access to information redacted from reports prepared as part of the approval process for the commissioning of the MOX plant in the UK Ireland also requested the ITLOS to adopt provisional measures that would prevent the operation of the plant and freeze the transport of radioactive materials associated with the MOX plant, and to take the necessary steps to ensure that no radioactive substances moved into or out of waters within UK sovereignty.

The ITLOS rejected Ireland's request for provisional measures, prescribing instead alternate provisional measures requiring Ireland and the United Kingdom to cooperate and consult in order to exchange information, risks or effects for the Irish Sea of the MOX plant operation and devise appropriate measures to prevent marine environmental pollution which might result from the plant's operation.[131] These measures were based on the duty to cooperate as "a fundamental principle in the prevention of pollution of the marine environment" under Part XII of UNCLOS, as well as general international law.[132] The Tribunal said that in its view "prudence and caution

---

[128] MOX Plant (Ir. v. U.K.) (Provisional Measures), Int'l Trib. for the Law of the Sea, Dec. 3, 2001, *reprinted in* 41 I.L.M. 405 (2001); Dispute Concerning Access to Information Under Article 9 of the OSPAR Convention (Ir. v. U.K.), 23 U.N.R.I.A.A. 59 (Decision of the Arbitral Tribunal, 2 July 2003).

[129] United Nations Convention on the Law of the Sea, Dec. 10, 1982, U.N. Doc. A/CONF.62/122, *reprinted in* 21 I.L.M. 1261 (1982).

[130] Convention for the Protection of the Marine Environment of the North-East Atlantic, Sept. 22, 1992, 2354 UNTS 67, *reprinted in* 32 I.L.M. 1069 (1992).

[131] ITLOS Provisional Measures, *supra* note 128, at para. 89.1(a)–(c).

[132] *Id.* at para. 82.

require that Ireland and the United Kingdom cooperate in exchanging information concerning risks or effects of operation of the MOX plant and in devising ways to deal with them as appropriate."[133] The Tribunal implicitly supported a state's duty to conduct transboundary environmental assessment and the obligation to consult and exchange information with states likely to be affected by its actions.

Subsequently, on July 2, 2003, the OSPAR Tribunal issued its opinion on the dispute. Pursuant to Article 9 of the OSPAR Convention, Ireland had requested access to information redacted from reports prepared for the approval process for the commissioning of the MOX plant. That article requires the contracting parties to make available "to any natural or legal person, in response to any reasonable request,...any available information...on the state of the maritime area [and] on activities or measures adversely affecting or likely to affect it." However, Article 9(3) allows the parties "in accordance with their national legal systems...to provide for a request for such information to be refused where it affects" certain matters requiring confidentiality, including "commercial and industrial confidentiality." The Tribunal narrowly interpreted Article 9. The information sought under the article, the majority said, must satisfy all the conditions, viz., "on the state of the maritime area"; on "activities or measures adversely affecting or likely to affect...the maritime area"; and "on activities or measures introduced in accordance with the Convention."[134] It dismissed Ireland's claims, holding that Ireland had failed to demonstrate that the redacted items are "'information...on the state of the maritime area' or, even if they were, are likely adversely to affect the maritime area."[135]

3.2.13 *Iron Rhine Railway Arbitration (Belg. v. Neth.)*[136]

The "Iron Rhine" is a railway that links Antwerp, Belgium, to the Rhine Basin in Germany, as it passes through two Netherlands provinces. During World War I commercial traffic was halted on the railway, and while it was resumed thereafter, the railway was destroyed during World War II and was later rebuilt. However, through traffic on the railway ceased in 1991. In 1998, the Belgian prime minister initiated discussions with the Netherlands about reactivating the railway. A memorandum of understanding in March 2000 called for environmental impact studies of the proposed reactivation and establishing a timeline for such reactivation. After the completion of

---

[133] *Id.* at para. 84.
[134] Decision of the Arbitral Tribunal, supra note 128, at para. 168.
[135] *Id.* at para. 179.
[136] Iron Rhine Railway Arbitration (Belg. v. Neth.), 27 U.N.R.I.A.A. 127 (Decision of the Arbitral Tribunal, 24 May 2005).

the environmental impact studies in 2001 there were disagreements on the cost allocation and the conditions on the use of the line. An 1839 treaty between the parties, pursuant to which the Iron Rhine was originally built provided for Belgium to bear the entire cost and expense up to the border of Germany.

The issues before the Tribunal were 1) whether the Netherlands' treaty obligation to allow construction and operation of the railway constrained its sovereign right to impose "'highly expensive' environmental protection measures as a condition to allow the reactivation," and 2) whether Belgium's obligation to bear the "cost and expense" of any "agreed works" on the line included an obligation to pay for environmental protection measures required by the Netherlands.[137]

In interpreting the treaty, the Tribunal noted that

> "environment" is broadly referred to as including air, water, land, flora and fauna, natural ecosystems and sites, human health and safety, and climate. The emerging principles, whatever their current status, make reference to conservation, management, notions of prevention and of sustainable development, and protection for future generations.[138]

The Tribunal referred to developments since the 1972 Stockholm Conference, on to the 1992 Rio Declaration, and observed:

> Importantly, these emerging principles now integrate environmental protection into the development process. Environmental law and the law on development stand not as alternatives but as mutually reinforcing integral concepts, which require that where development may cause significant harm to the environment, there is a duty to prevent, or at least mitigate, such harm.... This duty, in the opinion of the Tribunal, has now become a principle of general international law. This principle applies not only in autonomous activities but also in activities undertaken in implementation of specific treaties between the Parties.[139]

The Tribunal then referred to the ICJ's observation in the *Gabcikovo-Nagymaros Case* that the need to reconcile economic development with environmental protection "is aptly expressed in the concept of sustainable development," and to the Court's clarification there that "new norms have to be taken into consideration,...new standards given proper weight, not only when States contemplate new activities but also when continuing activities

---

[137] *See* JONATHAN CARLSON, SIR GEOFFREY PALMER, AND BURNS WESTON, DOC. SUPP. TO INTERNATIONAL ENVIRONMENTAL LAW AND WORLD ORDER – A PROBLEM ORIENTED COURSEBOOK 1450 (3d ed. 2011).

[138] Iron Rhine Arbitral Tribunal Decision, *supra* note 136, at para. 58.

[139] *Id.* at para. 59.

begun in the past," holding that the Court's dictum there "applies equally to the Iron Rhine railway."[140]

The Tribunal cited with approval the ICJ's earlier observation that "[t]he existence of the general obligation of States to ensure that activities within their jurisdiction and control respect the environment of other States or of areas beyond national control is now part of the corpus of international law relating to the environment."[141] The Tribunal observed that applying the principles of international environmental law it was faced in this case

> not with a situation of a transboundary effect of the economic activity in the territory of one state on the territory of another state, but with the effect of the exercise of a treaty-guaranteed right of one state in the territory of another state and a possible impact of such exercise on the territory of the latter state. The Tribunal is of the view that, by analogy, where a state exercises a right under international law within the territory of another state, considerations of environmental protection also apply. The exercise of Belgium's right of transit,...thus may well necessitate measures by the Netherlands to protect the environment to which Belgium will have to contribute as an integral element of its request. The reactivation of the Iron Rhine Railway cannot be viewed in isolation from the Environmental Protection Measures by the intended use of the railway line. These measures are to be fully integrated into the project and its costs.[142]

The Tribunal held that Belgium was obligated to fund the environment element of the overall costs of the reactivation as this was was integral to its exercise of its right of transit,[143] and as to the costs of an envisaged tunnel, it apportioned these equally between the parties.[144]

3.2.14 *Case Concerning Pulp Mills on the River Uruguay (Argentina v. Uruguay)*[145]

This environmental dispute between Argentina and Uruguay concerned Uruguay's construction of pulp mills on the banks of the Uruguay River, which forms the boundary between the two countries. Procedural as well as substantive issues were involved. In 1961 the parties had entered into a bilateral treaty which provided for the establishment of a "regime for the

---

[140] *Id.*

[141] *Id.* at para. 222.

[142] *Id.* at para. 223.

[143] *Id.* at para. 226.

[144] *Id.* at para. 234.

[145] Case Concerning Pulp Mills on the River Uruguay (Argentina v. Uruguay) (Merits), ICJ Apr. 20, 2010, *reprinted in* 49 I.L.M. 1118 (2010). *See generally* Cymie R. Payne, *International Decisions: Pulp Mills on the River Uruguay* (Argentina v. Uruguay), 105 Am. J. Int'l L. 94 (2011).

use of the river" covering various issues including the conservation of living resources and prevention of water pollution of the river. The "regime for the use of the river" was established by the 1975 Statute of the River Uruguay (1975 Statute), under which the Administrative Commission of the River Uruguay (CARU) was created. After unsuccessful negotiations to resolve the conflict Argentina submitted the dispute to the ICJ in May 2006, requesting also for provisional measures.[146] The Court declined to order the requested provisional measures to suspend authorization and construction of the pulp mills, on the ground that no harm would occur to Argentina by continued construction of the mills or by Uruguay's procedural breaches, and that if any harm occurred it could be reversed subsequently at Uruguay's cost provided Argentina prevailed on the merits.[147] The ICJ delivered its judgment on the merits on April 20, 2010,[148] finding that Uruguay had breached its procedural obligations of informing, notifying and negotiating with Argentina under the auspices of CARU under the 1975 Statute. However, the Court held that its declaration of this breach "constitutes appropriate satisfaction."[149]

On Uruguay's substantive obligation to prevent pollution and preserve the aquatic environment under Article 41 of the Statute, Argentina claimed that by allowing the discharge of additional nutrients into the river, Uruguay failed to prescribe appropriate measures regarding one of the mills to prevent pollution and thus failed to meet applicable international environmental agreements, which include the Biodiversity Convention and the Ramsar Convention, and further arguing that "the obligation to prevent pollution of the river is an obligation of result and extends not only to protecting the aquatic environment proper, but also to any reasonable and legitimate use of the river, including tourism and other recreational uses."[150] Uruguay contended that it "[had] complied with its duty to prevent pollution by requiring the plant to meet best available technology...standards."[151]

The Court recalled its holding in the 1996 Advisory Opinion on the Legality of the Threat or Use of Nuclear Weapons that there is now a customary international law obligation relating to the environment "to ensure that activities within [States'] jurisdiction and control respect the environment of other States or of areas beyond national control,"[152] and determined that Article 41 of the Statute requires the parties "to adopt appropriate rules and

---

[146] Pulp Mills on the River Uruguay (Arg. v. Uru) (Provisional Measures), ICJ, July 13, 2006.

[147] *Id.* at paras. 71–78.

[148] Pulp Mills Judgment on the Merits, *supra* note 145.

[149] *Id.* at para. 282.

[150] *Id.* at para. 191.

[151] *Id.* at para. 192.

[152] *Id.* at para. 193.

measures within the framework of their respective legal systems to protect and preserve the aquatic environment and to prevent pollution."[153]

Analyzing the application of the 1975 Statute to the controversy, the Court considerably furthered international environmental law. For example, the Court observed that

> the obligation to protect and preserve, under Article 41(a) of the Statute, has to be interpreted in accordance with a practice which in recent years had gained so much acceptance among States that it may now be considered a requirement under general international law to undertake an environmental impact assessment where there is a risk that the proposed industrial activity may have a significant adverse impact in a transboundary context, in particular, on a shared resource. Moreover, due diligence, and the duty of vigilance and prevention which it implies, would not be considered to have been exercised, if a party planning works liable to affect the regime of the river or the quality of its waters did not undertake an environmental impact assessment on the potential effects of such works.[154]

It added that

> it is for each State to determine in its domestic legislation or in the authorization process for the project, the specific content of the environmental impact assessment required in each case, having regard to the nature and magnitude of the proposed development and its likely adverse impact on the environment as well as to the need to exercise due diligence in conducting such an assessment. The Court also considers that an environment impact assessment must be conducted prior to the implementation of a project. Moreover, once operations have started and, where necessary, throughout the life of the project, continuous monitoring of its effects on the environment shall be undertaken.[155]

The Court referred in its analysis of Uruguay's EIA to the work of the UN Environment Program (UNEP) and to the guidelines and recommendations of international technical bodies, concluding that Uruguay did not breach its obligations under Article 41.[156]

3.3 Appraisal

One could argue that the agreements on which modern international environmental law is based are of little precedential value because of the limited perspective of the parties and hence the limited nature of the agreements. Similarly, the precedential value of some of the cases noted here can be

---

[153] *Id.* at para. 195.
[154] *Id.* at para. 204.
[155] *Id.* at para. 205.
[156] *Id.* at para. 265.

questioned on the ground that the claims were decided on rather limited bases, such as mootness in the Nuclear Tests cases, or on the basis of agreements between the parties.

Although the *sic utere* principle was often reiterated in the early days, cases dealt primarily with economic damages and only slowly evolved to recognize principles of broader international environmental responsibility. Several arbitral tribunals involved were not asked to determine whether the alleged state conduct violated principles of customary international law, but to interpret and enforce specific agreements. In the early stages of efforts to resolve bilateral or regional environmental disputes, decision-makers were setting the stage for the development of norms of international environmental law, for the principles enunciated in these agreements and cases can be extended to the problems currently at hand in the 21st century.

Chapter Four

The Next 40 Years: The Evolution of International Environmental Policy from 1972 to the Present

4.0 *Introduction*

This chapter initially focuses on two signal events that were instrumental in shaping the international environmental law and policy agenda in the late 20th century – the 1972 UN Conference on the Human Environment in Stockholm, Sweden, and, 20 years later, the 1992 UN Conference on Environment and Development (UNCED) in Rio de Janeiro, Brazil, popularly known as the "Earth Summit." It further discusses subsequent significant developments, including the 2002 World Summit on Sustainable Development (WSSD) in Johannesburg, and the events leading to the 2012 UN Conference on Sustainable Development (UNCSD) or "Rio+20," as a 20-year follow-up to the historic 1992 Rio Earth Summit. Highlighted are the activities of the United Nations Environment Programme (UNEP) and the Commission on Sustainable Development (CSD), the role of UNEP in the development of international environmental law norms and multilateral environmental agreements (MEAs), and the vexing issue of international environmental governance.

As Mostafa K. Tolba, former Executive Director of UNEP, has noted, the environment became a "top item on the world's political agenda" in 1988.[1] However, public awareness of global environmental concerns preceded this date by 25 years, as advances in science and technology led to a growing realization that human activities were damaging the environment at an accelerated pace. Two 1960s publications – Rachel Carson's book *Silent Spring*[2] and Garrett Hardin's article "Tragedy of the Commons"[3] – in particular

---

[1] UNEP, 1988 Annual Report of the Executive Director, at 1, U.N. Doc. UNEP/GC. 15/4 (1989) [hereinafter 1988 Annual Report].

[2] RACHEL CARSON, SILENT SPRING (1962).

[3] Garrett Hardin, *Tragedy of the Commons*, 162 SCIENCE 1243–48 (1968).

radicalized public and political thinking about the environment. By the late 1960s, concern over environmental degradation had catalyzed a proliferation of international conventions on transboundary air pollution,[4] the world's rivers,[5] and transportation of oil on the high seas.[6] In 1968, the UN General Assembly responded by calling for a world conference to address the human environment.[7]

Soon, world attention began to focus on providing a coherent management strategy for environmental issues, as there was a growing realization that existing environmental efforts were scattered, redundant, and insufficient to meet global needs. Two events in the early 1970s further spurred the growing global efforts. The first was the publication of the Club of Rome's controversial study, *The Limits to Growth*,[8] which presented a bleak picture of humanity's future if environmental degradation were to continue. The second was the UN Conference on the Human Environment, held at Stockholm in June 1972 (Stockholm Conference).

The Stockholm Conference was the most successful international meeting held to that time on the environment, for an agreement was reached among the nations participating that concerted international action was needed in order to meet the environmental challenge. The Conference adopted the Stockholm Declaration, a set of 26 guiding principles, which represented the first global consensus on the nature and scope of the environmental challenge confronting the world community.[9] It also produced an Action Plan containing 109 recommendations for environmental management and established a framework for a new international organization to implement it.[10] The Stockholm Declaration and the resulting UN Environment Program (UNEP) will be discussed next.

---

[4] *See* UNEP, Environmental Law: An In-Depth Review 5, UNEP Rep. No. 2, 1981 [hereinafter UNEP Rep. No. 2]. For a listing of conventions, *see* UNEP, *Register of International Conventions and Protocols in the Field of the Environment*, UNEP/GC./INFO.5 (1977), and accompanying supplements [hereinafter UNEP Register].

[5] *See* Developments in the Field of Natural Resources – Water, Energy and Minerals – Technical Aspects of International River Basin Development, U.N. Doc. E/C 7/35, at 13 (1972).

[6] *See generally* T. Mensah, *International Environmental Law: International Conventions Concerning Oil Pollution at Sea*, 8 CASE W. RES. J. INT'L L. 110 (1976).

[7] G.A. Res. 2398 (XXIII) (Dec. 3, 1968).

[8] D. Meadow, *et al.*, THE LIMITS TO GROWTH (Report to the Club of Rome, 1972).

[9] Report of the United Nations Conference on the Human Environment, U.N. Doc. A/CONF. 48/14/ and Corr. 1 (1972) [hereinafter Stockholm Report]; for the text of the Stockholm Declaration, *see id.* at 3–5.

[10] *See id.* at 6–28 (Action Plan).

4.1   *The Stockholm Conference and Declaration*

4.1.1   *Analysis*

The lasting monument of the 1972 Stockholm Conference was the adoption of the Stockholm Declaration.[11] Although legally nonbinding, its 26 environmental principles reflected general agreement that concerted global action would be required in order to preserve and enhance the human environment, and a number have come to be viewed as binding international law.[12] The preamble recognized the risk that humans "can do massive and irreversible harm to the earthly environment on which our life and well-being depend."[13] It proclaimed the goal to "defend and improve the human environment for present and future generations," along with the "fundamental goals of peace and of worldwide economic and social development."[14] Achievement of the environmental goal, it stated, would "demand the acceptance of responsibility by citizens and communities and by enterprises and institutions at every level, all sharing equitably in common efforts."[15]

Principle 1 declared an individual "right" to a quality environment and linked this right to a "responsibility" on the part of the individual "to protect and improve the environment for present and future generations." To assist the individual in fulfilling this responsibility, Principle 19 stated that education in environmental matters was "essential." Principles 2 through 7 provided a philosophical foundation – presaging the modern notion of sustainable development – as they called for the safeguarding of the natural resources "for the benefit of present and future generations through careful planning or management."[16] Specific suggestions included improvement of "the capacity of the earth to provide vital renewable resources,"[17] use of nonrenewable resources so as to "guard against the danger of their future exhaustion and to ensure that benefits from such employment are shared by all mankind,"[18] wise management of wildlife and its habitat,[19] control of pollution of the seas,[20] and protection from toxic and other dangerous

---

[11] *See generally* L. B. Sohn, *The Stockholm Declaration on the Human Environment*, 14 HARV. INT'L L.J. 423 (1973).

[12] Stockholm Declaration, *supra* note 9, preamble.

[13] *Id.* ¶ 6.

[14] *Id.* (emphasis added).

[15] *Id.* ¶ 7 (emphasis added).

[16] *Id.* Principle 2.

[17] *Id.* Principle 3.

[18] *Id.* Principle 5.

[19] *Id.* Principle 4.

[20] *Id.* Principle 7.

substances.[21] Science, technology, and research were seen as crucial instruments in protecting the environment.[22] An "integrated and coordinated approach" to development and environmental protection, environmental planning, management, and institutions, and international cooperation were also declared to be essential.[23] Such focus on the ends and means of environmental protection was noteworthy, but a major obstacle in the implementation of these principles lay in the rather vague and platitudinous language in which they were couched.

The Conference proceeded to address a variety of policy issues.[24] The key one was the differing roles of developed and developing countries in the implementation of environmental programs. Developing countries emphasized their need to continue to develop, while acknowledging that the environment should be protected and conserved.[25] This notion – that planned economic development can be pursued without detriment to the environment – has evolved into the modern concept of sustainable development. Furthermore, developing states emphasized that their environmental problems were much different from those of developed states: developed states were concerned primarily with pollution resulting from development, whereas developing states were primarily concerned with environmental problems that stemmed from poverty and underdevelopment.[26]

The outcome of this conflict was evident in the special treatment of developing states in the Stockholm Declaration. Principle 8 commenced with a broad statement that emphasized the importance of economic and social development – although it did not yet enunciate a right to development.[27] Principle 9 recognized the differentiated positions of developed and developing countries in regard to the environment. It stated that many environmental problems were the by-products of underdevelopment and poverty and provided for the transfer of technology and funds to the developing countries in an effort to stimulate economic development. Likewise, Principle 12 took into account the "circumstances and particular requirements of the

---

[21] *Id.* Principle 6.

[22] *Id.* Principles 18, 20.

[23] *Id.* Principles 13–15, 17, 24.

[24] *See* M. A. Gray, *The United Nations Environment Programme: An Assessment*, 20 Envtl. L. 291, 293 (1990).

[25] Stockholm Declaration, *supra* note 9, Principles 8–12. *See* J. Ntambirweki, *The Developing Countries in the Evolution of An International Environmental Law*, 14 Hastings Int'l & Comp. L. Rev. 905, 906 (1991).

[26] *See id.* at 907 (Ntambirweki cites a statement made by the Ugandan delegation to the Stockholm Conference).

[27] On the right to development, *see* generally V. Nanda, *A Right to Development: An Appraisal*, *in* World Debt And The Human Condition (V. Nanda ed., 1993).

developing countries" and reiterated the need to provide those states with financial assistance and technology in order that they might "incorporat[e] environmental safeguards into their development planning."

Due to the conflict presented by the developed and developing states at the Conference, the Declaration constituted a compromise.[28] This compromise detracted somewhat from the status of the Declaration as customary international law, but it simultaneously evidenced the need – as a result of the different perceptions and concerns of states at different levels of development – for a flexible approach in regard to environmental issues.

Stockholm's most important contribution is the often-cited Principle 21, which, while acknowledging the sovereignty right of states "to exploit their resources pursuant to their environmental policies," limited that sovereignty by linking it to "the responsibility to ensure that activities within their jurisdiction or control do not cause damage to the environment of other States or of areas beyond their national jurisdiction." This rule of "no transboundary harm" was a reiteration of the sic utere principle of state responsibility stated in the Trail Smelter arbitration[29] (*see* §§ 2.1.1 and 2.1.3).

A less successful declaration was Principle 22:

> States shall cooperate to develop further the international law regarding liability and compensation for the victims of pollution and other environmental damage caused by activities within the jurisdiction or control of such states to areas beyond their jurisdiction.

Unfortunately, this aspiration remains largely unfulfilled.

4.1.2   *Appraisal*

The Stockholm Declaration was certainly the most ambitious environmental undertaking of the international community of its time and is to be lauded as a collection of forward-looking principles accepted by many diverse international actors with competing agendas. Although not initially binding on states as a formal treaty, the Declaration represented and continues to represent an unprecedented international consensus on environmental issues and a strong international legal authority for a number of the provisions which have evolved and are evolving into customary international law.[30]

---

[28] *See* V. Nanda, *Trends in International Environmental Law*, 20 Ca. W. Int'l L.J. 187, 189 (1990).

[29] Trail Smelter (U.S. v. Can.), 3 R.I.A.A. 1905 (1938 & 1941).

[30] *See* I. Hodkova, *Is There a Right to a Healthy Environment in the International Legal Order?* 7 Conn. J. Int'l L. 65, 67 (1991).

4.2   *The Post-Stockholm Period – The Flowering of UNEP*

4.2.1   *Introduction*

Following the Stockholm Conference, the UN General Assembly established a number of bodies to implement the Conference's goals: the United Nations Environment Program (UNEP),[31] consisting of a Governing Council comprising representatives of 58 governments, to serve as a legislative body; the Environmental Fund, financed by voluntary contributions and used to support the cost of new environmental issues undertaken within the UN system; and the Environmental Secretariat, which would serve as a focal point for environmental action and coordination within the UN system, as well as a catalyst for environmental action. In the post-Stockholm period, mounting concern for the environment, coupled with UNEP as a catalyst, led to promising developments. Within a decade, over 100 countries had established ministries of environment, compared to ten prior to Stockholm.[32] An increasing number of developing states accepted the linkage between development and environmental protection.[33] At the international level, all UN specialized agencies and some UN organs began to include relevant environmental considerations in their policies and programs.

It was, however, only after the occurrence of the environmental disasters in Bhopal, Chernobyl, and Basel in the mid-1980s[34] and the 1987 discovery

---

[31] Institutional and Financial Arrangements for International Environmental Cooperation, G.A. Res. 2997, 27 U.N. GAOR Supp. (No. 30) at 43, U.N. Doc. A/8730 (1972). UNEP official documents are contained in UNEP, COMPENDIUM OF LEGISLATIVE AUTHORITY (1978).

[32] *See, e.g.,* J. Donohue, *Earthwatch*, 146 AMERICA 453 (1982).

[33] *See, e.g.,* R. CLARKE & L. TIMBERLAKE, STOCKHOLM PLUS TEN – PROMISES, PROMISES? THE DECADE SINCE THE 1972 UN ENVIRONMENT CONFERENCE (1982). *See* also then-Indian Prime Minister Indira Gandhi's comment at the 1981 UN Conference on New and Renewable Sources of Energy: "We do not attach priority to the environment. We have to make our people more alive to the fact that conservation is not something extra, but is essential in the counting of costs – social costs and even basic economic costs." Interview: Mrs. Gandhi, 6 UNITERRA, No. 5, at 5 (1981). At the Stockholm conference she advocated the position of developing states, saying:
> The rich countries may look upon development as the cause of environmental destruction, but to us it is one of the primary means of improving the environment of living....How can we speak to those who live in villages and in slums about keeping the oceans, rivers and air clean when their own lives are contaminated at the source?

Quoted in N.Y. TIMES, June 15, 1972, at 12, col. 3.

[34] *See generally* V. Nanda & B. Bailey, *Export of Hazardous Waste and Hazardous Technology: Challenge for International Environmental Law*, 17 DEN. J. INT'L L. & POL'Y 155 (1988).

of the hole in the ozone layer over the Antarctic[35] that the world community was roused to definitively confront environmental challenges. It was recognized that concerted global efforts were necessary,[36] and this realization led to an enhanced role for international organizations, especially UNEP, to work on international environmental problems and threats.

Two important documents on the environment appeared in 1987. One was the *Environmental Perspective to the Year 2000 and Beyond*, which cautioned that "despite noteworthy developments…, environmental degradation has continued unabated, threatening human well-being and, in some instances, the very survival of life on our planet."[37] The second was the seminal report of the World Commission on Environment and Development (WCED), entitled *Our Common Future*.[38] The WCED was convened by the UN specifically to address the growing conflict between the developed nations of "the North," with their focus on environmental protection, and the developing countries of "the South," with their emphasis on economic development and fear that environmental protection standards would impede their legitimate interest in economic betterment. The WCED's report advocated adoption of the compromise concept of "sustainable development," which is defined as "development that meets the needs of the present without compromising the ability of future generations to meet their own needs."[39] Adopted at Rio five years later, "sustainable development" will become the new international environmental legal paradigm (*see* § 2.1.4).

Although a large number of UN agencies and other IGOs have become active in the environmental field, UNEP remains the leading international body established to address environmental challenges. Envisioned as a vehicle for coordinating the goals of global environmental assessment and environmental management,[40] it performs this task through the coordination of environmental activities of the various UN agencies and the cooperation of governments, international scientific and professional communities, and nongovernmental organizations. Overall, it acts as "the environmental

---

[35] *See* R. W. Watson *et al., Present State of Knowledge of the Upper Atmosphere 1988: An Assessment Report* 18 (NASA Ref. Pub. 1208, Aug. 1988).

[36] *See generally* V. Nanda, *Stratospheric Ozone Depletion: A Challenge for International Law and Policy*, 10 MICH. J. INT'L L. 482 (1989); V. Nanda, *Global Warming and International Environmental Law: A Preliminary Inquiry*, 30 HARV. J. INT'L L. 375 (1989).

[37] 42 U.N. GAOR, Supp. No. 25, Annex 11, para. 1, U.N. Doc. A/42/25 (1987).

[38] WORLD COMMISSION ON ENVIRONMENT AND DEVELOPMENT, OUR COMMON FUTURE (Oxford University Press ed., 1987).

[39] *Id.* at 43.

[40] G.A. Res. 2997, 27 U.N. GAOR Supp. 30, at 43, U.N. Doc. A/8730 (1972).

conscience of the UN."[41] The Action Plan adopted at Stockholm outlined a three-part functional framework for UNEP consisting of Environmental Assessment, Environmental Management, and Supporting Measures.[42]

4.2.2   *Environmental Assessment*

To carry out its environmental assessment function, in 1977 UNEP established "Earthwatch," a program of evaluation and review, research, monitoring, and information exchange that has been hailed as a substantial achievement.[43] Earthwatch's major components included: (1) the Global Environmental Monitoring System (GEMS); (2) the International Referral System for Sources of Environmental Information (INFOTERRA); (3) the International Register of Potentially Toxic Chemicals (IRPTC); (4) the assessment of basic human needs in relation to outer limits of the tolerance of the biosphere, climactic changes, weather modification, risk to the ozone layer, and social outer limits; and (5) research and assessments.[44] Two of these components continue – GEMS and INFOTERRA – and will be described here.

GEMS encourages and coordinates the acquisition, analysis, storage, and dissemination of data by governments and international organizations. These activities are in keeping with UNEP's dual mandate to coordinate environmental programs within the United Nations system and to play a catalyst role in initiating action where there are program gaps. GEMS has also conducted long-term studies of trends in environmental changes. GEMS projects have focused on: (1) resource monitoring; (2) climate-related monitoring; (3) human health-related monitoring in relation to air quality, water quality and food; (4) long-range transport of pollutants; (5) ocean monitoring; and (6) research and publications.[45] In the 1980s and 1990s, its programs included coordination of environmental monitoring in Africa, delimitation of West African and Amazon forest areas, glacier research, monitoring of

---

[41] This is how UNEP describes itself. UNEP in Brief (UNEP Information and Public Affairs Branch, Nairobi, Kenya, 1989).

[42] *See* Stockholm Report, *supra* note 9, at 59.

[43] *See* Gray, *supra* note 24, at 297.

[44] UNEP, The Environment Programme: Medium-Term Plan 1982–1983, UNEP/GC.9/6, Mar. 1981, at 11–54 [hereinafter UNEP/GC.9/6]. In the following discussion under this section, we have relied on V. Nanda & P. Moore, *Global Management of the Environment: Regional and Multilateral Initiatives, in* WORLD CLIMATE CHANGE 93, 98–103 (V. Nanda ed., 1983).

[45] *See id.* at 14–21. *See also* UNEP, Report of the Governing Council of the United Nations Environment Programme on the Work of Its Ninth Session, Nairobi, May 13–26, 1981, UNEP/GC. 9/15, 5 June 1981, at 48–49 [hereinafter UNEP/GC.9/15]; UNEP, The Environment Programme: Programme Performance Report – Report of the Executive Director, UNEP/GC. 9/5, Feb. 25, 1981, at 8–12 [hereinafter UNEP/GC.9/5].

climate systems, development of methods to assess the impact of pollution on forest ecosystems, and study of the behavior of pollutants in air, water, soil, flora, and fauna.[46] The GEMS data management program, Global Resource Information Database (GRID), was established in order to translate the highly technical environmental data assessments into information useable by managers and planners, especially in developing countries.[47] For facilitating access to scientific and technical information on chemicals, the International Register of Potentially Toxic Chemicals (IRPTC) maintains records on more than 600 chemicals as well as experts' hazard assessments and risk evaluations.[48]

INFOTERRA provides a complementary referral network for the exchange of environmental information. To accomplish its overall objective of ensuring that "the information needed for rational decision-making and for achieving environmentally-sound development is available to those who need it,"[49] UNEP decided in the early 1980s that its future activities should be focused on enhancing cooperation and linkages with governments, international organizations and appropriate information systems.[50] INFOTERRA continues to grow and provide access to scientific and technical information on environmental and resource issues all over the world by compiling and supplying needed information for environmental problem-solving between and among nations.[51]

4.2.3   *Environmental Management*

UNEP's environmental management began with the development of frameworks for the preparation of environmental impact assessment statements and for the application of cost-benefit analysis to environmental protection measures.[52] In February 1980, at the United Nations Development Program (UNDP) headquarters in New York, nine multilateral development financing institutions signed a Declaration of Principles for incorporating environmental considerations into development policies, programs, and projects.[53]

UNEP management activities in its first decade included: (1) environmental aspects of human settlements planning and human health; (2) terrestrial ecosystems, including arid and semi-arid ecosystems and desertification,

---

[46] 1988 Annual Report, *supra* note 1, at 22.

[47] UNEP/GCSS.1/7/Add.1 (Nairobi 1988) at 74 [hereinafter 1988 UNEP 1990–1995 Program].

[48] 1988 Annual Report, *supra* note 1, at 34.

[49] UNEP/GC.9/6, *supra* note 44, at 22.

[50] *See id.* at 22–28.

[51] 1988 Annual Report, *supra* note 1, at 34.

[52] UNEP, Environmental Management – An Overview, 12–16 (UNEP Report No. 3, 1981).

[53] *Id.* at 17.

tropical woodlands and forest ecosystems, mountain, island, coastal and other ecosystems, soils, water, genetic resources, wildlife, and protected areas; (3) environment and development, including integrated approaches and environmentally sound and appropriate technology; (4) industry and environment; (5) oceans, including marine pollution, living marine resources, and the regional seas program; (6) energy; (7) natural disasters; and (8) the development of environmental law.[54]

Environmental management activities of UNEP in the late 1980s and 1990s evolved into: (1) oceans and coastal areas, including the global marine environment and the regional seas program; (2) water resources; (3) terrestrial ecosystems, including renewable resources, soils, forests, wildlife, and protected areas, genetic resources, bioproductivity research, and lithosphere; (4) desertification control; (5) environmental health, including agricultural chemicals; (6) peace, security, and the environment; and (7) technology and environment, including energy, industry and transportation, human settlements and natural disasters.[55]

4.2.4   *Environmental Law*

Developing international environmental law is a vital component of environmental management, although it can be argued that this task does not fall squarely within UNEP's express mandate. However, because UNEP has the primary responsibility for implementing the principles incorporated in the Stockholm Declaration on the Human Environment, it follows that it is obligated to formulate environmental rules.[56]

UNEP's early law-developing activities included draft principles for the guidance of states in the conservation and harmonious utilization of natural resources that they share in common.[57] At its 34th session, the General Assembly requested that all states use the draft principles in the formulation

---

[54] *Id.* at 53–67.

[55] 1988 Annual Report, *supra* note 1, at 39–58.

[56] The pertinent principle in the Stockholm Declaration, Principle 22, is unambiguous: "States shall co-operate to develop further the international law regarding liability and compensation for victims of pollution and other environmental damage caused by activities within the jurisdiction or control of such states to areas beyond their jurisdiction." Under Resolutions 2997 and 3129, the General Assembly assigned UNEP the responsibility of fulfilling the mandate stated in Principle 22. G.A. Res. 2997, 29 U.N. GAOR Supp. 30, at 43, U.N. Doc. A/8730 (1972); G.A. Res. 3129, 28 U.N. GAOR Supp. 30, U.N. Doc. A/9030 (1973). It should be noted that, since most of the conventions developed by UNEP do not relate to liability but rather establish regulatory regimes, this major UNEP activity of drafting conventions on environmental issues does not appear to be directly fulfilling Principle 22.

[57] Draft Principles of Conduct in the Field of the Environment for Guidance of States in the Conservation and Harmonious Utilization of Natural Resources Shared by Two or More

of bilateral or multilateral conventions regarding natural resources shared by two or more states.[58] Subsequently, in 1981, a team of environmental law experts met under UNEP auspices and recommended that UNEP give its highest priority to three areas: (1) marine pollution from land-based services; (2) protection of the stratospheric ozone layer; and (3) transport, handling, and disposal of toxic and dangerous wastes.[59] The experts also suggested other areas for UNEP action including: (1) international cooperation in environmental emergencies, (2) coastal zone management, (3) soil conservation, (4) transboundary air pollution, (5) international trade in potentially harmful chemicals, (6) protection of rivers and other inland waters against pollution, (7) legal and administrative mechanisms for the prevention and redress of pollution damage, and (8) environmental impact assessment.[60] They recommended that periodic review of environmental law be undertaken by UNEP,[61] and that in "codification, progressive development, and implementation of environmental law" special attention be given to the developing countries.[62]

The revised goals for UNEP for 1982 included "wide acceptance by Governments and application of international conventions and protocols in the field of the environment [both those now existing and those being developed]" and "[a]greement on the principles which should guide States in their relations with each other in respect of shared natural resources, the problems of liability and compensation for pollution and environmental damage, weather modification and risks to the ozone layer."[63] Although there were some delegates who objected to UNEP's initiatives in the development of environmental law,[64] UNEP continued to pursue this work vigorously.

UNEP also was concerned with the lack of environmental law administration skills faced by developing countries. It adopted specific goals and strategies to remedy the problem in a fourfold approach:[65] (1) promotion of national environmental law, (2) education and research, (3) acceptance and implementation, and (4) technical cooperation. Supporting measures included environmental education and training, communication of

---

States, approved by the UNEP Governing Council, May 19, 1978, U.N. Doc. UNEP/IG12/2 (1978); 17 I.L.M. 1097 (1978).

[58] G.A. Res. 3129, *supra* note 56.

[59] UNEP Rep. No. 2, *supra* note 4, at 28.

[60] UNEP, Programme Performance Report – Addendum, UNEP/GC. 1015 Add. 2, Dec. 7, 1981, at 2 [hereinafter GC 10/5/Add. 2].

[61] *Id.* at 4.

[62] *Id.*

[63] UNEP Rep. No. 2, *supra* note 4, at 15.

[64] UNEP/GC. 9/15, *supra* note 45, at 66.

[65] *Id.* at 195–98.

environmental information to decision-makers and the general public, and technical assistance.[66]

4.2.5   *Appraisal*

UNEP was established as a catalyst and focal point for coordinating environmental activities in the UN system. However, its ability to coordinate global environmental efforts and to combat environmental degradation was questioned in the 1990s primarily on two grounds. First, because of severe underfunding, UNEP must rely upon individual state contributions as its source of financing,[67] which causes some doubt that UNEP can have any substantial impact upon the policy development level of international environmental law.[68] Second, because of UNEP's lack of enforcement power, its inability to compel compliance by violators of its environmental principles, it is viewed in some quarters as lacking teeth.[69] However, despite these monetary and enforcement hindrances, UNEP's accomplishments during this period, especially in terms of assessment and monitoring of the global environment and acting as a catalyst, were notable.[70] Its activities since that time will be noted after a study of the Rio Summit in the next section.

4.3   *The Rio Conference on Environment and Development*

4.3.1   *Introduction*

The United Nations Conference on Environment and Development (UNCED or Rio) was held in Rio de Janeiro from June 3 to 14, 1992, to mark the 20th anniversary of the Stockholm Conference and address the North-South environment-development split. It attracted the largest attendance ever for an event of its kind – representatives from 175 countries and over 100 heads of state[71] – and represented the culmination of two years of intense preparatory committee (PrepComm) negotiations. During the 20 years between Stockholm and Rio, international environmental issues had indeed reached the forefront of the global political agenda. States had entered into a large

---

[66] UNEP/GC.9/5, *supra* note 45, at 41–45 & 68–70.

[67] *See* Gray, *supra* note 24, at 296; Developments in the Law – International Environmental Law (Part V. Institutional Arrangements), 104 Harv. L. Rev. 1580, 1585 (1991).

[68] *See id.*

[69] G. Palmer, *New Ways to Make International Environmental Law*, 86 Am. J. Int'l L. 259, 261 (1992).

[70] *See* Gray, *supra* note 24, at 294.

[71] *See Brazilian President Proud of UNCED*, 15 Int'l Env't Rep. (BNA), Curr. Rep. 395 (June 17, 1992).

number of international environmental conventions that contained binding legal obligations, many of which are still in force.[72] Equally important were the continuous development of soft law and the work of international organizations, publicists' writings, and judicial and arbitral decisions, which had resulted in the emergence of general legal principles on the international environment (*see* Chapter 2).[73]

Yet the environmental health of the planet – especially in the developing countries – had continued to deteriorate at an alarming rate. Maurice Strong, Secretary-General of both Stockholm and Rio Conferences, noted:

> Although progress was made in many individual areas after Stockholm, it had little effect on environment-development relationships in the policies and practices of governments and industry. Even more ominous is the fact that the underlying conditions driving the risks to the human future that had been perceived at Stockholm did not fundamentally change in the two decades that separated Stockholm from Rio.[74]

Strong graphically recounted the plight of the developing world:

> As I traveled to every region of the world, retracing my steps of twenty years ago, the extent and nature of this environmental degradation and its tragic human consequences were everywhere. The cities of the developing countries, growing at rates beyond anything ever before experienced, are now among the world's most polluted, many of them headed for environmental and social breakdown. The appalling destruction of natural resources, loss of forest cover, erosion and degradation of soils, and deterioration of supplies and quality of water are visible throughout the developing world. Economic losses in agriculture, fisheries, and tourism are tragically manifested in diminished livelihoods for already impoverished and struggling people. This forbidding drama is unfolding throughout the developing world, threatening a massive human

---

[72] *Environmental Law in UNEP* (UNEP Environmental Law No. 1, 1991); International Conventions and Protocols in the Field of the Environment, U.N. Doc. A/C. 2/46/3 (1991); UNEP/GC. 16/INF. 4 (Nairobi 1991); UNEP, *International Legal Instruments in the Field of the Environment*, Decision 15/31 of the Governing Council of the United Nations Environment Programme (May 25, 1989), *reprinted in* UNEP, Report of the Governing Council on the Work of Its Fifteenth Session, 44 U.N. GAOR Supp. No. 25, Annex 1, at 158, U.N. Doc. A/44/25. *See also* Decision 15/33 of the Governing Council of UNEP [hereinafter GC Decision 15/331], *reprinted in* GC Fifteenth Session Rep., at 160, noting the adoption of the Basel Convention on the Control of Transboundary Movements of Hazardous Wastes and Their Disposal, adopted and opened for signature Mar. 22, 1989, 28 I.L.M. 649 (1989) (entered into force May 5, 1992).

[73] *See generally* O. Schachter, *The Emergence of International Environmental Law*, 44 J. INT'L AFF. 457 (1991) [hereinafter Schachter].

[74] M. Strong, *Beyond Rio: Prospects and Portents*, 4 COLO. J. INT'L ENVTL. L. & POL'Y 21, 23 (1993).

ecotragedy beyond any ever before witnessed, the grim portents of which can be seen in the recurring famines in Africa.[75]

At Rio, World Bank President Lewis Preston proclaimed the magnitude of the environmental challenges that faced developing countries: over one billion people lacked safe drinking water, one-third of the world lacked adequate sanitation, and 1.3 billion people were exposed to indoor smoke and soot as a result of pollution. In addition, he expressed concern regarding soil erosion, loss of ecosystems and biodiversity, and climate change.[76]

Negotiations preceding the Conference revealed the chasm had deepened between the North and the South regarding the goals of UNCED. Northern states focused primarily on the environment, while Southern states sought answers to their development dilemmas. Developing countries believed that UNCED constituted an opportunity to receive an unequivocal endorsement of their right to development. They also sought increased financial and technical assistance from industrialized states in order to meet their environmental and development needs.[77] Negotiations on the set of principles to form the Rio Declaration became "so divisive that even the name of the document could not be agreed upon."[78]

Ultimately, however, Rio was a stunning success in terms of international consensus and new legal authorities. It produced three nonbinding documents – the Rio Declaration (*see* next section), the Agenda 21 plan of implementation (*see* § 4.3.3), and the Forest Principles (*see* § 8.2); established two new binding treaties of major continuing consequence – the Framework Convention on Climate Change (*see* § 10.3) and the Convention on Biological Diversity (*see* § 8.3); and led to the formation of the UN Commission on Sustainable Development (*see* § 4.3.4).

4.3.2   *The Rio Declaration on Environment and Development*

The Rio Declaration originally was envisioned as an "Earth Charter," modeled after the 1948 Universal Declaration of Human Rights,[79] that would set forth principles on sustainable development for the subsequent development of "hard law" conventions (*see* § 2.1.4). The document was anticipated to act

---

[75] *Id.*

[76] Reported in Earth Summit, 15 Int'l Env't Rep. (BNA), Curr. Rep. 395, 396 (June 17, 1992) [hereinafter Earth Summit].

[77] *See, e.g.*, L. Mouat, *Earth Summit in Rio Faces Complex Issues*, Christian Science Monitor, Mar. 27, 1992, at 7.

[78] J. Kirwin, *Nations to Rescue Talks on Environmental Action Plan at Earth Summit*, 15 Int'l Env't Rep. (BNA), Curr. Rep. 311, 311 (May 20, 1992).

[79] Adopted Dec. 10, 1948, G.A. Res. 217A(III), U.N. Doc. A/8 10, at 7 (1948).

as an "ideological umbrella" for Agenda 21,[80] the implementation plan for effectuating the Rio principles in the 21st century. The developing countries, however, were uneasy about the title "Earth Charter," which they viewed as placing too much emphasis on the environment. Hence the title was changed to the "Rio Declaration on Environment and Development."[81] There was controversy on every aspect of the document – its focus, precision, wording, and even its length. In reply to a statement by the US Ambassador to UNCED, Robert Ryan, that the United States would prefer a short text that could be printed on a poster and "used by children in their bedrooms," the negotiator for G-77 (which has a membership of over 120 developing states) said that many children in developing countries "don't have bedrooms."[82]

Eventually, UNCED representatives from 175 states adopted by consensus the Rio Declaration, which contains a preamble and 27 principles. At the conclusion of the Conference, Secretary-General Strong stated to the over 1,000 journalists in attendance,

> We need to take stronger action than what is in these documents. The negotiations were difficult. Hopefully this conference will have raised awareness levels of an impending disaster if things do not change.
>
>   ....
>
> But it is vitally important that we use the momentum created here to make changes. Basically, we squandered the last twenty years. If you went back and looked at the speeches I made in Stockholm 20 years ago, there is no difference in what I am saying now.
>
> We need to get on the fast track. If our economies don't make some fundamental changes we are headed for disaster in the next century. I'm at a stage of my life where probably none of this is going to affect me personally. But it will affect my children and your children and all of our grandchildren.[83]

The Rio Declaration incorporates Principle 21 of the Stockholm Declaration,[84] providing a delicate balance between recognition of the sovereign right of all states to "exploit their own resources pursuant to their own environmental and developmental policies," and their "responsibility to ensure that activities within their jurisdiction or control do not cause damage to the environment

---

[80] Kirwin, *supra* note 78.

[81] UNCED, *Rio Declaration on Environment and Development*, U.N. Doc. A/CONF. 51/26/ Rev. I (Vol. 1), Annex 1, at 3 (1992) [hereinafter I UNCED Rep.], 31 I.L.M. 874 (1992) [hereinafter Rio Declaration]. For a commentary, *see* generally J. D. Kovar, A Short Guide to the Rio Declaration, 4 COLO. J. INT'L ENVTL. L. & POL'Y 119, 119–22 (1993) [hereinafter Kovar]. Mr. Kovar was a participant in the drafting of the Declaration. We have relied on his insights in our analysis of the Rio Declaration that follows.

[82] *See* Kirwin, *supra* note 78.

[83] *See* Earth Summit, *supra* note 76, at 397.

[84] Stockholm Declaration, *supra* note 9.

of other States or of areas beyond the limits of national jurisdiction" (*see* § 2.1.3).[85] It explicitly links environmental protection to the development process by stating that the former constitutes an "integral part" of the latter and thus "cannot be considered in isolation from it."[86] It also expands on the Stockholm Declaration in its unambiguous recognition of the principle of intergenerational equity: "The right to development must be fulfilled so as to equitably meet developmental and environmental needs of present and future generations."[87]

While it obligates states to "cooperate in a spirit of global partnership to conserve, protect and restore the health and integrity of the Earth's ecosystem" (*see* § 2.1.2), the Rio Declaration recognizes states have "common but differentiated responsibilities" in view of their "different contributions to global environmental degradation."[88] Developed countries acknowledge their responsibility "in the international pursuit of sustainable development in view of the pressures their societies place on the global environment and of the technologies and financial resources they command."[89] It calls for wide application of the "precautionary approach," as well as application of the "polluter-pays" principle.[90] It particularly recognizes the vital role of women[91] and of indigenous people and local communities[92] in the achievement of sustainable development.

4.3.2.1   *Analysis*

The title of the Rio Declaration clearly linked environment and development, indicating acceptance by the negotiators of the G-77 desire that the title not emphasize the environment at the cost of development.[93] The Preamble reaffirms the Stockholm Declaration and seeks to build on it. While recognizing "the integral and interdependent nature of the Earth, our home" and the need to work towards international agreements "which respect the interests of all and protect the integrity of the global environment and development systems," it sets the goal of "establishing a new and equitable global partnership."

Principle 1 sets the tone of a human-centered focus for the Declaration, proclaiming that "[h]uman beings are at the centre of concerns for

---

[85] *Id.* Principle 2.
[86] *Id.* Principle 4.
[87] *Id.* Principle 3.
[88] *Id.* Principle 7.
[89] *Id.*
[90] *Id.* Principle 15.
[91] *Id.* Principle 20.
[92] *Id.* Principle 22.
[93] *See* Kovar, *supra* note 81, at 123.

sustainable development. They are entitled to a healthy and productive life in harmony with nature" (*see* § 2.1.6). Developing countries derailed the efforts mounted by some Western states and Western NGOs to steer the Rio Declaration away from the homocentric approach of previous UN pronouncements on the environment. Consequently, those who had wished to address "environmental concerns from a conceptual position within – as an integral part of the workings of the Earth's ecosystem, not from the outside looking in"[94] – were unable to do so.

Principle 5 of the Declaration reflects the primary concern of developing countries – the eradication of world poverty – calling on all states and all people to "cooperate in the essential task of eradicating poverty as an indispensable requirement for sustainable development, in order to decrease the disparities in standards of living and better meet the needs of the majority of the people of the world." Similarly, Principle 3 recognizes the "right to development,"[95] and that it "must be fulfilled so as to equitably meet developmental and environmental needs of present and future generations" (*see* §§ 2.1.5 and 2.1.7). This statement was a result of the developing countries' demand that equity be the standard for meeting intragenerational and environmental needs.[96] Throughout the negotiations, the United States consistently opposed the concept of the "right of development." Thus, the US added an interpretative statement to Principle 3 at the time of the Declaration's adoption:

> The United States does not, by joining consensus on the Rio Declaration, change its long-standing opposition to the so-called "right to development." Development is not a right. On the contrary, development is a goal we all hold, which depends for its realization in large part on the promotion and protection of the human rights set out in the Universal Declaration of Human Rights.
>
> The United States understands and accepts the thrust of Principle 3 to be that economic development goals and objectives must be pursued in such a way that the development and environmental needs of present and future generations are taken into account. The United States cannot agree to, and would disassociate itself from, any interpretation of Principle 3 that accepts a "right to development," or otherwise goes beyond that understanding.[97]

---

[94] *Id.* at 124, citing a proposal from Canada submitted at UNCED, a principle of a Draft Earth Charter presented by a working group of the U.S. Citizen's Network on UNCED.

[95] On the status of the right to development, *see generally* Nanda, *supra* note 27 at 41–61.

[96] *See, e.g., Agora: What Obligation Does Our Generation Owe to the Next? An Approach to Global Environmental Responsibility*, 84 Am. J. Int'l L. 190 (1990).

[97] UNCED, Report of the United Nations Conference on Environment and Development, U.N. Doc. A/CONF. 151/26 (Vol. IV), at 20 (1992) [hereinafter IV UNCED Rep.] *cited in* Kovar, *supra* note 81, at 126.

The new paradigm of "sustainable development" permeates the Declaration's principles, inextricably linking environment and development. Principle 4 is the clearest example of their reciprocity, stating that "environmental protection shall constitute an integral part of the development process" and that environmental protection "cannot be considered in isolation from" development.

Several Principles in the Rio Declaration that elaborate on the environment-development linkage represent negotiation achievements for developing countries.[98] The Declaration gives "special priority" to the needs of developing countries, "particularly the least developed and those most environmentally vulnerable" – although it adds that international efforts "should also address the interests and needs of all countries."[99] This addition was made at the insistence of former Soviet bloc European states with "economies in transition." The G-77 and China had blocked any reference to a priority status for them, believing that such recognition could initiate competition for international assistance levels between the two groups of states.[100]

The Rio Declaration explicitly recognizes the principle of "common and differentiated responsibilities" among states (*see* § 2.1.12) as follows:

> States shall cooperate in a spirit of global partnership to conserve, protect and restore the health and integrity of the Earth's ecosystem. In view of the different contributions to global environmental degradation, States have common but differentiated responsibilities. The developed countries acknowledge the responsibility that they bear in the international pursuit of sustainable development in view of the pressures their societies place on the global environment and of the technologies and financial resources they command.[101]

Neither the developing nor the developed countries were satisfied with the final wording.[102] The former considered the text inadequate insofar as it did not directly blame developed countries for the prevailing environmental problems, while the latter objected to the language that described their special role.[103] Although the text was not reopened for negotiation at Rio, the United States added the following interpretative statement on Principle 7: "The United States understands and accepts that Principle 7 highlights the special leadership role of the developed countries, based on our industrial

---

[98] *See, e.g.,* R. Panjabi, *From Stockholm to Rio: A Comparison of the Declaratory Principles of International Environmental Law,* 21 Denv. J. Int'l l. & Pol'y 215, 236–45 (1993).

[99] Rio Declaration, *supra* note 81, Principle 6.

[100] Kovar, *supra* note 81, at 127–28.

[101] Rio Declaration, *supra* note 81, Principle 7.

[102] *Id.* For an insightful discussion on the drafting difficulties regarding this Principle, *see* Kovar, *supra* note 81, at 128–30.

[103] *Id.*

development, our experience with environmental protection policies and actions, and our wealth, technical expertise and capabilities."[104]

Principle 8 declares that "States should reduce and eliminate unsustainable patterns of production and consumption"[105] This call to developed countries to reduce their production and consumption excesses was couched in the milder "should" language at their insistence, although some would have preferred to condemn the wealthier countries for such patterns and to call for radical reductions.[106] Principle 8 links this with a reciprocal call that states "should promote appropriate demographic policies."[107] This "should" was inserted at the insistence of developing nations, which initially had rejected any reference to the population challenge in the Declaration – a definite watering down of Stockholm Principle 16's more forceful language.[108]

The Rio Declaration provides clear guidance on environmental standards. Principle 11 notes states have the duty to "enact effective environmental legislation" (*see* § 2.2.6). This is qualified by the statement that environmental standards "should reflect the environmental and developmental context in which they apply." In order to further assuage the apprehension of developing states that failure to meet developed country standards would result in discrimination, it recognizes that environmental standards "may be inappropriate and of unwarranted economic and social cost to other countries, in particular developing countries."

The connection of international trade with sustainable development was of particular concern to the delegates. Principle 12 commences with a call for cooperation "to promote a supportive and open international economic system that would lead to economic growth and sustainable development in all countries, to better address the problems of environmental degradation." This was a response to the fear that environmental concerns might be used by developed countries in order to close their markets to developing countries' products. Principle 12 continues:

> Trade policy measures for environmental purposes should not constitute a means of arbitrary or unjustifiable discrimination or a disguised restriction on

---

[104] IV UNCED Report, *supra* note 97, at 20–21, *cited in* Kovar, *supra* note 81, at 129–30.

[105] Rio Declaration, *supra* note 81, Principle 8.

[106] Panjabi, *supra* note 98, at 240; Kovar, *supra* note 81, at 130.

[107] Rio Declaration, *supra* note 81, Principle 8; *see* Kovar, *supra* note 81, at 130; Panjabi, *supra* note 98, at 223–26.

[108] "Demographic policies, which are without prejudice to basic human rights and which are deemed appropriate by Governments concerned, should be applied in those regions where the rate of population growth or excessive population concentrations are likely to have adverse effects on the environment or development, or where low population density may prevent improvement of the human environment and impede development." Stockholm Principle 16.

international trade. Unilateral actions to deal with environmental challenges outside the jurisdiction of the importing country should be avoided. Environmental measures addressing transboundary or global environmental problems should, as far as possible, be based on an international consensus.

The interrelationship between international trade law and international environmental law has yet to be fully coordinated, and trade sanctions (illegal under the former) still constitute one of the most effective enforcement tools of the latter (*see* Chapter 14). The European Community, Mexico, and several Latin American countries sought to include such a principle because of US legislation to protect dolphins[109] and turtles[110] from certain tuna and shrimp fishing practices, respectively.[111] The US responded with the following interpretative statement on Principle 12: "The United States understands that, in certain situations, trade measures may provide an effective and appropriate means of addressing environmental concerns, including long-term sustainable forest management concerns and environmental concerns outside national jurisdiction, subject to certain disciplines."[112]

Several principles emphasize the importance of public participation in the process of sustainable development (*see* § 2.2.1). Principle 10 embodies all "three pillars" of public participation – access to information, access to participation in decision making, and access to justice. It calls for individuals to have "appropriate access to information...held by public authorities," information on hazards in their communities, "and the opportunity to participate in decisionmaking processes." States are obligated to make "information widely available" and to provide "[e]ffective access to judicial and administrative proceedings." Principle 20 acknowledges women's "vital role in environmental management and development," and states that their "full participation is essential to achieve sustainable development." Principle 21 similarly recognizes the role of youth. Principle 23 recognizes the importance of indigenous people and local communities in the achievement of sustainable development.

Two principles address issues of war and peace, and one principle functions as a political statement. Principle 24 calls warfare "inherently destructive of sustainable development," and calls upon states to respect the existing international law of war providing for protection of the environment, and to cooperate in its further development. Principle 25 states that peace is a prerequisite for development and environmental protection. As a political

---

[109] International Dolphin Conservation Act of 1992, Pub. L. No. 105–123, 100 Stat. 3425 (1992), codified at 16 U.S.C. §§ 952–953, 973r, 1361, 1411–1418 (1994 & Supp. III 1997).

[110] Pub. L. No. 101–162 § 609 103 Stat. 988 (1990).

[111] Kovar, *supra* note 81, at 132–33.

[112] IV UNCED Report, *supra* note 97, at 21.

statement, Principle 23 calls for the protection of the "environment and natural resources of people under oppression, domination and occupation." The United States made a deal with Israel (the obvious target of 23): Israel would lift its objection to this language in the Rio Declaration if all references to "people under occupation" were removed from Agenda 21.[113]

As mentioned previously, international cooperation is a pervasive theme in the Declaration (*see* § 2.1.2). Cooperation is essential "to decrease the disparities in standards of living;"[114] to "cooperate...to conserve, protect and restore the health and integrity of the Earth's ecosystem;"[115] "to promote a supportive and open international economic system;"[116] "to cooperate to strengthen endogenous capacity building...through exchange of scientific and technological knowledge, and by enhancing the development, adaptation, diffusion and transfer of technologies, including new and innovative technologies";[117] and to "discourage or prevent the relocation and transfer to other States of any activities and substances that cause severe environmental degradation or are found to be harmful to human health."[118]

Principles that make special reference to the emerging norms of international law include the reiteration in Rio Principle 2 of Stockholm Principle 21's no-harm rule – a state's duty not to cause environmental damage outside its borders, combined with its sovereign right to use its natural resources pursuant to its environmental policies (*see* § 2.1.3). The words "and developmental" have been added after the word "environmental" to reflect the South's developmental concerns.[119] Similarly, Stockholm Principle 22, which calls upon states to cooperate for further development of international law of liability and compensation, is reiterated with two minor additions: (1) the language calls for states to proceed "in an expeditious and more determined manner" for such development; and (2) states are also called upon to develop similar national laws (*see* § 2.1.14).[120] Finally, the Declaration calls for states and individuals to develop further "international law in the field of sustainable development."[121] The significance of this call is its subject matter, that is, not simply the development of international law of environment but that of sustainable development. However, given the unspectacular results achieved in the development of international environmental law on liability

---

[113] Kovar, *supra* note 81, at 137; *see* Panjabi, *supra* note 98, at 227–29.
[114] Rio Declaration, *supra* note 81, Principle 5.
[115] *Id.* Principle 7.
[116] *Id.* Principle 12.
[117] *Id.* Principle 9.
[118] *Id.* Principle 14.
[119] *Id.* Principle 2.
[120] *Id.* Principle 13.
[121] *Id.* Principle 27.

and compensation since the Stockholm Conference, one cannot be too optimistic as to the effect it will have on the international community.

Principle 26 obligates states to resolve their environmental disputes "peacefully and by appropriate means in accordance with the Charter of the United Nations." This broad statement is a reiteration of UN member states' obligations under the UN Charter itself,[122] and contains no specific methods of dispute settlement, which was a concession to developing nations.[123]

The Declaration enumerates the following specific state obligations, which are illustrative of evolving soft law on the environment:

1. Principle 15 calls for wide application of the "precautionary approach," defined as follows: where there is a threat of "serious or irreversible damage, lack of full certainty shall not be used as a reason for postponing cost-effective measures to prevent environmental degradation" (*see* § 2.2.4). This principle would resolve the problem of scientific uncertainty essentially by switching the burden of proof. Under it, questionable risks, substances, or activities should be prevented until proved safe by their development proponents – rather than permitted until proved harmful by their environmental opponents.

2. Principle 16 adopts the polluter-pays principle, which was first introduced by the European Community,[124] underscoring the importance of applying free market principles to address environmental problems. The United States and many other industrialized countries made clear early in the negotiations that reliance on market mechanisms was of major importance for the Declaration. This was considered particularly important given the information that emerged about the terrible environmental consequences of former Soviet bloc central economic planning.[125]

3. Principle 17 follows the model of the US National Environmental Policy Act,[126] calling upon nations to undertake environmental impact assessment "as a national instrument...for proposed activities that are likely to have a significant adverse impact on the environment [that] are subject to

---

[122] Article 2(4) of the UN Charter reads: "All members shall refrain in their international relations from the threat or use of force against the territorial integrity or political independence of any state, or in any other manner inconsistent with the Purposes of the United Nations."

[123] Kovar, *supra* note 81, at 139.

[124] *See generally* S. E. Gaines, *The Polluter-Pays Principle: From Economic Equity to Environmental Ethos*, 26 Texas Int'l L.J. 463 (1991).

[125] Kovar, *supra* note 81, at 135.

[126] National Environmental Policy Act of 1969, 42 U.S.C. §§ 4321–4370a.

a decision of a competent national authority." This practice quickly took hold in the international arena (*see* §§ 2.2.5 and 2.2.6).[127]

4. Principles 18 and 19 adopt the widely accepted notification and consultation principles (*see* § 2.2.2). Principle 18 reads: "States shall immediately notify other States of any natural disasters or other emergencies that are likely to produce sudden harmful effects on the environment of those States. Every effort shall be made by the international community to help States so afflicted." And Principle 19 reads: "States shall provide prior and timely notification and relevant information to potentially affected States on activities that may have a significant adverse transboundary environmental effect and shall consult with those States at an early stage and in good faith."

4.3.2.2 *Appraisal*

As a major statement on sustainable development, both in defining and clarifying the concept, the Rio Declaration reflects a profound change in thinking since the Stockholm Conference. No longer was the focus on the environment alone, but on the environment-development linkage and integration,[128] with priority given to development, as was sought by developing states. Because of the focus on development, the Declaration is a human-centered document that gives special attention to the needs and interests of developing countries. However, it avoided the confrontational North-South tone that marked the PrepComm meetings, especially the final New York meeting.[129]

Perhaps the Declaration can be criticized for not concentrating enough on conservation issues.[130] However, the Declaration does further refine concepts that pertain to environmental management. Thus, it did surpass the Stockholm Declaration in its inclusion, for example, of the environmental impact assessment, the precautionary approach, and the polluter-pays principle. Yet by no means did it constitute a bold and visionary step toward the development of international environmental law.

As a UN Declaration, the measure of the success of the Rio Declaration in the creation of international environmental law will be determined by how the principles are implemented by states and become reflected in future treaties and state practice. For it is only consistent state practice over a period

---

[127] *See, e.g.,* Convention on Environmental Impact Assessment in a Transboundary Context, Feb. 25, 1991 (a UN ECE Convention), 30 I.L.M. 800 (1991).

[128] *See* Strong, *supra* note 74, at 24–25.

[129] *See generally* Kovar, *supra* note 81, at 121–22.

[130] *See* Panjabi, *supra* note 98, at 251–52.

of time, combined with *opinio juris*, that gives rise to rules of customary international law.[131]

4.3.3   *Agenda 21*

Agenda 21 is a unanimously adopted, minutely detailed, nearly 500-page "action plan" for managing the environment in the 21st century. It lays out numerous policies, plans, programs, processes, and other guidance for IGOs and national governments to follow in order to actually implement the international legal documents produced at Rio.

Agenda 21 gives in-depth meaning to the concept of "sustainable development" in its four sections and 40 chapters. Section 1 (Chapters 2–8) covers "Social and Economic Dimensions." It includes recommended actions on sustainable development, cooperation in developing countries, poverty, consumption patterns, demographics, human health, human settlements, and integration of environment and development in decision-making.[132] Section 2 (Chapters 9–22), "Conservation and Management of Resources for Development," includes chapters on the protection of the atmosphere, land resources, combating deforestation, combating desertification and drought, mountain development, agriculture development, biological diversity, management of biotechnology, protection of the oceans, protection of fresh water resources, and management of toxic chemicals, hazardous wastes, solid wastes and radioactive wastes.[133] Section 3 (Chapters 23–32), "Strengthening the Role of Major Groups," includes ways to increase the participation of major groups in sustainable development efforts, including women, youth, indigenous peoples and their communities, nongovernmental organizations, local authorities, trade unions, business and industry, the scientific and technological community, and farmers.[134] Section 4 (Chapters 33–40), "Means of Implementation," comprises chapters on financial resources and mechanisms, technology transfer, cooperation and capacity-building, science, education, public awareness and training, international institutional arrangements, international legal instruments and mechanisms, and information for decision-making.[135]

This action plan makes recommendations for over 2,500 actions in almost 150 program areas, without providing any explicit priority, although implicitly a high priority is placed on policies that build on the links between

---

[131] *See* The North Sea Continental Shelf Cases, 1969 I.C.J. 3. For a discussion, *see* W. Friedmann, *The North Sea Continental Shelf Cases*, 64 Am. J. Int'l L. 229 (1970).

[132] UNCED Rep. U.N. Doc. A/CONF. 151/26, at 14–110.

[133] *Id.* at 111–372.

[134] *Id.* at 373–411.

[135] *Id.* at 412–79.

poverty reduction, economic efficiency, and sound environmental management. It establishes the environmental work program for the period beyond 1992 and into the 21st century.

In the chapter that specifically addresses international legal instruments and mechanisms,[136] four priority areas are identified. The first calls for review and assessment of previous performance and priorities for future lawmaking on sustainable development. Specifically mentioned are an examination of the feasibility of elaborating general rights and obligations of states regarding sustainable development, attention to differential obligations or gradual application, and designation of legal experts in order to carry out this task pursuant to earlier UNEP practice. Large-scale destruction of the environment in times of armed conflict and the possibility of drafting a nuclear safety convention in the framework of the International Atomic Energy Agency are referred to in particular. The second area concerns implementation mechanisms, calling for the establishment of efficient and practical reporting systems on the implementation of international legal instruments and appropriate ways to further develop these mechanisms. The third area addresses effective participation in international lawmaking, especially for developing countries. This section calls for scientific/technical expertise to ensure access to the necessary information and assistance in building up expertise in international law, particularly in relation to sustainable development. The fourth area calls for avoidance and settlement of disputes and arranging effective dispute resolution techniques.

The effectiveness with which Agenda 21 is actually funded and implemented will determine whether this ambitious document is successful.

4.3.4   *The Commission on Sustainable Development*

Following Rio, the UN General Assembly established a high-level Commission on Sustainable Development (CSD) to assist in the implementation of the recommendations and decisions of the Earth Summit.[137] With its headquarters in New York, it is composed of representatives of 53 states elected for three-year terms on a rotating basis and with representation on a geographical basis. Created to guide UN member nations toward sustainable development and environmental action, it acts as a central forum to review progress made in the implementation of Agenda 21 and to "advance global dialogue and foster partnerships for sustainable development."[138]

---

[136] *Id.* Chapter 39, at 469–72.

[137] *See General Assembly Approves Establishment of Commission on Sustainable Development,* 16 Intl Env't Rep. (BNA), Curr. Rep. 6 (Jan. 13, 1993).

[138] Programme for the Further Implementation of Agenda 21, U.N. Doc. A/RES/S-19/2, Annex, ¶ 16 (Sept. 19, 1997) [hereinafter Implementation Programme].

Its role is threefold:

- to review progress in the implementation of recommendations and commitments arising out of UNCED, *i.e.*, Agenda 21, the Rio Declaration, and the Statement of Principles on Forests;
- to elaborate policy guidance and options for activities in pursuance of the goals of Agenda 21; and
- to promote dialogue and build partnerships among governments, the international community and groups who have a significant role to play in bringing about sustainable development – including indigenous peoples, women, youth, nongovernmental organizations, scientists, labor, farmers, industry and business, and local authorities.[139]

Thus, the Commission's primary task is to facilitate the efforts being undertaken around the world to ensure that Agenda 21 is implemented and to review progress to that end. The CSD's work will be studied after an appraisal of UNCED in the next section.

4.3.5   *Appraisal*

The Rio Conference was a compromise between the developed and developing countries, between ecology and economics. As for the issue that caused the major tension – the financing of environmental and development programs in the developing world – the disappointment of the developing countries was evident in the words of a senior Colombian diplomat: "[W]e are leaving Rio with the same resources we had when we arrived."[140] This comment was a response to a compromise on the date by which industrialized countries should reach the target for providing 0.7 percent of their gross domestic product as aid to developing countries. The resultant text called on the wealthier nations to do so "as soon as possible," although the agreement also said that "some countries agree or have agreed to reach the target by the year 2000."[141] A senior Malaysian diplomat also reiterated developing countries' disappointment with the results of UNCED, saying, "[T]he commitments made by the developed countries' leaders signaled a lack of political commitment to sustainable development," adding that "[w]ith the lack of hard financial commitments it will be difficult to fund Agenda 21."[142] As feared by

---

[139] *See* United Nations Sustainable Development, *Mandate of the Commission on Sustainable Development*, Mar. 26, 2001, http://www.un.org/esa/sustdev/csdback.htm.

[140] *Earth Summit: Compromise Reached in Financing; Developing Nations Dismayed with Accord*, 15 Intl Env't Rep. (BNA), Curr. Rep. 395 (June 17, 1991).

[141] *Id.*

[142] *Id.* at 396.

these delegates, the target was not reached by the time of the Johannesburg Summit on Sustainable Development in 2002.

Despite these weaknesses, UNCED definitely enhanced awareness of environment and development issues and the inextricable link between them. It also focused the world's attention on the goal of achieving sustainable development. Equally important, the two conventions signed at Rio and the Rio Declaration, Agenda 21, and the Forestry Principles, constitute important steps in the development of international environmental law. Subsequent to the Rio Conference, the UN General Assembly also adopted a resolution establishing an intergovernmental negotiating committee modeled after the INC with the object of conducting negotiations on climate change and elaborating on a new international convention to combat desertification.[143]

4.4   *The Uneven Road from Rio to Rio (1992–2012)*

Attempting to build on the success of the 1992 Rio Conference, the UN has convened numerous meetings to review and stimulate progress in environment and sustainable development, with mixed success. The key meetings include the 1997 UNGA Special Session five years after Rio (dubbed "Rio+5"), the 2002 World Summit on Sustainable Development in Johannesburg, South Africa ("Rio+10"), and the 2012 UN Conference on Sustainable Development, symbolically held again in Rio de Janeiro ("Rio+20"). A discussion of these efforts and the changing work of the CSD and UNEP follows.

4.4.1   *The CSD and "Rio+5"*

The UN Commission on Sustainable Development (CSD), envisioned in Agenda 21, was promptly established by UNGA in December 1992 as a program of action to ensure effective follow-up of the Rio Summit accomplishments, enhance international cooperation, rationalize intergovernmental decision-making capacity, and examine and advise on progress in Agenda 21 implementation at the local, national, and international levels.[144] It is a body of the UN Economic and Social Council (ECOSOC), with 53 rotating country-members, that meets annually in New York City. The Division for

---

[143] *See* 30 UN Chronicle at 80, 81 (March 1993).

[144] UN Division for Sustainable Development (UNDSD), *About the UN Commission on Sustainable Development (CSD)* (2009) http://www.un.org/esa/dsd/csd/csd_aboucsd.shtml; International Institute for Sustainable Development (IISD), *A Brief Introduction to the UN Commission on Sustainable Development* (2010), http://www.iisd.ca/process/sustdevt-csd intro.htm.

Sustainable Development in the UN Department of Economic and Social Affairs (DESA) acts as its Secretariat. The CSD's first five annual sessions (1993–1997) focused on cross-sectoral issues including finance, technology transfer, trade and environment, and consumption and production.[145]

In June 1997, the UN convened a "Special Session of the UN General Assembly to Review Implementation of Agenda 21" (UNGASS) and what progress had been achieved in the five years since the Rio Summit. This "Rio+5" session observed that considerable work had been done by the CSD, UNEP, and others to promote sustainable development. However, while noting that some progress had been made, delegates concluded that much more remained to be done on the fundamental means of implementation set out in Agenda 21, particularly in the practical areas of finance, technology transfer, technical assistance, and capacity building.[146] The Special Session specifically targeted several areas requiring urgent action, including integration of economic, social, and environmental objectives; action on specific sectors and issues; and enhancing means of implementation.[147] Particularly important issues addressed under the first heading were the objectives of eradicating poverty,[148] changing consumption and production patterns,[149] making trade and environment mutually supportive,[150] promotion of decline in population growth rates,[151] health for all,[152] and sustainable human settlements.[153] The sectors and issues especially identified were fresh water,[154] oceans and seas,[155] forests,[156] energy,[157] transport,[158] atmosphere,[159] toxic chemicals,[160] hazardous and radioactive wastes,[161] land and sustainable agriculture,[162] desertification

---

[145] IISD, *supra* note 144, contains a summary of the CSD's meetings and output from 1993–2009.

[146] Programme for Further Implementation of Agenda 21, U.N. GAOR, 19th Special Sess. (June 23–28, 1997), Annex U.N. Doc. A/S: 19/29, ¶ 17 (1997), http://www.un.org/documents/ga/res/spec/aress19-2.htm.

[147] *Id.* ¶¶ 23–115.

[148] *Id.* ¶ 27.

[149] *Id.* ¶ 28.

[150] *Id.* ¶ 29.

[151] *Id.* ¶ 30.

[152] *Id.* ¶ 31.

[153] *Id.* ¶ 32.

[154] *Id.* ¶¶ 34–35.

[155] *Id.* ¶ 36.

[156] *Id.* ¶¶ 37–41.

[157] *Id.* ¶¶ 42–46.

[158] *Id.* ¶ 47.

[159] *Id.* ¶¶ 48–56.

[160] *Id.* ¶ 57.

[161] *Id.* ¶¶ 58–61.

[162] *Id.* ¶¶ 62–63.

and drought,[163] biodiversity,[164] sustainable tourism,[165] small island developing states (SIDS),[166] and natural disasters.[167] Among the means of implementation singled out were financial resources and mechanisms,[168] transfer of environmentally sound technologies,[169] capacity-building,[170] science,[171] education and awareness,[172] and information and tools for measuring progress.[173]

The Rio+5 Special Session set out a program of work for the CSD for the period 1998–2002 with the overriding issues being poverty and consumption and production patterns.[174] Initially, the CSD focused on energy for sustainable development, protection of the atmosphere, transport, information for decision-making and participation, and international cooperation for an enabling environment.[175] In addition, the CSD acted as the preparatory committee for the 2002 Johannesburg World Summit on Sustainable Development and hence was responsible for the plan of implementation for the Summit (*see* § 4.4.3). That "Rio+10" Summit caused the CSD to adopt a new approach – a multi-year work program for 2004–2017, consisting of two-year action-oriented "implementation cycles" with a "review session" the first year and a "policy session" the second year.[176] Each two-year cycle is devoted to a thematic cluster of issues, with the first year spent reviewing progress made in implementing sustainable development and identifying obstacles and the second year, planning measures to speed up implementation.[177]

The CSD has received increasing criticism for its lack of effectiveness.[178] "[T]here has been growing concern [whether] the CSD has succeeded in fulfilling its mandate and further advanced the sustainable development agenda.

---

[163] *Id.* ¶¶ 64–65.

[164] *Id.* ¶ 66.

[165] *Id.* ¶¶ 67–70.

[166] *Id.* ¶¶ 71–72.

[167] *Id.* ¶¶ 73–75.

[168] *Id.* ¶¶ 76–87.

[169] *Id.* ¶¶ 88–97.

[170] *Id.* ¶¶ 98–100.

[171] *Id.* ¶¶ 101–104.

[172] *Id.* ¶¶ 105–110.

[173] *Id.* ¶¶ 111–115.

[174] *Id.* Appendix.

[175] Commission on Sustainable Development – Report on the Ninth Session (May 5, 2000 and April 16–27, 2001), ESC Off. Rec., 2001, Supp. No. 9, U.N. Doc. E/2001/29, E/CN.17/2001/19, at 1–31 (2001), http://www.un.org/esa/sustdev/csd/ecn172001-19e.htm.

[176] IISD, *supra* note 144.

[177] UNDSD, *supra* note 144 (showing the thematic issues for each two-year cycle from 2004–2017).

[178] Stine Madland Kaasa, *The Commission on Sustainable Development: A Study of Institutional Design, Distribution of Capabilities and Entrepreneurial Leadership* (Fridtjof Nansen Institute, May 2005), http://www.fni.no/doc&pdf/FNI-R0505.pdf.

Some observers have even argued that the CSD is a 'talk shop' and a waste of time and money."[179] An independent 2005 study gave the CSD a "low score" on elaborating policy guidance and options for future initiatives and only a "medium score" on reviewing and monitoring progress on the implementation of Agenda 21, concluding that member states' positions and interests have a major impact on the low degree of accomplishment.[180] The Executive Director of UNEP, summarizing a 2008 report, stated that negative environmental "change was occurring at an unprecedented rate and...humanity had yet to turn the corner to sustainable development; all indicators were pointing to a worsening situation affecting both developed and developing countries...[and] the threshold of sustained action was yet to be crossed."[181]

4.4.2   UNEP Reforms for the New Century

During the 1990s, UNEP pursued its mandate as the principal UN body in the environmental field. Toward the end of the decade and into the beginning of the new millennium, however, it underwent a number of evolutionary changes leading to greater focus and efficiency. These changes were spurred by a lack of adequate resources, questions about UNEP's role following the establishment of the CSD, and concerns about UNEP's management and institutional structure. Responding to this, the UNEP Governing Council's 1997 "Nairobi Declaration"[182] revised UNEP's mandate by identifying the following tasks, among others:

- assessing environmental trends, providing policy advice and early warnings on environmental threats, and catalyzing and promoting international cooperation and action based on the available scientific and technical capabilities;
- furthering the development of international environmental law to promote sustainable development, "including the development of coherent inter-linkages among existing international environmental conventions;"
- advancing the implementation of agreed international norms and policies, monitoring and fostering compliance with environmental principles and international agreements, and stimulating cooperative action to respond to emerging environmental challenges;

---

[179] *Id.* at 1 (citations omitted).

[180] *Id.* at 56, abstract preceding page i.

[181] UNEP, *Proceedings of the Governing Council/Global Ministerial Environment Forum at its Tenth Special Session*, UNEP/GCSS.X/10, ¶ 38 (10 Mar. 2008), http://www.unep.org/gc/gcss-x/proceedings_docs.asp.

[182] UNEP Governing Council Decision 19/1, Annex of Feb. 7, 1997, endorsed by a special session of the UN General Assembly in June 1997, http://www.unep.org/resources/gov/prev_docs/97_GC19_proceedings.pdf.

- strengthening its role in the coordination of the UN system's environmental activities; and providing policy and advisory services to governments and other institutions in key areas of institution-building.

Subsequently, the UNEP Governing Council adopted the 2000 Malmö Declaration,[183] identifying major environmental challenges of the 21st century and pointing out ways for the international community to address them. In that Declaration, the Council recognized the growing trends of environmental degradation that threaten sustainability, notwithstanding the international community's commitment to halt them. It noted the discrepancy between commitment and action, and stressed "that the root causes of global environmental degradation are embedded in social and economic problems such as pervasive poverty, unsustainable production and consumption patterns, inequity in distribution of wealth, and the debt burden."[184] The Council also emphasized that, to combat environmental degradation, full participation of all actors in society would be required; that actions should be timely taken to implement the political and legal commitment entered into by the international community; and that the outcomes of such actions should be aimed at reversing the present trends of environmental degradation.

UNEP responded to both the Nairobi and Malmö Declarations by developing a functional approach rather than continuing the fragmented, sectoral approaches it had traditionally followed. In his report on the organization's proposed program of work for the Biennium 2002–2003, the UNEP Executive Director explained the agency's new seven-part, "functional" focus:

> The functions of environmental assessment and early warning, environmental policy development, policy implementation, regional cooperation and representation, building mutual support, coherence and greater effectiveness among conventions and communications and public information remain at the core of UNEP's programme planning and delivery. Together with the subprogramme on technology, industry and economics, these functions form the seven-subprogramme structure of UNEP's programme of work.[185]

Two of UNEP's areas of functional focus – environmental assessment and environmental conventions/international law – merit special attention. Regarding environmental assessment, UNEP is further enhancing and strengthening its capabilities and output. It has produced four impressive

[183] UNEP Governing Council decision SS.VI/1, Annex (2000), http://www.unep.org/malmo/malmo_ministerial.htm.

[184] *Id.*

[185] UNEP Governing Council/Global Ministerial Environment Forum, Report of the Executive Director, Programme, The Environment Fund and Administrative and Other Budgetary Matters, UNEP/GC. 21/16, Oct. 2, 2000, ¶ 68. *See also* G.A. Res. 56/6, U.N. Doc. A/56/6/ (Sect. 12) (Apr. 17, 2001), http://www.un.org/documents/ga/docs/56/a566s12.pdf.

reports on the state of the global environment – Global Environmental Outlook 1 (GEO-1)(1997),[186] GEO-2000 (1999),[187] GEO-3 (2002),[188] and GEO-4 (2007)[189] – and the new GEO-5 (2012).[190] The four GEOs first detailed dire assessments of the state of negative environmental change, the lack of progress toward sustainable development, and the need for prompt action. Other significant environmental assessment developments include the formal integration of the World Conservation Monitoring Center into UNEP,[191] enhancement of UNEP's early warning capability through its Global Resource Information Database Centers,[192] and the work of the reformed INFOTERRA, the global environmental information exchange network.[193]

Regarding environmental conventions and international law, UNEP is developing linkages among the various environmental treaty governing bodies and promoting their effective implementation. Its work on regional seas conventions and action plans exemplify its capacity to unite the focus of agencies and conventions. Moreover, the UNEP is strengthening linkages between the regional seas conventions and the chemicals-related conventions (particularly the Basel Convention on Hazardous Wastes, the Rotterdam Convention on Prior Informed Consent, and the Persistent Organic Pollutants (POPs) Convention (*see* Chapter 12)) and the biologic conventions (the Convention on Biological Diversity, CITES, the Convention on Migratory Species of Wild Animals, and conventions and programs on marine mammals, fisheries, and coral reef ecosystems (*see* Chapter 8)).[194]

UNEP's program for the development of environmental law for the first decade of the 21st century[195] has focused on three areas: effectiveness of

---

[186] UNEP, GEO-1: GLOBAL STATE OF THE ENVIRONMENT REPORT 1997, http://www.unep .org/geo/geo1/ch/toc.htm.

[187] UNEP, OVERVIEW GEO-2000: GLOBAL ENVIRONMENT OUTLOOK, http://www.unep.org/ geo/GEO2000.asp.

[188] UNEP, GEO-3, http://www.unep.org/geo/GEO3.asp.

[189] UNEP, GEO-4: ENVIRONMENT FOR DEVELOPMENT, http://www.unep.org/geo/GEO4.asp.

[190] UNEP GEO-5 ENVIRONMENT FOR DEVELOPMENT, http://www.unep.org/geo/Index.asp.

[191] UNEP WORLD CONSERVATION MONITORING CENTRE, http://www.unep-wcmc.org/.

[192] UNEP DEWA/GRID-GENEVA, http://www.grid.unep.ch/.

[193] UNEP-INFOTERRA: THE GLOBAL ENVIRONMENTAL INFORMATION EXCHANGE NETWORK, http://www.unep.org/infoterra/.

[194] UNEP Governing Council/Global Ministerial Environment Forum, Report of the Third Global Meeting of Regional Seas Conventions and Action Plans, UNEP/GC. 21/Inf/14, Annex, Jan. 21, 2001, ¶¶ 79–136, http://www.unep.org/GC/GC21/Documents/gc-21-INF-14/ E-21-INF-14.PDF.

[195] UNEP Governing Council/Global Ministerial Environment Forum, Report of the Meeting of Senior Government Officials Expert in Environmental Law to Prepare a Programme for the Development and Period Review of Environmental Law for the First Decade of the

environmental law,[196] conservation and management,[197] and relationship with other fields. Effectiveness comprises nine subheadings: implementation, compliance, and enforcement; capacity-building; prevention and mitigation of environmental damage; avoidance and settlement of international environment disputes; strengthening and development of international environmental law; harmonization and coordination; public participation and access to information; information technology; and innovative approaches to environmental law.[198] Conservation and management covers eight areas: freshwater resources; coastal and marine ecosystems; soils; forests; biological diversity; pollution prevention and control; production and consumption patterns; and environmental emergencies and natural disasters.[199] Relationship with other fields includes trade, security and the environment, and military activities and the environment.

UNEP is working to develop international environmental law by:

- encouraging international action to address gaps and weaknesses in existing international environmental law;
- responding to new environmental challenges;
- promoting and providing legal advisory services for the development or strengthening of regional and global multilateral environmental agreements;
- assisting governments, particularly those of developing countries and countries with economies in transition, in the developing of legal instruments;
- developing and promoting the development of soft law instruments, such as codes of conduct and guidelines.[200]

The list of focus areas, functions, and tasks under UNEP's authority is staggering. As the body responsible for achieving these objectives, UNEP clearly requires a tremendous amount of support from the UN system and the political will and support of member states. As with the CSD, however, political support for UNEP waxes and wanes. Nevertheless, UNEP enjoys a generally

---

Twenty-First Century, UNEP/GC.21/INF/3, Dec. 15, 2000. The document contains the report of the meeting of those experts, UNEP/Env't Law/4/4, Oct. 31, 2000, http://www.unep.org/gc/gc21/Documents/gc-21-INF-03/K0000295.E.PDF.

[196] UNEP/Env'tLaw 4/4, *supra* note 195, Annex I, § I, ¶¶ 1–9. *See also* UNEP ENVIRONMENT FOR DEVELOPMENT, *Montevideo Program*, http://www.unep.org/law/About_prog/montevideo_prog.asp.

[197] UNEP/Env'tLaw 4/4, *supra* note 195, § II., ¶¶ 10–17.

[198] *Id.*

[199] *Id.*

[200] UNEP, *Development of International Environmental Law*, http://www.unep.org/Law/Programme_work/Devt_international_law/index.asp.

positive image with the public in general and civil society and NGOs, and has not been the object of large-scale criticism as have other UN agencies.[201]

4.4.3   *The 2002 Johannesburg World Summit on Sustainable Development*[202]

"Betrayal,"[203] "disaster,"[204] "failure"[205] were but some of the negative assessments of the 2002 United Nations World Summit on Sustainable Development (WSSD, "Earth Summit," or "Rio+10"), held in Johannesburg, South Africa.[206] Even its UN promoters damned it with faint praise – for example UNEP Executive Director Klaus Toepfer admitted that "Johannesburg is less visionary and more workmanlike [than Rio]...,"[207] and UN Secretary-General Kofi Annan conceded, "We have to be careful not to expect conferences like this to produce miracles.... This is just a beginning...."[208]

A more accurate assessment of the 2002 Earth Summit lies between these extremes of acid and apologetics. At Johannesburg, the expanding field of international environmental law (IEL) ran into the hard reality of the world's existing economic order, and the economic order did not give much. What resulted was indeed a wasted opportunity for expanding IEL, but at least it avoided rolling back 30 years of progress, as at times it seemed it might. The US government and some other nations effectively worked against virtually

---

[201]   Socio-Ecological Union, *Enhancing Civil Society Engagement in the Work of UNEP* § 2.1(Draft IV, Oct. 23, 2001).

[202]   This section is based on George (Rock) Pring, *The 2002 Johannesburg World Summit on Sustainable Development: International Environmental Law Collides with Reality, Turning Jo'burg into "Joke'Burg,"* 32 DEN. J. OF INT'L L. & POL'Y 101 (2003).

[203]   Friends of the Earth International, *Friends of the Earth International Challenges UN Governments "Don't Let Big Business Rule the World" – Summit Wasted – the Time for Action is Now* (Nov. 13, 2002), http://www.foei.org/en/media/archive/2002/1113.html?searchterm=United+Nations+World+Summit+on+Sustainable+Development+betrayal.

[204]   Bill Rodgers, *Greenpeace Hangs Banner on Rio's Christ Statue in Protest of Johannesburg Summit,* WorldNewsSite.com (Sept. 6, 2002) http://worldnewssite.com/News/2002/September/2002-09-06-4-Greenpeace.html.

[205]   Heinrich Böll Foundation, *What Are the Outcomes of the World Summit?* (2002) (comment of Worldwatch Institute representative) http://www.worldsummit2002.org/guide/wssdoutcome.htm.

[206]   A valuable range of views and research tools on the Earth Summit can still be found on the web, including http://www.johannesburgsummit.org (the official UN web site); http://www.worldsummit2002.org (the Heinrich Böll Foundation); http://www.iisd.org/ (the International Institute for Sustainable Development), http://www.earthsummit2002.org/ (Stakeholder Forum Earth Summit 2002), and other websites footnoted herein.

[207]   James Dao, *Protesters Interrupt Powell Speech as UN Talks End,* N.Y. TIMES, Sept. 5, 2002, http://www.nytimes.com/2002/09/05/world/protesters-interrupt-powell-speech-as-un-talks-end.html.

[208]   John Sullivan, *World Summit Adopts Development Plan, Political Declaration as Meeting Concludes,* 33 Env't Rep. (BNA) 1909 (Sept. 6, 2002).

all positive change at Johannesburg, and even sought rollbacks in existing law.[209] The best view of the Summit is: it did not permanently give up serious ground; it exposed the naysayers to intense worldwide scrutiny; and the possibilities for progress in IEL remain open in the years to come.

World leaders started Rio+10 with good intentions. The UN General Assembly resolution authorizing the conference envisioned a "summit...to reinvigorate the global commitment to sustainable development" and to "focus on the identification of accomplishments and areas where further efforts are needed" to carry out the pledges made at the 1992 Rio Conference.[210] As 2002 loomed, "it was hardly a secret – or even a point in dispute – that progress in implementing sustainable development has been extremely disappointing since the 1992 Earth Summit, with poverty deepening and environmental degradation worsening."[211] In response, the UN specifically planned the forum to "reinvigorate" the process of implementing Agenda 21 and the Rio Declaration.[212]

However, a funny thing happened on the way to that forum – en route, the UN's vision was taken hostage by *both* the South and the North. The South reconceived Johannesburg in its own image. The South worked to make it a development rather than an environment summit, one that would focus on poverty alleviation and wealth redistribution for the betterment of the poorer nations.[213] Meanwhile, elements of the North, particularly the US and some other nations, sought to avoid the developmental focus by insisting the agenda produce no new multilateral goals, no new treaties, no mandatory agreements, no legal principles of substance, and no fixed targets, percentages, or timetables for accomplishing Agenda 21's ten-year-old promises. The US excuse for this negative stance was to assert that it would take "concrete programs" not "deadlines and targets" to get results,[214] but its approach

---

[209] *See, e.g.,* Rachel Swarns, *World Development Forum Begins with a Rebuke,* N.Y. Times, Aug. 27, 2002, http://www.nytimes.com/2002/08/27/world/world-development-forum-begins-with-a-rebuke.html; Rachel Swarns, *U.S. Summit Scapegoat: Nation Is Blamed for Opposing Deal, But It's Not Alone,* N.Y. Times, Aug. 31, 2002; and web sites *supra* note 206.

[210] *Ten-Year Review of Progress Achieved in the Implementation of the Outcome of the UN Conference on Environment and Development,* G.A. Res. 55/199, at §§ 1, 3, U.N. Doc. A/55/582/Add. 1 (Dec. 20, 2000), http://www.un.org/esa/sustdev/sids/res_55_199.htm.

[211] United Nations, *The Johannesburg Summit Test: What Will Change?,* http://www.johannes burgsummit.org/html/whats_new/feature_story41.html.

[212] G.A. Res. 55/199, *supra* note 210, at § 1 and 13th Preamble.

[213] Heinrich Böll Foundation, *The Jo'burg Memo – Fairness in a Fragile World – Memorandum for the World Summit on Sustainable Development* 6, http://www.boell-afghanistan .org/downloads/Joburg_Memo_engl..pdf.

[214] *See* Rachel L. Swarns, *U.S. Shows Off Aid Projects at U.N. Development Meeting,* N.Y. Times, Aug. 30, 2002, http://www.nytimes.com/2002/08/30/world/us-shows-off-aid-projects-at-un-development-meeting.html.

was widely viewed as complete obstructionism and provoked "a relentless storm of criticism."[215] This US retreat from multilateralism, cooperation, and international law, while more obvious during President George W. Bush's Administration,[216] was not an altogether new posture for the US. Of the 16 major global IEL treaties that entered into force from 1979–2002, the US had joined only half.[217] Even after Obama took office, critics still complain that the US has not acted quickly enough on the issue of climate change and other international issues.[218]

The Preparatory Committee negotiations for Johannesburg focused on "whether or not the rich nations of the world would come up with the cash to pay for the implementation of the Rio agreements" and broke down without final resolution.[219] This left the sponsors and delegates searching for a face-saving solution, and one was found by making a virtue of necessity –

---

[215] *Id.*

[216] Examples include abandoning the treaties on global warming and ballistic missile defense; rejecting agreements on banning germ warfare, creating an international criminal court, curtailing strategic nuclear weapons, banning all nuclear tests, biological weapons, land mines, and small arms; and threatening withdrawal from others such as the UN's landmark family planning agreement. *See* Bill Nichols, *Critics decry Bush stand on treaties*, USA TODAY, July 26, 2001, http://www.usatoday.com/news/washington/july01/2001-07-27-bush-treaties-usat.htm; Thom Shanker, *White House Says the U.S. Is Not a Loner, Just Choosy*, N.Y. TIMES, July 31, 2001, http://www.nytimes.com/2001/07/31/world/white-house-says-the-us-is-not-a-loner-just-choosy.html; James Dao, *U.S. May Abandon Support of U.N. Population Accord*, N.Y. TIMES, Nov. 2, 2002, http://www.nytimes.com/2002/11/02/international/asia/02ABOR.html.

[217] *See* J. W. Anderson, *U.S. Has No Role in U.N. Treaty Process; Senate Reluctant to Ratify*, RESOURCES 12 (Summer 2002) www.rff.org/RFF/Documents/RFF-Resources-148-treaty-process.pdf. The US had *not* become a party to 1979 Bonn Convention on Conservation of Migratory Species, 1982 Convention on the Law of the Sea, 1989 Basel Convention on Transboundary Movements of Hazardous Waste and Their Disposal, 1992 Convention on Biological Diversity, 1997 Kyoto Protocol to the Climate Change Convention, 1997 Convention on Non-navigational Uses of International Watercourses, 1998 Rotterdam Convention on Prior Informed Consent for Hazardous Chemicals and Pesticides, or the 2001 Stockholm Convention on Persistent Organic Pollutants. It has become a party to the 1972 London Convention on Prevention of Marine Pollution, 1973/78 MARPOL Convention for Prevention of Pollution from Ships, 1973 Convention on International Trade in Endangered Species, 1979 Convention on Long-Range Transboundary Air Pollution, 1985 Vienna Convention for the Protection of the Ozone Layer, 1987 Montreal Protocol to the same, 1992 Framework Convention on Climate Change, and 1994 Convention to Combat Desertification. *See id.* at 15.

[218] *See* David Jenkins, *Measuring Obama's Environmental Record, Republicans for Environmental Protection*, (2010) http://repamerica.org/opinions/op-eds/135B.html.

[219] GREENPEACE, *Rich Countries Refuse to Pay Their Environmental and Social Debt* (June 7, 2002) http://archive.greenpeace.org/earthsummit/news_june7b.html.

given the US opposition to goals, targets, and timetables. In an Orwellian turn of doublespeak, the delegates began calling those progressive steps "Type 1 deliverables" ("Type I outcomes") and denigrating them (since they were not going to happen). In their place, delegates began emphasizing "Type 2 deliverables" ("Type II outcomes"), defined as "action-oriented coalitions focused on deliverables."[220] Without admitting it, the conference was defaulting back to the former, failed system of uncoordinated "foreign aid" projects.[221] The UN sponsors themselves conceded this switch "marked a major departure from previous UN conferences...that could have a major effect on the way the international community approaches problem solving in the future."[222] US Johannesburg delegate John Turner, Assistant Secretary of State for Oceans and International Environmental and Scientific Affairs, attempted to justify the change: "I think goals are important, but they're only lofty rhetoric without the commitment of resources."[223] However, critics condemned it as a ruse to divert attention from the reluctance of wealthy nations to reduce trade subsidies and commit new resources, pointing out that most of the money would come from already existing programs.[224]

One environmental leader at Johannesburg pinpointed the problems with this shift:

> Some of the partnerships that were showcased in Johannesburg may not be so bad. Some are steps in the right direction, and involve good NGO's doing quality work on the ground....But many dangers exist with making partnerships the centerpiece of a once-every-ten-years Earth Summit. First among them: in the absence of any accountability or guidelines for partnerships...they provide an opportunity for multinationals [business entities] to continue with business as usual and wrap their operations in the flag of the UN and sustainability to inoculate themselves against criticism. The bigger threat, though, is the way that partnerships take the focus away from governmental agreements at the WSSD, and distract media and public scrutiny from the abject failures in that area. When it comes to issues like climate change, it's clear that partnerships are incapable of making the necessary global corrections. Commitments and leadership from governments are the only solution.[225]

---

[220] Linkages, *Background Information on Type II Outcomes*, http://www.iisd.ca/wssd/partnerships.html.

[221] Such "partnerships" have been sponsored or encouraged by the UN for nearly 20 years. *See* Eric J. Lyman, *State Department Proposes Partnerships to Address Environmental, Health Issues*, 33 Env't Rep. (BNA) 1913 (Sept. 6, 2002).

[222] *See* United Nations, *The Johannesburg Summit Test, supra* note 211.

[223] Swarns, *World Development Forum Begins with a Rebuke, supra* note 209.

[224] *See* Swarns, *U.S. Shows Off, supra* note 214.

[225] Steven Sanderson, *The Future of Conservation*, 81 Foreign Affairs 162, 164, 171 (2002).

The US delegation at Johannesburg rejected progressive initiatives on virtually every issue, from renewable energy, safe drinking water, sanitation, trade, and foreign aid to women's reproductive health, agricultural subsidies, and human rights. However, it was not alone. On renewable energy, Saudi Arabia, Canada, Japan, and Australia joined the US in opposing deadlines for a 10 to 15 percent conversion from fossil fuels to solar, wind, and other renewables; the European Union joined it in opposing elimination of agricultural subsidies that make it next to impossible for poor countries to export to the US and EU; developing countries joined it in watering down a commitment to reduce the threat of dangerous chemicals; and Australia joined it in initially refusing to support a timeline for reducing the number of people who lack adequate sanitation.[226]

So, what accomplishments can Johannesburg claim? Of the customary "Type 1 deliverables" (policy), there were two, but neither one produced substantive change. First, delegates produced a pious "Political Declaration"[227] (e.g., "We commit ourselves to build a humane, equitable and caring global society..."),[228] which avoided setting any standards or making any real commitments. Second, despite Agenda 21's existence and nonfulfillment, they drafted a new "Plan of Implementation"[229] (only 54 pages, compared to the detailed Agenda 21, which is almost ten times that long). The good news is that Rio and progeny survived, with the statement that the delegates "strongly reaffirm our commitment to the Rio principles, the full implementation of Agenda 21...the United Nations Millennium Declaration and...the outcomes of the major United Nations conferences and international agreements since 1992."[230]

The major "commitments"[231] in the Plan of Implementation included:

---

[226] Swarns, *U.S. Summit Scapegoat, supra* note 209.

[227] The Johannesburg Declaration on Sustainable Development (Sept. 4, 2002), http://www.un.org/jsummit/html/documents/summit_docs/0409_l6rev2_pol_decl.pdf.

[228] *Id.* ¶ 2.

[229] World Summit on Sustainable Development Plan of Implementation (revised, Sept. 23, 2002), http://www.johannesburgsummit.org/html/documents/summit_docs/2309_planfinal.htm.

[230] *Id.* ¶ 1.

[231] While there are many vague, contentless "commitments" in the Plan, this list contains the ones the UN thought serious enough to be mentioned in its 3-page *Highlights of Commitments and Implementation Initiatives*, initially posted on the official UN Johannesburg web site and revised on Sept. 12, 2002 (copy with author), but then removed and replaced by a much more face-saving 7-page *Key Outcomes of the Summit in October*, http://www.johannesburgsummit.org/html/documents/summit_docs/2009_keyoutcomes_commitments.doc. *See also* John Sullivan, *"Plan of Implementation" Seeks to Aid Poor, Spur Growth Without Harming Environment*, 33 Env't Rep. (BNA) 1909 (Sept. 6, 2002).

- Water and sanitation – to cut in half the proportion of the world's people who are without access to basic sanitation[232] and safe drinking water by 2015;[233]
- Energy – to increase access to modern energy services,[234] increase energy efficiency,[235] and renewable energy use,[236] phase out energy subsidies where appropriate,[237] and support access to energy for at least 35 percent of the African population by 2022;[238]
- Health – to aim to achieve use and production of chemicals that lead to minimization of significant adverse effects on human health and environment by 2020,[239] enhance cooperation to reduce air pollution,[240] and improve developing countries' access to environmentally sound alternatives to ozone-depleting chemicals by 2010.[241]
- Agriculture – to call on the Global Environmental Facility (GEF) to consider inclusion of desertification as a new focal area for funding[242] and develop food security strategies for Africa by 2005;[243]
- Biodiversity – to significantly reduce biodiversity loss by 2010,[244] reverse the current trend in natural resource degradation as soon as possible,[245] restore fisheries to their maximum sustainable yields by 2015,[246] establish representative marine protected areas by 2012,[247] undertake initiatives to reduce land-based ocean pollution by 2004;[248]
- Crosscutting issues – to recognize that opening up access to markets is a key to development,[249] support phase out of export subsidies,[250] establish a ten-year program on sustainable consumption and production,[251] promote

---

[232] WSSD Plan of Implementation, *supra* note 229, ¶ 7.

[233] *Id.*

[234] *Id.* ¶ 8.

[235] *Id.* ¶ 19(d).

[236] *Id.*

[237] *Id.* ¶¶ 19(p), (q).

[238] *Id.* ¶ 56(j)(i).

[239] *Id.* ¶ 22.

[240] *Id.* ¶ 37.

[241] *Id.* ¶ 37(d).

[242] *Id.* ¶ 39(f).

[243] *Id.* ¶ 61.

[244] *Id.* ¶ 42.

[245] *Id.* ¶ 23.

[246] *Id.* ¶ 30(a).

[247] *Id.* ¶ 31(c).

[248] *Id.* ¶ 52(e).

[249] *Id.* ¶¶ 6(i), 41(e).

[250] *Id.* ¶ 86(c).

[251] *Id.* ¶ 14.

corporate responsibility and accountability,[252] and improve natural disaster preparedness and response.[253]

This list is less impressive than it seems for three reasons. First, these are the same type of generalized promises that the same countries made ten years previously in Agenda 21 but never funded or implemented. Second, only two appear to be new promises, sanitation and marine reserves, the rest being existing commitments already made in previous post-Rio UN conferences.[254] Lastly, a number of the old promises that are included are subtly and not so subtly diluted, delayed, or denied. Examples of the latter include making it only an "aim" to eliminate dangerous chemicals by 2020 (contrary to the thrust of current chemical treaties; *see* Chapter 12),[255] backing off to just "a significant reduction" in loss of biodiversity (undercutting the 1992 Convention on Biological Diversity),[256] and promoting "clean" fossil fuels (despite the Climate Change treaty regime).[257]

As one disgusted environmental NGO put it: "We could go on, but the list of weasel words and lost promises is nearly endless. Do not believe Government spin doctors who claim success for the Summit. It is by any objective test a failure."[258] Another NGO evaluated the summit's performance in ten different categories (maximum 10 points each) and gave it a failing score of only 22 points out of a possible 100.[259]

Is the environmentalists' assessment overly harsh? Perhaps, but even the UN sponsors were tepid in their assessment:

> [T]here were no silver bullet solutions to aid the fight against poverty and a continually deteriorating natural environment....Johannesburg did not produce a particularly dramatic outcome – there were no agreements that will lead to new treaties....However, important new targets were established [citing the four targets for sanitation access, chemical safety, fish stocks maintenance, and biodiversity loss reduction].[260]

Certainly, Johannesburg was a sad conclusion for the first international sustainable development conference of the 21st century. The forthcoming

---

[252] *Id.* ¶¶ 45.ter, 122(f).

[253] *Id.* ¶¶ 35(g), 59, 99(e), 119.noviens.

[254] Friends of the Earth, *Earth Summit: Betrayal* (Sept. 3, 2002), http://www.foe.co.uk/resource/press_releases/0904wrap.html.

[255] WSSD Plan of Implementation, *supra* note 229, ¶ 22.

[256] *Id.* ¶ 42.

[257] *Id.* ¶ 19(e).

[258] Friends of the Earth, *supra* note 254.

[259] Friends of the Earth, *Earth Summit End of Term Report*, http://www.foe.co.uk/resource/press_releases/0902scor.html.

[260] *The Johannesburg Summit Test, supra* note 211.

"Rio+20," the 2012 UN Conference on Sustainable Development, symbolically to be held again in Rio de Janeiro will tell whether the outcome at Johannesburg represents the wave of the future of international environmental law or only an embarrassing temporary dip in our progress toward ensuring a safe, healthy environment, society, and economy for the world in the years ahead.

4.4.4   "Rio+20" – The Return to Rio

As this book goes to press, the world is gearing up for another international environmental summit, scheduled for June 20–22, 2012, to mark the 20th anniversary of the 1992 Rio Conference. Symbolically, UNGA has called for this UN Conference on Sustainable Development (UNCSD or "Rio+20") to be held again in Rio de Janeiro, Brazil.[261] The UNGA resolution calls for the conference to be held "at the highest possible level, including Heads of State and Government or other representatives."[262] The "objective" of the conference is "to secure renewed political commitment for sustainable development, assessing the progress to date and the remaining gaps in the implementation of the outcomes of the major summits on sustainable development and addressing new and emerging challenges."[263] Rio+20 is to have two "themes": (1) "a green economy in the context of sustainable development and poverty eradication" and (2) the institutional framework for sustainable development."[264]

Is there hope for a different and more productive outcome than at Rio+10 in Johannesburg? Possibly, since UNGA wants the conference to "result in a focused political document,"[265] perhaps suggesting a return to the "Type 1" deliverables – actual substantive policy negotiated and agreed on between states – that was significantly lacking at Rio+10. If this "focused political document" really tackles the transition to a global "green economy" and promotes reform of the "institutional framework" responsible for sustainable development, Rio+20 could be a success.

> This...could feasibly restructure everything ranging from the UN Environmental Program (UNEP) and the UN Development Program to the 500 different multilateral environmental treaties and agreements currently in place....Given the rising trends of global temperature, hunger, water scarcity, and biodiversity loss, the existing mishmash of eco-governance is clearly failing to deliver.

---

[261] G.A. Res. 64/236, U.N. GAOR, 64th Sess., U.N. Doc A/RES/64/236, ¶ 20 (Mar. 31, 2010), http://www.uncsd2012.org/rio20.

[262] *Id.*

[263] *Id.* ¶ 20(a).

[264] *Id.*

[265] *Id.* ¶ 20(b).

RIO+20 is a precious chance for decision-makers to take stock of where the world went wrong in the last 20 years and plan intelligently for the next 20. Hopefully RIO+20 will deliver a jolt of political will to the global environmental agenda, as well as a smart plan to get the planet back on track.[266]

However, criticism and pessimism were already mounting during the preparatory process.

Far from cooking up a plan to save the Earth, what may come out of the summit could instead be a deal to surrender the living world to a small cabal of bankers and engineers – one that will dump the promise of the first Rio summit along the way. Tensions are already rising between northern countries and southern countries over the poorly defined concept of a global "Green Economy" that will be the centerpiece of the summit.

What is a global green economy?...[S]uspicion is running high that the proposed prescriptions for a "green economy" are more likely to deliver a greenwash economy or the same old, same old "greed" economy.... The key words to focus on here are "markets" and "technology."...[Some] would like to steer the RIO+20 summit away from addressing the root causes of our ecological crises. They would like the emphasis to be on a "forward-looking" effort to establish new financial arrangements based on so-called "ecosystem services" while liberating funds for iconic "green technologies."[267]

It is true that UNEP has sponsored two study reports as background for Rio+20 that are highly economic in approach – "Green Economy Report" (GER)[268] and "The Economics of Ecosystems and Biodiversity" (TEEB).[269] The studies make an economic case that the environment can be precisely valued based on the "services" that it provides humans, such as nitrogen cycling, carbon sequestration, water purification, etc. The theory of this approach is that, once a value is set on the services provided by a rain forest, river, or mountain, then those values can be capitalized and traded to raise money for environmental protection and conservation. Also, new eco-friendly technologies can be developed to enhance the value of these services and generate income. The "most vocal" supporters of this monetizing or commoditizing approach to nature are "Fortune 500 companies and G8 diplomats."[270]

Will this monetization approach to a "green economy" be used to replace and discard Rio's paradigm of "sustainable development"? Will it divert

---

[266] Jim Thomas, *Will Rio+20 Squander Green Legacy of the Original Earth Summit?*, THE GUARDIAN, Mar. 31, 2011, http://www.guardian.co.uk/environment/2011/mar/31/rio-20-earth-summit.

[267] *Id.*

[268] UNEP, *Green Economy Report*, http://www.unep.org/greeneconomy/GreenEconomy Report/tabid/1375/Default.aspx.

[269] UNEP et al., *The Economics of Ecosystems and Biodiversity (TEEB)* http://www.teebweb .org/.

[270] Thomas, *supra* note 266.

attention from sustainable development's focus on protecting the environment, society, and human rights, eliminating poverty, and creating intragenerational and intergenerational equity? Will it focus government and business
leaders excessively on "technology cures" instead of precaution and prevention principles? Is it just a ruse to allow business-as-usual utilization of the
environment?

Only time – and Rio+20 – will tell.

4.5   *International Environmental Law, Multilateral Environmental Agreements, and International Environmental Governance*

We have already briefly noted that UNEP has been actively engaged in the
development and promotion of environmental law, and the negotiation,
adoption, and strengthening of global and regional multilateral environmental agreements (MEAs) since the early 1980s (*see* Chapter 4.2.4 and 4.4.4).
Here we discuss these contributions further, and also study international
environmental governance, one of the two themes selected for UNCSD and
a topic of great interest and concern at present.

4.5.1   *UNEP and International Environmental Law*[271]

When the United Nations General Assembly established UNEP in December
1972,[272] it delegated authority to its Executive Director to promote "international cooperation in the field of environment"[273] and "perform such other
functions as may be entrusted to him by the Governing Council."[274] Drawing
on this authority, UNEP initiated its program for the development of international law. Almost 20 years later, Agenda 21,[275] adopted at the Rio Summit,
in its chapter 38 underscored the role of UNEP in the further development

---

[271] The UNEP has an excellent series of websites describing its work in the field of international environmental law. *See Programme of Work*, UNEP, http://www.unep.org/law/
Programme_work/index.asp; *Development of International Environmental Law*, UNEP,
www.unep.org/law/Programme_work/Devt_international_law/index.asp; *Division of Environmental Law and Conventions*, UNEP, http://www.unep.org/delc/EnvironmentalLaw/
tabid/54403/Default.aspx; *Publications*, UNEP, http://www.unep.org/law/Publications_
multimedia/index.asp.

[272] G.A. Res. 2997, 27 U.N. GAOR Supp. (No. 30) at 43, U.N. Doc. A/8730 (1972), pt. II,
¶ 2(e) http://www.un-documents.net/a27r2997.htm.

[273] *Id.* pt. II, ¶ 2e.

[274] *Id.* ¶ 2(j).

[275] Agenda 21 is a plan of action for sustainable development adopted by UNCED on June 14,
1992. Its text appears in U.N. Doc. A/CONF.151/26 (3 vols. 1992), available at http://www
.un.org/documents/ga/conf151/aconf15126-1annex1.htm.

and implementation of international environmental law, as well as provision of technical, legal, and institutional advice to Governments in establishing and enhancing their national legal and institutional frameworks, and this role was subsequently affirmed as part of UNEP's mandate by the UNEP Governing Council in its 1997 Nairobi Declaration[276] and the 2000 Malmö Declaration.[277]

Guided by its Governing Council, UNEP has continued to perform these functions – contributing to the development of globally and regionally binding legal instruments as well as soft law instruments, such as guidelines, principles, standards, and codes of conduct, and administering the secretariats of several MEAs in biodiversity cluster and chemicals and hazardous waste cluster. It has also undertaken several other related activities, such as (1) training judges; (2) promoting environmental law education; (3) promoting compliance with, implementation, and enforcement of environmental law, including MEAs, by states; (4) preparing studies on environmental law issues; and (5) advising states in the development of national environmental legislation.

UNEP's environmental law activities began in 1982 with a series of 10-year programs (Montevideo Programs)[278] adopted by its Governing Council for the development and periodic review of environmental law, which have provided frameworks for the UNEP agenda. The latest such program is Montevideo IV,[279] with a broad strategy for charting UNEP's activities in the field of environmental law for the decade commencing in 2010. The following discussion presents the range and scope of these activities.

---

[276] *See* Nairobi Declaration *supra* note 182. The "Nairobi Declaration" revised UNEP's mandate, identifying as one of its specific tasks furthering the development of international environmental law to promote sustainable development.

[277] *See* Malmö Declaration *supra* note 183. The Malmö Declaration identified major environmental challenges of the 21st Century as well as ways for the world community to address them.

[278] UNEP, *Division of Environmental Law and Conventions, Montevideo Programme*, http://www.unep.org/delc/MontevideoProgramme/tabid/54416/Default.aspx.

[279] Proceedings of the Governing Council/Global Ministerial Environment Forum at its twenty-fifth session, document UNEP/GC.25/17, Decision 25/11: Environmental Law (I) – Fourth Programme for the Development and Periodic Review of Environmental Law, February 25, 2009: Report of the Meeting of Senior Government Officials Expert in Environmental Law to Prepare a Fourth Programme for the Development and Periodic Review of Environmental Law (Montevideo IV), document UNEP/Env.Law/MTV4/IG/2/2, October 22, 2008; Governing Council of the United Nations Environment Programme, Report by the Executive Director: Fourth Programme for the Development and Periodic Review of Environmental Law, document UNEP/GC.25/11, October 28, 2008 – Environmental Law, document UNEP/GC.25/17.

Montevideo Program I

The Governing Council of UNEP adopted Montevideo Program I on May 31, 1982,[280] for the decade of the 1980s. Three major subject areas of environmental law were selected for the development of agreements or guidelines and principles. Eight other subject areas with specific objectives were also identified. The three major areas were (1) marine pollution from land-based sources, (2) protection of the stratospheric ozone layer, and (3) toxic and hazardous wastes (*see* Chapter 4.2.4). UNEP was successful in accomplishing the goals set for all these subjects. The outcome for the first subject area was the adoption of the 1985 Montreal Guidelines for the Protection of the Marine Environment against Pollution from Land-Based Sources,[281] which subsequently formed the basis of several international and regional MEAs and plans of action for the development of national environmental laws.

On the second major subject area, UNEP succeeded initially in the negotiation and adoption of the 1985 Vienna Convention for the Protection of the Ozone Layer (*see* Chapter 10.2.7) and subsequently the 1987 Montreal Protocol on Substances that Deplete the Ozone Layer (*see* Chapter 10.2.8). On the third subject, toxic and hazardous wastes, a UNEP working group developed the Cairo Guidelines during the years 1982–1987,[282] which formed the basis for the 1989 Basel Convention on the Control of Transboundary Movement of Hazardous Wastes and their Disposal (*see* Chapter 12.2). Also, on other topics considered by UNEP during the decade, such as biological diversity and climate change, framework conventions were adopted at the 1992 UN Rio Conference – the Framework Convention on Climate Change (Chapter 10.3.4), and the Convention on Biological Diversity (Chapter 8.3.1).

Montevideo Program II

The UNEP Governing Council, by its Decision 17/25 of May 21, 1993, adopted the Program for the Development and Periodic Review of International Law for the 1990s (Montevideo Program II), which provided the strategy for UNEP activities in the field of international law. As in the preparation for Montevideo Program I, UNEP had organized meetings of senior government officials expert in environmental law during 1991–1992 to design the program, which was largely based upon the requirements contained in

---

[280] Programme for the Development and Periodic Review of Environmental Law, Decision 10/21 of the Governing Council of UNEP, May 31, 1982, *reprinted in* UNEP, Report of the Governing Council (session of a special character and tenth session), 37 U.N. GAOR Supp. (No. 25), Annex I at 108, U.N. Doc. A/37/25 (1982), http://www.unep.org/resources/gov/prev_docs/82_05_GC10_%20special_character_report_of_the_GC_10_1982.pdf.

[281] Adopted by UNEP Governing Council Decision 13/18, section 2, May 24, 1985.

[282] The Cairo Guidelines were approved by UNEP Governing Council Decision 14/30, June 17, 1987.

Agenda 21, as well as the relevant concepts and principles of the Rio Declaration. The Program consisted of 18 program areas and a few additional
subjects listed for possible consideration during the decade.[283] It is worth
noting that in contrast to Montevideo I, the focus in Montevideo II was
not on developing new principles and norms in a few selected areas but
instead on 18 diverse program areas UNEP was to pursue within the general
framework of established principles or agreements. In its decision the Governing Council requested the Executive Director to prepare and disseminate
analytical reports, organize intergovernmental meetings, and contribute to
capacity-building in the field of environmental law as part of the implementation of the program.

The areas selected spanned a wide range and scope. They were: (1) enhancing the capacity of states to participate effectively in the development and
implementation of environmental law; (2) implementation of international legal instruments in the field of the environment; (3) adequacy of
existing environmental instruments; (4) dispute avoidance and settlement;
(5) legal and administrative mechanisms for the prevention and redress
of pollution and other environmental damage; (6) environmental impact
assessment; (7) environmental awareness, education, information, and public participation; (8) concepts or principles significant for the future of international environmental law; (9) protection of the stratospheric ozone layer;
(10) transboundary air pollution control; (11) conservation management and
sustainable development of soils and forests; (12) transport, handling, and
disposal of hazardous wastes; (13) international trade in potentially harmful chemicals; (14) environmental protection and integrated management,
development, and use of inland water resources; (15) marine pollution from
land-based sources; (16) management of coastal areas; (17) protection of the
marine environment and the law of the sea; and (18) international cooperation in environmental emergencies.

The additional subjects for possible consideration were: (1) environmental
protection of areas beyond the limits of national jurisdiction; (2) use and
management of biotechnology, including the question of intellectual and
property rights with respect to genetic resources; (3) liability and compensation or restitution for environmental damage; (4) environment and trade;
(5) examination of the environmental implications of international agreements on subjects which do not relate directly to the environment;

---

[283] *See* the UNEP Governing Council Decision 17/25, Programme for the Development and
Periodic Review of Environmental Law, May 25, 1993. The program is contained in Annex
at 60, Programme for the Development and Periodic Review of Environmental Law: Programme Areas, Objectives, Strategies and Activities, http://www.unep.org/download_file
.multilingual.asp?FileID=13.

(6) environmental problems of human settlements, including their growth; and (7) transfer of appropriate technology and technical cooperation.

Two years after the adoption of Montevideo Programme II, the UNEP Governing Council decided in May 1995 to request the Executive Director to (1) prepare a position paper for international environmental law aiming at sustainable development, which should explore compliance/implementation mechanisms, dispute avoidance/settlement procedures and new concepts and principles, with reference to existing international legal instruments, and guidelines, and (2) prepare a study on the need for and feasibility of new international legal instruments aiming at sustainable development.[284]

On February 7, 1997, the UNEP Governing Council considered the Executive Director's Report on the mid-term review of the Program, which was undertaken by environmental law experts UNEP had convened.[285] It commended UNEP for the actions it had undertaken toward implementation of the Program.[286] It took note of the position paper UNEP had prepared on international environmental law aiming at sustainable development[287] as well as of the preliminary study UNEP had prepared on the need for and feasibility of new international environmental instruments aiming at sustainable development, and requested the Executive Director "to continue the work of identifying ways of better implementing existing and future international instruments aiming at sustainable and the need for and feasibility of such new instruments."[288]

Montevideo Program III
We have already briefly noted Montevideo Program III, the Programme for the Development and Periodic Review of Environmental Law for the First Decade of the Twenty-first Century, which was adopted by the UNEP Governing Council Decision 21/23 of February 9, 2001, and which provided the broad strategy for UNEP's activities for that period (*see* Chapter 4.4.4).[289]

---

[284] UNEP Governing Council Decision 18/9, May 26, 1995.

[285] UNEP Governing Council Decision 19/20, February 7, 1997.

[286] *Id.* op. para. 1.

[287] *Id.* op. para. 2.

[288] *Id.* op. para. 3.

[289] UNEP Governing Council Decision 21/23 of February 9, 2001. *See* UNEP Governing Council/Global Ministerial Environment Forum, 21st Sess., Nairobi, Feb. 5–9, 2001, Provisional Agenda item 4(a), Note by the Secretariat: Policy Issues: State of the Environment – Report of the Meeting of Senior Government Officials Expert in Environmental Law to Prepare a Programme for the Development and Periodic Review of Environmental Law for the First Decade of the Twenty-First Century, UNEP/GC.21/INF/3, 15 Dec. 2000 [hereinafter Secretariat's Note], http://www.unep.org/gc/gc21/Documents/gc-21-INF-03/K0000295.E.PDF. The Secretariat's Note contains the experts' report (Nairobi, Oct. 23–27, 2000), UNEP/Env'T. Law/4/4, Oct. 31, 2000.

The environmental law experts who prepared the report adopted as the Montevideo Program III "generally felt that emphasis should be laid more on implementing existing laws rather than creating new ones," and noted that "public participation could play a key role in ensuring that laws were enforced."[290] The experts organized their report under three broad headings – effectiveness of environmental law,[291] conservation and management,[292] and relationship with other fields – comprising 20 program areas.[293]

The strategy proposed to strengthen and further develop international environmental law was through encouragement of international action "to address gaps and weaknesses in existing international environmental law and to respond to new environmental challenges."[294] Under effectiveness of environmental law, specific action includes reviewing the existing application of the 1972 Stockholm Principles and the 1992 Rio Principles, assisting governments in the development of bilateral, regional, and global legal instruments in the environmental field, and strengthening collaboration within the UN system, as well as with other intergovernmental bodies.[295]

Effectiveness is furthered, the experts found, by innovative approaches to environmental law. This calls for assessing state practice "in utilizing tools such as eco-labeling, certification, pollution fees, natural resources taxes and emissions trading" and assisting in the use of such tools; promoting the development and assessing the effectiveness of "voluntary codes of conduct and comparable initiatives that promote environmentally and socially responsible corporate and institutional behavior, to complement domestic law and international agreements;" and encouraging the development of law and policy "for reducing the debt burdens of developing countries in ways that benefit the environment."[296]

To effectively prevent and mitigate environmental damage, the experts called for the promotion of state efforts "to develop and adopt minimum international standards at high levels of protection and best practice standards," and support of states' development of processes and procedures for victims and potential victims of environmentally harmful activities so as to "[e]nsure appropriate access to justice" and "[p]rovide appropriate redress, including the possibility of compensation, *inter alia*, through insurance and compensation funds."[297]

---

[290] Secretariat's Note, *supra* note 289, at 4.
[291] *Id.* at 5–11.
[292] *Id.* at 11–16.
[293] *Id.* at 16–18.
[294] *Id.* at 8.
[295] *Id.* at 8–9.
[296] *Id.* at 11.
[297] *Id.* at 7.

The experts' proposed strategy to achieve effective implementation of, compliance with, and enforcement of environmental law, included "the widest possible participation in multilateral environmental agreements" and the suggested action included provision of assistance to developing countries in establishing and strengthening domestic law to improve enforcement of international environmental obligations and to develop national and regional environmental action plans or strategies, including establishment of model laws, promoting the use of financial mechanisms, technology transfer, and economic incentives and disincentives, including effective civil liability mechanisms.[298] The proposed strategy for capacity-building was to provide: "appropriate technical assistance, education and training to those concerned, based on assessment of needs," and the suggested action included assisting "the development and strengthening of domestic environmental legislation, regulations, procedures and institutions," the production and dissemination of environmental law publications, and promotion of the teaching of domestic, international and comparative environmental law in universities and law schools.[299]

The first review of the Program was submitted by the Executive Director to the 23rd Session of the UNEP Governing Council held in Nairobi from February 21 to 25, 2005.[300] The Executive Director reported that in each of the 20 program areas UNEP had carried out significant activities, while devoting special attention to two areas: (1) "substantive work in the development and application of principles, regulations, and procedures of international and national environmental law in specific thematic subject areas," and (2) "the adoption of appropriate mechanisms for improving the delivery of the objectives and outcomes established in relation to those thematic subject areas."[301] He especially noted four achievements as deserving special mention: (1) UNEP's legal advice and support leading to the development and entry into force of a number of global and regional environmental agreements, including the 2001 Stockholm Convention on Persistent Organic Pollutants, and two regional agreements – the 2001 ASEAN Agreement on Transboundary Haze Pollution and the 2003 African Convention on the Conservation of Nature and Natural Resources; (2) UNEP's launching of the Global Judges Program, including the 2002 Global Judges Symposium; (3) UNEP's initiation

---

[298] *Id.* at 5–6.

[299] *Id.* at 6.

[300] Report of the Executive Director, UNEP Governing Council, State of the Environment and Contribution of the United Nations Environment Program to Addressing Substantive Environmental Challenges, Addendum: Implementation of the Program for the Development and Periodic Review of Environmental Law for the First Decade of the Twenty-First Century (Montevideo Program III), document UNEP/gc.23/3/Add.3, November 4, 2004.

[301] *Id.* at 3.

and support of the development of the Guidelines for the Enforcement of and Compliance with MEAs; and (4) UNEP's launching of its environmental law website and the joint UNEP-Food and Agriculture Organization-World Conservation Union database ECOLEX on the internet.[302]

The report on the final review of the Program was presented at the 25th Session of the UNEP Governing Council held in Nairobi from February 16 to 20, 2009.[303] The report noted that the issue of implementation of the existing internationally agreed environmental goals and objectives as contained in Agenda 21, the Johannesburg Plan of Implementation, the UN Millennium Declaration, the 2005 World Summit Outcome, and MEAs had been receiving increased attention since 2001. The report further noted that UNEP was responsive in supporting governments, especially developing countries and countries with economies in transition to facilitate compliance with and enforcement of MEAs, and also in providing legal and technical assistance.[304] UNEP had also initiated the preparation of a compilation of internationally agreed environmental goals and objectives.[305]

In addition, UNEP had continued its support for strengthening the regulatory and institutional capacity of developing countries and countries with economies in transition to develop and implement environmental law. UNEP's activities also included (1) preparing and widely disseminating publications on environmental law and strengthen the teaching of environmental law in universities, (2) raising awareness among judges through the Judges Program on environmental policies and law, and (3) conducting training programs on environmental law.[306]

The report noted UNEP achievements during the decade. These included the preparation of the Draft Guidelines for the Development of National Legislation on Liability and Compensation for Environmental Damage,[307] which reflect the Polluter-Pays Principle as a central conceptual principle, and the Draft Guidelines for the Development of National Legislation on Access to Information, Public Participation and Access to Justice in Environmental

---

[302] *Id.* at 3–4.

[303] UNEP Governing Council, Note by the Executive Director, Fourth Program for the Development and Periodic Review of Environmental Law, Addendum: Report on the Review of the Third Program for the Development and Periodic Review of Environmental Law, document UNEP/gc.25/INF/15/Add.1, February 13, 2009, http://www.unep.org/gc/gc25/info-docs.asp [hereinafter Report on the Review of Montevideo Program III].

[304] *Id.* at 3–4.

[305] *Id.* at 4.

[306] *Id.* at 4–6.

[307] *Id.* at 7.

Matters,[308] both of which were adopted by the Governing Council at its Eleventh Special Session in February 2010.[309] The latter guidelines implemented Principle 10 of the 1992 Rio Declaration, which reads:

> Environmental issues are best handled with participation of all concerned citizens, at the relevant level. At the national level, each individual shall have appropriate access to information concerning the environment that is held by public authorities, including information on hazardous materials and activities in their communities, and the opportunity to participate in decision-making processes. States shall facilitate and encourage public awareness and participation by making information widely available. Effective access to judicial and administrative proceedings, including redress and remedy, shall be provided.[310]

UNEP's support of the Strategic Approach to International Chemicals Management process, which "constitutes an overarching policy framework for the management of chemicals that support, among other things, strengthening the existing multilateral environmental agreements in field of chemicals and wastes" was another milestone.[311] Also noteworthy were several other achievements, including the Ad-hoc Joint Working Group on Enhancing Cooperation and Coordination among the Basel, Rotterdam and Stockholm Conventions established by the Conferences of the Parties to these conventions,[312] and the UN General Assembly's adoption in December 2007 of the Non-Legally Binding Instrument on all Types of Forests.[313] The number of global and regional conventions and protocols in the field of environment adopted during the period 2001–2008, was indeed impressive – 35 in all.[314]

Regarding relationship with other fields, UNEP's activities included studies on linkages between the legal regimes in the field of human rights and the environment, as well as on legal issues relating to trade and the environment, security and the environment, and military activities and the environment.[315]

---

[308] *Id.* at 8–10.

[309] UNEP, Guidelines for the Development of Domestic Legislation on Liability, Response Action and Compensation for Damage Caused by Activities Dangerous to the Environment, Document UNEP/GCSS/XI/11, Annex I, Decision GCSS XI/5 B, Annex, February 24–26, 2010; UNEP, Guidelines for the Development of National Legislation on Access to Information, Public Participation and Access to Justice in Environmental Matters, document UNEP/GCSS/XI/11, Annex I, Decision GCSS XI/5 A, Annex, February 24–26, 2010.

[310] UNCED, Rio Declaration on Environment and Development, U.N. Doc. A/CONF.151/26/ Rev.I (Vol. I), Annex I, at 3 (1992), *reprinted in* 31 I.L.M. 874 (1992).

[311] Report on the Review of Montevideo Program III, *supra* note 303, at 8 ¶ 33.

[312] *Id.* at 9 ¶ 38.

[313] *Id.* at 13 ¶ 61.

[314] *Id.* Annex at 17–18.

[315] *Id.* at 15–16.

Montevideo IV

The Governing Council, in its Decision 25/11, adopted the Fourth Program for the Development and Periodic Review of Environmental Law.[316] Montevideo IV comprises the following 27 program areas:

(a) Effectiveness of environmental law:
   (i)   Implementation, compliance and enforcement;
   (ii)   Capacity-building;
   (iii) Prevention, mitigation and compensation of environmental damage;
   (iv)   Avoidance and settlement of international disputes relating to the environment;
   (v)   Strengthening and development of international environmental law;
   (vi)   Harmonization, coordination and synergies;
   (vii) Public participation and access to information;
   (viii) Information technology;
   (ix)   Other means to increase the effectiveness of environmental law;
   (x)   Governance;
(b) Conservation, management and sustainable use of natural resources:
   (i)   Fresh, coastal and marine water and ecosystems;
   (ii)   Aquatic living resources, including marine living resources;
   (iii) Soils;
   (iv)   Forests;
   (v)   Biological diversity;
   (vi)   Sustainable production and consumption patterns;
(c) Challenges for environmental law:
   (i)   Climate change;
   (ii)   Poverty;
   (iii) Access to drinking water and sanitation;
   (iv)   Ecosystem conservation and protection;

---

[316] Proceedings of the Governing Council/Global Ministerial Environment Forum at its twenty-fifth session: UNEP/GC.25/17, http://www.unep.org/gc/gc25/working-docs.asp. For the text of the program, *see* UNEP Governing Council, Policy Issues: State of the Environment, Report by the Executive Director: Fourth Program for the Development and Periodic Review of Environmental Law, document UNEP/gc.25/11, October 28, 2008, http://www.unep.org/gc/gc25/working-docs.asp [hereinafter Montevideo Program IV]. *See also* UNEP, Report of the Meeting of Senior Government Officials Expert in Environmental Law to Prepare a Fourth Program for the Development and Periodic Review of Environmental Law (Montevideo Program IV), Nairobi, September 29–October 3, 2008, document UNEP/Env.Law/MTV4/IG/2/2, October 22, 2008, http://www.pnuma.org/gobernanza/documentos/Meeting_Report_Montevideo1V.pdf.

(v)   Environmental emergencies and natural disasters;
(vi) Pollution prevention and control;
(vii) New technologies;
(d) Relationships with other fields:
   (i)   Human rights and the environment;
   (ii) Trade and the environment;
   (iii) Environment and security;
   (iv) Environment and military activities.[317]

Montevideo Program IV is a continuation of the work begun in Montevideo Program III. However, the selection of program areas shows some differences. Under "effectiveness of environmental law," the program area "avoidance and settlement of international environmental disputes" in Montevideo Program III is changed in Montevideo Program IV to read "avoidance and settlement of international disputes relating to the environment," which was apparently done to sharpen the focus of inquiry. "Harmonization and coordination" is recast as "harmonization, coordination and synergies," and two program areas – "other means to increase the effectiveness of environmental law" and "governance" – replace "innovative approaches to environmental law." The "conservation and management" area in Montevideo Program III is given a new heading, "conservation, management and sustainable use of natural resources," in Montevideo Program IV, and the program area "fresh, coastal and marine water and ecosystems" in Montevideo Program IV combines two program areas – "freshwater resources" and "coastal and marine ecosystems" under the prior "conservation and management area" of Montevideo Program III; it also adds another program area under "fresh, coastal and marine water and ecosystems" heading.

Montevideo Program IV adds another heading, "challenges for environmental law," and new program areas are added under this heading: "climate change," "poverty," "access to drinking water and sanitation," "ecosystem conservation and protection," and "new technologies." The Program also adds under this heading "pollution prevention and control" as well as "environmental emergencies and natural disasters," which were formerly under the "conservation and management" heading in Montevideo Program III. "Production and consumption patterns" in Montevideo Program III is recast as "sustainable consumption and production patterns." Under "relationship with other fields," "human rights and the environment" is a new heading in Montevideo Program IV.

---

[317] Montevideo Program IV, *supra* note 316, at 4–5.

4.5.2   *UNEP and Multilateral Environmental Agreements*

International treaties and other instruments related to the environment have grown both in number and scope since the 1972 Stockholm Conference. UNEP has played a significant role in the development of multilateral environmental agreements (MEAs) and, as of the beginning of 2012 they number more than 1,100,[318] with over 600 registered with the United Nations – 61 related to atmosphere, 155 to biodiversity, 179 to chemicals and wastes, 46 to land, and 197 to water.[319]

While earlier agreements were restricted in scope to specific subject areas – such as selected chemicals, certain species of marine wildlife, and quarantine procedures for plants and animals – and their focus was regional, new clusters of such agreements have emerged since 1972. To illustrate, as of 2003, about seventy percent of the agreements developed since 1972 were regional in scope (especially the treaties and protocols related to the regional seas) and biodiversity related. However, since 1992 there has been exponential growth in both regional and global agreements, as well as development in new environmental realms.[320] While biodiversity continues to be an important subject area for the development of MEAs, new categories of MEAs have emerged, designed for the protection and safety of, among other things, the atmosphere, endangered species, chemicals and wastes, land, and oceans, seas, and waters.[321]

Among UNEP's activities in the creation of new MEAs, in 2012 it has been engaged in preparation of a global legally-binding instrument on mercury.[322] The plan is to complete the negotiation process by the 27th regular session of the UNEP Governing Council in February 2013.[323] UNEP has also undertaken

---

[318]   University of Oregon IEA Database Project, http://iea.uoregon.edu/page.php?file=home .htm&query=static. The database lists international environmental treaties, conventions, and other agreements comprising over 1,100 multilaterals, 1,500 bilaterals, and 250 "other," which includes environmental agreements between governments and international organizations or non-state actors, rather than two or more governments. *Id.*

[319]   UNEP Governing Council, Discussion Paper by the Executive Director, Background Paper for the Ministerial Consultations – Global Environment Outlook and Emerging Issues: Setting Effective Global Environmental Goals, document UNEP/GCSS.XII/13, January 5, 2012, at 2 ¶ 3, http://www.unep.org/gc/gcss-xii/docs/working_docs.asp [hereinafter Discussion Paper by the Executive Director].

[320]   *Id.*

[321]   UNEP Programme Work, http://www.unep.org/law/Programme_work/Devt_international_ law/index.asp.

[322]   UNEP Governing Council, Report of the Executive Director: Chemicals Management, Including Mercury, document UNEP/GC.26/5/Rev.1, January 25, 2011, http://www.unep .org/gc/gc26/working-docs.asp.

[323]   UNEP Governing Council, Report of the Executive Director: Chemicals Management, Including Mercury, Addendum – Outcome of the Second Session of the Intergovernmental

activities designed to implement the Strategic Approach to International Chemicals Management Efforts,[324] which include addressing risks posed to human health and the environment from exposure to lead and cadmium and reducing their human-caused uses in key products and industry.

It should be noted that many of the latest developments have been in the form of Amendments or Protocols to existing MEAs. Of special note, however, remain the energy/atmosphere related conventions, such as the 1995 Vienna Convention for the Protection of the Ozone Layer and its Montreal Protocol and the 1992 UN Framework Convention on Climate Change and the Kyoto Protocol (*see* Chapter 10), and biodiversity related MEAs.

An especially noteworthy feature of the post-1972 agreements is their common institutional components – a secretariat, a bureau, advisory bodies, and financial and clearinghouse mechanisms. Their decision-making bodies are Conferences and Meetings of the Parties (COPs and MOPs), with subsidiary bodies on scientific, technical or financial issues, or focused on progress in implementation. It is promising that there has been some closer collaboration in the programs of work between and among the various conventions, although, as will be discussed later, much more needs to be done to promote further collaboration and effectiveness. Also, NGOs have played a more active role as advisors or observers in the deliberations of many agreements.

The number of MEAs and their scope are indeed impressive. However, in December 2001 the then-UNEP Executive Director made several critical observations. He reported that "the agreements lack coherence with respect to a number of important new environmental policy issues such as the precautionary approach and scientific uncertainty, intergenerational and intra-generational equity, the life-cycle economy, common but differentiated responsibilities, and sustainable development."[325] He noted the lack of adequate coordination among existing MEAs as a major obstacle to implementation of these agreements and to effective international environmental

---

Negotiating Committee to Prepare a Global Legally-Binding Instrument on Mercury, document UNEP/GC.26/5/Rev.1/Add.1, February 4, 2011, http://www.unep.org/gc/gc26/working-docs.asp.

[324] UNEP Governing Council, Report of the Executive Director: Chemicals Management, Including Mercury, § III.B. Other United Nations Environment Programme Activities Relating to Lead and Cadmium, document UNEP/GC.26/5/Rev.1, January 25, 2011, http://www.unep.org/gc/gc26/working-docs.asp.

[325] UNEP Governing Council/Global Ministerial Environment Forum, Seventh Special Session, Cartagena, Colombia, Feb. 13–15, 2002, International Environmental Governance, Report of the Executive Director, UNEP/GCSS.VII/2, ¶ 51, Dec. 27, 2001 [hereinafter Executive Director's 2001 Report].

governance.[326] Several problem areas include too many MEAs; secretariats for conventions are located in different places – Montreal, Geneva and Bonn – as are the venues for conferences of parties and of their subsidiary bodies; and the large number of meetings causes difficulties in participation, much less implementation, especially for developing countries.[327] Also, the burdensome national reports required by MEAs are frequently either submitted late or not at all.[328] Lack of sufficient finances, uncertainty of appropriate technology transfer, and inadequate alternative dispute resolution mechanisms are among other major causes of ineffective implementation and monitoring.

In his 2001 report the Executive Director had suggested grouping a number of MEAs in order to promote efficiency and effectiveness, which could be done by clustering those that are related or overlapping at the sectoral level – for example, by grouping together biodiversity-related conventions – or at least clustering the meetings of conferences of parties and their subsidiary bodies. Or they could be clustered together at a functional level, for example, by grouping trade and finance related issues, or on a regional level.[329] Also, their secretariats could work together and their financial arrangements could also be coordinated.[330]

Since 2001, UNEP has taken several initiatives in response to the criticism so as to remedy the situation.[331] In March 2012, while the UNEP Governing

---

[326] See generally *id.*, ¶¶ 135–139. See also Konrad von Moltke, *On Clustering International Environmental Agreements* (International Institute for Sustainable Development), June 2001, http://www.iisd.org/pdf/trade_clustering_meas.pdf.

[327] Executive Director's 2001 Report, *supra* note 325, ¶ 136. In 2010, there were more meetings than days in the year. A world organisation for an equitable green economy, http://www.scidev.net/en/science-and-innovation-policy/science-at-rio-20/opinions/a-world-organisation-for-an-equitable-green-economy.html.

[328] Executive Director's 2001 Report, *supra* note 325, ¶ 137.

[329] *Id.* at ¶ 136.

[330] See generally Konrad von Moltke, *supra* note 326.

[331] To illustrate, at the eleventh special session of the UNEP Governing Council/Global Ministerial Environment Forum held in Bali from February 24–26, 2010, the ministers and heads of delegation of the Global Ministerial Environment Forum adopted the "Nusa Dua Declaration," where they welcomed

the activities undertaken by the United Nations Environment Programme and the secretariats of the multilateral environmental agreements, at the behest of the parties to those agreements, in particular the Basel Convention on the Control of Transboundary Movements of Hazardous Wastes and their Disposal, the Rotterdam Convention on the Prior Informed Consent Procedure for Certain Hazardous Chemicals and Pesticides in International Trade and the Stockholm Convention on Persistent Organic Pollutants, to enhance cooperation and coordination between the three conventions and to support Governments in their efforts to implement, comply with and enforce the multilateral environmental agreements.

Decisions adopted by the Governing Council/Global Ministerial environment Forum at its eleventh special session, Bali, February 24–26, 2010, GCSS.xi/9: Nusa Dua

Council acknowledged the progress made thus far and recognized "the importance of enhancing synergies, including at the national and regional levels, among the biodiversity-related conventions," it encouraged "the conferences of the parties to these conventions to strengthen efforts further in that regard,"[332] it asked the Executive Director to undertake activities "to improve the effectiveness of and cooperation among multilateral environmental agreements,"[333] and to "[explore] the opportunities for further synergies in the administrative functions of the multilateral environmental agreement secretariats administered by the United Nations Environment Programme and to provide advice on such opportunities to the governing bodies of those [MEAs]."[334] The Governing Council also requested the Executive Director to "facilitate and support an inclusive, country-driven consultative process on the challenges to and options for further enhancing cooperation and coordination in the chemicals and wastes cluster in the long term."[335]

In the President's summary of the discussions by ministers and heads of delegation at the twelfth special session of the Governing Council/Global Ministerial Environment Forum of the United Nations Environment Program, he said that reform of the system may include "enhanced synergies within multilateral environment agreement clusters to increase their effectiveness and efficiency,"[336] as such synergies "afford an opportunity to realize the more efficient of resources and to tackle environmental issues more effectively at the national and international levels and in delivering on the ground, among other things."[337]

Declaration, sec. C. international environmental governance and sustainable development, para. 10, document UNEP/GCSS.xi/11, annex I, http://www.uncsd2012.org/files/interagency/UNEP_GCSS_XI_REPORT240610.pdf.

They also welcomed "the outcome of the simultaneous extraordinary meetings of the conferences of the parties to the Basel, Rotterdam and Stockholm Conventions," and appreciated "the consultative process on financing options for chemicals and wastes...." *Id.* para. 11.

[332] UNEP, Decisions adopted by the Governing Council / Global Ministerial Environment Forum at its twelfth special session, advance copy, Decision No. SS.XII/3: International Environmental Governance, op. para. 1.

[333] *Id.* op. para. 2.

[334] *Id.* op. para. 3.

[335] *Id.* Decision No. SS.XII/5: Enhancing Cooperation and Coordination within the Chemicals and Wastes Cluster, op. para. 3, available at http://www.unep.org/gc/gcss-XII/docs/Decisions_summary_advance.pdf.

[336] UNEP, President's summary of the discussions by ministers and heads of delegation at the twelfth special session of the Governing Council/Global Ministerial Environment forum of the United Nations Environment Programme, (Advance Copy), at para. 41, March 8, 2012, http://www.unep.org/gc/gcss-xii/docs/Decisions_summary_advance.pdf [hereinafter President's Summary].

[337] *Id.* para. 42.

Multilateral environmental agreements require sustained funding. The Global Environment Facility, established in 1991 as a pilot program in the World Bank to promote environmentally sound and sustainable development, is a critical financial mechanism for several MEAs.[338] The World Bank, the United Nations Development Program, and the United Nations Environment Program initially became the GEF's implementing agencies and now the GEF partnership includes seven more agencies. It has allocated $9 billion, which is supplemented by over $40 billion in co-financing for more than 2,600 projects in over 165 countries. In implementation of MEAs its focal areas are climate change, biodiversity, international waters, ozone-depleting substances, persistent organic pollutants, land degradation, and multi-focal, out of which it has had considerable impact in achieving progress toward achieving global environmental benefits.[339] As of June 30, 2009, GEF funding for biodiversity focal area amounted to nearly $ 2.79 billion, and for climate change $ 2.74 billion.[340] The GEF is underfunded and funding levels need to rise substantially in order to address the increasingly urgent problems.[341]

4.5.3   UNEP and International Environmental Governance

As noted earlier, UNEP continues to provide environmental assessment, monitoring, and information for decision-makers and continues to serve as a global policy-making forum. UNEP's establishment of an annual Governing Council/Global Ministerial Environment Forum with universal participation at the ministerial level, which is aimed at promoting policy coherence on environmental issues, was a major development. Also, the UN General Assembly established the Environment Management Group to promote inter-agency cooperation within the UN system and to ensure closer cooperation and participation of multilateral environmental agreements with UN agencies.

Institutional developments have indeed been impressive since the 1972 Stockholm Conference.[342] Between 1972 and 1982, many new national environmental laws were adopted and over 100 countries established ministries

---

[338] Global Environment Facility, http://www.thegef.org/gef/.

[339] GEF, Evaluation Office, Progress Toward Impact – 4th Overall Performance Study of the GEF, Executive Version, at 26–29, 2010, http://www.thegef.org/gef/sites/thegef.org/files/documents/OPS4-Executive%20Version_ENGLISH_1.pdf.

[340] *Id.* at 10.

[341] This was recommendation no. 1 of the 4th Overall Performance Study of the GEF, released in March 2010, *id.* at 16.

[342] UNEP, GLOBAL ENVIRONMENTAL OUTLOOK, GEO 3, chapter 1, *Integrating Environment and Development 1972–2002*, at 4–5, http://www.unep.org/geo/GEO3/english/pdfs/chapter1.pdf.

or departments of the environment.[343] By the year 2000, the Organization of African Unity (now the African Union) and over 50 governments throughout the world had recognized a healthy environment as a fundamental human right in their national constitutions or through special legislation.[344]

For several years, however, there has been recognition that the prevailing environmental organizational structure does not allow for effective international environmental governance and there have been many suggestions for reform and for strengthening it. To illustrate, in 2001, the then-UNEP Executive Director noted several such suggestions, including: the mandates and functioning of the CSD, UNEP, and GEF need to be strengthened; the participation of environmental NGOs needs to be enhanced; the UNEP Governing Council/Global Ministerial Environment Forum and Environmental Management Group need to be utilized and their role enhanced for setting broad policy guidelines for environmental action on the international level; and improved coordination and synergies among the various environment-related organizations and between WTO and these organizations need to be developed.[345]

A major push for reform came following the September 14–16, 2005 World Summit of Heads of State and Government at the United Nations Headquarters in New York. In a resolution adopted by the United Nations General Assembly, entitled "2005 World Summit Outcome," the Heads of State and Government supported the achievement of "stronger system-wide coherence within the United Nations system" by implementing, among other measures:

Environmental activities

Recognizing the need for more efficient environmental activities in the United Nations system, with enhanced coordination, improved policy advice and guidance, strengthened scientific knowledge, assessment and cooperation, better treaty compliance, while respecting the legal autonomy of the treaties, and better integration of environmental activities in the broader sustainable development framework at the operational level, including through capacity-building, we agree to explore the possibility of a more coherent institutional framework to address this need, including a more integrated structure, building on existing institutions and internationally agreed instruments, as well as the treaty bodies and the specialized agencies.[346]

---

[343] *Id.* at 5.

[344] *Id.* at 4.

[345] *See generally* Executive Director's 2001 Report, *supra* note 325, at ¶¶ 129–134.

[346] U.N. General Assembly, Resolution adopted by the General Assembly, 60/1. 2005 World Summit Outcome, U.N. Doc. A/RES/60/1, October 24, 2005, http://daccess-dds-ny.un.org/doc/UNDOC/GEN/N05/487/60/PDF/N0548760.pdf?OpenElement.

Several gaps in the current system of international environmental governance have been identified, including the following:

(a) Lack of an authoritative voice to guide environmental policy effectively at the global level;
(b) Lack of coherence among global environmental policies and programs;
(c) High degree of financial fragmentation;
(d) Lack of coherence in the governance and administration of multilateral environmental agreements;
(e) Lack of a central monitoring, review and accountability system for commitments made under multilateral environmental agreements;
(f) Lack of sufficient, secure and predictable funding;
(g) Implementation gap experienced at the country level.[347]

In response, informal consultations under the auspices of the UN General Assembly led to a recommendation to the Governing Council of UNEP to "take stock and debate the course of action...to find a political compromise...which allow[s] improving the current system."[348] Following consultations under the UNEP Governing Council and further discussions by a selected group of environmental ministers, six key objectives of the international environmental governance system and their underlying functions were presented at the Governing Council's special session in February 2010:

• Creating a strong, credible and coherent science base;
• Developing a global authoritative and responsive voice for environmental sustainability;
• Achieving coherence within the United Nations system;
• Securing sufficient, predictable and coherent funding;
• Ensuring a responsive and cohesive approach to meeting country needs;
• Facilitating the transition towards a global green economy.[349]

---

[347] UNEP Governing Council, Discussion Paper Presented by the Executive Director: Background Paper for the Ministerial Consultations: International Environmental Governance in "The Future We Want," document UNEP/GCSS.XII/13/Add.2, January 24, 2012, at 2, ¶ 2, http://www.unep.org/gc/gcss-xii/docs/download.asp?ID=3553 [hereinafter January 2012 Background Paper].

[348] *Id.* ¶ 4.

[349] *Id.* at 3, ¶ 5. *See also* UNEP Governing Council, Report of the Executive Director: International Environmental Governance, document UNEP/GC.26/3, December 20, 2010, http://www.unep.org/gc/gc26/cow_details-docs.asp?DocID=UNEP/GC.26/3&CatID=10; UNEP Governing Council, Report of the Executive Director: International Environmental Governance, document UNEP/GCSS.xii/3, December 16, 2011, http://www.unep.org/gc/gcss-xii/

Following further consultation and debate, the preparatory committee for the United Nations Conference on Sustainable Development (UNCSD) was presented with five options for the broader institutional reform of international environmental governance:

(a) Enhancing UNEP;
(b) Establishing a new umbrella organization for sustainable development;
(c) Establishing a specialized agency such as a world environment organization;
(d) Reforming the United Nations Economic and Social Council and the United Nations Commission on Sustainable Development;
(e) Enhancing institutional reforms and streamlining existing structures.[350]

Further consultations with governments, civil society, and UN bodies led to the inclusion of several options in the January 10, 2010 Zero Draft of the proposed outcome document for the UNCSD (Rio+20), to be held in Rio de Janeiro from June 20–22, 2012 (for further discussion of Rio+20, *see* Chapter 16). Among the suggested reforms regarding the Commission on Sustainable Development (CSD) and UNEP are: a proposal to strengthen the CSD or transform it into a sustainable development council,[351] and another proposal to strengthen the capacity of UNEP by establishing universal membership for its Governing Council and significantly increasing its financial base or to establish a United Nations specialized agency that would operate on an equal footing with other UN specialized agencies "with universal membership of its governing council, based on UNEP, with a revised and strengthened mandate, supported by stable, adequate and predictable financial contributions."[352]

Subsequently, at the special session of the Governing Council held in Nairobi from February 20–22, 2012, environment ministers discussed this topic and the president of the Governing Council summarized their discussions as follows:

> The strengthening of the environmental component of the institutional framework for sustainable development found broad support among the ministers and other heads of delegation. Many expressed support for the establishment of a specialized agency for the environment. Others expressed support for strengthening UNEP but suggested that changing UNEP to a specialized agency could weaken it.[353]

---

docs/download.asp?ID=3346 (identifying the incremental changes in the set of options for international environmental governance reform).
[350] January 2012 Background Paper, *supra* note 347, ¶ 6.
[351] *Id.* ¶ 49.
[352] *Id.* ¶ 51.
[353] *Id.* ¶ 37.

The president further stated that there was general agreement at the meeting that the UNCSD must make a clear decision on both the institutional framework for sustainable development and on international environmental governance.[354] He noted that current shortcomings need to be addressed in an overall reform of the system, which should include:

> an anchor organization with universal membership; improving the science-policy interface; providing guidance to and coordinating multilateral environmental agreements; enhanced synergies within multilateral environmental agreement clusters to increase their effectiveness and efficiency; and the development of a United Nations system-wide strategy for the environment that sets priorities, decides on the division of labour and assigns roles to relevant actors..., and links private investment and public policy. The establishment of a system of assessed contributions for the international environmental governance anchor institution would increase the total volume of available resources.[355]

In the Outcome Document of the UNCSD the Heads of State and Government and high-level representatives invited the UN General Assembly to adopt a resolution strengthening and upgrading UNEP by establishing universal membership in the UNEP Governing Council, ensuring a more secure budget, and giving it broader powers to initiate scientific research and to "lead efforts to formulate United Nations system-wide strategies on the environment."[356] They also decided to establish a "high-level" forum to coordinate global sustainable development and subsequently replace the Commission on Sustainable Development, although the forum's format and organizational aspects have yet to be determined.[357]

---

[354] *Id.* ¶ 38.

[355] President's Summary, *supra* note 336, ¶ 41.

[356] Rio+20, Outcome of the Conference – The Future We Want, Rio de Janeiro, Brazil, June 20–22, 2012, ¶ 88, UN Doc. A/CONF.216/L.1, June 19, 2012, https://rio20.un.org/sites/rio20.un.org/files/a-conf.216l-1_english.pdf.pdf.

[357] *Id.* ¶¶ 84–86.

Chapter Five

International Environmental Institutions and Organizations

5.0 *Introduction*

The growth of international environmental law since 1970 has been paralleled by a proliferation of international institutions and organizations working on these issues. A veritable alphabet soup of international governmental organizations (IGOs) and nongovernmental organizations (NGOs), as well as multitudes of multistate, regional, national, and local level institutions, can now be found working on the world environment in the 21st century.

There is no central international authority on environmental issues. Sovereign states have been willing to give some, but by no means controlling, authority to the UN and other entities (*see* § 1.1). There is no international lawmaking body, no central enforcement authority, and international courts are few and their environmental rulings rare. In lieu of conventional lawmaking approaches, international environmental law is increasingly being "made" by a host of entities – IGOs, NGOs, international financial organizations (IFOs), international conferences, think-tanks, even private-sector corporations and their associations and trade groups (*see* § 1.1.6).

To provide a thorough description of all these institutions would take a book in itself. Good sources exist,[1] but the best research and reference

---

[1] They include Lyonette Louis-Jacques, *Legal Research on International Law Issues Using the Internet*, http://www.lib.uchicago.edu/~llou/forintlaw.html; George (Rock) Pring *et al.*, *Trends in International Environmental Law Affecting the Minerals Industry*, 17 J. Energy & Nat, Resources L. 39 (Part I) and 151 (Part II) (1999); Patricia w. Birnie & Alan E. Boyle & C. Redgwell, International Law & The Environment 58–105 (2009); David Hunter *et al.*, International Environmental Law and Policy 219–271 (3d ed. 2007); Edith Brown Weiss *et al.*, International Environmental Law and Policy 226–36 and Appx. II at 1169 (1998); United Nations, Basic Facts About the United Nations (1998); New Zealand Ministry of Foreign Affairs and Trade, United Nations Handbook 1998 (1998).

sources today are the Internet web sites of the institutions themselves. Rather than duplicate those good sources and web sites, the goal of this chapter is to provide an overview of the major players and current references to their web sites for the reader's further study.

5.1   *The United Nations "Family"*

The United Nations establishment is in the process of reforming all of its bureaucracy to conform to the new international mission of "sustainable development" (*see* § 2.1.4).[2] At the top, the UN General Assembly (UNGA)[3] gives "relatively scant attention" to the environment, compared with its peace and security issues,[4] but it is an important forum and has taken some significant actions in the field, including convening key law-developing conferences (like the 1972 Stockholm, 1992 Rio, and 2012 Rio+20 Conferences), establishing the UN Environment Programme (UNEP) and other environmental entities (below), issuing key resolutions and declarations (like the World Charter for Nature), and convening key negotiating processes (like those leading to the climate change, desertification, and fisheries treaties). The Economic and Social Council (ECOSOC) is the principal UN organ coordinating economic, social, cultural, environmental, human rights, and related issues, and it serves as a gatekeeper to UNGA on them, but rarely performs any significant work of its own in the field.[5]

Created by UNGA in 1972 to be "the environmental conscience of the UN system," UNEP is a major force in developing environmental law and promoting sustainable development, and despite "a smaller budget and staff than many national environment agencies, UNEP has accomplished a great

---

[2] Pring *et al., supra* note 1, at 170; George (Rock) Pring, *Sustainable Development: Historical Perspectives and Challenges for the 21st Century, in* UN DEVELOPMENT PROGRAMME & UN REVOLVING FUND FOR NATURAL RESOURCES EXPLORATION, PROCEEDINGS OF THE WORKSHOP ON THE SUSTAINABLE DEVELOPMENT OF NON-RENEWABLE RESOURCES TOWARD THE 21ST CENTURY 21 (James Otto & Hyo-Sun Kim eds., 1999).

[3] *General Assembly,* UN, http://www.un.org/en/ga/. The Secretariat has some environmental activities, such as the informational and promotional work of the Department of Economic and Social Affairs (DESA), but is "generally peripheral" to the mainstream of international environmental work. The Security Council has no direct environmental functions, but it has done one significant thing in the field – its resolution holding Iraq responsible for environmental damage it caused in the Kuwait invasion/Gulf War. S/RES/687, ¶ 16 (Mar. 2, 1991).

[4] WEISS ET AL., *supra* note 1, at 1173.

[5] *See id.; Development,* UN http://www.un.org/esa.

deal."[6] Headquartered rather remotely in Nairobi, Kenya, it has neverthe-less successfully sponsored negotiations leading to the adoption of numerous international environmental "hard" law treaties (including those on climate change, ozone, hazardous wastes, regional seas, nature, and wildlife). It has also spearheaded the adoption of numerous "soft" law guidelines that are commanding increasing respect over time (including those on shared natural resources, technical assistance, offshore mining and drilling, marine pollu-tion from land-based sources, EIAs, chemicals, etc.). Parallel to UNEP is the much larger UN Development Programme (UNDP).[7] The UNDP was origi-nally viewed as an environmental depredator for funding destructive projects, but more recently "greening" to integrate environmental and sustainable development considerations in its planning. To these was added in 1992 the Commission on Sustainable Development (CSD),[8] which has provided a forum on the issues, but has contributed little to actual legal development.

A host of other UN agencies of varying missions contribute to the devel-opment of law and policy in the environmental area, including the Food and Agriculture Organization (FAO),[9] International Labor Organization (ILO),[10] World Health Organization (WHO),[11] UN Educational, Scientific and Cultural Organization (UNESCO),[12] World Meteorological Organiza-tion (WMO),[13] International Maritime Organization (IMO),[14] International Atomic Energy Agency (IAEA),[15] UN Conference on Trade and Develop-ment (UNCTAD),[16] as well as numerous UN "Experts Groups."[17]

The International Court of Justice (ICJ or World Court)[18] is, of course, the preeminent UN judicial body. It issues relatively few rulings, and only in the last two decades has it decided any environmental cases, but, anticipat-ing more, in 1993 it created a seven-member standing Chamber for Envi-ronmental Matters. However, as states showed no enthusiasm, the initiative

---

[6] HUNTER ET AL., *supra* note 1, at 225; UN ENVIRONMENTAL PROGRAMME, http://www.unep.org.

[7] UN DEVELOPMENT PROGRAMME, http://www.undp.org.

[8] *Division for Sustainable Development,* UN, http://www.un.org/esa/dsd/csd/csd_aboucsd.shtml.

[9] FOOD AND AGRICULTURE ORGANIZATION, http://www.fao.org.

[10] INTERNATIONAL LABOR ORGANIZATION, http://www.ilo.org.

[11] WORLD HEALTH ORGANIZATION, http://www.who.int/home-page.

[12] UN EDUCATIONAL, SCIENTIFIC AND CULTURAL ORGANIZATION, http://www.unesco.org.

[13] WORLD METEOROLOGICAL ORGANIZATION, http://www.wmo.ch/index-en.html.

[14] INTERNATIONAL MARITIME ORGANIZATION, http://www.imo.org/index.htm.

[15] INTERNATIONAL ATOMIC ENERGY ASSOCIATION, http://www.iaea.org/worldatom.

[16] UN CONFERENCE AND TRADE AND DEVELOPMENT, http://www.unctad.org.

[17] *See, e.g.,* WEISS ET AL., *supra* note 1, at 1181.

[18] INTERNATIONAL COURT OF JUSTICE, http://www.icj-cij.org.

was scuttled. Established in 1947, the International Law Commission (ILC)[19] is a highly respected UN "think-tank" of international law experts representing the world's principal legal systems. It is specifically charged with the codification and progressive development of international law and has been enormously productive in the environmental area. Its work has included draft treaties and guidance on state responsibility and liability, freshwater resources, and other key areas. In addition, the UN has established several regional commissions active in the environmental law field (*see* § 5.4).

5.2   *International Financial Organizations*

The "greening" of IFOs is one of the major new trends of international environmental law.[20] IFOs – multilateral development banks (MDBs), bilateral development assistance agencies (DAAs), national export-import promotion agencies (Ex-Ims), export credit agencies (ECAs), and other public and private sector finance, insurance, and trade entities – are increasingly "conditioning" their aid, loans, underwriting, and other support or involvement on the environmental and sociocultural acceptability of the applicants, enterprises, and host governments. Following is a description of the key IFOs that are influencing the development and direction of international environmental law.

The World Bank Group (a cluster of four distinct IFOs) has been the leading IFO fostering this trend. Its International Bank for Reconstruction and Development (IBRD or World Bank)[21] lends billions to member governments, and its environmental sustainability rules, which have been evolving since the 1980s, are becoming a standard among IFOs. The International Financial Corporation (IFC)[22] provides financing for private sector entities engaging in projects in developing nations. The International Development Association (IDA)[23] is the high-risk lender of the Group, loaning funds on concessional terms to poorer countries that cannot meet the financial requirements of the other IFOs. The Multilateral Investment Guarantee Agency (MIGA)[24] is the Group's insurance arm, underwriting the risks of development projects in developing countries. The Global Environmental Facility (GEF)[25] is an independent IFO, created in 1990 by the World Bank, UNEP, and UNDP,

---

[19] INTERNATIONAL LAW COMMISSION, http://www.un.org/law/ilc/.
[20] Pring *et al.*, *supra* note 1, at 163–65.
[21] WORLD BANK, http://www.worldbank.org.
[22] INTERNATIONAL FINANCIAL CORPORATION, http://www.ifc.org.
[23] *International Development Association,* WORLD BANK, http://www.worldbank.org/ida.
[24] *Multilateral Investment Guarantee,* WORLD BANK GROUP, http://www.miga.org.
[25] GLOBAL ENVIRONMENT FACILITY, http://www.gefweb.org.

which focuses its financing on seven main areas – biodiversity, climate change, chemicals, international waters, land degradation, sustainable forest management / REDD, and ozone layer depletion – as well as several cross-cutting issues and programs.

A number of regional MDBs exist that are very active in promoting international environmental standards. The Asian Development Bank (ADB)[26] is noteworthy for its leadership on sustainable development standards and practices, as is the European Bank for Reconstruction and Development (EBRD),[27] which services Western, Central, and Eastern Europe, as well as the Newly Independent States (NIS) of the former Soviet Union.

In addition to MDBs, many countries have national agencies engaged in foreign aid (DAAs) or in promoting trade (Ex-Ims, ECAs), and these increasingly are being environmentally conditioned. Taking the US as an example, it has a for-profit government DAA called the Overseas Private Investment Corporation (OPIC)[28] that provides loans, guarantees, and insurance to US private companies investing in developing nations and emerging economies. Its bilateral DAA, the Agency for International Development (USAID)[29] dispenses aid to foreign governments and the Export-Import Bank (Ex-Im)[30] is its trade-promoting entity.

The leading free-trade entity globally is the World Trade Organization (WTO),[31] overseer of the General Agreement on Tariffs and Trade (GATT). The WTO has regional counterparts as well (*see* § 5.4). These are influential players in the field, often at odds with environmental protection aims, since their main mission is to prohibit any laws or actions that restrict trade (with few exceptions). This mission often brings the WTO and its regional counterparts into conflict with international and national environmental laws that use trade embargoes, export-import bans, and other economic sanctions to enforce provisions.[32]

5.3   Other International IGOS

A number of IGOs have been established both within and separate from the UN organization to protect particular aspects of the environment. Most often, they are created by a treaty which establishes an ongoing body with

---

[26]   Asian Development Bank, http://www.adb.org.
[27]   European Bank for Reconstruction and Development, http://www.ebrd.org.
[28]   Overseas Private Investment Corporation, http://www.opic.gov.
[29]   USAID, http://www.usaid.gov.
[30]   Export Import Bank of the United States, http://www.exim.gov.
[31]   World Trade Organization, http://www.wto.org.
[32]   Pring *et al.*, *supra* note 1, at 156–58.

some level of oversight or enforcement power, usually a Commission, Secretariat, or a "Conference of the Parties" (COP).

The leading examples of this type of IGO are:

- The International Whaling Commission (IWC),[33] set up to monitor the 1946 Convention on the Regulation of Whaling;
- The UN Framework Convention on Climate Change Secretariat (UNFCCC),[34] created by the Climate Change Treaty;
- The UNEP Ozone Secretariat,[35] established to oversee the Stratospheric Ozone Treaty regime;
- The Secretariat of the Convention on Biodiversity,[36] created under that treaty;
- The Secretariat of the Convention on International Trade in Endangered Species and related bodies,[37] set up to monitor the CITES wildlife regime;
- The Basel Convention Secretariat,[38] established by the Basel Convention on the Control of Transboundary Movements of Hazardous Wastes;
- The UN Secretariat of the Convention to Combat Desertification,[39] created pursuant to that treaty;
- The FAO/UNEP Secretariat on the Rotterdam Convention on Prior Informed Consent,[40] an "interim joint" Secretariat for the new PIC chemical safety treaty; and
- The UNEP Convention on Migratory Species Secretariat and related entities,[41] created by the Bonn Treaty.

Still another type of IGO is the international "conference," called to negotiate a new international treaty or other instrument or to address a particular environmental issue. Frequently, these conferences are not short-term affairs, but involve substantial years of preparatory committee meetings (prepcoms) and have a long life of influence afterward. The preeminent example certainly is the 1972 UN Conference on the Human Environment (UNCHE

---

[33] INTERNATIONAL WHALING COMMISSION, http://iwcoffice.org/.

[34] UN FRAMEWORK CONVENTION ON CLIMATE CHANGE, http://unfccc.int/2860.php.

[35] *Ozone Secretariat,* U.N.E.P., http://www.unep.org/ozone/index.shtml.

[36] *CBD Secretariat,* CONVENTION ON BIOLOGICAL DIVERSITY, http://www.cbd.int/secretariat.

[37] *The CITES Secretariat,* CITES, http://www.cites.org/eng/disc/sec/index.php.

[38] *The Basel Convention Secretariat,* BASEL CONVENTION, http://www.basel.int/Home/tabid/2202/Default.aspx.

[39] *The Secretariat,* UNCCD, http://www.unccd.int/en/about-the-convention/The-Secretariat/Pages/default.aspx.

[40] *The Rotterdam Convention Secretariat,* ROTTERDAM CONVENTION, http://www.pic.int/.

[41] *CMS Secretariat,* CONVENTION ON MIGRATORY SPECIES, http://www.cms.int/secretariat/index.htm.

or Stockholm Conference), the "birthplace" of international environmental law and the source of the famous Stockholm Declaration. Another is the 1984 World Commission on Environment and Development (WCED or Brundtland Commission), whose 1987 report, "Our Common Future," gave the world the "sustainable development" paradigm. A third is, of course, the 1992 UN Conference on Environment and Development (UNCED or Rio Conference), the source of today's guiding Rio Declaration as well as Agenda 21, the Climate Change and Biodiversity Treaties, and the Forest Principles. Rio also shows how such conferences can have a long institutional afterlife – there already has been a "Rio + 5" complete with a secretariat in 1997,[42] and a "Rio + 10" in 2002 in Johannesburg, South Africa (World Summit on Sustainable Development) (*see* Chapter 4), and a "Rio+20" United Nations Conference on Sustainable Development, again in Rio de Janeiro (*see* Chapters 4, 16).[43]

5.4 *Regional International IGOS*

Multilateral IGOs covering specific regions of the world also contribute significantly to international environmental law. The preeminent example of these is the European Union (EU),[44] formerly the European Community (EC), and before that the European Economic Community (EEC). The EU is the "most advanced form of international organization in the world"[45] because, unlike typical IGOs which can only suggest laws to their member states, the EU is a "supranational" legal entity. This means it has the ability to legislate law that is binding on its 27 member states, the power to enforce compliance, and compulsory-jurisdiction courts. As a world leader on environmental issues, what the EU does and wants significantly influences the direction and development of international law.

Three other very influential IGOs based in Europe are the Organization for Economic Co-operation and Development (OECD),[46] the UN Economic Commission for Europe (UN/ECE),[47] and the Council of Europe.[48] Not limited to Europe, their member states span all or most of the industrialized

---

[42] Rio + 5 Secretariat, http://www.ecouncil.ac.cr/rio.

[43] *Rio + 20 Dedicated Secretariat,* Rio + 20, http://www.uncsd2012.org/.

[44] Website at http://europa.eu.int.

[45] Lakshman D. Guruswamy, International Environmental Law in a Nutshell 65 (4th ed. 2012).

[46] OECD, http://www.oecd.org.

[47] UN Economic Commission for Europe, http://www.unece.org.

[48] Council of Europe, http://www.coe.int.

"North,"[49] giving these IGOs a huge power base. The OECD has been an innovator in developing international environmental law in water resource, air pollution, and hazardous waste among other issues (*see* Chapters 9, 10, and 12). The UN/ECE has produced treaty regimes for transboundary air pollution,[50] environmental impact assessment,[51] transboundary industrial accidents,[52] public participation,[53] and international freshwater resources (*see* further those chapters).[54] The Council of Europe has brought about treaties on wildlife protection, civil liability for environmentally dangerous activities, and criminal law protection for the environment, and many other environmental programs.[55]

Some of the UN's programs are regional, notably the very successful UNEP Regional Seas Program,[56] which has spawned environmental treaties and action programs for 14 different oceans, from the Mediterranean to the Caribbean. In addition to UN/ECE, the UN has created four other regional commissions, all active to one degree or another in the environment. They include the UN Economic Commissions for Africa (UN/ECA)[57] and for Latin America and the Caribbean (UN/ECLAC or CEPAL),[58] and UN Economic and Social Commissions for Asia and the Pacific (UN/ESCAP)[59] and for Western Asia (UN/ESCWA).[60]

For the most part, non-UN regional IGOs have not been very active in environmental lawmaking. However, there are exceptions such as the Organization of African Unity (OAU) which was replaced in 2002 by the

---

[49] The OECD has 34 members, including Western and Central Europe, US, Canada, Australia, New Zealand, South Korea, Japan, and Mexico. The UN/ECE is one of five UN regional commissions; it has 56 members, covering Western, Central, and Eastern Europe, Russia, US, Canada, and Israel. The Council of Europe has 47 member states, including most of Western and Central Europe, Russia and several of the former USSR republics; the U.S., Canada, Japan, and Mexico are not members, but have active "observer" status. In addition, many NGOs, business, and professional organizations take part in the IGOs' activities.

[50] *Convention on Long-Range Transboundary Air Pollution*, UNECE, http://www.unece.org/env/lrtap.

[51] *Convention on Environmental Impact Assessment*, UNECE, http://www.unece.org/env/eia.

[52] *Convention on the Transboundary Effects of Industrial Accidents*, UNECE, http://www.unece.org/env/teia/welcome.htm.

[53] *Convention on Public Participation*, UNECE, http://www.unece.org/env/pp/welcome.html.

[54] *Water Convention*, UNECE, http://www.unece.org/env/water.

[55] *Sustainable Development*, COUNCIL OF EUROPE, http://www.coe.int/what-we-do/culture-and-nature/sustainable-development.

[56] *Regional Seas*, UNEP, http://www.unep.org/regionalseas/.

[57] *Economic Commission for Africa*, UN, http://www.uneca.org.

[58] *ECLAC*, UN, http://www.eclac.org/default.asp?idioma=IN.

[59] *ESCAP*, UN, http://www.unescap.org.

[60] *ESCWA*, UN, http://www.escwa.un.org.

new, more powerful African Union,[61] the Organization of American States (OAS),[62] the Association for Southeast Asian Nations (ASEAN),[63] and the South Pacific Regional Environmental Programme (SPREP).[64] The OAU has been especially active in hazardous waste and desertification issues; the OAS has done notable recent work on public participation; ASEAN has put out treaties and guidance documents on the environment; and SPREP, on biodiversity and climate change. In addition to the UNEP Regional Seas Program, other geographically regional environmental treaties have spun off ongoing organizations, such as the OSPAR Commission,[65] created by the Convention for the Protection of the Marine Environment of the North-East Atlantic.

Regional free-trade agreements, paralleling GATT/WTO (*see* § 5.2), have created ongoing institutions. One with substantial environmental review powers is the North American Commission for Environmental Cooperation (CEC),[66] an offshoot of the "Environmental Side Agreement" (NAAEC) to the North American Free Trade Agreement (NAFTA) involving Canada, US, and Mexico. Others, such as Mercosur[67] (Argentina, Bolivia, Brazil, Chile, Paraguay, Uruguay), have not integrated environmental considerations to the same extent.

Some courts with regional jurisdictions will bear watching. The most obvious example is the International Tribunal for the Law of the Sea (ITLOS),[68] headquartered in Hamburg, Germany, which has jurisdiction over litigation arising under the UN Convention on the Law of the Sea (UNCLOS). However, other multistate regional courts could play significant future roles in international environmental protection, such as the very powerful Court of Justice of the European Community.[69]

---

[61] Rachel L. Swarns, *African Leaders Drop Old Group for One That Has Power*, N. Y. Times, July 9, 2002. For information on the old OAU, *see Organisation of African Unity*, South African History Online, http://www.sahistory.org.za/topic/organisation-african-unity-oau; for the web site of the new African Union, *see* http://www.au.int/en/.

[62] Organization of American States, http://www.oas.org.

[63] Association for Southeast Asian Nations, http://www.aseansec.org.

[64] SPREP, http://www.sprep.org/.

[65] OSPAR Commission, http://www.ospar.org/.

[66] Commission for Environmental Cooperation, http://www.cec.org.

[67] MERCOSUR, http://www.mercosur.int/msweb/Portal%20Intermediario/.

[68] International Tribunal for the Law of the Sea, http://www.itlos.org/.

[69] *Court of Justice for the European Union*, EU, http://europa.eu/about-eu/institutions-bodies/court-justice/index_en.htm.

5.5   *Nonstate Entities – NGOs and Business Interests*

Traditionally, international law was the "law of nations," a closed system in which only states (national governments) had standing, lawmaking power, rights, and responsibilities. All that changed in the last third of the 20th century with the vast growth in environmental and other public-interest-issue NGOs, the Internet, and the globalization of commerce, capital, and information. Today, NGOs and commercial enterprises alike are very active participants in lobbying for and formulating international and national environmental laws, monitoring and enforcing them, assisting states and IGOs with their programs, and taking issue with their projects and action plans.

5.5.1   *International NGOs*

Standing out among the environmental NGOs is the International Union for the Conservation of Nature and Natural Resources (IUCN or World Conservation Union).[70] The IUCN was founded in 1948 and is today a formidable network composed of 89 states, 124 government agencies, 976 NGOs, 42 affiliates, and almost 11,000 scientists and experts from 181 countries, with a staff of 1,000, in 45 regional and country offices and its headquarters in Gland, Switzerland. The IUCN directly helped draft, among other treaties, the World Heritage Convention, Ramsar, CITES, and the Biodiversity Treaty and now has quasi-official status assisting IGOs, national and local governments in their implementation. The World Wildlife Fund[71] is another very large NGO active in many countries in many treaty regimes including climate change, biodiversity, forests, oceans and rivers, and of course wildlife.

A number of large, membership-based US environmental action groups have expanded their international environmental law work – often employing lawyers, scientists, and economists – and have become very significant players in many IGO and national government venues. These include the Sierra Club,[72] Environmental Defense Fund,[73] Natural Resources Defense Council

---

[70] IUCN, http://www.iucn.org.
[71] WWF, http://www.wwf.org.
[72] Sierra Club, http://www.sierraclub.org.
[73] The Environmental Defense Fund, http://www.edf.org/.

(NRDC),[74] Friends of the Earth (FOE),[75] the National Wildlife Federation,[76] the National Audubon Society,[77] and the Earthjustice Legal Defense Fund.[78]

A wealth of respected research, educational, and consultative groups exist that provide programs, studies, draft legal instruments, and make other invaluable contributions to the development of international environmental law. The highly respected International Law Association (ILA)[79] has led in the drafting and adoption of numerous international environmental law treaties and other legal authorities, notably in the areas of freshwater, marine resources, and transfrontier pollution. Other notable "think-tanks" include the Environmental Law Institute (ELI),[80] World Resources Institute (WRI),[81] Worldwatch Institute,[82] the Center for International Environmental Law (CIEL),[83] and the Environmental Law Alliance Worldwide (E-LAW).[84]

Outside the US, numerous international law NGOs exist contributing at all levels of activism. Examples include Greenpeace,[85] headquartered in Amsterdam with offices throughout the world, which is controversial and activist (e.g., whaling boat blockades) but still highly respected by international authorities for its views; the Earth Council,[86] headquartered in San Juan, Costa Rica, which promotes sustainable development and other Rio Earth Summit principles; the International Institute for Environment and Development (IIED)[87] in London; the Foundation for International Environmental Law and Development (FIELD)[88] at the University of London; the Regional Environmental Center for Central and Eastern Europe (REC),[89] an impressive "nonadvocacy" regional environmental information and

---

[74] NRDC, http://www.nrdc.org.

[75] Friends of the Earth, http://www.foe.org.

[76] National Wildlife Federation, http://www.nwf.org.

[77] The National Audobon Society, http://www.audubon.org.

[78] Earthjustice, http://www.earthjustice.org. Formerly the Sierra Club Legal Defense Fund, the Earthjustice Legal Defense Fund works on U.S. and international environmental legal issues.

[79] International Law Association, http://www.ila-hq.org.

[80] Environmental Law Institute, http://www.eli.org.

[81] World Resources Institute, http://www.wri.org.

[82] Worldwatch Institute, http://www.worldwatch.org.

[83] Center for International Environmental Law, http://www.ciel.org.

[84] Environmental Law Alliance Worldwide, http://www.elaw.org.

[85] Greenpeace, http://www.greenpeace.org.

[86] Earth Council, http://www.ecouncil.ac.cr.

[87] International Institute for Environment and Development, http://www.iied.org.

[88] Foundation for International Environmental Law and Development, http://www.field.org.uk.

[89] Regional Environmental Center, http://www.rec.org.

participation group headquartered in Szentendre, Hungary; and the European Environmental Bureau (EEB)[90] headquartered in Brussels. Among numerous regional environmental groups those in Europe, South America, Asia, and parts of Africa are indeed thriving.[91] In addition to these broad-based issue groups, there are many effective NGOs focusing on a narrower range of issues, such as the Basel Action Network (BAN),[92] which concentrates on hazardous waste, and even more extremely focused ones, like the Bat Conservation International.[93]

5.5.2   *Multinational Corporations and Other Business Interests*

Private sector interests are equally active in lobbying, drafting, monitoring, and influencing the development and direction of international environmental law. Many multinational corporations have created sophisticated networks in the field.[94] However, many more rely on trade associations to do their international environmental law lobbying. Two generic giants are the International Chamber of Commerce[95] and the World Business Council for Sustainable Development.[96] Some industries have specialized associations active on the international legal front, such as the minerals industry's International Council of Mining and Metals (ICMM)[97] and the chemical industry's American Chemical Council (ACC) and International Council of Chemical Associations (ICCA).[98] The industries and their trade groups also sponsor studies of international environmental law, an impressive example being the Mining, Minerals and Sustainable Development Project (MMSD),[99] a multi-million-dollar effort to examine how the minerals industry can contribute to sustainable development.

Moreover, industry's international interests are supported by national governments, through ministerial or secretarial agencies. The US example is

---

[90] European Environmental Bureau, http://www.eeb.org.

[91] *See, e.g.*, Hunter et al., *supra* note 1, at 257–258.

[92] Basel Action Network, http://www.ban.org.

[93] Bat Conservation International, http://www.batcon.org.

[94] *See* Gareth Porter & Janet Welsh Brown, Global Environmental Politics 64–66 (1991).

[95] International Chamber of Commerce, http://www.iccwbo.org.

[96] WBCSD, http://www.wbcsd.org.

[97] International Council on Mining and Metals, http://www.icmm.com (until 2002, the more benignly named International Council of Mining and Environment (ICME)).

[98] International Council of Chemical Associations, http://www.icca-chem.org/.

[99] *Mining, Minerals, and Sustainable Development Project*, IIED, www.iied.org/mmsd. Between 2000 and 2002 this group carried out research, analysis and consultation on the mining industry and sustainable development. In 2012, the group issued a MMSD+10 examining the progress on original goals and identifying ongoing challenges.

the US Department of Commerce,[100] which often finds itself on the opposite side of the lobbying table from the US Environmental Protection Agency[101] international office.

Finally, mention should be made of the International Organization for Standardization (ISO),[102] a worldwide federation of standards organizations headquartered in Geneva. It is famous for creating the ISO 14000 Series Environmental Management Standards, which are fast becoming the international standards for corporate environmental planning and compliance monitoring.

5.5.3   *Corporate Social Responsibility*[103]

The profit-maximization requirement of corporations[104] creates tension between business and environmental interests.[105] Because the very survival of a corporation depends on its ability to reduce costs and increase profits, corporations have historically opposed environmental regulations and policies that they believed would impose significant new costs or reduce the demand for their product.[106] Thus, corporations have typically preferred lax environmental regulations because law regulations allow the corporation to externalize environmental costs.[107] Recently, however, corporations have begun to realize environmental and business goals may not always be at odds.[108]

---

[100] US Department of Commerce, http://www.commerce.gov/.

[101] *International Programs,* EPA, http://www.epa.gov/international/.

[102] International Organization for Standardization, http://www.iso.org/iso/home.htm.

[103] This section on Corporate Social Responsibility was prepared for this edition by Teresa (Tessa) Mendez (JD University of Denver Sturm College of Law 2011, MA University of Denver Korbel School of International Studies 2011, Editor-in-Chief of the *Denver Journal of International Law & Policy* 2010–2011), and member of the California Bar.

[104] Ian B. Lee, *Corporate Law, Profit Maximization and the "Responsible Shareholder,"* in Berkeley Electronic Press Legal Series, 2005, at 2, http://law.bepress.com/cgi/viewcontent.cgi?article=2238&context=expresso&sei-redir=1#search=%22corporation%20%2B%20profit%20%2B%20maximization%22; Celia R. Taylor, *United States Company Law as It Impacts Corporate Environmental Behavior, with Emphasis on Climate Change* at 1 (Univ. of Oslo, Norway, Sustainable Companies Workshop, Working Paper Aug. 2011), *available from author,* ctaylor@law.du.edu.

[105] While this section focuses on the environmental aspects of corporate social responsibility (CSR), CSR is by no means limited to environmental problems. It encompasses a broad range of social, cultural, ethical, and other public interest issues.

[106] *See* Aneel Karnani, *The Case Against Corporate Social Responsibility,* Wall St. J., Aug. 23, 2010, http://online.wsj.com/article/SB10001424052748703338004575230112664504890.html.

[107] *See* chapter 2.1.13 for definition and explanation of externalities.

[108] The role of business in society has been pondered for centuries, but has taken on special importance since the industrial revolution. While isolated philanthropic initiatives have

The "corporate social responsibility" (CSR) movement seeks to integrate environmental, social, and human rights awareness into the corporate business model.[109]

While there is no universal definition of CSR, it is generally understood as the adoption of corporate self-regulation to effectuate transparent business practices that respect ethical values, domestic and international legal norms, communities, and the environment.[110] Critically, this definition does not preclude profit maximization. First and foremost, a corporation is an economic unit in society. As such, the corporation has a responsibility to produce goods and to sell them for a profit.[111] Also, as a member of society, corporations have an obligation to perform their business function within the framework of the law.[112] The ethical responsibilities of CSR go above and beyond the profit-making and legal duties. CSR extends to actions, decisions, and practices which the corporation undertakes to improve its community and the environment.

Socially responsible business practices have attracted considerable controversy in both the academic and business worlds. Advocates of CSR argue that businesses make more long-term profit by adopting the CSR approach.[113] Critics of CSR argue that it is a distraction from the profit maximization goal of business and provides negligible social benefit.[114] Other critics of CSR in civil society argue that CSR is merely a tool that corporations use "greenwash"[115] their operations – using advertisements and public relations campaigns to mislead customers regarding environmental practices of the

---

been taking place throughout history, CSR has only gained widespread legitimacy in the last few decades. *See* JENNIFER ZERK, MULTINATIONALS AND CORPORATE SOCIAL RESPONSIBILITY 16 (2006).

[109] RAYMOND W. Y. KAO, SUSTAINABLE ECONOMY: CORPORATE SOCIAL AND ENVIRONMENTAL RESPONSIBILITY 3 (2010).

[110] For an excellent resource on CSR terms and programs, *see* WAYNE VISSER ET AL., THE A-Z OF CORPORATE SOCIAL RESPONSIBILITY 106 (2d ed. 2010).

[111] *Id.* at 107. *See also* the Harvard Kennedy School, Corporate Social Responsibility Initiative, which notes that: "Corporate social responsibility encompasses not only what companies do with their profits, but also how they make them," http://www.hks.harvard.edu/m-rcbg/CSRI/init_define.html.

[112] Opponents of corporate social responsibility maintain that profit-making and legal duties are the only responsibilities of corporations. "There is one and only one social responsibility of business – to use its resources and engage in activities designed to increase its profits so long as it stays within the rules of the game, which is to say, engages in open and free competition without deception or fraud." MILTON FRIEDMAN, CAPITALISM AND FREEDOM 133 (1962).

[113] Ron Robbins, *Does CSR Increase Profits?* ENVTL. LEADER, May, 26 2011, http://www.environmentalleader.com/2011/05/26/does-corporate-social-responsibility-increase-profits/.

[114] FRIEDMAN, *supra* note 112, at 133.

[115] *See Greenwashing*, GREENPEACE, http://stopgreenwash.org/.

company. These critics additionally argue that corporations adopt CSR in an effort to sideline government regulation over their industry.

CSR programs can be expensive, and they contradict some traditional business attitudes. Therefore, the question arises, why are so many corporations adopting CSR? Fundamentally, corporations voluntarily implement CSR programs because they believe that CSR creates a competitive advantage.[116] Specifically, corporations see the advantages as:

- enhanced reputation
- greater customer loyalty
- a more satisfied and productive workforce
- fewer regulatory or legal problems
- long term viability in the marketplace
- a stronger community
- increased revenues, and
- easier access to capital.[117]

Companies will also adopt CSR defensively – to prevent costly and embarrassing environmental scandals, consumer boycotts, loss of market share, and litigation. CSR is increasingly becoming a legitimate business practice today as corporate leaders begin to understand that CSR can increase profits and mitigate risk.[118]

Because CSR can be difficult to define and measure quantitatively, international organizations and institutions have attempted to codify CSR as a way of substantiating its fundamental principles. The first attempt at codification began in 1974 when the United Nations created the UN Commission on Transnational Corporations (the Commission) – "to provide a permanent intergovernmental forum for deliberations on issues related to TNCs [transnational corporations]" – and the UN Center on Transnational Corporations (UNCTC) – "to study TNCs and related policy issues" and to serve as the

---

[116] *See e.g.* Michael E. Porter & Mark R. Kramer, *Strategy and Society: The Link Between Competitive Advantage and Corporate Social Responsibility,* HARVARD BUSINESS REVIEW, Dec. 1, 2006, at 78–91.

[117] In 2002 PricewaterhouseCoopers conducted a survey CSR responsibility programs in large U.S. companies. At that time, 75 percent of the respondents said they had adopted some sustainable business practices. The list above contains some of their top reasons for doing so. *See* PRICEWATERHOUSECOOPERS, SUSTAINABILITY SURVEY REPORT 2002, http://www.basisboekmvo.nl/files/Sustainability%20survey%20report%20-%20PwC.pdf.

[118] *See* Tara Weiss *et al., CEOs On CSR,* FORBES, Oct. 16, 2008, http://www.forbes.com/2008/10/16/ceos-csr-critics-lead-corprespons08-cx_tw_mk_kk_1016ceos.html.

secretariat for the Commission.[119] The UNCTC and the Commission were marked by conflict between developing and developed countries from the very beginning.[120] Developing countries wanted a binding international code of conduct for multinational corporations that would impose compliance in the areas of: CSR, foreign direct investment, corruption, labor, competition, and the environment. Developed countries, however, insisted that the code had to be voluntary. Vigorous negotiations on a "Code of Conduct for Transnational Corporations" continued for over a decade,[121] but the code was never finalized, and both the UNCTC and the Commission were subsumed into UNCTAD in 1993.[122]

In 1976, the OECD responded to the UN's lack of progress in the area by drafting a corporate code of conduct, the "Declaration on International Investment and Multinational Enterprises," which adopts the developed countries' perspective on the rights and obligations of international corporations.[123] The Declaration is completely voluntary, and, rather than trying to enforce mandatory regulations, seeks to influence attitudes and behavior with fewer and more flexible rules. The three-page Declaration has been revised periodically, and now incorporates a detailed, 74-page set of OECD Guidelines for Multi-National Enterprises.[124] While all 34 OECD countries have subscribed to the Declaration,[125] it is difficult to determine what effect it has had in those developed countries, let alone in the rest of the world. Moreover, because the Declaration is voluntary, some commentators feel that its utility and efficacy is reduced.[126]

As the 20th century drew to a close, globalization was increasing corporate power to unprecedented levels, leading some to argue that corporate

---

[119] UNCTAD, *The United Nations Center on Transnational Corporations*, http://unctc.unctad. org/aspx/index.aspx; UNCTAD, *UNCTC Origins*, http://unctc.unctad.org/aspx/UNCTC-Origins.aspx.

[120] For a helpful historical analysis of corporate codes of conduct and the UN, *see* Tagi Sagafi-nejad, The UN and transnational Corporations: From Code of Conduct to Global Compact 89–124 (2008).

[121] *Id.* at 110.

[122] *Id.* at 111.

[123] Organization for Economic Co-Operation and Development (OECD), Declaration on International Investment and Multinational Enterprises, June 21, 1976, 15 I.L.M. 967, http://www.oecd.org/dataoecd/43/29/48004323.pdf at 5.

[124] *Id.* at 9. The latest amendments to the Guidelines were agreed to on May 25, 2011, and can be found at the link provided in the above citation.

[125] OECD, *About the Declaration on International Investment and Multinational Enterprises,* http://www.oecd.org/document/24/0,3746,en_2649_34887_1875736_1_1_1_1,00&&en-USS_01DBC.html.

[126] *E.g.*, Sagafi-nejad, *supra* note 120 at 112.

code of conduct was more necessary than ever. However, the frameworks proposed by the UN and OECD did not satisfactorily establish a widespread agreement on corporate behavior. Taking up this challenge, UN Secretary-General Kofi Annan challenged the world's business elite to meet their social responsibilities in a speech at the 1999 World Economic Forum in Davos, Switzerland. He called on international businesses to join a new UN policy initiative called the Global Compact.[127] The Global Compact is a voluntary code that enunciates ten principles in the areas of human rights, labor, anti-corruption and the environment.[128] The environmental principles are drawn from the Rio Declaration (*see* Chapter 4.3),[129] and include:

- Principle 7: Support a precautionary approach to environmental challenges;
- Principle 8: Undertake initiatives to promote greater environmental responsibility; and
- Principle 9: Encourage the development and diffusion of environmentally friendly technologies.[130]

In the years since Kofi Annan's initial call to action, the Global Compact has gained massive support. Over 8,700 corporations and civil society organizations in 130 countries have signed it, making it the largest voluntary corporate responsibility initiative in the world.[131] Nevertheless, this effort has been criticized for relying on self-monitoring and self-reporting. Environmental activists claim that the Global Compact is the ideal "greenwashing" instrument because it allows businesses to publicize their participation in an international initiative without actually implementing significant CSR reform.[132] Additionally, the principles lack specificity, which also allows businesses to claim commitment without making any significant changes. Despite these shortcomings, the voluntary Global Compact has gained the support

---

[127] UN, *United Nations Global Compact,* http://www.unglobalcompact.org/AboutTheGC/TheTenPrinciples/index.html. For an analysis of the history and criticisms of the Global Compact, *see* ELISA MORGERA, CORPORATE ACCOUNTABILITY IN INTERNATIONAL ENVIRONMENTAL LAW 88 (2009).

[128] *Id.*

[129] United Nations Conference on Environment and Development, Rio de Janeiro, Braz., June 3–14, 1992, *Rio Declaration on Environment and Development,* U.N. Doc. A/CONF.151/26/Rev. 1 (Vol. I) (Aug. 12, 1992).

[130] *UN Global Compact, supra* note 127.

[131] UN, *Overview of the UN Global Compact,* http://www.unglobalcompact.org/AboutTheGC/index.html.

[132] MORGERA, *supra* note 127, at 90.

of corporations, shareholders, governing boards, civil society and public-interest organizations, and governments – something which the previous UN efforts had not achieved.

CSR has not become an accepted business practice solely, or even chiefly, because of these top-down government initiatives. Rather, corporations themselves catalyzed the CSR revolution by creating individualized CSR codes of conduct governing their own operations and reporting systems. The first significant wave of individual businesses started defensively devising corporate codes in response to ethical scandals that shook the defense and financial industries in the 1980s.[133] While academics debated the theoretical implications of CSR, the movement gained strength as corporations realized that CSR has considerable advantages. Today almost every major corporation has some sort of CSR code, and many make it an integral part of their operations.

The widespread acceptance of CSR has generated a virtual "industry" of environmental-CSR entities that provide corporations with advice, forums, guidelines and standards, auditing and monitoring programs, best practices, and/or reporting systems.[134] Examples of these include:

- ISO 14000[135] and ISO 26000[136]
- AA1000 Series of Standards on Accountability[137]
- Carbon Disclosure Project[138]

---

[133] ENCYCLOPEDIA OF BUSINESS ETHICS AND SOCIETY 326 (Robert Kolb ed. 2008).

[134] VISSER ET AL., *supra* note 110.

[135] ISO 14000 is an "environmental management system" designed to identify and control the environmental impact of activities, products, or services; to improve environmental performance continually; to implement a systematic approach to setting environmental objectives and targets; and to achieve these and demonstrate that they have been achieved. International Organization for Standardization, *ISO 14000 essentials,* http://www.iso.org/iso/iso_14000_essentials.

[136] ISO 26000 is a system of "guidance for social responsibility," a CSR system that is "intended to assist [private and public] organizations in contributing to sustainable development through seven core subjects – organizational governance, environment, labor, human rights, community involvement and development, consumer issues, and fair operating practices. International Organization for Standardization, *ISO 26000 – Social Responsibility,* http://www.iso.org/iso/social_responsibility.

[137] AA1000 are reporting standards that aim "to help organizations become more accountable, responsible and sustainable." ACCOUNTABILITY, *Setting the Standard for Corporate Responsibility and Sustainable Development,* http://www.accountability.org/index.html.

[138] CDP is a database where "thousands of organizations from across the world's major economies measure and disclose their greenhouse gas emissions, water use and climate change strategies." CARBON DISCLOSURE PROJECT, *Carbon Disclosure Project,* https://www.cdproject.net/en-US/Pages/HomePage.aspx.

- Dow Jones Sustainability Indexes[139]
- European Union Emissions Trading System[140]
- Earthcheck[141]
- Forest Stewardship Council[142]
- Global Reporting Initiative's Sustainability Reporting Guidelines[143]
- International Chamber of Commerce, Business Charter for Sustainable Development[144]
- World Business Council for Sustainable Development[145]
- Institute of Environmental Management and Assessment[146]

---

[139] Dow Jones Indexes provides "global indexes tracking the financial performance of the leading sustainability-driven companies worldwide." DOW JONES INDEXES, *Dow Jones Sustainability Indexes,* http://www.sustainability-index.com.

[140] The EU ETS claims to be "the first and biggest international scheme for the trading of greenhouse gas emission allowances" and covers 30 countries. EUROPEAN COMMISSION, *Climate Action – Emissions Trading System (EU ETS),* http://ec.europa.eu/clima/policies/ets/index_en.htm.

[141] Earth Check states that it is "the largest environmental management system used by the travel and tourism industry." It tracks and measures resource use and waste output, enhances design and operational efficiencies, and encourages corporate social responsibility. EARTHCHECK, *Why Earth Check,* http://www.earthcheck.org/Default.aspx.

[142] FSC is "an independent, non-governmental, not-for-profit organization established to promote the responsible management of the world's forests." FOREST STEWARDSHIP COUNCIL, *About FSC,* http://www.fsc.org.

[143] GRI states that is "the world's most widely used sustainability reporting framework" and is dedicated to "the mainstreaming of disclosure on environmental, social and governance performance." GLOBAL REPORTING INITIATIVE, *What Is GRI?,* http://www.globalreporting.org/AboutGRI/WhatIsGRI/.

[144] The ICC's "Charter" consists of 16 principles that "provide businesses worldwide with a basis for sound environmental management." INTERNATIONAL CHAMBER OF COMMERCE, *Business Charter for Sustainable Development,* http://www.iccwbo.org/policy/environment/id1309/index.html.

[145] The WBCSD is "a CEO-led, global association of some 200 companies dealing exclusively with business and sustainable development" that leads in the development of policy, best practices, and advocacy in the fields of energy and climate, development, business role, and ecosystems. WORLD BUSINESS COUNCIL FOR SUSTAINABLE DEVELOPMENT, *WBCSD,* http://www.wbcsd.org/templates/TemplateWBCSD5/layout.asp?type=p&MenuId=NjA&doOpen=1&ClickMenu=LeftMenu.

[146] The IEMA states that it is "the largest professional membership body for the environment with over 15,000 members." INSTITUTE OF ENVIRONMENTAL MANAGEMENT & ASSESSMENT, http://www.iema.net. It serves as an environmental auditing body that works toward "promoting best practice standards in environmental management, auditing and assessment for all industry sectors."

- Marine Stewardship Council[147]
- Mining, Minerals for Sustainable Development project[148]

The near collapse of the global financial system in 2007 and the continuing economic instability in the years that followed challenged the viability of the growing CSR movement.[149] While some companies contracted or even slashed their CSR programs as they sought to cut costs, many other CSR programs remained viable.[150] In fact, some companies saw the recession as an opportunity to expand their CSR credentials at cut-rate prices.[151] Because CSR can bolster a company's reputation, many companies proved willing to invest in CSR during the economic recession to foster a competitive advantage over rival companies.[152]

Some analysts have even argued that the financial crisis highlighted the need for more responsible business practices, contending CSR must become standard corporate practice to prevent future crises.[153]

> The financial crisis was triggered by a bout of corporate social irresponsibility on a massive scale that has tarnished the reputations of even the bluest of blue-chip companies. Now corporate leaders have a chance to show that they are not just motivated by short-termism after all.[154]

The global financial crisis has revealed that transparent, accurate, and responsible business practices are essential to the functioning of domestic and international markets,[155] a revelation that may bolster the CSR movement and lead to its further expansion.

---

[147] The MSC professes itself "the world's leading certification and ecolabelling program for sustainable seafood" in order to recognize and reward sustainable fishing. Marine Stewardship Council, *About Us,* http://www.msc.org/about-us.

[148] The MMSD was a huge stakeholder-engaged study project to develop "sustainability" standards for the mining industry; it published its research and recommendations and concluded work in 2002. International Institute for Environment and Development, *MMSD – Introduction,* http://www.iied.org/sustainable-markets/key-issues/business-and-sustainable-development/mmsd-introduction.

[149] Lilia Dvorakova and Marcela Srchova, *Corporate Social Responsibility During the Financial Crisis and Economic Recession,* Annals of DAAAM & Proceedings, 2010.

[150] *A Stress Test for Good Intentions,* The Economist, May 14, 2009, http://www.economist.com/node/13648978.

[151] Philippe Gohier, *A Conscience Choice: Why Companies Didn't Scale Back on Social Responsibility Efforts During the Downturn,* 123 Maclean's 38, Jun. 21, 2010.

[152] *Id.*

[153] *Id.*

[154] *A Stress Test for Good Intentions, supra* note 150.

[155] Alyson Warhurst, *The Future of Corporate Philanthropy,* Bloomberg Businessweek, Dec. 8, 2008, http://www.businessweek.com/globalbiz/content/dec2008/gb2008128_757524.htm.

A dichotomy lies at the heart of CSR. On the one hand, countless environmental problems can be directly traced to corporate behavior. On the other hand, the prevention and cure of environmental problems can only be achieved with the support of business interests. In many cases, corporations are in a better position to promote environmental responsibility than either governments or civil society organizations because of the resources, infrastructure, and human capital at their disposal. Corporations are usually smaller and more efficient than government bureaucracies and may also be less corrupt.[156] Corporations also typically possess greater access to financial and technical support than most not-for-profit organizations.[157] Thus, while at first it may seem paradoxical, it makes perfect sense for the sector most responsible for anthropogenic environmental damage to take the lead in environmental protection.

It is axiomatic that, for the most part, international law governs state actors, and the private sector is outside the normal sphere of international law regulation. The international community has responded to this gap by encouraging businesses to engage in self-regulation of CSR. While many skeptics both inside and outside the corporate world doubt the wisdom of self-regulation,[158] the recent proliferation of independent CSR auditing, reporting, and certification entities may represent a solution to corporate "greenwashing."

---

[156] Reuven S. Avi-Yonah, *The Cyclical Transformations of the Corporate Form: A Historical Perspective on Corporate Social Responsibility*, 30 Del. J. Corp. L. 767, 768 (2005).

[157] *Id.*

[158] Undoubtedly, the most famous critic of self-regulation is Dr. Garrett Hardin, whose scathing debunking of "voluntary" standards, in his seminal essay on "Tragedy of the Commons," was a major factor in the USA's development of command-control environmental regulation. Garrett Hardin, *Tragedy of the Commons,* 162 Science 1243 (Dec. 13, 1968), http://www.sciencemag.org/content/162/3859/1243.full#ref-3.

Part Three: The Key Issues

Chapter Six

Environmental Impact Assessment

6.0   *Introduction*

The United States made a momentous change in its relationship with the environment in 1969, with little appreciation of the profound consequences it would continue to have today. That year marked the beginning of the "Environmental Law Revolution" in the United States, and did so with an entirely new kind of law – a paradigm shift in the way humans interact with the world around them – the National Environmental Policy Act (NEPA).[1]

NEPA, for the first time, required the government in advance to evaluate and consider the consequences of major national government actions and projects likely to have significant impacts on the environment. The goal of the law is to force such advance examination specifically to "prevent or eliminate damage to the environment and biosphere and stimulate the health and welfare of man...."[2] To implement this precautionary approach, NEPA requires a "detailed statement" of environmental impacts and alternatives to be prepared at the recommendation (pre-decisional) stage by the government official responsible for the action.[3] This "environmental impact statement" (EIS) has multiple purposes: to serve as an "action-forcing device" to insure that NEPA policies and goals are made part of federal government

---

[1] 42 U.S.C. § 4321 *et seq.*, http://www.law.cornell.edu/uscode/42/usc_sup_01_42_10_55.html. NEPA regulations are contained in 40 C.F.R. §§ 1500.1–1517.7, http://ecfr.gpoaccess.gov/cgi/t/text/text-idx?c=ecfr&tpl=/ecfrbrowse/Title40/40cfr1500_main_02.tpl. A detailed website for NEPA can be found at USEPA, *National Environmental Policy Act (NEPA),* http://www.epa.gov/compliance/nepa/index.html.

[2] 42 U.S.C. § 4321.

[3] Section 102(2)(C), 42 U.S.C. § 4332(2)(C), http://www.law.cornell.edu/uscode/42/usc_sec_42_00004332----000-.html; Kleppe v. Sierra Club, 427 U.S. 390 (1976), http://supreme.justia.com/us/427/390/case.html. Interestingly, the EIS concept was not added to NEPA until very late in its consideration by Congress and then based on the testimony of one person, Political Science Professor Lynton K. Caldwell, "the father of the EIS," who pointed out to Congress that they had put no "action-forcing" mechanism into their law.

programs and actions, to inform the government and lead to better decisions, to integrate environmental considerations into mission planning, to
serve as an environmental full disclosure document for the public and other
decision-makers, and to evince that the law has been complied with.[4]

From this beginning, the international environmental impact assessment
(EIA) process has evolved:

> Born in the United States, it was initially ignored then (in turn) caused great
> disturbance and antagonism, began to change people's lives for the better, set-
> tled down and learned from experience, became respectable and, eventually,
> was extensively imitated all over the world.[5]

Australia was the next country to adopt an EIA policy in 1972, with Canada,
New Zealand, Columbia, Thailand, France, West Germany, and other countries following suit later in the 1970s.[6] In the mid-1980s, the EU's EIA Directive imposed the process on European countries, UNEP began its role of
actively promoting EIAs,[7] numerous developing countries instituted the study
procedures, and "the diffusion of EIA…has continued unabated" since.[8]

Today, EIA requirements appear to be the most widely adopted environmental requirements of all, worldwide.[9] Many nations, subnational regions
and units, and institutions now require EIAs.[10] While the majority of EIA

---

[4] *See* 40 C.F.R. § 1502.1, http://ceq.hss.doe.gov/nepa/regs/ceq/1502.htm#1502.1; Calvert
Cliffs' Coordinating Committee, Inc. v. US Atomic Energy Commission, 449 F.2d 1109
(DC Cir. 1971); James W. Spensley, *National Environmental Policy Act, in* ENVIRONMEN-
TAL LAW HANDBOOK 583 (Gov't Instits., 20th ed., 2009); George (Rock) Pring, *Evaluación
de Impacto Ambiental en los Estados Unidos de América de Conformidad con la Ley Nacio-
nal de Politicas Ambientales de 1969, in* LA NATURALEZA JURÍDICA DE LA EVALUACIÓN DE
IMPACTO AMBIENTAL: ANÁLISIS DE DERECHO COMPARADO (José Juan González ed., 2010).

[5] CHRISTOPHER WOOD, ENVIRONMENTAL IMPACT ASSESSMENT: A COMPARATIVE REVIEW
XIV (1995).

[6] *Id.* at 3.

[7] In 1987, UNEP adopted *Goals and Principles of Environmental Impact Assessment,*
UNEP/GC.14/25, Annex III (1987), http://www.unep.org/download_file.multilingual
.asp?FileID=28 at ¶ 31, and since has actively produced a number of conferences, resources,
and guidance documents. For more, see http://www.unep.org and its webpages related to
"EIA" and "environmental impact assessment."

[8] WOOD, *supra* note 5, at 4. Another good source on national EIA laws is ENVIRONMEN-
TAL LAW NETWORK INTERNATIONAL (ELNI), INTERNATIONAL ENVIRONMENTAL IMPACT
ASSESSMENT: EUROPEAN AND COMPARATIVE LAW AND PRACTICAL EXPERIENCE (1997)
(hereafter ELNI).

[9] Cheryl Wasserman, *Enforcement of Environmental Impact Assessment Requirements* at 1 (back-
ground paper for the International Network for Environmental Enforcement and Compliance
(INECE) INTERNATIONAL CONFERENCE ON ENVIRONMENTAL COMPLIANCE AND ENFORCE-
MENT, June 20–24, 2011, http://inece.org/conference/9/proceedings/57_Wasserman.pdf.

[10] DAVID HUNTER, JAMES SALZMAN & DURWOOD ZAELKE, INTERNATIONAL ENVIRONMENTAL
LAW AND POLICY 499 (2011).

requirements appear in national laws, they have also emerged in international law. A number of the newer international treaties require EIAs and international financial institutions (IFIs), like the World Bank, have begun to require EIAs as a precondition of financial support. This chapter focuses on these international EIA legal authorities.

6.1   *EIA Procedures: The Common Requirements*

An EIA is a formal process for studying a project, program, plan, or other action with potentially significant environmental impact in order to (1) predict and evaluate environmental effects (and possibly social[11] and economic[12] impacts as well), (2) examine alternative approaches that may be environmentally preferable, and (3) avoid or mitigate negative impacts. The goal of the EIA process is to ensure that problems are foreseen, alternatives considered, and environmentally informed decisions and plans result. The process is, as one authority summarizes it, "an anticipatory, participatory, integrative environmental management tool...."[13] An EIA is anticipatory in that the analysis should be completed, in theory, before irrevocable decisions and commitments are made, so that environmentally unacceptable actions can be avoided, abandoned or reconfigured. An EIA is participatory, in that the government is expected to make it public and to seek the involvement and input of the public, developers, investors, regulators, planners, citizens, local communities, NGOs, IGOs, and other affected government entities (*see* § 2.2.1). Finally, an EIA is integrative, in that it requires the systematic input and coordination of many different disciplines, perspectives, and types of expertise from ecologists, planners, and mitigation specialists to lawyers, engineers, and economists.

Not all national or international EIA systems have the same requirements, but most follow a fairly similar pattern. The general goal is to promote the implementation of sustainable development, that is development with the greatest short-and long-term environmental, social, cultural, and economic benefits and the least detriments. In sequence, the steps in the EIA process[14] generally include:

---

[11] *See* Wasserman, *supra* note 9.

[12] Antonio Massarutto, *Integrating the Economic Dimension in EIA*, in ELNI, *supra* note 8, at 189.

[13] Wood, *supra* note 8, at xiv.

[14] For more detailed discussion of the procedural steps the specific controlling law should be consulted. Additional detail can be found in the UNEP documents, *supra* note 7; Wood, ELNI, *supra* note 8, at 12; Wasserman, *supra* note 9.

1. *Screening*: The first step, performed ideally at the earliest "concept stage," is to determine if the proposal is likely to cause sufficient environmental problems to require EIA review. This can be done by measuring the proposal against set physical criteria (size, location, etc.), by project type (mines yes, schools no, etc.), by impact levels (based on past experience), and so on.[15] Typical EIA laws have two profoundly important limitations: (a) they only require EIAs for government (usually national level) decisions, thus omitting a host of private development initiatives that are not government-involved in some way, and (b) they only require EIAs for proposals with "significant" or "substantial" impacts, thus setting a threshold that eliminates review of many intermediate-size or cumulatively significant small actions.

2. *Organization*: Once it has been determined that an EIA is necessary, the proposing government authority should commission an expert study team to prepare the EIA. With some laws, this is done in-house by government employees, while other laws allow the preparation to be done by outside, independent experts.

3. *Scoping*: The EIA study team's first job is "scoping" the EIA, that is deciding what breadth and depth of topics, geographic area, and impacts will be covered. A frequent issue of contention at this stage is geographic scope, for generally the larger the area studied the greater the impacts. Ideally, public participation begins at this definitional stage.

4. *Impact analysis*: The first stage in preparing the study is to assess the proposal's impacts. This normally entails three separate inquiries: (a) identification of the impacts which should be assessed in detail, including direct, indirect, cumulative, and synergistic impacts;[16] (b) prediction of the extent of the changes; and (c) evaluation of the changes to determine if they are adverse enough to require mitigation, a fundamental project change, or outright denial of the action. This step can be done by evaluating the impacts relative to existing laws and standards, consistency with government policies, acceptability to the affected public, etc.

5. *Alternatives analysis*: This is the "heart" of the EIA, in the words of the US regulations.[17] Here, the EIA study team should rigorously identify and analyze all "reasonable" alternative ways of achieving the same goal(s) as the original proposal, always including the "no action" or *status quo*

---

[15] Concrete criteria or checklists have proved much more effective than the use of vague "threshold" words like "major action" or "significant effects on the environment," as was done in the US law, and which has led to countless lawsuit challenges.

[16] On the difficulty of identifying let alone analyzing "cumulative" environmental impacts, *see* Wasserman, *supra* note 9. Alaric Sample, *Assessing the Cumulative Environmental Impacts: The Case of National Forest Planning*, 21 ENVTL. L. 839 (1991).

[17] 40 C.F.R. § 1502.14, http://law.justia.com/cfr/title40/40-31.0.3.5.3.0.29.14.html.

alternative. In the case of a mainstream dam for water supply, for example, reasonable alternatives might include smaller tributary dams, water conservation, watershed management, underground storage, no action, etc. Similarly, a proposal to build a dam for flood control purposes might require examining alternatives such as land use planning, floodplain zoning, flood insurance or other compensation, movement of people and structures, no action, etc. The impacts of each reasonable alternative should be presented so that reviewers can evaluate the comparative merits of the alternatives against those of the original proposal.

6. *Mitigation planning*: In reviewing the impacts of the proposal and alternatives, the next question is "What can and should be done about them?" Mitigation measures are steps that can be taken to prevent, reduce, remedy, or compensate for each significant impact. Examples might include changing the project site or route, altering the process or operation, changing project design, developing pollution control measures, landscaping, training, conducting off-site programs, compensating individuals, etc. Since mitigation measures often profoundly influence the decision to approve or reject the proposal, this step should lead to a "mitigation plan" which will be funded and monitored over the life of the proposal to assure that the mitigation measures are implemented and effective.[18]

7. *Action plan*: The proposal and alternatives should then be compared by the study team, trade-offs between them analyzed, a cost-benefit analysis made (if required), political-value judgments expressly applied, and a final recommendation made. In some systems, this is not incorporated in the EIA but is left to other government decision-makers.

8. *Public participation*: This step is often considered the "most important feature of the EIA process."[19] For maximum public and political acceptability, public review and comment on a "draft" EIA is advisable (*see* § 2.2.1). For most developed countries, EIA laws require the input of those affected – local communities, NGOs, indigenous peoples, key decision-makers, etc. – but some countries and international entities omit this step.[20]

---

[18] This is a particularly notable problem with the US NEPA, which requires mitigation analysis but has no provision for assuring the mitigation will be carried out; for a classic example of this, see Robertson v. Methow Valley Citizens Council, 490 U.S. 332 (1989), http://supreme.justia.com/us/490/332/case.html. As a result, some of the more farsighted US government agencies have mandated such a plan requirement in their own EIA regulations.

[19] Hemantha Withanage, *Advocacy Guide to ADB EIA Requirement* at 45 (2006), http://www.forum-adb.org/docs/EIA-guidebook.pdf. *See* George (Rock) Pring & Susan Y. Noé, *The Emerging International Law of Public Participation Affecting Global Mining, Energy, and Resources Development, in* HUMAN RIGHTS IN NATURAL RESOURCE DEVELOPMENT: PUBLIC PARTICIPATION IN THE SUSTAINABLE DEVELOPMENT OF MINING AND ENERGY RESOURCES 11 (Donald Zillman, Alastair Lucas & George (Rock) Pring eds., 2002).

[20] Pring & Noé, *supra* note 19, at 12, 21, 25–26.

9. *Decision*: A transparent process should be in place so that a competent government official or entity may evaluate the EIA information, public input, and other factors and make a decision on the proposal, communicating the decision and its reasoning to all interested parties and the public.

10. *Follow-through*: Finally, a system should be in place to oversee the implementation of the proposal during its lifetime. This should include monitoring the proposal's compliance with all laws and standards and approval conditions, evaluating the accuracy of the EIA in its impacts, ensuring the success of its mitigation plan, and enforcing compliance and any additional requirements that are needed. Needless to say, this is the weakest link in the EIA process in practice.[21]

How effective are EIA systems? Although there has been criticism that the EIA system is "flawed"[22] as well as "paper rich and information poor,"[23] it is generally accepted that the EIA process is effective and that, if properly done, it does influence proposal selection, design, and (dis)approval, does provide greater environmental protection and mitigation, and does achieve greater public approval.[24] However, the process can vary considerably from law to law and country to country and may be much less effective, depending on the extent to which environmental values are ingrained in the law and national cultures. Additional factors influencing EIA success include transparency, accountability, clear procedures, government support, and public participation.[25]

Today, EIAs have joined the more familiar engineering and economic feasibility studies as an equally important tool in designing a viable project, plan, program, or action. So much so that, by the 1980s, it had already become "clearly very risky to undertake, finance, or approve a major project without first taking into account its environmental consequences – and then siting and designing the project so as to minimise adverse impacts."[26]

With current technological advances, compliance with EIA has become easier. New online/web tools are providing information quicker and more efficiently. Two examples of new tools are NEPAssist, currently deployed in six countries; and an EIA tracking system deployed in five countries by

---

[21] As mentioned above, this is an area of profound weakness in the US law; few government agencies effectively monitor their own post decisional, implementation phase.

[22] *Environmental Activists Urge Overhaul of EIA Process*, TAIPEI TIMES, Apr. 21, 2011, http://www.taipeitimes.com/News/taiwan/archives/2011/04/21/2003501308.

[23] Wasserman, *supra* note 9, at 12.

[24] For a detailed analysis of EIA system effectiveness and the various authorities, *see* WOOD, *supra* note 5, at 5.

[25] *See* WOOD, *supra* note 5, at 7–8.

[26] UNEP, ENVIRONMENTAL IMPACT ASSESSMENT: BASIC PROCEDURES FOR DEVELOPING COUNTRIES at 3 (1988).

USAID's Environmental and Labor Excellence consultants.[27] NEPAssist allows reviewers to do the following:

> Map a proposed project; manipulate project boundaries and provide distance information; accesses and instantaneously map distributed date from different sources; visualize project setting using satellite imagery; generate a pre-programmed report on a series of yes-no questions on presence or proximity key features; enable user to change parameters and assumptions; enable user to go behind data and identify names and locations of particular features.[28]

6.2 *The Development of EIA Requirements in International Law*

EIA provisions can now be found in four different forms at the international level. First, they emerged and can still be found in international treaties, declarations, and other authorities that commit states to implement EIA at their own national level. Second, EIA appears as the central tool in treaties dealing with transboundary environmental impacts. Third, the process is increasingly being used in treaties dealing with global environmental problems. Fourth, international institutions, particularly IFIs like the World Bank, are requiring EIA as a condition of their lending and other financial decisions. This section surveys the first three EIA uses, and the following section looks at its use by IFIs.

EIA-type provisions began appearing in international legal instruments in the 1970s, shortly after the adoption of the US NEPA. Without mentioning it literally, the 1972 Stockholm Declaration foreshadows the EIA process with its provisions calling for an "integrated and coordinated approach to... development planning... to protect and improve the human environment"[29] and the application of "[s]cience and technology... to the identification, avoidance and control of environmental risks and the solution of environmental problems...."[30] A 1974 treaty, the Nordic Convention,[31] while not using the term EIA, sets up an elaborate notification, documentation, and investigation process for "environmentally harmful activities" with transboundary effects in other states.

---

[27] Wasserman, *supra* note 9, at 12–13.

[28] *Id.* at 19.

[29] Stockholm Declaration of the United Nations Conference on the Human Environment, June 16, 1972, Principle 13, U.N. Doc. A/CONF.48/14/Rev. 1 at 3, (1973), 11 I.L.M. 1416 (1972), http://www.unep.org/Documents.Multilingual/Default.asp?documentid=97&article id=1503; *see also* Principles 14 and 15 on "rational planning."

[30] *Id.* Principle 18.

[31] Convention on the Protection of the Environment Between Denmark, Finland, Norway and Sweden, Feb. 9, 1974, 1092 U.N.T.S. 279, 13 I.L.M. 591 (1974), http://untreaty.un.org/unts/1_60000/30/16/00058775.pdf.

EIA's first major international endorsement came in 1974, when the Organization for Economic Cooperation and Development (OECD, consisting chiefly of the industrial nations of the "North") recommended that its member countries adopt EIA processes, which some promptly did. Also in the 1970s, UNEP began its role of "global environmental watchdog," and, among other things, became a major promoter of EIA. The UNEP Governing Council's 1978 Draft Principles for Shared Natural Resources,[32] while nonbinding, elevated the EIA concept by asserting that "[s]tates should make environmental assessments" for any activity with respect to a shared resource which "may create a risk of significantly affecting the environment of another State...."[33]

The watershed year for EIA was 1982. "Should" became "shall" for EIA in the UN General Assembly's nonbinding but authoritative World Charter for Nature in 1982.[34] Also that year, both the UN Convention on the Law of the Sea (*see* Chapter 11)[35] and the ILA Rules of Transfrontier Pollution (*see* Chapter 9) set forth EIA requirements for activities that might cause significant environmental harm, and other UN agencies began to adopt and promote EIA in their work and guidelines.[36]

In 1987, UNEP issued its authoritative "Goals and Principles" for EIA[37] and the prestigious Experts Group on Environmental Law of the UN World Commission on Environment and Development (WCED or Brundtland Commission) put its considerable weight behind the existence of an EIA requirement as a principle of international law.[38] Also, in those years leading up to the Rio Conference, EIA requirements began appearing in a number of international legal authorities as national obligations,[39] transboundary

---

[32] Draft Principles of Conduct in the Field of the Environment for Guidance of States in the Conservation and Harmonious Utilization of Natural Resources Shared by Two or More Countries, May 19, 1978, U.N. Doc. UNEP/IG12/2 (1978), 17 I.L.M. 1097 (1978).

[33] *Id.* Principle 4.

[34] World Charter for Nature, Oct. 28, 1982, ¶ 11(c), G.A. Res. 37/7 (Annex), U.N. GAOR, 37th Sess., Supp. No. 51, at 17, U.N. Doc. A/37/51, 22 I.L.M. 455 (1983), http://www.un.org/documents/ga/res/37/a37r007.htm.

[35] Granted, the Law of the Sea Treaty's EIA provisions are considerably weakened by phrases such as "reasonable grounds for believing" and "as far as practicable."

[36] HUNTER, *supra* note 10, at 498–99.

[37] *Goals and Principles of Environmental Impact Assessment, supra*, note 7.

[38] Experts Group on Environmental Law of the World Commission on Environment and Development, Legal Principles for Environmental Protection and Sustainable Development, Aug. 4, 1987, art. 5, U.N. Doc. WCED/86/23/ADD. 1 (1986), http://habitat.igc.org/open-gates/ocf-a1.htm.

[39] *E.g.*, UNEP Montreal Guidelines for the Protection of the Marine Environment Against Pollution from Land-Based Sources, May 24, 1985, art. 12, UNEP/GC.13/9/Add. 3, UNEP/GC/DEC13/1811, UNEP ELPG No. 7, http://www.pnuma.org/deramb/actividades/gobernanza/cd/Biblioteca/Derecho%20ambiental/28%20UNEPEnv-LawGuide&PrincN07.pdf.

requirements,[40] and conditions for protecting global commons.[41] One of the most significant, the 1991 Convention on Environmental Impact Assessment in a Transboundary Context (also called the Espoo Treaty), was sponsored by the UN Economic Commission for Europe and now has 45 parties.[42]

Influenced by the work of the WCED, participants at the 1992 Rio Conference made EIA a central part of the Rio Declaration in Principle 17:

> Environmental impact assessment, as a national instrument, shall be undertaken for proposed activities that are likely to have a significant adverse impact on the environment and are subject to a decision of a competent national authority.[43]

Agenda 21 implements the EIA requirement by, among other things, calling for adoption of EIA and cost-benefit and risk assessment[44] and making "[f]urther development and promotion of the widest possible use" of EIA a priority area for UNEP and other UN agencies.[45] The three other Rio outputs – the Biodiversity Convention,[46] the Framework Convention on Climate Change,[47] and the Forest Principles[48] – all incorporate EIA procedures. The use of EIAs continued throughout the start of the new millennium, and in April 2010 the International Court of Justice ruled that EIA is required

---

[40] *E.g.*, UNECE Convention on Environmental Impact Assessment in a Transboundary Context (Espoo Convention), Feb. 25, 1991, 30 I.L.M. 800 (1991), http://live.unece.org/env/eia/about/eia_text.html.

[41] *E.g.*, Protocol on Environmental Protection to the Antarctic Treaty, Oct. 4, 1991, art. 8, XI ATSCM/2, 30 I.L.M. 1461 (1991), http://www.ats.aq/e/ep.htm; Convention for the Protection of the Natural Resources and Environment of the South Pacific Region (SREP Convention), Nov. 25, 1986, art. 16, 26 I.L.M. 38 (1987), http://sedac.ciesin.org/entri/texts/natural.resources.south.pacific.1986.html.

[42] Espoo Convention, *supra* note 40; parties listed at http://treaties.un.org/Pages/ViewDetails.aspx?src=TREATY&mtdsg_no=XXVII-4&chapter=27&lang=en.

[43] Rio Declaration on Environment and Development, June 13, 1992, Principle 17, U.N. Doc. A/CONF.151/26 (vol. I) (1992), 31 I.L.M. 874 (1992), http://www.un.org/documents/ga/conf151/aconf15126-1annex1.htm.

[44] Agenda 21, June 13, 1992, ¶ 8.5(b), U.N. Doc. A/CONF. 151/26 (vols. I–III) (1992), http://www.un.org/esa/dsd/agenda21/.

[45] *Id.* ¶ 38.22(i).

[46] Convention on Biological Diversity, June 5, 1992, art. 14, 31 I.L.M. 818 (1992), http://www.cbd.int/convention/text/.

[47] UN Framework Convention on Climate Change, May 29, 1992, art. 4(1)(f), 31 U.N. Doc. A/CONF.151/26, I.L.M. 849 (1992), http://unfccc.int/essential_background/convention/background/items/2853.php.

[48] Non-Legally Binding Authoritative Statement of Principles for a Global Consensus on the Management, Conservation and Sustainable Development of All Types of Forests, June 13, 1992, Principle 8(h), U.N. Doc. A/CONF. 151/26 (Vol. III) (1992), 31 I.L.M. 881 (1992), http://www.un.org/documents/ga/conf151/aconf15126-3annex3.htm.

"where there is a risk that a proposed industrial activity may have a significant adverse impact in a transboundary context."[49]

6.3   *International Financial Institutions' EIA Requirements*

The "greening" of IFIs, led by the World Bank, is one of the most significant trends in all recent international environmental law.[50] Stung by environmental disasters, widespread criticism, lack of standards, and concerns about their own potential liability, IFIs – multilateral development banks (MDBs), development assistance agencies (DAAs), national export-promotion agencies (Ex-Ims), and other public and private-sector finance, insurance, and trade entities – are becoming more environmentally proactive. Increasingly, IFIs are "conditioning" their loans, aid, insurance underwriting, and other involvement on the environmental, social, and cultural acceptability of the project or enterprise, the applicant, and the host country. New development ventures, particularly in developing countries, are a major focus of these toughened environmental conditions.

This IFI "green conditionality" chiefly manifests itself in EIA requirements for advance screening of projects and (to a much lesser extent so far) in on-going operating standards to promote sustainable development.[51] The significance of this quasi-law-creating trend is three-fold: (1) new international environmental law standards are being imposed not by traditional public law-making bodies but by financial institutions; (2) the new rules are "raising the bar" for environmental protection above existing national and international law requirements; and (3) they are in turn stimulating upward revision of national laws. Currently, IFI's are working together to "harmonize" their EIA requirements, environmental policies, and assistance to make them less cumbersome for the countries being served.[52]

All MDBs now impose some environmental/sustainable development criteria on their lending and other supports. The acknowledged leader in

---

[49] Cymie Payne, *World Court Recognizes EIA is a Duty Under International Law*, Legal Planet, Apr. 23, 2010, http://legalplanet.wordpress.com/2010/04/23/world-court-recognizes-eia-is-a-duty-under-international-law/.

[50] George (Rock) Pring, James Otto & Koh Naito, *Trends in International Environmental Law Affecting the Minerals Industry*, 17 J. Energy & Nat. Resources L. 39, 67–70 (1999); William T. Onorato & Peter Fox, *The Role of the World Bank and Other Multilateral and Private Sector Finance Institutions in Resources Development in Developing Countries*, 41 Rocky Mtn. Min. L. Inst. 7–1 (1995).

[51] *See Life as Commerce: International Financial Institutions, Payments for Environmental Services and Carbon Finance* (2008), http://www.cbd.int/doc/external/cop-09/gfc-impact-en.pdf.

[52] *See* Withanage, *supra* note 19, at 15.

this area is the World Bank, which lends money to its 187 member countries, and its environmental-sustainability rules are becoming the standard within the international community.[53] To get a sense of its scope, in 2009 the World Bank sponsored 767 projects with a total commitment of US$58.8 billion.[54] In 1989, the World Bank first made EIA standard operating procedure for its investment projects.[55] In 2001, it adopted the "Environment Strategy" to integrate environmental management into its operations.[56] Following that, it created "Safeguard Policies" covering EIA, physical cultural resources, disputed areas, forests, indigenous peoples, international waterways, involuntary settlement, natural habitats, pest management, and dam safety.[57] What is striking about these rules is that they are applied to raise the bar for countries with inadequate laws or enforcement,[58] in effect creating new "law" through site-specific agreements. While the Bank has made progress, it has also been criticized for insufficient environmental attention in its work. In 2012, the World Bank responded to this criticism by creating a new Environment Strategy that it hopes will guide the bank through 2022.[59]

Like most IFIs, the World Bank has created EIA categories based on the nature, size, importance, and sensitivity of a project.[60] "Category A" projects – those likely to have significant environmental impacts (e.g., mining, ports and harbors, large-scale power plants, dams, large-scale industry, irrigation, timbering, mass transit, roads, etc.) – require detailed EIAs. "Category B" projects – a less adverse category that may potentially be an environmental hazard for the human population or environmental areas (e.g., impacts on wetlands, forests, grasslands, and other natural habits. "Category C" projects – those that have either minimal to no adverse impacts (e.g., protected area establishment and management, geological or mineral surveys, family planning, forestry research, education, investigative studies) for which EIAs are not

---

[53] *See* THE WORLD BANK, http://www.worldbank.org/.

[54] *Youthink,* WORLD BANK, http://youthink.worldbank.org/about/inside-world-bank.

[55] World Bank, Operational Directive (OD) 4.00, Annex A: Environmental Assessment (1989), http://go.worldbank.org/9MIMAQUHN0. The newest EIA rules, OD 4.01, are at http://go.worldbank.org/0BM4HLLCB0. THE WORLD BANK GROUP, POLLUTION PREVENTION AND ABATEMENT HANDBOOK: TOWARD CLEANER PRODUCTION (1998) (hereinafter WORLD BANK HANDBOOK), http://go.worldbank.org/E6G093QFZ1.

[56] *Environmental Assessment,* WORLD BANK, http://go.worldbank.org/AHIKU7O7H0.

[57] *Id.*

[58] WORLD BANK HANDBOOK, *supra* note 55, at v.

[59] *Introduction to the WBG's Environment Strategy,* WORLD BANK, http://go.worldbank.org/R0OUDEBT00; *A New Environment Strategy for the World Bank Group,* WORLD BANK, http://go.worldbank.org/NLP85UZ8X0.

[60] *Advanced Search: Environmental Categories,* WORLD BANK, http://go.worldbank.org/UWS18NE640.

required. Lastly, "Category F" projects – those involving a financial intermediary in subprojects that may have an adverse affect towards the environment

The World Bank Group has three other members. The International
Finance Corporation (IFC), which finances private-sector projects in developing nations,[61] the International Development Association (IDA), the high-risk
entity that loans to the poorest developing countries on a no-interest basis,[62]
and the Multilateral Investment Guarantee Agency (MIGA), which is the
insurance arm of the group.[63] Critics view the IFC's, IDA's, and MIGA's application of environmental rules as "lower" than the World Bank's; something
which may change with the new Environment Strategy for 2012–2022.[64]

A number of other international and regional MDBs are incorporating
EIA processes. The Global Environmental Facility (GEF), an independent IFI
created in 1990 by the World Bank, UNEP, and UNDP to finance environmental efforts on climate change, stratospheric ozone depletion, biodiversity,
persistent organic pollutants, land degradation, and international waters, is
raising international performance standards with its EIA-centered lending
rules. The Asian Development Bank (ADB), which finances projects in the
Asia-Pacific region in infrastructure, health care, administration, and climate
change,[65] is viewed as a leader in EIA.[66] Likewise, the European Bank for
Reconstruction and Development (EBRD), which finances the transition to
market economies and democracy in 29 countries from central Europe to
central Asia,[67] applies EIA through all stages of its projects.[68]

Development assistance agencies (DAAs) have also begun to condition
their "foreign aid" on EIA. As an example, the Overseas Private Investment
Corporation (OPIC),[69] an independent for-profit US government agency
engaged in financing and facilitating US private investment in emerging
economies and developing nations, has extensive EIA processes.[70] Currently,
both the US foreign aid program, the Agency for International Development

---

[61] INTERNATIONAL FINANCE CORPORATION, http://www.ifc.org/.

[62] INTERNATIONAL DEVELOPMENT ASSOCIATION, http://www.worldbank.org/ida/.

[63] MULTILATERAL INVESTMENT GUARANTEE AGENCY, http://www.miga.org/.

[64] *E.g., World Bank Breaks Rules in Lending to Palm Oil Companies,* ECOLOGIST, Aug. 27, 2009,
http://www.theecologist.org/News/news_round_up/309965/world_bank_breaks_rules_
in_lending_to_palm_oil_companies.html. *See* sources cited in Pring, Otto & Naito, *supra*
note 50, at 164.

[65] ASIAN DEVELOPMENT BANK, http://adb.org.

[66] *See* Pring, Otto & Naito, *supra* note 50, at 165.

[67] *Our History,* EUROPEAN BANK OF RECONSTRUCTION AND DEVELOPMENT, http://www.ebrd
.com/pages/about/history.shtml.

[68] *Environmental Procedures,* EUROPEAN BANK OF RECONSTRUCTION AND DEVELOPMENT,
http://www.ebrd.com/pages/about/policies/environmental.shtml.

[69] OVERSEAS PRIVATE INVESTMENT CORPORATION, http://www.opic.gov.

[70] *E.g., Annual Environmental Report* (2007), OPIC, http://www.opic.gov/sites/default/files/
docs/environmental_report_fy06.pdf.

(USAID), and the US export-promotion agency, the Export-Import Bank (Ex-Im Bank), are required by US law to observe EIA and environmental protection procedures.[71] The OECD has published DAA environmental guidelines for its member states, and most benchmark their environmental requirements against those of the World Bank, but vary in their commitment to enforcing sustainable development.[72]

Nevertheless, EIA still has not been thoroughly integrated into international finance. Not only are the "green conditions" evolving and variable, but they remain fairly weak in comparison to developed country EIA standards, like the USA's NEPA. The IFIs' chief problem is their near-exclusive reliance on EIAs, which are of somewhat limited utility in either predicting or controlling development impacts by themselves. Just as a few disasters embarrassed IFIs into instituting EIAs, it can be predicted that the next round of crises at development projects that have done EIAs will propel the financial institutions to incorporate the next logical steps beyond EIAs: (1) monitoring actual operations and (2) evaluating on-going project performance. Given the significance these two measures will have both for new projects and for reform of legal standards worldwide, their development should be closely watched. As one authority concludes: "Increasingly financial institutions... are seen as a means of harnessing commercial forces to propel implementation of the international environmental agenda. This is facilitated by the increasing use of liability and compensation provisions in international conventions as a means of enforcement."[73]

6.4   *The Future of EIA*

While there is as yet no way to measure the effectiveness of the EIA process or its net benefit to society and the environment, the general consensus is that the process works. EIAs involve many types of expertise and the public in decision-making in order to protect environmental, social, cultural, and economic values and to integrate environmental and development planning.[74] However, as it has been practiced thus far, EIA has four obvious flaws: reliability, comparability, objectivity, and enforceability. From a *reliability* standpoint, humans

---

[71] For a sampling of these rules, see *Environmental Compliance,* USAID, http://www.rmportal .net/library/content/tools/environmental-regulations-compliance-tools/tool-environmental-compliance-regulation-216-faa; and Export Import Bank Act of 1945, Pub. L. No. 173-7, http://fraser.stlouisfed.org/docs/historical/martin/12_01_19450731.pdf.

[72] *DAC Guidelines on Aid and Environment,* OECD, http://www.oecd.org/document/26/0,33 43,en_2649_34421_1887578_1_1_1_1,00.html.

[73] INTERNATIONAL AND COMPARATIVE MINERAL LAW AND POLICY: TRENDS AND PROSPECTS 132 (Elizabeth Bastida ed. 2005).

[74] WOOD, *supra* note 5, at 5–11.

lack the ability to predict all of the direct impacts of a development proposal in advance, let alone the complex indirect, secondary, cumulative, and synergistic impacts. From a *comparability* standpoint, development "benefits" will typically be easy to quantify while environmental "costs" will not (e.g., the new dam will provide millions of dollars in hydropower, but the loss of the pristine wilderness canyon is not quantifiable in dollars). From an *objectivity* standpoint, EIAs are sometimes criticized for being "post-facto justifications" for decisions already made by government officials or ignored when they are not.[75] Most problematic, from an *enforceability* standpoint, frequently EIAs are ignored and no follow-on monitoring is done to assure project compliance, mitigation accomplishment, and EIA accuracy.

Other recognized weaknesses of the EIA practice include:

- *Technical shortcomings*, exhibited by the poor quality of many EIA reports. The accuracy of impact predictions, the utility of mitigation and management measures, and the relevance of reports for decision-making often fall short of internationally accepted standards.
- *Procedural limitations*, including inconsistencies in process administration and guidance. Time delays and costs of applying EIAs remain a serious concern for project proponents. Affected communities are more concerned with the lack of quality control of EIA studies or enforcement of mitigation measures.
- *Structural issues*, stemming from the application of EIA as a separate process, unrelated to the project cycle or the larger context of decision-making.
- *System faults,* if a coherent policy-planning frame and systematic follow-up procedures are not well established, EIA cannot be effective.[76]

The EIA process also suffers from perception problems. Even its proponents privately admit that it can seem anti-development, narrowly project-focused, encumbered with technical expertise incomprehensible to decision-makers and the public, lacking integration of social, cultural, human rights, and other considerations of sustainable development. EIA needs to be part of a larger, more holistic process of sustainable development planning and implementation. Clearly, UNEP and other supporters of EIA must work to further develop EIA procedures, uniform standards, credibility, transparency, accountability, and enforceability. Nevertheless, the goal of sustainable development is to bring about intragenerational and intergenerational economic, social, and environmental betterment, and the EIA process is proving to be one of the necessary means to that end.

---

[75] *See* Joseph Sax, *The (Unhappy) Truth About NEPA*, 26 Okla. L. Rev. 239 (1973).

[76] United Nations University, *et al.*, *Environmental Impact Assessment Course Module: Key Elements of the EIA Process*, http://eia.unu.edu/course/?page_id=101.

Chapter Seven

Energy and the Environment: An International Perspective

*By Don C. Smith**

7.0   *Introduction*

Energy is fundamental to modern society. It has been referred to as representing "the heart of modern life"[1] as well as being the "lifeblood"[2] of contemporary living. Many sectors of the modern economy, including agriculture, heating, lighting, industry, and transport, are heavily dependent on access to energy.[3] And, looking ahead, this is extremely unlikely to change. Well known energy researcher and author Daniel Yergin has observed in relation to one key energy sector – electricity – that, "The prospects for electric power in the 21st century can be summarized in a single word: growth."[4]

For much of history, energy was readily available to a relatively few people and most of those were in the global West. However, that is changing rapidly and some three billion additional people in countries extending from China to Brazil and India to Vietnam now aspire to have the living standards

---

* Don C. Smith is a Lecturer and Director of the Environmental & Natural Resources Law & Policy Graduate and J.D. Programs at the University of Denver Sturm College of Law. He is the Editor-in-Chief of the International Bar Association's Journal of Energy & Natural Resources Law and specializes in environmental law with particular emphasis on the European Union. B.S. with distinction University of Kansas; J.D. Washburn University School of Law; LL.M. with distinction University of Leicester (England) Faculty of Law.

[1] Stephen M. Schwebel, *Foreward, in* INTERNATIONAL ENERGY INVESTMENT LAW – THE PURSUIT OF STABILITY vii (Peter D. Cameron ed., 2010).

[2] DRIES LESAGE, THIJS VAN DE GRAAF, KISTEN WESTPHAL, GLOBAL ENERGY GOVERNANCE IN A MULTIPOLAR WORLD 15 (2010).

[3] Schwebel, *supra* note 1, at vii.

[4] DANIEL YERGIN, THE QUEST: ENERGY, SECURITY, AND THE REMAKING OF THE MODERN WORLD 396 (2011).

so long associated with the West such as electricity, air conditioned homes, refrigerators, automobiles, computers, and so on.[5] As Václav Bartuska, the Czech Republic's Ambassador at Large for Energy Security, has observed, the West's "record in spreading democracy is patchy, but success in proselytizing consumerism is undeniable. At least in this aspect the West has won: the world measures its well-being in things it can buy, use, accumulate – and burn."[6]

And yet for hundreds of years it has been evident that environmental degradation has often been associated with the generation of and combustion related to energy.[7] In fact, legislation banning coal burning in certain locales dates as far back as the 13th century.[8]

With the steadily increasing need for energy on one hand and the environmental degradation associated with energy on the other hand, energy is poised "to become one of the major international political issues of the 21st century."[9] In short, the world economy depends largely on fossil fuels, which are limited in character, often located in the same areas, and are linked to enormous streams of pollution. Meanwhile, alternative energy sources such as bio-fuels, hydroelectricity, and nuclear have their own negative aspects insofar as the environment is concerned.[10] It has been suggested that failing to generate energy in an environmentally benign way "will have dramatic consequences in various spheres of human life."[11]

With that background in mind, this chapter assesses international environmentally related legal and policy issues associated with energy from several perspectives. In section 7.1, consideration is given to the intertwined relationship among energy, economic development, and the environment. The evolution of energy and environmental law in an international context is analyzed in section 7.2. Current international law relating to energy and the environment is explored in section 7.3. In this section three specific topics are considered: nuclear energy regulation; marine oil pollution regulation; and a unique treaty that aims to foster energy development along with environmental protection. Section 7.4 looks ahead and contemplates a new scheme for regulating energy, global energy governance. Finally, conclusions are offered in section 7.5.

---

[5] Václav Bartuska, *Energy for survival, in* Green, Safe, Cheap – Where next for EU energy policy 98 (Katinka Barysch ed., 2011).

[6] *Id.*

[7] Roger Fouquet, *A Brief History of Energy, in* International Handbook on the Economics of Energy 1 (Joanne Evans and Lester C. Hunt eds., 2009).

[8] *Id.* at 14.

[9] Lesage, *supra* note 2, at 2.

[10] *Id.* at 2.

[11] *Id.* at 2.

7.1 Energy, Economic Development, and the Environment

7.1.1 Energy Availability and Usage and Economic Development

The relationship between the availability and usage of energy and economic development is undisputed.[12] Producing, exchanging, and consuming services and goods are "driven by refinements in ways of capturing and harnessing energetic resources."[13] Put another way, economic growth is linked inextricably with "the availability, extraction, distribution, and use of energy."[14] One energy expert has gone so far as to assert that the key aspect of successful economic development is "improved access to energy services…"[15]

An energy policy expert has written, "Energy is crucial to the improvement of social and economic welfare. It is necessary to continued economic activity in modern industrialized nations, and its absence would result in cessation of economic growth and diminishing standards of living."[16] From this perspective, the absence of what is often characterized as modern energy services[17] "is a principal cause of low levels of economic and social development. Access to electricity promotes social development and improved welfare by allowing greater access to information via computer, radio and television, cleaner means of storing and preparing food, and the attainment of heating and cooling services."[18]

Globally, in the 20th century there was a "very close secular lockstep" between commercial energy consumption and a "reconstruction" of the world's gross economic product.[19] Using calculations that accounted for constant monies and purchasing power parities, "The growth rates of the

---

[12] *See* Fouquet, *supra* note 7, at 1. There is a casual link "running from electricity consumption to economic growth in…most studies. Consequently, we may conclude that [the lack of electricity] is a limiting factor to economic growth…" Ilhan Ozturk, *A Literature Survey on Energy-Growth Nexus*, ENERGY POL'Y 38, 340, at 347 (2010).

[13] *See* Fouquet, *supra* note 7, at 1.

[14] *Id.*

[15] Ann Florini and Benjamin K. Sovacool, *Bridging the Gaps in Global Energy Governance*, Vol. 17 No. 1 GLOBAL GOVERNANCE, 57, 66 (2011).

[16] Kenneth B. Medlock III, *Energy Demand Theory*, *in* INTERNATIONAL HANDBOOK ON THE ECONOMICS OF ENERGY 89 (Joanne Evans and Lester C. Hunt eds. 2009).

[17] Modern energy services have been defined as "household access to electricity and clean cooking facilities." *See* International Energy Agency, UN Development Program, UN Industrial Development Organization, ENERGY POVERTY: HOW TO MAKE MODERN ENERGY ACCESS UNIVERSAL 8 (2010), http://content.undp.org/go/cms-service/stream/asset/?asset_id=2822269.

[18] *See* Medlock, *supra* note 16, at 89.

[19] VACLAV SMIL, ENERGY AT THE CROSSROADS 65 (2003).

global commercial [total primary energy supply][20] coincide almost perfectly with those of the [gross world product], indicating a highly stable elasticity near 1.0. Each variable shows approximately a 16-fold increase in 100 years, with energy consumption rising from about 22 to 355 [exajoules], and the economic product [in constant 1990 US dollars] going from about $2 to $32 trillion [over the century]."[21] The same relationship between energy consumption and the gross national product of nation states holds true as well.[22]

The United Nations has underscored the role that access to modern energy services will play in the achievement of the UN Millennium Development Goals,[23] especially as it relates to poverty eradication. According to the UN, "It is an alarming fact that today – in the 21st century – there are still billions of people without access to electricity...The ambitious goals that have been set to eradicate poverty can never be fully realized without acknowledging and confronting this fact."[24] By the UN's count, the number of people without access to electricity is 1.4 billion, and of those about 85 percent live in rural settings.[25]

7.1.2   *Tension Between Energy Generation and Consumption and the Environment*

Increased energy generation and consumption results in economic growth. The consequence of that economic growth is "the rising affluence of a broader part of the urban middle-income population. Globally, households become smaller but more energy intensive. Life-styles increasingly reflect energy...intensive consumption patterns."[26]

---

[20] Total primary energy supply, often abbreviated as TPES, refers to the total of all global energy sources including coal, oil and gas, nuclear, and hydro.

[21] SMIL, *supra* note 19, at 65.

[22] CLAUDE DUVAL, HONORÉ LE LEUCH, ANDRÉ PERTUZIO, JACQUELINE LANG WEAVER, INTERNATIONAL PETROLEUM EXPLORATION AND EXPLOITATION AGREEMENTS: LEGAL, ECONOMIC & POLICY ASPECTS (2d ed., 2009).

[23] In 2000, the United Nations Millennium Declaration was adopted by world leaders. The declaration included a commitment to "eradicate extreme poverty" by 2015. *See* MILLENNIUM DEVELOPMENT GOALS, http://www.un.org/millenniumgoals/. It is worth noting, however, that the goals do not include specific targets on access to electricity or energy more broadly. International Energy Agency, UN Development Program, UN Industrial Development Organization, ENERGY POVERTY: HOW TO MAKE MODERN ENERGY ACCESS UNIVERSAL, OECD/IEA 3, http://content.undp.org/go/cms-service/stream/asset/?asset_id= 2822269.

[24] *Id.*

[25] *Id.* at 7.

[26] European Environment Agency, THE EUROPEAN ENVIRONMENT STATE AND OUTLOOK 2010: ASSESSMENT OF GLOBAL MEGATRENDS 18 (2010), www.eea.europa.eu/soer.

However, as the use of energy increases so do the consequent environmental impacts. One key impact involves carbon dioxide emissions and climate change. The World Energy Outlook 2011[27] puts it starkly: "We cannot afford to delay further action to tackle climate change if the long-term target of limiting the global average temperature increase to 2°C. ... is to be achieved at reasonable cost."[28] Another impact involves land use. "... [E]xtraction of fossil fuels and generation of hydroelectricity are major causes of land use changes caused by surface mines, hydrocarbon fields and large water reservoirs. Transportation of fuels and transmission of electricity contribute to this problem due to extensive rights-of-way for railways, roads, pipelines, and high-voltage lines."[29]

In addition, there are immense issues related to natural gas venting and flaring, handling and disposal of nuclear waste, spillage of oil, and the degradation of forests.[30] There are energy system failures that occasionally attract the public's attention,[31] perhaps the "gravest of all ecological risks" is the atmospheric accumulation of greenhouse gases.[32]

In short, the "environmental consequences of producing, moving, processing, and burning coal and hydrocarbons and generating nuclear electricity and hydroelectricity embrace an enormous range of undesirable changes."[33] At the same time economic growth generally depends on increasing energy usage, which in turn is the "main [driver] of environmental impacts."[34]

7.1.3   Energy and Related Trends

Despite the economic downturn of recent years, all projections call for increased energy consumption in the future.[35] For example, the International

---

[27] The World Energy Outlook is produced by the International Energy Agency. The agency, also called the IEA, is "an autonomous organization which works to ensure reliable, affordable and clean energy for its 28 member countries...Founded in response to the 1973/74 oil crisis, the IEA's initial role was to help countries co-ordinate a collective response to major disruptions in oil supply through the release of emergency oil stocks to the market." *What is the International Energy Agency,* INTERNATIONAL ENERGY AGENCY, http://www .iea.org/journalists/faq.asp.

[28] International Energy Agency, WORLD ENERGY OUTLOOK 2011, Executive Summary 2, http://www.worldenergyoutlook.org/media/weowebsite/2011/executive_summary.pdf.

[29] SMIL, *supra* note 19, at 64.

[30] LESAGE, *supra* note 2, at 30.

[31] E.g., the 1986 implosion of the Chernobyl nuclear plant, the 2010 massive Gulf of Mexico oil spill in 2010, or the 2011 Fukushima nuclear plant disaster.

[32] LESAGE, *supra* note 2, at 30.

[33] SMIL, *supra* note 19, at 105–106.

[34] European Environment Agency, *supra* note 26, at 34.

[35] See, e.g., *Id.*; International Energy Agency, WORLD ENERGY OUTLOOK 2011, Executive Summary 1, *supra* note 28; US Energy Information Administration, INTERNATIONAL ENERGY OUTLOOK 2011, Highlights 1, http://205.254.135.7/forecasts/ieo/pdf/0484(2011).pdf.

Energy Outlook 2011[36] has predicted that assuming policies and laws currently in place are not changed between now and 2035, the world will consume 53 percent more energy.[37] Energy consumption is expected to grow 18 percent in Organization for Economic Co-operation and Development (OECD)[38] countries and 85 percent in non-OECD countries.[39] This differential in rates is linked to the expected "strong long-term economic growth" in non-OECD countries.[40] Moreover, the "dynamics of energy markets" will be increasingly determined in the future by non-OECD countries.[41] For example, in 2035 it is projected that energy consumption in China will be 70 percent more than in the US despite the fact that Chinese per capita consumption will still lag the US by 50 percent.[42]

Global electricity demand is predicted to grow more rapidly than other forms of energy. In the World Energy Outlook 2010 report,[43] produced by the International Energy Agency, the "new policies scenario"[44] projects that electricity demand will increase by 2.2 percent annually between 2008 and 2035.[45] China alone, during the next 15 years, "is projected to add generating capacity equivalent to the current total installed capacity of the United

---

[36] The International Energy Outlook is produced by the US Energy Information Administration. It forecasts the outlook of the international energy market. *See* INTERNATIONAL ENERGY OUTLOOK, http://www.eia.gov/oiaf/ieo/.

[37] *See* US Energy Information Administration, *supra* note 33, at 1.

[38] The Organization for Economic Co-operation and Development, also referred to as the OECD, "promotes policies that will improve the economic and social well-being of people around the world. The OECD provides a forum in which [its 34 country members] can work together to share experiences and seek solutions to common problems. [It works] with governments to understand what drives economic, social and environmental change." *About the Organization for Economic Co-operation and Development,* OECD, http://www.oecd.org/pages/0,3417,en_36734052_36734103_1_1_1_1_1,00.html. Among member countries are Australia, Canada, Chile, France, Germany, Japan, Mexico, Spain, Turkey, the United Kingdom, and the United States. OECD, *Members and Partners,* http://www.oecd.org/document/25/0,3746,en_36734052_36761800_36999961_1_1_1_1,00.html.

[39] *See* US Energy Information Administration, *supra* note 35, at 1.

[40] *Id.*

[41] *See* International Energy Agency, *supra* note 28, at 1–2.

[42] *Id.* at 2.

[43] International Energy Agency, WORLD ENERGY OUTLOOK 2010, Executive Summary 8, available from author.

[44] The "new policies scenario" referred to in the World Energy Outlook 2010 report "takes account of the broad policy commitments and plans that have been announced by countries around the world, including the national pledges to reduce greenhouse-gas emissions and plans to phase out fossil-energy subsidies even where the measures to implement these commitments have yet to be identified or announced. These commitments are assumed to be implemented in a relatively cautious manner, reflecting their non-binding character and, in many cases, the uncertainty shrouding how they are to be put into effect." *Id.*, at 4.

[45] *Id.* at 8.

States."[46] The other large energy consumer – the United States – also faces an electricity demand challenge in the near term. "Even with increased energy efficiency over the next two decades, growing demand for power in the US could require the equivalent of 540 new coal plants or 200 new nuclear plants."[47]

The changes in overall energy type consumption over the next several decades is instructive in considering the international environmental challenges that may lie ahead. Despite the impressive annual growth rate of three percent from 2007 to 2035 in global use of renewable energy, the share of energy associated with renewables will increase only to 23 percent in 2035 from 18 percent in 2007.[48] However, the World Energy Outlook 2011 projects that non-hydro renewables, as a share of total power generation, will grow substantially to 15 percent in 2035 from three percent in 2009.[49] On the other hand the European Environment Agency predicts, "Fossil fuels will remain the most important energy source, at least until 2030, and the use of oil, gas, and coal is expected to grow in volume over this period."[50] Looked at another way, the IEA forecasts that fossil fuel use will decline only slightly from 2010 to 2035, from 81 percent to 75 percent.[51]

Improvements in energy efficiency are expected to reduce, to some extent, the overall consumption of energy.[52] It has been observed that in the European Union "energy efficiency (if not quite yet absolute energy savings) enjoys a level of political attention not seen since the oil price shocks of 1973 and 1979."[53] There is general agreement that "energy intensity"[54] "almost invariably rises during the early stages of industrialization and its peak is often fairly sharp and hence relatively short."[55] However, the "sustained reduction in energy use (especially oil use) per unit of output" while steadily improving in developed countries "has not yet materialized in the same scale in

---

[46] *Id.*

[47] Daniel Yergin, *"Stepping on the Gas,"* WALL ST. J., April 2–3, 2011, C1.

[48] *See* US Energy Information Administration, *supra* note 35, at 4.

[49] International Energy Agency, World Energy Outlook 2011, *supra* note 28, at 4. This projection assumes that renewables-related subsidies grow by nearly 500 percent to $180 billion. *Id.*

[50] European Environment Agency, *supra* note 26, at 42.

[51] International Energy Agency, WORLD ENERGY OUTLOOK 2011, *supra* note 28, at 2.

[52] DUVAL, *supra* note 22, at 3.

[53] Pernille Schiellerup, *Energy Saving is the Key to EU Energy and Climate Goals, in* GREEN, SAFE, CHEAP: WHERE NEXT FOR EU ENERGY POLICY 53 (Katinka Barysch ed., 2011).

[54] The ratio between the amount of total primary energy consumed and gross domestic product is referred to as energy intensity. J. W. Sun, *Three Types of Decline in Energy Intensity – an Explanation for the Decline of Energy Intensity in Some Developing Countries*, 31 ENERGY POL'Y 519, at 519 (2003).

[55] SMIL, *supra* note 19, at 68.

developing countries, such as China, where energy consumption is projected to continue to rise at high rates…"[56] Moreover, the World Energy Outlook 2011 reported that "global energy intensity worsened for the second straight year."[57]

The increased energy consumption will be driven by a variety of demographic and market-related reasons. One observer has written, "As population growth increases, energy must be applied more intensively to drive up labor productivity…The revolution in telecommunications and transportation during the last 30 years has made possible a global assembly line that has intensified the use of energy and labor as it both serves an expanded population and feeds its growth."[58] Moreover, nearly one billion "new consumers" from the developing world will enter the world market place before 2020.[59] "Although these consumers will have less power than their counterparts in the developed world, they will still have similar demands,"[60] including an increasing appetite for consuming energy. Looked at another way, by 2030 the size of the world's middle class is anticipated to be five billion, nearly double today's number, a surge described as "unseen since the Industrial Revolution."[61] Some of this growing middle class will happen in China, in which currently the per capita energy usage is only 1/12th of the US per capita usage and 1/6th of Japan's.[62]

Alongside the increasing use of energy, and its concomitant impacts on the environment, is the notion that as societies and their economies become more prosperous those societies ultimately demand more emphasis on environmental protection. This notion, which is called the Kuznets Curve, is a "hypothesized relationship between various indicators of environmental degradation and income per capita. In the early stages of economic growth degradation and pollution increase, but beyond some level of income per capita (which will vary for different indicators) the trend reverses, so that at high-income levels economic growth leads to environmental improvement."[63]

---

[56] Duval, *supra* note 22, at 3.

[57] International Energy Agency, World Energy Outlook 2011, *supra* note 28, at 1.

[58] Sheila D. Collins, *Closing the Boxes, Enlarging the Circles: Toward a New Paradigm of Global Governance and Economy, in* Climate Change and Environmental Ethics 79, at 83 (Ved P. Nanda ed., 2011).

[59] Ivo J. H. Bozon, Warren J. Campbell, and Mats Lindstrand, Global Trends in Energy 2 (February 2007), http://www.mckinseyquarterly.com/Global_trends_in_energy_1923.

[60] *Id.* at 2.

[61] Christa Case Bryant, *Surging BRIC Middle Classes are Eclipsing Global Poverty*, Christian Science Monitor, May 18, 2011.

[62] Chris P. Nelson and Mun S. Ho, Clearing the Air: The Health and Economic Damages of Air Pollution in China 9 (2007).

[63] David I. Stern, *The Environmental Kuznets Curve, in* the International Society for Ecological Economics Internet Encyclopaedia of Ecological Economics 1, http://www.ecoeco.org/pdf/stern.pdf.

However, there are key exceptions to this notion, not least of which are carbon dioxide emissions that continue to climb even as other environmental indicators are improving.[64]

7.2   The Evolution of Energy and Environmental Law in an International Context

The very nature of environmental problems is often underscored by the fact that they extend beyond national borders.[65] And yet, traditionally states have "opposed cross-border regulatory measures and have invoked doctrines of state sovereignty – such as permanent sovereignty over natural resources – as bulwarks against cross-border regulatory efforts relating to environmental matters."[66]

Moreover, the regulation of energy has historically been done at a national level[67] including in the supranational-based European Union.[68] Despite the state-centric manner in which this sector has been regulated, however, "the energy and electricity sectors have become international...."[69]

---

[64] James David Fahn, A LAND ON FIRE: THE ENVIRONMENTAL CONSEQUENCES OF THE SOUTHEAST ASIAN BOOM 36 (2003).

[65] Michael Faure, Morag Goodwin, Franziska Weber, *Bucking the Kuznets Curve: Designing Effective Environmental Regulation in Developing Countries*, 51 VA. J. INT'L LAW 95 (2010).

[66] *Id.*

[67] THOMAS W. WÄLDE, INTERNATIONAL ENERGY LAW: CONCEPTS, CONTEXT AND PLAYERS 1 (2001) (provisional first draft for book), http://www.dundee.ac.uk/cepmlp/journal/html/vol9/article9-21.pdf.

[68] Dieter Helm, *What Next for EU Energy Policy*, GREEN, SAFE, CHEAP – WHERE NEXT FOR EU ENERGY POLICY 13 (Katinka Barysch ed., 2011). Notwithstanding the fact that much regulation in the EU continues at member state level one observer has suggested, "The European Union constitutes at present the most developed laboratory for international regulation of energy. It is not really possible to study international energy law without familiarity with EU energy law. Here, all the themes of the global economy have been played out: The dialectical tension between narrow and often myopic national self-interests and the interest of everybody to activate the wealth machine of regional economic integration has been producing, in particular since 1985 (start of the internal market programme) a large array of EU legislation...which address free-trade, free investment, non-discriminatory access to energy resources by licensing, free cross-border transit, access to energy transport facilities, non-discriminatory procurement by state agencies, enterprises and energy utilities and the application of competition law against predatory behavior based on dominant market power." Thomas W. Wälde, *International Energy Law – An Introduction to Modern Concepts, Context, Policy, and Players*, in HANDBUCH RECHT DER ENERGIEWIRTSCHAFT 1127, at 1135 (Dr. Jens-Peter Schneider and Dr. Christian Theobald eds., 2003).

[69] Nick Butler and Ian Pearson, *The Water Industry Must Take on the World*, FIN. TIMES, August 17, 2011.

To grasp international law as it relates to energy and the environment, it is necessary to understand that international energy law – as a discreet subject – did not exist until about 1970. One prominent writer has suggested that until that time, "There were nationally segregated electricity, coal, and nuclear industries. Oil was the only exception as it had to be shipped from far-away producing countries.... As there was no substance matter for international law to regulate, such international law did not exist. What existed were general rules of mainly customary international law which impacted on the industry's international investment [practices]...."[70]

On the other hand, in more recent years there have been developments indicating that a state's total independence to develop energy resources may be limited by international law. In other words, "Within the state-centric paradigm, environmental problems become legally relevant when activities within one state inflict significant harm within the territory of another."[71] One observer has written, "It is now a settled rule of international law that state sovereignty over natural resources is subject to a corresponding responsibility to ensure that activities within their jurisdiction or under their control do not cause damage to the environment of other states or areas beyond the limits of national jurisdiction."[72] The aim of international environmental law in this context is to "strike a balance between territorial integrity and territorial sovereignty, since neither can be absolute in the environmental context. This goal is reflected in the obligation not to cause significant transboundary harm, which represents a 'cornerstone' of international environmental law."[73] Moreover, on occasion states may accept voluntarily "restrictions on their sovereignty over natural resources by ratifying instruments which require them to pursue defined environmental objectives and/or to minimize environmental degradation."[74]

In summary, states obviously remain central in today's governance scheme. Nevertheless, it has been suggested that states now are "more porous not only economically but also environmentally. Consequently, it is increasingly difficult to draw a clear separation between international and domestic environmental policy."[75] Issues related to climate change present a stark reminder of

---

[70] Wälde, *supra* note 68, at 1129.

[71] Daniel Bodansky, Jutta Burnnée, Ellen Hey, The Oxford Handbook of International Environmental Law 9 (2007).

[72] Clare Shine, *Environmental Protection Under the Energy Charter Treaty, in* The Energy Charter Treaty 520, at 520 (Thomas W. Wälde ed., 1996).

[73] Bodansky, *supra* note 71, at 9.

[74] Shine, *supra* note 7, at 523.

[75] Bodansky, *supra* note 71, at 18.

this: "[Climate change] has implications for virtually ever aspect of domestic policy [including] energy, transportation, construction, land use."[76]

A significant problem involving energy and environmental law in an international context is how to prevent one state from harming another state through the former's energy policies. This may be reflected in a number of ways, perhaps most strikingly in the concept of environmental externalities.[77] In this regard several experts have asserted, "To the extent that a country is able to 'externalize' the costs of polluting, it has no economic incentive to stop. The no-harm rule is meant to address this problem, by prohibiting one state from imposing significant environmental costs on another. Although the no-harm principle has...achieved canonical status, in practice it is not consistently applied to resolve specific environmental disputes by courts or tribunals...Even the massive transboundary pollution caused by [the] Chernobyl and Sandoz accidents did not lead to legal claims by the victim states."[78]

7.3   *International Law Related to Energy and the Environment*

7.3.1   *Introduction*

This section will explore three sectors where international law has begun playing a role vis-à-vis energy and the environment. While international regulation in these sectors is relatively new, consideration of them provides context in which to understand how concern about how energy-related pollution can be the basis for a multinational regulatory framework. The three

---

[76] *Id.*

[77] "Environmental externalities refer to the economic concept of uncompensated environmental effects of production and consumption that affect consumer utility and enterprise cost outside the market mechanism. As a consequence of negative externalities, private costs of production tend to be lower than its 'social' cost." United Nations, GLOSSARY OF ENVIRONMENT STATISTICS, Studies in Methods, Series F., No. 67 (1997). In the context of a coal-fired electricity plant, externalities have been described in this manner: "The emission of pollutants such as sulfur dioxide, nitrogen oxides and particulate matter from [coal-fired power plants] causes damages to the environment and society not only in the vicinity of the [power plant] but also in distant areas, even in other countries, that are in the trajectory of pollutants dispersion. The term 'externalities' is widely used to express the costs of these damages. Nowadays, external costs resulting from certain damages [such as these] are not reflected in the market prices of the [electricity]." Lucyna Czarnowska, Christos A. Frangopoulos, *Dispersion of Pollutants, Environmental Externalities Due to a Pulverized Coal Power Plant and their Effect on the Cost of Electricity*, Vol. 41 Issue 1 ENERGY 212 (2012).

[78] BODANSKY, *supra* note 71, at 9.

sectors are nuclear power, marine oil spills from tanker vessels, and investment in energy facilities bearing in mind environmental considerations.

7.3.2   *Nuclear Energy*

7.3.2.1   *Overview*

Nuclear generated electricity plays a major role in meeting global power
demands. Looked at in context, in 2008 nuclear power generated about 14
percent of the world's electricity; in 2020 it is projected to generate about
14.6 percent before declining slightly to 13.9 percent in 2035.[79] The electricity provided by nuclear energy is considered reliable and continuous
available "base-load" power.[80] In April 2011, 437 nuclear reactors were operating around the globe.[81] As of late 2011, 65 nuclear reactors were under
construction,[82] the highest number since 1988.[83] In 2010 alone, work began
on 15 new nuclear plants in what has been described as "the largest new
construction starts since 1985."[84]

However, the industry has always been plagued by doubts about its safety
and impact on the environment. The Three Mile Island accident, which took
place in the US in 1979, "served notice on the nuclear authorities in many
countries that a major nuclear accident at a large nuclear power plant was
not simply a remote contingency suitable for theoretical studies, but a real
possibility that nuclear authorities must do everything in their power to
avoid..."[85] Seven years later, the Chernobyl nuclear accident in the former
Soviet Union raised questions once more about "the adequacy of national
and international regulation of nuclear facilities. It showed how limited were
the powers of the International Atomic Energy Agency [*see* Section 7.3.2.3

---

[79] US Energy Information Administration, INTERNATIONAL ENERGY OUTLOOK 2011 86,
http://www.eia.gov/forecasts/ieo/pdf/0484%282011%29.pdf (Table 11: OECD and non-
OECD Net Electricity Generation by Source 2008–2035).

[80] World Nuclear Association, Nuclear Power in the World Today (February 2011), http://
www.world-nuclear.org/info/inf01.html.

[81] MYCLE SCHNEIDER, ANTONY FROGGATT, STEVE THOMAS, THE WORLD NUCLEAR INDUSTRY
STATUS REPORT 2010–2011 – NUCLEAR POWER IN A POST-FUKUSHIMA WORLD 7 (2011),
http://www.worldwatch.org/system/files/WorldNuclearIndustryStatusReport2011_%20
FINAL.pdf.

[82] *Power Reactor Information System,* IAEA http://www.iaea.org/programmes/a2/.

[83] Mycle Schneider, Antony Froggatt, and Steve Thomas, *2010–2011 World Nuclear Industry
Status Report,* 67(4) BULLETIN OF THE ATOMIC SCIENTISTS 60, at 60 (2011).

[84] Board of Governors, Annual Report 2010, International Atomic Energy, Association (2011),
Overview 1, http://www.iaea.org/Publications/Reports/Anrep2010/overview.pdf.

[85] DAVID FISCHER, HISTORY OF THE INTERNATIONAL ATOMIC ENERGY AGENCY – THE FIRST
FORTY YEARS, INTERNATIONAL ATOMIC ENERGY AGENCY 191 (1997), http://www-pub.iaea
.org/MTCD/publications/PDF/Pub1032_web.pdf.

below] and how little agreement existed on questions of liability and state responsibility."[86] In reaction to the Chernobyl accident, two international treaties[87] were agreed to, although neither directly addressed the energy-environment nexus.

In the mid-1990s the international community came together to agree on two nuclear power-related treaties that did have environmental protection as a centerpiece. As one observer has noted, "... [I]t was not until the adoption of the Conventions on Nuclear Safety [*see* Section 7.3.2.3.1 below] and the Safety of Spent Fuel and Radioactive Waste Management [*see* Section 7.3.2.3.2 below] in 1994 and 1997 that binding minimum standards for environmental protection could be... assured. These treaties have codified much of the customary international law relating to nuclear activities..."[88]

Between the late 1980s and early 2011, nuclear power was viewed as a cornerstone in some countries' energy strategy. It still is in countries such as France, which derives more than 75 percent of its power from nuclear generation.[89] As recently as three years ago, energy experts wrote that one of the diversification strategies that energy consuming countries had developed was "the promotion and use of nuclear energy for power generation in the wake of high oil prices and global warming concerns."[90]

Until the March 2011 nuclear power plant disaster at Fukushima Daiichi[91] in Japan, many speculated that nuclear power was about to enjoy a significant upswing. A report in the Financial Times said, "With fossil fuels become more expensive, concern about the threat of global warming remaining high, and many renewable methods still unproven as large sources of electricity, this should have been nuclear's moment. Reactor suppliers... were looking forward to a 'nuclear renaissance' of investment in new reactors..."[92] However, the disaster at Fukushima may dim that slightly. For example, the German government decided in 2011 to phase out all nuclear generation

---

[86] Patricia Birnie, Alan Boyle, Catherine Redgwell, International Law and the Environment 3rd Edition 492 (2009).

[87] They were the Convention on Assistance in the Case of a Nuclear Accident or Radiological Emergency, http://www.iaea.org/Publications/Documents/Infcircs/Others/infcirc336.shtml and the Convention on the Early Notification of a Nuclear Accident, http://www.iaea.org/Publications/Documents/Infcircs/Others/infcirc335.shtml.

[88] Birnie, *supra* note 86, at 493.

[89] *See* World Nuclear Association, *Nuclear Power in France,* http://www.world-nuclear.org/info/inf40.html.

[90] Duval, *supra* note 22, at 11.

[91] A detailed review of what happened at Fukushima is provided in the IAEA Mission report of June 16, 2011, http://www-pub.iaea.org/MTCD/Meetings/PDFplus/2011/cn200/documentation/cn200_Final-Fukushima-Mission_Report.pdf.

[92] Ed Crooks and Sylvia Pfeifer, *Nuclear Power: Atomised Approach,* Fin. Times, June 6, 2011.

by 2022.[93] However, this decision has not been without its own problems. "Less nuclear power also means [Germany's] grid is less stable – authorities narrowly averted a blackout in February [2012] that could have had consequences across Europe," according to the Financial Times.[94] Nevertheless, the long-term impact of Fukushima seems negligible [*see* Section 7.3.2.3.3 below].

7.3.2.2   *International Environmental Law in Relation to Nuclear Energy*

Addressing nuclear safety in an international context is essential because of the underlying risks associated with a nuclear accident as well as the potential of radiation from an accident spreading indiscriminately over a large area. "Nuclear accidents respect no borders," International Atomic Energy Agency Director General Yukiya Amano has said.[95] Looked at another way "…[N]uclear power creates unavoidable risks for all states, whether or not they choose to use this form of energy…International law is capable of moderating these ultra-hazardous risks by assuring stronger regulation, more effective multilateral oversight, and enhanced provision for liability and compensation in cases of transboundary damage. Such a policy entails limitations on the freedom of states to conduct hazardous activities within their own territory which they have sometimes been reluctant to endorse, but it represents a price which may have to be paid if nuclear energy is to remain internationally accepted."[96]

7.3.2.3   *The International Atomic Energy Agency*

The International Atomic Energy Agency (IAEA) was founded in 1956. It is "an independent intergovernmental, science and technology-based organization, in the United Nations family, that serves as the global focal point for nuclear cooperation" including in the area of electricity generation.[97] It has 154 member states.[98]

At the time of the founding of the IAEA "it was widely believed that the benefits [of nuclear energy] outweighed the risk and could be shared by all.

---

[93] Melissa Eddy, *Merkel Defends Germany's Nuclear Power Deadline*, N.Y. Times, March 13, 2012, http://www.nytimes.com/2012/03/13/world/europe/merkel-offers-defense-of-her-policy-on-energy.html.

[94] Joshua Chaffin, *Clean Power Needs Serious Investment*, FT Report: The Future of the European Union, Fin. Times, May 9, 2012, at 4.

[95] Speech by IAEA Director General Yukiya Amano, June 20, 2011, http://www.iaea.org/newscenter/statements/2011/amsp2011n013.html.

[96] Birnie, *supra* note 86 at 488.

[97] *Mission Statement*, IAEA http://www.iaea.org/About/mission.html.

[98] *Member States*, IAEA, http://www.iaea.org/About/Policy/MemberStates/.

This optimistic view was reflected in international policy."[99] One of the IAEA's objectives was, and continues to be to facilitate and encourage the adoption of nuclear power.[100] As one expert has written, "The prevalent belief [at the IAEA's founding] was that the health and environmental risks could be managed successfully by governments and the IAEA through cooperation on safety matters."[101]

As early as in the 1960s, the Agency's Secretariat began trying to persuade nuclear regulators as well as the industry to adopt a nuclear power safety-related international convention to establish "minimum uniform and global standards for an activity that lay at the centre of the civilian uses of nuclear energy."[102] However, it would not be until the mid-1990s when the Convention on Nuclear Safety[103] was adopted.

Despite the fact that the amount of nuclear powered electricity has grown substantially since the 1950s, the work of the IAEA came under scrutiny even before the Fukushima Daiichi disaster. One observer wrote, "The IAEA is already badly overstretched and needs to be considerably strengthened to address the need for monitoring and safeguarding what is likely to be an explosion in the number and size of nuclear energy programs, particularly in Asia."[104]

The IAEA serves as the secretariat for the Contracting Parties to the Convention on Nuclear Safety[105] and to the Joint Convention on the Safety of Spent Fuel Management and on the Safety of Radioactive Waste Management.[106] In addition, under the two conventions the IAEA plays a major role in establishing standards for nuclear safety and nuclear waste management. Despite having been characterized as "relatively conservative"[107] in terms of regulating nuclear risks, one observer has written that, "Their most

---

[99] BIRNIE, *supra* note 86, at 489.

[100] *See* Statute of the International Atomic Energy Agency, Art. II Objectives, http://www.iaea .org/About/statute_text.html#A1.2. It is also worth noting, however, that another key IAEA objective is to "ensure that nuclear power [is] used for peaceful purposes only." BIRNIE, supra note 77, at 490. *See also* Statute of the International Atomic Energy Agency, Arts. II, III. For the purposes of this chapter, discussion will focus on nuclear power.

[101] BIRNIE, *supra* note 86, at 489.

[102] FISCHER, *supra* note 85, at 216–217.

[103] Convention on Nuclear Safety, http://www.iaea.org/Publications/Documents/Infcircs/ Others/inf449.shtml.

[104] Florini, *supra* note 15, at 60.

[105] Convention on Nuclear Safety, Art. 28, http://www.iaea.org/Publications/Documents/ Infcircs/Others/inf449.shtml.

[106] Joint Convention on the Safety of Spent Fuel Management and on the Safety of Radioactive Waste Management, Art. 37, http://www.iaea.org/Publications/Documents/Infcircs/1997/ infcirc546.pdf.

[107] BIRNIE, *supra* note 86, at 500.

important feature, however, is that for the first time they give binding treaty status to some of IAEA's most fundamental standards of nuclear safety law affecting most aspects of civil nuclear reactors, radioactive waste management, and spent fuel disposal and reprocessing."[108]

7.3.2.3.1   1994 Convention on Nuclear Safety

The Convention on Nuclear Safety (the "Convention") was adopted June 17, 1994, following an IAEA-organized diplomatic conference. It entered into force in 1996.[109] The convention was "the first international document that legally binds its parties to ensure the safety of land-based civilian nuclear reactors."[110] However, equally as important is the convention's admonition that "responsibility for nuclear safety rests with the State having jurisdiction over a nuclear installation."[111]

The Convention has been described as taking "a significant step towards defining the obligations of states operating nuclear installations, but only in fairly general terms."[112] On the other hand, in terms of recognizing the IAEA's safety standards "it can be seen as an elaboration of the general rule of customary international law regarding diligent regulation and control of potentially harmful activities in accordance with Principle 2 of the Rio Declaration and other precedents..."[113]

One of the Convention's key objectives is to "maintain a high level of nuclear safety in civil nuclear power plants and related facilities" through "enhancing national measures and international cooperation."[114] In this regard, the Statute of the IAEA provides that the agency "establish or adopt...standards of safety for protection of health and minimization of danger to life and property" associated with radiation exposure.[115] However, the Statute does not mandate that member states implement or comply with these standards.[116]

Despite the non-mandatory nature of the safety standards, "In practice...many IAEA standards are relied upon by states in developing and

---

[108] BIRNIE, *supra* note 86, at 500.
[109] Convention on Nuclear Safety, http://www.iaea.org/Publications/Documents/Conventions/nuclearsafety.html.
[110] FISCHER, *supra* note 85, at 217.
[111] Convention on Nuclear Safety, Preamble iii, http://www.iaea.org/Publications/Documents/Infcircs/Others/inf449.shtml.
[112] BIRNIE, *supra* note 86, at 501.
[113] *Id.*
[114] *Id.*
[115] Statute of the IAEA, Art. III A. 6, http://www.iaea.org/About/statute_text.html#A1.3.
[116] BIRNIE, *supra* note 86, at 495.

implementing national legislation and standards."[117] Moreover, the standards have "resulted in an appreciable degree of harmonization" as well as made "a significant contribution to controlling the risks of nuclear energy."[118] One observer has said, "…IAEA nuclear safety standards are considered to be the cornerstone for an international nuclear safety and security mechanism [that] provides the basis for states to perform their duties relating to nuclear safety."[119]

If an installation is operated by a private firm, the responsibility – such as it is – for nuclear safety and damage to the environment remains with the state.[120] However, the issue of whether a state might be liable for the breach of its obligations under the Convention "regarding nuclear safety under public international law is conspicuously left open."[121]

Interestingly enough, following the Chernobyl disaster IAEA member states considered requiring minimum reactor safety standards in order to strengthen international nuclear power regulation. However, agreement on this idea could not be reached for practical and political reasons.[122] On one hand, anticipated financial burdens associated with minimum safety standards loomed, while on the other was a reluctance to relinquish any national sovereignty.[123] In more recent times, Russia has unsuccessfully asserted that the safety standards be made mandatory.[124]

According to the IAEA, the obligation set forth in Articles 5 and 20 of the Convention for the contracting parties to submit for peer review reports explaining measures they have taken to implement the Convention's obligations "is the main innovative and dynamic element of the Convention."[125] This is in keeping with the IAEA's view that the Convention "is an incentive instrument" rather than an agreement "designed to ensure fulfillment of obligations by parties through control and sanction…"[126] Among other things, the purpose of the peer review meetings is to "identify problems,

---

[117] PHILIPPE SANDS, PRINCIPLES OF INTERNATIONAL ENVIRONMENTAL LAW 641 (2d ed., 2003).

[118] BIRNIE, *supra* note 86, at 496.

[119] Sayed Zeidan, *The Procedural Rules and Obligations Under International Law for Construction of a Nuclear Installation: Prevention and Reduction of Environmental Damage*, 23 GEO. INT'L ENVTL. L. REV. 263, 286 (2011).

[120] *Id.* at 287.

[121] *Id.* at 288.

[122] BIRNIE, *supra* note 86, at 499.

[123] *Id.*

[124] Crooks, *supra* note 92.

[125] *International Conventions & Agreements*, IAEA, http://www.iaea.org/Publications/Documents/Conventions/nuclearsafety.html.

[126] *Id.*

concerns, uncertainties, or omissions in national reports, focusing on the most significant problems or concerns in order to ensure efficient and fruitful debate at the meetings; and identify technical information and opportunities for technical cooperation in the interest of resolving safety problems identified."[127] However, this "mechanism" has been criticized for a lack of transparency. First, non-governmental organizations are omitted from the process.[128] Second, "Although a summary of discussions and conclusions must be made public, individual countries will not be named and the content of peer reviews must remain confidential."[129]

Finally, the IAEA has little authority to perform the role of a nuclear safety inspectorate unless it is asked to by a member state.[130] The Convention contains "no explicit obligations relating to the inspection of nuclear installations."[131] As a result, "Compulsory inspections are possible only where an assistance agreement with the [IAEA] is in force, and in practice this power is rarely used."[132] However, governments can find the inspections quite useful when they are undertaken because of their "independence and reassurance."[133]

7.3.2.3.2   1997 Joint Convention on the Safety of Spent Fuel Management and on the Safety of Radioactive Waste Management

The Joint Convention on the Safety of Spent Fuel Management and on the Safety of Radioactive Waste Management (the "Joint Convention"),[134] which entered into force June 18, 2001,[135] "is the only multilateral international agreement concerning the safety of the management of radioactive waste and spent fuel."[136] As stated by the IAEA, "The Joint Convention applies to spent fuel and radioactive waste resulting from civilian nuclear reactors and applications and to spent fuel and radioactive waste from military or defense

---

[127] Convention on Nuclear Safety, Annex to the Final Act of the Diplomatic Conference, paragraph 3, http://www.iaea.org/Publications/Documents/Infcircs/Others/inf449a1.shtml.

[128] Birnie, *supra* note 86, at 502–503.

[129] Statute of the IAEA, Art. XII, http://www.iaea.org/About/statute_text.html#A1.12.

[130] Birnie, *supra* note 86, at 502–503.

[131] Zeidan, *supra* note 119, at 287.

[132] Birnie, *supra* note 86, at 497–498. *See* IAEA Statute, Art. 12, http://www.iaea.org/About/statute_text.html#A1.12.

[133] Birnie, *supra* note 86, at 498.

[134] Joint Convention on the Safety of Spent Fuel Management and on the Safety of Radioactive Waste Management, Art. 37, http://www.iaea.org/Publications/Documents/Infcircs/1997/infcirc546.pdf.

[135] *International Conventions & Agreements*, IAEA, http://www.iaea.org/Publications/Documents/Conventions/jointconv.html.

[136] Ana Stanič, *A Step Closer to EU Law on the Management of Radioactive Waste and Spent Fuel*, Issue 29 No. 1 J. Energy & Nat. Resources L. 117, 124 (2011).

programs if and when such materials are transferred permanently to and managed with exclusively civilian programs...The [Joint] Convention also applied to planned and controlled releases into the environment of liquid or gaseous radioactive materials from regulated nuclear facilities."[137] The Joint Convention's objectives include "ensuring high safety standards and prevention of accidents."[138]

The Joint Convention "gives somewhat greater effect to IAEA...soft law in setting minimum standards for national regulation" than the Nuclear Safety Convention.[139] In this regard, "Not only must national law provide 'effective' protection for individuals, society, and the environment, it must also give 'due regard to international endorsed criteria and standards.' This formulation does not make IAEA...soft law binding on parties to the Joint Convention, but it strengthens the view that nuclear soft law is particularly relevant in deciding whether states have taken the 'appropriate steps' required by the principal provision of the Convention."[140]

Despite the fact that the Joint Convention has "resulted in a significant harmonization of national rules" related to managing spent fuel and radioactive waste, the requirements and standards developed by the IAEA "are binding for the IAEA's own activities and a contracting state's activities in operations assisted by the IAEA. However, neither the Joint Convention for the IAEA guides, standards, and principles provide for any sanctions for non-compliance and contain no mechanism for enforcement..."[141] Moreover, there is no requirement about how long-term management of waste should be handled by national programs or for decision-making to involve the public.[142]

Notwithstanding the Joint Convention's shortcomings in relation to lack of an enforcement mechanism, the situation is changing in the European Union. In September 2011, legislation requiring binding standards for managing radioactive waste entered force.[143] European Commissioner for Energy

---

[137] *International Conventions & Agreements*, IAEA http://www.iaea.org/Publications/ Documents/Conventions/jointconv.html.

[138] Birnie, *supra* note 86, at 503.

[139] *Id.* at 504.

[140] *Id.*

[141] Stanič, *supra* note 136, at 132–133.

[142] *Id.*

[143] European Union Council Directive 12142/11 (July 12, 2011), http://register.consilium .europa.eu/pdf/en/11/st12/st12142.en11.pdf. It is worth noting that the directive was adopted by the Council of the EU based on the European Atomic Energy Community (Euratom) Treaty, not the Treaty of Lisbon. As a consequence, the European Parliament played only a limited legislative role. Stephen Gardner, *EU Finalizes Requirements for National Plans on Management, Disposal of Nuclear Waste*, 34 Int'l Env't Rep. (BNA) (August 17, 2011).

Günther Oettinger said, "With this directive, the EU becomes the most advanced region for the safe management of radioactive waste and spent fuel."[144] The legislation has two key elements: First, IAEA safety standards are legally binding on EU member states; second, member states are required to regularly undertake "peer reviews," the results of which will be made available to the European Commission.[145]

7.3.2.3.3   Post-Fukushima Daiichi Disaster

In the wake of the Fukushima Daiichi disaster – that IAEA Director General Yukiya Amano described as having "caused deep public anxiety throughout the world and damaged confidence in nuclear power"[146] – the role of nuclear energy looks different than it did the day before the disaster. But perhaps not that much different. As one expert has noted, "In the aftermath of the Japanese nuclear incident...countries around the world have started to reconsider their stance towards nuclear power...Another de facto nuclear moratorium would make the task of controlling climate change even more difficult. Nuclear power is not risk free, but the associated risks are lower and more manageable than the risk of uncontrolled climate change."[147] Moreover, IAEA Director General Amano told the 55th Regular Session of the IAEA General Conference in the autumn of 2011, "It is clear that there will, in fact, be continuous and significant growth in the use of nuclear power in the next two decades, although at a slower rate than our previous projections." He went on to predict that the number of reactors worldwide would increase somewhere between 90 and 350 by 2030.[148] On the other hand, some in the industry characterized Fukushima as a "visible, visceral setback."[149]

The matter of whether there should be some type of global regulation of the industry and whether the IAEA should be a nuclear safety inspectorate remain highly disputed ones. An official with the World Nuclear Association, an industry advocacy group, said in the summer of 2011 that global

---

[144] European Commission, Nuclear waste: Commission welcomes adoption of radioactive waste directive (July 19, 2011), http://europa.eu/rapid/pressReleasesAction.do?reference=IP/11/906&format=HTML&aged=0&language=EN&guiLanguage=en.

[145] *Id.*

[146] Yukiya Amano, Statement to the 55th Regular Session of the IAEA General Conference 2011 (September 19, 2011), http://www.iaea.org/newscenter/statements/2011/amsp2011n021.html.

[147] Stephen Tindale, *Europe Needs Nuclear Power, in* GREEN, SAFE, CHEAP – WHERE NEXT FOR EU ENERGY POLICY 73 (Katinka Barysch ed., 2011).

[148] Amano, *supra* note 146.

[149] Crooks, *supra* note 92 (quoting Jim Ellis, president of the Institute of Nuclear Power Operations, a US-based industry group).

regulation would result in "the worst common system."[150] Meanwhile, an executive with a nuclear fuel supplier noted during the same timeframe, "I'm not saying that the IAEA doesn't have a role, but I find it hard to see that it could be a regulator."[151]

7.3.2.3.4   Summary
Despite the fact that most of the IAEA's standards are not mandatory, "In practice...many IAEA standards are relied upon by states in developing and implementing national legislation and standards."[152] Moreover, in September 2011 the IAEA General Conference endorsed an IAEA Action Plan on Nuclear Safety,[153] a first-ever document that was the direct result of the Agency's reaction to Fukushima. However, whether individual member states actually implement the plan, which emphasizes nuclear safety transparency,[154] remains to be seen.

7.3.3   *Marine Oil Pollution From Ships*

7.3.3.1   *Overview*
Oil tanker accidents or spillage represent a major risk to the oceans of the world. This is especially so since "the vast majority of oil transported on the world's oceans is shipped via tankers..."[155] The amount of crude oil carried on tankers is staggering. For example, 1.8 billion tons of crude oil was shipped across the oceans in 2010.[156] The largest "loading area" was Western Asia. The oil was destined for the "major unloading areas" including Europe, Japan, North America, and East and South Asia.[157] Moreover the growth in world oil demand is expected to continue to grow,[158] thus necessitating even more oceanic oil shipping. The size of the fleet of oil tankers at the end of the

---

[150]   *Id.*

[151]   *Id.*

[152]   SANDS, *supra* note 117, at 641.

[153]   IAEA, IAEA Nuclear Safety Action Plan Approved by General Conference (Sept. 22, 2011), http://www.iaea.org/newscenter/news/2011/actionplan.html.

[154]   *Id.*

[155]   Michael A. de Gennaro, *Oil Pollution Liability and Control Under International Maritime Law: Market Incentives as an Alternative to Government Regulation*, 37 VAND. J. TRANSNAT'L L. 265, 266 (2004).

[156]   UNITED NATIONS CONFERENCE ON TRADE AND DEVELOPMENT, REVIEW OF MARITIME TRANSPORT 2011, 14, http://unctad.org/en/docs/rmt2011_en.pdf.

[157]   *Id.*

[158]   *See, e.g.*, Ed Crooks, *Shell Chief Warns of Year of Energy Volatility*, FIN. TIMES, September 21, 2011; US Energy Information Administration, *supra* note 35, at 1–2.

last century was also daunting as well, with nearly 7,000 vessels ranging from 76,000 tons to 175,000 tons of capacity traversing the world's oceans.[159]

The international community's response to the high risks associated with marine oil pollution as well as the on-going demand for seaborne oil has been the enactment of two "super statutes," known collectively as the International Convention on Civil Liability for Oil Pollution Damage, 1992.[160] In addition, there is corresponding law dealing with claims for marine oil pollution damage, the International Convention on the Establishment of an International Fund for Compensation for Oil Pollution Damage.[161]

7.3.3.2   Developments Leading Up to International Regulation of Marine Oil Spills

Enactment of oil pollution regulation is hardly a new phenomenon. In the 19th century countries in Europe as well as the United States regulated oil pollution.[162] Modern-day regulation would not be put into place, however, until the late 1960s following the 1967 Torrey Canyon spill.[163] Torrey Canyon, which was transporting crude oil from the Persian Gulf to southwest England, encountered a reef, ran aground, and leaked 30,500 tons of oil,[164] which was the largest marine oil spill – at that time – in history.[165]

At the time of the Torrey Canyon spill no comprehensive liability or compensation scheme at international level was in place to address oil tanker spillage. William O'Neil, former Secretary General of the International Maritime Organization, has written, "If an accident occurred the question as to whether any person or government could sue for resulting damage was a matter solely regulated by the internal law, if any, of the state affected by the incident."[166] Moreover, legal obligations to insure against pollution liability did not exist thus making even a successful claim for damages potentially

---

[159] de Gennaro, *supra* note 155, at 266.

[160] International Convention on Civil Liability for Oil Pollution Damage, 1992, http://www .iopcfund.org/npdf/Conventions%20English.pdf.

[161] International Convention on the Establishment of an International Fund for Compensation for Oil Pollution Damage, 1992, http://www.iopcfund.org/npdf/Conventions%20 English.pdf.

[162] de Gennaro, *supra* note 155, at 269.

[163] Robin J. Law, *The Torrey Canyon Oil Spill 1967, in* OIL SPILL SCIENCE AND TECHNOLOGY 1103 (Mervin Fingas, ed., 2011).

[164] *Id.*

[165] de Gennaro, *supra* note 155, at 269.

[166] William O'Neil, *The International Compensation Regime from an IMO Perspective, in* THE INTERNATIONAL OIL POLLUTION COMPENSATION FUNDS 2010 ANNUAL REPORT 29 (2010).

unrecoverable if the ship owner lacked sufficient resources to pay the injured party.[167]

The Torrey Canyon accident thus revealed "that no proper legislation governing liability and compensation for such events existed either nationally or internationally."[168] Environmental organizations, shipping interests, and governments all generally agreed on the need for a "uniform international regime" to handle oil spills at sea.[169] The alternative – no international regulation – would mean "a system of unilateral national legislation under which ships, cargoes, and insurers might be subjected to different and uncoordinated laws in different countries. This was clearly undesirable for an industry as global as shipping…"[170]

The ultimate consequence was the adoption of two laws, the 1969 International Convention on Civil Liability for Oil Pollution Damage[171] and subsequently the 1971 International Convention on the Establishment of an International Fund for Compensation for Oil Pollution Damage.[172]

7.3.3.3   *International Environmental Law in Relation to Marine Oil Spills*

The 1982 UN Convention on the Law of the Sea Article 235[173] establishes the duty of states to cooperate "in the development of international law relating to liability and compensation for pollution damage and criteria and procedures to ensure adequate compensation for such damage."[174] The International Convention on Civil Liability for Oil Pollution Damage and the International Convention on the Establishment of an International Fund for Compensation of Oil Pollution Damage have been described as "…two

---

[167] *Id.*

[168] Mans Jacobsson, *The International Liability and Compensation Regime for Oil Pollution From Ships – International Solutions for a Global Problem*, 32 TUL. MAR. L.J. 1, 2 (2007).

[169] Thomas Mensah, The IOPC Funds: How it All Started, The International Compensation Regime 25 Years On 45, at 45–46 (2003), http://www.iopcfund.org/npdf/jub_en.pdf.

[170] *Id.*

[171] 1969 International Convention on Civil Liability for Oil Pollution Damage, http://www.admiraltylawguide.com/conven/civilpol1969.html. For further background *see also CLC*, http://www.imo.org/About/Conventions/ListOfConventions/Pages/International-Convention-on-Civil-Liability-for-Oil-Pollution-Damage-(CLC).aspx.

[172] 1971 International Convention on the Establishment of an International Fund for Compensation for Oil Pollution Damage, http://www.admiraltylawguide.com/conven/oilpolfund1971.html. For further background *see also FUND*, http://www.imo.org/about/conventions/listofconventions/pages/international-convention-on-the-establishment-of-an-international-fund-for-compensation-for-oil-pollution-damage-(fund).aspx.

[173] UN Convention on the Law of the Sea, http://www.un.org/depts/los/convention_agreements/texts/unclos/unclos_e.pdf.

[174] Jacobsson, *supra* note 168, at 32.

well-developed and well-applied international instruments…"[175] These two conventions principally regulate civil liability arising from marine oil pollution.[176] Meanwhile, with respect to the "Compensation" Conventions, "Through the decisions of member states in the governing bodies of the [Compensation] Funds on matters of principle relating to the admissibility of compensation claims and the adoption of admissibility criteria, the Funds contribute to the development of international law."[177] Thomas Mensah, former Assistant Secretary-General of the IMO, has gone so far as to say that the Compensation Funds are "the first practical implementation of this provision"[178] of the Law of the Sea Convention.

7.3.3.4   *International Maritime Organization*

The International Maritime Organization (IMO), which was established in 1948, is a United Nations agency responsible for shipping-related security and safety as well preventing ship-caused marine pollution.[179] The IMO's Mission Statement, as set out in its Strategic Plan for the period 2010–2015, includes promoting "…environmentally sound…shipping through cooperation. This will be accomplished by…prevention and control of pollution from ships, as well as through consideration of the related legal matters and effective implementation of IMO's instruments with a view to their universal and uniform application."[180]

The IMO oversees or was directly involved in the development of a number of oil pollution-related conventions including the International Convention on Oil Pollution Preparedness, Response and Co-operation,[181] which entered into force in 1995, as well as the International Convention on Civil Liability for Oil Pollution Damage [*see* Section 7.3.4.1] and the International Convention on the Establishment of an International Fund for Compensation of Oil Pollution Damage [*see* Section 7.3.4.2].

---

[175] SANDS, *supra* note 117, at 913.

[176] *Id.*

[177] Jacobsson, *supra* note 168, at 32.

[178] Mensah, *supra* note 169, at 48–49.

[179] International Maritime Organization, Introduction to the IMO, http://www.imo.org/About/Pages/Default.aspx.

[180] Strategic Plan for the [IMO], Resolution A.1011(26) Annex 3 (2010), http://www.imo.org/About/strategy/Documents/1011.pdf.

[181] *See* International Convention on Oil Pollution Preparedness, Response, and Co-operation, http://www.imo.org/about/conventions/listofconventions/pages/international-convention-on-oil-pollution-preparedness,-response-and-co-operation-(oprc).aspx.

7.3.3.4.1   International Convention on Civil Liability for Oil Pollution Damage, 1992[182]

In 1969, in the wake of the Torrey Canyon oil spill, the Intergovernmental Maritime Consultative Organization (now called the International Maritime Organization) convened a gathering that resulted in the adoption of the first international civil liability code for damage caused by oil pollution from tankers. In that measure, the International Convention on Civil Liability for Oil Pollution Damage of 1969 (CLC 1969), "…basic principles for oil pollution compensation were decided, mainly the imposition of strict liability on the ship owner to a certain limit, a requirement for compulsory insurance, and liability channeled exclusively to the ship owner and its insurer."[183] In 1992, the Civil Liability Convention of 1969 was replaced by a similar measure that is now known as the Civil Liability Convention of 1992 (CLC 1992).[184] As of June 1, 2012, CLC 1992 had been acceded to or ratified by 129 states.[185]

There are a number of key elements to the Civil Liability Convention of 1992 that are worthy of consideration. First, the measure "applies to oil pollution resulting from spills of persistent oil from tankers."[186] However, damages as the result of non-persistent oil (e.g., kerosene, gasoline, light diesel) are not recoverable under the Convention.[187] Second, the Convention "covers pollution damage suffered in the territory, territorial sea or exclusive economic zone…or equivalent area of a state party to the Convention. The flag State of the tanker and the nationality of the ship-owner are irrelevant for determining the scope of application."[188] Third, pollution damage covers harm to the environment. However, the IMO has noted that, "In the case of environmental damage (other than loss of profit from impairment of the environment) compensation is restricted to costs actually incurred or to be incurred for reasonable measures to reinstate the contaminated environment."[189] Moreover, the concept of pollution damage also "includes measures, wherever taken, to

---

[182] Liability and Compensation for Oil Pollution Damage: Texts of the 1992 Conventions and the Supplementary Fund Protocol, International Convention on Civil Liability for Oil Pollution Damage, 1992, http://www.iopcfund.org/npdf/Conventions%20English.pdf.

[183] Michael Faure and Wang Hui, *Economic Analysis of Compensation for Oil Pollution Damage*, 37 J. Mar. L. & Com. 179, 195 (2006).

[184] *See* International Convention on Civil Liability for Oil Pollution Damage (CLC), http://www.imo.org/About/Conventions/ListOfConventions/Pages/International-Convention-on-Civil-Liability-for-Oil-Pollution-Damage-(CLC).aspx.

[185] Secretariat of the International Oil Pollution Compensation Funds, The International Regime for Compensation for Oil Pollution Damage 1 (June 2012), http://www.iopcfund.org/npdf/genE.pdf.

[186] *Id.*

[187] *Id.*

[188] *Id.*

[189] *Id.* at 1–2.

prevent or minimize pollution damage...Expenses incurred for preventative measures are recoverable even when no spill of oil occurs, provided that there was a grave and imminent threat of pollution damage."[190] Fourth, the registered owner of an oil tanker is exclusively liable under the measure. In this regard, "Compensation claims may not be pursued against the servants or agent of the owner, the members of the crew, the pilot, any other person performing services for the ship..., any charterer...manager or operator of the ship, or any person performing salvage operation or taking measures to prevent or minimize pollution."[191] However, this provision may not apply if the damage resulting from the pollution was the result of a person's act or omission "committed with the intent to cause such damage, or recklessly and with knowledge that such damage would probably result."[192]

Another key aspect of the Civil Liability Conventions of both 1969 and 1992 was the adoption of strict liability as applied to oil tankers. As one observer noted, the adoption of strict liability "was contrary to the traditional maritime liability rules based on fault. This strict liability of the ship-owner has been widely accepted nowadays even in other areas of maritime law, and it remains one basic principle of the CLC."[193] Another observer has written, "The imposition of strict liability is a very welcome approach: expecting a victim to rely on a regime based on negligence, delictual responsibility or even presumed fault may lead to the unsuccessful pursuit of claims and uncompensated damage. The strict liability method...accords with the principle that the carrying out of an abnormally dangerous activity that causes harm should trigger the imposition of liability without the need to prove negligence."[194] Klaus Töpfer, former Executive Director of the UN Environment Program, has written that the inclusion of the strict liability concept "was a major step forward and cleared up many problems in the civil law."[195]

In most instances liability always attaches to the registered owner of the tanker.[196] In this regard, "compensation claims may not be pursued against the servants or agent of the owner, the members of the crew, the pilot, any other person performing services for the ship..., any charterer...manager or operator of the ship, or any person performing salvage operation or taking

---

[190] *Id.* at 2.

[191] Jacobsson, *supra* note 168, at 19.

[192] 1992 Civil Liability Convention, Art. IV(4).

[193] Faure, *supra* note 183, at 197.

[194] Gotthard M. Gauci, *Protection of the Marine Environment through the International Ship-Source Oil Pollution Compensation Regime*, Vol. 8 Issue 1 1999, RECIEL 29, at 30.

[195] Klaus Töpfer, *Beyond the Marketplace: The IOPC Funds and the Environment, in* THE IOPC FUNDS' 25 YEARS OF COMPENSATING VICTIMS OF OIL POLLUTION INCIDENTS 37, 40–41 (2003).

[196] 1992 Civil Liability Convention, Art. III.

measures to prevent or minimize pollution."[197] However, an oil tanker owner may be exempt from liability where it can be established that, "(a) the damage resulted from an act of war or a grave natural disaster, or (b) the damage was wholly caused by sabotage by a third party, or (c) the damage was wholly caused by the negligence of public authorities in maintaining lights or other navigational aids."[198]

The CLC 1992 generally provides a limitation of liability. For incidents occurring after November 1, 2003, the limits are as follows: for tankers of 5,000 gross tonnage units or less, $7.3 million; for tankers with tonnage ranging from 5,000 to 140,000 gross tonnage units, $7.3 million in addition to $1,016 for additional tonnage units; for tankers of more than 140,000 gross tonnage units, $144.5 million.[199] One observer has written that the ship owner's limitation of liability "has a long tradition in maritime law...The limitation mechanism emerges in maritime law because it was needed to encourage ship owners to invest in highly risky maritime adventures...Moreover, limitation of liability was considered necessary to offset the heavy burden imposed on the ship owner via strict liability."[200]

The CLC of 1992 also requires oil tanker owners of ships registered in contracting states and transporting 2,000 tons of bulk oil or more "...to maintain insurance or other financial security...to cover his liability for pollution damage under this Convention."[201]

Despite the acceptance of the CLC of 1992, criticisms have been aimed at the scheme. For example, it has been suggested that the 1992 CLC could be made stronger by the availability of punitive damages for "egregious abuses and irresponsible action that jeopardizes marine ecosystems, instead of continuing to treat the environment as having no market value."[202] Moreover, the use of strict liability combined with a limit on liability may not be entirely effective at preventing future accidents. One observer has written, "...[T]he economic literature [shows] that a strict liability rule is efficient only if the potential tortfeasor is fully exposed to the potential damage which may result from his activity. A financial limit on the (strict) liability of the tanker owner will have the same effect as the insolvency of the tanker owner: underdeterrence."[203] Another criticism relates to jurisdiction. The 1992 CLC does not apply "out of CLC's water. Therefore, if a spill occurs in a non CLC

---

[197] Jacobsson, *supra* note 168, at 19.
[198] Secretariat, *supra* note 185, at 2.
[199] *Id.*
[200] Faure, *supra* note 183, at 199.
[201] 1992 Civil Liability Convention, Art. VII.
[202] Tőpfer, *supra* note 195, at 40–41.
[203] Faure, *supra* note 183, at 206.

state's territorial waters, such as the United States, then CLCs provisions do not apply. Finally, CLCs judgments will not necessarily be enforceable if a ship owner travels to a non-CLC's jurisdiction to escape liability."[204]

One observer has suggested that instead of applying the CLC scheme, a better approach would be to establish "market-based" incentives to encourage more oil spill prevention. Under this approach, oil tanker transporters would buy permits similar to those sold under the US Clean Air Act. "...[I]ndividual governments...would determine an environmental standard specifying the total number of gallons per year that could be spilled in the world's oceans without incurring the need for monetary compensation or remediation. Each government then would establish a pool of permits and allocate them to relevant oil transporting firms. Every firm would be required to hold these permits to account for potential spills occurring during the transport of oil, but they would be allowed to freely buy, sell, and trade the permits amongst themselves; those most able to create and implement pollution control technology would be able to sell their permits to those who have less ability and financial resources. Each government would retain overall control over the process by specifying how much pollution could occur, and by issuing a set number of permits according to its determination."[205]

Despite participating in the negotiations leading up to adoption of the 1969 Convention, the US chose not to join, citing "inadequate damage liability caps."[206] Instead the US enacted a similar scheme, the Oil Pollution Act of 1990.[207]

Another measure, that is modeled after the CLC 1969, is beyond the scope of this chapter but it nonetheless deserves to be mentioned. The International Convention on Civil Liability for Bunker Oil Pollution Damage[208] was adopted in 2001 and entered into force in 2008. The legislation's aim is to ensure the provision of prompt and adequate compensation to those suffering damage related to oil spills involving fuel located in the bunkers of ships.[209]

---

[204] de Gennaro, *supra* note 155, at 276–277.

[205] *Id.* at 284–285.

[206] *Id.* at 269.

[207] Oil Pollution Act of 1990, 33 USC 2701–2761, http://www.law.cornell.edu/uscode/text/33/chapter-40.

[208] International Convention on Civil Liability for Bunker Oil Pollution Damage (2001), http://www.imo.org/About/Conventions/ListOfConventions/Pages/International-Convention-on-Civil-Liability-for-Bunker-Oil-Pollution-Damage-(BUNKER).aspx.

[209] *Id.*

7.3.3.4.2   International Convention on the Establishment of an International Fund for Compensation for Oil Pollution Damage, 1992[210]

While the Civil Liability Convention 1969 provided some level of compensation for victims of tanker oil spills, it was soon realized that it "did not offer a satisfactory solution to provide adequate compensation... [Thus] the idea of an international compensation fund was proposed as a compromise to solve the unresolved dispute."[211] The result was the International Convention on the Establishment of an International Fund for Compensation of Oil Pollution Damage, 1971, which was superseded by the 1992 Protocol (known as the 1992 Fund).[212] Despite operating alongside various Conventions associated with the IMO, the 1992 Fund is an intergovernmental organization independent from the UN.[213] As of June 1, 2012, 110 states had acceded to or ratified the 1992 Convention.[214] The 1992 Fund, the 1971 fund, and the new Supplementary Fund [*see* Section 7.3.4.3] are administered by the International Oil Pollution Funds (IOPC).[215]

The objective of the 1992 Fund is to "provide compensation for pollution damage which is inadequately compensated by the 1992 CLC"[216] for one of several reasons: "(a) the ship owner is exempt from liability under the 1992 Civil Liability Convention because he can invoke one of the exemptions under that Convention; or (b) the ship owner is financially incapable of meeting his obligations under the 1992 Civil Liability Convention in full and his insurance is insufficient to satisfy the claims for compensation for pollution damage; or (c) the damage exceeds the ship owner's liability under the 1992 Civil Liability Convention."[217]

To make a claim for compensation as the result of oil pollution, the claimant must be able to establish "a quantifiable economic loss. The claimant must be able to show the amount of his loss or damage by producing accounting records or other appropriate evidence" according to the Fund.[218]

---

[210] International Convention on the Establishment of an International Fund for Compensation for Oil Pollution Damage, 1992, http://www.iopcfund.org/npdf/Conventions%20English.pdf.

[211] Faure, *supra* note 183, at 202.

[212] *See* http://www.imo.org/About/Conventions/ListOfConventions/Pages/International-Convention-on-the-Establishment-of-an-International-Fund-for-Compensation-for-Oil-Pollution-Damage-(FUND).aspx.

[213] International Oil Pollution Compensation Funds, Annual Report 2010 4, http://www.iopcfund.org/npdf/AR2010_e.pdf.

[214] International Regime for Compensation for Pollution Damage, http://www.iopcfund.org/npdf/genE.pdf.

[215] *See* International Oil Pollution Compensation Funds, http://www.iopcfund.org/.

[216] SANDS, *supra* note 117, at 916.

[217] Secretariat, *supra* note 185, at 3.

[218] International Oil Pollution Compensation Funds, *supra* note 213, at 22.

There are generally five types of damage that can serve as the basis of a claim: property; on shore and sea-based cleanup; losses suffered by those engaged in the fishing or mariculture business; tourism-related economic losses; and environmental reinstatement costs."[219]

The 1992 Fund has published a claims manual that explains how compensation claims should be presented.[220] With respect to cleanup costs or efforts to minimize or prevent damages from pollution, the 1992 Fund will provide compensation if the costs are reasonable. The governing body – the 1992 Fund Assembly – "has decided that the concept of reasonableness is an objective and technical one. The question of whether or not the costs of certain measures are reasonable is to be assessed on the basis of objective criteria. That a government or other public body decides to take certain measures does not in itself mean that the measures are reasonable for the purpose of compensation under the Conventions."[221] Meanwhile, economic loss claims are admissible but only to the extent that the damage or loss was caused by contamination.[222] "... [I]n order for a claim to qualify for compensation, the basic criterion is that a sufficiently close link of causation exists between the contamination and the loss or damage sustained by the claimant. A claim is not solely admissible solely because the loss or damage would not have occurred but for the oil spill in question."[223] In determining whether a "sufficiently close link" has been established, the 1992 Fund will consider: the proximity between the contaminated area and the claimant's business; the economic relationship between a claimant's business and the contaminated resource; whether there were alternative supply sources for the claimant; and how integral the claimant's business was to the affected area's economic activity.[224] Environmental claims are compensable "for the costs of reasonable reinstatement measures aimed at accelerating natural recovery of environmental damage. Contributions may be made to the costs of post-spill studies provided that they relate to damage which falls within the

---

[219] *Id.*

[220] International Oil Pollution Compensation Fund, Claims Manual (December 2008 Edition; adopted by the Assembly in October 2004 and amended in June 2007), http://www .iopcfund.org/npdf/2008%20claims%20manual_e.pdf; *see also*, International Oil Pollution Compensation Fund 1992, Guidelines for presenting claims in the fisheries, mariculture and fish processing sector, December 2008 Edition (adopted by the Assembly in June 2008), http://www.iopcfund.org/npdf/Fisheries%20Guidelines%20-%20Claimants_e.pdf (provides guidelines for making compensation claims specifically for claimants involved with farming, catching, and processing seafood).

[221] Jacobsson, *supra* note 168, at 27.

[222] *Id.* at 26.

[223] *Id.*

[224] International Oil Pollution Compensation Funds, Claims Manual 2008 Edition, *supra* note 220, at 29.

definition of pollution damage under the Conventions, including studies to establish the nature and extent of environmental damage caused by an oil spill and to determine whether or not reinstatement measures are necessary and feasible."[225] In 2005, a 1992 Fund working group considered a proposal to include "damage to the marine ecosystem and its resources" in the definition of "pollution damage," but the idea was turned down.[226]

The highest amount of compensation that is payable under the tanker owner's insurer and the 1992 Fund is about $322 million; it is about $1.19 billion if the incident is also covered by the Supplementary Fund.[227]

Contributions to the 1992 Fund are "levied on those who received in a calendar year more than 150,000 tons of 'contributing oil' (including crude oil and fuel oil) in a port or terminal in the territory of a member state after sea transport. The amount of the contribution of a specific oil receiver is directly related to the quantity of oil he has received in a calendar year."[228] In 2010, contributions to the 1992 Fund were Japan 16 percent, India 11, Republic of Korea 8.5, Italy 8.5, Netherlands 6, Singapore 6, France 6, Canada 5, U 5, Spain 4, others 24.[229]

About 140 incidents from around the globe have been handled by the 1971 and 1992 Funds. In most of these, the claims were settled without going to court.[230]

7.3.3.4.3   Protocol of 2003 to the International Convention on the Establishment of an International Fund for Compensation of Oil Pollution Damages

In 2003, a "third-tier" compensation scheme – known as the Supplementary Fund – was established by the Protocol of 2003 to the International Convention on the Establishment of an International Fund for Compensation of Oil Pollution Damages[231] As of 2010 the Supplementary Fund had neither been involved nor was potentially likely to be involved in any oil spill incidents.[232] It is funded entirely by the oil industry.[233]

---

[225] *Id.* at 13.

[226] Jacobsson, *supra* note 168, at 18.

[227] INCIDENTS INVOLVING THE IOPC FUNDS 20101 3, http://www.iopcfund.org/npdf/ incidents2011_e.pdf.

[228] Faure, *supra* note 183, at 203.

[229] International Oil Pollution Compensation Funds, *supra* note 213, at 20.

[230] *Id.* at 4.

[231] Liability and Compensation for Oil Pollution Damage: Texts of the 1992 Conventions and the Supplementary Fund Protocol 53, http://www.iopcfund.org/npdf/Conventions%20 English.pdf.

[232] International Oil Pollution Compensation Funds, *supra* note 213, at 4.

[233] Jacobsson, *supra* note 168, at 17.

7.3.4   *Energy Charter Treaty*

7.3.4.1   *Overview*

The Energy Charter Treaty (ECT),[234] which was signed in 1994 and entered into force in 1998,[235] is a unique multilateral agreement "limited in scope to the energy sector...which establishes within that sector legal rights and obligations with respect of a broad range of investment, trade and other subjects such as...the environment...and which, in most cases provides for the enforcement of those rights and obligations."[236] The inclusion of environmental considerations "has broken new ground by coupling...trade and investment provisions with emphasis on the importance of environmental protection in all aspects of the energy industry..."[237]

The ECT is a legally-binding instrument, "the only one of its kind dealing specifically with inter-governmental cooperation in the energy sector."[238] The ECT has been acceded to or signed by more than 50 countries as well as the European Union."[239] Potentially the ECT has "worldwide vocation."[240]

The diplomatic process leading to the establishment of the ECT followed in the wake of the disbanding of the Soviet Union. Many of the former Soviet republics, not least of which was Russia, enjoy enormous energy resources. Western European countries needed access to energy resources. On the other hand, many of the new states needed direct investment from foreign interests so as to improve their energy development infrastructure. Consequently, "Nowhere were the prospects for mutually beneficial cooperation between East and West clearer than in the energy sector."[241] One observer has written, "In general terms, the hope was to use energy integration as an organizing mechanism to establish norms and procedures that would promote economic and political development and stabilize the post Cold War relations in much the way that the original European Coal and Steel Community (ECSC) helped promote economic and political development and integration in the

---

[234] Energy Charter Treaty and Related Documents 11, at 13, http://www.encharter.org/fileadmin/user_upload/document/EN.pdf.

[235] *Id.*

[236] Craig S. Bamberger, Jan Linehan and Thomas Wälde, *Energy Charter Treaty in 2000: in a New Phase*, Vol. 18 No. 4 J. ENERGY & NAT. RESOURCES L. 331 (2001).

[237] Shine, *supra* note 72, at 545.

[238] Energy Charter Treaty and Related Documents, *supra* note 234, at 13; *see also* Andrei Konoplyanik and Thomas Wälde, *Energy Charter Treaty and its Role in International Energy*, Vol. 24 No. 4 J. ENERGY & NAT. RESOURCES L. 523, at 526 (2006).

[239] The Energy Charter Treaty and Related Documents, *supra* note 234, at 13.

[240] Graham Coop, *Energy Charter Treaty and the European Union: Is Conflict Inevitable?* Vol. 27, No. 3 J. ENERGY & NAT. RESOURCES L. 404, at 405 (August 2009).

[241] The Energy Charter Treaty and Related Documents, *supra* note 234, at 13.

years following World War II."[242] It is no surprise then that the European Union, one of the successor bodies that followed the ECSC, was the "principal driving force" involving the ECT's establishment.[243] Today, the ECT "has been integrated into the *acquis communautaire* of the EU."[244]

The ECT is particularly noteworthy since it is the "largest multilateral investment treaty in terms of the number of states and the combined populations [885 million] and GDP [\$26 trillion in 2008] encompassed."[245] Moreover, one observer has suggested that "...[I]n a legal sense, it incorporates a wide range of commitments, both of the 'hard' and 'soft' law variety."[246]

The ECT focuses on five themes: "...[T]he protection and promotion of foreign energy investments, based on the extension of national treatment, or most-favored national treatment (whichever is more favorable); free trade in energy materials, producing and energy-related equipment, based on WTO rules; freedom of energy transit through pipelines and grids; reducing the negative environmental impact of the energy cycle through improving energy efficiency; and mechanisms for the resolution of State-to-State or Investor-to-State disputes."[247]

Perhaps the most notable objective of the ECT is to promote the attraction of "capital to the treaty parties by limiting the potential for host government interference with foreign investors."[248] In this regard, "The fundamental aim of the [ECT] is to strengthen the rule of law on energy issues, by creating a level playing field of rules observed by all participating governments, thus minimizing the risks associated with energy-related investments and trade."[249]

---

[242] Matthew D. Slater, *The Energy Charter Treaty: A Brief Introduction to its Scope and Initial Arbitral Awards, in* ALTERNATIVE DISPUTE RESOLUTION IN THE ENERGY SECTOR 15, at 16 (Association for International Arbitration, ed. 2010).

[243] LESAGE, *supra* note 2, at 67.

[244] *Id.* at 66. The term *acquis communautaire* "refers to the rights and obligations deriving from EU treaties, laws, and regulations." ENCYCLOPEDIA OF THE EUROPEAN UNION UPDATED VERSION 2 (Desmond Dinan, ed. 2000). Put another way, the ECT is considered part of the EU's "legal order in the energy sector." PETER D. CAMERON, INTERNATIONAL ENERGY INVESTMENT LAW – THE PURSUIT OF STABILITY 153–154 (2010).

[245] Slater, *supra* note 242, at 15.

[246] CAMERON, *supra* note 244, at 153–154.

[247] The Energy Charter Treaty and Related Documents: A Legal Framework for International Energy Cooperation 13, 14, http://www.encharter.org/fileadmin/user_upload/document/EN.pdf.

[248] Justin R. Marlles, *Public Purpose, Private Losses: Regulatory Expropriation and Environmental Regulation in International Investment Law*, 16 J. TRANSNAT'L L. & POL'Y 275, at 277 (2007).

[249] The Energy Charter Treaty and Related Documents, *supra* note 234, at 14.

While the ECT clearly has strong ties to Europe – one observer has written that it is "politically 'owned'" by the European Union[250] – its reach has broadened considerably – especially into Eurasia. "Japan, Australia, and the state of Central Asia signed the Treaty in 1994–1995. They were subsequently joined by Mongolia, which acceded to the Treaty in 1999. The Asian dimension...was further strengthened when Observer status was granted to the People's Republic of China in 2001, to the Republic of Korea in 2002, and to the ASEAN Centre for Energy in 2003. The Islamic Republic of Iran became an Observer in 2002."[251] Pakistan was granted Observer status in 2005 as was Afghanistan in 2006.[252] Despite playing an active role in the ECT negotiations, the US chose not to sign the treaty and asserted "that the ECT did not provide additional protection to investments to that already provided or to be provided by [bilateral investment treaties] between the US and the states concerned."[253]

Thus far the number of arbitration awards, available to the public and undertaken as a result of the ECT, has been described as "rather paltry."[254] Through 2009 only six arbitration awards had been issued and none involved Article 19 [*see* Section 7.3.4.3], which deals with environmental issues.[255] Looking ahead, one commentator has said that the "strategic value" of the ECT "is likely to increase in the context of efforts to build a legal foundation for global energy security, based on principles of open, competitive markets, and sustainable development."[256]

7.3.4.2   *Energy Charter Treaty Article 18: Sovereignty Over Energy Resources*

Notwithstanding the fact that the ECT calls attention to the environmental aspects of energy generation, Article 18(1) clearly states, "The contracting parties recognize state sovereignty and sovereign rights over energy resources" subject to the exercise of those rights "in accordance with and subject to the rules of international law." Article 18(2) also provides that the Contracting Parties shall maintain their own rules with respect to "governing the system of property ownership of energy resources." Moreover, Article 18(3) confirms that Contracting Parties continue "to hold in particular the rights to decide the geographical areas within its area to be made available

---

[250] *See* Wälde, *supra* note 68, at 1135.
[251] The Energy Charter Treaty and Related Documents, *supra* note 234, at 19.
[252] Konoplyanik, *supra* note 238, at 550.
[253] CAMERON, *supra* note 246, at 153.
[254] Marlles, *supra* note 248, at 320.
[255] Slater, *supra* note 242, at 47–54.
[256] Konoplyanik, *supra* note 238, at 527.

for exploration and development of its energy resources, the optimalization of their recovery and the rate at which they may be depleted or otherwise exploited…, and to regulate the environmental and safety aspects of such exploration, development, and reclamation within its area…"

7.3.4.3 *Energy Charter Treaty Article 19: Environmental Aspects*
Article 19 of the ECT states, "In pursuit of sustainable development and taking into account its obligations under those international agreements concerning the environment to which it is party, each Contracting Party shall strive to minimize in an economically efficient manner harmful Environmental Impacts occurring either within or outside its Area from all operation within the Energy Cycle[257] in its Area, taking proper account of safety. In doing so each Contracting Party shall act in a Cost-Effective manner."

Furthermore, Article 19 encourages Contracting Parties to "strive to take precautionary measures to prevent or minimize environmental degradation" as well as notes that they should "in principle, bear the cost of pollution, including transboundary pollution, with due regard to the public interest and without distorting Investment in the Energy Cycle or international trade."

Other notable provisions of Article 19 include that Contracting Parties shall bear in mind the following concepts in the context of "energy cycle" decisions and operations: enhance energy efficiency as well as develop and use more renewable energy and other clean fuels;[258] raise the public's knowledge about energy system impacts on the environment;[259] encourage "the transparent assessment at an early stage and prior to decision" of how major energy projects will impact the environment.[260] However, it is important to note that these provisions "do not create enforceable commitments, but function rather as indicators of good practice."[261]

It has been noted that while the ECT may appear overall "heavily [skewed] towards the side of foreign investors, consequently disfavoring state regulation, this is in fact not the case. Particularly in the area of environmental

---

[257] In the context of Article 19 of the Energy Charter Treaty, the term energy cycle "means the entire energy chain, including activities related to prospecting for, exploration, production, conversion, storage, transport, distribution, and consumption of the various forms of energy, and the treatment and disposal of wastes, as well as the decommissioning, cessation or closure of these activities, minimizing harmful environmental impacts." Energy Charter Treaty, Article 19(3)(a).

[258] *Id.* at 19(d).

[259] *Id.* at 19(f).

[260] *Id.* at 19(i).

[261] Shine, *supra* note 72, at 528.

regulation, the ECT [through Article 19] presents a much more level playing field for states than most [bilateral investment treaties].[262]

While Article 19 has been described as "potentially far-reaching,"[263] it has also been characterized as largely "horatory."[264] In regard to the latter characterization, it is worth bearing in mind Article 19's significant limitations. First, it is not mandatory. As one observer has stated, "It is arguable that the negotiators were simply being realistic when they placed such emphasis upon the cost element inherent in pollution control, tacitly acknowledging the degree to which Governments must take account of commercial imperatives when determining whether to commit themselves to stringent environmental obligations under international agreements."[265] Moreover, the phrase cost effective "leaves Contracting Parties free to choose whether priority should be given to cost parameters or environmental objectives."[266] This has led one writer to say Article 19 contains "a mainly programmatic good-practices set of principles on environment."[267]

Article 19's impact is also "somewhat circumscribed by Article 27(2), which removes disputes regarding the 'application or interpretation' of Article 19 from the purview of the ECT's dispute resolution mechanisms."[268] Thus the key provisions in Article 27 that require "Contracting Parties to endeavor to settle disputes through diplomatic channels and, where this fails, to submit the matter to an ad hoc arbitral tribunal" do not apply to Article 19 disputes.[269] The procedures that are set out in Article 19(2) are "notably weaker."[270]

7.3.4.4   *Energy Charter Protocol on Energy Efficiency and Related Environmental Aspects*

At the same time the ECT was signed in 1994, the Energy Charter Protocol on Energy Efficiency and Related Environmental Aspects (PEEREA)[271] was also signed. PEEREA came into force in 1998 at the same time as the Energy Charter Treaty.[272]

---

[262] Marlles, *supra* note 248, at 319.

[263] Shine, *supra* note 72, at 526.

[264] Bamberger, *supra* note 236, at 335 (footnote 11).

[265] Shine, *supra* note 72, at 526.

[266] *Id.*

[267] Konoplyanik, *supra* note 238, at 539.

[268] Marlles, *supra* note 248, at 319.

[269] Shine, *supra* note 72, at 536.

[270] *Id.*

[271] Energy Charter Protocol on Energy Efficiency and Related Environmental Aspects (Annex 3 to the Final Act of the European Energy Charter Conference) 139–155, http://www.encharter.org/fileadmin/user_upload/document/EN.pdf#page=141.

[272] The Energy Charter Treaty and Related Documents, *supra* note 234, at 13.

The protocol "defines policy principles for the promotion of energy efficiency as a considerable source of energy and for consequently reducing adverse environmental impacts of energy systems."[273] PEEREA's implementation alongside the ECT is aimed at providing "transition economies with a menu of good practices and a forum in which to share experiences and policy advice on energy efficiency issues with leading OECD states. Within this forum, particular attention is paid to such aspects of a national energy efficiency strategy as taxation, pricing policy in the energy sector, environmentally-related subsidies and other mechanism for financing energy efficiency objectives."[274] PEERA has emphasized "in-depth energy efficiency reviews, designed to produce concrete recommendations for individual governments" to improve strategic energy efficiency plans at national level.[275]

7.3.4.5 *Environmentally-Based Regulatory Takings*

One matter that has been raised in the context of the ECT involves the concept of environmentally based regulatory takings.[276] On one hand, it has been suggested that the "environmental provisions [of the ECT] may be relied upon by an international tribunal in interpreting other provisions of the treaty (e.g., the expropriation or sanctity-of-contract provisions). Since the distinction between normal 'regulation and a compensable regulatory taking' is not easy and requires a balancing process, the environmental standards recognized in a treaty are suitable to serve as factor to be taken into account in such a balancing process."[277] However, it has also been stated that, "Because international law does not yet recognize an unlimited right for states to engage in environmental regulation without compensating foreign investors for resulting regulatory expropriation...multi-lateral investment treaties...risk 'freezing the development of sound environmental regulations, as well as other public welfare protection measures.'"[278]

---

[273] Energy Charter Protocol on Energy Efficiency and Related Environmental Aspects, *supra* note 271, at 143.

[274] The Energy Charter Treaty and Related Documents, *supra* note 234, at 16.

[275] *Id.*

[276] A regulatory taking or expropriation "is a term describing any scenario in which a capital-importing state uses its regulatory powers to deprive foreign investors of their property or the effective enjoyment thereof...While customary international law recognized early on that governments engaging in expropriation had a duty to compensate foreign investors for their losses, there were few limits on how government expropriation of foreign investments might take place, or even a clear notion of what expropriation constituted." Marlles, *supra* note 248, at 277.

[277] Thomas W. Wälde and Abba Kola, *Environmental Regulation, Investment Protection and Regulatory Taking in International Law*, 50 INT'L & COMP. L.Q. 811, 817 (2001).

[278] Marlles, *supra* note 248, at 330. *See also* Howard Mann and Konrad von Moltke, *Working Paper: NAFTA's Chapter 11 and the Environment – Addressing the Impacts of Investor-State Process on the Environment* 47 (1999), http://www.iisd.org/publications/pub.aspx?id=409.

There is also the issue of how to handle a situation where stricter regulation to protect the environment results in a foreign investor's legally compensable financial losses. Where the investor is entitled to compensation, the consequence, according to one observer writing about the ECT and its environmental provisions, is that "...[T]he economic burden of pollution is shifted to the general taxpayer, and the external environmental cost of pollution is not internalized with the investor...Such a practice seems in direct conflict with the 'polluter pays' principle, according to which the cost of environmental protection measures should be reflected in the cost of goods and services that cause pollution in production and consumption. Interestingly, then," the observer says, "Article 19...[states] that...'the polluter...should, in principle bear the cost of pollution...'"[279] In a somewhat related sense, there has also been concern expressed about the "dark side to environmental regulation" where governments use such regulation to "chip away at the value of foreign investments in their country for the purpose of benefitting domestic competitors, or appeasing anti-foreigner populist sentiments."[280]

7.3.4.6   *A Fundamental Shortcoming: The Absence of Key Nation States*
Despite the unique character of the ECT, there is a fundamental shortcoming involving the absence from membership of important energy importing and exporting countries. For example, among the important importers who are not part of the treaty are China and the United States. In regard to the US and Russia – also not a member – it has been suggested that, "Countries with a traditional emphasis on national sovereignty have great problem accepting the authority and jurisdiction of an international tribunal outside its control..."[281] On the other hand, significant exporters such as Norway and the OPEC countries are not members.[282] One observer has noted that, "As long as these key players are not integrated into the ECT regime, the treaty's role as a central institution for governing global energy and investment issues is seriously undermined."[283]

The European Commission has said that the ECT "should seek to extend membership towards North Africa and [the] Far East" and that Russia should

---

[279] Gaetan Verhoosel, *Foreign Direct Investment and Legal Constraints on Domestic Environmental Policies: Striking a "Reasonable" Balance Between Stability and Change*, 29 Law & Pol'y Int'l Bus. 451, 466 (1998).

[280] Marlles, *supra* note 248, at 332.

[281] Konoplyanik, *supra* note 238, at 546. Along these same lines it has been said that by comparison "EU countries may be somewhat more accepting [which they have been in the context of the ECT, which they have all ratified], mainly because they are used to having to account to the European Court of Justice and the European Court of Human Rights." *Id.*

[282] Lesage, *supra* note 2, at 67–68.

[283] Lesage, *supra* note 2, at 68.

play "a full role" in the treaty.[284] Despite the EU's entreaties to Russia, however, such a development seems unlikely for the time being. In the summer of 2009 – in the wake of the Russia's gas dispute with the Ukraine[285] – the Russian cabinet voted to terminate its "provisional application" of the ECT.[286] The termination took effect October 18, 2009.[287]

7.4 Looking Ahead

7.4.1 Introduction

The demands of modern societies in terms of industrial activities – as well as maintaining general patterns of life in an increasingly developed world – have resulted in "the emergence of international environmental politics as a major concern of the post-war era...the sheer magnitude and cumulative effects of industrial activities have extended their environmental consequences from local to global scales."[288] Put another way, "[T]he metabolic throughput of industrial society has, for the first time in human history, begun to stretch the carrying capacity of the global biosphere."[289] This is clearly the case in terms of global energy generation and consumption.

---

[284] Communication from the Commission to the European Parliament, the Council, the European Economic and Social Committee and the Committee of the Regions, COM(2011) 539 final, at 13 (September 7, 2011), http://eur-lex.europa.eu/LexUriServ/LexUriServ.do?uri= SEC:2011:1022:FIN:EN:PDF. One observer has suggested that, "As long as the ECT remains unratified...by Russia, this country will be at a disadvantage when it comes to attracting capital and to cross-border energy trade." Konoplyanki, *supra* note 238, at 554–555.

[285] In 2008 and 2009, Russia shut off gas supplies to the Ukraine because of "the now customary dispute over pricing between Ukraine and Russia which...led the latter to cut supplies to the Ukrainian domestic market." *The Customary Gas Stand-Off*, Economist (January 5, 2009).

[286] Lesage, *supra* note 2, at 67. In 1994 Russia signed the ECT and agreed to provisionally apply it while considering ratification. That meant that Russia agreed to application of ECT "to the extent that [it was] consistent with Russia's constitution, laws, and regulations," according to the Energy Charter secretariat. The lack of ratification did not "present an obstacle to the practical and technical work of the Energy Charter process, in which Russia [was] an active participant. It [did], however leave ambiguity about the extent of Russia's legal rights and obligations under the treaty." Energy Charter FAQ, http://www.encharter .org/index.php?id=18.

[287] Energy Charter FAQ, *supra* note 286.

[288] Nathan Pelletier, *Of Laws and Limits: An Ecological Economic Perspective on Redressing the Failure of Contemporary Global Environmental Governance*, 20 Global Envtl. Change 220, 220 (2010).

[289] *Id.*

And yet, the current forms of "environmental diplomacy" have largely been ineffective in addressing the environmental issues the world is facing due to a combination of restricted national concerns along with a demand for respect for national sovereignty often enshrined in multilateral environmental agreements. In short, many observers are calling for new governance schemes to address "the most serious contemporary environmental problems that are trans border and/or global"[290] in nature.

7.4.2   A New Paradigm for Regulating Energy? Global Energy Governance

7.4.2.1   Introduction
Historically energy issues have generally been handled at the nation state level. This has largely been the case for at least two reasons. First, the principle of national sovereignty "asserts that each of the roughly 200 countries in the world is entitled to do whatever it pleases within its national boundaries."[291] Second, national governments have tended to view "energy services as crucial to national security and national power," thus leading governments to intervene in and endorse the concepts of energy-related independence or security of supply.[292] The result has been, for example in the context of global climate change, "a failure to adequately recognize 21st century realities, notably rapidly expanding numbers of new consumers in the developing world that are adding greatly to the greenhouse gas pollution that has long come from the developed world."[293]

Despite the world's nearly universal acceptance of energy regulation by nation states (with some exceptions as described in Section 7.3 above), there are several fundamental pollution-related problems with the current system. They involve the concepts of public goods[294] and externalities.[295] In both cases, a strong argument can be made that the current system is simply not up to the task of handling the challenges at hand. Notwithstanding the market's general success in matching goods and service producers with the desire

---

[290] *Id.* at 225.
[291] Ann Florini, Benjamin K. Sovacool, *Who Governs Energy? The Challenges Facing Global Energy Governance*, 37 ENERGY POL'Y 5239, 5341 (2009).
[292] *Id.* at 5239.
[293] Paul G. Harris, *Cosmopolitan Diplomacy and the Climate Change Regime: Moving Beyond International Doctrine, in* ETHICS AND GLOBAL ENVTL. POL'Y (Paul G. Harris ed., 2011) 175, 175.
[294] The definition of public goods is those services and products "that are non-excludable and non-rival in consumption – i.e., once they exist, no consumer can be excluded from consuming them, and no one's consumption interferes with the ability of other consumers to consume them." Florini, *supra* note 291, at 5240.
[295] United Nations, *supra* note 77.

and need for humans to consume those goods and services, there is often a failure for those same markets to deliver "certain categories of goods and services that people want."[296] Examples of such goods – often referred to as public goods – are illustrated by national defense or public education. "No one has an individual incentive to produce such goods, because once they are produced everyone gets the benefits of them, even if they do not pay for the goods. Thus, the 'consumers' can free-ride. 'Producers,' knowing the consumers will not pay, do not produce."[297] This is a particularly major issue in the context of environmental governance at a global level "since the countries refusing to cooperate in environmental regimes cannot be excluded from the benefits of common property resources such as a stable climate…"[298]

The second problem relates to negative externalities such as environmental pollution.[299] When a manufacturing plant discharges polluted water into a stream it is not doing so to harm anyone downstream. Instead it undertakes this approach to rid itself of the pollution. Simply put this "is just the cheapest way of dealing with its waste."[300]

In both cases – that is providing for public goods while also dealing with negative externalities – some form of governance has to address the underlying issues. But whether the appropriate level is nation state governance is another matter. Among other things, these challenges are often marked by the cross-border nature of the issues. In the context of negative externalities, climate change is a glaring example of an "energy-related" issue that requires "extensive border-crossing governance."[301] In summary, "The energy field is replete with public goods problems and externalities, many of which cross borders and thus are beyond the scope of individual national governments to address on their own."[302]

There are three additional concerns that cannot easily be handled at a nation state level, but are enormous global issues – the "geopolitical challenges of [the] global oil trade," providing modern energy services to those who lack access to it,[303] and finally energy security of supply.[304]

Meanwhile, there is an increasing acceptance that the world's energy markets are becoming more integrated, just as is the world economy.[305]

---

[296] Florini, *supra* note 291, at 5240.
[297] *Id.*
[298] Pelletier, *supra* note 288, at 226.
[299] Florini, *supra* note 291, at 5240.
[300] *Id.*
[301] *Id.* at 5241.
[302] *Id.*
[303] *Id.* at 5246.
[304] *Id.* at 5241.
[305] Fouquet, *supra* note 7, at 17.

Consequently, "Coal, petroleum and increasingly natural gas and even electricity markets are dependent on the dynamics of supply and demand around the world. It is probable that phases of abundance and scarcity of energy resources that have implied periods of wealth and strife in individual cities, countries, or continents of the past will now affect the whole world."[306] In many respects, "The focus on the world economy is even more pertinent in relation to environmental problems" since the globalized rate of pollution "is beyond the planet's assimilation capacity."[307]

Notwithstanding the attention called to all of the above matters, however, nation state governments, among others, "have proven remarkably ineffective at coordinating across borders on energy issues."[308] The result has been a growing interest in the idea of "global governance"[309] or, in this context, "global energy governance." The term governance, in this regard, "refers to any of the myriad processes through which a group of people set and enforce rules needed to enable that group to achieve desired outcomes."[310]

7.4.2.2   *Current Actors in Global Energy Governance*

The general inability of nation states to regulate cross border energy-related pollution is documented above. But international efforts have been to date hardly more successful, leading one observer to comment that, "Internationally, the [energy] governance picture is even more incoherent. Energy is governed piecemeal, mostly in ad-hoc responses involving specific countries or groups of countries and any of a wide number of non-governmental actors."[311]

International "cross-border energy governance," if it exists at all, is often organized by energy sector or source[312] in intergovernmental organizations. But none of these organizations has truly global reach over the entire of range of energy issues. Nuclear power, for instance, is governed by the International Atomic Energy Agency. However, "as its work is strictly confined to atomic energy it cannot be qualified as a complete and comprehensive global energy regime that is able to address the diverse energy pressures in today's

---

[306] *Id*. at 16.

[307] *Id*. at 17.

[308] Florini, *supra* note 291, at 5239.

[309] The debate regarding "global governance" is "one of the most absorbing in political science, and the political importance of the concept is also increasing." Ulrich Brand, *Order and Regulation: Global Governance as a Hegemonic Discourse of International Politics?* 12:1 Rev. Int'l Pol. Econ. 155, 155 (Feb. 2005).

[310] Florini, *supra* note 291, at 5239.

[311] *Id*.

[312] *Id*. at 5246.

world."[313] Another example is the Energy Charter Treaty, which regulates a few gas and oil pipelines running from Europe to Asia.

Despite the international reach of the UN, its energy-related activities "remain fragmented and piecemeal. Few of [its] competent agencies address the energy issue per se...Neither the 2002 Johannesburg Summit, nor the recently erected coordination mechanism, UN-Energy, have really succeeded in bringing more coherence and depth to the fragmented energy activities within the UN system."[314]

The International Energy Forum (IEF), which has about 90 member countries, provides a global forum for energy ministers from energy exporting and importing countries.[315] However, it remains "rather constrained as it still lacks a firm structure or a clear mission statement...The Forum has no decision-making authority. Its usefulness primarily lies in the opportunity it creates for bi-lateral contacts...Overall, the IEF has failed to eliminate the deep-rooted mutual suspicion between oil consumers and producers."[316]

There are also organizations made up of energy consumers or producers. The Organization of the Petroleum Exporting Countries (OPEC) represents oil producers. On the other hand, the International Energy Agency (IEA) takes account of energy consumers. These groups have been called the world's "two most important [energy related] institutions."[317] And yet it has been suggested that "OPEC cannot be considered as a driving force for sustainable development"[318] while the IEA has "been hobbled by the requirement that the agency's members also belong to the Organization for Economic Cooperation, or OECD."[319] Among the key energy consuming countries that do not belong to OECD include China and India.[320]

The Energy Charter Treaty, discussed above in Section 7.3.4, has been described as having "no practical impact on energy markets, despite its bold vision for integrating the energy systems of eastern and western Europe. One

---

[313] LESAGE, *supra* note 2, at 53.

[314] *Id.* A series of UN sponsored meetings on the environment has devoted little attention to energy-related issues. For example, the 1972 UN Conference on Human Environment included almost nothing on energy; similarly the 1992 UN Conference on Environment and Development did not include energy on the agenda, and its final product, Agenda 21, only "indirectly touched on energy matters." *Id.* at 54. On the other hand while the UN Framework Convention on Climate Change and the Kyoto Protocol do address energy, progress in reaching their goals has been extremely limited.

[315] *What is the IEF?*, IEF, http://www.ief.org/Pages/_about.aspx.

[316] LESAGE, *supra* note 2, at 62.

[317] *Id.* at 72.

[318] *Id.* at 58.

[319] David G. Victor and Linda Yueh, *The New Energy Order: Managing Insecurities in the Twenty-first Century*, Vol. 89 No. 1 FOREIGN AFF. 61, 66 (2010).

[320] LESAGE, *supra* note 2 at 60.

problem is that the treaty violates the first rule of effective institution building: it alienates the most important player. Russia, Europe's pivotal energy
supplier, sees no benefit in subjecting itself to oversight by an intrusive Western institution and so has ensured the treaty's irrelevance."[321]

A sometimes over-looked example of a form of global governors is reflected
in multilateral development banks. These organizations typically provide technical and economic help to national governments in the developing world.[322]
Examples include the World Bank[323] and the Asian Development Bank, "which
is helping to shape Asia's rapidly growing energy infrastructure."[324] However,
"their roles in marshaling investment and influencing policy remains highly
controversial, with long-standing debates over the equity of their internal
decision-making processes, their legitimacy and accountability to the people
whose lives are affected by their funding and policy preferences, their competence, and the appropriateness of their agendas."[325]

Summit-based organizations, such as the G8, "represent a halfway house
between the formal institutionalization of [international governmental orga-
nizations] and the everyday processes of diplomacy among governments."[326]
Some observers have suggested that organizations like the G8 "are the most
plausible solution to the conundrums of global governance – small enough
to provide space for real discussions and meeting of minds, but large enough
to include powerful national leaders that exert significant influence on global
problems."[327] Nevertheless the G8 has been criticized for having done little
"beyond issuing grand and often empty proclamations"[328] on energy-related
matters as well as for "its extremely exclusive, and therefore illegitimate,
nature..."[329]

In summary, the existing governance structure when it comes to global
energy matters is "fragmented and underdeveloped. None of the international institutions dealing with energy has a truly universal mission."[330] As a
consequence, the "nature and scope of global energy challenges" cannot be
effectively addressed by the current actors.[331] On the other hand, whether a
system of global energy governance is the answer by itself is quite another

---

[321] Victor, *supra* note 319, at 67.
[322] Florini, *supra* note 291, at 5244.
[323] LESAGE, *supra* note 2, at 64.
[324] Florini, *supra* note 291, at 5244.
[325] *Id.* at 5247.
[326] *Id.* at 5243.
[327] *Id.* at 5247.
[328] Victor, *supra* note 319, at 68.
[329] Florini, *supra* note 291, at 5247.
[330] LESAGE, *supra* note 2, at 72.
[331] Florini, *supra* note 291, at 5247.

matter. As one commentator has written, "The dramatic description of the situation – which prevails in most Global Governance contributions – is answered by very moderate political ideas, which is due to the fact that the constitution of the problems is paid scarcely any attention. The postulated comprehensive claim to produce changes exists alongside the broad acceptance of social relations as they are. Political ideas therefore often correspond to a rather naïve wishful thinking."[332]

7.4.2.3   A Different Approach: Regional Energy Governance

The idea of shifting sovereignty from nation state level to a supranational entity is already underway, perhaps seen most clearly in the establishment of the European Union.[333] That said, a nation state's security of energy supply "is central to its economic growth, employment, and quality of life, and national governments are extremely risk adverse when signing away accountability."[334]

Examples are generally lacking of supranational entities having authority to make enforceable decisions about the energy distribution and generation of nation states, with perhaps the only one being OPEC. This has historically even been the case with the EU "where delegation of national sovereignty has arguably progressed the furthest."[335] With the Lisbon Treaty now in force, however, that may change slightly since for the first time the EU has official competence in the energy field. Specifically, the Treaty on the Functioning of the European Union[336] Article 194, which is premised on the economic and environmental dimensions of energy,"[337] provides: "1. In the context of the establishment and functioning of the internal market and with regard for the need to preserve and improve the environment, Union policy on energy shall aim, in a spirit of solidarity between Member States, to: (a) ensure the functioning of the energy market; (b) ensure security of energy supply in the Union; (c) promote energy efficiency and energy saving and the development of new and renewable forms of energy; and (d) promote the interconnection of energy networks." Notwithstanding the provisions in Article 194(1), a significant level of national control remains in effect pursuant to Article 194(2) which states that each Member State retains the "right to determine the

---

[332] Brand, *supra* note 309, at 168.

[333] Anthony G. Patt, *Effective Regional Energy Governance – Not Global Energy Governance – Is What We Need Right Now for Climate Change*, 20 GLOBAL ENVTL CHANGE 33, 33 (2010).

[334] *Id.*

[335] *Id.*

[336] Treaty on the Functioning of the European Union, http://eur-lex.europa.eu/LexUriServ/LexUriServ.do?uri=OJ:C:2010:083:0047:0200:EN:PDF.

[337] PAUL CRAIG, THE LISBON TREATY: LAW, POLITICS, AND TREATY REFORM 321 (2010).

conditions for exploiting its energy resources, it choice between different energy sources and the general structure of its energy supply…"

Even with the above caveats in mind, it has been suggested that it may be "very likely" that a form of regional energy governance should be explored because of its "positive net benefits."[338] Such a regional structure will not be established quickly because of the matter of national reluctance to give up sovereignty on energy issues, the difference in energy needs for post-industrial countries and those that are quickly growing industrial capacities, and the current absence of trust in undertaking such a major effort.[339] On the other hand, development and investment in new technologies such as concentrated solar power (CSP) and wind lend themselves nicely to a regional governance approach.[340] "To implement the two renewable energy technologies on a scale that could replace fossil fuels will require extensive regional electricity transmission, crossing jurisdictional boundaries, and requiring international planning. In the case of wind, this will be to balance out the intermittency across atmospheric pressure systems, and in the case of CSP, it will be to build and link large generation facilities in the world's deserts to service population centers a thousand kilometers away."[341] The fact that such an effort would be regionally, rather than globally based might work to the advantage of the approach. "With fewer states involved, asymmetries are less and negotiations become tractable. Furthermore, the institutions to enforce regional cooperation – such as the European Commission – are already much stronger than are the global institutions set up by the [United Nations Framework Convention on Climate Change]."[342]

As a consequence of the regional approach, the costs of implementing wind and concentrated solar power would become competitive with coal and the scale of available capacity would be enhanced.[343] Such an effort could conceivably begin in Europe, the Middle East, and North America.[344]

A somewhat related energy governance concept has been termed "polycentric climate and energy governance."[345] This governance concept involves "multiple scales (local, regional, national, and global), mechanisms (centralized command and control regulations, decentralized and local policies, and the free market), and actors (government institutions, corporate and

---

[338] Patt, *supra* note 333, at 33.

[339] *Id.* at 34.

[340] *Id.*

[341] *Id.*

[342] *Id.*

[343] *Id.*

[344] *Id.*

[345] Benjamin K. Sovacool, *An International Comparison of Four Polycentric Approaches to Climate and Energy Governance*, 39 ENERGY POL'Y 3832, 3833 (2011).

business firms, civil society, and individuals and households)."[346] One of the key benefits of a polycentric governance system, according to one observer, is that it "recognizes that climate and energy problems differ substantially by region...but also [ensures] that a common standard motivates all communities to act...It appreciates that policy preferences tend to be more homogeneous within smaller units than across broader areas."[347] On the other hand, polycentric systems "are so complex that there is no guarantee they will produce effective solutions or optimal forms of governance."[348]

7.5   Conclusion

Despite the uncertainty about how to address the environmental challenges related to future energy production and consumption, two trends seem clear. First, the amount of energy the world needs to maintain a healthy global economy is going to increase. The often discussed concept of "decoupling" economic development from energy consumption has simply not come to pass and it may never do so. While energy efficiency has improved, that improvement has generally made little impact in a world that continues to consume energy – often involving fossil fuels – in ever greater quantities.[349] Second, trepidation about the energy system's environmental impact is increasing enormously.[350]

Set against these trends are challenges related to governance issues involving energy and the environment. Many of these challenges arise from the simple fact that "energy issues transcend national borders," with one consequence being "environmental cross-border impacts."[351] On the one hand no individual nation (or more likely small handful of nations) can effectively regulate the overall global energy system in a manner that prevents "a tragedy of the commons" inherent in issues such as global warming. Put simply, "protection of the commons requires collective action."[352] On the other hand, traditional intergovernmental sectoral-based schemes related to matters such as marine oil pollution from tankers and nuclear power safety are also lacking. Too often these schemes are merely descriptive best practices, but lack any real enforcement provisions.

---

[346] *Id.*

[347] *Id.* at 3843.

[348] *Id.* at 3842.

[349] European Environment Agency, *supra* note 26, at 42.

[350] Victor, *supra* note 319, at 61.

[351] Wälde, *supra* note 68, at 1132.

[352] *See* Bodansky, *supra* note 71, at 11.

Consequently, as the 21st century begins there is a growing awareness that current forms of "energy governance" are simply not effective or efficient for the problems the world faces. This conclusion is based on a number of factors, not least of which are energy insecurity, the changing nature of pollution (e.g., carbon emissions), how to protect and promote "global public goods" related to a healthy environment, addressing energy poverty, and the need to encourage huge investments in new and modern energy infrastructure. The result, as one observer has commented, is that, "... [T]he world is currently on an unsustainable and conflict-prone energy track of volatile and unreliable energy supply, brittle and vulnerable energy infrastructure, massive environmental degradation, and failure to deliver energy services..."[353]

The solution is unlikely to involve establishing a new "super institution." Rather, "What is needed...is a mechanism for coordinating hardnosed initiatives focused on delivering energy security and environmental protection."[354] Such a mechanism – perhaps to be called the "World Energy Community"[355] (WEC) – would promote measures "to advance the interests of the most important governments, of importers and exporters alike, ...and align with the needs of private and state firms that provide most of the investment in energy infrastructure."[356] The over-arching goal would be to establish "a practical strategy for setting effective norms to govern the global energy economy."[357]

Taking its lead from the communal-based spirit embodied in the European Coal and Steel Community,[358] the predecessor of today's European Union, and which dealt in part with energy issues,[359] the WEC would begin "with a practical focus on filling the most important governance vacuums in the world's energy system: those regarding how to promote investment to develop urgently needed supplies of today's main energy sources, oil and

---

[353] *See* Florni, *supra* note 15, at 57.

[354] *See* Victor, *supra* note 319, at 63.

[355] The author's idea based on the notion of promoting the concept of a communal response to a global-wide problem. Other authors have referred to this concept as the Energy Stability Board. *See* Victor, supra *note* 319, at 64.

[356] *See* Victor, *supra* note 319, at 63.

[357] *Id.* at 67.

[358] The European Coal and Steel Community was established in 1951 by Belgium, France, Germany, Italy, Luxembourg, and the Netherlands. "The plan was not only economically inspired, but represented an attempt to restabilize relations between France and Germany after [World War II], to allay French fears about any German military threat, and to bind them within a limited framework of peaceful co-operation in order to avert a rivalry over coal production." PAUL CRAIG AND GRÁINNE DE BÚRCA, 5 EU LAW (5th ed. 2011).

[359] Ian H. Rowlands, *Promotion of Renewable Electricity in the United States and the European Union: Policy Progress and Prospects, in* TRANSATLANTIC ENVT & ENERGY POL. 145, 149 (Miranda A. Schruers, Henrik Selin, and Stacy D. Vandeveer eds., 2009).

gas, and how to support the climate-friendly technologies that will transform the energy system over the next several decades."[360] This focus would
take account of today's situation in which the money needed to invest in
new energy sources is not being committed because of a combination of
risks. "The problem is not geology: technological innovation is more than
amply offsetting the depletion of convention fossil fuels," two observers have
suggested.[361] "The problem lies in the massive economic and political risks
inherent in new projects, particularly those that supply energy across national
borders and thus face a multitude of political uncertainties."[362]

Two initial projects are worth considering. First, the WEC could convene
a global gathering to study the matter of addressing the international challenges related to energy and continued world economic development. One
aspect of this gathering might be to address energy-related environmental
externalities. This would not be, of course, an easy matter to resolve, but
there would be nearly uniform agreement on the need for the world to have
enough energy to drive forward future economic development. Second, it is
unlikely that any sort of overall progress can be made without China and its
suppliers of energy as well as the other "large players in the world energy
market" establishing standards of investment "that align China's interest
in securing steady energy supplies with Western norms of well-functioning
markets and good governance."[363] Again, this discussion might be fraught
with difficulties and challenges – in fact to expect anything less would be
naïve. However, it would represent a practical step towards building trust
and predictability in the world's energy governance system.

Will this new approach work? Perhaps. Perhaps not. But what is not disputed is that the current governance system is not really suited to handle the
rapidly growing problem of environmental degradation related to contemporary energy systems.

Reverting again to the establishment of the European Coal and Steel
Community, it is worth considering the words of French Foreign Minister Robert Schuman who on May 9, 1950, proposed the concept underlying
the Community when he said, "Europe will not be made all at once, or
according to a single plan. It will be built through concrete achievements
which first create a de facto solidarity."[364] Of course, the world's current
energy problems cannot be precisely compared with the aftermath of World

---

[360] Victor, *supra* note 319, at 68.
[361] *Id.*
[362] *Id* at 68–69.
[363] *Id.* at 69–70.
[364] Robert Schuman, Declaration of 9 May 1950, http://europa.eu/abc/symbols/9-may/decl_
en.htm.

War II. But what can be said is that the world coming to realistic terms with its energy challenges is no less an opportunity to completely reexamine and consider a new governance system. Consequently a new world energy system "will not be made all at once, or according to a single plan." But establishing a WEC will allow for the opportunity of "concrete achievements which first create a de facto solidarity."

Chapter Eight

Preservation

8.0 *Introduction*

The legal concept of preservation – prohibiting human development or destruction of natural areas, spectacular scenery, open space, paleontological-cultural-historic sites, wildlife and plant species, habitat and ecosystems, biological diversity, global commons, even outer space – is a relatively new phenomenon in international law. The concept has been slow to emerge because preservation often conflicts with traditional notions of development.[1] Governments that are primarily concerned with enhancing growth rates and economic improvement have established policies and strategies that encourage intensive use of natural resources with little or no oversight; however, because unregulated use of natural resources often results in inefficient and inequitable exploitation, both governments and citizens have begun to advocate preservation.[2]

Even as the concept of preservation has gained legitimacy in both domestic and international law, population growth and the resource intensive lifestyle led by many citizens in developed countries has put significant pressure on states to limit preservation efforts. This pressure is exemplified in the debate between preservation and conservation. Preservation connotes "nonuse" while conservation connotes "wise use" by and for humans. This debate is by no means new. It divided noted environmentalists John Muir and Gifford Pinchot and remains a contentious issue both domestically and internationally.[3]

---

[1] Michael Jeffery, *Biodiversity Conservation in the Context of Sustainable Human Development: A Call to Action, in* IUCN Academy of Environmental Law Research Studies, Biodiversity, Conservation, Law and Livelihoods 69 (Michael Jeffery *et al.* eds. 2008).

[2] *Id.*

[3] On the preservation-conservation dichotomy, *see* Bill Devall & George Sessions, Deep Ecology: Living As If Nature Mattered (1985); Bryan g. Norton, Toward Unity Among Environmentalists (1991).

While the legal framework accompanying systematic preservation is relatively recent, isolated examples of preservation can be found throughout history. The world's earliest known park (in what is now Iraq) dates from the third millennium BC;[4] monarchs traditionally protected wildlife (usually for their own ends, as Robin Hood could attest);[5] "sacred groves" of forests and other natural sites are central to some of the world's oldest religions;[6] ancient buildings and antiquities have been venerated by most cultures;[7] even the very idea of wilderness is an "intellectual legacy of the Old World to the New."[8]

The modern movement to preserve resources through law did not take hold until the 19th century, however, when the youthful United States pioneered the first preservation legislation. In 1872, the US Congress passed legislation creating "the first national park in the world"[9] – Yellowstone Park – which became the catalyst for the entire international preservation effort. The US followed that with the first system of reserved land management in 1891[10] (now the National Forests), the first prehistoric and historic preservation laws in 1906,[11] the first national system of parks beginning in 1916,[12] the first wilderness act in 1964,[13] the first wild rivers act in 1968,[14] and the first

---

[4] On this dichotomy relative to national parks, *see* the landmark book JOSEPH SAX, MOUNTAINS WITHOUT HANDRAILS: REFLECTIONS ON THE NATIONAL PARKS (1980).

[5] On international wildlife preservation, *see* MICHAEL BOWMAN, PETER DAVIES, & CATHERINE REDGWELL, LYSTER'S INTERNATIONAL WILDLIFE LAW 3–23 (2d ed. 2010).

[6] *See* J. Donald Hughes & M. D. Subash Chandran, *Sacred Groves Around the Earth: An Overview, in* CONSERVING THE SACRED FOR BIODIVERSITY MANAGEMENT 69–86 (P. S. Ramakrishnan *et al.* eds., 1998). In 2011, scientists at Oxford University were working on a world map showing all of the land owned or revered by world religions – estimated at about 15 percent of all land on earth – and determining its value in terms of biodiversity, http://www.enn.com/top_stories/article/43012; the scientists' website is at http://www.biodiversity.ox.ac.uk/.

[7] On historic/cultural preservation, *see generally*, THOMAS KING, CULTURAL RESOURCE LAWS AND PRACTICE (3d ed. 2008). DIANE BARTHEL, HISTORIC PRESERVATION: COLLECTIVE MEMORY AND HISTORICAL IDENTITY (1996); PRESERVATION AND CONSERVATION: PRINCIPLES AND PRACTICES: PROCEEDINGS OF THE NORTH AMERICAN INTERNATIONAL REGIONAL CONFERENCE (Sharon Timmons ed., 1976).

[8] RODERICK NASH, WILDERNESS AND THE AMERICAN MIND 8 (3d ed. 1982).

[9] An Act to set apart a certain Tract of Land lying near the Head-waters of the Yellowstone River as a public Park, U.S. Statutes at Large, Vol. 17, Chap. 24, pp. 32–33 (Mar. 1, 1872), http://www.yellowstone-online.com/history/yhfour.html. MARION CLAWSON, THE FEDERAL LANDS REVISITED 28 (1983).

[10] Forest Reserve Act, Oct. 1, 1890, ch. 1263, 26 Stat. 650.

[11] Antiquities Act of 1906, 16 U.S.C. § 431–433.

[12] National Park Service Organic Act of 1916, 16 U.S.C. § 1.

[13] The Wilderness Act of 1964, 16 U.S.C. § 1131.

[14] Wild and Scenic Rivers Act, 16 U.S.C. § 1271.

Endangered Species Act in 1973.[15] In total some 40 national laws mandate various types of resource preservation in the US[16] and, through their example, inspired the huge expansion of today's international preservation laws.

The earliest international "conservation" treaties, of the late 19th and early 20th centuries, were little more than agreements "dividing the spoils" of commercial hunting and fishing. This early focus on exploitation has evolved through a number of more progressive modern focuses, first on species protection, then on habitat for those species, then ecosystems for their own sake, to the latest focus on biological diversity. In 1940, the preservation philosophy first made its appearance in international law, and the 1970s produced a watershed of major treaties, creating the framework that today supports a growing network of international environmental law, IGOs, and NGOs working to preserve nature and other resources. The rest of this chapter will track the genesis of international preservation laws, beginning with pre-1970 laws, next taking on the "Stockholm Era" of 1972–1992, and finally tackling the "Rio Era" of 1992 until present day.

8.1   Preservation Laws Prior to the 1970s

8.1.1   The Early Wildlife Laws

There have doubtless been agreements on the sharing of game and harvesting rights since our ancestors first emerged as hunter-gatherers. Prior to the 1970s, the great bulk of international agreements on biological resources, reflected only that utilitarian concern. One of the leading compendiums of international law instruments lists scores of such bilateral and multilateral treaties since 1880 dealing with such topics as "convention on fishing," "preservation and protection of fur seals," "protection of game animals," "protection of birds useful to agriculture," regulation of whaling, tuna commissions, and fishing in transboundary waters.[17]

Africa's wildlife first became the subject of an international treaty in 1900, when the colonial powers (France, Germany, Great Britain, Italy, Portugal, and Spain) signed the London Convention for the Preservation of Wild

---

[15] Endangered Species Act, 16 U.S.C. § 1531.

[16] *See* George W. Pring & Stephen Miller, *Wilderness and Natural Area Preservation in the United States: A Survey of National Laws, in* PROCEEDINGS OF THE SINOAMERICAN CONFERENCE ON ENVIRONMENTAL LAW 52 (U. Colo. Sch. of Law 1987).

[17] EDITH BROWN WEISS, PAUL C. SZASZ & DANIEL B. MAGRAW, INTERNATIONAL ENVIRONMENTAL LAW: BASIC INSTRUMENTS AND REFERENCES 52–72 (1972).

Animals, Birds and Fish in Africa.[18] Embarrassing to read now, that treaty and its 1933 successor[19] had as their main objective the protection of species of economic or "trophy" value for big game hunters.

An early exception to the exploitation treaties is the 1916 Migratory Bird Treaty between the US and Canada[20] (still in effect and now including Mexico). In the 19th century, migrating flocks of songbirds, waterfowl, and other avifauna used to "darken the skies" for hours, even days, at a time, but rampant, indiscriminant "meat" and "sport" hunting (including firing cannons filled with scrap metal into the flocks) decimated these species in a few short decades. When the last known passenger pigeon (*Ecopistes migratorius*) died in captivity in 1914, the huge public outcry resulted in this treaty, which pledges the parties to protect hundreds of listed migratory birds. In furtherance of the treaty, the US adopted the Migratory Bird Treaty Act of 1918,[21] still one of the strictest preservation laws on the books. It prohibits the "taking" (hunting, killing, possessing, or interfering with) of treaty-listed birds and provides substantial criminal and civil penalties.

8.1.2   *The Western Hemisphere Conservation Convention*

In 1940, a score of North and South American nations gathered in Washington, DC, to sign the first treaty designed to provide comprehensive protection to natural areas and biologic resources, the Convention on Nature Protection and Wildlife Preservation in the Western Hemisphere.[22] The Convention pledges the parties to "explore the possibility" of establishing national parks, national reserves, nature monuments, and strict wilderness reserves, with varying levels of protection for the scenery, flora, and fauna in each category.[23] It also commits parties to adopt laws to preserve flora and fauna and "natural scenery, striking geological formations, and regions and natural objects of aesthetic interest or historic or scientific value" throughout

---

[18] Convention for the Preservation of Wild Animals, Birds and Fish in Africa, May 19, 1900, 94 Brit. and Foreign St. Papers 715, http://iea.uoregon.edu/texts/1900-PreservationWild AnimalsBirdsFishAfrica.EN.htm.

[19] Convention Relative to the Preservation of Fauna and Flora in Their Natural State, Nov. 18, 1933, 172 L.N.T.S. 241, http://www.ecolex.org/server2.php/libcat/docs/TRE/ Multilateral/En/TRE000069.txt.

[20] Canada-US Convention for the Protection of Migratory Birds in the United States and Canada, Aug. 16, 1916, 39 Stat. 1702, T.S. No. 628.

[21] 16 U.S.C. § 703 *et seq.*

[22] Convention on Nature Protection and Wildlife Preservation in the Western Hemisphere, Oct. 12, 1940, 161 U.N.T.S. 193, 56 Stat. 1354, T.S. No. 981, http://www.oas.org/juridico/ english/treaties/c-8.html.

[23] *Id.* arts. I–IV.

their countries,[24] protect migratory birds and prevent extinction of species,[25] control hunting, killing, capturing, or taking of species listed in the annex,[26] and control the import and export of protected flora or fauna.[27]

While "visionary for [its] time," the Western Hemisphere Conservation Convention has had limited effect since it has been ratified by only 19 nations and did not create either a compliance-monitoring secretariat or any enforcement means.[28] Still, its provisions foreshadowed and influenced the Convention on International Trade in Endangered Species (CITES), a third of a century later, and it has inspired many countries to develop quite impressive national parks and reserves systems – a praiseworthy extreme being Costa Rica, where over 25 percent of the entire country is preserved in one of these categories.[29]

8.2   *Preservation Efforts – The Stockholm Era: 1972–1992*

The 20-year period from 1972–1992 was a highly formative era in the history of international environmental law. The 1960s brought a huge increase in public concern over the environment and particularly over the progressive loss of endangered species, habitat, ecosystems, natural areas, and cultural sites to population expansion, war, and development. This translated into the influential 1972 Stockholm Declaration, which called for preservation in three key Principles, 2, 4, and 12:

> The natural resources of the earth including the air, water, land, flora and fauna and especially representative samples of natural ecosystems must be safeguarded for the benefit of present and future generations through careful planning or management, as appropriate.[30]
>
> Man has a special responsibility to safeguard and wisely manage the heritage of wildlife and its habitat which are now gravely imperiled by a combination of

---

[24] *Id.* art. V(2).

[25] *Id.* art. VII.

[26] *Id.* art. VIII.

[27] *Id.* art. IX.

[28] Weiss *et al.*, *supra* note 17, at 211–12.

[29] Sean T. McAllister, *Community-Based Conservation: Restructuring Institutions to Involve Local Communities in a Meaningful Way*, 10 Colo. J. Int'l Envtl. L. & Pol'y 195, 198 (1999).

[30] United Nations Conference on the Human Environment, Stockholm, Swed., June 5–16, 1972, *Stockholm Declaration of the UN Conference on the Human Environment*, Principle 2, UN Doc. A/CONF.48/14/Rev. 1 at 3, UN Doc. A/CONF.48/14 at 2–65 and Corr. 1 (June 16, 1972), http://www.unep.org/Documents.Multilingual/Default.asp?documentid=97&article id=1503.

adverse factors. Nature conservation including wildlife must therefore receive importance in planning for economic development.[31]

Resources should be made available to preserve and improve the environment, taking into account the circumstances and particular requirements of developing countries....[32]

These aspirations were rewarded with an outpouring of new international preservation initiatives in the 1970s, which continues today. In particular, preservation regimes were established to protect (1) ecosystems, (2) natural and cultural resources, (3) endangered species, and (4) the global commons, a discussion of each of which follows.

8.2.1   *Ecosystems*

8.2.1.1   *Wetlands*

Wetlands – including streams, lakesides, mangrove swamps, marshes, fens, peat bogs, prairie potholes, tropical river systems, estuaries, tidal flats, coastal beaches, and shallow coral reefs – are among our most important, productive, and diverse ecosystems. While wetlands only cover 9 percent of the earth's landmass,[33] they play a vital role in fish and wildlife habitat, commercial foodstocks, pollution filtration, natural flood control, and recreation. Wetlands are perhaps the ecosystems most threatened by human development.[34] Fittingly, the oldest global treaty for the protection of ecosystems focuses on them, the Convention on Wetlands of International Importance Especially as Waterfowl Habitat,[35] signed in Ramsar, Iran, in 1971.

The Ramsar Convention is designed to protect wetlands from human destruction, drainage, pollution, dumping, filling, and the like. It uses a "listing" approach, requiring state parties to list or designate their areas of wetlands that have "international significance in terms of ecology, botany, zoology, limnology, or hydrology" especially for waterfowl.[36] By 2012, 160

---

[31] *Id.* Principle 4.

[32] *Id.* Principle 12.

[33] *See* David Hunter, James Salzman & Durwood Zaelke, International Environmental Law And Policy 1136 *et seq.* (2011). An "ecosystem" is a unit of plants, animals, and their physical and chemical environment, in which no one part exists independently of the others.

[34] *See* President's Council on Environmental Quality, Our Nation's Wetlands 1 *et seq.* (1978).

[35] Ramsar Convention on Wetlands of International Importance Especially as Waterfowl Habitat, Feb. 2, 1971, 996 U.N.T.S. 245, 11 I.L.M. 969 (1972), http://www.ramsar.org/cda/en/ramsar-documents-texts/main/ramsar/1-31-38_4000_0__.

[36] *Id.* art. 2. Although rarely used, the Ramsar Convention also allows parties to delete or restrict listings at will. *Id.* art. 2(5).

countries had joined as parties and over 1,971 sites had been listed, covering 190,737,919 hectares (over 471 million acres).[37] The convention further pledges the parties to "promote the conservation" of the listed wetlands,[38] advise of any actual or potential "change" in the wetlands as a result of "human interference,"[39] establish nature reserves on wetlands,[40] compensate for net loss of deleted or restricted wetlands,[41] and endeavor through management to increase waterfowl populations.[42]

Ramsar creates a "Conference of the Parties" (COP) to oversee and advise on implementation (but without enforcement powers, except that of moral suasion). The COP requires annual monitoring reports on listed sites, and also keeps a list of Ramsar sites that are "under threat" (such as the US Everglades). An innovative aspect of the treaty is that it makes an NGO an integral part of its ongoing operation: the respected International Union for Conservation of Nature and Natural Resources (IUCN or World Conservation Union) serves as the "continuing bureau" (or staff) for the COP, maintaining the list, assisting in convening COP meetings, and advising of changes to the list, changes in character of wetlands, and other monitoring activities.[43]

The treaty contains an early example of the protection-development contradiction found in modern "sustainable development" treaties, like the Convention on Biologic Diversity (below). Ramsar requires that parties plan so as to make "wise use" of their wetlands,[44] which the COP's guidelines interpret as "sustainable utilization." Although there is no sanction if a party fails to protect a listed wetland, the embarrassment of a negative COP report has proved a reasonably effective pressure. Although wetlands continue to deteriorate internationally, Ramsar has already achieved a measure of success. In the future, it will work toward securing the resources necessary to achieve its mission and progress towards universal membership.[45]

8.2.1.2   *Other Ecosystems*

The preeminent example of an ecosystem-focused law (although it is also much more than that) is the 1982 United Nations Convention on the Law

---

[37] *Id.*

[38] *Id.* art. 3(1).

[39] *Id.* art. 3(2).

[40] *Id.* art. 4(1).

[41] *Id.* art. 4(2).

[42] *Id.* art. 4(4).

[43] *Id.* art. 8.

[44] *Id.* art. 3(1).

[45] Bowman, Davies, Redgwel *supra* 5, note at 405–6.

of the Sea (*see* § 8.2.4.1 and Chapter 11). Bilateral and multilateral treaties abound for freshwater rivers and lakes, but they typically focus more on resource allocation than ecosystem preservation (with notable exceptions, like the US-Canada Great Lakes Agreement, *see* § 8.2.2.4).[46] Ecosystems receive some secondary attention in the various natural and cultural area preservation treaties (next section below). Efforts in the 1990s to adopt a comprehensive international treaty for the world's forest ecosystems foundered (*see* § 8.3.2), while a treaty on "preventing" the spread of desert ecosystems succeeded (*see* § 8.3.3).

8.2.2   *Natural and Cultural Resources*

The most widespread of all preservation conventions is the 1972 Convention for the Protection of the World Cultural and Natural Heritage, which had been ratified by 188 countries as of the beginning of 2012.[47] Two separate campaigns were woven together in this one treaty – UNESCO's work to save important buildings, archaeological sites, and other cultural properties (after the destruction of World War II) and the IUCN's and USA's efforts to create international protection for natural parks, wildlife areas, and other sites. The treaty uses a three-fold approach: a positive listing process,[48] a negative list of sites "in danger"[49] (the US Everglades are also listed here), and funding, including emergency assistance.[50]

States nominate outstanding "cultural and natural heritage" properties within their borders, which (unlike Ramsar) must be approved by a 21-country elected intergovernmental committee before being placed on the "World Heritage List."[51] By 2012, 936 sites had been listed (183 natural, 725 cultural, and 28 mixed), including Yellowstone Park and the Grand Canyon in the US, Australia's Great Barrier Reef, Nepal's Mount Everest region, the Galapagos Islands, the Great Wall of China, the Acropolis, the Vatican, the Kremlin, and the Auschwitz Concentration Camp.[52] A permanent secretariat within

---

[46] For a collected list of these, *see* WEISS ET AL., *supra* note 17, at 40–50.

[47] United Nations Educational, Scientific & Cultural Organization (UNESCO) Convention for the Protection of the World Cultural and Natural Heritage, Nov. 16, 1972, 27 U.S.T. 37, 1037 U.N.T.S. 151, http://whc.unesco.org/archive/convention-en.pdf; parties are listed at *States Parties: Ratification Status,* UNESCO, http://whc.unesco.org/en/statesparties.

[48] *Id.* arts. 1–3.

[49] *Id.* art. 11(4); threatened list at *World Heritage in Danger,* UNESCO, http://whc.unesco.org/en/danger.

[50] *Id.* arts. 15–16.

[51] *Id.* arts. 8, 11(2).

[52] *World Heritage List,* UNESCO http://whc.unesco.org/en/list.

UNESCO serves as staff, and several prominent NGOs, including IUCN, are made integral parts of the monitoring and implementation process.[53]

Listing obligates parties to protect their sites from damage,[54] but enforcement is left up to each state. The only express sanctions are the power of the committee to "delist" a site that a state has failed to preserve adequately[55] or to place the site on the "in danger" list. Despite the lack of external enforcement, these have proved strong motivators, since most countries seek heritage listing because it confers added prominence to their sites and attracts income from tourism.[56] The listing-prevents-development aspect of this and similar conventions has also been used as an offensive weapon by environmentalists, indigenous peoples, and local communities.[57] The Windy Craggy mine proposal in the Tatshenshini-Alsek region of British Columbia, Canada, was defeated in part by successful government and NGO efforts to list the area as a World Heritage Site;[58] Yellowstone Park's status as a listed site was a factor in the US government's opposition to the New World mine near the park boundary;[59] and Australia's denial of the Coronation Hill mine was partially over concerns that increased mining might threaten the World Heritage listing of downstream Kakadu National Park.[60] Simply the prospect of having a UNESCO/World Heritage inspection team come to examine an allegedly threatened listing can create a political furor, as happened in Australia with the Kakadu site in 1998.[61]

In 2001, UNESCO dove into yet another heritage treaty, adopting the Convention on the Protection of the Underwater Cultural Heritage.[62] The treaty protects "all traces of human existence having a cultural, historical or archaeological character which have been partially or totally under water,

---

[53] World Cultural and Natural Heritage Convention, *supra* note 47, art. 14. For full details on parties, sites, organizations, meetings, etc., *see About World Heritage,* UNESCO, http:// whc.unesco.org/en/about/.

[54] *Id.* arts. 4–6.

[55] *Id.* art. 11(2).

[56] *See* Ken Miller, *A U.N. Occupation of American Parks?,* GANNETT NEWS SERV., Sept. 12, 1996, reprinted in HUNTER ET AL., *supra* note 33, at 1135.

[57] *See* George Pring, Jim Otto & Koh Naito, *Trends in International Environmental Law Affecting the Minerals Industry,* 17 J. ENERGY & NAT. RESOURCES L. 39, 51 (1999).

[58] *See Update: B.C. Preserves Vast Tat Watershed,* 23 INTERNATIONAL WILDLIFE 31 (September 1993).

[59] *See Yellowstone Values, Wildlife Defended,* 69 NATIONAL PARKS 10 (1995).

[60] *See* Peter Pockley, *Australians Seek International Allies in Battle Over Uranium Mine,* 399 NATURE, MAY 6, 1999, at 7 (1999).

[61] *Id.*

[62] Convention on the Protection of the Underwater Cultural Heritage, November 6, 2001, 41 I.L.M. 40, http://unesdoc.unesco.org/images/0012/001260/126065e.pdf. Four states voted against and 15 abstained.

periodically or continuously, for at least 100 years," including sites, structures, artifacts, human remains, vessels, and prehistoric objects.[63] It generally obligates parties to cooperate in preserving the underwater cultural heritage, preferably *in situ* and without commercial exploitation.[64] The treaty entered into force on January 2, 2009.

8.2.3   Endangered Species

For most of the 20th century, both national and international wildlife preservation efforts have focused on preventing the killing of animal species that are endangered or threatened with extinction.[65] Less attention has been paid to the equally (some would say more) important issues of preserving the necessary habitat for wildlife and preserving biodiversity – two quite different approaches to the common problem of permanent biotic loss. Concededly, extinction is a natural part of the process of evolution, for, as critics of preservation like to point out, as much as 99 percent of all animals and plants that have ever existed on the earth are extinct.[66] What that statistic fails to take into account, however, is that human beings, with our vast population growth and technology, have enormously accelerated the process of extinction.[67]

One staggering estimate is that we are permanently losing 27,000 species each year, 74 species per day, three every hour.[68] The IUCN, the international NGO which officially declares species threatened or extinct, created "shock waves" with its 2004 report on the world's biodiversity, which calculated that extinctions had reached 1,000 times the rate before humans.[69] The rate is increasing, and it is possible that the dramatic predictions of experts like Harvard biologist E. O. Wilson, the father of modern biodiversity science,

---

[63] *Id.* art. 1(1)(a).

[64] *Id.* art. 2.

[65] For an in-depth study of international wildlife agreements, *see* LYSTER, *supra* note 5.

[66] *Has Earth's Sixth Mass Extinction Already Arrived?* SCIENCEDAILY, Mar. 5, 2011, http://www.sciencedaily.com/releases/2011/03/110302131844.htm.

[67] Although extinction is a natural phenomenon, it occurs at a natural "background" rate of about one to five species per year. *The Extinction Crisis*, CENTER FOR BIOLOGICAL DIVERSITY, http://www.biologicaldiversity.org/programs/biodiversity/elements_of_biodiversity/extinction_crisis/index.html. *See also* PAUL EHRLICH & ANNE EHRLICH, EXTINCTION: THE CAUSES AND CONSEQUENCES OF THE DISAPPEARANCE OF SPECIES 6–8 (1981).

[68] EDWARD O. WILSON, THE DIVERSITY OF LIFE 280 (1992).

[69] Juliette Jowit, *Humans Driving Extinction Faster Than Species Can Evolve, Say Experts,* THE GUARDIAN, Mar. 7, 2010, http://www.guardian.co.uk/environment/2010/mar/07/extinction-species-evolve.

will prove true: the rate of loss could reach 10,000 times the background rate a few years from now.[70]

Some scientists are calling our human-caused losses "the sixth mass extinction," but, unlike the natural mass extinctions that have occurred five times during the past 540 million years, caused by asteroid strikes, volcanic eruptions, and natural climate change, this one is human-induced.[71] The causes are easy to see, if difficult to control. Humans are causing extinctions directly through over-consumption (food, clothing, pets, products, hunting) and indirectly through climate change (increased global temperatures, rising sea levels, changing weather patterns) and destruction of habitat (logging, slash-and-burn agriculture, dams, the draining of wetlands, and pollution).[72] Unfortunately, scientists are only beginning to realize that human induced climate change represents at least as great a threat to the number of species surviving on Earth as habitat-destruction and over-consumption.[73] Moreover, because it is difficult to predict the effect of climate change on future landscapes, researchers are still trying to determine the best ways to mitigate the effects for wildlife.[74]

The arguments for "preservation of our fellow travelers on Spaceship Earth" are many, and include those based on ethics/compassion, human aesthetics, scientific interest, direct economic benefits, and unknown future utility.[75] However, conservation can be costly, particularly for the economically disadvantaged rural populations in developing countries who might otherwise benefit in the short term from exploitation of these resources.[76] An argument can be made that protection of endangered species has now become customary international law, but the overwhelming focus of the field is on conventional law,[77] and a number of international environmental treaties exist seeking to find a rational balance for the conflicting issues surrounding species extinction.

---

[70] *Id.*

[71] *Has Earth's Sixth Mass Extinction Already Arrived?*, Science Daily, Mar. 5. 2011, http://www.sciencedaily.com/releases/2011/03/110302131844.htm; Center for Biological Diversity, *The Extinction Crisis, supra* note 67.

[72] HUNTER ET AL., *supra* note 33, at 7.

[73] John Roach, *By 2050 Warming to Doom Million Species, Study Says*, NATIONAL GEOGRAPHIC, http://news.nationalgeographic.com/news/2004/01/0107_040107_extinction.html.

[74] Cornelia Dean, *Preservation and Climate Change: The Preservation Predicament*, N.Y. TIMES, Jan. 29, 2008 at F1, http://www.nytimes.com/2008/01/29/science/earth/29habi.html?pagewanted=1.

[75] WILSON, *supra* note 68, at 7.

[76] FRANCES CAIRNCROSS, COSTING THE EARTH: THE CHALLENGE FOR GOVERNMENTS, THE OPPORTUNITIES FOR BUSINESS 131 (1992–93).

[77] Michael Glennon, *Has International Law Failed the Elephant?*, 84 AM. J. INT'L L. 1, 10 (1990).

8.2.3.1   *African Wildlife*

It was the newly independent nations of Africa, in 1968, that showed the world the path to preservation of endangered species, five years before the US and international endangered species laws came into existence. Meeting under the auspices of the Organization of African Unity (OAU), African countries rejected the "trophy hunting" treaties of the colonial powers (*see* § 8.1.1) and adopted the world's first endangered species preservation treaty, the African Convention on the Conservation of Nature and Natural Resources,[78] now ratified by some 30 countries as of 2012. A truly comprehensive approach to conservation, the convention covers not only animals but conservation of soil,[79] water,[80] flora[81] and habitat areas.[82] Its principal goal is preservation of "protected species" (animals and plants "threatened with extinction, or which may become so") and their necessary habitat.[83] It does this by creating two lists – a highly protected "Class A" list and a less protected (managed) "Class B" list, which includes most of the "big game" animals.[84] Setting the stage for future treaties like CITES (*see* § 8.2.3.2), the African convention employs a "trade-control" approach to preservation, requiring parties to strictly regulate "traffic" (trade, transport, export, import) in "specimens" (alive) and "trophies" (dead) of both listed and non-listed species.[85] Limiting its effectiveness are numerous qualifying phrases[86] and exceptions.[87]

---

[78] African Convention on the Conservation of Nature and Natural Resources, Sept. 15, 1968, 1001 U.N.T.S. 3, http://www.africa-union.org/root/au/Documents/Treaties/Text/Convention_Nature%20&%20Natural_Resources.pdf.

[79] *Id.* art. IV.

[80] *Id.* art. V.

[81] *Id.* art. VI.

[82] *Id.* art. X. These "conservation areas" may be "strict nature reserves," somewhat less protected "national parks" and "partial reserves," and "game reserves" (for hunting).

[83] *Id.* art. VIII(1).

[84] Species on the "Class A" list must be "totally protected" (killing, capture, etc., allowed "only on authorization in each case of the highest competent authority" and "only if required in the national interest or for scientific purposes"); species on the "Class B" list must also be "totally protected" (but killing, capture, etc., may be authorized by lower authority and without the national-interest/scientific purpose limitation). The Class A list includes, as examples, chimpanzees, gorillas, cheetahs, pygmy hippos, flamingos, vultures, marine turtles, and several plants; the Class B list includes all monkeys (except common baboons), some hyaenas, crocodiles, ostriches, and "big game" animals such as lions, leopards, elephants, black rhinoceroses, hippos, and most of the antelope species.

[85] *Id.* art. IX.

[86] *E.g.,* "with due regard to the best interests of the people" (art. II), "if required in the national interest" (art. VIII(1)(1)), conservation areas "where appropriate" (art. X(1)).

[87] *E.g.,* contrary measures may be taken if in the "paramount interest of the State," "in time of famine," "for the protection of public health," "in defense of property," *etc.* (art. XVII).

8.2.3.2 *CITES*

The international effort to preserve endangered species is centered on the 1973 Convention on International Trade in Endangered Species (CITES),[88] to which 175 countries are parties as of 2012. Unlike the US Endangered Species Act,[89] CITES does not directly prohibit killing of wildlife or destruction of habitat. Instead its approach is to regulate the commercial trade in endangered species, restricting the passage across national borders of "specimens" (listed animals or plants, alive or dead, and parts thereof).[90] Unquestionably, wildlife trade is big business. It is estimated that over 350 million animals and plants are traded each year.[91] While the exact figures on the value generated from this "industry" vary widely, it is generally agreed that wildlife trade involves billions of dollars each year. Unfortunately, a large percentage of that trade takes place illegally and threatens the survival of wild animals and plants.[92]

Animals are killed and traded for a myriad of reasons. Elephants across Africa and Asia are killed for their ivory tusks. Between 1977 and 1997, the 1.3 million elephants in Africa were reduced to 600,000, and the slaughter continues.[93] Rhinoceros horns, shark fins, tiger bones, bear gall bladders, and other animal parts are coveted for oriental and traditional medicines, aphrodisiacs, and tourist trinkets. Tropical fish and fowl are captured and sold as exotic pets. Rare trees are in demand for furniture or household items. Furs are sold as luxury items. Some animals, such as sea turtles, whales, or abalone, are considered delicacies and are prized for their meat. Because wildlife is put to such a wide range of uses, it can be difficult to effectively tackle the root causes of illegal trafficking.

---

[88] Convention on International Trade in Endangered Species of Wild Fauna and Flora, Mar. 3, 1973, 27 U.S.T. 1087, T.I.A.S. No. 8249, http://www.cites.org (hereinafter CITES); parties listed at http://www.cites.org/eng/disc/parties/index.php.

[89] 16 U.S.C. §§ 1531–1534.

[90] CITES, *supra* note 88, art. 1(b).

[91] Amy Wagner, *Endangered Species: Traded to Death*, EARTHTRENDS 2001, http://earthtrends .wri.org/features/view_feature.php?theme=7&fid=25.

[92] *Wildlife Trade*, WORLD WILDLIFE FUND, http://www.worldwildlife.org/what/globalmarkets/ wildlifetrade/whyitmatters.html; INTERNATIONAL WILDLIFE TRADE: A CITES SOURCEBOOK vii (Ginette Hemley ed., 1994).

[93] Public Broadcasting Service, *Nature: The Elephants of Africa: The Poaching Problem* (2010), http://www.pbs.org/wnet/nature/elephants/poaching.html. Other resources dealing with animal and plant poaching and trade can be found in sources such as Wagner, *supra* note 91; The Humane Society of the United States, *Poaching*, http://www.humanesociety.org/ issues/poaching/; Dominic Dyer, *Poaching is now the greatest threat to many endangered species*, The Sunday Times (London), Mar. 21, 2010, http://www.timesonline.co.uk/tol/ news/environment/article7069944.ece.

CITES protection relies on three lists or "appendices" of species, establishing three different levels of protection depending on the degree to which the species is threatened. The highest level of protection is provided by Appendix I, which lists "all species threatened with extinction which are or may be affected by trade"[94] (over 800 species, including American alligators, several rhinos, all sea turtles, great apes and some other primates, tigers, whale species covered by the International Whaling Commission moratorium, numerous parrots, mollusks, and some orchids and cacti). Appendix II provides an intermediate level of protection for species which "may become" threatened with extinction unless trade regulated[95] (this list contains over 25,000 species, including chimpanzees and other primates, mountain lions, numerous birds, American crocodiles, polar bears, boas and pythons, and gila monsters). Appendix III provides the least protection for species voluntarily identified by any party as being regulated by them and needing the cooperation of other parties to be effective[96] (including water buffaloes, mongooses, and Canadian walruses). Species may be added to or removed from Appendices I and II by a 2/3 vote of parties present and voting at any meeting[97] of the COP.

CITES then operates through a permit system requiring export and import permits for Appendix I species[98] and export permits only for species on Appendix II[99] and III.[100] CITES provisions require exporting and importing countries to make numerous strict findings before granting the permit (key among these being that the permit "will not be detrimental to the survival of the species" and "was not obtained in contravention of the laws" of the producer state).[101] The treaty also grants parties the power (and responsibility) to "take appropriate measures" to enforce the convention and prohibit violations.[102] Taken together, these permit requirements prohibit producer states, middleperson states, and consumer states from trading Appendix I species, restrict exporters but not importers of Appendix II species, and rely primarily on the laws of the exporting state for Appendix III species.

Despite the fact that CITES revolutionized the protection of endangered species, it has several serious defects. CITES is undermined by numerous self-weakening exemptions. For example, it tolerates trade for household use

---

[94] CITES, *supra* note 88, art. II(1).
[95] *Id.* art. II(2).
[96] *Id.* art. II(3).
[97] *Id.* art. XV.
[98] *Id.* art. III.
[99] *Id.* art. IV.
[100] *Id.* art. V.
[101] *Id.* art. III(2)–(5).
[102] *Id.* art. VIII(1).

and with captive-bred stock,[103] allows reservations,[104] and permits trade with nonparties[105] – all of which are prone to abuse. The treaty also faces a major ideological split between those who believe in the effectiveness of prohibition and those who do not.[106] This split is best exemplified by the debate over elephant ivory. East and Central African states generally favor an "ivory ban" as the best means for the elephant's survival, while Southern African states favor a "safari policy" that funds preservation through limited paid hunting.[107] At this point, many believe that CITES has proved ineffective at halting a new boom in poaching fueled by increased demand for ivory from a growing middle class in east Asia.[108] It is estimated that more poaching took place in 2006 than took place before the ban was put in place.[109] As one CITES representative noted: "Bans are popular and easy to adopt by enacting legislation, but they do not work everywhere."[110] Given these obstacles, the general view is that CITES has made a large contribution to resolving the problem, but will need to improve remedies and enforcement to keep up with new surges in poaching.

8.2.3.3   *Migratory Wildlife*

Migratory animals are among the most vulnerable of all species, for if even one country in their migration range does not protect them, they can be threatened with extinction. The global treaty addressing this problem is the 1979 Convention on the Conservation of Migratory Species of Wild Animals (CMS or Bonn Convention),[111] with 116 parties by 2012, and for which

---

[103] *Id.* art. VII.

[104] *Id.* arts. XV, XVI, XXIII.

[105] *Id.* art. X.

[106] *See* WILLIAM ADAMS, AGAINST EXTINCTION: THE STORY OF CONSERVATION, 199–200 (2004).

[107] Since 1989, CITES has relaxed the ban on the sale of ivory to permit three one-time sales of stockpiled ivory confiscated by African governments. These sales have further fueled the debate over whether legitimate sales encourage the ivory market and lead to more poaching. After the last one-time sale was completed in 2008, CITES put a nine-year moratorium on such trades. Alan Cowell, *Bid to Relax International Ban on the Sale of Ivory Is Rejected*, N.Y. TIMES, Mar. 22, 2010, http://www.nytimes.com/2010/03/23/world/africa/23ivory.html. *See also* Bijal P. Trivedi *UN Body OK's One-Time Ivory Sale, Sparks Controversy*, NATIONAL GEOGRAPHIC, Nov. 14, 2002, http://news.nationalgeographic.com/news/2002/11/1114_021114_TVIvoryTrade.html.

[108] Samuel Wasser, *et al. The Ivory Trail*, 301 SCIENTIFIC AMERICAN, 68–76 (2009).

[109] *Id.*

[110] Juan Carlos Vasquez, CITES Legal and Trade Policy Officer *quoted in*: *Call of the Wild*, 386 ECONOMIST, Mar. 8, 2008, at 85.

[111] Convention on the Conservation of Migratory Species of Wild Animals, June 23, 1979, 1980 Misc. 11, 19 I.L.M. 15 (1980), http://www.cms.int/documents/convtxt/cms_convtxt_

UNEP provides the Secretariat. The Bonn Convention also employs the listing approach, with Appendix I for "endangered" migratory species[112] and Appendix II for those with an "unfavorable conservation status" (threatened).[113] For Appendix I species "range state" parties must endeavor to conserve and restore habitats of importance, minimize impeding activities and obstacles, control future endangerment, and, with some exceptions, prohibit takings.[114] However, the similarity to CITES and other conventional wildlife treaties ends there, as the Bonn Convention utilizes a very innovative framework for protecting Appendix II species by encouraging parties to enter into cooperative agreements to "benefit the species."[115] After a slow start, in which only a few such formal agreements were forthcoming, the COP has recommended that parties use more informal "memoranda of understanding" (MOUs), which has greatly increased the pace of cooperative efforts since the early 1990s.[116]

A problem with the Bonn Convention is that some major migratory states have not joined, feeling their bilateral and multilateral migratory species and regional conventions are adequate. For example, neither the US nor Canada has become a party, presumably because of their 1916 Migratory Bird Treaty (*see* § 8.1.1). This short-sighted approach overlooks the threats to all of the other Bonn-protected species and the need for a global perspective on migrations.[117]

8.2.3.4   *Regional Wildlife Treaties*
In addition to the more global wildlife treaties, quite a number of multilateral regional wildlife treaties have been developed. The first of the modern era was the 1940 Western Hemisphere Conservation Convention (*see* § 8.1.2), followed by the 1968 OAU African Convention (*see* § 8.2.2.1). One of the most significant ones is the 1979 Conservation of European Wildlife and Natural Habitats (Berne Convention),[118] which has fostered a host of EU directives and regulations and UN/ECE codes of conduct and other agreements.

---

english.pdf; parties listed at *About CMS,* Convention on Migratory Species, http://www.cms.int/about/part_lst.htm.

[112] *Id.* arts. I(1)(e), III.

[113] *Id.* arts. I(1)(c)–(d), IV.

[114] *Id.* art. III(4)–(5).

[115] *Id.* arts. IV, V.

[116] Bowman, Davies, Redgwell *supra* 5, note at 235–36; CMS, *Introduction to the Convention on Migratory Species,* http://www.cms.int/about/intro.htm.

[117] *See id.* at 562.

[118] Conservation of European Wildlife and Natural Habitats, Sept. 19, 1979, E.T.S. No. 104 (hereafter Berne Convention).

The countries of Southeast Asia were also affected by the environmental movement beginning in the 1970s. In 1985 the Association of South East Asian Nations (ASEAN) created the Agreement on the Conservation of Nature and Natural Resources[119] which illustrates that regional treaties may be evolving from their traditional narrow focus on endangered species and trade controls into more holistic ecosystem protection. While the agreement covers trade in both endangered and endemic species,[120] it goes beyond that to include conservation of ecosystems, biological diversity, reserve establishment, environmental impact assessment, scientific research, and public participation. Modern ecosystem preservation approaches can also be found in treaties focused on issues other than wildlife. A major example is the 1978 US-Canada Great Lakes Water Quality Agreement[121] which expressly "recogniz[es] that restoration and enhancement of the boundary waters cannot be achieved independently of other parts of the Great Lakes Basin Ecosystem,"[122] meaning "the interacting components of air, land, water and living organisms, including humans, within the drainage."[123] Accordingly, it calls for sweeping programs dealing broadly with direct water pollution discharges, land uses, shipping, dredging, on- and off-shore facilities, and airborne toxics.[124]

8.2.3.5 *Species-Specific Wildlife Laws*

At the opposite end of the spectrum from these holistic-ecosystem approaches, are species-specific preservation treaties that protect certain "charismatic megafauna" like whales, seals, polar bears, dolphins, and sea turtles, the treatment of which has galvanized public opinion sufficiently to warrant special attention. Ironically, specific-species protections originated to benefit their commercial exploiters and have only slowly evolved into preservation laws. Moreover, a number of these species are found in shared areas outside national jurisdiction, such as the high seas and Antarctica, adding to the ever-problematic nature of international law enforcement. The travails of

---

[119] ASEAN Agreement on the Conservation of Nature and Natural Resources, July 9, 1985, 1985, 15 E.P.L. 64 (not yet in force).

[120] *Id.* art. 5.

[121] Great Lakes Water Quality Agreement, Nov. 22, 1978, 30 U.S.T. 1383, T.I.A.S. No. 9257, as amended Oct. 16, 1983, T.I.A.S. No. 10798, and Nov. 18, 1987, http://www.ijc.org/en/background/treat_trait.htm.

[122] *Id.* preamble, para. 8.

[123] *Id.* art I(g).

[124] *Id.* art. VI.

each of these creatures and their human defenders and exploiters is a book unto itself.[125]

8.2.4   *The Global Commons*

Vast areas lie outside the limits of national jurisdiction – the international seas, Antarctica, outer space, and some would argue the Arctic – and are viewed by many as "global commons" (as discussed in § 2.1.10). Although they may seem remote, each of these areas has development potential that is already receiving serious attention, in particular for mineral resources. There is growing international support for recognition of these areas as "the common heritage of humankind" – a principle that creates an obligation for states to use these common areas in a way that benefits humankind as a whole[126] – but whether "common heritage" means developmental profit-sharing or preservation of nature is still subject to great debate, as a review of these common heritage laws shows.

8.2.4.1   *The High Seas*

The 1982 United Nations Convention on the Law of the Sea (UNCLOS or Law of the Sea Treaty)[127] is a comprehensive framework for regulating human use, development, and preservation of the nearly 75 percent of the earth's surface which is ocean (*see* full discussion in Chapter 11). It has enormous future significance in the preservation-development debate, obviously in its "deep seabed mining" provisions and less obviously in its environmental preservation-protection provisions. The latter, if effectively implemented and enforced, could well make it the marine equivalent of the terrestrial Convention on Biological Diversity (*see* below). Furthermore, as a comprehensive "framework" treaty, it provides the basis for adoption of the Global Plan of Action for the Marine Environment and linkages to other international and regional treaties preventing degradation of the marine environment from ships, dumping, land-based sources, and development activities.

Generally, UNCLOS leaves mineral resources within 200 miles of shore under the exclusive control and sovereignty of the coastal state.[128] The vast remainder of the ocean is outside national jurisdiction. Its surface and waters

---

[125] For good background summaries with citations to the controlling laws, *see* WEISS ET AL., *supra* note 17, at 1014–30.

[126] HUNTER ET AL., *supra* note 33, at 452–53.

[127] United Nations Convention on the Law of the Sea, Dec. 10, 1982, 1833 U.N.T.S. 3, 397; 21 I.L.M. 1261 (1982), http://www.un.org/Depts/los/convention_agreements/texts/unclos/closindx.htm.

[128] *Id.* arts. 2–16 (territorial sea), 55–75 (exclusive economic zone), and 76–85 (continental shelf).

are the "high seas"[129] and its sea-bed and subsoil are "the Area."[130] The Area is specifically designated as "the common heritage of mankind"[131] and targeted for "development of resources"[132] "for the benefit of mankind as a whole."[133] An International Seabed Authority (ISA or the Authority),[134] headquartered in Kingston, Jamaica, has the power to control all mining and mineral-related activities in the Area and share the profits among all nations. This is the UNCLOS concept successfully pushed by developing nations and most opposed by the US and other industrialized nations that favor a "freedom of the high seas" rather than a "common heritage" approach to mining.[135] The ISA has legislated regulations on prospecting and exploration for certain minerals and is working on others that combined will be the UNCLOS "Mining Code."[136] Since deep sea mining has yet to become commercially viable, it remains to be seen how Japanese, Australian, and other leading marine mining entities will fare within or without this common heritage regime.

The Convention's numerous provisions for protecting and preserving the marine environment contain some of the strongest language of any treaty, and the trend appears to be toward the development of strong implementing standards and programs to effectuate them (even in the view of nations, like the US, which oppose the ISA mining regime). UNCLOS creates a general obligation on states to "protect and preserve the marine environment,"[137] has detailed requirements for the adoption of needed laws, measures, and enforcement programs to that end,[138] calls for "conservation and management of the living resources" of the exclusive economic zone and the high seas,[139] and even directs the ISA to adopt rules and enforcement procedures "to ensure effective protection for the marine environment from harmful effects which may arise from ['exploitation of resources']" in the Area.[140] UNCLOS tackles the sovereignty issue head on, expressly qualifying states' "sovereign right to exploit their natural resources pursuant to their environmental policies" with the restriction that all such development must be "in accordance with

---

[129] *Id.* arts. 86–120.

[130] *Id.* arts. 1(1)(1), 133–191.

[131] *Id.* art. 136.

[132] *Id.* art. 150.

[133] *Id.* art. 140.

[134] *Id.* arts. 1(1)(2), 156.

[135] For a good overview of seabed mining *see* Michael W. Lodge, *Environmental Regulation of Deep Seabed Mining, in* INTERNATIONAL MARINE ENVIRONMENTAL LAW: INSTITUTIONS, IMPLEMENTATION, AND INNOVATIONS 49–59 (Andree Kirchner ed. 2002).

[136] ISA, *Mining Code*, http://www.isa.org.jm/en/documents/mcode.

[137] UNCLOS, *supra* note 127, art. 192.

[138] *E.g., id.* arts. 192–237.

[139] *Id.* arts. 61–75, 116–120.

[140] *Id.* art. 145.

their duty to protect and preserve the marine environment."[141] Moreover, the Convention calls for the establishment of "international rules, regulations and procedures" to protect the marine environment,[142] which cannot help but increase the level of national regulation since national laws must be "no less effective" than the international rules.[143]

Authorities differ in predicting how restrictive these UNCLOS preservation regulations will be, with some believing they will impose strong "sustainable development" standards (*see* Chapter 11) and others believing they will fall short of that protective level.[144] Nevertheless, many scholars view UNCLOS to be one of the most successful preservation regimes to be developed, substantively advancing the development of international environmental law.[145] Today, many analysts believe that UNCLOS's provisions on protection and preservation of the marine environment constitute generally applicable customary law.[146] Whether preservation or development prevails, the trend is for more, not less, regulation of the marine environment and its resources.

8.2.4.2   *Antarctica*

Larger than the US and Mexico combined and twice the size of Australia, our fifth largest continent contains some of the most unique and fragile ecosystems on earth. Far from a wasteland, Antarctica and its ocean are almost unmatched in bio-productivity, in populations of whales and other critically endangered marine mammals and birds and in tonnage of the microscopic plants and animals that form the base of the marine food chain. The continent plays a critical role in regulating the world's climate and sea levels.[147] It may also contain large reserves of iron, copper, molybdenum, coal, uranium, gold, and other minerals.[148]

---

[141] UNCLOS, *supra* note 127, art. 193.

[142] *Id*. art. 216.

[143] *Id*. art. 210(6).

[144] Philippe Sands, Principles of International Environmental Law 179 (2d ed. 2003).

[145] *See id*. 396.

[146] *Id*. (citing the Preamble to the 1992 OSPAR Convention, Agenda 21 paras. 17.1 and 17.22, and widespread state practice as evidence of this fact). *See also* Ted L. Dorman, Salt Water Neighbors: International Ocean Law Relations Between the United States and Canada 24 (2009) (citing as evidence US President Reagan's March 1983 Oceans Policy Statement and a 2004 statement by the Legal Advisor to the US Department of State).

[147] *See* Jacques-Yves Cousteau & Bertrand Charrier, *The Antarctic: A Challenge to Global Environmental Policy, in* The Antarctic Environment and International Law 5–6 (Joe Verhoeven *et al.* eds., 1992).

[148] E. Sahurie, The International Law of Antarctica 352–58 (1992).

A handful of developed nations have controlled the treaty processes in Antarctica, with developing nations largely objecting to the regime.[149] In 1959, the Antarctic Treaty[150] was drafted by the 12 countries with territorial and other usage claims to the continent – Argentina, Australia, Belgium, Chile, France, Japan, New Zealand, Norway, South Africa, the then-USSR, the UK, and the US ("the Contracting Parties," later the "Consultative Parties"). Since that time, 16 additional countries have attained Consultative Party status, and another 20 nations have acceded to (agreed to be legally bound by) the Treaty. The Treaty stipulates that Antarctica shall only be used for peaceful purposes, deliberately postpones the decision as to who has territorial sovereignty, leaves practical control in the hands of the Consultative Parties to the exclusion of other nations, and allows scientific uses without expressly forbidding developmental uses (such as mining).[151]

A Convention on the Conservation of Antarctic Marine Living Resources (Canberra Convention or CCAMLR)[152] was added in 1980, largely designed to control the commercial harvesting of fish, mollusks, and crustaceans by non-Contracting Parties. In 1988, a Convention on the Regulation of Antarctic Mineral Resource Activities (Wellington Convention or CRAMRA)[153] was drafted by the Consultative Parties, but this pro-mining treaty has not yet been ratified by enough states to go into force, and probably never will be.

Preservation forces prevailed in Antarctica with the 1991 Environmental Protection Protocol,[154] a strong environmental protection framework, finally ratified by enough countries to go into force in 1998. It specifically states: "Any activity relating to mineral resources, other than scientific research,

---

[149] The "Question of the Antarctic" has frequently been put on the agenda of the UN General Assembly by developing nations and others that are not among the controlling "Contracting Parties" under the treaty regime. *See, e.g.,* G.A. Res. 44/124, U.N. GAOR, 44th Sess., Supp. No. 49, at 91, U.N. Doc. A/44/49 (Dec. 15, 1989).

[150] Antarctic Treaty, Dec. 1, 1959, 12 U.S.T. 794, 402 U.N.T.S. 71, 19 I.L.M. 860 (1980), http://www.nsf.gov/od/opp/antarct/anttrty.jsp.

[151] *See generally,* Jonathan Weiss, Comment, *The Balance of Nature and Human Needs in Antarctica: The Legality of Mining,* 9 TEMP. INT'L & COMP. L.J. 387 (1995).

[152] Convention on the Conservation of Antarctic Marine Living Resources, May 20, 1980, 33 U.S.T. 3476, T.I.A.S. No. 10240, 19 I.L.M. 841 (1980), http://www.ccamlr.org/pu/e/gen-intro.htm.

[153] Convention on the Regulation of Antarctic Mineral Resource Activities, June 2, 1988, U.N. Doc. AMR/SCM/88/78, 27 I.L.M. 859 (1988) (not entered into force). It would set up a commission of the Consultative Parties with power to designate approved mining areas, grant permits, and regulate operations, much like the UNCLOS International Sea-Bed Authority, http://www.state.gov/documents/organization/15282.pdf.

[154] Protocol on Environmental Protection to the Antarctic Treaty, Oct. 4, 1991, 30 I.L.M. 1461 (1991), http://www.antarctica.ac.uk/about_antarctica/geopolitical/treaty/update_1991.php.

shall be prohibited."[155] While the majority of the world's nations object to the Consultative Parties' monopoly and advocate a common heritage regime, there appears to be widespread support for banning mining and other large-scale or commercial development[156] in one of the earth's last great places.

8.2.4.3   *The Arctic*

Unlike Antarctica, the Arctic is typically not treated as a global commons area, although some would argue it should be.[157] Having no landmass, the Arctic is treated as an ocean and generally governed accordingly by the eight states with territory above the Arctic Circle – Canada, Denmark (because of its sovereignty over Greenland), Finland, Iceland, Norway, Russia, Sweden, and the US.[158] Despite its foreboding appearance, the Arctic is a very sensitive ecosystem; its extreme low temperatures, limited species diversity, low biological productivity, and long-lived organisms with high fat levels (capable of storing pollutant chemicals) make it extremely vulnerable to human damage.[159] Yet, until the 1990s, there were no serious national or international protection efforts.[160]

International concern for the Arctic began mounting in the 1980s, with reports of pollutant contamination (chiefly oil, heavy metals, persistent organic contaminants (POPs), noise, radioactivity, and acidification from carbon dioxide), Russian military nuclear waste dumping, development pressures, and impacts on the indigenous populations.[161] In 1991, the eight nations signed a detailed regional agreement, the Arctic Environmental Protection Strategy, that, while nonbinding soft law, sets goals and creates a framework for international cooperation on "the protection, enhancement and restoration of environmental quality and the sustainable utilization of natural resources…in the Arctic."[162] This was followed by progressively

---

[155] *Id.* art. 7.

[156] *See* G.A. Res. 44/124, *supra* note 149.

[157] Kathryn Milun, *Reclaiming a True Global Commons in the Arctic Melt,* May 9, 2007, http://onthecommons.org/reclaiming-true-global-commons-arctic-melt.

[158] *See* the parties' web site, Arctic Council, http://www.arctic-council.org; David Caron, *Toward an Arctic Environmental Regime,* 24 Ocean Dev. & Int'l L. 377 (1993). One of the creative aspects of this regime is its involvement of indigenous peoples and scientists as official "observers."

[159] For a detailed description of the Arctic environment and its problems, see the Arctic Environmental Protection Strategy (AEPS), June 14, 1991, 30 I.L.M. 1624 (1991), http://www.arctic-council.org/index.php/en/about/documents/category/4-founding-documents.

[160] Technically some ocean and wildlife treaties include the area, as discussed on the website of the World Wildlife Fund Arctic Programme, http://wwf.panda.org/what_we_do/where_we_work/arctic/.

[161] *See, id.*

[162] *Id.* at ¶ 2.1(ii).

more firm and detailed agreements for joint protection measures[163] and the creation in 1996 of the Arctic Council as a "high level forum" of the eight Arctic states and indigenous peoples for cooperation in protection efforts.[164]

Since the creation of Arctic Council, however, scientists have determined that global warming is transforming the Arctic landscape, a fact that dramatically alters the area's geopolitical significance. Rising global temperatures are melting the region's thick ice packs, and leading scientists to project that the Arctic sea routes will open up to seasonal shipping within this century.[165] Similarly, less ice in the Arctic means that the region is more open to oil, gas, and mineral extraction.[166] As countries scramble to exert sovereignty over the area, preservation efforts will need to be reinforced to protect this vulnerable region.

8.2.4.4   *Outer Space*

Outer space may seem a farfetched environment for concern, but that has not stopped mineral speculators[167] and international law from considering it. The UN's work in this area dates from shortly after Sputnik in 1957.[168]

---

[163] *E.g.*, Nuuk Declaration on Environment and Development in the Arctic, Sept. 16, 1993, 1993, http://arcticcircle.uconn.edu/NatResources/Policy/nuuk.html; Agreement Between the Government of the United States of America and the Government of the Russian Federation on Cooperation in the Prevention of Pollution of the Environment in the Arctic, Dec. 16, 1994, U.S. State Dept. No. 95–28, 1994 WL 761204, http://iea.uoregon.edu/pages/MarineMammals/engine/Documents/1-0889-0892.htm; Declaration Among the Royal Ministry of Defence of the Kingdom of Norway, the Ministry of Defense of the Russian Federation, and the Department of Defense of the United States of America on Arctic Military Environmental Cooperation (AMEC), Sept. 26, 1996 (from which the US withdrew in 2006), in Guruswamy et al., Supplement of Basic Documents to International Environmental Law and World Order 258 (2d ed. 1999); Agreement Between the Government of the Kingdom of Norway and the Government of the Russian Federation on Environmental Cooperation in Connection with the Dismantling of Russian Nuclear Powered Submarines, May 26, 1998, *id.* at 267.

[164] Joint Communique and Declaration on the Establishment of the Arctic Council, Sept. 19, 1996, 35 I.L.M. 1382, searchable at http://www.arctic-council.org/index.php/en/about/documents/category/4-founding-documents.

[165] *See e.g.* Clifford Krauss, Steven L. Myers, Andrew C. Revkin & Simon Romero, *As Polar Ice Turns to Water, Dreams of Treasure Abound*, N.Y. Times, Oct. 10, 2005, at A1. Mark Jarashow, Michael B. Runnels, & Tait Svenson, Note, *UNCLOS and the Arctic: the Path of Least Resistance*, 30 Fordham Int'l L.J. 1587, 1587 (2007).

[166] *See e.g.*, Alun Anderson, *Arctic Drilling: The Big Picture*, 207 New Scientist, Sept. 4, 2010, at 1.

[167] *See, e.g.*, Louis Sahagun, *Which Asteroid Will Host the First Mine?*, Denver Post, Feb. 8, 1998, at J-3.

[168] As detailed in Weiss et al., *supra* note 17, at 459.

The resulting 1967 Outer Space Treaty[169] provides a framework for peaceful uses of outer space and for developing further international law on the subject. Significantly, this early treaty provides that space endeavors shall not cause "harmful contamination" of space or earth[170] and recognizes the common heritage principle to some extent.[171] Several other outer space treaties have followed,[172] the most significant being the 1979 Moon Treaty,[173] which specifically establishes a common heritage regime deoted to peaceful, scientific purposes and environmental protection,[174] yet contains a provision for future creation of an international regime "to govern the exploitation of the natural resources of the moon" without providing any details.[175]

A momentous event took place in 1998, making such concerns more tangible. Human beings began building their first permanent settlement away from the earth. The International Space Station moves other worlds within human grasp and makes the balance between preservation and exploitation of those worlds all the more pressing. Even though the United States ended its Space Shuttle program in July 2011,[176] the International Space Station is scheduled to remain in operation through at least 2020.[177] The end of the Space Shuttle era may open the door for commercial space flight and a host of new preservation concerns.[178]

---

[169] Treaty on Principles Governing the Activities of States in the Exploration and Use of Outer Space, Including the Moon and Other Celestial Bodies, Jan. 27, 1967, 18 U.S.T. 2410, 610 U.N.T.S. 205, http://treaties.un.org/doc/Publication/UNTS/Volume%20610/volume-610-I-8843-English.pdf.

[170] *Id.* art. IX.

[171] *Id.* art. I ("exploration…shall be carried out for the benefit and in the interests of all countries").

[172] WEISS *ET AL.*, *supra* note 17, at 459–60.

[173] Agreement Governing the Activities of States on the Moon and Other Celestial Bodies, Dec. 5, 1979, U.N. Doc. A/RES/34/68 (1979), 18 I.L.M. 1434 (1979), http://untreaty.un.org/cod/avl/ha/tos/tos.html.

[174] *Id.*

[175] *Id.* art. 11(5).

[176] *Space Shuttle*, N.Y. TIMES, July 8, 2011, http://topics.nytimes.com/top/news/science/topics/space_shuttle/index.html.

[177] Marcia Smith, *ESA Formally Agrees to Continue ISS Through 2020*, SPACE POLICY ONLINE, http://www.spacepolicyonline.com/pages/index.php?option=com_content&view=article&id=1538:esa-formally-agrees-to-continue-iss-through-2020&catid=67:news&Itemid=27.

[178] *See e.g.*, Seth Borenstein, *Future of Spaceflight? NASA is Outsourcing the Job*, ASSOC. PRESS, July 21, 2011, http://abcnews.go.com/Technology/wireStory?id=14119444.

8.3   *Preservation Efforts – Rio and the 21st Century*

The 1992 Rio Declaration[179] did very little to advance the international law of preservation. Despite the 1972 Stockholm Declaration's emphasis on preservation (*see* § 8.2) and despite the increase in international preservation law and practice in the 20 years between Stockholm and Rio, Rio actually says very little directly about preservation or conservation. Granted, the Rio Declaration is replete with principles for protection of the "environment" and promotion of "sustainable development," both of which implicitly encompass preservation; however, it contains only one principle expressly on the subject, Principle 7: "States shall cooperate in a spirit of global partnership to conserve, protect and restore the health and integrity of the Earth's ecosystem."[180] While a significant statement given both its scope and mandatory language, it pales in comparison to the multiple Stockholm provisions mandating the safeguarding of natural resources and ecosystems, human responsibility for wildlife and habitat, the integration of nature conservation in economic development, etc.

Clearly, developing nations at Rio were less interested in preservation than in economic development and protection of human health. Some of this sentiment is reflected in the controversial remainder of Rio Principle 7 which states that nations have "common but differentiated responsibilities" with regard to environmental protection and that developed countries have greater responsibility, negatively because of the "pressures" they have placed on the environment and positively because of the "technologies and financial resources" they have to contribute. This position has been basically rejected by the US and some other developed countries (as discussed in § 2.1.12).

However, other Rio Conference products – Agenda 21,[181] the Convention on Biodiversity, and the Forest Principles (below) – more than make up for the Declaration's shortcomings on preservation. Agenda 21's longest section, Section 2, expressly covers "Conservation and Management of Resources for Development." It contains preservation-relevant chapters calling for "Combating Deforestation,"[182] "Managing Fragile Ecosystems,"[183] "Conservation

---

179   United Nations Conference on Environment and Development, Rio de Janiero, Braz., June 3–14, 1992, *Rio Declaration on Environment and Development*, Principles 5, 7, 9, 12, 14, 26, 27, UN Doc. A/CONF.151/26/Rev. 1 (Vol. I) (Aug. 12, 1992) [hereinafter Rio Declaration].

180   *Id.* Principle 7.

181   Agenda 21, June 13, 1992, U.N. Doc. A/CONF. 151/26 (vols. I–III) (1992); an excellent annotated copy is in AGENDA 21 & THE UNCED PROCEEDINGS (Nicholas Robinson ed., 1992).

182   *Id.* ch. 11.

183   *Id.* chs. 12 and 13.

of Biological Diversity,"[184] "Protection of the Oceans...and...Their Living Resources,"[185] and "Protection of...Freshwater Resources."[186] Agenda 21 in numerous provisions recognizes the need for "open spaces,"[187] "sinks for greenhouse gases,"[188] and "protected areas,"[189] with the following recommendation being one of the clearest examples:

> Establishing, expanding and managing, as appropriate to each national context, protected area systems, which includes systems of conservation units for their environmental, social and spiritual functions and values, including conservation of forests in representative ecological systems and landscapes, primary old-growth forests, conservation and management of wildlife, nomination of World Heritage Sites under the World Heritage Convention, as appropriate, conservation of genetic resources, involving *in situ* and *ex situ* measures and undertaking supportive measures to ensure sustainable utilization of biological resources and conservation of biological diversity and the traditional forest habitats of indigenous people, forest dwellers and local communities.[190]

In addition, "soft" law developments leading up to Rio provide further support for preservation principles. The World Charter for Nature,[191] adopted overwhelmingly by the UN in 1982 (111 votes for, with only the USA voting against), sets forth 24 principles for the preservation and conservation of nature. One of its "general principles" is that "special protection shall be given to unique areas, to representative samples of all the different types of ecosystems and to the habitats of rare or endangered species."[192] The Legal Principles for Environmental Protection and Sustainable Development adopted by the Experts Group on Environmental Law of the influential World Commission on Environment and Development (WCED or Brundtland Commission), which led to the Rio UNCED Conference, pronounce that "States shall ensure that the environment and natural resources are conserved and used for the benefit of present and future generations."[193] The

---

[184] *Id.* ch. 15.

[185] *Id.* ch. 17.

[186] *Id.* ch. 18.

[187] *Id.* ¶ 7.27.

[188] *Id.* ¶ 9.20(a)(ii).

[189] *Id.* ¶ 10.7(c).

[190] *Id.* ¶ 11.13(b) (emphasis added).

[191] World Charter for Nature, G.A. Res. 37/7 (Annex), U.N. GAOR, 37th Sess., Supp. No. 51, at 17, U.N. Doc. A/37/51, (Oct. 28, 1982), http://www.un.org/documents/ga/res/37/a37 r007.htm.

[192] *Id.* ¶ 3.

[193] Experts Group on Environmental Law of the World Commission on Environment and Development, Legal Principles for Environmental Protection and Sustainable Development, U.N. Doc. WCED/86/23/Add. 1, art. 2 (1986), http://habitat.igc.org/open-gates/ocf-a1.htm.

Experts Group further posited as an international law principle that "States shall maintain ecosystems and related ecological processes... [and] maintain maximum biological diversity by ensuring the survival and promoting the conservation in their natural habitat of all species of fauna and flora, in particular those which are rare, endemic or endangered."[194] A number of other treaties[195] and nonbinding but authoritative international declarations[196] in the last three decades further support the existence of the principle of preservation, as do Rio's Convention on Biological Diversity, its Forest Principles, and the Desertification Treaty, each of which is discussed in turn below.

8.3.1 *The Convention on Biological Diversity*

8.3.1.1 *Introduction and Background*
The 1992 Convention on Biological Diversity[197] (CBD or Biodiversity Convention) is not just the latest example of wildlife preservation. It is an entirely new direction in preservation – a direction that in some ways contradicts and rejects the endangered-species focus that has occupied ecology and the law for most of the 20th century.

In the 1970s, ecologists began to be concerned that conservation focused on endangered and migratory species, trade, and "megafauna" was too restrictive an approach and ignored the greater issue of what was happening to the overall *richness* of life on earth. The new approach was to focus instead on "biological diversity," defined sweepingly in the Biodiversity Convention as "the variability among living organisms from all sources including, *inter alia*, terrestrial, marine and other aquatic ecosystems and the ecological complexes of which they are part; this includes diversity within species, between species and of ecosystems."[198] This means focusing on all three levels of "life": the genetic diversity within each species, the species diversity within each ecosystem, and the ecosystem diversity worldwide.[199] As can be explained in reverse order, Earth is vulnerable to weakness in its pool of ecosystems;

---

[194] *Id.* art. 3(a)–(b).

[195] *E.g.*, African, Caribbean and Pacific States – European Economic Community Convention (Lomé IV), Dec. 15, 1989, arts. 33, 35–36, 1990 E.C. 120, 29 I.L.M. 783 (1990).

[196] *E.g.*, The Langkawi Commonwealth Heads of Government Declaration on Environment, Oct. 29, 1989, http://www.thecommonwealth.org/shared_asp_files/GFSR.asp?NodeID=171727.

[197] Convention on Biological Diversity, June 5, 1992, 1760 U.N.T.S. 79, 143; 31 I.L.M. 818 (1992), http://www.biodiv.org.

[198] *Id.* art. 2.

[199] *See* WILSON, *supra* note 68; KATRINA BROWN ET AL., ECONOMICS AND THE CONSERVATION OF GLOBAL BIOLOGICAL DIVERSITY (1993); WORLD RESOURCES INSTITUTE (WRI) ET AL., GLOBAL BIODIVERSITY STRATEGY: GUIDELINES FOR ACTION TO SAVE, STUDY, AND USE EARTH'S BIOTIC WEALTH SUSTAINABLY AND EQUITABLY (1992).

ecosystems are vulnerable to weakness in their pool of species; and species are vulnerable to weakness in their gene pools.

The value of biodiversity is both enormous and enormously hard to quantify:

> Biodiversity has value to humans for a variety of reasons. These include use values (direct use, indirect use, and option values) and nonuse values. Direct use values include food, fibers, forest products, pharmaceuticals and other chemicals, and opportunities or education and recreation. Indirect use values include the services provided by biodiversity and the natural ecosystems on which we depend: water purification and flood control, climate control, regulation of air quality, photosynthesis, pollination, pest control, soil maintenance, decomposition, and disposal of wastes. Option value is the discounted present value of the potential of biodiversity to lead to the development of new goods, such as pharmaceuticals.
>
> Non-use values include aesthetic, intrinsic, ethical, spiritual, existence, and bequest values. Existence value is the satisfaction some individuals derive from knowing that certain species or ecosystems exist even though they may never actually spend money to visit them. Bequest value captures the desire to leave a natural legacy for future generations.... Existing techniques of economic valuation are, however, incapable of fully evaluating the contributions of biodiversity to human and non-human society.[200]

The "father of biodiversity," Harvard professor E. O. Wilson, explains why human economic valuation misses the mark:

> What then is biodiversity worth? The traditional econometric approach, weighing market price and tourist dollars, will always underestimate the true value of wild species. None has been totally assayed for all of the commercial profit, scientific knowledge, and aesthetic pleasure it can yield. Furthermore, none exists in the wild all by itself. Every species is part of an ecosystem, an expert specialist of its kind, tested relentlessly as it spreads its influence through the food web. To remove it is to entrain changes in other species, raising the populations of some, reducing or even extinguishing others, risking a downward spiral of the larger assemblage.... If species composing a particular ecosystem begin to go extinct, at what point will the whole machine sputter and destabilize?[201]

Three of the richest areas of the planet in terms of biodiversity are tropical rain forests, wetlands, and coral reefs. Tropical forests (*see* § 8.3.2) are some of the most diverse places on earth, but they cover less than 5 percent of the earth's surface area.[202] Wetlands provide crucial breeding and feeding areas for countless birds and aquatic species. Coral reefs contain 25 percent of all

---

[200] Dana Clark & David Downes, What Price Biodiversity? 5–6 (Center for International Environmental Law 1995).

[201] Wilson, *supra* note 68, at 308–09.

[202] *Tropical Rainforests of the World*, MongaBay, http://rainforests.mongabay.com/0101.htm.

known marine species. The chief threat to each of these habitats is human development and exploitation.[203]

8.3.1.2 *The Convention*

The Biodiversity Convention was developed under UNEP auspices and opened for signature at the 1992 Rio Conference. By 2012, an impressive 193 states had ratified or otherwise joined it as parties.[204] The US is one of the only countries that has not ratified the Convention, arguing that it finds "particularly unsatisfactory the text's treatment of intellectual property rights; finances…; technology transfer and bio-technology."[205] Other issues with which the US is "disappointed" included those "related to environmental impact assessments, the legal relationship between this Convention and other international agreements, and the scope of obligations with respect to the marine environment."[206] The Convention covers many subjects, and its approach to preservation of biodiversity is general, befitting a "framework" treaty. It emphasizes, *inter alia*, development of national strategies, plans, and programs for the conservation and sustainable use of biological diversity;[207] inventorying and monitoring;[208] the establishment of "protected areas";[209] "protection of ecosystems, natural habitats and…viable populations of species in natural surroundings";[210] and other "in-situ" (in natural habitats) and "ex-situ" (not in natural habitats, as in zoos) conservation techniques.[211] Parties are obliged to protect biodiversity within their jurisdictions and outside if affected by processes and activities from within their jurisdictions.[212] Procedural requirements include environmental impart assessments;[213] notification, exchange of information, and consultation;[214] and emergency responses.[215] A Conference of the Parties is established for reviewing its

---

[203] HUNTER ET AL., *supra* note 33, at 7.

[204] *See List of Parties,* CONVENTION ON BIOLOGICAL DIVERSITY, http://www.cbd.int/information/parties.shtml.

[205] Declaration of the United States of America, ¶ 4, attached to the Nairobi Final Act, 31 I.L.M. 848 (1992).

[206] *Id.* ¶ 5.

[207] Biodiversity Convention, *supra* note 197, art. 6(a), 10–14.

[208] *Id.* art. 7.

[209] Described as "a geographically defined area which is designated or regulated and managed to achieve specific conservation objectives." *Id.* arts. 2 and 8.

[210] *Id.* art. 8(d).

[211] *Id.* arts. 8 and 9.

[212] *Id.* art. 4.

[213] *Id.* art. 14.

[214] *Id.* arts. 14, 17–18.

[215] *Id.* art. 14(1).

implementation.[216] No reservations are permitted under the Convention.[217] Means for the settlement of disputes[218] include negotiation, arbitration and conciliation procedures established under the Convention,[219] and submission to the International Court of Justice.[220]

Other noteworthy provisions relate to access to genetic resources;[221] access to and transfer of technology;[222] handling of biotechnology and distribution of its benefits;[223] financial resources,[224] financial mechanisms,[225] and interim financial arrangements.[226] These provisions makes it clear who is to pay the bill for this: "The developed country Parties shall provide new and additional financial resources to enable developing country Parties to meet the...costs to them of implementing measures which fulfill the obligations of this Convention...."[227]

Intellectual property rights were the source of the greatest tension between developing countries (many of whom possess considerable genetic resources) and developed countries (who possess the majority of the patents and other property rights).[228] As expressed by Anil Aggarwal of India: "The North cannot have free access to the South's biomaterial. The value of the South's germ plasm [to] pharmaceutical industries of the North runs into billions of dollars a year."[229] Hence the developing states negotiated for insertion of provisions in the Convention which would confer benefits on them – sharing of profits, technology, research and knowledge – in return for the use of such resources by the developed states. On the other hand, developed countries, especially the United States, insisted that intellectual property rights not be compromised.

Articles 15–21 seek to resolve that tension with a *quid pro quo* compromise. That compromise begins with Article 15's recognition of state sovereignty over access to natural resources, but with the general obligation to grant

---

[216] *Id.* art. 23.

[217] *Id.* art. 37.

[218] *Id.* art. 27.

[219] *Id.* Annex 11.

[220] *Id.* art. 27(3)(b).

[221] *Id.* art. 15.

[222] *Id.* art. 16.

[223] *Id.* art. 19.

[224] *Id.* art. 20.

[225] *Id.* art. 21.

[226] *Id.* art. 39.

[227] *Id.* art. 20(2).

[228] *Id.* art. 8(a)–(e).

[229] Quoted in M. Chandler, *The Biodiversity Convention: Selected Issues of Interest to the International Lawyer*, 4 COLO. J. INT'L ENVTL. L. & POL'Y 141, 161 (1993).

access.[230] In return, the resource states are to "shar[e] in a fair and equitable way the results of research and development and the benefits arising from the commercial and other utilization of genetic resources with the Contracting Party, providing such resources…upon mutually agreed terms."[231] The Convention requires states to cooperate to ensure that "patents and other intellectual property rights" are "supportive of and do not run counter to" the above objectives,[232] which could be interpreted to mean that intellectual property rights must not stand in the way of the Convention's objective of transferring technology and sharing profits with developing countries. Thus, this provision has been criticized as "the source of the highly objectionable language on intellectual property rights."[233]

8.3.1.3 *Appraisal*

What this hastily drafted treaty will mean for preservation in the 21st century is still unclear. Expanding the preservation focus to all three levels – ecosystems, species, and gene pools – could very well lead us to different and more successful conservation strategies and accomplishments compared to the past. Emphasizing ecosystem diversity logically could lead to the protection of more, and larger land areas. For example, the US National Wilderness System of over 109 million acres contains only 157 of the 261 distinct ecosystems found in the US.[234] Emphasizing species diversity could lead to less concern over the loss of an endangered species, if it were known to be not essential to maintaining the stability of the ecosystem.[235] Emphasizing genetic diversity could lead to fundamental changes in agriculture (monoculture-dependent as it is) or change our priorities one way or the other about genetically inbred species (like the cheetah).

However, the flaws and inconsistencies in the treaty, its dominant emphasis on the financial *quid pro quo* for access to genetic resources, and the refusal of the US to accept the treaty make it unlikely that it will be dramatically successful, without changes. Still, considering that 20th century national and international wildlife preservation laws have not been notably successful in dealing with the exponentially increasing loss of species and habitat, we

---

[230] Biodiversity Convention, *supra* note 197, art. 15(1).

[231] *Id.* art. 15(7).

[232] *Id.* art. 16(5).

[233] Chandler, *supra* note 229, at 164.

[234] *See* Pete Morton, *The Economic Benefits of Wilderness: Theory and Practice*, 76 DENV. U.L. REV. 465 (1999); *see also* G. D. DAVIS, ECOSYSTEM REPRESENTATION AS A CRITERION FOR WORLD WILDERNESS DESIGNATION (1987). For more information, visit the U.S. Forest Service's web site, available at http://www.fs.fed.us.

[235] *See* HUNTER ET AL., *supra* note 33, at 984.

can only hope that the more holistic Biodiversity Convention approach does not have too high a price tag or is not too little too late.

8.3.2   *Forests*

Forests cover almost one third of the Earth's total land area, excluding Antarctica and Greenland, and are our richest terrestrial ecosystems in both a biodiversity and an economic sense. Therein lies the problem.[236] Until early this century, most forest loss occurred in the temperate and boreal forests of Europe, North Africa, and North America, which have been largely stripped of their original cover (95–98 percent of all forests in the continental US having been logged at least once, and in Europe two thirds of the forests are gone).[237] Now, the focus has shifted to the tropical forests, where nearly half of the timber in developing countries has been logged in the 20th century. Every year, an area of tropical forests as large as Switzerland and Austria combined is lost.

Deforestation – from commercial logging, slash-and-burn agriculture, fuel-wood-gathering, road building, mining, population growth/migration, drought, and natural and human-induced wildfires – is accelerating "at rates that will be difficult, perhaps impossible, to reverse."[238] Trade in forest products (timber, pulp, and paper) is a huge economic force, and demand is growing. The legal trade alone reaches over US $100 billion a year, making it one of the world's richest economic sectors; the illegal trade is inestimable. Unfortunately, deforestation is only one of the dangers to global forests: in addition, the quality of forests is declining markedly due to air pollution (such as acid rain), the spread of monocultures (even-age tree plantations), human population pressures, disease, invading species, etc.

Forests are too valuable to treat so cavalierly. Experts point out five classes of benefits that forests confer on present and future generations: (1) direct commercial benefits such as timber, forest products (gums, medicines, fibers, fruits, nuts, etc.), and other agricultural and industrial materials; (2) direct

---

[236] Good background references on forest issues include EDWARD ELGAR, DEFORESTATION AND CLIMATE CHANGE: REDUCING CARBON EMISSIONS FROM DEFORESTATION AND FOREST DEGRADATION (2010); LAWRENCE CHRISTY, FOREST LAW AND SUSTAINABLE DEVELOPMENT: ADDRESSING CONTEMPORARY CHALLENGES THROUGH LEGAL REFORM (2007); JANET ABRAMOVITZ, STATE OF THE WORLD (1998); DAVID HARRIS, THE LAST STAND (1995); ANS KOLK, FORESTS IN INTERNATIONAL ENVIRONMENTAL POLITICS: INTERNATIONAL ORGANIZATIONS, NGOS, AND THE BRAZILIAN AMAZON (1996); CHARLES LITTLE, THE DYING OF THE TREES: THE PANDEMIC IN AMERICA'S FORESTS (1995).

[237] U.S. FISH AND WILDLIFE SERVICE, CATCH THE MIGRATION SENSATION (1999), http://library.fws.gov/pubs/mbd_habitat_loss.pdf.

[238] EDITH BROWN WEISS, IN FAIRNESS TO FUTURE GENERATIONS: INTERNATIONAL LAW, COMMON PATRIMONY, AND INTERGENERATIONAL EQUITY 219 (1989).

life-support benefits like fuelwood,[239] livestock fodder, food, shelter, and homes for indigenous peoples; (3) amenity benefits such as recreation, hunting and fishing, ecotourism, education, scientific research, etc.; (4) essential environmental services, such as conserving surface and groundwater, preventing soil erosion, maintaining soil productivity, wildlife habitat, and buffering climate through their roles in the hydrologic cycle and as "sinks" for greenhouse gases; and (5) direct economic benefits downstream in the form of increased hydroelectric production, irrigation water supplies, flood protection, and navigation (due to reduced siltation of downstream waterways and dams).[240]

Given the immense values offered by forests and the threats to their continued existence, it would seem logical for preservation to play a dominant role in forest management; however, that has not been the case. The developed countries of the North and developing countries of the South are polarized on this issue, with the North schizophrenically advocating preservation and sustainable management of forests while avidly consuming their products, and the South viewing its ability to exploit and export its timber resources as crucial to its economic development.[241] Environmentalists too are split (in the same way and for the same reason as they are in wildlife issues like the elephant, above) over whether saving forests is best achieved through preservation or though the promotion of sustainable commercial use.[242]

As yet, there is no comprehensive, binding international agreement on forest management, nor even any agreement on whether there should be one. Starting in the 1980s, some binding forest trade agreements, nonbinding management principles, and initiatives began to develop, but they contain very little agreement on preserving the resource. In 1983, producer countries (primarily developing countries in Latin America, Africa, and Asia) and consumer countries (primarily developed countries in North America, Europe, and Asia) negotiated the International Tropical Timber Agreement (ITTA)[243] to promote trade in tropical timber. Tellingly, it was negotiated under the auspices, not of the UN Environment Program (UNEP), but the UN Conference on Trade and Development (UNCTAD). The ITTA now governs 90 percent of the world's tropical forests and 90 percent of the tropical timber

---

[239] In developing countries, up to 90 percent of the population relies exclusively on wood for cooking and heating LAKSHMAN GURUSWAMY & BRENT HENDRICKS, INTERNATIONAL ENVIRONMENTAL LAW IN A NUTSHELL 118 (2007). Recall that the United States was a wood-based energy culture at the time of its War of Independence.

[240] *See* EDITH BROWN WEISS, *supra* note 238, at 219.

[241] HUNTER ET AL., *supra* note 33, at 1145.

[242] *Id.*

[243] International Tropical Timber Agreement (ITTA), Nov. 25, 1983, U.N. Doc. TD/TIMBER/11/Rev.1 (1984), as amended, Jan. 26, 1994.

trade.[244] The original ITTA was superseded by new agreements in 1994 and 2006, and the new agreements move beyond trade promotion to embrace sustainable development and forest conservation.[245] This is reflected in provisions that include abjurations for "contributing to sustainable development and poverty alleviation," "promoting increased...processing of tropical timber from sustainable sources," and "reforestation."[246] Nevertheless, the ITTA still has not produced an effective sustainable forestry regime.

The 1990s brought renewed attention – and controversy – to forest issues. In the leadup to the 1992 Rio Conference, the US and other G-7 developed countries advocated negotiation of a treaty to protect tropical forests, which led to one of the most divisive disputes at Rio. The G-77 developing countries, led by timber producers like Malaysia and Brazil, saw this as a disguised trade restriction, suppressing their economic development by shutting down the South's logging while permitting the North's to continue. They also saw such a treaty as a device to preserve carbon sinks in the South that would permit the North to continue greenhouse gas emissions unabated. In a deft example of diplomatic "turn-about-is-fair-play," the developing countries counter-proposed expanding the treaty to cover the North's temperate and boreal forests,[247] successfully dampening developed country support (particularly of the US and Russian Federation with their vast forests).

Ultimately, the best the warring factions could do was to agree on non-binding principles, specifically titled the Non-legally Binding Authoritative Statement of Principles for a Global Consensus on the Management, Conservation and Sustainable Development of All Types of Forests (Forest Principles).[248] The Forest Principles are not really "global" in outlook, emphasizing national sovereignty over forest resources rather than international interests.[249] They do reiterate the need for "forest conservation and sustainable development" in numerous places, but generally with an emphasis on economic "use."[250] Preservation is addressed once, with the call for "protection of ecologically viable representative or unique examples of forests, including primary/old-growth forests, cultural, spiritual, historical, religious

---

[244] Micahel Allaby, Tropical Forests 235 (2005).

[245] Hunter et al., *supra* note 33, at 1164.

[246] ITTA *supra* note 238 at arts. 1(c), (i), (j).

[247] Kolk, *supra* note 236, at 159–60.

[248] Non-legally Binding Authoritative Statement of Principles for a Global Consensus on the Management, Conservation and Sustainable Development of All Types of Forests, June 13, 1992, U.N. Doc. A/CONF.151/26 (Vol. III) (1992), 31 I.L.M. 881 (1992), http://www.un-documents.net/for-prin.htm.

[249] *E.g., id.* Principles 1(a), 2(a).

[250] *E.g., id.* Principles 1(b), 2(b), 6.

and other unique and valued forests," but the call is specifically for this to be done by "national policies and/or legislation," not international ones.[251]

Commendably, the Principles do deal with some of the important underlying problems in preservation, giving recognition to "the vital role" forests play,[252] the need for financial assistance and technology transfer to the South to support forest conservation,[253] and the need for full participation of all stakeholders, particularly indigenous people, local communities, and women.[254] Among other noteworthy principles are the need for sustainable forest management, afforestation, reforestation, and forest conservation;[255] financial support to developing countries "to enable them to sustainably manage, conserve and develop their forest resources, including through afforestation, reforestation and combating deforestation and forest and land degradation,"[256] and specific financial support to developing countries for the conservation of forests;[257] environmental impact assessments;[258] the need for international cooperative efforts;[259] the strengthening of scientific research[260] and national and international institutional capability;[261] enhancement of international exchange of information;[262] facilitation of open and free international trade;[263] and control of pollutants.[264]

On the negative side, the Forest Principles are nonbinding, set forth no concrete standards, and break no new ground. Nevertheless, they are the first comprehensive international consensus on forest conservation and may lead to future binding international law, if the issues of economics between North and South can be worked out.

Several other initiatives could potentially positively affect forest preservation. The most important of these is the Framework Convention on Climate Change (*see* § 10.3), which places great emphasis on the world's forests

---

[251] *Id.* Principle 8(f).
[252] *Id.* Principle 4.
[253] *E.g., id.* Principles 7(b), 9(a), 10, 11.
[254] *Id.* Principles 5, 12(d).
[255] *Id.* Principles 6(a), 8(a).
[256] *Id.* Principle 10.
[257] *Id.* Principle 7(d).
[258] *Id.* Principle 8(h).
[259] *Id.* Principles 3(b) and 9(a).
[260] *Id.* Principle 12(a).
[261] *Id.* Principles 3(b) and 12(b).
[262] *Id.* Principle 12(c).
[263] *Id.* Principles 13 and 14.
[264] *Id.* Principle 15.

as "sinks" for removing greenhouse gases from the atmosphere;[265] this will mean that the preservation of large forest areas in the South will now have direct economic value as an offset to the North's emissions. Another positive force could be Agenda 21, which devotes an entire chapter to "Combating Deforestation,"[266] with strong preservation components, such as the establishment and expansion of "protected area systems" (discussed above).[267] A third could be the interaction of treaties on other preservation topics, like those discussed above. For example, CITES lists mahogany as an endangered species, the Biodiversity Convention will require preservation of sufficient forests to preserve their biodiversity, and the World Heritage Convention invites the listing of natural and old-growth forests. Each of these examples suggests that forest preservation could emerge from these other directions, as well.

8.3.3   *Desertification*

Desertification presents yet another perspective on the issue, that of preserving agricultural and human productivity by preserving nature. Desertification is one of our world's most serious socio-environmental problems, the result of natural and human actions causing such land and vegetative degradation that the agricultural/biological productivity of a region is destroyed.[268] Put another way, desertification is the transformation of productive "drylands" (arid, semi-arid, or dry sub-humid plains and grasslands) into deserts, causing loss of soil fertility and moisture retention, destruction of vegetative cover, erosion, exhaustion of surface and groundwaters, salinization of soil

---

[265] UN Framework Convention on Climate Change, May 29, 1982, arts. 1(8), 4, and 8, 1771 U.N.T.S. 107; 31 I.L.M. 849 (1992), http://unfccc.int/key_documents/the_convention/items/2853.php.

[266] Agenda 21, *supra* note 181, ch. 11. In addition, a number of other chapters deal with land use and other practices also having bearing on forest preservation, such as the chapters on agriculture, biological diversity, freshwater resources, etc.

[267] *Id.* art. 11.13(b).

[268] Background resources include: Governing Global Desertification: Linking Environmental Degradation, Poverty, and Participation (Pierre Marc Johnson *et al.* eds. 2006); Land Degradation and Desertification: Assessment, Mitigation and Remediation (Pandi Zdruli *et al.* eds. 2010). R. L. Heathcote, The Arid Lands: Their Use and Abuse (1983); UNEP, Fact Sheet 3: United Nations Convention to Combat Desertification (1995), http://www.unccd.int/publicinfo/factsheets/showFS.php?number=3; Executive Director UNEP, *Status of Desertification and Implementation of the United Nations Plan of Action to Combat Desertification*, UNEP/GCSS.111/3 (1992); William Burns, *The International Convention to Combat Desertification: Drawing a Line in the Sand?*, 16 Mich. J. Int'l L. 831 (1995); M. Kassas *et al.*, *Desertification and Drought: An Ecological and Economic Analysis*, 20 Desertification Control Bull. 19 (1991).

and water, loss of wildlife habitat, forced human migrations, urbanization, and social unrest.

Dryland agriculture produces more than 20 percent of the world's food supply, and desertification has affected 70 percent of our drylands (one fourth of the world's entire land area). Over 250 million people are directly dependent on these lands for subsistence, and more than a billion people in over 110 developed and developing countries are indirectly affected, including large portions of Africa, the Middle East, South America, southern Russia, Australia, and even the US.[269] Desertification has occurred throughout human history (at the height of the Roman Empire, it was possible to travel across North Africa in the shade of trees),[270] and it is not to be confused with the results of natural droughts or the natural expansion-contraction of deserts.

This calamity is caused by humans to humans, principally through over-cultivation, overgrazing, deforestation, and irrigation practices that do not adequately drain salts out of the soil. Behind these immediate causes are other more deeply rooted ones: population growth, land ownership patterns, trade practices, poverty, war, etc.

Efforts to preserve drylands and prevent desertification began with a 1974 UN resolution urging "international action," which lead to a nonbinding 1977 Plan of Action to Combat Desertification and some planning efforts,[271] but by the early 1990s it was clear that greater action was needed. In 1992, Agenda 21 devoted an entire chapter to "Managing Fragile Ecosystems: Combating Desertification and Drought,"[272] with a wealth of conservation recommendations. Two years later, a binding treaty was concluded, the Convention to Combat Desertification in Those Countries Experiencing Serious Drought and/or Desertification, Particularly in Africa (CCD or Desertification Convention).[273] The Desertification Convention takes a number of new directions rarely seen in preservation laws to date. First, it emphasizes a "bottom-up" approach, relying on local people and communities to develop and implement the necessary conservation programs, instead of the "top-down" central government planning/aid-dispensing approach of most treaties.[274] Second, it emphasizes process, planning, and partnerships over

---

[269] *See* HUNTER ET AL., *supra* note 33, at 1172.

[270] WILSON, *supra* note 68, at 39.

[271] Burns, *supra* note 268, at 849.

[272] Agenda 21, *supra* note 181, ch. 12.

[273] Convention to Combat Desertification in Those Countries Experiencing Serious Drought and/or Desertification, Particularly in Africa, June 17, 1994, 1954 U.N.T.S. 3, 33 I.L.M. 1328 (1994), http://www.unccd.int/convention/text/convention.php?annexNo=0 [hereinafter Desertification Convention].

[274] *Id.* art. 3(a). *See* Kyle Danish, *International Environmental Law and the "Bottomup" Approach: A Review of the Desertification Convention*, 3 IND. J. GLOBAL LEG. STUD. 133 (1995).

the traditional creation of new rules and standards.[275] Third, it commits parties to "address the underlying causes of desertification and pay special attention to the socio-economic factors contributing" to it.[276] Its other provisions are less unusual (which is not to say less useful), including "national action programs" for combating desertification,[277] as well as the now familiar trio of technology transfer,[278] capacity building,[279] and financial mechanisms.[280]

As developed countries have not been as forthcoming with financing as the developing countries had hoped (here as elsewhere),[281] it remains to be seen whether the combination of innovative and traditional approaches to preservation in the Desertification Convention will be successful in halting humans' propensity to over utilize the commons and convert it to wastelands. As desertification is really a symptom of depressed human conditions and expectations, its solution hinges on solving even more basic societal issues, just as every preservation issue inevitably does.

8.4   Conclusion

In many ways, the preservation movement is at the heart of international environmental law because it seeks to protect the most cherished wonders of the natural world. People become upset when an awe-inspiring landscape is destroyed or when an animal is driven to extinction because nature holds immense and unquantifiable value. At the same time, however, it is easy to overlook this value or take it for granted. Vulnerable landscapes are often exploited in the name of more pressing human needs – such as food, shelter, and fuel. With world population projected to increase from 7 billion in 2011 to 8.9 billion by 2050, the human impact on the environment will reach new heights.[282] This expansion will test the carrying capacity of the world's resources, and put even more stress on already fragile ecosystems.

Global warming will add to the pressure, changing the environment in ways that are difficult to predict.[283] For example if global warming precipitates a rise in sea levels, then many sensitive coastal areas and river deltas

---

[275] Desertification Convention, *supra* note 273, art 3(a).

[276] *Id.* art. 5(c).

[277] *Id.* arts. 9–10.

[278] *Id.* art. 18.

[279] *Id.* art. 19.

[280] *Id.* arts. 20–21.

[281] The primary funding source will be through the Global Environmental Facility (GEF).

[282] U.N. Dep't of Econ. & Soc. Affairs, World Population 2300, ST/ESA/SER.A/236 (2004), http://www.un.org/esa/population/publications/longrange2/WorldPop2300final.pdf.

[283] Roach, *supra* note 73.

will be submerged. Changing weather patterns may make habitats unlivable for the species that evolved to thrive in that specific area. Oceanic acidification, caused by the absorption of carbon dioxide, may kill large swaths of coral reefs, which act as the bastions of life in the ocean. Because carbon dioxide remains in the atmosphere for years, future climate change cannot be averted at this point. Therefore, scientists will have to focus their efforts on mitigating the effects of climate change on the landscape and the species that live there.

Chapter Nine

International Freshwater Resources

9.0 *Introduction*[1]

All life is dependent upon water. Civilization itself is aquatic, rising around and dependent upon water sources. Yet the increasing scarcity and contamination of the world's freshwater – rivers, streams, lakes, wetlands, and underground aquifers – may be the most underestimated resource crisis we face in the 21st century.[2]

Viewed from space, Earth is a "water planet," with nearly 70 percent of its surface covered by water, twice the area of the land.[3] However, that liquid resource is limitedly utilizable, unevenly distributed, and often

---

[1] Portions of this chapter draw on the authors' earlier works, including: Ved P. Nanda, *The Law of Non-Navigational Uses of International Watercourses: Draft Articles on Protection and Preservation of Ecosystems, Harmful Conditions and Emergency Situations, and Protection of Water Installations*, 3 Colo. J. Int'l L. & Pol'y 175 (1992); Ved P. Nanda, *Emerging Trends in the Use of International Law and Institutions for the Management of International Water Resources*, 6 Denv. J. Int'l l. & Pol'y 239 (1977); George (Rock) Pring *et al.*, *Trends in International Environmental Law Affecting the Minerals Industry*, 17 J. Energy & Nat. Resources L. 39, and 151 (1999); George W. Pring & Karen Tomb, *License to Waste: Legal Barriers to Conservation and Efficient Use of Water in the West*, 25 Rocky Mtn. Min. l. Inst. 25-1 (1979).

   Web sites of interest on International Freshwater Resources include the University of Denver College of Law Natural Resources web site, http://law.du.edu/forms/enrgp/weblinks/index2.cfm, as well as the following: *Program in Water Conflict Management*, Oregon State University, http://www.transboundarywaters.orst.edu, International Water Law Project, http://www.internationalwaterlaw.org, *Centre for Water Law, Policy and Science,* University of Dundee, http://www.dundee.ac.uk/water/, World Water Council, http://www.worldwatercouncil.org, and *Water Science,* Environment Canada, http://www.cciw.ca/gems/intro.html.

[2] *Freshwater Crisis*, National Geographic, http://environment.nationalgeographic.com/environment/freshwater/freshwater-crisis/. *See generally* Peter H. Gleick, et al., The World's Water: The Biennial Report on Freshwater Resources (2012).

[3] *Id.*

unreliable. Over 97 percent of it is salt water, in the oceans and other saline water bodies.[4] Of the barely 3 percent that is fresh, most is locked up in polar ice caps, glaciers, and deep underground aquifers, so that only 0.3 percent of all freshwater reserves on Earth is easily accessible for humans and terrestrial ecosystems.[5] Still, that figure represents an enormous amount of water – approximately 14,000 cubic kilometers (almost 3,360 cubic miles) of accessible freshwater by UN estimate – and so far humans are using only about half of that.[6]

Water's properties approach the magical, and a basic grasp of its attributes is necessary to understand the laws that have evolved around it. Water is one of the few substances that can be found in nature in all three states of matter: liquid, solid, and gas. It is stable, yet unstable – stable in that the amount of water on earth has basically not changed for billions of years; unstable in that it is always in motion, nonstatic, not confined by national borders. Water is an extremely effective solvent, and almost the entire periodic table can be found dissolved or suspended in natural waters. Its saving grace, for us, is that it is renewable, daily cleansed through evapo-transpiration from liquid/solid on land into gas in the air and back again to liquid/solid on land through the world's largest "distillery" – the solar-powered hydrologic cycle. Water's infinite linkages require us to think holistically in terms of entire "watercourse systems" ("watersheds," "drainages," or "basins") so that our laws must recognize the interconnectedness of the surface water channels with the tributaries, lakes, reservoirs, canals, glaciers, wetlands, and

---

[4] *Water Basics*, US GEOLOGICAL SURVEY (USGS), http://ga.water.usgs.gov/edu/mwater .html; *The Water Cycle: Freshwater Storage*, USGS, http://ga.water.usgs.gov/edu/watercycle freshstorage.html; *Interesting Ocean Facts*, SAVE THE SEA, http://savethesea.org/STS%20 ocean_facts.htm.

[5] *Water Cycle, supra* note 4; UNEP, THE GREENING OF WATER LAW: MANAGING FRESHWATER RESOURCES FOR PEOPLE AND THE ENVIRONMENT 1 *et seq.* (2010), http://international waterlaw.org/bibliography/UN/UNEP_Greening_water_law.pdf. *See further* STEPHEN C. MCCAFFREY, THE LAW OF INTERNATIONAL WATERCOURSES chs. 1–2 (2d ed. 2007) [hereinafter MCCAFFREY, WATERCOURSES]; Stephen C. McCaffrey, *The Coming Fresh Water Crisis: International Legal and Institutional Responses*, 21 VT. L. REV. 803, 805 (1997) [hereinafter McCaffrey, *Crisis*]; UNESCO, UN WORLD WATER DEVELOPMENT REPORT: WATER IN A CHANGING WORLD (2009), http://www.unesco.org/water/wwap/wwdr/wwdr3/pdf/ WWDR3_Water_in_a_Changing_World.pdf.

[6] UN, *Assessment of the Freshwater Resources of the World*, E/CN.17/1997/9 (Feb. 4, 1997) [hereinafter UN Freshwater Assessment], http://www.un.org/ecosocdev/geninfo/sustdev/ waterrep.htm; David Hunter, *Special Report: Global Environmental Protection in the 21st Century – Filling the Environmental Policy Gaps*, *in* GLOBAL FOCUS: U.S. FOREIGN POLICY AT THE TURN OF THE MILLENNIUM (2000).

groundwaters that link to those surface water channels and form the water-course system.[7]

So, what is the "global water crisis" recently declared by the UN?[8] Increasing human population, expanding economic activity, and rising per capita human consumption are increasing water shortages for humans and aquatic ecosystems, and the situation is only expected to worsen:

> The world's population is growing by about 80 million people a year, implying increased freshwater demand of about 64 billion cubic meters a year. An estimated 90% of the 3 billion people who are expected to be added to the population by 2050 will be in developing countries, many in regions where the current population does not have sustainable access to safe drinking water and adequate sanitation.[9]

Water consumption has been "escalating at alarming rates," doubling every 21 years and increasing at more than twice the rate of population.[10] If this pattern continues, little quantity or quality of water will remain "instream" in many areas, with potentially disastrous results for natural ecosystems, recreation, navigation, or hydropower.[11] Average water availability per capita has fallen from 17,000 cubic meters per person per year (m3/person/yr) in 1950 to 7,000 in 1995.[12] By 2025, water availability is estimated to decrease to less than 5,100 cubic meters per person.[13]

However, averages are misleading. Water consumption is by no means evenly distributed. People in developed countries, like the US, consume disproportionate amounts compared to people elsewhere; for example, the US utilizes 70 times more water per person than residents of Ghana.[14] Law itself contributes to "the unequal and inequitable distribution of water . . . including access to domestic water supplies, maintenance of water and sewage infrastructure, contamination of drinking water, and safe levels of floodplain

---

[7] *Water Properties: Facts and Figures About Water,* USGS, http://ga.water.usgs.gov/edu/waterproperties.html; McCAFFREY, WATERCOURSES, *supra* note 5, ch. 2.

[8] *The Global Water Crisis,* UN, http://www.un.org/works/sub2.asp?lang=en&s=19. See *International Decade for Action "Water for Life" 2005–2015,* UN, http://www.un.org/waterforlifedecade/.

[9] McCaffrey, *Crisis, supra* note 5, at 805.

[10] *Id.* at 808; UN Freshwater Assessment, *supra* note 6.

[11] DAVID HUNTER, JAMES SALZMAN & DURWOOD ZAELKE, INTERNATIONAL ENVIRONMENTAL LAW AND POLICY 838 (2011).

[12] UN Freshwater Assessment, *supra* note 6.

[13] *Id.* An interesting resource for calculating personal water consumption can be found at: WATER FOOTPRINT NETWORK, http://www.waterfootprint.org/?page=cal/waterfootprint calculator_indv.

[14] McCAFFREY, WATERCOURSES, *supra* note 5, at 5.

occupancy" in ways that are racially and ethnically discriminatory, throughout both the developed and developing world.[15]

Average water consumption below 1,000 m3/person/yr is defined as "water scarcity," and consumption between 1,000–1,700 m3/person/yr is defined as "water stress." Today, about one-third of the world's people are already living in countries of water stress; by 2025, as many as two thirds of all people on Earth will be living under stress conditions;[16] and, worse, by that year over 30 countries may drop below the minimum life needs and fall into scarcity.[17] The most acute water problems are in Africa and West Asia, typically in the poorest countries.[18]

Four factors drive this increasing water scarcity:

- Increased population growth,
- Increased urbanization that focuses the demand for water among an ever more concentrated population,
- Increased per-capita consumption as the world becomes more developed,
- Decreased water resources resulting from climate change.

Climate change will affect both water availability and water demands for all uses, as it will increase hydrologic variability as well as extreme weather events, such as floods, droughts, and storms (*see* Section 10.3).[19]

Quantity is not the only problem. Water quality represents an equally great challenge. Water is one of the most efficient solvents on Earth, and its natural ability to dissolve and transport pollutants is increasingly being augmented by human contamination from sewage, industrial sources, agricultural runoff, tree and ground-cover destruction, urban sprawl, overdrafts leading to saline intrusion, etc.[20] Shockingly, almost 1 billion people in this world today do not have safe water to drink and 2.6 billion lack adequate sanitation, problems the UN's Millennium Development Goals are seeking to address.[21]

---

[15] Tom I. Romero II, *The Color of Water: Observations of a Brown Buffalo on Water Law & Policy in Ten Stanzas*, 15 U. DENVER WATER L. REV (forthcoming).

[16] UN Freshwater Assessment, *supra* note 6; UN, *Water for Life, supra* note 8.

[17] McCaffrey, *Crisis, supra* note 5, at 805.

[18] *Hot Issues: Water Scarcity*, FAO, http://www.fao.org/nr/water/issues/scarcity.html; *Coping with Water Scarcity: Challenge of the Twenty-First Century* (2007), FAO, http://www.fao .org/nr/water/docs/escarcity.pdf.

[19] UN-WATER, THE UNITED NATIONS WORLD WATER DEVELOPMENT REPORT 4: MANAGING WATER UNDER UNCERTAINTY AND RISK 2 (March 2012), (hereafter UN-WATER 4), http:// www.unesco.org/new/en/natural-sciences/environment/water/wwap/wwdr/wwdr4-2012/.

[20] UN Freshwater Assessment, *supra* note 6.

[21] *We Can End Poverty 2015 – Millennium Development Goals*, UN, http://www.un.org/ millenniumgoals/pdf/MDG_FS_7_EN.pdf.

Poor water quality fosters disease; it is estimated that one half of all the people in developing countries suffer from life-shortening water- and food-related diseases.[22] Moreover, a growing number of the world's rivers, lakes, and groundwater basins are being severely contaminated by human pollution inputs and pure-water withdrawals. Due to the interconnectivity of water resources, this pollution is causing widespread and increasing harm to our natural ecosystems, including the Earth's oceans, into which much of the freshwater ultimately flows.[23]

The World Commission on Water for the 21st Century reports that more than half the world's major rivers are going dry or have become severely polluted, creating millions more refugees than war does.[24] Key international examples include:

- The Amu Darya (Oxus) River (Afghanistan, Kyrgyzstan, Tajikistan, Turkmenistan, Uzbekistan) and Syr Darya River (Kazakhstan, Kyrgyzstan, Tajikistan, Uzbekistan) have had their flow into the Aral Sea cut by three fourths with catastrophic drops in the level of this inland freshwater sea.
- The Colorado River (Mexico, US) is so degraded by agriculture that its downstream delta has turned from lush green to desolate salt marshes.
- The Nile River (Burundi, Democratic Republic of the Congo, Egypt, Eritrea, Ethiopia, Kenya, Rwanda, Sudan, Tanzania, Uganda), with 90 percent of its natural flow used for irrigation or lost through evaporation, is heavily polluted when it reaches the Mediterranean Sea.
- The Ganges River (Bangladesh, India, Nepal) is so depleted and polluted that downstream wetlands and users are severely threatened.
- The Jordan Basin (Israel, Jordan, Lebanon, Syria) is a tinderbox of the Middle East with only one third of its water reaching the Dead Sea and projected upstream development threatening downstream Israel's heavy dependence on the river.[25]

---

[22] UN Freshwater Assessment, *supra* note 6; *Water Crisis*, WORLD WATER COUNCIL, http://www.worldwatercouncil.org/index.php?id=25.

[23] UN Freshwater Assessment, *supra* note 6. In round numbers, about 8 percent of the freshwater resource is used for human consumption and sanitation, 67–70 percent for agriculture, and 20 percent for industry, "leav[ing] precious little for freshwater ecosystems that nourish countless species of plants and animals and constitute a vital part of the human life-support system." McCaffrey, *Crisis*, *supra* note 5, at 808. In addition, *see World Water Quality Facts and Statistics*, PACIFIC INSTITUTE, http://www.pacinst.org/reports/water_quality/water_quality_facts_and_stats.pdf.

[24] World Water Council, *supra* note 23.

[25] *See Problem: Fresh Water and Oceans in Danger*, WEB OF CREATION, http://www.webofcreation.org/Earth%20Problems/water.htm.

Water is the one resource that is essential for all forms of human enterprise and, unlike oil and other resources, there is no substitute for water for most of its uses.[26] Our major consumptive uses are agriculture (70 percent of humans' water use), domestic-municipal, industrial, and electricity (thermoelectric and hydroelectric).[27] Our major non-consumptive uses include navigation, fishing, recreation, and environment. Municipal and industrial uses generate far more direct economic return per unit used than agriculture and other uses, so, in the witticism of US water lawyers, "Water flows uphill toward money."

Water is the prime example of a shared natural resource, and its international character makes dealing with these crises even more complex. Over 260 river basins are shared by two or more countries. These international water basins cover almost half the world's landmass (excluding Antarctica), are home to some 40 percent of its population, and contain some 60 percent of global freshwater.[28] Indeed, thirteen river basins are shared by five to eight countries,[29] and there are five basins shared between nine to eleven countries.[30] Those shared primarily by developed countries typically have extensive international treaty regimes in place, while those shared by developing countries have few or no agreements.[31]

The 2012 UN World Water Development Report highlights this issue:

> Greater recognition is needed of the fact that water is not solely a local, national or regional issue that can be governed at any of those levels alone. On the contrary, global interdependencies are woven through water, and decisions relating to water use on a local, national, river basin or regional level often cannot be isolated from global drivers, trends and uncertainties.... [W]ater cuts across all social, economic and environmental activities.... [I]ts governance requires cooperation and coordination across diverse stakeholders and sectoral "jurisdictions."[32]

---

[26] *Is Clean Water the New Oil?*, THE FLETCHER SCHOOL OF TUFTS UNIVERSITY, http://fletcher.tufts.edu/MIB/Ten-Questions/Q6-Is-clean-water-the-new-oil.

[27] *Web of Creation, supra* note 26.

[28] MCCAFFREY, WATERCOURSES, *supra* note 5, at 16–17; Sandra L. Postel & Aaron T. Wolf, *Dehydrating Conflict*, FOREIGN POLICY, Sept. 2001, http://www.foreignpolicy.com/articles/2001/09/01/dehydrating_conflict?page=full.

[29] *Water for Life, supra* note 8.

[30] *Id.*

[31] ROBIN CLARKE, WATER: THE INTERNATIONAL CRISIS 92 (1993). Europe has four major river basins shared by four or more countries, regulated by some 175 treaties; Africa has 12 great river basins shared by four or more countries, with 34 treaties regulating their use; Asia has five basins shared by four or more countries, with 31 treaties.

[32] UN-WATER 4, *supra* n. 19, at 2.

Human history and today's disputes have been profoundly affected by hydrology. The earliest known international water treaty dates from the third millennium BCE and was negotiated to settle a war between two independent Mesopotamian city-states, in what is now Iraq, over Euphrates River irrigation water.[33] Extensive international regulation of freshwaters through bilateral and multilateral treaties started in the late 18th century, with border delimitation and navigation being the early focuses. Beginning early in the 20th century, the treaties began evolving into a more comprehensive focus on so-called "non-navigational uses" (every use except navigation) and on pollution. Today, international water treaties number in the thousands.[34]

More often than not, downstream areas of river basins tend to be arid and flat and develop irrigated agriculture civilizations early, while upstream areas typically are more humid and rugged and develop intensive-water-use cultures much later.[35] What happens when late-developing upstream states begin major water withdrawals, depriving earlier-developed downstream states of their accustomed water supplies and increasing downstream pollution concentrations? What happens when the poorest developing countries, wherever located in the basin, want to develop water supplies that might erode existing water monopolies of their developed neighbors? What happens to "instream flow" uses – natural ecosystems, navigation, fishing, and the like – as water withdrawals increase up and down the basins?

Does the answer lie in "sovereignty" or in its very opposite, the notion that resources are shared in a "community of interests," a Garrett Hardin commons? Sovereignty leads to "the most infamous legal view yet espoused" in the water field – the "Harmon Doctrine."[36] It arose in 1895 when complaints from downstream Mexico of US overuse of the shared Rio Grande River (Rio Bravo del Norte in Mexico) led to a legal opinion by then US Attorney General Judson Harmon that concluded a state had "absolute territorial sovereignty" over resources within its borders allowing an upstream

---

[33] J. BRUHÁCS, THE LAW OF NON-NAVIGATIONAL USES OF INTERNATIONAL WATER-COURSES 9 (1993); Postel & Wolf, *supra* note 29.

[34] Renata D'Aliesio, *Chrétien's Call to Canada: Don't Fear Water-Export Debate,* THE GLOBE AND MAIL, Mar. 23, 2011 (quoting Professor Patricia Wouters, Director of the UNESCO IHP-HELP Center for Water Law), http://www.theglobeandmail.com/news/politics/ chrtiens-call-to-canada-dont-be-afraid-of-water-exporting-debate/article578411/.

[35] Stephen C. McCaffrey, The Global Freshwater Crisis and International Environmental Law, Address at the University of Denver College of Law (Feb. 27, 1999) (notes available with authors) [hereinafter McCaffrey, *Address*]. International rivers like the Nile, Colorado, Euphrates, Jordan, etc., are examples that come to mind.

[36] *See* Stephen McCaffrey, *The Harmon Doctrine One Hundred Years Later: Buried, Not Praised,* 36 NAT. RESOURCES J. 549 (1996) [hereinafter, McCaffrey, *Harmon*], http://law library.unm.edu/nrj/36/3/05_mccaffrey_harmon.pdf.

state complete freedom of action with regard to international watercourses within its territory irrespective of downstream consequences.[37] (The western states in the USA and other arid regions of the world still use a comparable "first-in-time-first-in-right" approach internally, but not in an interstate context.) However, the US Secretary of State essentially ignored the AG's opinion and negotiated a treaty with Mexico based on equitable sharing of the Rio Grande.[38] Sovereignty works both ways, and downstream states counter the "absolute territorial sovereignty" notion with the assertion of "absolute territorial integrity," according to which downstream states had the sovereign right to receive the same natural-flow quantity and quality of water they always had. Obviously, either extreme version of "absolute" sovereignty rights has disastrous consequences for basin harmony, and these two theories, while frequently asserted in negotiations still today, have never been accepted in international customary or conventional law.[39]

Not only does sovereignty not work efficiently or equitably as a basis for water distribution, but also, being focused only on the *temporary* geographic location of liquid water, it actually ignores the reality of the hydrologic cycle. Water is constantly in motion, so that any one country's control over it is accidental and temporary.[40] The same water molecules cut by the prow of Columbus' ships may be in Bangladesh today; clouds taking up moisture from rice paddies in China may rain in Canada days later; water in the Mississippi could have evaporated from the Pacific Ocean or some other water body a world away, and when it evaporates again it may not reliquify until it is over Africa. In short, it can be argued that it is hydrologic folly not to treat water as a global commons, potentially belonging to all.[41]

Of course, this view is still gross heresy in water law. Customary and conventional international water laws have developed two less drastic steps away from "absolute sovereignty." The first is a more flexible, shared distribution principle (borrowed from US legal practice), called "equitable and reasonable use" (also known as "equitable apportionment" or "proportionality").[42] This

---

[37] McCaffrey, Watercourses, *supra* note 5, at ch. 4.

[38] McCaffrey, *Harmon, supra* note 36, at 579.

[39] McCaffrey, Watercourses, *supra* note 5, at 125–26, 133–35.

[40] *Id.* at 25.

[41] This is not such a far-fetched concept. It has already been done with deep seabed mineral resources in the UN Convention on the Law of the Sea, Dec. 10, 1982, Part XI, U.N. Doc. A/CONF.62/122; 21 I.L.M. 1261 (1982), http://www.un.org/Depts/los/convention_agreements/texts/unclos/unclos_e.pdf.

[42] *See generally,* George William Sherk, Dividing the Waters: The Resolution of Interstate Water Conflicts in the United States (2000); Elizabeth Burleson, *Equitable and Reasonable Use of Water Within the Euphrates-Tigris Basin,* 35 Envtl. L. Rep. 10041 (2005), http://www.internationalwaterlaw.org/bibliography/articles/general/BurlesonTigris-Euphrates.pdf.

principle is based on a balancing analysis of all relevant factors, such as need, alternatives, efficiency, and not just maximization of those first-in-time. The second is a sustainability approach called the "ecosystem concept."[43] The ecosystem concept requires consideration of the natural environment, not just maximization of *human* consumptive uses. The development of these two modern concepts will be traced in international customary and conventional law in the following sections.

9.1   Development of Customary International Law

9.1.1   The Major Cases

Given the vital role of water in civilization, multinational water bodies have long been a subject of international law, developing over the centuries a relatively rich body of international customary law. While the late 20th century has seen the successful codification of most of these principles into global and regional treaties, a brief look first at the building blocks of customary law will provide context for these developments. Initially, the customary law coalesced around two macro issues – use allocation and procedural rights and duties. The 20th century introduced a third – environmental protection.

Although judicial cases have not contributed much to the development of international water law until recently,[44] a sextet of 20th and 21st century cases have laid out several major principles. The equitable and reasonable use concept, long a part of international practice, was first judicially recognized in the 1929 *River Oder Case*, in which the Permanent Court of International Justice (PCIJ) applied general principles of "international fluvial law" on that international river to rule that navigable tributaries of the Oder wholly inside Poland were open to traffic from other "riparian" states (states through or along whose land the river flowed).[45] The Court broadly ruled for the first time:

---

[43] *The Ecosystem Concept*, WORLD INSTITUTE FOR CONSERVATION & ENVIRONMENT, http://www.ecosystems.ws/ecosystem_concept.htm.

[44] BRUHÁCS, *supra* note 33, at 13. For a relatively exhaustive bibliography of 25 judicial and arbitration cases involving international waters, *see* p. 239.

[45] Case Relating to the Territorial Jurisdiction of the International Commission of the River Oder (Czech., Den., Fr., Ger., Swed., UK/Pol.), 1929 P.C.I.J. (ser. A) No. 23, at 5, http://www.worldcourts.com/pcij/eng/decisions/1929.09.10_river_oder.htm. Technically, the Court was called upon to decide whether the commission created by the World War I Versailles Peace Treaty had jurisdiction over the tributaries, but, as the treaty was silent on this point, the Court was obliged to look to international customary law.

> [w]hen...a single waterway traverses or separates the territory of more than one State...a solution of the problem has been sought [by States] not in the idea of a right of passage in favour of upstream States, but in that of a community of interest of riparian States...a common legal right, the essential features of which are the perfect equality of all riparian States in the user of the whole [navigable] course of the river...."[46]

Equitable utilization plus an early hint of the great sovereignty compromise of Stockholm Principle 21 were evident in the 1937 *River Meuse Case*, in which downstream Netherlands sued upstream Belgium for alleged excessive diversions from their shared river.[47] The PCIJ ruled in favor of Belgium, holding that its new diversion would not affect "the normal level and flow," invoking the customary rule that a state is at liberty to develop its resources as it sees fit provided it does not endanger the physical well-being of other states.

The "no harm" rule took a forward leap in the 1946 *Corfu Channel Case*.[48] There, two British destroyers were hit by mines while engaged in "innocent passage" through the Corfu Channel in Albanian territorial waters. The International Court of Justice found that the mines could not have been laid (presumably by Germany) without Albania's knowledge, holding that Albania should have warned Britain, because, under international law principles, states have an obligation not to knowingly allow their territories to be used for acts contrary to the rights of other states.

Procedural rights and duties were the issue in the precedent-setting 1957 *Lac Lanoux Arbitration*.[49] In that case, downstream Spain unsuccessfully sought to block a water development in upstream France. France's planned hydroelectric project, while diverting much of the natural flow of their shared river, would pump back replacement waters of equal quantity and quality before the river crossed into Spain. Since Spain faced no substantive injury to quantity or quality, it claimed procedural injury, arguing that international customary law required "prior agreement" of co-riparians before one state could substantially alter the course of transboundary waters. The arbitrators rejected this claim and ruled that under international customary law (1) a state is required to notify other potentially affected states of such plans, but

---

[46] *Id.* at 27.

[47] Diversion of Water from the Meuse Case (Neth. v. Belg.), 1937 P.C.I.J. (ser A/B) No. 70, at 4, http://www.worldcourts.com/pcij/eng/decisions/1937.06.28_meuse.htm. Here too a treaty was involved but did not cover the diversions in question, requiring application of customary law.

[48] Corfu Channel Case (U.K. v. Alb.), 1949 I.CJ. at 4, http://www.icj-cij.org/docket/files/1/1645.pdf.

[49] Summary of Lac Lanoux Arbitration (Spain v. Fr.), 12 R.I.A.A. 281 (1957), http://www.lfip.org/laws666/lakelanoux.htm.

(2) is not required to obtain their prior consent (no "right of veto"), but (3) is required to take into consideration in a reasonable manner the interests of those other states.

With the *Gabcikovo-Nagymoros Dam Case,*[50] the International Court of Justice in 1997 produced the most important transboundary water decision of the modern era, one recognizing the vital importance of environmental protection in today's world. In 1977, Hungary and then-Czechoslovakia entered into a Soviet-era treaty to construct a massive joint system of hydropower dams, canals, and industrial sites on the Danube River between Bratislava and Budapest, where the Danube forms part of their common border. During the downfall of the Iron Curtain and the vast political changes of 1989, Hungary – avowedly for environmental reasons – refused to build its downstream dam (Nagymaros) and unilaterally terminated the 1977 treaty, citing its potential for silting up of the river, pollution of groundwater, extinction of ecosystems, and damage to drinking water supplies. Unpersuaded, Czechoslovakia (succeeded by Slovakia) continued by building an alternate dam on its own territory (Gabcikovo), which diverted virtually the entire flow of the Danube from a 31-mile shared reach of the river.

In a very mixed opinion for the environment and the parties (both sides claimed victory), the ICJ began from an excellent premise:

> The Court is mindful that, in the field of environmental protection, vigilance and prevention are required on account of the often irreversible character of damage to the environment and of the limitations inherent in the very mechanism of reparation of this type of damage.
>
> Throughout the ages, mankind has, for economic and other reasons, constantly interfered with nature. In the past, this was often done without consideration of the effects upon the environment. Owing to new scientific insights and to a growing awareness of the risks for mankind – for present and future generations – of pursuit of such interventions at an unconsidered and unabated page, new norms and standards have been developed, set forth in a great number of instruments during the last two decades. Such new norms have to be taken into consideration, and…given proper weight, not only when States contemplate new activities but also when continuing with activities begun in the past. This need to reconcile economic development with protection of the environment is aptly expressed in the concept of sustainable development.[51]

---

[50] Case Concerning the Gabcikovo-Nagymoros Project (Hung.-Slovakia), Sept. 25, 1997, 1997 I.C.J. 7, http://www.icj-cij.org/docket/files/92/7375.pdf. For a more detailed treatment of the history and 8,500 pages of submissions in the case, *see* Afshin A-Khavari, *The Danube Dam Case: The World Court and the Development of Environmental Law,* 3 ASIA-PACIFIC J. ENVTL L. 101 (1998); Institute for Peace Research and Security Policy, *The Hungarian Slovakian Conflict Over the Gabcikovo-Nagymoros* Project, http://ece.columbia.edu/research/intermarium/vol6no2/furst3.pdf.

[51] *Id.* ¶ 140.

However, in holding the 1977 treaty was still in force and ordering the parties to go forward with negotiations on some form of implementation, its specific rulings were a mixed bag for the environment, including:

- Safeguarding the ecological balance has come to be considered an "essential interest" of all states;[52]
- States have a general obligation to respect and protect their natural environment and avoid transboundary harm to the environment of other states;[53]
- "Ecological necessity" can be a defense to violation of a treaty;[54]
- However, Hungary's evidence was insufficient to prove the "imminent peril" requirement of that defense because it was "mostly of a long-term nature and…uncertain";[55] thus, sadly, the Court refused to apply the "precautionary principle" in precisely the circumstances for which it was intended;
- On the other hand, Czechoslovakia violated Hungary's "right to an equitable and reasonable share of the natural resources of the Danube" – the "proportionality" requirement of international law – by unilaterally assuming control of a shared resource;[56]
- The emergence of new peremptory norms of international law requiring protection of the environment is "relevant," and these peremptory norms must be taken into account in future interpretation and implementation of prior treaties;[57]
- Consequently, the parties should reexamine the project and its environmental impacts and seek a "solution," taking into account and balancing their treaty obligations with the current norms of international environmental law and the law of international watercourses.[58]

---

[52] *Id.* ¶ 53.

[53] *Id.*, citing and relying on the ICJ's Advisory Opinion on the Legality of the Threat or Use of Nuclear Weapons, ¶ 29, July 8, 1996, U.N. Doc. A/51/218, 35 I.L.M. 809 (1996), http://www.icj-cij.org/docket/files/95/7495.pdf?PHPSESSID=cad3afae4c75012a36e3f651af7a10a7.

[54] *Id.*

[55] *Id.* ¶¶ 54–57.

[56] *Id.* ¶ 85.

[57] *Id.* ¶ 112. The opinion suggests that post-1970 international environmental law could constitute "changed circumstances" justifying abrogation of a treaty, but would not in this case because the 1977 treaty (surprisingly for its time) contained express provisions for protection of nature, water quality, and fisheries, which the Court felt would obligate these parties to take the new international environmental law norms into account in renegotiating the project.

[58] *Id.* ¶ 141.

The *Gabcikovo-Nagymoros Dam Case* thus is strong support for principles of equitable apportionment and environmental protection, yet the majority decision is disappointing in the latter arena by not applying the precautionary principle to avoidance of long-term impacts and refusing to recognize "sustainable development" as a binding legal principle, instead relegating it to the category of mere "concept."[59]

In 2010, the ICJ handed down its most recent international environmental and water decision in the *Case Concerning Pulp Mills on the River Uruguay (Argentina v. Uruguay).*[60] The dispute involved water pollution from two wood pulp mills proposed in Uruguay on the Uruguay River, an already polluted watercourse forming the boundary between Uruguay and Argentina. Argentina alleged extensive procedural and substantive violations of a 1975 bilateral treaty between the two countries that establishes the regime for the shared use and protection of the river and its environment. Based on a detailed examination of the treaty, the Court ruled that Uruguay had breached its procedural obligations (to notify and consult), but that Argentina's evidence failed to prove substantive violations of the treaty (regarding potential pollution and damage to the environment). As to reparations, the Court concluded its declaration of the procedural breaches was sufficient satisfaction in the case.[61]

While largely based on treaty interpretation, the judgment is most notable for its elaborations on *customary* international law.[62] For the first time, the Court ruled that an environmental impact assessment (EIA) is *required* by customary international law in advance of any proposed activity that presents a risk of significant transboundary environmental harm;[63] disappointingly, however, the Court held that international customary law does not provide requirements about the scope, content, and adequacy of such an EIA and that such requirements depend on the domestic law of the state involved.[64] Second, "continuous monitoring" of the on-going operations must be performed and, where necessary, throughout the life of the project.[65]

---

[59] *See* dissenting opinion of ICJ Vice President Weeramantry objecting to this, http://www.icj-cij.org/docket/files/92/7383.pdf.

[60] Pulp Mills on the River Uruguay (Arg. v. Uru.), 2010 I.C.J. 135 (Apr. 20) *reprinted in* 49 I.L.M. 1118 (2010), http://www.icj-cij.org/docket/index.php?p1=3&p2=1&k=88&case=135&code=au&p3=4.

[61] An excellent summary analysis of the Court's reasoning is Donald K. Anton, *Case Concerning Pulp Mills on the River Uruguay (Argentina v. Uruguay) (Judgment) [2010]*, 17 Austl. Intl L. J. 213 (2010), http://papers.ssrn.com/sol3/papers.cfm?abstract_id=1705810##.

[62] *See id.* at 213–14.

[63] Judgment, *supra* note 60, ¶ 204.

[64] *Id.* ¶ 205.

[65] *Id.*

Third, the Court reconfirmed that the prevention principle is a customary international law requirement, based on the no significant transboundary harm rule.[66] Fourth, the judgment and a number of the separate opinions focused on the increasingly frequent problem of expert evidentiary proof in environmental cases; all felt it would have been better to have actual testimony from expert witnesses, rather than the written and oral "reports" of experts which did not allow for cross-examination or judicial questioning.[67] In summary, the ICJ judgment in the *Pulp Mills Case* advanced international law with respect to EIAs and prevention, but missed notable opportunities to advance international environmental law otherwise or to apply the precautionary principle to the pollution issues in that case. Given the ICJ's disappointing performance in the case, one astute analyst has noted:

> [O]ne wonders if it might not be apropos for the Court to begin holding elections again for the Chamber for Environmental Matters (discontinued in 2006). ... [An] habitual use [of the chamber] could see the ICJ develop specialist environmental expertise essential to justly resolving cases like *Pulp Mills* involving difficult balancing between the environment, human health and economic development.[68]

9.1.2   *The Key "Soft Law" Developments*

More significant than judicial cases in the development of the law of international waters have been the many "soft law" declarations of rules and principles by leading international organizations and conferences.[69] That body of work, from the 1960s through 1990s, helped coalesce agreement and led to the most recent "hard law" advance – the 1997 UN Convention on the Law of the Non-Navigational Uses of International Watercourses (next section). This body of soft law continues to evolve even today, and informs both international conventions and national laws and actions.

But first, two significant early 20th century treaties involving the US and its neighbors ushered in new legal approaches for the use of shared watercourses. In 1906, ignoring its Attorney General Harmon's opinion (section

---

[66] *Id.* ¶ 101.

[67] *Id.* ¶ 169.

[68] Anton, *supra* note 61, at 223. *See also* George Pring & Catherine Pring, Greening Justice: Creating and Improving Environmental Courts and Tribunals (2009), http://www.law.du.edu/ect-study.

[69] For a comprehensive list, starting with the 1911 Madrid Resolution on Non-Navigation Uses of International Watercourses, *see* Edith Brown Weiss, Paul C. Szasz & Daniel B. Magraw, International Environmental Law: Basic Instruments and References 40–50 (1992), and Edith Brown Weiss, Daniel B. Magraw & Paul C. Szasz, International Environmental Law: Basic Instruments and References 1992–1999, 189–210 (1999).

9.0 above), the US entered into its first international water treaty, agreeing to an "equitable distribution" with Mexico of the Rio Grande/Rio Bravo River.[70] Three years later, the US and Canada negotiated the precedent setting 1909 Boundary Waters Treaty,[71] covering all lakes, rivers, bays, and other waters along their 2,000-mile common border; its pioneering provisions include one of the earliest treaty commitments to prevention of pollution, as well as freedom of navigation, controls on dams and diversions, and the creation of the International Joint Commission through which the two countries today work on water, air, and related transboundary issues.[72]

The Institute of International Law (IIL) or Institut de Droit International (IDI), a respected NGO "think tank" for the codification and progressive development of international law, first took up the water issue in 1911 and, 50 years later, produced the non-binding 1961 Salzburg Rules on international watercourses.[73] Very much a product of their times, the Salzburg Rules declared that there was a common interest in "maximum utilization" of natural resources[74] (scarcely consistent with today's view of "optimizing" resources or of "sustainable development"). Somewhat more progressively, the Salzburg Rules recognized that every state's right to use international waters was "limited" by the reciprocal rights of other states in the watershed;[75] they also adopted "equity" as the preferred basis for sharing international waters[76] and required advance notice, negotiations, adequate compensation, and dispute resolution for water projects or uses that may affect other states.[77]

Much more influential was the landmark articulation of soft law principles five years later by another respected NGO, the International Law Association (ILA). In 1966 it drafted the Helsinki Rules on the Uses of the Waters of

---

[70] Convention for the Equitable Distribution of the Waters of the Rio Grande River, U.S.-Mexico, May 21, 1906, T.S. 455, 9 Bevans 924, http://www.ibwc.state.gov/Files/1906Conv .pdf.

[71] Treaty Relating to Boundary Waters and Questions Arising Along the Boundary Between the United States and Canada, Jan. 11, 1909, 36 Stat. 2448, T.S. No. 548, http://laws.justice .gc.ca/eng/acts/I-17/page-6.html. *See also, About Us,* INTERNATIONAL JOINT COMMISSION, http://www.ijc.org/rel/agree/water.html.

[72] *See* HUNTER ET AL., *supra* note 14, at 888 *et seq.*

[73] Resolutions adopted by the Institute of International Law at its Session at Salzburg, ANNU-AIRE DE L'INSTITUT DE DROIT INTERNATIONAL, vol. 49–II, Salzburg Session, Sept. 1961, at 381 (1961), http://www.idi-iil.org/idiE/resolutionsE/1961_salz_01_en.pdf.

[74] *Id.* 2d preamble.

[75] *Id.* art 2.

[76] *Id.* art. 3.

[77] *Id.* arts. 4–8.

International Rivers,[78] which became the first authoritative statement of the customary law of international watercourses. The Helsinki Rules' definition of "international drainage basin" – the watershed limits of both surface and underground waters[79] – was hydrologically more accurate and inclusive than the Salzburg Rules, but limited just to international rivers and the underground aquifers specifically connected to them. The Helsinki Rules' basis for distribution was more comprehensive, giving each basin state "a reasonable and equitable share" for "beneficial uses."[80] The rules' specification of the 11 "relevant factors" to be considered in determining each state's share was the first attempt at a detailed codification of the "equitable and reasonable utilization" doctrine. The "multifactor analysis" items included geography, hydrology, climate, past use, economic and social needs, dependent population, costs of alternatives, availability of other resources, avoidance of unnecessary waste, practicability of compensation, and the substantiality of injury to a co-basin state.[81] The Helsinki Rules further required abatement and prevention of water pollution if it would cause "substantial injury,"[82] and their dispute prevention-settlement provisions were highly detailed.[83]

Other significant 20th century soft law contributions to the development of the international law of watercourses include:

- The 1972 Stockholm Declaration, which advanced a number of general principles relevant to freshwater (largely without mentioning it specifically), including protection of the environment, safeguarding of natural resources (including water), maintaining renewable resources, assuring economic and social development, integrated planning, prevention of transboundary harms, etc.[84]
- The 1978 UNEP Draft Principles on Natural Resources Shared by Two or More States, which incorporate the standards of "equitable utilization," protection of the environment, prevention of transboundary harms,

---

[78] Helsinki Rules on the Uses of the Waters of International Rivers, Aug. 20, 1966, 52 I.L.A. 484 (1967), http://www.mpil.de/shared/data/pdf/pdf/8helsinki_rules_on_the_waters_of_international_rivers_ila.pdf.

[79] *Id.* art. II.

[80] *Id.* art. IV.

[81] *Id.* art. V.

[82] *Id.* art. X.

[83] *Id.* arts. XXVI–XXXVII.

[84] United Nations Conference on the Human Environment, Stockholm, Swed., June 5–16, 1972, Stockholm Declaration of the UN Conference on the Human Environment, Principles 1, 2, 3, 5, 8, 13, 21, and 22, UN Doc. A/CONF.48/14/Rev. 1 at 3, UN Doc. A/CONF.48/14 at 2–65 and Corr. 1, (June 16, 1972) (hereinafter Stockholm Declaration), http://www.unep.org/Documents.Multilingual/Default.asp?DocumentID=97&ArticleID=1503.

environmental assessments, information exchange, notification, consultation, cooperation, and principles of responsibility and liability.[85]

- The 1986 work of the highly regarded World Commission on Environment and Development (WCED), the UN-created group which paved the
way for the 1992 UN Rio Conference. The WCED's legal subcommittee,
called the "Experts Group," produced Legal Principles for Environmental Protection and Sustainable Development, which, in addition to codifying and progressively developing "general principles," specifically focus
on "transboundary natural resources." The principles call for allocation of
transboundary water in a "reasonable and equitable manner," as well as
for prevention of transboundary harms, responsibility and liability rules,
cooperation, information exchange, notice, consultation, and environmental assessments.[86]

- In 1982, the ILA updated the Helsinki Rules with respect to water quality
in its Montreal Rules on Water Pollution in an International Drainage
Basin.[87]

- In 1986, the ILA tackled groundwater in its somewhat limited Seoul Rules
on International Groundwaters.[88]

- In 1990, the International Law Commission (ILC) adopted its seminal
Draft Articles on the Law of Non-Navigational Uses of International
Watercourses, which would form the basis for the 1997 Convention on the
Law of the Non-Navigational Uses of International Watercourses (both
discussed in section 9.2 below).

- The 1992 Rio Declaration advanced most of the same general principles
about freshwater as did the predecessor Stockholm Declaration, adding
a right to develop that "equitably" meets the needs of present and future
generations, express recognition of the "special situation and needs" and
"common but differentiated responsibilities" of developing countries, the

---

[85] UN Environment Programme, Draft Principles of Conduct in the Field of the Environment for Guidance of States in the Conservation and Harmonious Utilization of Natural
Resources Shared by Two or More States, approved by the UNEP Governing Council, May
19, 1978, U.N. Doc. UNEP/IG12/2 (1978); 17 I.L.M. 1097 (1978) http://www.unep.org/
Documents.Multilingual/Default.Print.asp?DocumentID=65&ArticleID=1260&l=en.

[86] Experts Group on Environmental Law of the World Commission on Environment and
Development, Legal Principles for Environmental Protection and Sustainable Development, June 18–20, 1986, U.N. Doc. WCED/86/23/Add.1 (1986), http://www.un-documents
.net/ocf-a1.htm.

[87] International Law Association, Report of the Sixtieth Conference, Montreal Rules on Pollution, Sept. 4, 1982, 60 I.L.A. 535 (1983), http://www.fao.org/DOCREP/005/W9549E/
w9549e08.htm#bm08..4.10.9.

[88] International Law Association, Report of the Sixty-second Conference, Seoul Complementary Rules, Aug. 30, 1986, 62 I.L.A. 251 (1987), http://www.mpil.de/shared/data/pdf/
pdf/9seoul.pdf.

need to halt "unsustainable patterns of production and consumption," the "precautionary approach," the "polluter pays principle," and other progressive improvements.[89]

- By comparison, the water resources chapter of Agenda 21,[90] the action plan adopted at the 1992 Rio Conference, is rather disappointing on international freshwater. Agenda 21 focused chiefly on actions at the national level; moreover, it simplistically states that transboundary water resources are "of great importance to riparian States" and so "cooperation among those States *may be desirable*"[91] (emphasis added) – a statement that seems woefully inadequate, given the critical importance of such cooperation).

- Finally, in 1997, UNGA adopted the Convention on the Law of the Non-Navigational Uses of International Watercourses, the first global treaty on the subject, and proposed it for ratification by states, but ratifications have been slow in coming (as discussed in section 9.2 below).

A number of these soft law pronouncements succeeded in codifying or hardening into international customary law by the start of the 21st century. Key among them are the principles of "good neighborliness" or "cooperation" (with its components of prior notification, consultation, and negotiation, *see* §§ 2.1.2 and 2.2.2), "equitable utilization" (§ 2.1.8), and the "no harm" rule (§ 2.1.3).[92] However, the extent to which they would be recognized and apply in different contexts remained situational and vague. These disparate pronouncements plus the gaps in their coverage prompted the ILA to create a more comprehensive summary of modern international law applicable to all freshwater resources. The drafting process incorporated "the experience of the nearly four decades since the Helsinki Rules were adopted, taking into account the development of important bodies of international environmental law, international human rights law, and the humanitarian law relating to the war and armed conflict...."[93]

---

[89] Rio Declaration on Environment and Development, June 13, 1992, Principles 3, 6, 7, 8, 15, and 16, U.N. Doc. A/CONF.151/26 (vol. I) (1992), 31 I.L.M. 874 (1992), http://www.un.org/documents/ga/conf151/aconf15126-1annex1.htm.

[90] Agenda 21, June 13, 1992, U.N. Doc. A/CONF. 151/26/Rev. 1 (Vol. I), ¶¶ 18.1–18.90, http://www.un.org/esa/dsd/agenda21; reprinted in AGENDA 21 & THE UNCED PROCEEDINGS 357–411 (Nicholas A. Robinson ed., 1993).

[91] *Id.* ¶ 18.4.

[92] *See* Stephen McCaffrey, *The 1997 United Nations Convention on International Watercourses*, 92 AM. J. INT'L L. 97, 106 (1998), http://untreaty.un.org/cod/avl/pdf/ha/clnuiw/clnuiw_e.pdf [hereinafter McCaffrey, *Convention*]; *see* LAKSHMAN GURUSWAMY & BRENT HENDRICKS, INTERNATIONAL ENVIRONMENTAL LAW IN A NUTSHELL 380–93 (2007).

[93] Berlin Rules on the Uses of the Waters of International Rivers, Aug. 21, 2004, I.L.A. (2004), http://internationalwaterlaw.org/documents/intldocs/ILA_Berlin_Rules-2004.pdf.

The resulting Berlin Rules on Water Resources, were adopted by the ILA in 2004 specifically to replace their Helsinki Rules.[94] The new rules codify customary international law and propose progressive developments beyond existing law, in ways significantly different from the Helsinki Rules. For the first time, these rules include both international and *national* waters to the extent that customary international law has developed around them. Chapter II covers general principles for all fresh waters, including the right of public participation and the duty to manage waters to achieve sustainability and minimization of environmental harm. Article 12 obliges states to manage the waters in an equitable and reasonable "manner," a significant departure from the Helsinki Rules, which emphasized the right of states to have a reasonable and equitable "share." Article 16 couples shared management with the obligation not to cause significant harm. The rules break new ground in addressing human rights, including the individual right to equal access to water to sustain life in Article 17. Chapter V details obligations to protect the aquatic environment, and Chapter VI covers EIAs. Chapter VIII is the first comprehensive presentation of customary international law relating to groundwater. Other provisions cover the issues addressed in the Helsinki Rules and do so in greater detail.

The Berlin Rules are not themselves enforceable international law. They are also considered controversial since some significant ILA members did not agree with many of the progressive development features.[95] However, in going beyond established customary international law and incorporating new principles, these efforts show that soft law continues to be a significant source of development in the field of international water law today.

9.2   *The 1997 UN Convention on International Watercourses*

In 1970, the UN General Assembly recommended that the International Law Commission (ILC) address the "progressive development and codification" of the law of the non-navigational uses of international watercourses.[96] The ILC is the official UN organ of international law experts created in 1947 to encourage "the progressive development of international law and

---

[94] *Id.*

[95] The dissenters' views can be found at *Dissenting Opinion*, INTERNATIONAL WATER LAW CONFERENCE, http://internationalwaterlaw.org/documents/intldocs/ila_berlin_rules_dissent .html.

[96] G.A. Res. 2669 (XXV), 1970 U.N. JURID. Y.B. 209, UN Sales No. E.72 I.1, http://www .un.org/documents/ga/res/25/ares25.htm.

its codification."[97] The ILC began deliberations in 1974 and, after two decades' work, adopted its groundbreaking 1994 Draft Articles on the Law of Non-Navigational Uses of International Watercourses.[98] In 1997, UNGA adopted the Convention on the Law of the Non-Navigational Uses of International Watercourses (also known as the UN Convention on International Watercourses),[99] the first global treaty on the subject, generally following the text of the ILC Draft Articles.

The UN Convention is intended to be a "framework" treaty (5th preamble), establishing general legal principles which could lead to further refinement in protocols and multilateral agreements on specific watercourses. The convention is divided into seven parts:

- Part I ("Introduction") includes articles on the convention's scope (Article 1), definitions (2), and relation to other watercourse agreements (3–4).
- Part II ("General Principles") contains the core rules on "equitable and reasonable utilization" (5–6), "obligation not to cause significant harm" (7), "cooperation" (8–9), and the principle that no type of use has inherent priority over any other (10).
- Part III ("Planned Measures") details obligations of states when they plan new or changed water uses, including information exchange (11), prior notification (12–16, 18), consultation and, negotiation (11, 17), and overriding urgency (19).
- Part IV ("Protection, Preservation and Management") contains the key provisions on protection and preservation of the ecosystem (20) and the marine environment (23), pollution prevention, reduction, and control (21), introduction of alien or new species (22), joint institutional management (24), regulation of water flow (25), and safety and best management practices for dams and other water installations (26).
- Part V ("Harmful Conditions and Emergency Situations") consists of provisions on prevention and mitigation of natural or human-caused harmful conditions (27) and emergency situations (28).

---

[97] G.A. Res. 174 (II) (1947); United Nations, Basic Facts About the United Nations 261–62 (1998); *Introduction*, International Law Commission, http://www.un.org/law/ilc/.

[98] Draft Articles with Commentaries, http://untreaty.un.org/ilc/texts/instruments/english/commentaries/8_3_1994.pdf. For an overview, *see* Stephen McCaffrey, *Background and Overview of the International Law Commission's Study of the Non-Navigational Uses of International Watercourses*, 3 Colo. J. Int'l Envtl. L. & Pol'y 17 (1992).

[99] Convention on the Law of the Non-Navigational Uses of International Watercourses, May 21, 1997, G.A. Res. A-RES-51-229, U.N. Doc. A/51/869, 36 I.L.M. 700 (1997), http://untreaty.un.org/ilc/texts/instruments/english/conventions/8_3_1997.pdf. For convenience, specific citations to its provisions will be made in the text, without repeated footnotes.

- Part VI ("Miscellaneous Provisions") adds procedures for armed conflict (29) and other situations where direct state-to-state contacts face obstacles (30), protection of national defense/security data (31), nondiscrimination in judicial or other procedural access (32), and dispute settlement (33).
- Part VII ("Final Clauses") contains typical provisions on signature, ratification, entry into force (35 parties), and authentic texts (33–37).

In addition, there is an Annex on "Arbitration" and an interesting addendum of "Statements of Understanding Pertaining to Certain Articles of the Convention," commenting on the meaning of nine of the articles as well as indicating that the ILC's commentaries on its draft articles can be used to clarify the convention's provisions.

The treaty has not entered into force, and may never do so. Ratifications have been slow: as of the start of 2012, only 24 states had become parties (including only a few major powers), leaving 11 more still needed for it to enter into force.[100] Despite that, the convention is viewed as "the essential basis of international law on fresh waters," since it is a "codification convention" generally expressing agreed customary international law.[101] Moreover, it does clarify a number of very significant forward-looking concepts, as discussed in the following sections.

9.2.1 Adoption of the "Ecosystem" Concept

Article 20 of the 1997 Convention prescribes a general obligation that "[w]atercourse States shall, individually and, where appropriate, jointly, protect and preserve the ecosystems of international watercourses."[102] This reflects the generally modernizing nature of the treaty, incorporating a "holistic" ecosystem-focused approach into the law of non-navigational uses of international watercourses and bringing it more into line with modern international environmental law and policy. "Ecosystem" is not defined in the convention, but the definitions do employ the "system" concept, defining "watercourse" broadly as "a system of surface waters and ground waters constituting by virtue of their physical relationship a unitary whole and normally flowing into a common terminus."[103] The ILC's commentary on Article 20

---

[100] *Status of the Convention on Non-Navigational Uses of International Watercourses,* UN, http://treaties.un.org/pages/ViewDetails.aspx?src=TREATY&mtdsg_no=XXVII-12& chapter=27&lang=en.

[101] A. C. KISS & DINAH SHELTON, INTERNATIONAL ENVIRONMENTAL LAW 402 (3d ed. 2004).

[102] *See generally* Connie S. Singh, *The International Law Commission and State Responsibility: Application of Comparative Paradigm on Oil and Watercourses,* FORUM ON PUBLIC POLICY, http://www.forumonpublicpolicy.com/summer08papers/archivesummer08/singh.pdf.

[103] UN Convention, *supra* note 99, art. 2(a).

defines "ecosystem" as "an ecological unit consisting of living and non-living components that are interdependent and function as a community."[104] Earlier versions used the phrase "the environment of an international watercourse," until the ILC became persuaded that ecosystem has "a more precise scientific and legal meaning" than environment.[105]

The ecosystem concept first came into general use in the scientific literature in the mid-1930s;[106] an early definition, hard to improve on, was Raymond Lindeman's: "the system composed of physical-chemical-biological processes active within a space-time unit of any magnitude, i.e., the biotic community plus its abiotic environment."[107] Modern scientific writing mirrors this definition, as in the Ehrlichs' statement that an ecosystem is "the functional unit that includes both biotic (living) and abiotic (nonliving) elements."[108] (One could fault the ILC and Lindeman definitions only in that an "ecosystem" today is not viewed as one "community," but as multiple communities, so that community is a subset of ecosystem and represents a different level of biological analysis.[109])

There has been slow and uneven acceptance of the ecosystem concept in environmental law, both nationally and internationally. Some criticisms are that the concept is too broad and it fails to identify criteria "for testing ecosystem theories and models."[110] While its use was urged in US environmental law as early as 1970 – by the "father of the National Environmental Policy Act (NEPA)," political science Professor Lynton Caldwell[111] – 20 years later it was still only "emerging" as a US legal concept.[112]

---

[104] ILC Draft Articles and Commentaries, *supra* note 98, text at n. 322.

[105] *Id.*

[106] *See, e.g.,* A. G. Tansley, *The Use and Abuse of Vegetational Concepts and Terms,"* 16 ECOLOGY 284, 299 (1935), http://karljaspers.org/files/tansley.pdf.

[107] Raymond L. Lindeman, *The Trophic-Dynamic Aspect of Ecology,* 23 ECOLOGY 399, 400 (1942) (emphasis in original), http://www.fcnym.unlp.edu.ar/catedras/ecocomunidades/Lindman_1942.pdf.

[108] PAUL EHRLICH, ANNE EHRLICH & J. P. HOLDREN, ECOSCIENCE: POPULATION, RESOURCES, ENVIRONMENT 97 (1977).

[109] *See generally,* UNU/IAS, DEFINING AN ECOSYSTEM APPROACH TO URBAN MANAGEMENT AND POLICY DEVELOPMENT (2003), http://www.ias.unu.edu/binaries/UNUIAS_Urban Report1.pdf.

[110] Kevin de Laplante & Jay Odenbaugh, *What Isn't Wrong with Ecosystem Ecology,* at 2, *in* PHILOSOPHY AND THE LIFE SCIENCES: A READER (Robert A. Skipper *et al.,* eds. 2004), http://legacy.lclark.edu/~jay/What%20Isn't%20Wrong%20with%20Ecosystem%20 Ecology.pdf.

[111] Lynton K. Caldwell, *The Ecosystem as a Criterion for Public Land Policy,* 10 NAT. RESOURCES J. 203 (1970).

[112] *See, e.g.,* R. B. Keiter, *NEPA and the Emerging Concept of Ecosystem Management on the Public Lands,* 25 LAND & WATER L. REV. 43, 44 (1990).

In the context of international law, there have been increasing calls for eco-system management of international waters;[113] yet it is only in the last decade that the concept has begun to appear in the language of international documents and resolutions.[114] Early examples include use of the term "ecosystem" in the 1978 Canada-US Great Lakes Water Quality Agreement,[115] in the 1980 Convention on the Conservation of Antarctic Marine Living Resources,[116] the 1982 World Charter for Nature,[117] and a few regional agreements.[118] Article 20 of the UN Convention on International Watercourses is indicative of the trend toward more comprehensive, ecosystem-based resource management efforts that recognize the necessity of protecting ecological processes, rather than just individual species or discrete resources found in the environment.[119] Under such a broadened definition, the emphasis on navigation, flood control, apportionment of water, and hydropower generation which has historically dominated international water agreements would no longer be the only focus, but this greater breadth causes both increased applicability and increased complexity in application. The breadth of the "ecosystem" intended by the ILC is illustrated in its commentary on Article 20. It notes that "an external impact affecting one component of an ecosystem causes reactions among other components and may disturb the equilibrium of the entire ecosystem" and "may impair or destroy the ability of an ecosystem to function as a life-support system."[120]

Three comments are in order here. First, the concept of an ecosystem does not distinguish between the human species and other species, whether plant

---

[113] *See, e.g.,* ORGANIZATION FOR ECONOMIC CO-OPERATION AND DEVELOPMENT (OECD), THE STATE OF THE ENVIRONMENT 69 (1991). UNEP noted that in the 1970s and early 80s, there was "increasing recognition of the need for better management of water resources by treating river basins as unitary systems." UNEP, THE WORLD ENVIRONMENT 1972–1982: A REPORT BY THE UNITED NATIONS ENVIRONMENT PROGRAM 124 (M. Holdgate *et al.* eds., 1982).

[114] A glaring example of this is the absence of the term in the ENCYCLOPEDIA OF PUBLIC INTERNATIONAL LAW (North-Holland 1986).

[115] U.S.-Canada, Nov. 22, 1978, arts. I(g), II, 30 U.S.T. 1383. *See generally, About Us,* INTER-NATIONAL JOINT COMMISSION, http://www.ijc.org/rel/agree/quality.html.

[116] Convention on the Conservation of Antarctic Marine Living Resources, May 20, 1980, art. I(3), L252 O.J.E.C. 27 (1981), T.I.A.S. No. 10240, 19 I.L.M. 841 (1980), www.ccamlr.org/pu/e/e_pubs/bd/pt1.pdf.

[117] World Charter for Nature, G.A. Res. 37/7 (Annex), art. I(3), I(4), U.N. GAOR, 37th Sess., Supp. No. 51, at 17, UN Doc. A/37/51, 22 I.L.M. 455 (1983), http://www.un.org/documents/ga/res/37/a37r007.htm.

[118] *E.g.,* the 1989 Amazon Declaration, ¶ 9, http://www.jstor.org/pss/20693361; also in WEISS ET AL., INTERNATIONAL ENVIRONMENTAL LAW: BASIC INSTRUMENTS AND REFERENCES, *supra* note 69, at 553.

[119] The ILC Commentaries reflect this, *supra* note 98, art. 22, ¶ 2, at 57.

[120] *Id.,* art. 20, ¶ 2, at 123.

or animal. All merit consideration, and the ILC wording about "components" is consistent with this view, repositioning humans relative to the rest of the biosphere and emphasizing the importance of the non-human components. Such a readjustment parallels changes in US environmental law and policy,[121] and is a positive step toward treating causes rather than symptoms of environmental degradation.

Second, the focus of Article 20 on ecological processes draws attention to the dynamic, changing nature of ecosystems and of the interactions between their human and nonhuman components. Change is the paradox of ecosystems – both central to their continued existence (evolution) and, at too extreme a level, their biggest threat. As Aldo Leopold's visionary work reminds us:

> In the beginning, the pyramid of life was low and squat; the food changes short and simple. Evolution has added layer after layer, link after link.... Science has given us...at least one certainty: the trend of evolution is to elaborate and diversify the biota.... When a change occurs in one part of the ["biotic pyramid"], many other parts must adjust themselves to it.... [E]volution is a long series of self-induced changes, the net result of which is to elaborate ["and diversify the biota"].... Evolutionary changes, however, are usually slow and local. Man's [sic] invention of tools has enabled him to make changes of unprecedented violence, rapidity, and scope.... The combined evidence of history and ecology seems to support one general deduction: the less violent the man-made changes, the greater the probability of successful readjustment of the pyramid.[122]

Article 20 thus requires states to both "protect and preserve" international watercourse ecosystems. "Protect" looks to the future in its application and implies that the current condition of an ecosystem is desirable to maintain.[123] "Preserve" looks to the present and implies that the current condition needs protection.[124] This potentially presents two problems. One is how to determine what Leopold would consider the "natural changes" which contribute to "biodiversity" and distinguish them from the extreme "man-made changes" which threaten the ecosystem. Another is how to deal with ecosystems which are already in highly degraded states – suffering soil erosion as a

---

[121] For example, the Spotted Owl controversy in the US Pacific Northwest revolves around both the protection to be afforded an animal species and an old-growth forest ecosystem, and the extent to which these nonhuman species' requirements should impact human communities and economies. For a good overview and sources, *see* Zygmunt J. B. Plater et al., Environmental Law and Policy: Nature, Law, and Society 788–794 (2004).

[122] Aldo Leopold, A Sand County Almanac, 215–20 (1948).

[123] The ILC Commentaries state that the requirement is to "shield" the ecosystems from harm or damage. ILC Commentaries, *supra* note 98, art. 20, ¶ 3, at 123.

[124] Although the ILC notes that it intends the obligation to apply "in particular" to "pristine or unspoiled" ecosystems. *Id.* art. 20, ¶ 3, at 123.

result of deforestation, or loss of biodiversity from habitat development, or desertification from excessive water withdrawals, or other impacts of spiraling human population and poverty. These uncertainties hopefully will be worked out in future protocols or policy development.

Third, given the generally thorough discussion in the commentary on the meaning and intent of Article 20, it is puzzling that "water quantity" is not mentioned, since fluctuations in the amount of water in a watercourse have significant consequences for its ecosystem. Construction of a dam, for example, can be the most significant negative impact on a watercourse ecosystem.[125] Impoundments and withdrawals of water can have multiple and multiplying effects – (1) increasing concentrations of pollutants downstream (reducing the "pollution dilution" power of a watercourse), (2) decreasing flows and flow rates to the detriment of flood-dependent or other dependent downstream ecosystems, (3) changing water temperatures, and of course (4) curtailing water supplies needed in the immediate area and downstream by human and nonhuman components of the ecosystem. In this context, it is worth remembering the OECD's recommendation that "[t]he quantitative relationship between water quality and quantity must be thoroughly evaluated prior to a management decision."[126] It is not clear why there is no explicit discussion of water quantity in the commentaries; however, if the language of Article 20 is to be taken seriously, as it must, then the expected physical consequences of a project or management decision, such as a dam or diversion, would need to be carefully examined in terms of the mandate to "protect and preserve" the ecosystems of international watercourses.

The term "ecosystem," while broadening, is a narrower and more precise term than "environment," the latter being a word that troubled some delegates because it "could be interpreted quite broadly to apply to areas 'surrounding' the watercourses that have minimal bearing on the protection and preservation of the watercourse itself"[127] (and possibly stretch the treaty controls too far away from the watercourse for some states' comfort). The use of the ecosystem concept appears responsive to those concerns, since the focus on ecosystems correctly places the emphasis on (usually observable) interrelationships rather than possibly unrelated geography. Still, "ecosystem" is not

---

[125] *See generally* LAWRENCE J. MACDONNELL, FROM RECLAMATION TO SUSTAINABILITY: WATER, AGRICULTURE, AND THE ENVIRONMENT IN THE AMERICAN WEST (1999); SANDRA POSTEL, PILLAR OF SAND: CAN THE IRRIGATION MIRACLE LAST? (1999); Marc Reisner & Ronald H. McDonald, *The High Cost of High Dams, in* BORDERING ON TROUBLE: RESOURCES & POLITICS IN LATIN AMERICA 270 (A. Maguire & Janet W. Brown eds., 1986); T. Scudder, *The Need and Justification for Maintaining Transboundary Flood Regimes: The Africa Case*, 31 NAT. RESOURCES. J. 75 (1991).

[126] OECD Environment, *supra* note 113, at 65.

[127] ILC Commentaries, *supra* note 98, art. 20, ¶ 2, at 123.

so precise as to make defining boundaries of one easy; for example: Is a plant community 1,000 meters from a stream sufficiently dependent to be part of the stream system? Are groundwaters in the area sufficiently connected to the surface waters? Is a particular migratory bird part of the ecosystem, if only resident seasonally or temporarily?

Perhaps the appropriate response in such cases is that the question of the boundaries of an ecosystem must be viewed in light of the extent to which there may be "significant harm" under Article 7 (next section). The convention defines harm as a factual standard "capable of being established by objective evidence and not...trivial in nature,"[128] so, to the extent the location of the ecosystem boundary is not determinable, the likelihood that the harm can be established as significant will diminish correspondingly. Nevertheless, caution seems in order with regard to the hope that increased precision in defining area limits will result from the use of the ecosystem concept.

9.2.2   Conflict Between the Principles of "Equitable Utilization" and "No Significant Harm"

The first "General Principle" in the International Watercourse Convention and a "cornerstone" of the law in this field[129] is human-use-focused: Article 5's mandate that watercourse states "utilize an international watercourse in an equitable and reasonable manner" and "with a view to attaining optimal and sustainable utilization thereof." Efforts by a number of delegates to update this rather homocentric-utilitarian focus to better match modern environmental views and the ecosystem concept resulted in only one change from the draft articles – but a significant one – the insertion of the words "and sustainable."[130] That, coupled with the requirement at the end of Article 5(1) that allocation be "consistent with adequate protection of the watercourse," is certainly sufficient to make "equitable and reasonable utilization" include considerations other than human consumption. The second paragraph of the article calling for equitable participation is the first of a number of sections of the treaty emphasizing that cooperation in watercourse "use, development and protection" is essential.

Article 6 presents a non-exhaustive list of the "relevant factors" for determining whether a particular use is "equitable and reasonable utilization." Included are natural factors (geographic, hydrographic, hydrological,

---

[128] Statements of Understanding Pertaining to Certain Articles of the Convention, "as regards article 3," at 5, in Report of the Sixth Committee Convening as the Working Group of the Whole, U.N. Doc. A/51/869 (1997) *reprinted* in 36 I.L.M. 719, http://www.undemocracy .com/A-51-869.pdf.

[129] McCaffrey, Watercourses, *supra* note 5, at 363.

[130] *Id.*

climatic, ecological, etc.), social and economic factors, dependent populations, effects on other states, existing and potential uses, water conservation
and its costs, and available alternatives.[131] As guidance on how to do such a
complex, multifactoral analysis, Articles 6's paragraphs 2 and 3 merely advise
cooperation, weighting factors based on their comparative importance, and
considering all factors together as a whole.

The key additional factor in or limitation on "equitable and reasonable
utilization" is the most controversial provision in the convention:[132] Article
7's obligation to "take all appropriate measures to prevent the causing of
significant harm to other watercourse States." Illustrating its importance,
the "no harm" rule appears in various guises in no less than seven other
articles, including Articles 12 ("Notification concerning planned measures
with possible adverse effects"), 21(2) ("Prevention, reduction and control
of pollution" (*see* § 9.2.3)), 22 ("Introduction of alien or new species"),
26 ("Installations"), 27 ("Prevention and mitigation of harmful conditions"),
28 ("Emergency situations"), and 32 ("Non-discrimination").

The tensions between the "equitable utilization" Articles 5–6 and the "no
significant harm" Article 7 are obvious. Upstream states, with existing or
contemplated water uses that may harm downstream states' development
plans, naturally can be expected to argue that prohibitory Article 7 is "subordinate," by its own terms,[133] to permissive Articles 5–6, and consequently
that significant transboundary harm is just one of the many factors to be
weighed in that flexible multifactoral balance. Just as naturally, for self-
protective reasons downstream states can be expected to argue that Article
7 is an independent, overriding obligation, and consequently that significant harm automatically is not "equitable and reasonable" under Article 5.[134]
The convention does not expressly resolve this conflict, and authorities are
divided on whether Article 7 overrides or not.

The weight of authority resolves the conflict in favor of the equitable and
reasonable utilization principle. As ILC Rapporteur McCaffrey states:

> [T]he available authorities indicate that while the no-harm principle does
> qualify as an independent norm, it neither embodies an absolute standard nor
> supersedes the principle of equitable utilization where the two appear to con-
> flict with each other. Instead ... [the no-harm principle] plays a complementary

---

[131] Efforts to add sustainable development, needs of future generations, and contribution
to the watercourse by each state were rejected. McCaffrey, *Convention, supra* note 92, at
100.

[132] *Id.*

[133] Article 7(2) obliges states to take appropriate measures to eliminate or mitigate significant
harms, but qualifies that with the phrase "having due regard for the provisions of Articles
5 and 6...."

[134] McCaffrey, *Convention, supra* note 92, at 102.

role, triggering discussions between the states concerned and perhaps, in effect, proscribing certain forms of serious harm.[135]

Viewed in this light, the Convention's no-harm principle does not prohibit all *factual* harm but only harm to the *legally* protected equitable and reasonable share of a state. So the Convention and customary international law now protect a riparian state against deprivation of its equitable share of the uses and benefits of an international watercourse.[136]

In any case, the phrase "take all appropriate measures" makes no-harm not a strict obligation of result, but instead an obligation of conduct, and thus leaves unresolved tensions between Articles 5–6 and 7 for future resolution by protocol, individual watercourse agreements, cooperative negotiations, or adjudication. Furthermore, not all harm is proscribed by Article 7 and the other harm provisions, only that harm which rises to the level of "significant." The threshold for the level of harm required was a focus of considerable debate, as it is throughout international environmental law, and in this convention "significant" won out in the adjectivial debate over most provisions (*see* Articles 3(4), 7, 12, 21(2), 22, 26, 32).

Four escalating harm thresholds typically are advanced, as they were here:

1. No stated level, simply a proscription against harm without a limiting adjective, obviously the most protective and also, equally obviously, rarely used except in nonbinding declarations;[137]
2. "*Appreciable*" harm, the lowest harm threshold (most protective) seen in binding instruments, typically favored by downstream states fearful of upstream states' pollution, and the threshold chosen by the ILC in its Draft Articles;[138]

---

[135] McCaffrey, Watercourses, *supra* note 5, at 408.

[136] *Id.*

[137] A notable exception being Article 27 of this Convention which obligates states to take all appropriate measures to prevent or mitigate natural or human-caused conditions that "may be harmful" (no limiting adjective) to other states. Another of the rare treaty examples being the UN Convention on the Law of the Sea, art. 194 ("prevent, reduce and control pollution") (*see* Chapter 11). More typical of this approach are aspirational soft law documents like Stockholm Principle 21 and Rio Principle 2, both of which speak of the responsibility to "not cause damage" to the environment outside one's borders, without stating a limiting threshold level.

[138] ILC Draft Articles, *supra* note 98, art. 21(2). Other examples of the use of the "appreciable" threshold include the ILC Draft Articles on International Liability for Injurious Consequences Arising Out of Acts Not Prohibited by International Law, May 30, 1989, arts 2(a), 9, Report of the International Law Commission on the Work of its Forty-First Session, U.N. GAOR, 44th Sess., Supp. No. 10, at 222, U.N. Doc. A/44/10 (1989).

3. *"Significant"* harm, generally viewed as a higher threshold (allowing some-what more harm), a compromise level most widely used in international environmental legal authorities,[139] and the one chosen in this Convention and in the 2004 Berlin Rules; and

4. *"Substantial"* harm, the highest (least protective) threshold, typically favored by upstream states desiring the least possible limitations on their (ab)use of shared freshwaters, and the one chosen in the pre-environmen-tal-era 1966 ILA Helsinki Rules.[140]

So, what is "significant"? Threshold-establishing terms like these are always slippery to define (think about legal terms like "reasonableness," "appropri-ate," "good faith," "due diligence," etc.). The UNGA drafting committee for the Convention made the following observation:

> The term "significant" is not used…in the present Convention in the sense of "substantial." What is to be avoided are…[agreements or actions] which have a significant adverse effect upon third watercourse States. While such an effect must be capable of being established by objective evidence and not be trivial in nature, it need not rise to the level of being substantial.[141]

This circular explanation actually advances our understanding in two ways: (1) as to means, by setting a factual standard of proof ("objective evidence") and (2) as to ends, by setting a *de minimus* floor ("not…trivial"). However, this differs very little from the definition of "appreciable" given in commen-taries to the ILC Draft Articles, which also set an "objective evidence" stan-dard and a de minimus standard of "not insignificant or barely detectable, but…not necessarily 'serious.' "[142] The ILC commentaries go on to require "a real impairment of use, i.e. a detrimental impact of some consequence upon, for example, public health, industry, property, agriculture or the environ-ment in the affected State."[143]

There is the obvious eye-of-the-beholder problem with a word like "significant." What might appear to be a "significant" level of pollution to a downstream victim might be declared "insignificant" by its upstream

---

[139] *E.g.*, Convention on Environmental Impact Assessment in a Transboundary Context, Feb. 25, 1991, art. 2, 30 I.L.M. 800 (1991), http://live.unece.org/fileadmin/DAM/env/eia/documents/legaltexts/conventiontextenglish.pdf.

[140] Helsinki Rules, *supra* note 78, art. X ("prevent…pollution…which would cause substan-tial injury"). Another example is the WCED Experts Group Legal Principles, *supra* note 86, art. 11(1) ("significant risk of substantial harm").

[141] Statements of Understanding, in Rep. of the Sixth Comm. convening as the Working Group of the Whole at ¶ 8 "As regards article 3," April 11, 1997, U.N. Doc. A/51/869, GAOR, 51st Sess., Agenda item 144, http://www.un.org/law/cod/watere.htm.

[142] ILC Commentaries, *supra* note 98, art. 7, ¶ 5, at 52 (footnote omitted).

[143] *Id.*

perpetrator. On another level entirely, wealth disparities between the perpetrator and the victim could well cause disputes over what is significant, as, for example, if the upstream polluter were an impoverished developing nation and the downstream complaining state were a wealthy developed nation, or vice versa.[144]

Also helpful is the choice of word "harm" over "injury," which has the commendable result of reframing the debate on what impacts are "significant" into a factual standard of harm, not the murkier legal concept of injury.[145] It is clear that what is intended is an application of the most basic "good neighborliness" principle – *sic utere tuo ut alienum non laedas* (use your property so as not to injure the property of others)[146] – and that it applies not only to sovereigns but to the private entities operating within their borders as well.[147] It is also reasonably clear that the "precautionary" or anticipatory-action principle has been incorporated into the Article 7 no-significant-harm rule, through the use of the word "prevent" (*see* further discussion of this in the next section).

9.2.3   *Pollution Control*

While the main emphasis in the UN Watercourse Convention is quantitative – rules governing human uses (*see* § 9.2.2) – water quality was also addressed. Water quality issues are extremely important because surface and groundwater are being polluted at the highest level known in history.[148]

Article 21 requires states to "prevent, reduce and control the pollution of an international watercourse that may cause significant harm...." Its provisions find broad support in customary international law, according to the ILC commentaries.[149] "Harm" can be "to other watercourse States or to their environment" and specifically includes harm to human health or safety, to other beneficial uses, or to the "living resources of the watercourse." Use of the term "environment" here is thus intended to make the pollution control articles even broader in their protection than the "ecosystem concept" used

---

[144] *See generally* Anita Halvorssen, Equality Among Unequals in International Environmental Law: Differential Treatment for Developing Countries (1999).

[145] *See* Rep, of the Int'l Law Comm'n on the Work of its Fortieth Session, [1988] 2 Y.B. Int'l L. Comm'n 22, 28, U.N. GAOR Supp. No. 10, U.N. Doc. A/43/10; Stephen McCaffrey, *The Law of International Watercourses: Some Recent Developments and Unanswered Questions*, 17 Denv. J. Int'l l & Pol'y 505, 518 (1989).

[146] ILC Commentaries, *supra* note 98, art. 7, ¶ 1, at 51.

[147] *Id.* ¶ 4, at 52.

[148] *See* Meena Palaniappan, *et al.*, *Water Quality, in* The World's Water, *supra* note 2, at 45 *et seq.*

[149] Rep. of the Comm'n to the G.A. on the Work of Its Forty-Second Session, in [1990] 2 Y.B. Int'l l. Comm'n, pt. 2, art. 23 ¶ 9, at 63.

earlier in Article 20. "Pollution" is also broadly defined in Article 21(1) as "any detrimental alteration in the composition or quality of the waters… which results directly or indirectly from human conduct." Article 21(3) obligates watercourse states to consult, inter alia, on implementing measures, water quality objectives, and lists of prohibited substances.

Not all pollution is proscribed by Article 21(2), only that which causes "significant" harm, raising all of the issues of determining thresholds discussed in § 9.2.2. It appears that the "precautionary" or anticipatory-action principle has been incorporated into Article 21. While explicit anticipatory words like "threat of" or "risk of" are not included in the definition of pollution ("any detrimental alteration"), Article 21(2) uses the terms "prevent" and "may cause," justifying the ILC commentary that "the principle of precautionary action is applicable, especially in respect of dangerous substances such as those that are toxic, persistent or bioacccumulative.[150]

Also, while not dealt with in express terms in Article 21, there is state practice and soft law indicating a distinction to be made between new and existing pollution. The convention's affirmative obligation to "prevent, reduce and control" pollution causing significant harm applies with full force to new pollution (from planned new or expanded existing facilities), according to the ILC commentaries.[151] However, with regard to existing pollution, only the "reduce and control" obligations apply with full force in existing state practice:

> That practice indicates a general willingness to tolerate even appreciable pollution harm, provided – and this is an important proviso – that the watercourse State of origin is making its *best efforts* to reduce the pollution to a mutually acceptable level. A requirement that existing pollution causing such harm be abated immediately could, in some cases, result in undue hardship, especially where the detriment to the watercourse State of origin was grossly disproportionate to the benefit that would accrue to the watercourse State experiencing the harm. On the other hand, failure by the watercourse State of origin to exercise due diligence in reducing the pollution to acceptable levels would entitle the affected State to claim that the State of origin had breached its obligation to do so.[152]

Again, it is worth noting the criticism that the convention in Article 21 fails to refer to diminution in the *quantity* of water as potentially constituting pollution, since such changes in volume, velocity, turbulence, etc., certainly can. As Professor Davis explains:

---

[150] ILC Commentaries, *supra* note 98, art. 21, ¶ 3, at 139 (footnote omitted). Article 27 ("Prevention and mitigation of harmful conditions") reinforce this with similar language.

[151] *Id.*, art. 21, ¶ 3.

[152] *Id.* (emphasis added; footnote omitted).

> Diversion of water for irrigation, manufacturing, and public water supply can reduce the flow available to an amount less than the minimum required for natural waste assimilative processes. Unless the volume and concentration of treated and untreated waste discharges can be reduced or the streamflow increased, the wastes will overwhelm the assimilative processes of the stream. That process will result in insufficient or zero oxygen levels in the water, fish kills and odors. An appropriate balance between streamflow and waste discharges is essential to a healthy stream.[153]

Failure to require consideration of the interplay between quantity and quality explicitly is a typical discontinuity between earlier water rights laws and more modern water pollution laws worldwide (*see* § 9.2.1). However, the quantity-quality nexus is implicit in some subsequent articles, such as Article 25 dealing with "regulation of the flow of the waters" and Article 26 dealing with the "operation and maintenance of installations."

9.2.4 *Other Important Provisions of the International Watercourses Convention*

It is hard to imagine a convention that focuses more on the principle of "good neighborliness," given the many provisions here that stress procedural cooperation and consultation among states sharing freshwater resources. The general obligation to cooperate in good faith "to attain optimal utilization and adequate protection" of international watercourses is housed in Article 8, and Article 9 supports this with a requirement of regular exchange of information. Articles 3 and 4 specifically encourage states to develop additional "watercourse agreements" which "apply and adjust the provisions of the present Convention" to cover particular watercourses. Article 5(2) balances the "right to utilize the watercourse" with an explicit "duty to cooperate in the protection and development" of it. Article 6(2) urges states to "enter into consultations in a spirit of cooperation" in determining what is "equitable and reasonable utilization." Where significant harm cannot be avoided, Article 7(2) urges "consultation" on issues of control and compensation. Part III (Articles 11–19) contains detailed procedures for "planned measures" (such as new water diversions, dams, and the like), including timely prior notification, information exchange, consultations, and negotiations. States are to "consult" and "harmonize" their pollution control policies to reduce conflicts, under Article 21(2) and (3), and hold consultations to deal with regulating water flow and maintaining water installations, under Articles 25 and 26. Other provisions also have explicit and implicit "contact"

---

[153] Peter N. Davis, *Protecting Waste Assimilation Streamflows by the Law of Water Allocation, Nuisance, and Public Trust, and by Environmental Statutes*, 28 NAT. RESOURCES J. 357, 358 (1988) (footnote omitted).

requirements. One very significant aspect of this multiplicity of information-communication requirements is that "it provides further evidence that the international community as a whole emphatically rejects the notion that a state has unfettered discretion to do as it alone wishes with the portion of an international watercourse within its territory…,"[154] thus, laying to rest the notorious "Harmon Doctrine."

Similarly, Article 10 extinguishes the notion that there is any inherent "priority" or preference hierarchy of water uses. (Some national and local legal systems do this, giving, for example, later-developing domestic withdrawals priority or preemption over established agricultural, hydropower, or vice versa.) Article 10(2) makes clear that "no use…enjoys inherent priority," unless there is agreement or custom to the contrary, except that "special regard" must be given to "vital human needs."[155]

The "no harm" rule is expanded in Articles 27 and 28, dealing respectively with "Harmful conditions and emergency situations." Article 27 contains the anticipatory requirement to "take all appropriate measures to prevent or mitigate conditions…that may be harmful to other watercourse states," whether human-caused or natural. Specific (nonexhaustive) examples include "flood or ice conditions, water-borne diseases, siltation, erosion, salt-water intrusion, drought or desertification." The mandatory language is intended to focus attention on problems of "serious" consequence.[156] The softening "all appropriate measures" language is intended to set a "reasonableness" or "due diligence" standard (reasonable in view of the circumstances of the watercourse state in question), according to the ILC commentaries,[157] which then go on to state a seemingly higher standard of "best efforts."[158] This is an anticipatory, precautionary requirement,[159] but obviously highly contextual in nature, given the "reasonableness" test. It should also be noted that Article 24 is not limited to harmful conditions directly acting on the watercourse; the conditions need only be "related to" the watercourse, so conceivably could apply to much broader problems – such as global climate change, acid deposition, Chernobyl-type radioactive fallout, cross-media pollution,

---

[154] McCaffrey, *Convention, supra* note 92, at 103.
[155] This is explained in the "Statements of Understanding," *supra* note 148, as including "sufficient water to sustain human life, including both drinking water and water required for production of food in order to prevent starvation."
[156] ILC Commentaries, *supra* note 98, art. 24, ¶ 1, at 152. (ILC Draft Article 24 became Convention Article 27.)
[157] *Id.* ¶ 2, at 152.
[158] *Id.* at 153.
[159] *Id.* ¶ 1, at 152.

etc. – which are "related to" water in the sense that they potentially affect its quantity or quality.[160]

Article 28 addresses the instances in which the anticipatory prevention or mitigation called for in Article 26 has not been effective, resulting in an "emergency" that "causes, or poses an imminent threat of causing, serious harm" to other states. This is a responsive, as opposed to anticipatory, obligation.[161] Paragraph 1 broadly defines "emergency," again presumably transcending water-only situations; paragraphs 2 and 3 establish notification, cooperation, and action responses, and paragraph 4 urges contingency planning.

Article 33 introduces an elaborate new set of provisions for "settlement of disputes," augmented by an Annex on arbitration. The ten paragraphs start with "negotiation," then move unsettled disputes through the progression of mechanisms of increasing third-party involvement set out in the UN Charter Article 33 on "pacific settlement of disputes."

9.3   *Bilateral, Multilateral, and Regional Regimes of International Freshwater Regulation*

With over 260 river basins shared by two or more countries (draining nearly half the world's landmass),[162] not surprisingly hundreds of bilateral, multilateral, and regional agreements have been adopted during the last two centuries governing these shared resources.[163] However, many international watercourses still lack any cooperative agreements and remain trouble spots as their development progresses, particularly in the turbulent areas of the Middle East, Asia, Central Europe, and the former Soviet republics. A brief sample of some of the existing multistate agreements will illustrate their commonalities and diversity.

One of the oldest continuing bilateral efforts and one of the most respected models for others is the US-Canada Boundary Waters regime, covering the Great Lakes, Saint Lawrence Seaway, and all shared transboundary rivers, constituting one fifth of the world's surface freshwater.[164] It started with a

---

[160] *See generally*, Gretta Goldenman, *Adapting to Climate Change: A Study of International Rivers and Their Legal Arrangements*, 17 Ecology L.Q. 741 (1990).

[161] ILC Commentaries, supra note 98, art. 25, ¶ 1, at 156. (ILC Draft Article 25 became Convention Article 28.)

[162] *See* Clarke, *supra* note 32.

[163] *See* Bruhács, *supra* note 33; Clarke, *supra* note 32, at 91.

[164] The website of the US-Canada International Joint Commission provides the treaties and other legal authorities and information, at International Joint Commission, http://ijc.org. *See also* the Great Lakes Commission, http://www.glc.org; James Davidson,

1909 framework treaty, supplemented with multiple additional agreements, annexes, appendices, rules, plans, programs, and studies from the 1970s to the present. The two countries have created an International Joint Commission (IJC) which serves as a sophisticated forum not only for the expected issues of water transportation, quantity, and quality, but also for the inextricably connected issues of land use, air pollution, facilities construction, etc. Undoubtedly, part of the success of this international legal regime stems from the fact that the two countries are both upstream and downstream neighbors of each other.

With regard to the US's other neighbor, Mexico, the US is predominately the upstream state and the controller of the two major shared rivers – the Colorado and the Rio Grande Rivers – resulting in a very "troublesome" relationship over that resource for more than a century.[165] Starting with navigation treaties in the 1880s, the US grudgingly began to guarantee water shares to Mexico in subsequent Rio Grande (1906) and Colorado River (1944) treaties, subsequent "Minutes" (sub-agreements) including a key one in 1973 on Colorado River water quality, and a 1983 agreement to cooperate on environmental issues. A radical change in their relationship occurred with the 1993 signing of the North American Free Trade Agreement (NAFTA) and its two sub-agreements, which led to an increase in environmental cooperation – the US-Mexico-Canada "Environmental Side-Agreement" (creating the tri-national Commission for Environmental Cooperation (CEC))[166] and the special US-Mexico agreement (creating the Border Environment Cooperation Commission (BECC)[167] and the North American Development Bank (NADBank),[168] controlling and funding a growing variety of environmental programs and infrastructure projects in the border area).

Europe, with many more centuries of watercourse-related development, has an immense array of international freshwater treaties. One of the oldest and most complex governs the Rhine River, Western Europe's longest international watercourse, the source of water for nearly 50 million people in nine countries (including tributaries), and one of the most polluted rivers in one

---

Resolution of Transboundary Pollution Disputes: The Great Lakes Experience, 3 ASIA PACIFIC J. ENVTL. L. 233 (1998).

[165] INTERNATIONAL BOUNDARY AND WATER COMMISSION, http://www.ibwc.gov/home.html. *See also* Lenard Milich & Robert G. Varady, *Managing Transboundary Resources: Lessons from River-Basin Accords*, 40 ENV'T 8 (1998); KISS & SHELTON, *supra* note 105, at 415, 427–32.

[166] COMMISSION FOR ENVIRONMENTAL COOPERATION, http://www.cec.org; NORTH AMERICAN AGREEMENT ON ENVIRONMENTAL COOPERATION (the "side-agreement), http://www.cec.org/Page.asp?PageID=1226&SiteNodeID=567.

[167] BORDER ENVIRONMENT COOPERATION COMMISSION, http://www.becc.org/.

[168] NORTH AMERICAN DEVELOPMENT BANK, http://www.nadbank.org.

of the most industrialized regions on earth.[169] Beginning with a navigation treaty in 1815, the state parties have developed a regime of multiple, complex utilization and pollutant-specific control agreements, two international commissions, and numerous action programs. While these efforts have been a model for many other river basins, the regime's commissions lack power and can conflict with each other, national powers predominate, a host of national and local water agencies still make and execute policy, and overall coordination has been lacking. In 1999, a more comprehensive international convention was signed aimed at achieving sustainable development of the entire river ecosystem, not just focusing on pollution, which bodes well for the future.[170]

The Danube River presents even more complex hydrologic, economic, and social problems, flowing over 1,780 miles through Western, Central, and Eastern Europe to the Black Sea. The Danube drains portions of 17 countries ranging from wealthy, highly industrialized, environmentally concerned upstream nations (e.g. Germany, Austria) to some of the poorest, war-torn former Iron Curtain nations in the lower basin (Bosnia & Herzegovina, Croatia, Serbia, Romania). Efforts at international agreements and institution-building began in the 1850s and were chiefly focused on navigation and hydropower-project treaties until modern times,[171] with one of these provoking the *Gabcikovo-Nagymoros Dam Case* in 1997 (*see* § 9.1.1). More recent agreements on water pollution have been hampered in their accomplishments by the tremendous developmental and economic disparities in the region. In 1994, 11 of the basin states and the European Community adopted the Convention on Cooperation for the Protection and Sustainable Use of the Danube River,[172] which generally follows closely the 1992 UNECE Helsinki Convention (discussed below).

In yet another important layer of European law, the UN Economic Commission for Europe (UNECE) in 1992 developed the regional Convention on the Protection and Use of Transboundary Watercourses and International Lakes (the Helsinki Convention),[173] covering its member states throughout

---

[169] INTERNATIONAL COMMISSION FOR THE PROTECTION OF THE RHINE, http://www.iksr.org; KISS & SHELTON, *supra* note 105, at 408–11.

[170] Convention on the Protection of the Rhine, Jan. 22, 1998, http://ec.europa.eu/world/agreements/downloadFile.do?fullText=yes&treatyTransId=1435.

[171] For further details and references, *see* Milich & Varady, *supra* note 165; KISS & SHELTON, *supra* note 105, at 411–13.

[172] Convention on Cooperation for the Protection and Sustainable Use of the Danube, June 29, 1994, http://ec.europa.eu/world/agreements/downloadFile.do?fullText=yes&treatyTransId=1406; http://internationalwaterlaw.org/documents/regionaldocs/danube1994.html.

[173] *UNECE Water Convention*, UNECE, http://www.unece.org/env/water.

the Northern Hemisphere. The Helsinki Convention, while compatible with the 1997 UN Convention on International Watercourses (discussed in § 9.2), is both narrower and broader. It is narrower, in that it focuses essentially on protections against transboundary impacts, while the UN Convention focuses on all non-navigational uses and protections. It is broader, in that it includes additional rules such as the precautionary and polluter-pays principles, more detailed management requirements, and best-available-technology standards. In 1999, the UNECE added a Protocol on Water and Health[174] to the Helsinki Convention, expanding requirements for drinking water and sanitation to prevent waterborne diseases, and effort is underway to establish a protocol on liability and responsibility.

In addition to the above, other European water basins have treaty regimes, like the Elbe (Czech Republic, EC, and Germany), Meuse (France, Netherlands, and the three Belgian regions), and Tornealven Rivers (Finland, Sweden).[175] The EU has also adopted a broad range of water-pollution directives, starting in 1976.[176]

In Sub-Saharan Africa, there are 54 multinational watercourses, and every country shares at least one river basin with another.[177] One of the earliest and still one of the most ambitious treaties on paper is the 1987 Zambezi River Agreement[178] (between Botswana, Mozambique, Tanzania, Zambia, and Zimbabwe), which spells out an integrated management approach to planning and environmental protection in a way still rare in the developing world. Additional African treaty systems are in existence, including ones for the nine-state Niger River Basin (Burkina Faso, Cameroon, Chad, Benin, Guinea, Ivory Coast, Mali, Niger, and Nigeria), Gambia River Basin (Gambia, Guinea, and Senegal), Lake Victoria (Kenya, Tanzania, and Uganda), and the shared watercourses of the 15-state Southern Africa Development Community.[179]

Some of Asia's great international river basins have developed treaty systems, including the Ganges (Bangladesh, India, Nepal), Mahakali (India, Nepal), and the Mekong (Burma, Cambodia, China, Laos, Thailand, Vietnam), the latter being the most comprehensive, except for upstream China's

---

[174] *About the Protocol on Water and Health*, UNECE, http://www.unece.org/?id=2975.

[175] *See* KISS & SHELTON, *supra* note 105, at 411, 414; Milich & Varady, *supra* note 165, at 6–8.

[176] *See* KISS & SHELTON, *supra* note 105, at 406–08.

[177] Milich & Varady, *supra* note 165, at n. 1.

[178] Agreement on the Action Plan for the Environmentally Sound Management of the Common Zambezi River System, May 28, 1987, http://www.fao.org/docrep/W7414B/w7414b0j .htm.

[179] *See* KISS & SHELTON, *supra* note 105, at 416–17.

failure to join.[180] South American countries likewise share some common rivers, and international agreements have been concluded on several, including treaties in 1975 for the Uruguay River (Argentina, Brazil, Uruguay) and 1995 for the Rio Pilcomayo (Argentina, Bolivia, and Paraguay), which are principally focused on water pollution.[181]

The Middle East has two major river systems with no binding comprehensive arrangements for water and environmental management, the Jordan River (Israel, Jordan, Lebanon, Syria, and the West Bank) and the Euphrates River (Iraq, Syria, and Turkey), and these basins are fraught with tensions over water development. In the Jordan Basin, a few limited agreements involving water have been reached between Israel, Jordan, and the Palestine Liberation Organization (PLO).[182] Peace in the Middle East may well be dependent on the negotiation of successful water-sharing agreements, in addition to the political and territorial sovereignty issues that receive more media attention.[183]

Beyond the work of these treaty states, international financial organizations (IFOs) – like the World Bank, Global Environmental Facility (GEF), and other multilateral development banks (MDBs) – actively promote international watercourse agreements, policies, and projects. The World Bank actively takes water resource strategies into account when funding projects, linking environment, poverty alleviation, and sustainable development.[184] Similarly, international waters is one of the GEF's seven primary areas of work.[185] Regional MDBs likewise focus on water, particularly from a human-health perspective, as evidenced by the work of the Asian Development Bank's farsighted agenda in its report, "Water in the 21st Century."[186] UNEP, in cooperation with other IGOs contributes through the water quality

---

[180] *See id.* at 417–18; Jonathan Chenoweth, *International River Basin Management: Data and Information Exchange Under International Law and the Case of the Mekong River Basin*, 18 J. ENERGY & NAT. RESOURCES L. 142 (2000); Salman M. A. Salman & Kishor Uprety, *Hydro-Politics in South Asia: A Comparative Analysis of the Mahakali and the Ganges Treaties*, 39 NAT. RESOURCES J. 295 (1999).

[181] *See* KISS & SHELTON, *supra* note 105, at 415–16.

[182] *See id.* at 417–18.

[183] *See* Miriam R. Lowi, *Rivers of Conflict, Rivers of Peace – Continuity and Transformation: The Modern Middle East*, J. INT'L. AFF., June 22, 1995; Cat Lazaroff, *Israeli, Palestinian Ecologists Partner to Solve Land and Water Problems*, ENV'T NEWS SERV., Jan. 26, 2000, http://www.ens-newswire.com/ens/jan2000/2000-01-26-06.asp; CLARKE, *supra* note 32, at 100–105.

[184] WORLD BANK, *Water Program*, http://water.worldbank.org/water/; *see also* Pring *et al.*, *Trends, supra* note 1, at 163–66.

[185] GLOBAL ENVIRONMENTAL FACILITY, http://www.thegef.org/gef/Areas_work.

[186] *Water in the 21st Century*, ASIAN DEVELOPMENT BANK, http://www.adb.org/documents/reports/water/default.asp.

component of its Global Environmental Monitoring System (GEMS/Water), a monitoring and capacity-building program currently focusing on world river basins, land-based sources of marine pollution, toxic chemicals, and water quality management.[187]

9.4   *Groundwater*

Groundwater constitutes 99 percent of available freshwater,[188] yet, compared to surface water, it has been almost a forgotten step-child of international water law until recently. The delay in developing an integrated legal regime for groundwater is understandable; it is a classic "out-of-sight-out-of-mind" resource, typically last to be developed for technical and economic reasons, and scientifically far less understood than surface water. Yet underground aquifers account for more than 70% of the water used in the EU and are often the only, or one of the only, sources in arid and semi-arid zones, for example constituting 100 percent of water used in Saudi Arabia and Malta, 95 percent in Tunisia, and 75 percent in Morocco.[189] Many aquifers are multinational; UNESCO has inventoried 273 transboundary aquifers so far.[190]

Cinderella-like, groundwater is now seen as "the water of the future," because of the quantity-quality problems with surface waters in many areas and because groundwater is so plentiful, tends to be more pure, and tends to purify itself in some geologic structures.[191] On the other hand, it presents new problems: being more static, it is more vulnerable to contamination and depletion, and human impacts take longer to be noticed and to be cured.[192]

An underground "aquifer" may best be defined as "a subsurface water-bearing geologic formation from which significant quantities of water may be extracted."[193] Five potential aquifer configurations should be considered "international" or transboundary groundwaters:

---

[187] GEMS/Water, http://www.gemswater.org.

[188] USGS, *Water Basics, supra* note 4, http://ga.water.usgs.gov/edu/earthwherewater.html.

[189] UNESCO, *UN General Assembly adopts resolution on the Law of Transboundary Aquifers* (Dec. 11, 2008), http://www.unesco.org/water/news/transboundary_aquifers.shtml.

[190] *Id.*

[191] McCaffrey, Watercourses, *supra* note 5, at 483.

[192] *Id.* at 483–85.

[193] Bellagio Draft Treaty Concerning the Use of Transboundary Groundwaters, 1989, *reprinted* in 1 Basic Documents of International Environmental Law 42 (H. Hohmann ed., 1992); also at *Seol Rules on Groundwater*, ILA, http://www.fao.org/docrep/008/y5739e/y5739e0h.htm.

1. A "tributary" or "unconfined" aquifer underlying an international border and hydraulically linked to transboundary surface waters;
2. A "confined aquifer" underlying an international border, but not hydraulically linked to the surface waters;
3. An aquifer entirely under one state but hydraulically linked:
   (a) with transboundary surface waters (with the surface waters either influent or effluent as to the groundwater), or
   (b) with an aquifer in another state, or
   (c) with a surface recharge zone in another state for an aquifer in that latter state.[194]

While all of these configurations should be managed in an integrated fashion, (2) and possibly (3)(c) do not appear to fall under current international law, as discussed below.

International treaties on groundwater actually began to appear almost a century ago.[195] Soft law modernizations began with the 1966 ILA Helsinki Rules, which took a tentative step by including "underground water," but limited it to groundwater that was either connected to the surface waters (configuration 1 above) or flowed into a common terminus with them (the latter being hydrologically unlikely).[196] The ILA corrected this limitation two decades later in its 1986 Seoul Rules on International Groundwaters.[197] This brief, four-article effort chiefly served to bring more groundwaters under the Helsinki Rules. Thus, Article I defines covered waters as being any "aquifer that is intersected by the boundary between two or more States...whether or not the aquifer and its waters form with surface waters part of a hydraulic system flowing into a common terminus" (configurations 1 and 2). This was an improvement, but still left groundwaters subject to the management provisions of the rather dated Helsinki Rules and failed to cover configurations 3(a), (b), and (c).

A big improvement in soft law came later that same decade, when a multidisciplinary group of international experts in law, geohydrology, and other disciplines came together to draft a comprehensive treaty for groundwater as a model for states to adopt, the 1989 Bellagio Draft Agreement Concerning the Use of Transboundary Groundwaters.[198] Article I contains detailed modern

---

[194] *See* JULIO A. BARBERIS, INTERNATIONAL GROUNDWATER RESOURCES LAW 36, FAO Legislative Study No. 40 (1986); MCCAFFREY, WATERCOURSES, *supra* note 5, at 30–31.

[195] *See* INTERNATIONAL GROUNDWATER LAW 189 *et seq.* (Ludwick Teclaff & Albert Utton eds., 1981) for lists of several dozen bilateral and multilateral groundwater treaties.

[196] Helsinki Rules, *supra* note 78, at Annex II, art. II.

[197] Rules on International Groundwaters, Aug. 30, 1986, ILA Report of the 62nd Conference 251 (1987), http://www.fao.org/docrep/008/y5739e/y5739e0h.htm.

[198] Bellagio Draft Agreement, *supra* note 193.

definitions. Article II sets forth its twin purposes of ensuring "reasonable and equitable development and management" of shared groundwaters and "to protect the underground environment." Subsequent articles provide for an oversight commission, enforcement, water quality protection, conservation areas, comprehensive management plans, emergencies, planned depletions, transfers, drought, public interest protection, and dispute resolution. All in all, the Bellagio Draft, while not adopted by states, represents the high water mark to date in international groundwater rules.

Urged to include unconnected groundwaters in its Draft Articles, the ILC balked and in 1994 adopted a compromise "Resolution on Confined Transboundary Groundwater" that merely "commends" states to apply the Draft Articles to transboundary groundwater, including confined groundwater, but only "where appropriate."[199] Not surprisingly, the 1997 UN Watercourse Convention suffers from the same oversights, being a bit better than the 1966 Helsinki Rules but not as good as the 1986 Seoul Rules or the 1989 Bellagio Draft proposal. Article 2(a) of the UN Convention includes groundwaters connected to surface waters (configuration 1) but not unconnected transboundary groundwaters (configuration 2) or configurations 3(a), (b), and (c).

Finally, in 2008, the ILC adopted its Draft Law of Transboundary Aquifers.[200] It promptly received UNGA's consensus recommendation in the form of a resolution encouraging states "to make appropriate bilateral or regional arrangements for the proper management of their transboundary aquifers, taking into account the provisions of these draft articles."[201] While there are some issues with some of the draft's provisions, it represents an enormous positive step forward in codifying and progressively developing international groundwater law.

Article 2 of the Law of Transboundary Aquifers makes it clear that it covers only confined or unconnected aquifers (clearly configurations 2 and 3(b) and arguably 3(c) above), but not aquifers hydraulically connected with surface waters (configurations 1 and 3(a)), presumably because those aquifers are covered by the 1997 UN Watercourse Convention. Unfortunately, Article 3 unnecessarily injects a statement that individual states have "sovereignty" over the portion of a transboundary aquifer within their own territory; this

---

[199] ILC Resolution on Confined Transboundary Groundwater, 2 Y.B. Int'l L. Comm'n 135 (1994); http://internationalwaterlaw.org/documents/intldocs/ilc_gw_resolution.html.

[200] ILC, Draft Articles on Transboundary Aquifers, 2008 Supp. No. 10 (A/63/10), http://untreaty.un.org/ilc/texts/instruments/english/draft%20articles/8_5_2008.pdf; G.A. Res. 63/124, U.N. Doc. A/RES/63/124 (Jan. 15, 2009), http://www.isarm.org/dynamics/modules/SFIL0100/view.php?fil_Id=227.

[201] G.A. Res. 63/124, U.N. GAOR, 63rd Sess. (Dec. 11, 2008, distributed Jan. 15, 2009), http://www.isarm.org/dynamics/modules/SFIL0100/view.php?fil_Id=227.

statement is partly ameliorated by the following sentence that each state "shall exercise its sovereignty in accordance with international law and the present articles." Article 4 further softens the "sovereignty" statement by imposing the principle of "equitable and reasonable utilization" on transboundary aquifers, defining it to mean equitable and reasonable "accrual of benefits," "maximizing long-term benefits," subject to "a comprehensive utilization plan," and not using "a recharging transboundary aquifer...at a level that would prevent continuance of its effective functioning." Article 5 lists the factors relevant to determining equitable and reasonable utilization; these factors largely track the comparable Article 6 in the 1997 UN Watercourse Convention, while adding two interesting new factors – "contribution to the formation and recharge of the aquifer" (5(1)(d)) and the aquifer's "role...in the related ecosystem" (5(1)(i)).

Article 6 of the ILC's Law of Transboundary Aquifers imposes the no significant harm rule, with a new element: it applies to "activities other than utilization" of an aquifer, so that it covers activities other than direct withdrawal, such as interference with a recharge zone. Other articles generally reflect applicable articles in the 1997 UN Watercourse Convention, including requirements of cooperation (7); information exchange (8); protection and conservation of aquifer-dependent ecosystems (10); prevention and control of pollution (12); procedures for planned measures (15), emergency situations (17), and armed conflict (18). There are impressive new provisions, including requirements to employ best efforts to collect and generate new data and information (8); protect recharge and discharge zones (11); use the precautionary approach for pollution (12); establish joint monitoring (13), joint management plans (14), and technical cooperation (16).

The ILC's Law of Transboundary Aquifers has received much deserved praise. On the occasion of its 2008 recognition by UNGA, UNESCO stated: "Until today there was no instrument of international law that could provide a complete set of recommendations and guidelines for the sustainable and peaceful management of transboundary aquifers."[202] "Complete" seems an overstatement in light of the several issues with its coverage and provisions mentioned above, or in comparison with provisions of the Bellagio Draft. However, the ILC's effort does represent a very positive high-water mark in official restatements of the international law of groundwater.

---

[202] Press Release, UN General Assembly Adopts Resolution on Law of Transboundary Aquifers (2009), http://www.unesco.org/water/news/transboundary_aquifers.shtml.

9.5   *Conclusion*

International environmental law and policies are slowly but surely being integrated into international water law. Surface and underground freshwater resources are now recognized as far too valuable and scarce to continue to be treated as mere consumptive commodities, without a broader consideration of their importance to ecosystems, sustainable development, and intra- and inter-generational futures.

Customary international law and the modern treaties now recognize a number of important principles with regard to internationally shared water resources:

- *The right to equitable and reasonable use*: There is no more widely accepted water principle than that each state sharing a water basin has an equal right, based on sovereignty, to put the waters to beneficial use. This principle is limited by the resources, however, such that if the water is insufficient for all basin states' needs, they must share and apportion it on the basis of equity factors (absent a different agreement).
- *The no-significant-harm rule*: The equitable-reasonable utilization principle is paralleled by the rule that states are under an obligation not to use water in a way that causes "significant" transboundary harm – in quality or quantity – to other basin states' interests. This is really just an extension to the water field of the Stockholm 21/Rio 2 prohibition against transboundary damage. Through the growing acceptance of the "ecosystem concept," the definition of harm is being expanded beyond homocentric health and economic well-being to encompass harm to all elements of the ecosystem and values related to the watercourse.
- *The duty to inform, consult, and negotiate in good faith*: A "cardinal" rule[203] in the field of shared water resources is the duty to communicate in advance with other affected states about water development projects and plans which could have significant transboundary impacts. That entails a three-part obligation: to inform or notify (one-way information without a mutual exchange), to consult (mutual dialog without an obligation of negotiation or compromise), and to negotiate in good faith (mutual dialog with an obligation of compromise, if good faith reasonableness so requires, but without an obligation of result). Notification and

---

[203] S. Schwebel, Special Rapporteur, International Law Commission, Third Report on the Law of the Non-Navigational Uses of International Watercourses ¶ 154, U.N. Doc. A/CN.4/348 (1981), http://untreaty.un.org/ilc/documentation/english/a_cn4_348.pdf.

consultation are widely recognized customary international law rules, while negotiation is less universally recognized. The *Lac Lanoux* principle (section 9.1.1 above) still means that other states do not hold a "veto" power over other states' uses, but they must be allowed adequate opportunity to evaluate and respond, and the informing state must give reasonable consideration to their views.

- *The duty to prevent and control pollution*: A subset of the no-significant-harm rule specifically applies to the harms of pollution. Here, customary international law recognizes different rules, depending on whether the pollution targeted is new or existing. With regard to new or potential sources of significant pollution, the rule is to prevent. With regard to existing pollution, a more relaxed rule of "due diligence" applies – consisting of best efforts to control, taking into account a state's capacity.

- *The duty to protect and preserve ecosystems*: Much less universally recognized than the above, but an emerging principle (in progressive development), is the "ecosystem concept." This is the extension of the no-significant-harm rule to all aspects of the environment – human and nonhuman, biotic and abiotic, monetizable and nonmonetizable values – potentially affected by water resource use.

- *The anticipatory obligation to prevent or mitigate harmful conditions*: The "precautionary principle" is also working its way into international water law through the treaty route, although it is too soon to claim it exists broadly as customary law, given present levels of state practice. Still, the 1997 UN Convention and the 2008 ILC Law of Transboundary Aquifers have included it, at least as an obligation to prevent or mitigate harmful conditions, even expanding it to include natural conditions like floods, disease, siltation, erosion, saltwater intrusion, drought, desertification, and the like.

The Earth is a shared natural system defined and shaped by water. We predict the 21st century will see international freshwater law finally become defined and shaped by the realities of Earth.

Chapter Ten

International Air Pollution

10.0 *Introduction*

The earth's atmosphere – the "delicate membrane"[1] of gases that makes life on earth possible – is undergoing dramatic changes due to human activities. Because life on earth's surface has evolved to survive at very specific atmospheric conditions, these anthropogenic (human-caused) atmospheric alterations directly affect nearly every ecosystem on the planet. Human life and health and many populations may be threatened due to the damage currently being inflicted on the atmosphere.[2] Airsheds, winds, and chemical transport are no respecters of national borders, so, to paraphrase John Donne, no state is an island. The atmosphere is, in fact, our largest shared natural resource,[3] and much air pollution transcends national controls, making it a problem that international law must address.

Nature itself is an air polluter, releasing "background" solid, liquid, and gaseous contaminants through such events as volcanic activity, physical and chemical weathering, the emission of biologic gases, lightning-sparked forest fires, and other processes of nature.[4] Because these events are so difficult to predict and prevent, however, international environmental law focuses on the human activities that humans can control. We produce air pollution through virtually every form of agricultural, industrial, commercial, and residential development activity, including, mining, farming, slash and burn

---

[1] Lester R. Brown et al., State of the World 2000 32 (2000).

[2] *See* UN Framework Convention on Climate Change Secretariat, *Feeling the Heat: Climate Science and the Basis of the Convention*, http://unfccc.int/essential_background/the_science/items/6064.php.

[3] *See* Patricia W. Birnie & Alan E. Boyle, International Law & The Environment 338 (2001).

[4] National Park Service, *Air Pollution: Its Nature, Sources and Effects*, http://www.nps.gov/shen/naturescience/airpollution.htm. *See* Iain Thornton, Metals In The Global Environment: Facts And Misconceptions 10, 48 (1995).

agriculture, human-caused forest fires, energy generation, fossil fuel combustion, waste disposal, and other means.

From an international perspective, there are three air pollution "megaproblems": (1) transboundary air pollution, (2) stratospheric ozone depletion, and (3) climate change.[5] Each is dealt with by a separate regime of international law, as discussed in the three following sections.

10.1   *Transboundary Air Pollution*

10.1.1   *Introduction*

The fact that air pollution does not stop at national boundaries may seem obvious, but, until quite recently, air pollution was considered a "local problem," to be addressed by national and local regulation, if at all.[6] Although early warning signs caught the attention of some countries a century ago,[7] it would take decades for the world to *see* transboundary air pollution as an international problem. In the US, for example, air quality control was viewed as only a state or local government concern until 1970, when the federal government "nationalized" air pollution control. Even then, the national Clean Air Act did little to regulate interstate, let alone international, pollution for some years. Since that time, more controls have been put in place, but transboundary air pollution remains a concern in both the US and abroad.

Transboundary air pollution is defined as anthropogenic introduction of substances or energy into the atmosphere from a physical origin situated wholly or in part within the national jurisdiction of one state that has adverse effects in the area under the jurisdiction of another state. Transboundary air pollution is an insidious problem because airborne contaminants are both difficult to measure and to trace. As will be discussed below, air contaminants come from a variety of sources that are not always strictly regulated, making them difficult to measure. Moreover, because these contaminants readily disperse upon introduction to the atmosphere, individual sources are difficult to trace. One legal regime (LRTAP, *see* § 10.1.3.3) limits the definition to contaminants that come from "such a distance that it is not generally possible to distinguish the contribution of individual emission sources or

---

[5] *See* Agenda 21, June 13, 1992, ch. 9 ("Protection of the Atmosphere)," U.N. Doc. A/CONF. 151/26 (vols. I–III), copy in Agenda 21 & The UNCED Proceedings 137 (Nicholas A. Robinson ed. 1993), http://www.un.org/esa/dsd/agenda21/.

[6] Alexandre Kiss & Dinah Shelton, International Environmental Law 555 (3d ed. 2003).

[7] As in the famed *Trail Smelter Arbitration, see* § 10.1.2.

groups of sources."[8] The term is also used, however, for pollution from readily identifiable sources...if it crosses a border, as in the *Trail Smelter* case, involving pollution from a smelter in Canada that blew across the border into the US (*see* § 10.1.2 below).

The pollutants most associated with transboundary air pollution include: sulphur dioxide (SO_2), nitrogen oxides (NO_x), particulate matter (PM), volatile organic compounds (VOCs), and persistent organic pollutants (POPs).[9] The main sources of SO_2 are the burning of fossil fuels, the smelting of metals, and other industrial processes[10] in which sulphur is oxidized (that is, combined with oxygen, typically by burning), forming SO_2.[11] Motor vehicle emissions and industrial processes are the main anthropogenic sources of NOx, the oxidization of nitrogen.[12] Natural processes, such as forest fires, decomposition of organic material, and volcanic eruptions, also emit SO_2 and NOx into the atmosphere.[13]

VOCs cover hundreds of unstable, readily vaporizing compounds emitted by motor vehicles and industrial processes (for example, benzene and formaldehyde and other potentially carcinogenic compounds), which in the presence of sunlight vaporize (volatilize) and contribute to the creation of ground-level ozone (O_3) or "smog."[14] VOCs began receiving serious international attention in the late 1980s, when increased scientific research of ground-level ozone revealed their significant impacts on human health and ecosystems.[15] POPs are synthetic organic chemicals which share four common properties: they are toxic, accumulate in the food chain, are persistent (do not decompose readily) in the environment, and can travel long distances.[16]

---

[8] Convention on Long-Range Transboundary Air Pollution (LRTAP), art. 1, Nov. 13, 1979, 1302 U.N.T.S. 217, T.I.A.S. No. 1054, 18 I.L.M. 1442 (1979), http://live.unece.org/env/lrtap/status/lrtap_s.html.

[9] David Hunter, James Salzman & Durwood Zaelke, International Environmental Law and Policy 506–07 (4th ed. 2011).

[10] Jutta Brunnée, Acid Rain and Ozone Layer Depletion: International Law and Regulation 11–14 (1988).

[11] Mark L. Glode & Beverly Nelson Glode, *Transboundary Pollution: Acid Rain and United States-Canadian Relations*, 20 B.C. Envtl. Aff. L. Rev. 1, 3 (1993).

[12] *Id.*

[13] *Id.* at 4.

[14] David Novello, *Introductory Note, Protocol to the 1979 Convention on LRTAP Concerning the Control of Emissions of VOCs or their Transboundary Fluxes*, 31 I.L.M. 568 (1992).

[15] The Effectiveness Of International Environmental Regimes 157 (Oran Young ed., 1999).

[16] The World Bank, *Persistent Organic Pollution*, http://web.worldbank.org/WBSITE/EXTERNAL/COUNTRIES/EASTASIAPACIFICEXT/EXTEAPREGTOPENVIRONMENT/0,,contentMDK:20318848~menuPK:502915~pagePK:34004173~piPK:34003707~theSitePK:502886~isCURL:Y,00.html.

POPs include well-known pesticides (such as DDT), polychlorinated byphe-
nols (PCBs), dioxins, furans, polycyclic aromatic hydrocarbons (PAHs), and
other industrial byproducts which are used in a variety of widely used industrial and consumer products such as dyes, detergents, plastics, paints, and
biocides.[17] Some POPs can cause reproductive and behavioral abnormalities
in wildlife and humans and may be associated with increased incidence in
humans of cancer and neurological and respiratory problems.[18]

The most pervasive form of transboundary air pollution is acid deposition,
caused primarily by SO_2 and NO_x emissions.[19] Acid deposition occurs when
automobile and industrial emissions react with water in the atmosphere to
form acids, such as sulfuric and nitric acid.[20] These acids precipitate to the
earth in rain or snow or in dry form.[21] Precipitation is considered acidic
when its pH level is lower than 5.6, the level of "pure" rain – but even this
is not "pure," being 25 times more acidic than distilled water (which is 7.0
or "neutral" on the pH scale).[22] Some areas in North America have recorded
precipitation with a pH as low as 2.3, which is more than 10,000 times more
acidic than distilled water.[23] Depending on its concentration, acid deposition
can have devastating effects on aquatic life,[24] forests, plants, soil, buildings,
and historic monuments.[25]

Acid deposition was first studied scientifically in the late 1800s in British
industrial areas.[26] A Scottish scientist named Robert Angus Smith, recognizing the link between the sulphur emissions of the nearby coal-burning industry and the acidity of the water, was the first to use the term "acid rain."[27] In

---

[17] *Id.*

[18] *See* UNEP Chemicals, Persistent Organic Pollutants, http://www.chem.unep.ch/
pops/.

[19] M. Soroos, The Endangered Atmosphere 38–42 (1997); Ecological Society of America,
Acid Deposition, (2000) http://www.esa.org/education_diversity/pdfDocs/aciddeposition
.pdf.

[20] Ecological Society of America, *supra* note 19.

[21] *Id.* Approximately half of the acidity in the atmosphere falls back to earth through dry
deposition, hence the older term "acid rain" has fallen into disuse.

[22] Glode & Glode, *supra* note 11, at 4; *see* James L. Regens & Robert W. Rycroft, The Acid
Rain Controversy 35 (1989).

[23] Royal British Columbia Museum & Okanagan University College, Living Landscapes,
Land Use and Environmental Change in the Thompson-Okanagan (Michael Pidwirny ed.),
http://www.livinglandscapes.bc.ca/thomp-ok/env-changes/index.html.

[24] Jon Ricci, *Transboundary Air Pollution Between Canada and the United States: Paper Solutions to a Real Problem*, 5 J. Int'l L. & Prac. 305, 306 (1996).

[25] Environmental Action Programme for Central and Eastern Europe, Sec. VI.
Transboundary Issues: Regional and Global Concerns (Apr. 1993).

[26] The Effectiveness International Law Regimes, *supra* note 15, at 158.

[27] John McCormick, *Acid Pollution: The International Community's Continuing Struggle*,
Env't, Apr. 1998, at 16.

response, factories installed taller smokestacks, but, while this relieved some of the local pollution, tall stacks only succeeded in dispersing the pollutants farther across the North Sea and Europe.[28] In the 1950s, Scandinavian countries found pink and yellow snow on hillsides that faced England[29] and linked the disappearance of fish to decreased pH levels in their lakes and rivers.[30]

Acid deposition became a *cause célèbre* during the 1970s, seizing the attention of the public and world leaders who feared widespread loss of forests, architectural works, and aquatic wildlife.[31] By 1977, it was found that Canadian emissions were causing acid deposition in the US, and, conversely, that US emissions from as far away as the Ohio-Mississippi River valley were depositing acid in eastern Canada.[32] In 1982, it was estimated that 8% of German forests were showing significant signs of disease, and two years later that number grew to 50%.[33] Since that time, many developed countries have achieved a modicum of success in curbing acid deposition. For example, between 1990 and 2000 New England experienced a 25% decrease in NO_x emissions from all sources (from approximately 897,000 tons to 668,000 tons).[34] Between 2000 and 2006, NO_x emissions from power plants in the region further decreased by more than 31,000 tons.[35] Nevertheless, acid deposition promises to be a problem in newly industrializing countries, with scientists predicting that future SO_2 and NO_x emissions will substantially increase in the developing world, especially in Asia (*see* § 10.1.3.4).[36] For example, in 2006, the Chinese government reported that one third of the country (the southern, most industrialized region) was suffering from serious acid deposition. The nation's power plants, which rely mainly on coal, were emitting 25.5 million tons of SO_2 – up 27% from 2000.[37]

---

[28] Glode & Glode, *supra* note 11, at 7.

[29] *Id.* at 6–7.

[30] Hunter et al., *supra* note 9, at 520.

[31] McCormick, *supra* note 27, at 1.

[32] Edith Brown Weiss, Stephen C. McCaffrey, Daniel b. Magraw, Paul C. Szasz & Robert E. Lutz, International Environmental Law and Policy 578 *et seq.* (1998).

[33] Hunter et al., *supra* note 9, at 520.

[34] *Acid Rain in New England: A Brief History*, EPA, http://www.epa.gov/region1/eco/acidrain/history.html; *see Overview of the Acid Rain Program*, EPA, http://www.epa.gov/airmarkt/progress/ARP_4.html, for emission level statistics by region in the US.

[35] *Id.*

[36] Ecological Society of America, *supra* note 19.

[37] China has been somewhat successful at curbing the massive sulphur emissions since that time. "Between 2006 and 2009, China's sulphur dioxide emissions *decreased* more than 13 percent, even as construction of new coal-fired power plants expanded rapidly." Christina Larson, *China Takes First Steps in the Fight Against Acid Rain*, Yale Env't 360, Oct. 28, 2010, http://e360.yale.edu/feature/china_takes_first_steps_in_the_fight_against_acid_rain/2333/.

The following sections discuss the various international law regimes created to address transboundary air pollution and its damaging effects, beginning with the development of the customary international rule forbidding transboundary environmental harms, then examining four major examples of bilateral and multilateral agreements to abate transboundary air pollution.

10.1.2   *Customary International Law Governing Transboundary Air Pollution*

The legal basis for control of transboundary air pollution rests on the most fundamental of all international legal concepts, indeed the starting point of all international environmental law: "the general principle of good neighborliness" (*see* § 2.1.2). This principle is often expressed by the Latin maxim *sic utere tuo ut alienum non laedas* (use your own property so as not to injure that of another),[38] or, if one prefers, simply the Golden Rule of "do unto others as you would have others do unto you."

Not every state is equally affected by transboundary air pollution nor is every state equally capable of controlling it. In many cases pollution is emitted in one state ("exporter" state) and prevailing winds carry it to another state ("importer" state). In a region such as North America, generally it is easy to recognize the exporter state and solve problems with bilateral agreements and/or economic compensation. However, in Europe, where a number of countries share one region and the importer and exporter states are so intermingled they defy tracing, multilateral international cooperation is required to address transboundary air pollution effectively.[39] International cooperation is also necessary because some exporter states have little incentive (and/or little financial ability) to contribute to reaching a solution.[40]

Sovereignty was the major legal obstacle to the development of a customary international law norm prohibiting transboundary pollution. The doctrine of state sovereignty (*see* § 2.1.1) has traditionally espoused that individual states have largely unfettered control over what activities occur within their borders and have, in the words of the first part of Stockholm Principle 21, "the sovereign right to exploit their own resources pursuant to their own environmental policies."[41] Based on the concept of sovereignty, states have taken the

---

[38] Franz Xaver Perrez, *The Relationship Between "Permanent Sovereignty" and the Obligation Not to Cause Transboundary Environmental Damage*, 26 ENVTL. L. 1187, 1201 (1996).

[39] John McDonald, *Air Pollution Knows No Political Boundaries*, INTERNATIONAL JOINT COMMISSION FOCUS, Dec. 1998, http://www.ijc.org/rel/focus/v23i3/feat03.html.

[40] Thomas W. Merrill, *Golden Rules for Transboundary Pollution*, 46 DUKE L.J. 931, 980 (1997).

[41] United Nations Conference on the Human Environment, Stockholm, Swed., June 5–16, 1972, *Stockholm Declaration of the UN Conference on the Human Environment*, Principle

position that they have discretion over whether or not to control pollution and sometimes argue that they bear no responsibility for what effects that decision has on other countries. Thus, an international prohibition against transboundary pollution acts as an exception to or a limitation on state sovereignty and needs to be supported by sufficient state practice with *opinio juris* (customary international law), by voluntary agreement (conventional international law), or through recognition as a *jus cogens* (overriding or peremptory moral norm).[42]

The catalyst for limiting sovereignty with regard to transboundary pollution was the most famous and fundamental case in all of international environmental law – the *Trail Smelter Arbitration*.[43] The case involved SO_2 emissions from a huge, privately owned smelter located in Trail, British Columbia, a few miles over the border from and upwind of northeastern Washington State in the US. The smelter's emissions gradually rose to over 300 tons of sulphur per day, which caused visible damage to Washington's agriculture. The US government finally intervened diplomatically on the US growers' behalf in 1927.[44] Ultimately, the two countries agreed to refer the matter to a three-member arbitral tribunal that handed down its final decision in 1941,[45] with one of the most famous rulings in all of international environmental law:

> [U]nder the principles of international law, as well as of the law of the United States, no State has the right to use or permit the use of its territory in such a manner as to cause injury by fumes in or to the territory of another or the properties or persons therein, when the case is of serious consequence and the injury is established by clear and convincing evidence.[46]

The circumstances of the case made it somewhat unique. The pollution source, pathway, and impacts were clear; the international arbitrators relied heavily

---

21, U.N. Doc. A/CONF.48/14/Rev. 1 at 3 (1973), U.N. Doc. A/CONF.48/14 at 2–65 and Corr. 1 (1972); 11 I.L.M. 1416 (1972), also at http://www.unep.org/Documents.Multilingual/Default.asp?documentid=97&articleid=1503. Note that while the "first part" of Stockholm Principle 21 acknowledges state sovereignty, the "second part" provides that states have "the responsibility to ensure that activities within their jurisdiction or control do not cause damage to the environment of other States or of areas beyond the limits of national jurisdiction." Thus it incorporates the concept of good neighborliness or the no-harm rule.

[42] Perrez, *supra* note 38, at 1088; *see also* MARK W. JANIS, AN INTRODUCTION TO INTERNATIONAL LAW 71 (4th ed. 2003).

[43] Trail Smelter Arbitration, U.S. v. Can. (1941), 3 R.I.A.A. 1911 (1941), http://untreaty.un.org/cod/riaa/cases/vol_III/1905-1982.pdf.

[44] HUNTER ET AL., *supra* note 9, at 509.

[45] *Id.*

[46] Trail Smelter Arbitration, *supra* note 43.

on US law; and the defendant country Canada had already conceded liability, which left only the amount of damages and future remedies at issue.[47]

Nevertheless over the next 30 years, *Trail Smelter's* "no significant harm" rule gained ever-increasing acceptance until it was finally expressed as a principle of international law in the seminal 1972 Stockholm Declaration, signed by 103 nations and considered a major catalyst for the development of international environmental law.[48] Stockholm Principle 21 clearly limits sovereignty by requiring transboundary environmental protection:

> States have, in accordance with the Charter of the United Nations and the principles of international law, the sovereign right to exploit their own resources pursuant to their own environmental policies, and *the responsibility to ensure that activities within their jurisdiction or control do not cause damage to the environment of other States or of areas beyond the limits of national jurisdiction.*[49]

Although the Stockholm Declaration was not intended to be binding at the outset, Principle 21 today is viewed as expressing agreed customary international law,[50] and continues to be restated in international legal authorities, such as Principle 2 of the 1992 Rio Declaration.[51]

Many other "soft law" legal authorities now espouse the principle of *sic utere* in regard to transboundary pollution – including the 1982 ILA Rules on International Law Applicable to Transfrontier Pollution[52] and the 1987 Restatement (Third) of the Foreign Relations Law of the United States.[53] Versions of it are appearing in "hard law" treaties as well – for example, the 1992 Convention on Biological Diversity[54] and the UN Convention on the

---

[47] Merrill, *supra* note 40, at 948.

[48] *See* Brian R. Popiel, *From Customary Law to Environmental Impact Assessment: A New Approach to Avoiding Transboundary Environmental Damage Between Canada and the United States,* 22 B.C. ENVTL. AFF. L. REV. 447 (1995); *see also* Philippe Sands, *European Community Environmental Law: The Evolution of a Regional Regime of International Environmental Protection,* 100 YALE L.J. 2511 (1991).

[49] Stockholm Declaration, *supra* note 41, Principle 2 (emphasis added).

[50] HUNTER ET AL., *supra* note 9, at 515.

[51] United Nations Conference on Environment and Development, Rio de Janiero, Braz., June 3–14, 1992, *Rio Declaration on Environment and Development,* U.N. Doc. A/CONF.151/26 (1992), 31 I.L.M. 874 (1992), http://www.unep.org/Documents.Multilingual/Default.asp?documentid=78&articleid=1163.

[52] 1982 ILA Rules on International Law Applicable to Transfrontier Pollution, Art. 3, Sept. 4, 1982, 60 I.L.A. 158 (1983); Int'l Law Assn., Rep. 60th Conf. (1982).

[53] RESTATEMENT OF THE LAW (THIRD) OF THE FOREIGN RELATIONS LAW OF THE UNITED STATES §§ 601–04 (1987).

[54] Convention on Biological Diversity, art. 3, June 5, 1992, 1760 U.N.T.S. 79, 31 I.L.M. 818 (1992), http://www.cbd.int/convention/text/.

Law of the Sea.[55] Thus, one can safely argue that the prevention of trans-boundary air pollution is an accepted principle of customary international law,[56] even though a number of states have preferred to enunciate the principle specifically (rather than risk any lingering disagreement over universal state practice) by creating treaties giving it concrete authority. Key examples of this "concretizing" approach are treaties between the US and Canada, the US and Mexico, the EU and other "northern" states, and countries in Asia (next section).

10.1.3   *Regional Treaty and Planning Regimes*

Transboundary air pollution has not yet been brought under any global treaty regime, as stratospheric ozone depletion has been and climate change is seeking to accomplish (*see* §§ 10.2 and 10.3). The closest to a "global" approach appears, surprisingly, in the UN Convention on the Law of the Sea, which requires states to adopt domestic laws and establish international rules "to prevent, reduce and control pollution of the marine environment from or through the atmosphere."[57] Needless to say, this provision has been largely ignored. Instead, the significant steps in controlling transboundary air pollution have been negotiated directly between countries on a bilateral basis (as §§ 10.1.3.1 and 10.1.3.2 on the US and its neighbors Canada and Mexico illustrate) or on a regional basis (as §§ 10.1.3.3 and 10.1.3.4 on LRTAP and Asia show).

10.1.3.1   *US-Canada*

Since the precedent-setting *Trail Smelter* decision, Canada and the US have set the example for handling issues of transboundary air pollution, perhaps more than any other countries. They share the world's longest border covering 5,525 miles (8,892 km) of land and water (including the Alaska-Canada

---

[55] United Nations Convention on the Law of the Sea, arts. 193, Dec. 10, 1982, 1833 U.N.T.S. 3, 397; 21 I.L.M. 1261(1982), http://www.un.org/depts/los/convention_agreements/conven tion_overview_convention.htm.

[56] Daniel Bodansky, *Customary (and Not So Customary) International Environmental Law*, 3 IND. J. GLOBAL LEGAL STUD. 105 (1995).

[57] UNCLOS *supra* note 55, art. 212. In August 2001 the ILC adopted draft articles on the Prevention of Transboundary Harm from Hazardous Activities which directly address the obligation of one state to prevent transboundary damage (including damage from air pollution) to the environment of other states as a result of its own activities even though the polluting state has not violated international law. The Commission has recommended that the General Assembly draft a convention on the basis of the draft articles. *See* Report of the International Law Commission on the Work of Its Fifty-Third Session, 56 U.N. GAOR, Supp. (No. 10) and U.N. Doc. A/56/10 (2001) at 366–436, http://untreaty.un.org/ilc/reports/2001/2001report.htm (hereafter 53rd Session Report).

border)[58] and the area on either side contains some of the finest wilderness, national parks, forests, rivers, lakes, and wetlands in the world, as well as some of the most intense industrialization, agriculture, and urbanization. Each country produces millions of tons of air and water pollutants per year, a large portion of which blows or flows across the border into the other. By the late 1980s, Canada charged that acid deposition from US air pollutants had made 14,000 lakes and nine salmon-producing rivers "dead" to the point that they could no longer support aquatic life and had acidified 150,000 other lakes below a pH of 6.0, the threshold for detrimental biologic effects.[59]

Negotiations to address transboundary pollution between the two countries began in the early 20th century and resulted in the groundbreaking 1909 Boundary Waters Treaty.[60] The very general language of that framework agreement focused on resolution of water quality and quantity disputes but left the door open for it to serve as a vehicle for a broader range of transboundary environmental issues.[61] The treaty created the International Joint Commission (IJC), consisting of three members from each country,[62] exercising both investigatory and adjudicative functions in referred disputes involving transboundary issues.[63] Although originally formed to address water quality issues, the Commission has since been used by both states to negotiate emission reductions.[64]

In addition to negotiating regional agreements, the US and Canada each enacted national Clean Air Acts in the 1970s which placed limits on the acid deposition precursors, SO_2 and NO_x.[65] However, the governments originally encouraged tall stacks as controls, which only led to the increased spread

---

[58] Popiel, *supra* note 48, at 447.

[59] *See* WEISS ET AL., *supra* note 32, at 580.

[60] *See* Shawn M. Rosso, *Acid Rain: The Use of Diplomacy, Policy and the Courts to Solve a Transboundary Pollution Problem*, 8 J. NAT. RESOURCES & ENVTL. L. 421, 422 (1992–1993).

[61] *Id.* at 423. *See* International Air Quality Advisory Board, *Special Report on Transboundary Air Quality Issues* (Nov. 1998), http://www.ijc.org/php/publications/html/spectrans/cover.html.

[62] Rosso, *supra* note 60.

[63] *Id.*

[64] The Canada-United States Agreement on Air Quality, U.S.-Canada, art. 5, 30 I.L.M. 676 (1991), http://www.epa.gov/airmarkets/progsregs/usca/index.htm.

[65] Both the US and Canadian Clean Air Acts (CAAs) have been amended to specifically address acid deposition and the main pollutants associated with it. See Ricci, *supra* note 24, at 310. The US CAA includes a provision which addresses transboundary pollution; § 115 calls for the Environmental Protection Agency (EPA) Administrator to notify emitting states that emissions from their sources are causing adverse effects on a foreign country. 42 U.S.C. § 7415; *see* Rosso, *supra* note 60, at 429. The Canadian version of § 115 is § 21.1 of the Canadian Clean Air Act. Rosso, *id.* at 430.

of acid deposition.[66] Further scientific evidence that the problems had not been solved led to the negotiation of a nonbinding Memorandum of Intent (MOI) in 1980,[67] acknowledging the seriousness of transboundary air pollution and calling for both states to develop and enforce domestic environmental regulations, establish a committee for further negotiations, notify each other of activities that might harm the environment of the other state, and exchange information.[68] Although the MOI was not binding, it paved the way for future binding actions.

Eventually, increased pressure to solve transboundary air pollution resulted in the binding 1991 Canada-United States Agreement on Air Quality[69] which created specific obligations for control of transboundary air pollutants, including SO$_2$ and NO$_x$, required advance assessment and notice of the air quality impacts of proposed new activities,[70] established joint research and information exchange processes,[71] and established a bilateral Air Quality Committee to oversee compliance.[72] In 2000, they signed an annex to the treaty in order to abate transboundary ground-level ozone from electric utilities.[73] 2011 marked the 20th anniversary of the treaty – a model of successful bilateral international environmental law, according to the parties, by which "emissions causing acid rain have been cut in half and emissions causing smog have been cut by one-third in the region."[74]

10.1.3.2   US-Mexico

The situation between the US and its southern neighbor, Mexico illustrates how different and difficult transboundary air pollution control can be between a developed and developing country. Also a long border, at 1,933 miles (3,093 km), it has experienced a substantial increase in development in the late 20th century and, consequently, a substantial increase of transboundary air, water, and solid waste pollution.[75] On the Mexican side, damage to

---

[66] Weiss et al., *supra* note 32, at 579.

[67] Memorandum of Intent Between the Government of the United States of America and the Government of Canada Concerning Transboundary Air Pollution, 20 I.L.M. 690 (1981), http://iea.uoregon.edu/pages/MarineMammals/engine/Documents/0-2796-2801.htm.

[68] *Id.*

[69] Canada-U.S. Air Agreement, *supra* note 64.

[70] *Id.* art. 5.

[71] Glode & Glode, *supra* note 11, at 31.

[72] Hunter et al., *supra* note 9, at 524.

[73] A copy of the annex can be found at *Can-US Air Quality Agreement*, Environment Canada, http://www.ec.gc.ca/air/default.asp?lang=En&n=83930AC3-1.

[74] Press Release, EPA, 20th Anniversary of U.S. Canada Air Quality Agreement (Mar. 14, 2011), http://www.epa.gov/airmarkets/progsregs/usca/docs/anniversary.pdf.

[75] *See* M. Grace Giorgio, *Transboundary Pollution Disputes Under the North American Free Trade Agreement*, 3 S.C. Envtl. L.J. 166, 177 (1994).

human health and nearby national parks has been accelerated by severe economic limitations, minimal environmental enforcement, and a 300+ percent increase in population as workers migrate north to the "maquiladora" zones (tax-preference industrial areas of mixed Mexican-foreign enterprises on the Mexican side of the border).[76] Emissions from Mexican factories have decreased visibility in Big Bend National Park in Texas up to 60 percent[77] and Mexican metal smelter pollution can be traced as far as lakes in the Rocky Mountains in Colorado.[78]

Although bilateral boundary water agreements between the two countries began in the 1940s,[79] the first concrete step to address transboundary air pollution did not come until the 1983 Border Agreement.[80] That bilateral framework treaty recognizes the need for mutual cooperation to solve environmental problems[81] and obligates the parties to prevent transboundary pollution "to the fullest extent practical."[82] The agreement is supplemented by annexes, which describe more concrete objectives.[83] The 1989 Annex V to the Border Agreement[84] specifically addresses transboundary air pollution, but lacks any enforcement mechanism[85] and is dependent on (US) funding for implementation.[86]

Subsequent agreements supplement the environmental provisions of the Border Agreement, including the Integrated Environmental Plan for the US-Mexico Border Area and the North American Free Trade Agreement (NAFTA) regime.[87] The North American Agreement on Environmental Cooperation (NAAEC) – the "Environmental Side Agreement" which was a

---

[76] *See* Cameron A. Grant, *Transboundary Air Pollution: Can NAFTA and NAAEC Succeed Where International Law Has Failed?*, 5 COLO. J. INT'L ENVTL. L. & POL'Y 439, 440 (1994).

[77] Nicole Mikulas, *An Innovative Twist on Free Trade and International Environmental Treaty Enforcements: Checking in on NAFTA's Seven-year Supervision of the U.S.-Mexico Border Pollution Problems*, 12 TUL. ENVTL. L.J. 497, 499 (1999).

[78] James Coates, *Acid Rain Spreads Its Cloud to West*, CHI. TRIB., Apr. 14, 1985, at 14.

[79] *See* Mikulas, *supra* note 77, at 500–01.

[80] Agreement Between the United States of America and the United Mexican States on Cooperation for the Protection and Improvement of the Environment in the Border Area, 22 I.L.M. 1025 (1983), http://www.epa.gov/Border2012/docs/LaPazAgreement.pdf; *see generally US-Mexico Border 2012*, USEPA, http://www.epa.gov/usmexicoborder.

[81] *See* Giorgio, *supra* note 75, at 181.

[82] Border Agreement, *supra* note 80, art. 2.

[83] Mikulas, *supra* note 77, at 502.

[84] Agreement of Cooperation Regarding International Transport of Urban Air Pollution, 29 I.L.M. 29 (1990). This Agreement is Annex V to the Agreement on Cooperation for the Protection and Improvement of the Environment in the Border Area, *supra* note 80.

[85] Giorgio, *supra* note 75, at 181.

[86] *Id.*

[87] Mikulas, *supra* note 77, at 503.

condition of NAFTA's approval by the US – includes provisions specifically addressing transboundary air pollution related to trade.[88] NAFTA purports to be the world's first environmentally friendly trade treaty, but whether these environmental provisions have successfully curbed pollution remains controversial.[89] As part of its NAFTA requirements, Mexico has passed environmental laws similar to those of the United States and Canada, and has established an environment ministry.[90] Air pollution and other environmental concerns may be referred by the parties or by individual citizens and groups to the NAFTA Commission for Environmental Cooperation (CEC), which has the power to investigate, hear, and make nonbinding recommendations.[91] While the CEC provides a forum for airing of environmental issues, its enforcement mechanisms are severely limited and its accomplishments to date have been minimal.[92] In conclusion, the current regulatory scheme needs improvement and the US and Mexico must still work to reduce transboundary air pollution.

10.1.3.3 *LRTAP – Europe and the Developed "North"*

Significant progress has been achieved in transboundary air pollution control at the regional level in Europe.[93] Soon after the Scandinavian countries discovered the acid damage to their lakes and rivers in the 1950s, described above, scientific studies confirmed that the pollution originated outside of their borders.[94] It was found that over half the SO_2 and NO_x emissions of European countries were being deposited outside the border of the state of origin, and, in the case of some industrial countries like Switzerland and the Netherlands, upwards of 80% of their pollution was being exported to their neighbors.[95]

As net importer "victims," the Scandinavian states led the way in seeking international action to deal with acid deposition.[96] After an unsuccessful

---

[88] Grant, *supra* note 76, at 447.

[89] *A Greener or Browner Mexico?* THE ECONOMIST, Aug. 5, 1999, http://www.economist.com/node/230188.

[90] *Id.*

[91] Grant, *supra* note 76, at 448.

[92] *Id.* The author argues that despite the seemingly comprehensive language, the agreement lacks the power to produce any significant results because it is left to the Commission's discretion to address a specific issue. *Id.* at 449.

[93] KISS & SHELTON, *supra* note 6, at 573.

[94] Glode & Glode, *supra* note 11, at 7.

[95] SOROOS, *supra* note 19, at 531.

[96] THE EFFECTIVENESS OF INTERNATIONAL ENVIRONMENTAL REGIMES, *supra* note 13, at 166. In Finland, Norway, Sweden, Austria and Switzerland, more than half of the total deposition of sulphur was estimated to have come from foreign sources. McCormick, *supra* note 27, at 2.

attempt to bring acid deposition to the table at the 1972 Stockholm Conference, they sought additional scientific confirmation that it was a serious problem. Several seminal studies, including one by the Organization for Economic Cooperation and Development (OECD), confirmed that air pollutants such as SO_2 could travel thousands of miles before being deposited, and that in half of the European countries the majority of the acid deposition came from outside of their borders.[97]

Thus bolstered, in 1975 the Scandinavian states persuaded their neighbors to call upon the UN Economic Commission for Europe (UN/ECE) to prepare an international treaty on air pollution control, which it did,[98] resulting in the 1979 UN/ECE Long-Range Transboundary Air Pollution Treaty (LRTAP).[99] LRTAP came into force in 1983 and at the beginning of 2012 had been ratified by 51 states, including the EU, Russia, and states as far-flung as the US, Canada, and Kyrgyzstan.[100] Indeed, it was the first international environmental treaty signed by both East and West, potentially contributing to an easing of tensions during the Cold War era.[101] The initial LRTAP was decidedly a framework treaty with no mandatory controls on emissions. Instead it called on states to "endeavour to limit and, as far as possible, gradually reduce and prevent air pollution including long-range transboundary air pollution"[102] as much as economically feasible, and to consult, exchange information, and engage in research and development.[103]

Today, LRTAP anchors an international legal regime of considerable effectiveness, led by a central organ of the parties, the Executive Body, and numerous working groups to oversee compliance with the treaty and its protocols.[104] It implements a cooperative program for the Monitoring and Evaluation of the Long-Range Transport of Air Pollutants in Europe (EMEP), which collects emissions and ambient air data at some 100 monitoring stations in 24 nations.[105]

---

[97] Amy Fraenkel, *The Convention on Long-Range Transboundary Air Pollution: Meeting the Challenge of International Cooperation*, 30 Harv. Int'l L.J. 447, 454 (1989).

[98] Fraenkel, *supra* note 97, at 454.

[99] LRTAP, *supra* note 8; George (Rock) Pring, James Otto & Koh Naito, *Trends in International Environmental Law Affecting the Minerals Industry* (Part II), 17 Energy & Nat. Res. L. 151, 152 (1999).

[100] *Status of Ratification*, UNECE LRTAP, http://live.unece.org/env/lrtap/status/lrtap_st.html.

[101] *See* Hunter et al., *supra* note 9, at 526.

[102] LRTAP, *supra* note 8, art. 2.

[103] *Id.* arts. 3–9.

[104] *About the Convention*, UNECE, http://live.unece.org/env/lrtap/lrtap_h1.html.

[105] *Id.*

Since its entry into force, LRTAP has been extended by eight protocols that have given substantial regulatory force to the regime. The first was the 1984 Protocol for funding the EMEP system (above).[106] That was followed in 1985 by the Protocol on Sulphur Emissions,[107] which took the interesting approach of requiring an across-the-board 30% reduction in each country's sulphur emissions (rather than end-of-the-pipe, technology-based emission standards, as urged by the US). By 2012, the protocol had 25 ratifying parties and had entered into force.[108] All parties met their 30% reduction goal by 1993,[109] resulting in a 50% decrease in total SO_2 emissions in Europe between 1980 and 1995.[110]

The third protocol came in 1988 and focused on NO_x,[111] aiming to stabilize NO_x emissions at the 1987 level by 1995, with 12 of the 25 parties also agreeing to a 30–percent cut below 1980–86 levels. This third protocol has 34 ratifications and has entered into force.[112] However, it has been considerably less successful than the SO_2 Protocol, largely because motor vehicles are the principal source of NO_x, and these are backed by a political constituency – motorists – considerably less willing to be regulated than owners of factories producing SO_2.[113] Thus, overall emissions of NO_x in Europe have decreased only a small percentage.[114]

VOCs were the subject of the fourth LRTAP protocol in 1991,[115] which offers parties three different compliance options: (1) a 30% reduction in emissions of VOCs by 1999 using 1988 as the base year; or (2) the same

---

[106] Protocol on Long-term Financing of the Cooperative Programme for Monitoring and Evaluation of the Long-range Transmission of Air Pollutants in Europe (EMEP), *entered into force* Jan. 28 1988, 27 I.L.M.701 (1988). The EMEP has been ratified by 44 states and gone into force. The latest texts of this and the other seven protocols, as well as lists of ratifiers and other information, may be found at: UNECE, *Protocols to the Convention*, http://www.unece.org/env/lrtap/status/lrtap_s.html.

[107] The 1985 Protocol on the Reduction of Sulphur Emissions or Their Transboundary Fluxes by at Least 30 Per Cent, July 8, 1985, EB.AIR/12, 27 I.L.M. 707 (1988), at the website *supra* note 106.

[108] *Protocols to the Convention, supra* note 106.

[109] E. Berge *et al., Long-term Trends in Emissions and Transboundary Transport of Acidifying Air Pollution in Europe*, 57 J. ENVTL. MGMT. 31, 32 (1999).

[110] *Id.* at 33.

[111] Sofia Protocol Concerning the Control of Emissions of Nitrogen Oxides or their Transboundary Fluxes, Oct. 31, 1988, 28 I.L.M. 212 (1988), http://live.unece.org/env/lrtap/nitr_h1.html.

[112] *Id.*

[113] KISS & SHELTON, *supra* note 6, at 574.

[114] McCormick, *supra* note 27, at 7.

[115] Protocol Concerning the Control of Emissions of Volatile Organic Compounds or Their Transboundary Fluxes, *entered into force* Sept. 29 1997, 31 I.L.M. 573 (1992), http://live.unece.org/env/lrtap/vola_h1.html.

30% reduction using any base year between 1984 and 1990 if the VOCs originate only from specified areas; or alternatively (3) for Central and Eastern European countries ("economies in transition"), stabilization at 1988 levels by 1999. It has 24 ratifications and has entered into force.[116] As a result of its implementation, 1996 VOC emissions in Europe were approximately 20% lower than in 1990, with success credited in part to the flexibility of the compliance options.[117]

By the early 1990s, studies showed that acid precipitation was still a problem, despite the success in meeting the 30% goal of the first SO_2 Protocol, so a fifth protocol – the second SO_2 Protocol – was adopted in 1994,[118] using an effects-based approach instead of relying on percentage reductions.[119] A "critical load" was set, representing the highest amount of acid deposition that will not lead to long term harmful effects on the ecosystem, and this becomes the control measure.[120] This flexible approach considered best available technology (BAT), economics, and other factors to differentiate obligations of the parties,[121] but still proposed deep reductions of 62% below 1980 levels for the EU by 2000, with the UK vowing an 80% reduction by 2010.[122] By 2012, it had 29 ratifications and had entered into force.[123]

In the 1990s, the LRTAP parties began to expand their focus beyond acidification precursors to encompass a much wider range of contaminants potentially affecting human health and the environment and began to look at regulating not only process gases but products as well.[124] The sixth LRTAP protocol – the 1998 Heavy Metals Protocol[125] – is a good example of this. It is designed to control anthropogenic emissions of "heavy metals"[126] subject to transboundary transport with significant human health or environmental effects. As a first step, the protocol focuses on emissions of only three metals – lead, cadmium, and mercury – by industrial sources (ferrous and nonferrous

---

[116] *Id.*

[117] Andrzej Jagusiewicz, *The History of the Convention on Long-range Transboundary Air Pollution*, POLLUTION ATMOSPHERIQUE, Dec. 1991, at 18.

[118] Protocol on Further Reduction of Sulphur Emissions, *entered into force* Aug. 5 1998, 33 I.L.M. 1618 (1994), http://live.unece.org/env/lrtap/fsulf_h1.html.

[119] McCormick, *supra* note 27, at 11.

[120] BERGE ET AL., *supra* note 109, at 46.

[121] LRTAP, *supra* note 8.

[122] *See* KISS & SHELTON, *supra* note 6, at 574. At the time of this publication, it is unclear whether the UK met that target, but there have been significant reductions.

[123] *Protocols to the Convention, supra* note 106.

[124] Pring *et al., supra* note 99, at 152.

[125] Protocol on Heavy Metals, *entered into force* Dec. 29, 2003, http://live.unece.org/env/lrtap/hm_h1.html.

[126] All metals being by nature "heavy" (except for lithium), it should be recognized that the redundant adjective is an intentional or unconscious pejorative.

metals industries), combustion processes (power generation, road transport, etc.), and waste incineration. It requires parties to: (1) cut emissions below 1990 levels, (2) adopt stringent emission limits and BAT, (3) phase out lead in petrol, and (4) begin to ban certain products using lead, cadmium, or mercury (such as mercury in batteries).[127] The drafters are also considering measures to expand the protocol to include other emissions and to reduce or ban metals in a wide range of products – such as electrical components (thermostats, switches), measuring instruments (thermometers, barometers, etc.), fluorescent lamps and bulbs, dental amalgam, pesticides, and paints, suggesting that the Heavy Metals Protocol could become an on-going vehicle for bans on many common uses and products.[128] By 2012, it had 31 parties and had entered into force.[129]

A seventh protocol, focused on persistent organic pollutants (POPs), was likewise signed in 1998.[130] It seeks to eliminate or reduce emissions and other discharges of 16 POPs – chiefly human-made organic substances which are toxic, persistent, bioaccumulative, and can travel long distances, including 11 pesticides and industrial by-products like dioxins, furans, and polycyclic aromatic hydrocarbons (PAHs). The 1998 POPs Protocol has significance for agriculture, as it bans production and use of many popular agricultural bio-cides (aldrin, chlordane, mirex, etc.), as well as for a variety of mineral pro-duction processes, waste incineration, and other industries in which dioxins and furans are byproducts. By 2012, it had 31 parties and had entered into effect.[131] Additional substances, like DDT, other pesticides, and PCBs are scheduled for elimination later. The POPs Protocol has served as a model for the Stockholm POPs treaty that is global in scope.[132]

Finally, in 1999, the LRTAP parties produced an eighth protocol, return-ing to their original focus on acid precursors and seeking even greater reduc-tions in the Protocol to Abate Acidification, Eutrophication and Ground-level Ozone.[133] This protocol has 26 state parties by 2012 and has entered into force. It takes a multipollutant-multieffects approach, setting ceilings and

---

[127] Pring *et al., supra* note 99, at 152–53.

[128] *Id.* at 153, 160–61.

[129] Heavy Metal Protocol, *supra* note 125.

[130] 1998 Aarhus Protocol on Persistent Organic Pollutants (POPs), *entered into force* Oct. 23 2003, 37 I.L.M. 505 (1998), http://live.unece.org/env/lrtap/pops_h1.html. *See* Pring *et al., supra* note 99, at 153; 1998 Y.B. INT'L ENVTL. L. Vol. 9, at 176 (Jutta Brunnée & Ellen Hey eds.).

[131] *Protocols to the Convention, supra* note 106.

[132] *See* Stockholm Convention on Persistent Organic Pollution, May 22, 2001, 40 I.L.M. 531 (2001), http://chm.pops.int/Convention/ConventionText/tabid/2232/language/en-US/Default.aspx. The Convention entered into force May 17, 2004.

[133] *Protocols to the Convention, supra* note 106.

limit values designed to further reduce emissions of sulphur (by 63 percent below 1990 levels), NO_x (41 percent), VOCs (40 percent), and ammonia (17 percent), in order to reduce acidification, eutrophication (nutrient-loading of water bodies causing excessive growth of aquatic plants and resultant deoxygenation), and ozone concentration. Among the affected sources are electricity production, combustion plants, dry cleaning, motor vehicles, paints, aerosols, and agriculture (ammonia). It is estimated that implementation of the protocol will reduce the area in Europe with excessive levels of acidification from 93 million hectares to 15; reduce areas with excessive levels of eutrophication from 165 to 108 million hectares; and cut the number of days with excessive ground-level ozone in half (with some 47,500 fewer premature deaths per year).[134]

In addition to its regional commitments under LRTAP, the European Union (EU) has also adopted a number of air pollution directives binding on its member states. These include both general-scope directives and directives applicable to specific pollutants, processes, and products. A number of these have transboundary effect.

The LRTAP treaty regime remains the major focus for transboundary air pollution control for a growing body of nations (51 by January 2012) that, broadly speaking, represent the industrialized, developed nations of "the North." It is also the world's most important forum for expansion of air pollution regulation and a "laboratory" for new techniques, requirements, and regulated substances.

10.1.3.4   *Asia*

Air pollution is extremely high in many places in Asia.[135] The combination of rapid industrial growth, economic crises, heavy reliance on fossil fuels and leaded gasoline, disastrous forest fires, and relatively weak environmental enforcement[136] presents Asia with nearly overwhelming national and transboundary air pollution problems, and the region is still struggling to arrive at a solution. The issue of transboundary air pollution was first highlighted regionally in the 1990 Kuala Lumpur Accord on Environment and

---

[134] *Id.*

[135] Attempts to accumulate a worldwide database of pollution have proven unsuccessful because many cities where pollution is believed to be the highest do not monitor or keep statistics. World Health Organization, *Air Quality & Health Questions and Answer* at Q.3, http://www.who.int/phe/air_quality_q&a.pdf. *See also* Alan McDonald, *Combating Acid Deposition and Climate Change*, ENV'T, Apr. 1999, at 6.

[136] *See, e.g.,* James Otto, Koh Naito & George (Rock) Pring, *Environmental Regulation of Exploration and Mining Operations in Asian Countries*, 23 UN NAT. RES. F. 323 (1999).

Development,[137] which led to a series of ministerial agreements and declarations with little binding effect. The most notable of these is the ASEAN Cooperation Plan on Transboundary Pollution of 1995,[138] the air pollution component of which focused exclusively on forest fire prevention (with a "long term strategy" of "zero burning") to the exclusion of other transboundary air pollution sources, although it does commit the state parties to cooperate in the development of an air quality index, harmonization of sampling, information exchange, etc.

In 2002, the ASEAN nations, with the guiding hand of UNEP, created an Agreement on Transboundary Haze Pollution[139] in response to the major episodes of fire and transboundary haze pollution that occurred in the region during the 1980s and 1990s.[140] Transboundary haze pollution was particularly damaging during 1997 and 1998 when forest fires raged in Indonesia, burning over one million hectares of forest, blanketing Southeast Asia with smoke, forcing businesses, schools, and airports to close,[141] and causing over $4 billion in damage.[142] Occasioned by the long-standing practice of clearing lands for agricultural and other development by uncontrolled burning,[143] the fires were declared a "global disaster" by UNEP.[144] El Niño and global warming trends are expected to exacerbate this problem in the future.[145] ASEAN nations responded to this "haze disaster" with a Regional Haze Action Plan, which calls for ASEAN members to control the "slash and burn" method of clearing land for agriculture in order to prevent forest fires.[146]

---

[137] The Association of Southeast Asian Nations (ASEAN) maintains a very detailed web site with texts or summaries of the key currently operating international instruments and detailed histories, at http://www.aseansec.org (click on "Resources").

[138] *ASEAN Cooperation Plan on Transboundary Pollution*, ASEAN, http://www.aseansec.org/8926.htm.

[139] *ASEAN Agreement on Transboundary Haze Pollution*, ASEAN, http://www.aseansec.org/6086.htm.

[140] *Combating Haze in ASEAN: Frequently Asked Questions* (2007), ASEAN, http://www.aseansec.org/Fact%20Sheet/ASCC/2007-ASCC-001.pdf.

[141] Simon S. C. Tay, *Southeast Asian Fires: The Challenge for International Environmental Law and Sustainable Development*, 11 Geo. Int'l Envtl. L. Rev. 241, 245 (1999). This is a highly conservative estimate; other estimates calculate the damage at over seven million hectares. *Id.*

[142] 1998 Yearbook, Air and Atmosphere: Forest Fires, 1998 Colo. J. Int'l Envtl. L. & Pol'y 263.

[143] Tay, *supra* note 141 at 248.

[144] *Id.* at 241.

[145] *Id.* at 248.

[146] *ASEAN Cooperation Plan on Transboundary Pollution*, ASEAN, http://www.aseansec.org/9059.htm.

Even more problematic than Asian forest fires, however, is the pollution coming from industrial and civilian sources. Rapid economic growth in Asia, and especially in China, has accelerated air and water pollution in the region. In the words of one commentator, "China is choking on its own success."[147] For example, to fuel to its economic boom, China's power sector has been expanding at a rate roughly equivalent to three to four new coal-fired, 500-megawatt plants coming on line every week.[148] China currently uses more coal than the United States, the European Union, and Japan combined,[149] and the coal typically used in these power plants is locally mined, low-grade coal, which produces high levels of sulphur emissions.[150] Thus, even though many power plants in China use new, state-of-the-art equipment, pollution is still at dangerous levels in many cities.

The devastating effect of this air pollution has only become obvious in the last several years. The 2008 Beijing Olympics helped draw international attention to the issue, as many athletes feared the ill effects associated with breathing the highly polluted air of the host city during the competition. Only one percent of China's 560 million city dwellers breathe air considered safe by the European Union.[151] Ambient air pollution is blamed for hundreds of thousands of deaths each year, and pollution has contributed to making cancer China's leading cause of death.[152] Haze and acid precipitation travel as far as Tokyo, Japan, and Seoul Korea.[153] It is even believed that much of the particulate pollution over Los Angeles originates in China.[154]

Thus far, China has proved unwilling or unable to rein in pollution. The country's government is tied to maintaining high growth rates as a perceived antidote to social and political unrest.[155] At the same time, however, high pollution levels are sparking incidents of social unrest throughout the country.[156] Thus, the future of pollution in the region remains uncertain as ASEAN's general policy of nonintervention in member states' "domestic"

---

[147] Joseph Kahn & Jim Yardley *As China Roars, Pollution Reaches Deadly Extremes*, N.Y. Times, Aug. 26, 2007, http://www.nytimes.com/2007/08/26/world/asia/26china.html.

[148] David Chandler, *MIT Report Debunks China Energy Myth*, MIT News, Oct. 6, 2008, http://web.mit.edu/newsoffice/2008/china-energy-1006.html.

[149] Keith Bradsher & David Barboza, *Pollution from Chinese Coal Casts a Global Shadow*, N.Y. Times, June 6, 2006, http://www.nytimes.com/2006/06/11/business/worldbusiness/11chinacoal.html?pagewanted=all.

[150] Chandler, *supra* note 148.

[151] Kahn & Yardley, *supra* note 147.

[152] *Id.*

[153] *See* Henry Fountain, *Observatory*, N.Y. Times, Dec. 21, 1999, at F5. Bradsher & David Barboza, *supra* note 149.

[154] Kahn & Yardley, *supra* note 147.

[155] *Id.*

[156] *Id.*

affairs coupled with lack of internal resources, foreign aid, and technical assistance and training has curbed the ability of Asian nations to deal with transboundary air pollution.[157] The involvement of UNEP should put some substance behind ASEAN's numerous environmental initiatives, however dramatic changes in internal policies will probably be necessary to effectuate any meaningful reductions.

Asia is but one example. South America, Africa, and Central Europe also have laws and economic policies that are only beginning to deal with air pollutants and where any effective regional focus on the full range of transboundary industrial pollutants is yet to come.

10.2   *Stratospheric Ozone Depletion*

10.2.1   *Introduction*

The 1985 Vienna Convention for the Protection of the Ozone Layer[158] and its 1987 Montreal Protocol on Substances that Deplete the Ozone Layer[159] created a regime for the protection of the earth's ozone layer and are the only universally ratified UN treaties, with 197 parties as of 2012.[160] This unprecedented accomplishment has resulted in the phasing out of over 98 percent of the ozone depleting substances (ODSs) controlled by the Montreal Protocol by the end of 2010,[161] and is indeed one of the great success stories of international environmental law.

---

[157] *See* Tay, *supra* note 141, at 260.

[158] 1985 Vienna Convention for the Protection of the Ozone Layer, opened for signature Mar. 22, 1985, effective September 22, 1988, 1513 U.N.T.S. 293, reprinted in 26 I.L.M. 1516 (1987), http://ozone.unep.org/new_site/en/Treaties/treaty_text.php?treatyID=2 [hereinafter Vienna Ozone Convention].

[159] Protocol on Substances That Deplete the Ozone Layer, opened for signature Sept. 16, 1987, effective January 1989, S. Treaty Doc. No. 100–10, 1522 U.N.T.S. 3, reprinted in 26 I.L.M. 1541 (1987), http://www.UNEP.org/ozone/pdfs/montreal-protocol2000.pdf [hereinafter Montreal Protocol].

[160] Timor-Leste was the final ratification, done on September 16, 2009. *See* United Nations Environment Programme, Ozone Secretariat, Status of Ratification / Accession / Acceptance / Approval of the Agreements on the Protection of the Stratospheric Ozone Layer, May 18, 2012, http://www.montreal-protocol.org/new_site/en/treaty_ratification_status .php [hereinafter Status of Ratification].

[161] *Id. See also* UNEP, Report of the Combined ninth meeting of the Conference of the Parties to the Vienna Convention on the Protection of the Ozone Letter and the Twenty-third Meeting of the Parties to the Montreal Protocol on Substances that Deplete the Ozone Layer, Bali, Indonesia, November 21–25, 2011, at § 1, ¶ 4, doc. UNEP/OzL.Conv.9/7-UNEP/OzL.Pro.23/11, December 9, 2011 [hereinafter Vienna Ozone Convention-Montreal Protocol 2011].

A study of the legal framework devised to address the challenge of the ODSs is the focus of this chapter. The following discussion first addresses the phenomenon of stratospheric ozone depletion, noting significant recent developments and highlighting their ramifications. Next, global responses to ozone depletion are examined. The adequacy of these responses is then assessed, followed by the concluding section.

10.2.2   *The Problem*

Ozone is a pollutant at ground level and low altitudes.[162] However, in the upper part of the atmosphere, known as the stratosphere, it acts as a barrier against the ultraviolet rays of the sun, effectively absorbing them and thus protecting the earth from their harmful effects on human health, agricultural productivity, and fisheries.[163] That is why ozone loss in the stratosphere is critical.

Ozone occurs in the stratosphere as ultraviolet solar radiation causes photochemical reactions, continuously converting oxygen (O_2) to ozone (O_3) and back to oxygen.[164] Human activities are disturbing this production-and-loss balance: they cause ozone layer modification through the chemical catalytic processes resulting from emissions of nitrogen, chlorine, and hydrogen oxides.[165] For instance, chlorine is a catalytic agent that destroys ozone by promoting the following reactions:[166] a chlorine (Cl) atom reacting with ozone (O_3) forms ClO and O_2. ClO then reacts with another O_3 molecule, forming two molecules of O_2 and releasing the chlorine atom. After converting two molecules of ozone to three molecules of oxygen, the chlorine is ready to restart the process. Consequently, a single chlorine atom is capable

---

[162] *See, e.g.*, M. Russell, *Ozone Pollution: The Hard Choices*, 241 Sci. 1275–76 (1988).

[163] *See* R. T. Watson, M. A. Geller *et al.*, *Present State of Knowledge of the Upper Atmosphere: An Assessment Report* 19 (NASA Ref. Publ. 1162, May 1986) [hereinafter 1986 Assessment Report].

[164] *See generally* 1986 Assessment Report, *supra* note 163, at 22–23; F. Stordal & I. Isakson, *Ozone Perturbations Due to Increases in N20, Ch4, and Chlorofluorocarbons: Two-Dimensional Time-Dependent Calculations*, 1 Effects of Changes in Stratospheric Ozone and Global Climate 83 (J. Titus ed., 1986) (an EPA and UNEP study) [hereinafter 1986 Ozone and Climate Study].

[165] *See* 1986 Assessment Report, *supra* note 163, at 6–8; Stordal & Isakson, *supra* note 164, at 84; R. Kerr, Ozone Hole Bodes Ill for the Globe, 241 SCI. 785, 785–786 (1988) [hereinafter Kerr I].

[166] This simple model is taken from Titus & Seidel, Overview of the Effects of Changing the Atmosphere, 1986 Ozone and Climate Study, *supra* note 164, at 4. *See also* M. Tolbert *et al.*, *Antarctic Ozone Depletion Chemistry: Reactions of N2O3 with H2O and HCl on Ice Surfaces*, 240 Sci. 1018 (1988); M. Molina *et al.*, *Antarctic Stratospheric Chemistry of Chlorine Nitrate, Hydrogen Chloride, and Ice: Release of Active Chlorine*, 238 Sci. 1253 (1987); M. Tolbert *et al.*, *Reaction of Chlorine Nitrate with Hydrogen Chloride and Water at Antarctic Stratospheric Temperatures*, 238 Sci. 1258 (1988).

of destroying thousands of ozone molecules before returning to the lower atmosphere – the troposphere – to be rained out as hydrochloric acid (*see* § 10.0).

Scientists have discovered a rapid increase in atmospheric concentrations of a number of these depleting substances, gases that affect atmospheric ozone.[167] These include CFCs, halons, methane, nitrous oxide, and carbon dioxide, to name a few. The challenge, therefore, is to prevent further increase of these gases in the atmosphere. Additionally, scientists have confirmed that the release of chemicals containing chlorine and bromine (CFCs and halons, respectively), for which human activities are responsible, threatens the stability of the ozone layer in the polar vortex.[168] Consequently, the challenge is for decisionmakers to initiate appropriate preventive and remedial steps. The 1985 Vienna Convention for the Protection of the Ozone Layer,[169] the Montreal Protocol on Substances that Deplete the Ozone Layer,[170] and efforts to find substitutes for CFCs are such steps. Additionally, several amendments to the Montreal Protocol – the 1990 London Amendment,[171] the 1992 Copenhagen Amendment,[172] the 1997 Montreal Amendment,[173] and the 1999 Beijing Amendment[174] – are examples of the international community's willingness to take action.[175] The pertinent question concerning the adequacy of these measures will be discussed below.[176]

10.2.3   *Evidence of Loss*

The major concern lies in ozone loss in the stratosphere, which extends from about eight kilometers at the poles and seventeen kilometers at the equator to about 50 kilometers above the Earth's surface and is home to most

---

[167] *See* Kerr I, *supra* note 165 at 785.

[168] *See generally* R. W. Watson, *et al.*, *Present State of Knowledge of the Upper Atmosphere 1988: An Assessment Report* 3, 4, 9 (NASA Ref. Pub. 1208, August 1988) [hereinafter Ozone Trends Panel Report].

[169] Vienna Ozone Convention, *supra* note 158.

[170] Montreal Protocol, *supra* note 159.

[171] Report of the Second Meeting of the Parties to the Montreal Protocol on Substances that Deplete the Ozone Layer, U.N. Doc. UNEP OzL.Pro.2/3 (June 29, 1990), effective Aug. 10, 1992, reprinted in 30 I.L.M. 537 (1991) [hereinafter London Amendment].

[172] Report of the Fourth Meeting of the Parties to the Montreal Protocol on Substances that Deplete the Ozone Layer, reprinted in 332 I.L.M. 874 (1993) [hereinafter Copenhagen Amendment].

[173] Report of the Ninth Meeting of the Parties to the Montreal Protocol on Substances that Deplete the Ozone Layer, Annex IV (1997) [hereinafter Montreal Amendment].

[174] Report of the Eleventh Meeting of the Parties to the Montreal Protocol on Substances that Deplete the Ozone Layer, Annex V (1999) [hereinafter Beijing Amendment].

[175] *See infra* § 10.2.8.

[176] *See infra* § 10.2.8.5.

of the ozone in the atmosphere.[177] In 1974 two scientists, M. J. Molina and F. S. Rowland, revealed that CFCs caused atmospheric ozone destruction, as they, reported that "[p]hotodissociation of the chlorofluoromethanes in the stratosphere produces significant amounts of chlorine atoms and leads to destruction of atmospheric ozone."[178]

This report was followed by two reports released in September 1976 by the National Academy of Sciences (NAS) on the emissions of chlorofluoromethanes (CFMs) and the associated health and biological effects of such emissions.[179] The NAS sounded an ominous warning: "Selective regulation of CFM uses and releases is almost certain to be necessary at some time and to some degree of completeness."[180] However, the study noted that, at the time, "[n]either the needed timing or the needed severity can be reasonably specified."[181] The following month, several US federal agencies announced a proposed reduction over the next 18 months in the uses of certain CFCs in aerosol sprays.[182]

---

[177] R. T. Watson, *Atmospheric Ozone*, 1986 OZONE AND CLIMATE STUDY, *supra* note 164, at 69. Scientists have been studying changes both in the total column amount of atmospheric ozone and in its vertical distribution since the 1970s, using data from the ground-based Dobson spectrophotometer network, and since 1978, using data from NASA's Nimbus-7 satellite-based instruments, Solar Backscatter Ultraviolet (SBUV) and Total Ozone Mapping Spectrometer (TOMS), the Stratospheric Aerosol and Gas Experiment (SAGE) spectrometers, and the Solar Mesospheric Explorer (SME) spectrometers. *See* Ozone Trends Panel Report, *supra* note 168, at 3, 16. A new ozone sensor, costing US $5 million, to monitor changes in ozone concentrations, is now carried on a NOAA-11 a spacecraft launched on Sept. 24, 1988. *See* W. Broad, *Satellite to Improve Monitoring of Ozone Loss*, N.Y. TIMES, Oct. 25, 1988, at B 11, col. 1.

[178] M. Molina & F. Rowland, *Stratospheric Sink for Chlorofluoromethanes: Chlorine Atom-Catalyzed Destruction of Ozone*, 249 NATURE 810 (June 1974). *See also* F. Rowland & M. Molina, *Chlorofluoromethanes in the Environment*, 13 REV. GEOPHYS. SPACE PHYS. 1 (1975).

[179] NATIONAL ACADEMY OF SCIENCES (NAS), HALOCARBONS: EFFECTS ON STRATOSPHERIC OZONE (1976); NAS, HALOCARBONS: ENVIRONMENTAL EFFECTS OF CHLOROFLUOROME-THANE RELEASES (1976).

[180] NAS, HALOCARBONS: ENVIRONMENTAL EFFECTS OF CHLOROFLUOROMETHANE RELEASES 7 (1976).

[181] *Id.*

[182] *See Stratospheric Ozone Depletion and Chlorofluorocarbons: Joint Hearing Before the Subcomms. on Environmental Protection and Hazardous Wastes and Toxic Substances of the Senate Comm. on Environment and Public Works*, 100th Cong., 1st Sess., at 63, 66 (1987) (statement of F. S. Rowland, in which he notes this development) [hereinafter *Stratospheric Ozone Depletion and CFCs*]. For the U.S. action banning the use of CFCs in aerosols by 1978, *see* Toxic Substances Control Act, 15 U.S.C. §§ 2601–2629 (1976).

The NAS followed its 1976 studies by releasing two more in 1979,[183] and several in the 1980s.[184] It was clear that continued use of CFCs could cause a substantial depletion of ozone. In October 1980, the United States Environmental Protection Agency (EPA) issued an Advance Notice of Proposed Rulemaking that discussed the possibility of an immediate freeze on the production of some CFCs, and of using a system of marketable permits for the allocation of CFC consumption among those industries which use CFCs.[185]

It is significant that the United States was not alone in conducting these studies, issuing the warning, and taking action. Among other states that participated most were from Europe. Individually, as well as in agreements with other states, they acted to regulate the use of CFCs.[186]

Internationally, in the early 1980s, the United Nations Environment Programme (UNEP) and the World Meteorological Organization (WMO) took the initiative to actively pursue the issue, conducting studies and a series of workshops.[187] Negotiations to resolve differences between the United States, which sought stricter controls, and several of its trading partners, which

---

[183] *See* NAS, PROTECTION AGAINST DEPLETION OF STRATOSPHERIC OZONE BY CHLOROFLU-OROCARBONS (1979); NAS, STRATOSPHERIC OZONE DEPLETION BY CHLOROFLUOROCAR-BONS – CHEMISTRY AND TRANSPORT (1979).

[184] *See* NAS, CHANGING CLIMATE (1983); NAS, CAUSES AND EFFECTS OF CHANGES IN STRATOSPHERIC OZONE: UPDATE 1983 (1984). For an important study by NASA, *see* 1986 Assessment Report, *supra* note 164. Another study of note is by EPA, *see* Ozone Trends Panel Report, *supra* note 168.

[185] *See* 45 Fed. Reg. 66,726 (1980).

[186] *See, e.g.*, Edith Brown Weiss, *A Resource Management Approach to Carbon Dioxide During the Century of Transition, in* WORLD CLIMATE CHANGE: THE ROLE OF INTERNATIONAL LAW AND INSTITUTIONS 167, 184–85 (V. Nanda ed., 1983); Agreement Among the United States, France, and the United Kingdom, 27 U.S.T. 1437, T.I.A.S. No. 8255, reprinted in 1 Intl Env't Rep. (BNA) sec. 21: 2501 (1978 Reference File); P. Sand, *Protecting the Ozone Layer: The Vienna Convention is Adopted,* ENV'T, June 1985, at 18, 41.

[187] *See generally* UNEP, Environmental Law: An In-Depth Review 15 (UNEP Rep. No. 2, 1981) [hereinafter UNEP Rep. No. 2]; UNEP, Program Performance Report-Addendum, UNEP/GC. 1015 Add. 2, at 2–4 (Dec. 7, 1981); UNEP, *Nowhere to Hide, in Stratospheric Ozone Depletion and CFCs,* 57 (statement by M. K. Tolba, Executive Director, UNEP) [hereinafter Nowhere to Hide]; Sand, *supra* note 186, at 40–43; UNEP/GC 8/70 (Apr. 29, 1980); UNEP/GC. 13/16 91985; R. Benedick, *International Cooperation to Protect the Ozone Layer,* 86 DEP'T ST. BULL., June 1986, at 48; R. Benedick, *Protecting the Ozone Layer,* 85 DEP'T ST. BULL., Apr. 1985, at 63; M. Tolba, *The State of the World Environment: The 1980 Report of the Executive Director of the United Nations Environment Program* (1980), The State of the World Environment, 1972–1982, UNEP/GC (SSQ/INF. 2 (Jan. 29, 1982); G. Taubes & A. Chen, *Made In The Shade?* DISCOVER, Aug. 1987, at 62; World Meteorological Organization, Atmospheric Ozone: 1985 – Assessment of Our Understanding of the Processes Controlling its Present Disruption and Change (Global Ozone and Monitoring Project, Rep. No. 16, 1986); V. Wasermann, UNEP: Protection of the Ozone Layer, 17 J. WORLD TRADE L. 182 (1983).

favored more lax standards and controls,[188] culminated in the adoption of the 1985 Vienna Convention and subsequently the 1987 Montreal Protocol. According to the 1988 International Ozone Trends Panel Report, there was a measurable decrease in the average total column ozone of 1.7 to 3 percent "in all latitude bands from thirty to sixty-four degrees in the northern hemisphere from 1969 to 1986."[189]

The most dramatic discovery, however, was that of the Antarctic ozone hole, an unusual loss of 50 percent of ozone in the total column in the Antarctic springtime in 1987.[190] Data showed that, during the prior decade, the loss of total column ozone over Antarctica in the springtime (September through November) had ranged between 30 and 40 percent.[191] This loss was accompanied by a discovery that chlorine monoxide levels at certain altitudes reached 500 times normal concentrations.[192] In October 1987, the decline in

---

[188] UNEP's legal adviser discussed the negotiations leading to the adoption of the convention in Rummel-Bulaska, *The Protection of the Ozone Layer Under the Global Framework Convention, in* Transboundary Air Pollution 281 (C. Flinterman ed., 1986). *See also* UNEP, *Nowhere to Hide, supra* note 186; R. Benedick, *International Cooperation to Protect the Ozone Layer, supra* note 187; Sand, *supra* note 187, at 41–42; 10 Int'l Env't Rep. (BNA), Curr. Rep. 195–96 (May 13, 1987); 10 Int'l Env't Rep. (BNA), Curr. Rep. 273 (June 10, 1987); 10 Int'l Env't Rep. (BNA), Curr. Rep. 315–16 (July 8, 1987); 10 Int'l Env't Rep. (BNA), Curr. Rep. 451 (Sept. 9, 1987).

[189] Ozone Trends Panel Report, *supra* note 168 at 11. During the winter months, December through March, these decreases ranged from 2.3 to 6.2 percent. Between 1978 and 1985, the TOMS satellite data showed a decline of total ozone column in all latitude zones, the range being 1.1 to 3.7 percent in the Northern hemisphere, and 1.1 to 9 percent in the Southern hemisphere. The Panel also reported the depletion in the vertical distribution of ozone during 1979 and 1985 to maximize near 40 kilometers, from 5 to 12 percent. The decrease over this time period was estimated 4 to 9 percent in response to the increased abundance of trace gases, and only 1 to 3 percent in response to the reduced solar ultraviolet output.

   According to the Panel, there was evidence that natural events had affected this trend significantly. These events include natural cycle geophysical changes such as the annual cycle of the seasons, the quasi-biennial oscillation of the stratospheric winds, the 11-year solar sunspot cycle, and natural effects of irregular transient phenomena, such as the El Niño Southern Oscillation or volcanic eruptions. *Id.* at 11–13, 14–17. For earlier data, *see* 1986 Assessment Report, note 163, at 14–15.

[190] *See* R. W. Watson *et al.*, Ozone Trends Panel Report, *supra* note 168, at 86. *See also* P. Shabecoff, *Antarctic Ozone Loss Is Worsening*, N.Y. Times, Oct. 1, 1987, at 16, col. 4. For a thorough research source, *see* the U.N. Environment Programme's Ozone Secretariat web site, http://ozone.unep.org/new_site/en/index.php.

[191] K. Bowman, *Global Trends in Total Ozone*, 239 Sci. 48 (1988).

[192] E. Shell, *Solo Flights into the Ozone Hole Reveal Its Causes*, Smithsonian, Feb. 1988, at 142, 154 (reported by J. Anderson, Philip S. Weld Professor in Atmospheric Chemistry at Harvard University).

ozone concentrations between 15 and 20 kilometers was over 95 percent compared with their values in August 1987.[193]

In 1988, two reports by scientists, one based on "long-term, ground-based observations,"[194] and the other on total ozone mapping spectrometer (TOMS) data,[195] claimed springtime-level ozone losses during the polar winter as well. Following this disquieting discovery, the authoritative International Ozone Trends Panel,[196] a creation of the National Aeronautics and Space Administration (NASA) in collaboration with other federal agencies and international organizations, including the United Nations Environment Programme (UNEP), reported a global loss of ozone during the previous 17 years.[197] A few months later, in May 1988, a group of scientists at the Polar Ozone Workshop in Snowmass, Colorado, reported the first evidence of ozone destruction in the Arctic.[198] A consensus had emerged in the scientific community that humanly induced chemical change in the stratosphere is responsible, in whole or in part, for the rapid depletion of Antarctic ozone.[199] Then, an Arctic expedition, which operated out of Norway from January 1 to February

---

[193] Ozone Trends Panel Report, *supra* note 168, at 87. Dense stratospheric clouds form in the Antarctic and the ozone hole occurs within the polar vortex because of special conditions there, caused by weather, an isolated air mass, and very cold temperatures, which are prerequisites for perturbed chemistry. The reaction of chlorine under these conditions is especially destructive of ozone. *Id.* Furthermore, scientists found substantial ozone depletion, for compared with October 1979, the monthly mean amount of total ozone concentration at latitudes 50, 60, 70, and 80 degrees south in October 1987 was about 8 percent, 20 percent, 40 percent, and 50 percent lower, respectively. *Id.* It was estimated that during spring, there was now a 15-percent ozone depletion in southern Chile and Argentina in 1987 compared with pre-1979 values. J. K. Angell, 13 Geophys. Res. Letters 1240 (1986). According to TOMS data, in 1987 total column ozone had declined since 1979 by over 5 percent at all latitudes south of 60 degrees throughout the year. Ozone Trends Panel Report, *supra* note 168 at 98–99.

[194] *See* R. Kerr, Evidence of Arctic Ozone Destruction, 240 Sci. 1144, 1145 (1988) [hereinafter Kerr, II].

[195] *See* Kerr I, *supra* note 165.

[196] In the fall of 1986 NASA decided to coordinate and sponsor with the Federal Aviation Administration (FAA), the National Oceanic Atmospheric Administration (NOAA), the World Meteorological Organization (WMO) and the United Nations Environment Program (UNEP), a review of all ground-based and satellite-based data on the issue. It established the Ozone Trends Panel, comprising eminent scientists from federal agencies, research institutions, private industry, and universities. Ozone Trends Panel Report, *supra* note 168, at 2.

[197] *Id.* at 4.

[198] *See* Kerr II, *supra* note 194, at 1144. *See also Scientist Fears Hole in Ozone Is Developing Over the Arctic*, N.Y. Times, May 18, 1988, at 10, col. 5; Browne, *New Ozone Threat: Scientists Fear Layer Is Eroding at North Pole*, N.Y. Times, Oct. 11, 1988, at B7, col. 1.

[199] *See* Ozone Trends Panel Report, *supra* note 168, at 3.

15, 1989,[200] confirmed the fear that the unusual, perturbed chemistry found in the Antarctic also occurs in the North Polar stratosphere.[201] It was also considered probable, based upon the existing analyses of global ozone data, that ozone losses would not be confined to the Polar Regions.[202]

Subsequently, in 1993, the UN World Meteorological Organization (WMO) announced that ozone levels over Antarctica depleted sharply in the second and third weeks of August 1993, far earlier than in 1992.[203] The 1992 prediction by NASA scientists that an ozone hole would develop over the Northern Hemisphere, given the high levels of ozone-destroying chemicals, was subsequently borne out.[204] The situation continued to cause concern, as according to an April 2000 report of a European Commission-sponsored study in which NASA participated, there was a 60 percent ozone depletion in the Arctic atmosphere during the 1999–2000 winter.[205] The study also found that "the average or mean 'amounts of column ozone over Europe' were 15 percent below those in the early 1970s."[206]

On the related phenomenon of global warming, in November 1988, a joint intergovernmental panel of UNEP and the WMO considered global warming "the most important environmental concern of our day."[207] Implications of these trends – stratospheric ozone loss and global warming (*see* § 10.3) – are far-reaching.[208] They prompted scientists to further test and refine their

---

[200] P. Shabecoff, *Arctic Expedition Finds Chemical Threat to Ozone*, N.Y. TIMES, Feb. 18, 1989, at 1, col. 3. *See, e.g., Stratospheric Ozone Depletion and CFCs, supra* note 182, at 6 (statement of F. S. Rowland). *See also id.* at 34–41; S. Weisburd, *One Ozone Hole Returns, Another is Found*, 130 SCI. NEWS 215 (1986); *Ozone Hole Found Over Europe*, New Sci., Oct. 6, 1986, at 21.

[201] *Id.*

[202] *Id.*

[203] *Ozone Levels Over Antarctic Region Sharply Reduced in August, WMO Reports*, 16 Int'l Env't Rep. (BNA) 645 (Sept. 8, 1993) [hereinafter Antarctic Region].

[204] *NASA Predicts Ozone Hole over Parts of North*, WASH. TIMES, Feb. 4. 1992, at A-4 [hereinafter Ozone Hole].

[205] *Ozone Depletion*, 23 Int'l Env't Rep. (BNA) 311 (Apr. 12, 2000) (also noting that global warming has affected the increase of depletion).

[206] *Id.* Column ozone is the measurement used to monitor ozone concentrations.

[207] For a brief report on the 30-country panel's November 9–11 meeting in Geneva, *see* 11 Int'l Env't Rep. (BNA) 644 (Dec. 14, 1988).

[208] INTERGOVERNMENTAL PANEL ON CLIMATE CHANGE (IPCC), CLIMATE CHANGE: THE IPCC SCIENTIFIC ASSESSMENT, at xi (J. T. Houghton *et al.* eds., 1990); IPCC, 1992 IPCC Supplement 6, 25 (1992) (reaffirming the 1990 report, but noting the net rate of global warming is likely to be less than predicted in 1990).

models and theories,[209] and challenged decisionmakers to explore policy options with an unprecedented urgency.[210]

Data collected in 2001 from the TOMS/NASA satellite instruments showed that the ozone hole over Chile and Argentina was approximately 26 million square kilometers,[211] compared with two million square kilometers in 1981.[212] Earlier, in 1998, the WMO had reported that the ozone layer deficiency over latitudes 60 degrees south and lower was 25 percent greater than the average for the 1990s.[213] According to a 1998 Greek study, the ozone layer above Greece diminished by 10 percent between 1990 and 1998.[214] Environment Canada reported that ozone layers in the Canadian Arctic in March 1997 were 45 percent below normal values expected at that time of the year.[215] Also, NASA announced in 1997 that the Arctic had holes in its stratospheric layer like the Antarctic.[216]

Predictions of future ozone loss varied, depending upon the chemical and atmospheric models used.[217] However, between 1969 and 1987, such depletions at northern mid-latitudes were two to three times greater than those predicted.[218] Consequently, while scientists were uncertain what the global ramifications of the Antarctic ozone hole might be, decisionmakers had to weigh the risk of inadequate action, which in the long view might be very costly, against taking strong measures while scientific assessment continued. This use of the precautionary principle in the Montreal Protocol was exemplary. Without the action taken under the Protocol, UNEP has estimated that by 2050 ozone depletion would have increased by at least 50 percent

---

[209] *See generally* R. Kerr, *Is the Greenhouse Here?* 239 Sci. 559, 561 (1988).

[210] In the 100th Congress, two related bills were introduced in the U.S. Senate: Senate Bill 2663/2666, entitled the "Global Environment Protection Act of 1988," introduced on July 27, 1988, by Senators Stafford, Baucus, Chafee, Durenberger, and Gore (S. Res. 2663, 2666, 100th Cong., 2d Sess., 134 Cong. Rec. S 10 112, 10282 (1988)) [hereinafter Stafford Bill], and Senate Bill 2667, to establish a national energy policy to reduce global warming and for other purposes, introduced on July 28, 1988, by Senators Wirth, Johnston, Bumpers, Fowler, Matsunaga, Pell, Melcher, Sanford, Gore, Stafford, Baucus, Chafee, Danforth, Bingham, Inouye, Heinz, Eans, and Harkin, (S. Res. 2667, *id.* at S10282 (1988)) [hereinafter Wirth Bill]. In the 101st Congress, several more bills on the topic were introduced. For further developments, *see infra* § 10.2.9.2.

[211] *Ozone Depletion*, 24 Int'l Env't Rep. (BNA) 1104 (Dec. 5, 2001).

[212] *Ozone Depletion*, 21 Int'l Env't Rep. (BNA) 961 (Sept. 30, 1998).

[213] *Climate Change*, 22 Int'l Env't Rep. (BNA) 14 (Jan. 6, 1999).

[214] *Ozone Depletion*, 21 Int'l Env't Rep. (BNA) 636 (June 24, 1998).

[215] 20 Int'l Env't Rep. (BNA) 365 (Apr. 18, 1997).

[216] 20 Int'l Env't Rep. (BNA) 655 (June 11, 1997).

[217] *See* Ozone Trends Panel Report, *supra* note 168, at 103–27. A WMO/UNEP study does not expect Ozone recovery until the middle of the 21st century. *Ozone Depletion*, 21 Int'l Env't Rep. (BNA) 624 (June 24, 1998).

[218] Ozone Trends Panel Report, *supra* note 168, at 103.

in the northern hemisphere's mid-latitudes and 70 percent in the southern mid-latitudes, which is about ten times worse than current levels.[219] UNEP estimates that the implications of inaction would have included 19 million more cases of non-melanoma cancer, 1.5 million more of melanoma cancer, and 130 million more cases of eye cataracts.[220]

10.2.4   Long-Term Consequences

Depletion in the total column of stratospheric ozone – the amount of ozone found throughout the world – allows harmful solar ultraviolet radiation to penetrate to the surface of the Earth, since ozone is the only gas in the atmosphere to provide a barrier to such radiation.[221] Additionally, changes in vertical distribution of atmospheric ozone contribute to regional and perhaps global climatic changes.[222] Consequently, unless a proper balance of stratospheric ozone is maintained, adverse effects on human and animal health,[223] and harmful effects on plants[224] and aquatic systems[225] are likely to result from ultraviolet radiation exposure at the earth's surface.[226]

---

[219] *Backgrounder – Basic Facts and Data on the Science and Politics of Ozone Protection*, September 2008, at §4, http://ozone.unep.org/Events/ozone_day_2009/press_back grounder.pdf [hereinafter Backgrounder].

[220] *Id.*

[221] *See* J. Frederick, The Ultraviolet Radiation Environment of the Biosphere, 1986 Ozone and Climate Study, *supra* note 164, at 121.

[222] *See* J. Hansen *et al.*, The Greenhouse Effect: Projections of Global Climate Change, 1986 Ozone And Climate Study, *supra* note 164, at 199.

[223] *See, e.g.*, U.S. Environmental Protection Agency, Ultraviolet Radiation and Melanoma (Office of Air and Radiation, 1987). *See* Frederick, *supra* note 221, at 121; E. Emmett, *Health Effects of Ultraviolet Radiation*, 1986 Ozone and Climate Study, *supra* note 164, at 129; M. Waxler, *Ozone Depletion and Ocular Risks From Ultraviolet Radiation*, 1986 Ozone and Climate Study, *supra* note 164, at 147.

[224] *See* A. Teramura, *Overview of Our Current State of Knowledge of UV Effects on Plants*, 1986 Ozone and Climate Study, *supra* note 164, at 165.

[225] *See* R. C. Worrest, *The Effect of Solar UV-13 Radiation on Aquatic Systems: An Overview*, 1986 Ozone and Climate Study, *supra* note 164, at 175.

[226] Ultraviolet (UV) radiation is usually divided into three wave bands, UV-A, UV-B, and UV-C. While UV-A is not carcinogenic at usual levels of exposure, it causes most photosensitive reactions; that is, it exacerbates the symptoms of a number of skin diseases from sun exposure in those who are excessively sensitive to UV radiation. These diseases include infectious diseases such as herpes simplex, altered metabolic states, nutritional deficiency states, and some hereditary genetic and immunologically mediated diseases. Although UV-A is not absorbed by ozone, it is reflected back to space, away from the Earth's surface. UV-C, which can cause skin and eye cancers and skin inflammations, is at present absorbed almost entirely by stratospheric ozone. *See* E. Emmett, Health Effects of Ultraviolet Radiation, 1986 Ozone and Climate Study, *supra* note 164, 1 at 129–30, 137–38. UV-B is at present partially absorbed by ozone, and its exposure is of greatest

Along with potential increased incidence of skin cancer as an area of major concern, changes caused by long-term exposure to UV radiation in the cornea, ocular lens, and retina are three main areas of concern for adverse effects on the eye.[227] In 1999 it was reported that the WHO would study the impact of ozone depletion and resulting increased ultraviolet radiation on reducing the effectiveness of human vaccinations because of likely suppressive effects of ultraviolet radiation on the human immune system.[228] The United States

---

concern since it is usually responsible for sunburn and skin cancer, and has a potentially adverse effect on the body's immune system. *Stratospheric Ozone Depletion and CFCs, supra* note 182, at 42. Thus, the effectiveness of this shield is likely to be reduced if levels of ozone continue to decline in the future. Although other factors, including exposure to solar radiation, individual susceptibility, personal behavior, and land elevation also influence the nature and gravity of the chronic effects of ultraviolet radiation (*id.* at 5, 126, 143), it is estimated that every 1 percent decrease in total column ozone in the atmosphere results in a 2 percent increase in UV-B radiation, causing in turn a 4 percent increase in nonmelanoma skin cancer. *Id.* at 35, 44; 52 Fed. Reg. 47494 (1987), codified at 40 C.F.R. pt. 82. *See also Ozone Depletion*, 21 Int'l Env't Rep. (BNA) 636 (June 24, 1998) (WMO estimates 3- to 4-percent increase). Thus, lowered ozone levels are likely to result in an increasing number of deaths from skin cancer, as well. A Dutch study reported in 1996 that, without controls on ozone-depleting substances, excess skin cancer cases would have increased about 325 percent in the United States and 315 percent in Northwestern Europe. *See* 19 Int'l Env't Rep. (BNA) 1081 (Nov. 27, 1996) (the study appeared in the journal Nature).

[227] *See* Stratospheric Ozone Depletion and CFCs, *supra* note 182, at 46. Since both UV-B and UV-A are able to penetrate the interior of the eye, they both can damage the eye. Potential health problems include cataracts, stable vertical disorders, retinal degeneration, and aging and developmental disorders. *See* Waxler, *supra* note 223, at 147–48. In the late 1980s it was estimated that the number of cataracts cases for the United States population alive at that time and born by the year 2075, would increase by 18.2 million based upon a moderate growth rate in CFC levels in 1987. 52 Fed. Reg. 47495 (1987). To mitigate the potential carcinogenic effects of increased UV radiation exposure, humans could perhaps take particularly effective measures relying upon medical advancement and adapting their lifestyles to an increased UV intensity by using sunscreen and becoming more aware of the hazards of UV radiation. There are some scientists, however, who consider it unlikely that people will change their lifestyles in response to an increased UV radiation intensity. *See Stratospheric Ozone Depletion and CFCs, supra* note 182, at 46.

[228] *Ozone Depletion*, 22 Int'l Env't Rep. (BNA) 271 (Mar. 31, 1999). After screening about 200 species of plants and different varieties within species, scientists reported in 1986 that two out of every three plants tested showed some degree of UV sensitivity. *See* Teramura, *supra* note 224; Stratospheric Ozone and CFCs, *supra* note 181, at 48–49. UV-irradiated plants suffer from reduced leaf areas, plant stunting, a reduction in total dry weight of the plant, and increased plant diseases. *See* Teramura, *supra* note 224, at 170. Harmful effects of UV-B radiation on marine organisms and the marine food web include damage to fish larvae and juveniles, shrimp larvae, crab larvae, and other small animals and plants which are essential to sustain the marine food chain. Zooplankton, tiny animals that drift in water and live primarily close to the surface of the water, would be exposed to UV radiation. Similarly, phytoplankton, tiny drifting plants that live near the water's surface in order

Environmental Protection Agency's statement of December 14, 1987, provides an apt conclusion:

> Based on the WMO's assessment and EPA's recently completed risk assessment, the Agency believes that the current rate of growth in atmospheric levels of ozone-depleting gases is likely to result in substantial depletion of ozone which would lead to significant harm to human health and the environment.[229]

The conclusion of a 1991 EPA study that ozone loss over the northern-mid-latitudes was twice as great as previously estimated, supporting the notion that ozone depletion is occurring globally, rather than in an isolated region over Antarctica,[230] has subsequently been confirmed.[231]

10.2.5   *Policy Implications*

The ozone hole has presented a unique set of challenges to decision-makers. As scientists have found that atmospheric concentrations of ozone-modifying gases are on the rise, and since the emissions from CFCs and halons liberate chlorine atoms in the stratosphere through chemical actions with UV radiation and cause ozone depletion, policymakers have had no option but to regulate the manufacture and use of ozone-depleting chemicals.

---

to promote photosynthesis, would be exposed. Since almost every aquatic species relies directly or indirectly on either of these two plants for food, the food chain would be broken without these two planktons and the higher species which depend upon them for food would starve, thereby beginning the cycle of starvation through the aquatic food chain. Phytoplanktons and zooplanktons would probably swim deeper under water to escape the UV radiation, and since they are dependent upon sunlight, the likelihood is that they would grow less and thus would be of less nutritional value. *See* Worrest, *supra* note 225, at 179–83; *Stratospheric Ozone Depletion and CFCs, supra* note 182, at 47; 52 Fed. Reg. 47495 (1987). The long-term result could be an unstable ecosystem and an adverse effect on higher levels of the food chain, such as shellfish and finfish. *See Stratospheric Ozone Depletion and CFCs, supra* note 182, at 47. *See also Research*, 22 Int'l Env't Rep. (BNA) 816 (Sept. 21, 1999) (Argentine study on the adverse impact of ozone loss on aquatic environments); *Ozone Depletion*, 24 *id.* at 113 (Dec. 5, 2001) (impact on all marine life, including a decline in fish stocks). The conclusion is unavoidable that ozone depletion adversely affects the world's food supplies.

[229] 52 Fed. Reg. 47495 (1987).

[230] R. A. Kerr, *Ozone Destruction Worsens*, 252 Sci. 204 (1991).

[231] *See supra* notes 156–57; *see also* EU, *NASA Report Severe Losses of Stratospheric Ozone in Arctic*, 23 Int'l Env't Rep. (BNA) 311 (Apr. 12, 2000) (noting also the impact of global warming as an unanticipated factor in the depletion of Arctic stratospheric ozone); *but see Ozone Depletion in Northern Hemisphere Less than Earlier Years, U.N. Agency [World Meteorological Organization] Says*, 24 Int'l Env't Rep. 357 (May 9, 2001) (noting cause was "seasonal," not attributable to the efforts being made to reduce ozone-depleting emissions).

Emissions of CFCs (CFC-11, -12 and -13) increased during the 1970s and 1980s. CFC-11 is used primarily as a foam-blowing agent and CFC-12 as a refrigerant in the United States; both are used as aerosol propellants abroad; and CFC13 is used primarily as a solvent by the electronics and metal cleaning industries. These chemicals have extremely long atmospheric lifetimes (about 75 years for CFC-11 and about 120 years for CFC-12).[232] Thus, it was clear that the existing atmospheric levels of CFCs would decrease very slowly, even if emissions were reduced considerably, because the long lifetimes of these chemicals ensure that they will continue to be added to the atmosphere much faster than they are destroyed. It was estimated that (other things being equal, such as atmospheric temperatures) it would take an immediate 85-percent emissions reduction to stabilize CFC and ozone concentrations.[233]

Crucial questions for policymakers were on the nature of regulations on the manufacture and use of ozone-depleting chemicals and the efficacy of their implementation. A detailed discussion of these questions follows (in § 10.2.8.1–8.2). In a summary fashion, however, it should be noted that the drafting of the 1985 Vienna Convention[234] and subsequently the 1987 Montreal Protocol[235] attest to the selection of a formal multilateral treaty route as appropriate to accomplish the objective of bringing about emissions reduction. Furthermore, the 1990 London Amendments[236] and 1992 Copenhagen Amendments[237] evidence a continued reliance upon treaties to regulate emissions by creating a more stringent regulatory regime.

The treaty route was appropriate for prescribing control measures on both production and consumption of selected chemicals,[238] because the problem could not have been addressed effectively in an informal manner through measures such as information exchanges and technical aid. However, even before the entry into force of the 1985 and 1987 measures, they were found wanting in their ability to prevent further ozone depletion.[239] The subsequent 1990 and 1992 amendments to the Montreal Protocol were made to remedy

---

[232] *See Stratospheric Ozone Depletion and CFCs, supra* note 182, at 5 (Statement of F. S. Rowland).

[233] *See* U.S. ENVIRONMENTAL PROTECTION AGENCY, AN ASSESSMENT OF THE RISKS OF STRATOSPHERIC MODIFICATION (Office of Air and Radiation, 1986).

[234] *See* Vienna Ozone Convention, *supra* note 158.

[235] *See* Montreal Protocol, *supra* note 159.

[236] *See* London Amendment, *supra* note 171.

[237] *See* Copenhagen Amendment, *supra* note 172.

[238] *See infra* §§ 10.2.8.1 and 10.2.8.2.

[239] Under the Protocol, parties decide about further adjustments and reductions in production and consumption of the controlled substances, if necessary. Montreal Protocol, *supra* note 159, art. 2, ¶ 9.

this and prevent further ozone depletion by targeting an increased number of substances, especially CFCs, for a complete phaseout.[240] These amendments also advanced many of the deadlines established in the Montreal Protocol.[241] Lastly, these amendments added new ozone-depleting compounds to the list of controlled substances. Thus, the international community recognized at least some of the weaknesses in the Montreal Protocol and acted rather quickly to make it a more effective tool to slow, and eventually stop, ozone depletion. Of course, the control measures provide built-in flexibility to address special situations, such as those of developing countries, and are susceptible to manipulation by the parties.[242]

Implementation in the international arena always raises difficult questions. In the setting of a multilateral convention – even when the prescriptions are unambiguous and parties are clearly aware of their obligations and rights as well as of the available remedies under the agreement – how is the international community to ensure effective implementation? The first requirement, of course, is that there be wide ratification of the instrument. The second is that an effective institutional structure be in place to inform, to oversee and monitor, to invoke and apply the norms, and to provide the available remedies. The third is that appropriate procedures be established in order to provide reasonable access to those who seek a remedy under the agreement. The fourth is that there be sufficient incentives and penalties to encourage observance. The fifth requirement is that there be a compulsory dispute-settlement mechanism provided under the agreement.

As the following discussion will show, some of these requirements were met under the Montreal Protocol, while others were addressed in the subsequent amendments. Other problems have yet to be resolved completely. For instance, at their first meeting after the Protocol went into effect in 1989, the parties agreed to establish institutional mechanisms and procedures in order to determine non-compliance.[243] An interim noncompliance procedure was not established until the second meeting, at which time the London Amendments were made. This interim noncompliance procedure was still seen as inadequate to oversee and enforce the Protocol's control measures.[244] The current procedure, which will be discussed below, seems to be working.

---

[240] *See generally* D. M. Friedland & D. G. Isaacs, *Worldwide Community Takes Action on Ozone*, NAT'L L.J., June 14, 1993, at 30.

[241] *Id.*

[242] *See* Montreal Protocol, *supra* note 159, at art. 5.

[243] *Id.* art. 8.

[244] *See generally* I. H. Rowlands, *The Fourth Meeting of the Partners to the Montreal Protocol: Report and Reflection*, 35 ENV'T 25 (1993).

The amendments to the Protocol – the 1990 London Amendments, the 1992 Copenhagen Amendments, the 1997 Montreal Amendments, and the 1999 Beijing Amendments – added new substances to the list of ozone-depleting compounds regulated under the treaty, and require greater reductions in a shorter time. The amendments, however, retain exceptions for developing nations and "essential use" substances.[245] Another equally critical question is whether the policy undertaken has provided the needed incentives for the development and deployment of safe chemicals as replacements and substitutes for CFCs, halons, and other ODSs. One observation is clear: the evolution of international treaties that address ozone depletion is driven by scientific data, which has steadily revealed a genuine threat to the world community. With each new revelation, the nations of the world are increasingly willing to create a more stringent system to reduce the level of ODSs. Fortunately, the agreements addressing ozone depletion have proven to be flexible enough for the international community to take action in response to new scientific data.

10.2.6   *Prior to the 1985 Vienna Convention*

As discussed earlier (*see* Chapters 1 and 4) the horizontal nature of the world community, which generally lacks a centralized authority to prescribe norms, is reflected in a lack of effective international norms and mechanisms to address questions of the global environment, especially its management.[246] The first major international effort to remedy this situation, the 1972 UN Conference on the Human Environment, adopted the Stockholm Declaration. Three principles contained in the Declaration are of special note for the present discussion.

Principle 21 is a clear enunciation of a state's "responsibility to ensure that activities within...[its] jurisdiction or control do not cause damage to the environment of other States or of areas beyond the limits of national jurisdiction."[247] Principle 22 obligates states to cooperate in the further development of international environmental law on "liability and compensation" for victims of transnational pollution and other environmental damage. Principle 6 explicitly refers to the emission of substances such as CFCs: "The discharge of toxic substances and the release of heat, in such quantities and concentrations as to exceed the capacity of the environment to render them

---

[245] *See, e.g.*, Copenhagen Amendment, *supra* note 172, at annex 11, arts. 2C–2E.
[246] *See generally* UNEP Rep. No. 2, *supra* note 187, at 5–6.
[247] *See generally* L. B. Sohn, *The Stockholm Declaration of the Human Environment*, 14 Harv. Int'l L.J. 423, 485–93 (1973) (discussing this principle thoroughly).

harmless, must be halted in order to ensure that serious or irreversible damage is not inflicted upon ecosystems."[248]

Several pertinent recommendations made at Stockholm, especially those related to "[i]dentification and control of pollutants of broad international significance,"[249] are noteworthy. Governments are asked to "[c]arefully evaluate the likelihood and magnitude of climatic effects and disseminate their findings to the maximum extent feasible before" undertaking polluting activities, and to "[c]onsult fully other interested States when activities carrying a risk of...effects [on climate] are being contemplated or implemented."[250] Also, in another recommendation, the international community is asked to support large-scale testing programs "for evaluation of the environmental impact potential of specific contaminants or products,"[251] and a monitoring program to study "long-term global trends in atmospheric constituents and properties which may cause changes in meteorological properties, including climatic changes."[252] Under the auspices of UNEP, which was established pursuant to the Stockholm Conference and has functioned as a catalyst, international efforts initially were launched to address the ozone depletion problem.[253]

The Conference Principles and Recommendations spurred further action by UNEP,[254] and state governments,[255] as well as regional organizations.[256] In 1974, the Organization for Economic Cooperation and Development

---

[248] Stockholm Declaration, *supra* note 41 principle 6.

[249] *Id.* at 1449–53 (recommendations 70–85).

[250] *Id.* at 1449 (recommendation 70).

[251] *Id.* at 1450 (recommendation 74 (d)(ii)).

[252] *Id.* at 1452 (recommendation 79(a)).

[253] *See Stratospheric Ozone Depletion and CFCs, supra* note 182, at 57 (statement of Dr. Mostafa K. Tolba, then Executive Director, UNEP).

[254] *See generally* Peter Sand, *Environmental Law in the United Nations Environment Programme, Hague Academy of International Law/UN University, in* The Future of the International Law of the Environment 51 (R. Dupuy ed., 1985).

[255] *See generally Ten Years After Stockholm – International Environmental Law*, 77 Proc. Am. Soc'y Int'l L. 411–35 (1983). State interest in environmental issues was enhanced after Stockholm. *Id.* at 412. *Developments, The United Nations Environmental Programme After a Decade: The Nairobi Session of a Special Character, May 1981*, 12 DENV. J. INT'L L. & POL'Y 269 (1983); H. Wood, *The United Nations World Charter for Nature: The Developing Nations' Initiative to Establish Protections of the Environment*, 12 Ecology L.Q. 977 (1985). For another survey of environmental laws of a few selected countries in the EEC, Japan and Mexico, *see* T. Smith & R. Falzone, *Foreign Environmental Legal Systems – A Brief Review*, 11 Int'l Env't Rep. (BNA) 621 (Nov. 9, 1988).

[256] For example, in 1973, the European Economic Community adopted its own program of action on the environment. *See Declaration on the Environmental Action Program*, 16 O.J. Eur. Comm. (NO. C 112) 1 (1973), reprinted in 13 I.L.M. 164 (1974).

(OECD) adopted principles concerning transfrontier air pollution.[257] And in 1979, the UN Economic Commission for Europe (UN/ECE) succeeded in achieving the adoption of the Convention on Long-Range Transboundary Air Pollution at Geneva.[258]

In 1976, the International Law Commission adopted its Draft Articles on State Responsibility.[259] One article defined the breach of an international obligation that is essential for the protection and preservation of the human environment – such as obligations that prohibit massive pollution of the atmosphere or of the seas – as an international crime.[260] The Commission continues to develop rules of international environmental law. Among scholarly organizations, the work of the International Law Association[261] and the American Law Institute deserves special mention.

The major significance of these developments is that, in addition to the establishment of substantive norms of international environmental law on specific issues such as transboundary air pollution,[262] marine pollution,[263]

---

[257] This included the principles of notification and consultation; equal access to foreign nationals to seek administrative and judicial remedies as to the state's subjects; and non-discrimination, which requires states to control transboundary pollution as stringently as pollution remaining within the state. *See generally* OECD, A TENTATIVE ANALYSIS OF SOME DATA CONCERNING LONG-RANGE TRANSPORT OF AIR POLLUTANTS IN EUROPE 58 (1978), OECD Doc. ENV/TFP/78; OECD, *Legal Aspect of Transfrontier Pollution* (1977); OECD, *The Polluter Pays Principle* (1975); OECD, *Environmental Policies for the 1980s* (1980); OECD, *Non-Discrimination in Relation to Transfrontier Pollution: Leading OECD Documents* 35 (1978) (on financing the monitoring and evaluation of air pollutants in Europe).

[258] The Convention obligates contracting parties to consult upon request concerning activities affecting or posing a "significant risk" of long-range transboundary air pollution, and provides for information exchange and continued monitoring of pollutants, as well as collaborative research toward the objective of mitigating sulfur dioxide emissions. *See generally* G. Wetstone & A. Rosencranz, *Transboundary Air Pollution: The Search for an International Response*, 8 HARV. ENVTL. L. REV. 89, 100–106 (1986); Protocol to the 1979 Convention on Long-Range Transboundary Air Pollution, on Financing the Monitoring and Evaluation of Air Pollutants in Europe, arts. 4–7, 9, Sept. 28, 1984, reprinted in 24 I.L.M. 484 (1985).

[259] ILC Draft Articles on State Responsibility, 31 U.N. GAOR Supp. (No. 10) at 170, U.N. Doc. A/31/10 (1976), reprinted in 2 Y.B. INT'L L. COMM'N 73 (1976), U.N. Doc. A/CN.4/Ser.A/ I 976/Add. 1.

[260] *Id.* art. 19(3)(d).

[261] *See, e.g., Legal Aspects of Long-Distance Air Pollution*, INT'L L. ASS'N 198 (1987) (Report of the Sixty-Second Conference at Seoul); *see also Water Resources Law*, INT'L L. ASS'N at 231.

[262] *See* § 10.1.

[263] *See* Chapter 11. *See generally* RESTATEMENT, *supra* note 251, at §§ 603–604 (1987); UN Convention on the Law of the Sea, Dec. 10, 1982, at arts. 192–237, reprinted in 21 I.L.M. 1261 (1982); The Law of the Sea, official text of the United Nations Convention on the

and utilization of international waters,[264] several procedural norms emerged which have been gaining general acceptance. These include a state's duty to cooperate, to notify, to exchange information, to consult and negotiate regarding activities on its territory which may have extraterritorial environmental effects,[265] and the emerging regime of equal right of access and non-discrimination under OECD guidelines.[266]

10.2.7   *The 1985 Vienna Ozone Convention*

Eventually, in March 1985, a diplomatic conference adopted the Vienna Convention for the Protection of the Ozone Layer.[267] Recalling Principle 21 of the UN Conference on the Human Environment and UNEP's World Plan of Action on the Ozone Layer,[268] the Convention promoted the global cooperation necessary in order to protect the ozone layer. It established a framework for concerted action in the future, while limiting itself to providing general measures for international cooperation in research, monitoring, and information exchange. No concrete obligations were undertaken by states to limit the production or use of ODSs, but the Convention envisaged further

---

Law of the Sea with Annexes and Index (UN Sales No. E.83 V.5 (1983); V. Nanda, *Protection of the Internationally Shared Environment and the United Nations Convention on the Law of the Sea, in* Consensus and Confrontation: The United States and the Law Of The Sea Convention 403 (J. Van Dyke ed., 1985).

[264] *See* Chapter 9.

[265] *See generally* OECD, *OECD and the Environment* 106–26 (1979); G.A. Res. 2995, 27 U.N. GAOR Supp. (No. 30) 42 (1972); U.N. Doc. A/CN. 4/402, para. 14 (1986) (Report of J. Barboza to the International Law Commission.); UN Survey of State Practice Relevant to International Liability for Injurious Consequences Arising Out of Acts Not Prohibited by International Law 180–182, U.N. Doc. A/CN.4/394 (1984); M. Bothe, *Transfrontier Environmental Management, in* International Union – For Conservation of Nature and Natural Resources, Trends in Environmental Policy and Law 391 (1980); OECD, *Recommendations of the Council on Water Management Policies and Instruments*, Paris, Apr. 5, 1978. No. 7, OECD Doc. C. (78) 4 (Final); M. Bothe, *International Legal Problems of Industrial Siting in Border Areas and National Environmental Policies, in* OECD, Transfrontier Pollution and the Role Of States 79, 85–92, 95–97 (1981).

[266] *See, e.g.*, OECD, Recommendation of the Council for Implementation of Regime of Equal Right of Access and Non-Discrimination in Relation to Transfrontier Pollution, May 17, 1977, OECD Doc. C (77) 28 (Final (1977) (*see especially* Annex, Introduction, subpara. (a)); OECD, OECD and the Environment 115–116 (1979); OECD, 1974 Recommendation for Equal Right of Access in Relation to Transfrontier Pollution, OECD Doc. C(76) 55 (1976); Scandinavian Convention on the Protection of the Environment, 1974, art. 11, reprinted in 13 I.L.M. 591, 595 (1974). 257 Vienna Ozone Convention, *supra* note 158; UNEP, U.N. Doc. UNEP/IG 53/3,4 and 5/Rev. 1 (1985).

[267] Vienna Ozone Convention, *supra* note 158.

[268] *Id.* preamble.

negotiations and adoption of necessary international regulatory measures in the future.

Thus, although the Vienna Ozone Convention did not specify strategies, the parties would be obligated to cooperate in several ways: (1) by adopting appropriate legislative and administrative measures; (2) "in harmonizing appropriate policies" to control, limit, reduce, or prevent human activities under their jurisdiction that adversely affect the ozone layer; (3) "in the formulation of agreed [implementation] measures, procedures, and standards"; and (4) by working "with competent international bodies to implement effectively this Convention and protocols to which they are party."[269] The parties also undertook the obligation "to initiate and cooperate in, directly or through competent international bodies, the conduct of research and scientific assessments" on processes that may affect the ozone layer and on effects of modifications of the ozone layer.[270] Similarly, the parties agreed to promote or establish joint or complementary programs "for systematic observation of the state of the ozone layer," and to cooperate "in ensuring the collection, validation and transmission of research and observational data...in a regular and timely fashion."[271]

Other obligations include those to cooperate in the legal, scientific, and technical fields,[272] and to transmit pertinent information on the measures adopted by them in implementation of the Convention[273] to the Conference of the Parties, which was established under the Convention.[274] The Convention also established a secretariat[275] and a dispute settlement procedure, which includes negotiation, good offices, mediation, and conciliation, but does not obligate parties to resort to arbitration or litigation before the International Court of Justice if a settlement is not reached through negotiation or mediation.[276]

Although the Vienna Ozone Convention failed to provide for controls on the manufacture or use of ODSs, it was a promising first step, for it signified that the world community realized that it had to respond to this environmental challenge promptly – before any actual damage occurred. The remarks of Mostafa K. Tolba, then Executive Director of UNEP, are pertinent:

---

[269] *Id.* art. 2, ¶ 2.
[270] *Id.* art. 3, ¶ 1.
[271] *Id.* art. 3, ¶¶ 2–3.
[272] *Id.* art. 4.
[273] *Id.* art. 5.
[274] *Id.* art. 6.
[275] *Id.* art. 7.
[276] *Id.* art. 11.

This is the first global convention to address an issue that for the time being seems far in the future and is of unknown proportions. This Convention, as I see it, is the essence of the anticipatory response so many environmental issues call for: to deal with the threat of the problem before we have to deal with the problem itself.[277]

The period between the signing of the Vienna Ozone Convention and the adoption of the Montreal Protocol was still marked by a continuing debate on whether CFCs and trace gases were responsible for the depletion of ozone, or if such depletion could be attributed to natural atmospheric variations.[278] Those who believed in the dynamic theory of the ozone hole continued to argue that there was still uncertainty as to the effects of chlorine in the stratosphere.[279] Studies and further negotiations continued in the meantime.[280]

In 1986, the USEPA released a report on an assessment of the risks of stratospheric modification.[281] Then, at a Senate hearing in May 1987, David Doniger, Senior Attorney at the Natural Resources Defense Council, stated:

We should all remember that the 95% phase-down policy [for CFCs and 2 halons in 10–14 years] was developed on the basis of a broad scientific analysis, but without taking into account such phenomena as the passive and unexpected Antarctic ozone hole. As Ambassador Richard Benedick [chief US negotiator] stated at a CFC conference on March 25, "We have simply excluded that disturbing phenomenon from our equations." Now, however, scientists from the National Ozone Expedition who have directly investigated the causes of the Antarctic hole have testified that it is probably linked to CFC's. While many scientific issues remain to be explored, these developments reinforce an inevitability of the 95% phase-down policy for policymakers with any sense of prudence in the face of potentially catastrophic global consequences.[282]

---

[277] Excerpt from Dr. Tolba's statement at the Vienna Convention, reprinted in Sands, *supra* note 186, at 20.

[278] *See generally* Taubes & Chen, *supra* note 187, at 68–69.

[279] *See, e.g., Stratospheric Ozone Depletion and CFCs, supra* note 182, at 36–37 (statement of A. Tuck, Environmental Research Laboratories, National Oceanic and Atmospheric Administration, U.S. Department of Commerce).

[280] *See Nowhere to Hide, supra* note 187; *Stratospheric Ozone Depletion and CFCs, supra* note 182, at 472 (statement of L. M. Thomas, administrator EPA), 475 (statement of R. Benedick, Deputy Assistant Secretary for Environment, Health, and Natural Resources, Department of State), 477 (statement of A. Calio, Undersecretary of Commerce for Oceans and the Atmosphere, Department of Commerce); EPA, EFFECTS OF CHANGES IN STRATOSPHERIC OZONE AND GLOBAL CLIMATE (1986); R. Benedick, *International Efforts to Protect the Stratospheric Ozone Layer, in* CURRENT POLICY No. 931 (U.S. Dep't State, Mar. 1987).

[281] U.S. Environmental Protection Agency, *An Assessment of the Risks of Stratospheric Modification* (Office of Air and Radiation 1986).

[282] *Stratospheric Ozone Depletion and CFCs, supra* note 182, at 431, 433–34.

Eventually, with the active participation and support of the United States, UNEP's efforts paid off – the negotiations culminated in the adoption of the Montreal Protocol.[283]

10.2.8   *The 1987 Montreal Protocol and Subsequent Amendments*

On September 16, 1987, 24 states signed the Montreal Protocol on Substances that Deplete the Ozone Layer, which expanded the purpose of the Vienna Convention by upholding a state's obligation "to take appropriate measures to protect human health and the environment against adverse effects resulting or likely to result from human activities which modify or are likely to modify the ozone layer."[284] The recognition of scientific uncertainty reflected in the phrases "likely to result" and "likely to modify" emphasizes the position that preventive action must be taken in order to avert continued ozone depletion. The basis for such action must be the existing state of scientific knowledge, with sufficient flexibility to change if dictated by future scientific data.[285]

This scientific data – including a WMO report stating that "the 1991–1992 winter [could] be classified among those with the most negative deviation of systematic ozone observations" – led to subsequent amendments to the original Protocol.[286] The amendments to the Montreal Protocol took advantage of the assumption that the regulatory regime created under the Montreal Protocol would be modified as scientific data progressed. It should be noted at the outset, however, that while no limits were placed on any of the controlled substances that are specified in the Protocol, a separate limit was placed on the total ozone depletion caused by a group of controlled substances[287] that a party may produce and consume. Of course, if the "group" consists of only one controlled substance, it is in effect limited to a single compound.[288] These

---

[283] *See* J. Negroponte, *Montreal Protocol: Controlling Substances that Deplete the Ozone Layer*, 87 Dep't St. Bull., Dec. 1987, at 60, 61–62.

[284] Montreal Protocol, *supra* note 159, Preamble (emphasis added to highlight the addition to the Preamble of the Vienna Convention).

[285] *See id.* art. 2, ¶¶ 9–10, art. 6 (sufficient flexibility is provided).

[286] World Meteorological Organization, *On the State of the Ozone Layer in 1992*, UNEP/OzL. Pro.4/lnf2, pt. 6 (Nairobi, 1992).

[287] These ozone-depleting potentials are estimates based on existing knowledge and will be reviewed and revised periodically. *Id.* Annex A. Different CFCs have different depletion levels. CFC-11 and CFC-12 have been assigned an ozone depletion level of 1.0. All other controlled substances have an ozone depletion level that corresponds with CFC11 and CFC-12 depletion levels. Thus, a level less than 1.0 would have lower depletion effects than CFC-11 or CFC-12.

[288] *See, e.g.*, Copenhagen Amendment, *supra* note 172, annex III, art. 2H (regulating methyl bromide).

controlled substances are classified and enumerated in tables attached to the Protocol as annexes.[289] It was up to each party to determine how it would remain within the limits established in the Protocol and its amendments.

10.2.8.1   *Control Measures*

The basic order of the control measures created under the Montreal Protocol was first to place a cap on each party's production and consumption of CFCs and halons at their respective 1986 levels of production and consumption.[290] Then a control schedule called for a 20-percent reduction, and eventually a 50-percent reduction of consumption and production of CFCs and halons based on each party's 1986 levels. The 1990 London Amendments built upon the control measure framework created under the original Protocol, mandating greater reductions of CFCs and halons, and eventually their complete elimination by 2000. The base level is calculated on 1989 levels under the London Amendments and 1992 Copenhagen Amendments, rather than 1986 levels, for all controlled substances newly added to the annexes. Under the amendments, however, the base level year for CFCs and halons remained 1986.

These amendments added new compounds to the list of controlled substances – the London Amendments added methyl chloroform, carbon tetrachloride, and a further range of CFCs – and the Copenhagen Amendments added hydrochlorofluorocarbons (HCFCs), hydrobromofluorocarbons (HBFCs), and methyl bromide to the phaseout schedules, as well as accelerated phaseout schedules for substances already controlled and greater reductions at a faster rate than the original Protocol. Finally, the amendments strive for an eventual zero level of production and consumption.

The 1997 Montreal Amendment,[291] which entered into force November 10, 1999,[292] obligated parties to establish licensing systems for international trade in ODSs – CFCs, halons, carbon tetrachloride, methyl chloroform, HCFCs, HBFCs, and methyl bromide. The purpose was primarily to address the challenge of growing illegal trade in controlled substances. The Amendment also banned the import or export of ethyl bromide from states not parties to the Amendments. And the 1999 Beijing Amendments, which entered into force

---

[289] The Montreal Protocol included only Annex A, but the 1990 London Amendments added Annexes B and C. London Amendment, *supra* note 171, 30 I.L.M. at 552–53. The Copenhagen Amendment replaced Annex C and added Annex E. Copenhagen Amendment, *supra* note 172.

[290] Montreal Protocol, *supra* note 159, art. 2, paras. 1, 2.

[291] *See Amendment Considered to Restrict Trade in Methyl Bromide, List Solvent for Phaseout,* 25 Int'l Env't Rep. (BNA) 522 (May 22, 2002) [hereinafter Amendments Considered].

[292] *See Ozone Depletion,* 22 Int'l Env't Rep. (BNA) 707 (Sept. 1, 1999).

February 25, 2002,[293] further tightened the controls on production levels of HCFCs, revised controls on their consumption, and banned the production, consumption and international trade of bromochloromethane.

A multilateral fund to provide financial and technical assistance to developing country parties was also established in 1992. At several of the annual meetings of the parties, at which decisions are made on amending the Protocol and adjusting its control schedules, adjustments were also made to the control measures, thus accelerating the schedules for phasing out ODSs.[294]

There are several exceptions created under the Protocol and subsequent amendments. For instance, one exception allows for a 10-percent, and sometimes 15-percent, increase in production based upon 1986 levels, in order to satisfy the basic domestic needs of developing countries specially identified under the Protocol. The subsequent amendments also allowed developing nations to exceed their 1989 production levels by up to 10 percent,[295] and sometimes 15 percent,[296] depending on the substance and phaseout schedule. In addition, the Copenhagen Amendments made another exception, whereby the parties may agree to permit a higher level of production or consumption if they deem it "essential."[297] This new exception was potentially all-encompassing: the control measures will apply "save to the extent that the Parties decide to permit the level of production or consumption that is necessary to satisfy uses agreed by them to be essential."[298]

Other exceptions to these levels of production under the original Protocol included allowing a party whose 1986 level of production was less than 25 kilotons to transfer or receive production abilities in excess of the limits set for CFCs during any time period for purposes of industrial rationalization, provided that the combined production levels of all parties do not exceed applicable production limits.[299] "Industrial rationalization" is an economic

---

[293] *See Beijing Amendment*, UNEP Ozone Secretariat, http://ozone.unep.org/Ratification_status/beijing_amendment.shtml. *See* Amendments Considered, *supra* note 291.

[294] UNEP, Action on Ozone – 2000 Edition 11 (2000) [hereinafter 2000 Ozone Action].

[295] London Amendment, *supra* note 171, annex I, art. 2B, ¶¶ 1–2.

[296] *Id.* para. 3; Copenhagen Amendment, *supra* note 172, annex I, art. 213, ¶ 2.

[297] Copenhagen Amendment, *supra* note 172, annex I, arts. 2A and 213, annex II, arts. 2C–2E, annex III, art. 2G.

[298] *Id.* It is too early to know exactly what effect the essential use exception will have, but commentators are generally critical of it. *See, e.g.*, Friedland & Isaacs, *supra* note 240, at 31; Rowlands, *supra* note 244.

[299] Montreal Protocol, *supra* note 159, art. 2, ¶ 5. Except for developing countries covered in Article 5, any party which had contracted for or is constructing facilities to produce controlled substances prior to September 16, 1987, and had provided for the same in national legislation prior to January 1, 1987, could add the production capability from such facilities to its 1986 production base level, provided that such facilities were completed by December 31, 1990, and that such production would not raise a party's annual level of

solution which would allow one party to transfer some or all of its level of production to another party in order to achieve economic efficiency or meet anticipated supply shortages as a result of plant closures. Thus, if one party did not use all of its controlled substances production allotment, it could sell its rights to produce the controlled substances to another party, one that already may have reached its production level for controlled substances for a particular year, and wished to produce more.

Thus, a developed country such as the United Kingdom could acquire the production rights of a developing country such as Ghana and produce more CFCs than its allotted quota, insofar as the total does not exceed the applicable production limits of the two countries. Also, if the United Kingdom decided not to produce CFCs any longer, it could transfer its quota to Ghana. Under the London Amendments, the availability of such production transfers was actually broadened by removing the 25 kiloton limitation, thereby allowing "any party" to transfer production.[300] Furthermore, the Copenhagen Amendments added the possibility of consumption transfers for HCFCs.[301] Other exceptions include facilities under construction or contract for production of controlled substances[302] and the manner of implementation of the Protocol by states members of regional economic organizations, such as the European Union.[303] Yet another exception under the original Protocol allowed for a 10-percent increase above 1986 production levels for the purposes of "industrial rationalization" between parties.[304]

---

consumption of the controlled substances above 0.5 kilograms per capita. This provision seems to cater to special interests, such as the then-Soviet Union and other countries with planned economies, so that a nation's or industry's initial investment of financing new production facilities was not lost. It may have led, however, to increases in production capability, which is not what the Protocol was designed to do.

[300] London Amendment, *supra* note 171, annex II, art. 2, ¶ 5.

[301] Copenhagen Amendment, *supra* note 172, annex III, art. 2, ¶ 5 bis.

[302] *Id.* art. 2, ¶ 6. According to the provision, except for developing countries covered in Article 5, any party which had contracted for or was constructing facilities to produce controlled substances prior to September 16, 1987, and had provided for the same in national legislation prior to January 1, 1987, could add the production capability from such facilities to its 1986 production base level, provided that such facilities were completed by December 31, 1990, and that such production would not raise a party's annual level of consumption of the controlled substances above 0.5 kilograms per capita. This provision, too, seems to cater to special interests, such as the then-Soviet Union and other countries with planned economies, so that a nation's or industry's initial investment of financing new production facilities was not lost. It could, however, lead to increases in production capability, which is not what the Protocol was designed to do.

[303] *Id.* art. 2, ¶ 8.

[304] Montreal Protocol, *supra* note 159, art. 1, ¶ 8.

The industrial rationalization scheme under the Protocol was further modified by subsequent amendments, including removal of the 10-percent increase exception, but a signatory state was still free to transfer a given amount of its production of ozone-depleting controlled substances (under Articles 2A to 2E and 2H) to another signatory state, provided that the combined total of the two states' production did not exceed the limit set out for that group.[305] The Copenhagen Amendments also allow for a transfer of consumption in certain circumstances.[306] However, it is neither desirable nor appropriate to allow the economic marketplace to determine which controlled substances are produced; a supply and demand mechanism is not concerned with, nor will it reflect, potential environmental impacts (external costs) that may result in the long run in a "tragedy of the commons."

An even graver problem with the original Protocol was the fact that it set production and consumption levels at 1986 base levels. It later became clear that maintenance of such high levels (as existed in 1986) of production and consumption would allow ozone depletion to continue to increase well into the 21st century, along with its potentially deleterious effects. Also, calculation and verification of 1986 control baseline levels were seen as difficult in the absence of accurate records, thus adding uncertainty.[307] Some of these problems are addressed by the amendments, which use 1989 as the base level year for all ozone-depleting substances newly added to the annexes; however, 1986 remains the base level year for CFCs and halons.

10.2.8.2 *Developing Nations*

The Protocol recognizes that developing nations are not economically in a position to make many sacrifices. Thus, it provides a grace period of ten years for the compliance of developing nations, which are identified as those whose annual level of consumption of controlled substances is less than 0.3 kilograms per capita on or before January 1, 1999.[308] The only limitation

---

[305] London Amendment, *supra* note 171, annex II, art. 2, ¶ 5.

[306] Copenhagen Amendment, *supra* note 172, annex III. art. 2, ¶ 5 bis.

[307] *Id.* art. 2, para. 6. According to the provision, except for developing countries covered in Article 5, any party which had contracted for or was constructing facilities to produce controlled substances prior to September 16, 1987, and had provided for the same in national legislation prior to January 1, 1987, could add the production capability from such facilities to its 1986 production base level, provided that such facilities were completed by December 31, 1990, and that such production did not raise a party's annual level of consumption of the controlled substances above 0.5 kilograms per capita. This provision seems to cater to special interests, such as the then-Soviet Union and other countries with planned economies, so that a nation's or industry's initial investment of financing new production facilities was not lost. It may have led, however, to increases in production capability, which was not what the Protocol was designed to do.

[308] *Id.* art. 5.

is that the developing nation's consumption level of Annex A controlled substances (CFCs and halons) was not to exceed 0.3 kilograms per capita; while consumption of Annex B controlled substances (other fully halogenated CFCs and carbon tetrachloride) was limited to 0.2 kilograms per capita under the London Amendments.[309]

In order to reduce the need to produce such substances, the parties are to attempt to make alternative substances, technology, and financial subsidies available to developing nations.[310] It is true that developing nations have less impact on the overall levels of production and consumption of controlled substances, but this exception still allows for significant production growth rates. It is noteworthy that, among developing countries, India did not participate in the conference,[311] and the People's Republic of China participated in the conference but did not sign the Protocol.[312] Although developing nations were initially reluctant to sign the Protocol, they have now joined in its universal ratification.[313]

The London Amendments go further than the Montreal Protocol in devising a method of equitable burden sharing between developed nations and developing nations.[314] Here the common but differentiated responsibilities principle was put into practice.[315] Specific guidelines in Article 10 replaced ambiguous promises of technical assistance. Financial assistance and technology transfer were to be provided to developing nations, as defined under paragraph 1 of Article 5.[316] Additionally, Article 10A of the London Amendments ensures "[t]hat the best available, environmentally safe substitutes and related technologies are expeditiously transferred to developing nations."[317] These transfers must "occur under fair and most favourable conditions."[318]

---

[309] London Amendment, *supra* note 171, annex II, art. 5, ¶ 2.

[310] *Id.* art. 5 (replacing art. 5 under the Montreal Protocol).

[311] *See* M. Weisskopf, *Nations Sign Agreement to Guard Ozone Layer*, WASH. POST, Sept. 17, 1987, sec. A, at 2, cols. 4, 6.

[312] *Id.*

[313] Status of Ratification, *supra* note 160.

[314] *See* J. M. Patlis, *The Multilateral Fund of the Montreal Protocol: A Prototype for Financial Mechanisms in Protecting the Global Environment*, 25 CORNELL INT'L L.J. 181, 191–97 (1992).

[315] *See, e.g.*, WORLD BANK OPERATIONS EVALUATION DEPARTMENT, THE MULTILATERAL FUND FOR THE IMPLEMENTATION OF THE MONTREAL PROTOCOL, ADDRESSING CHALLENGES OF GLOBALIZATION: AN INDEPENDENT EVALUATION OF THE WORLD BANK'S APPROACH TO GLOBAL PROGRAMS, 2–3 (2004), http://www.worldbank.org/oed.

[316] London Amendment, *supra* note 171, annex II, art. 10, ¶ 1.

[317] *Id.* at art. 10A(a).

[318] *Id.* at art. 10A(b). *See* UNEP, *NGOs to Help Developing Nations to Reduce Use of Methyl Bromide on Crops*, 24 Int'l Env't Rep. 195 (Mar. 14, 2001).

The primary mechanism for implementing financial aid and technological assistance is the Multilateral Fund for the Implementation of the Montreal Protocol, initially created in 1991 as an interim fund under Article 10 of the London Amendments and made permanent at the fourth meeting of the parties in Copenhagen.[319] With the combination of technological assistance, financial assistance and control measures, developing nations have a better chance of achieving compliance. Article 5 under the London Amendments specifically recognized that the ability of developing countries to comply with the control measures is dependent upon financial cooperation and technology transfer provided for in Articles 10 and 10A, respectively.[320] Even the preamble recognized the necessity of special provisions for "additional financial resources and access to relevant technologies" in order to meet the needs of developing countries.[321]

The Multilateral Fund is dedicated to assisting developing countries to meet their Montreal Protocol commitments.[322] It has two primary goals: (1) to strengthen the control measures by creating incentives for developing nations to comply, and (2) to increase the number of parties to the Montreal Protocol by making it more attractive to developing nations.[323] The fund is financed by nations that are not considered developing nations, under paragraph 1 of Article 5, on the basis of the United Nations scale of assessments.[324] It finances three types of expenses. First, grants or concessions are paid to Article 5 countries in order to meet incremental costs.[325] Second, clearinghouse functions are funded in order to assist Article 5 countries in drafting country-specific studies, facilitating technical cooperation, distributing information, and facilitating other types of cooperation available to developing countries.[326] Third, the fund finances its own administrative costs.[327] Thus, the Multilateral Fund provides a structure in which developing nations have more incentive and ability to comply with control measures.

Critics, however, pointed to several problems with the establishment of the Fund. First, it is difficult to define and identify the incremental costs.[328] Second, technology transfer still occurs without any guidelines, creating

---

[319] *Id.* at art. 10, para 3. *See* Patlis, *supra* note 314, at 197–203.

[320] London Amendment, *supra* note 171, at annex II, art. 5, ¶ 5.

[321] *Id.* at art. 1, para. 2.

[322] *See* MULTILATERAL FUND FOR THE IMPLEMENTATION OF THE MONTREAL PROTOCOL http://www.multilateralfund.org/default.aspx.

[323] Patlis, *supra* note 314, at 197.

[324] London Amendment, *supra* note 171, at annex II, art. 10, ¶ 6.

[325] *Id.* at ¶ 3(a).

[326] *Id.* at ¶ 3(b).

[327] *Id.* at ¶ 3(c).

[328] Patlis, *supra* note 314, at 203.

problems over patents and ownership rights.[329] Third, developing nations are free to take advantage of funding requests, due to the lack of precise compliance measures.[330] In the final analysis, the ultimate effectiveness of the Multilateral Fund depends largely on its capitalization.[331] The amount of funding since its establishment has been generous: $240 million for 1991–1993, $455 million for 1994–1996, $466 million for 1997–1999, and $440 million for 2000–2002, a total of $1.5 billion over the first 12 years.[332] $474 million for 2003–2005, $400.4 million for 2006–2008, $400 million for 2009–2011, and $400 million for 2012–2014. It has approved activities worth over $2.8 billion. The fund has had an excellent record, with almost 90 percent of its promised funding achieved during its first six years.[333]

10.2.8.3   *Import/Export Restrictions*

Under the Montreal Protocol, each party must ban the import of controlled substances from any state that is not a party to the 1987 Protocol.[334] The London Amendments call for a ban on the importation of controlled substances under Annex A.[335] The importation of Annex B substances from nonparty states is to be banned within one year after the effective date of the London Amendments (August 10, 1992).[336] The Copenhagen Amendments ban the importation of Group II of Annex C (hydrobromofluorocarbons) substances from nonparty states within one year after the effective date of the amendments.[337] The Copenhagen Amendments also add a provision whereby the parties will consider whether or not to amend the Protocol to regulate the trade of controlled substances under Annex C, Group I (hydrochlorofluorocarbons) and Annex E (methyl bromide).[338]

No party may export any controlled substance (CFCs and halons) to a nonparty state by January 1993 under the Protocol.[339] This restriction remains for Annex A substances under the London Amendments.[340] The exportation of Annex B substances to nonparty states was banned one year after the effective

---

[329] *Id.*

[330] *Id.* at 205.

[331] *Id.* at 206–08.

[332] 2000 Ozone Action, *supra* note 294, at 14.

[333] *Id.*

[334] Montreal Protocol, *supra* note 159, art. 4, ¶ 1.

[335] London Amendment, *supra* note 171, annex II, art. 4. ¶ 1.

[336] *Id.* ¶ I bis.

[337] Copenhagen Amendment, *supra* note 172, annex III, art. 4., ¶ 2 ter.

[338] *Id.* para. 10.

[339] Montreal Protocol, *supra* note 159, art. 4, ¶ 2.

[340] London Amendment, *supra* note 171, annex 11, art. 4, ¶ 2.

date of the London Amendments.[341] Furthermore, both the Protocol and its subsequent amendments discourage parties from exporting technology that is useful for utilizing controlled substances to nonparties.[342] These provisions also provide an incentive for a state to sign the Protocol, especially if it is dependent upon foreign CFC production. All of the nonparties to the Protocol are developing nations, and thus were subject to several disadvantages, including the inability to import controlled substances from parties after January 1993 and export certain controlled substances to parties after May 1993.[343]

The Protocol and subsequent amendments further restricted the trade of controlled substances by creating mechanisms to list and prohibit the trade of products containing certain controlled substances. Under the London Amendments, lists of products containing controlled substances under Annex A and Annex B are made by the parties.[344] Any party that fails to object to the list within one year of the list's effective date must ban the import of those products from nonparty states.[345] The Copenhagen Amendments added products containing Group II of Annex C controlled substances to those that may be put on a list and eventually banned from import from nonparty states.[346] Furthermore, the London Amendments allow parties to determine the feasibility of banning or restricting the importation of products "produced with, but not containing controlled substances" under Annexes A and B to nonparty states.[347]

The Copenhagen Amendments also added products produced with, but not containing, substances under Group 11 of Annex C to be considered for future regulation.[348] Again, states that did not object to products placed on this list within one year of the effective date would be banned or restricted from importing such products from nonparty states.[349] These import bans and restrictions further prevent nations from profiting by not being a part of the controlled substances reductions. Parties to the Protocol are also to refrain from financing exports to nonparties of "products, equipment, plants, or technology that would facilitate the production of controlled substances."[350]

---

[341] *Id.* ¶ 2 bis.

[342] *See, e.g., id.* ¶ 5.

[343] Rowlands, *supra* note 244.

[344] London Amendment, *supra* note 171, ¶¶ 3. 3 bis.

[345] *Id.*

[346] Copenhagen Amendment, *supra* note 172, annex Ill. art. 4, ¶ 3 ter.

[347] London Amendment, *supra* note 171, annex II. art. 4, ¶¶ 4, 4 bis.

[348] Copenhagen Amendment, *supra* note 172, annex III, art. 4, ¶ 4 ter.

[349] *Id.*

[350] Montreal Protocol, *supra* note 159, art. 4, ¶ 6.

As new substances were subsequently added to the control schedules under the Montreal and Beijing Amendments, the trade restrictions have also been extended to cover them. However, these restrictions do not apply to non-parties otherwise in compliance with the control schedules. The 1997 Montreal Amendments obligated parties to introduce a licensing system for both imports and exports of ODSs, including "new, used, recycled and reclaimed controlled substances in Annexes A, B, C and E."[351] The licensing system was designed to address the problem of illegal trade in ODSs.

Economic disincentives and trade penalties were appropriately seen by parties as highly persuasive for convincing nations to join the Protocol (*see* Chapter 14). Also, these measures encourage development of substitute processes so that controlled substances are no longer used in the manufacturing process. Of course, the development of substitutes depends in turn on the development of appropriate new technologies. From the beginning, industrial reports on the introduction of technologies to develop substitutes for CFCs – as well as devices to capture and remove CFCs from automotive air conditioning systems – showed great promise.[352]

10.2.8.4   *Noncompliance*

The Montreal Protocol's predecessor, the 1985 Vienna Convention, which applies to the Montreal Protocol as well, aptly encompasses a workable compulsory dispute settlement mechanism. It provides that parties engaged in disputes concerning the Convention (or subsequent protocols to the Convention) shall first seek resolution by negotiation.[353] If a negotiated settlement is not reached, the parties may jointly seek the good offices of or request mediation by a third party.[354] A party may also declare in writing that, for a dispute not resolved by negotiation or mediation, it accepts compulsory arbitration as a means of dispute settlement.[355] Alternatively, the dispute may be submitted to the International Court of Justice (ICJ).[356] If neither

---

[351] New Article 4B(1) added to the Protocol.

[352] *See, e.g.*, 11 Int'l Env't Rep. (BNA), 520 (Oct. 12, 1988) (producers announce their replacement plans for CFCs); Int'l Env't Rep. (BNA), 158 (Mar. 9, 1988) (a joint statement by several U.K. companies on CFC phaseout and replacements); Int'l Env't Rep. (BNA), 109 (Feb. 10, 1988) (announcement on a substitute for CFC-113); Int'l Env't Rep. (BNA), 667 (Dec. 14, 1988) (announcement on the removal of coolants from automotive air conditioning systems); R. Koenig, *Carbide Says New Chemicals Can Wean Foam Makers From Chlorofluorocarbons*, WALL ST. J., Aug. 5, 1988, at 26, col. 5 (announcement on developing chemicals which will allow manufacturers to produce foam without using CFCs).

[353] Vienna Ozone Convention, *supra* note 158, art. 11, ¶ 1.

[354] *Id.* ¶ 2.

[355] *Id.* ¶ 3(a).

[356] *Id.* ¶ 3(b).

arbitration nor ICJ jurisdiction is agreed to by the parties involved, a Conciliation Commission is to be created upon the request of one of the parties to the dispute, whose "final and recommendatory award" the parties must consider in good faith.

The Protocol does not define noncompliance, nor did it establish the necessary institutional machinery[357] to determine noncompliance with the control measures.[358] It obligated the parties to create the necessary institutional mechanisms and procedures for the determination of noncompliance. An interim noncompliance procedure was adopted at the second meeting of the parties to the Montreal Protocol, which was the same meeting at which the London Amendments was implemented.[359]

This procedure lacked specificity and relied on the Ad Hoc Working Group of Legal Experts on the Noncompliance Procedure to make additional refinements.[360] Under the procedure, a party or parties may submit in writing to the Secretariat a complaint and supporting information alleging that another party has failed to comply with the Protocol.[361] The alleged violating party receives a copy of the complaint and has a reasonable opportunity to reply.[362] The reply is sent to both the complaining party and the Secretariat.[363] All the information is then forwarded to an Implementation Committee, which consists of ten parties who have been elected by all other parties to the Protocol based on "equitable geographic distribution."[364] The Implementation Committee then serves as an informal mediator by attempting to obtain an amicable resolution to the dispute, in light of the provisions of the Protocol.[365] The Implementation Committee reports at the subsequent meeting of the parties, when the parties may decide to call for measures to bring about compliance with the Protocol.[366] The disputing parties then report back to the meeting of the parties regarding the implementation of any measure to achieve compliance.[367]

---

[357] *Id.* ¶¶ 4, 5.

[358] Montreal Protocol, *supra* note 159, art. 8.

[359] This may require removing a controlled substance from the controlled list if it is found not to be a potential cause of ozone depletion. Two thirds majority vote of the parties would be needed for such a modification. *Id.* art. 2, ¶ 10.

[360] *Id.*

[361] *Id.*

[362] *Id.*

[363] *Id.*

[364] *Id.*

[365] *Id.*

[366] *Id.*

[367] *Id.*

Currently, representatives of ten state parties, two from each of the five UN regions, constituting the Implementation Committee of the Protocol, are responsible for implementation. The Committee reports cases of noncompliance to the meeting of the parties and recommends measures to be taken. These include providing financial or technical assistance from the multilateral fund and the Global Environment Facility (GEF),[368] cautioning noncompliant parties, or, as a last resort, suspending the party from the Protocol.[369]

10.2.8.5   *The Protocol's Contribution in Addressing the Ozone Depletion Problem*

The Protocol took an important and promising step toward international commitment to rectify the ozone depletion problem. Perhaps no "tougher" agreement could have been reached in September 1987, and the subsequent amendments have remedied many of the Protocol's initial weaknesses.

The Protocol is a landmark in the development of international environmental law, primarily because the world community showed a rare consensus in accepting the imposition of strict controls on states for activities potentially harmful, but having caused no proven specific damage or harm. As Mostafa Tolba said after the adoption of the Protocol, "Never before in the history of science and law has the international community agreed to take such radical steps to avert a problem they anticipate, before that problem has begun to take its toll."[370] Another major strength of the Protocol lies in the formula on its entry into force,[371] and its provisions on review and amendment.[372]

First, the Protocol recognized the special interest of the European Economic Community (now European Union – EU) as a distinct entity, capable of becoming a party in its own right. Prolonged negotiations on this point led to a resolution of the initial objection by the United States that it would set a "dangerous international precedent."[373] Second, it ensured that states that become parties were not likely to face unfair competition from nonparties

---

[368] *See generally* GEF, Global Environment Facility – Investing in our Planet: Behind the Numbers – A Closer Look at GEF Achievements – Protecting the Ozone Layer 16 (2012) (noting GEF's support of the Montreal Protocol and its investment in projects to phaseout substances that deplete the ozone layer, and in cofinancing such projects), http://www .thegef.org/gef/sites/thegef.org/files/publication/GEF_Behind_the_Numbers_CRA.pdf.

[369] 2000 Ozone Action, *supra* note 294, at 14.

[370] P. Menyasz, *International Agreement to Protect the Ozone Layer Hailed as Precedent for Global Environmental Solutions*, 10 Int'l Env't Rep. (BNA) 531 (Oct. 14, 1987).

[371] *See* Montreal Protocol, *supra* note 159, art. 16.

[372] *See id.* arts. 2, 6.

[373] *See* Menyasz, *supra* note 370, at 533. As a party in its own right the EU brings the total of parties to 197. *Supra* note 3.

to the Protocol, for it required ratification or accession by at least 11 states and international economic entities (such as the EU), representing two thirds of global consumption of CFCs and halons. Third, it appropriately mandated compliance by the parties, without reservations, with the Protocol's control measures, as well as its restrictions on trade with nonparties.[374] Fourth, the Protocol allows special treatment for developing countries[375] and those with planned economies.[376] The objective, obviously, is to seek wider participation. Finally, the Protocol provisions on review and amendment[377] allow the parties to revise their control measures by adding new compounds or changing emissions reductions in response to further research and scientific evidence.[378]

10.2.9   Developments in the United States and the European Union

10.2.9.1   US Action Prior to the 1990 London Amendments

To its credit, the United States took its role seriously in implementing the Protocol and the subsequent amendments, for the most part staying ahead of international regulations by enacting domestic laws in the form of both statutes and EPA rules more stringent than the Protocol and its amendments. Perhaps more importantly, a distinct enforcement mechanism exists in the United States to implement its obligations under the Protocol.[379]

The signing of the Montreal Protocol was a signal to industry to move swiftly in their efforts to recycle CFCs, chemically modify them, or find suitable replacements to meet the reductions called for by the Protocol.[380] In contrast with its earlier position, which was marked by combative responses to its critics,[381] DuPont, the world's largest manufacturer of CFCs, announced in March 1988 its plans to phase out all production of the chemicals.[382] Although no target date was set for ending production of CFCs, a company official said that "reducing output by at least ninety-five percent by the beginning of the

---

[374] Montreal Protocol, *supra* note 159, arts. 16–18.

[375] *Id.* arts. 2–5, 16–19. (Although most of the articles have been amended to some extent, developing nations still receive special consideration.)

[376] *Id.* art. 2, ¶ 6. (Amended to specify Annex A or Annex B controlled substance.)

[377] *Id.* art. 2, ¶ 10(a). (Amended by deleting 10(b), thereby making 10(a) simply 10.)

[378] *Id.*

[379] EPA's rule-making statutory authority is pursuant to the 1977 Clean Air Act Amendment, § 157(b), 42 U.S.C. § 7457(b) (1977). For the Act, *see* 42 U.S.C. §§ 7450–59 (1977).

[380] *See, e.g.*, Maugh, II, and L. Stammer, *Depletion Greater Than Thought; Loss of Ozone Calls for Speedy Action, Experts Say*, L.A. TIMES, Mar. 21, 1988, at 16, cols. 2–3.

[381] *See, e.g.*, W. Glaberson, *Behind DuPont's Shift on Loss of Ozone Layer*, N.Y. TIMES, Mar. 26, 1988, at 17, col. 3.

[382] *See* P. Shabecoff, *DuPont to Stop Making Chemicals that Peril Ozone*, N.Y. TIMES, Mar. 25, 1988, at A-1, col. 2.

next century was a 'reasonable goal,'"[383] demonstrating industry's readiness and ability to comply with the Protocol.[384]

The United States was among the first states to ratify the Montreal Protocol,[385] which took effect on January 1, 1989.[386] While the EPA and the US Congress actively pursued the issue, states and cities also began to take the initiative.[387]

10.2.9.1.1   EPA Rulemaking

As early as 1978, the EPA and the Food and Drug Administration banned the use of CFCs as aerosol propellants in most aerosol products, such as spray cans.[388] After the ban went into effect, CFC manufacturers found new applications for their product, obviating much of the efforts to reduce total CFC production. With the signing of the Montreal Protocol, however, a new opportunity arose to reduce production and consumption of ODSs such as CFCs and halons. As part of the US obligation to implement the 1987 Montreal Protocol, the EPA required all US firms in the industry to report by January 14, 1988, the amount of CFCs that they produced, exported, or imported in 1986.[389]

Furthermore, the EPA proposed regulations under Section 157(b) of the Clean Air Act[390] to implement and correspond to the terms of the Montreal Protocol.[391] The terms of Section 157(b) authorized the EPA Administrator to promulgate regulations to control any substance, process, practice, or activity that may reasonably be anticipated to affect the stratosphere, "if such

---

[383] *Id.* For a representative earlier position of the industry, *see Stratospheric Ozone Depletion and CFCs, supra* note 182, at 273 (statement of Chemical Manufacturers Association), 360, 384, 394, 402, 412, 499, 584, 657, 660 (statements of several industry representatives).

[384] *See* P. Shabecoff, *Industry Acts to Curb Peril in Ozone Loss*, N.Y. TIMES, Mar. 21, 1988, at A 11, col. 1.

[385] 88 DEP'T ST. BULL. 68 (June 1988).

[386] 12 Int'l Env't Rep. (BNA) 3 (Jan. 11, 1989).

[387] *See, e.g.,* N.Y. TIMES, Aug. 26, 1988, at 11, col. I (a foam producer settles a lawsuit brought by the State of Massachusetts to stop CFC emissions in a violation of state regulations); 11 Int'l Env't Rep. (BNA) 333 (June 8, 1988) (action by Minnesota); Int'l Env't Rep. (BNA) 457 (Aug. 10, 1988) (action by the City of Los Angeles).

[388] *See* 43 Fed. Reg. 11301, 11318 (1978). The EPA also calculated the costs and benefits of the proposed regulation. The costs would total approximately US $27 billion for the period 1987–2075, while the benefits were estimated to range from US $29 billion to US $340 trillion for the same time period. *See* 52 Fed. Reg. 47513 (1987).

[389] 52 Fed. Reg. 47488 (1987) (to be codified at 40 C.F.R. pt. 82).

[390] 42 U.S.C. § 7457(b) (1977).

[391] 52 Fed. Reg. 47498 (1987). According to EPA's estimates, compliance with the Protocol by most states would reduce ozone depletion to 1.3 percent by the year 2075. The EPA also had evaluated the risks of ozone depletion in EPA, Assessing the Risks of Trace Gasses that Can Modify the Stratosphere (Dec. 1987).

effect may reasonably be anticipated to endanger public health or welfare." Essentially, the Administrator was not required to prove that a substance, process, practice, or activity does in fact deplete stratospheric ozone levels before enacting such regulation.[392]

The EPA considered control strategies such as regulatory fees, auctioned rights, engineering controls, and chemical bans.[393] It subsequently considered adding a regulatory fee to supplement the allocated quota system.[394] The United States also imposed an excise tax on each pound of ozone-depleting substance used or sold by an importer, producer, or manufacturer in order to induce the use of substitutes.[395] In May 1988, following a public hearing on its proposed rules, the EPA issued a supplementary proposal setting forth company-specific apportionments of production and consumption rights.[396] Then on August 12, 1988, the EPA promulgated its final rule on protection of stratospheric ozone,[397] which took effect the day the Montreal Protocol entered into force.[398]

However, while proclaiming the final rule, it gave advance notice of proposed rulemaking, which discussed replacing allocated quotas with an auction system, supplementing the final rule with a regulatory fee, and/or engineering controls or bans on specific uses of CFCs and halons.[399] With its efforts to meet the ambient air quality standard under the Clean Air Act, the EPA, by virtue of its experience with emissions trading,[400] its research on economic

---

[392] Pursuant to § 113b of the Clean Air Act, 42 U.S.C. § 7413 (1977), the EPA can also impose penalties for noncompliance of up to US $25,000 per day per violation. Each kilogram of control substance produced or imported beyond a firm's allocated rights would be considered to be a separate violation. EPA also has the authority to seek injunctive relief to halt further production or imports if a firm has already reached its allocated rights limit for the year.

[393] *See* 52 Fed. Reg. 47499–47500 (1987).

[394] 53 Fed. Reg. 30605–36010 (1988).

[395] *See* Friedland & Isaacs, *supra* note 240, at 31.

[396] 53 Fed. Reg. 1880 (1988).

[397] 53 Fed. Reg. 30566 (1988). *See also* EPA, Regulatory Impact Analysis: Protection of Stratospheric Ozone (Aug. 1988).

[398] 53 Fed. Reg. 30566 (1988).

[399] *Id.* at 30604.

[400] *See generally* J. A. del Calvo and Gonzales, *Markets in the Air: Problems and Prospects of Controlled Trading*, 5 HARV. ENVTL. L. REV. 377, 396–430 (1981); J. Landau, *Economic Dream or Environmental Nightmare? The Legality of the "Bubble Concept" in Air and Water Pollution Control*, 8 B.C. ENVTL. AFF. L. REV. 741 (1980); D. Mandelkar & T. Sherry, *Emission Quota Strategies as an Air Pollution Control Technique*, 5 ECOLOGY L.Q. 401 (1976); Comment, *Regulating with a Carrot: Experimenting with Incentives for Clean Air*, 31 BUFF. L. REV. 193, 201–31 (1982); Note, *The EPA's Bubble Concept After Alabama Power*, 32 STAN. L. REV. 943 (1980).

and legal issues involved in ozone regulatory schemes,[401] and solicited public comments it receives from concerned parties,[402] was well suited to devise a workable, equitable, and efficient scheme.

10.2.9.1.2 Congressional Action

The US Congress was willing to act quickly to implement the Protocol and address the problem of ozone depletion. The Committee on Science, Space, and Technology of the US House of Representatives held a hearing in October 1987 to review the results of the 1987 Antarctic Ozone expedition.[403] Those testifying included representatives from the US Department of State,[404] EPA,[405] NASA,[406] NOAA,[407] and National Science Foundation.[408] The focus was on the "very clear chemical signature" in the evolution of the Antarctic ozone hole,[409] and on the adoption and ratification of the Montreal Protocol.[410] Assistant Secretary of State John Negroponte surmised that with the signing of the Montreal Protocol, "we have entered into a new era of global environmental management," for changes in the ozone layer affect the entire world.[411]

In July 1988, US Senators Robert Stafford and Timothy Wirth each introduced a broad piece of legislation,[412] primarily addressing the questions of stratospheric ozone depletion and the greenhouse effect, respectively. Senator Wirth's bill called for a reassessment of the control measures within a year of the enactment of the bill.[413] It also required the US Secretary of State to actively encourage the adoption of additional control measures requiring

---

[401] 53 Fed. Reg. at 30606 (EPA initiated two studies of its own to examine the issues of quotas and regulatory fees). For citations to these studies by S. Decaino & Sobotkin and Co., Inc., *see id.* at 30619.

[402] *See id.* at 30607–30619.

[403] Review of the Results of the Antarctic Ozone Expedition, Hearings before the Committee on Science, Space, and Technology of the House of Representatives, Oct. 29, 1987, 100th Cong., 1st Sess. 77 (1988).

[404] *Id.* at 12–18 (testimony and statement of John D. Negroponte, Assistant Secretary for Oceans and International Environment and Scientific Affairs, US Department of State).

[405] *Id.* at 19–26 (testimony and statement of A. J. Barnes, Deputy Administrator, EPA).

[406] *Id.* at 340–60 (testimony and statement of R. T. Watson, Chief, Upper Atmosphere Research Program, NASA).

[407] *Id.* at 361–372 (testimony and statement of A. Tuck, Aeronomy Lab, NOAA).

[408] *Id.* at 373–382 (testimony and statements of NSF representatives).

[409] *See, e.g., id.* at 340–60, 361, 362–63 (testimony of A. Tuck, a strong advocate of dynamism and "meteorological signatures").

[410] *See generally id.* at 3–4, 12–26.

[411] *Id.* at 12.

[412] Stafford Bill and Wirth Bill, *supra* note 210.

[413] Wirth Bill, *supra* note 210, § 1503(a).

the virtual elimination of emissions of all substances identified in the Montreal Protocol within five to seven years from the date of enactment of this title and appropriate control measures for other ozone-depleting chemicals not identified in the Montreal Protocol.[414] Senator Wirth reintroduced the bill, with slight modifications, on February 2, 1989.[415] Senator Stafford's bill – The Global Environmental Protection Act of 1988[416] – proposed stringent controls, providing for a virtual elimination of halogenated CFC use and sale by 1999.[417] While the bill was not enacted by the 100th Congress, it was reintroduced in the 101st Congress by Senator Patrick Leahy.[418] Another noteworthy bill introduced in the 101st Congress was the Global Environment Research and Policy Act of 1989, which provided a mechanism for planning and coordinating long-term research efforts on global climate change involving more than two federal agencies.[419]

On May 9, 2011, the United States, Canada, and Mexico submitted a joint North American proposal to phase down the use of hydrofluorocarbons (HFCs) under the Montreal Protocol.[420] The proposal calls upon all countries to take action to reduce their production and consumption of HFCs, asking developed countries to begin in 2015 gradually phasing down to 15 percent of baseline levels by 2033. Developing countries could begin in 2017 to phase down to 15 percent of baseline levels by 2043.

10.2.9.1.3 EPA Findings

In August 1988, the EPA released a report entitled "Future Concentrations of Stratospheric Chlorine and Bromine,"[421] which related rates of emissions to stratospheric levels of chlorine and bromine. It also examined the

---

[414] *Id.* § 1503(b).

[415] Senate Bill 324, cosponsored by 30 Senators, 135 Cong. Rec., sec. 1036 (daily ed., Feb. 2, 1989).

[416] Stafford Bill, *supra* note 210, at 10112, 10282.

[417] *Id.* §§ 102(6), 103, 107(f). Section 107(f) provides: "Effective January, 1999, it shall be unlawful for any person to produce or release [substances to be phased out and regulated, including halogenated CFCs] for any use other than medical uses." Section 103(b) states the national goal:

> [T]o eliminate atmospheric emissions of manufactured substances with ozone depleting potential, including chlorofluorocarbons and other halogenated carbons with ozone-depleting potential, and to reduce significantly emissions of other gases caused by human activities that are likely to affect adversely the global climate.

[418] Senate Bill 333, 135 Cong. Rec. S1069 (daily ed., Feb. 2, 1989).

[419] 135 Cong. Rec. E362 (daily ed., Feb. 9 1989); 135 Cong. Rec S522 (daily ed., Jan. 25, 1989).

[420] EPA, Ozone Layer Protection: Recent International Developments in Saving the Ozone Layer: North American Amendment Proposal to Phase-Down HFCs Under the Montreal Protocol, http://www.epa.gov/ozone/intpol/mpagreement.html.

[421] EPA, *Future Concentration of Stratospheric Chlorine and Bromine* (Office of Air and Radiation, Aug. 1988).

reductions required in order "to stabilize the atmosphere at current levels of chlorine and bromine.[422]

The report states that "chlorine and bromine levels will increase substantially from current levels" even with substantial global participation in the Montreal Protocol.[423] The report summary noted:

> The very large increase in CL and halon abundances would have been expected if the use and emissions of chlorine-containing compounds and halons had been allowed to increase without limit. The provisions of the Montreal Protocol will reduce the amount of the increase significantly, but will not keep the levels of CL and halons in the stratosphere from increasing. Significant additional reductions in emissions are required to keep the levels from increasing, possibly including a complete phaseout of the fully-halogenated compounds and a freeze on methyl chloroform. The rate of substitution with partially-halogenated chlorine-containing compounds will also influence future chlorine levels.[424]

Subsequently, in September 1988, the EPA Administrator called for a strengthening of the Protocol, "with a near-total phaseout of chlorofluorocarbons as the goal."[425] He stated that, persuaded by recent scientific data of the need to do more, he had written the UNEP and "his international counterparts, urging them to consider tightening the agreement."[426] Thus, the reaction in both the Congress and the EPA to the original Protocol was that it needed to be further strengthened to combat ozone depletion.

10.2.9.2   *US Action since the 1990 London Amendments*

Prior to the effective date of the London Amendments (August 10, 1992), the United States Senate was already adding a new title (Title VI) to the Clean Air Act, entitled Stratospheric Ozone Protection.[427] This progressive piece of legislation made it national policy to eliminate ozone-depleting substances "as expeditiously as possible."[428] The EPA was empowered to implement a more aggressive phaseout schedule than the one in the bill, if circumstances required.[429] Although the bill regulated CFCs in the same manner as under

---

[422] *Id.* at 1.

[423] *Id.*

[424] *Id.* at 27.

[425] 19 Int'l Env't Rep. (BNA) 985 (Sept. 16, 1988).

[426] *Id.*

[427] S. 1630, 101st Cong., 1st Sess. (1990) [hereinafter Clean Air Act Amendment]. *See Clean Air Act Amended*, 20 Envtl. Pol'y & L. 95 (1990). *See also* L. B. Talbot, *Recent Developments in the Montreal Protocol on Substances that Deplete the Ozone Layer: The June 1990 Meeting and Beyond*, 26 Int'l Law 145, 164 (1992).

[428] Clean Air Act Amendment, *supra* note 427.

[429] *Id.*

the Montreal Protocol, it required their elimination by the year 2000.[430] Furthermore, the phaseout schedule included halons and carbon tetrachloride with the most harmful CFCs;[431] and the production of methyl chloroform was to be reduced by 50 percent by 1996, and totally banned by 2000.[432] New production of HCFCs was to be frozen at 2014 levels by 2015, and new production prohibited by 2030.[433]

In addition to phaseout production, the legislation allowed the enactment of regulations to achieve significant and immediate reduction in ozone-depleting substances.[434] Finally, the bill included trade sanctions aimed at both parties and nonparties who engaged in activities that violated the Protocol,[435] and empowering the President to ban imports of products made with, but not containing, controlled substances.[436]

As the June 1990 London Amendments meetings came to a close, the US Department of Justice and the EPA filed suits against five US companies, alleging that they violated both the Clean Air Act and the Protocol.[437] EPA requirements direct producers and importers of CFCs to obtain allowances from the Agency, which these companies had failed to obtain.[438] One company quickly settled the case when it realized millions of dollars in penalties were at stake.[439] Consent decrees issued in the other four cases.[440] The importance of these cases lies in the signal that the United States sent to domestic industries that it takes seriously the obligations under the Montreal Protocol.

The 1990 Clean Air Act Amendment, which includes Title VI, works in conjunction with the EPA's rulemaking authority to implement the Montreal Protocol and its amendments in the United States. The trend has been toward creating stricter standards and regulations than required under international environmental treaties.[441] Additionally, both the statute and the EPA

---

[430] *Id.* (codified at 42 U.S.C. § 7671c(b) (1993)).

[431] *Id.* (codified at 42 U.S.C. § 767la(a) (1993)).

[432] *Id.*

[433] *Id.*

[434] *Id.* (codified at 42 U.S.C. § 767le (1993)).

[435] *Id.*

[436] *Id.*

[437] *Five Companies Sued by Justice, EPA over Violations of Montreal Protocol on CFCs*, 21 Env't Rep. (BNA) 441 (July 6, 1990). *See* Talbot, *supra* note 427, at 165–66.

[438] 40 C.F.R. §§ 82.5, .6, .13 (1991); Five Companies Sued, *supra* note 423; Talbot, *supra* note 427, at 165.

[439] *Id.* at 165.

[440] *Id.*

[441] *See generally* Friedland & Isaacs, *supra* note 240. Section 606 of the statute empowers the EPA to accelerate the phaseout of ozone-depleting substances under the Protocol as necessary, based on new scientific data (4 U.S.C. § 7671e (1993)) based on a recognition of the

have established labeling requirements for products made with, or containing, certain ODSs.[442]

The deadline for phasing out methyl bromide, initially set by the EPA at 2001, has been an issue of major concern since mid-1995, due to farmers' concerns that the chemical's use in pest control is so essential that, unless acceptable alternatives are available, US agriculture will suffer serious adverse consequences. The General Accounting Office, an arm of the US Congress, recommended in 1996 that the deadline be extended.[443] Also, US administration officials sought an amendment to the Clean Air Act to authorize exemptions to this ban.[444] Similar proposals to delay the deadline were subsequently offered by US officials and agricultural interests in 1997.[445] In June 1999, the EPA finalized a rule requiring a 25-percent reduction in production and consumption of methyl bromide for the two-year period 1999 and 2000.[446] The rule incorporated a 1997 renegotiation of the Protocol on the schedule for industrialized countries to phase out methyl bromide.[447] The Clean Air Act further called for a 50-percent phaseout by 2001 and 70 percent by 2003 from 1991 baseline levels and the Protocol calls for total phaseout in industrialized countries by 2005.[448] US farmers again pleaded with Congress to extend these deadlines because they were already facing stiff competition from foreign producers.[449] But under a final rule published in November 2001, EPA banned the use of prohibited substances, including methyl bromide, in the manufacture of all foam products, except those used for providing

---

importance of scientific data as a catalyst to creating more stringent regulations. The EPA proposed a rule under its acceleration authority to add methyl bromide and hydrobromofluorocarbons to the list of Class I substances, and to ban specified trade of these substances in accordance with Article 4 of the Protocol (58 Fed. Reg. 15104 (Mar. 18, 1993)). To further illustrate the active role of the EPA, it proposed a recycling program for ozone-depleting refrigerants recovered during servicing (58 Fed. Reg. 28660 (May 14, 1993)), and a program for evaluating and regulating substitutes for substances being phased out under Title VI (58 Fed. Reg. 29094 (May 12, 1993)), including the production and use of methyl bromide after 2001. An EPA rule prohibits the sale, distribution, or offer to sell certain products containing CFCs in interstate commerce after specified dates (58 Fed. Reg. 4768 (Jan. 15, 1993)).

[442] 42 U.S.C. § 767lj (1993); 58 Fed. Reg. 8136 (Feb. 11, 1993).

[443] *Ozone Depletion*, 19 Int'l Env't Rep. (BNA) 17 (Jan. 10, 1996).

[444] *Ozone Depletion*, 19 Int'l Env't Rep. (BNA) 86 (Feb. 7, 1996).

[445] *Ozone Depletion*, 20 Int'l Env't Rep. (BNA) 905 (Oct. 1, 1997).

[446] *Ozone Depletion*, 22 Int'l Env't Rep. (BNA) 490 (June 9, 1999).

[447] *Id.*

[448] *See Ozone Depletion*, 23 Int'l Env't Rep. (BNA) 573 (July 19, 2000).

[449] *See id.*

thermal protection to external tanks used for space vehicles.[450] The US phased out methyl bromine by January 1, 2005, pursuant to the Montreal Protocol and the Clean Air Act.[451]

As another example of the United States' vigorous observance of its obligations under the Protocol, it has acted to eliminate several "essential-use" exemptions from Clean Air Act regulations which limit the use of Class I ozone-depleting substances. This includes eliminating all remaining uses of CFCs in air conditioners and refrigerators.[452] It has continued to support the Multilateral Fund of the Montreal Protocol to help developing countries phase out ODSs,[453] and it also continues to take action against those involved in illicit trade of ODSs. For example, violators are subject to criminal charges by the Department of Justice.[454]

10.2.9.3 *European Union Action*

The European Commission confirmed earlier similar findings in its 2002 analysis that a "possibility of severe ozone losses over the Arctic and Europe remains high, due to slow chlorine decreases and the current increase of bromine concentrations, which will ultimately contribute to this loss," thus, mini ozone holes continue to increase over Europe.[455] However, the major ODSs' concentrations in the atmosphere had slowed, because, without the Protocol there would have been a far greater concentration of ODSs in the atmosphere – five times the value existing in 2002 and nine times the value projected for 2050 of chlorine.[456] This would cause ozone depletion amounting

---

[450] *See EPA Kills 'Nonessential Substances Exemptions,'* 24 Int'l Env't Rep. (BNA) 1058 (Nov. 21, 2001).

[451] EPA, Ozone Layer Protection – Regulatory Programs: The Phaseout of Methyl Bromide, http://www.epa.gov/ozone/mbr/.

[452] *See id.*

[453] *See Senate Approves $7.3 Billion in Spending for EPA, Restores Montreal Protocol Funds,* 22 Int'l Env't Rep. (BNA) 803 (Sept. 29, 1999); *Montreal Protocol Multilateral Fund Operates Cost-Effectively, Congress Told,* 20 Int'l Env't Rep. (BNA) 755 (Aug. 6, 1997).

[454] *See DOJ Files Five More Smuggling Cases, Including First Involving Halon1301,* 21 Int'l Env't Rep. (BNA) 236 (Mar. 4, 1998); *CFC Smugglers Charged as Crackdown on Illegal Market Announced by U.S. Officials,* 20 Int'l Env't Rep (BNA) 52 (Jan. 22, 1997); EPA, *Customs Service Cracking Down on Smuggling of CFCs, Hazardous Waste,* 19 Int'l Env't Rep. (BNA) 219 (Mar. 20, 1996).

[455] Joe Kirwin, *E.U. Expects Continued Increase in "Mini" Ozone Holes Over Europe,* 25 Int'l Env't Rep. (BNA) 107 (Jan. 30, 2002). The report was based on analysis of EU research between 1996 and 2000 as part of the Third European Stratospheric Experiment on Ozone.

[456] *See id.* at 17.

to at least 50 percent at northern and 70 percent at southern mid-latitudes, doubling or quadrupling surface UV-Bs, all of which figures would be growing, with substantial adverse impact on human health and wellbeing.[457] The EU has taken initiatives going beyond its obligations under the Montreal Protocol – its consumption of ozone depleting substances has been reduced to zero since 2010, a decade before the international target of 2020.[458]

10.2.10   *Appraisal and Recommendations*

The ozone regime established under the Vienna Convention and the Montreal Protocol is an historic success story.[459] Note the remarkable change in production and consumption figures for the various controlled substances. By the beginning of 1999, production of the originally controlled CFCs was almost eradicated in industrialized countries, having fallen by 95 percent, with the remaining 5 percent devoted to essential use exemptions and permitted exports to developing countries.[460] By 2000, production of the originally controlled halons for industrialized countries had similarly fallen by 99.8 percent and, despite the increase in developing countries as allowed under the Protocol, overall world production had reportedly declined by about 88 percent for CFCs and 84 percent for halons from 1996, the base year.[461] In 1986 the total consumption of CFCs globally was about 1 million tons of ozone depletion potential (ODP), but by 2006 this had gone down to about 35,000 tons,[462] and by 2011, with 197 parties to the Vienna Ozone Convention and the Montreal Protocol, 98 percent of ODSs controlled by the Montreal Protocol had been phased out.[463]

This success story is coupled with several challenges. The first is one of compliance.[464] The Multilateral Fund – whose implementing agencies are

---

[457] *See id.*

[458] European Commission, Climate Action – Protection of the Ozone Layer, March 11, 2011, http://ec.europa.eu/clima/policies/ozone/index_en.htm.

[459] *See generally* Vienna Ozone Convention-Montreal Protocol 2011, *supra* note 161; Elizabeth R. DeSombre, *The Experience of the Montreal Protocol: Particularly Remarkable and Remarkably Particular*, 19 UCLA J. Envtl. L. & Pol'y 49 (2000/2001).

[460] 2000 Ozone Action, *supra* note 294, at 16.

[461] *Id.*

[462] Backgrounder, *supra* note 219.

[463] Vienna Ozone Convention-Montreal Protocol 2011 Report, *supra* note 161, at §1, ¶ 4. For an earlier report, *see also* UNEP, Note by the Secretariat, Synthesis Report of the 2010 Assessments of the Montreal Protocol Assessment Panels, at 5 (The Success of the Montreal Protocol), Doc. UNEP/OzL.Pro.WG.1/31/3, June 6, 2011, http://ozone.unep.org/Meeting_Documents/oewg/31oewg/OEWG-31-3E.pdf.

[464] Initially the challenge was that of compliance by Russia, several Eastern European countries and former Soviet states, and developing countries. *See* Kirwin, *supra* note 455. at 18. *See*

UNEP, the United Nations Development Program, the United Nations Industrial Development Organization, and the World Bank – and the Global Environment Facility, have provided substantial financial assistance to developing countries, Russia, and former Soviet states, so that they can meet their compliance obligations.[465] Compliance by developing countries – as they agreed to a 1999 freeze on CFCs production and consumption, followed by a freeze on halons and methyl bromide by 2002 and a complete phaseout of CFC use by 2010 and of methyl bromide by 2015 – was of special attention as early as 2001 at the Sri Lanka Meeting of the Parties.[466] This challenge still remains as at the November 2011 meeting of the Conference of the Parties to the Vienna Convention and meeting of the Parties to the Montreal Protocol. Several countries including the Russian Federation, Libya, Iraq, Yemen, and the European Union, were found to be in noncompliance or facing potential noncompliance, and fourteen other countries requested revision of their baselines.[467]

The second challenge is that of illicit trade in CFCs and other substances banned under the Protocol. To illustrate, the September 2008 UNEP report, Backgrounder – Basic Facts and Data on the Science and Politics of Ozone Protection, lists among the remaining challenges the issue of illegal trade, stating, "As the continuing phase-out of ozone depleting substances further constrains their supply, the temptation to make money through illegal trade in such substances often increases; the Parties need to redouble their efforts

---

generally Timothy T. Jones, *Implementation of the Montreal Protocol: Barriers, Constraints and Opportunities*, 3 ENVTL. LAW 813 (1997). *See also Implementation Issues Top Agenda of Annual Montreal Protocol Ozone Meeting*, 24 Int'l Env't Rep. (BNA) 907–08 (Oct. 24, 2001) (the Protocol's Implementation Committee found that 23 of the treaty's 136 parties were not in compliance for either 1999 or 200 or both – 19 developing countries and four of the former Soviet republics).

[465] *See* 2000 Ozone Action, *supra* note 294, at 18; *Implementation Issues Top Agenda of Annual Montreal Protocol Ozone Meeting*, 24 Int'l Env't Rep. (BNA) 908 (Oct. 24, 2001) ($1.2 billion has been disbursed for ODS phase-out projects in nearly 120 developing countries since 1991 and the Fund's replenishment for the 2003–2005 period is essential for facilitating compliance).

[466] *See Implementation Issues Top Agenda of Annual Montreal Protocol Ozone Meeting*, 24 Int'l Env't Rep. (BNA) 908 (Oct. 24, 2001).

[467] Vienna Ozone Convention-Montreal Protocol 2011 Report, *supra* note 161, at XXIII/ 23–29, pp. 47–50.

to address this issue."[468] Several countries, however, have taken appropriate enforcement actions.[469]

The third challenge identified by UNEP is to ensure control of new chemicals which might pose a threat to the ozone layer, as UNEP notes:

> The same creative entrepreneurial spirit that inspired the development of alternatives to ozone depleting substances may spark the invention of new substances with ozone depleting properties. The Parties must be vigilant in the testing of new chemicals, lest new ozone depleters gain a foothold in the marketplace.[470]

---

[468] Backgrounder, *supra* note 219, at § 8, The Remaining Challenges. For earlier reports, *see generally* Frederick Poole Landers Jr., *Note: The Black Market Trade in Chlorofluorocarbons: The Montreal Protocol Makes Banned Refrigerants a Hot Commodity*, 26 GA. J. INT'L & COMP. L. 457 (1997); *Experts Urge UNEP to Take Lead in Efforts to Combat Environmental Crimes*, 22 Int'l Env't Rep. (BNA) 648 (Aug. 4, 1999) (the UN paper cites estimates by government and industry of the global total of smuggled ODSs at between 16,000 and 38,C00 tons in 1995, which represented up to 15 percent of worldwide ODS consumption); *G-8 Environment Ministers Vow Crackdown on Illegal Trade in ODS, Hazardous Wastes*, 21 Int'l Env't Rep. (BNA) 357 (Apr. 15, 1998); *U.S. Official Predicts CFC Shortage, Increased Smuggling as Phaseout Proceeds*, 23 Int'l Env't Rep. (BNA) 917 (Nov. 22, 2000) (increased smuggling predicted unless steps are taken to reduce demand); Environmental Investigation Agency (EIA), *A Crime Against Nature: The Worldwide Illegal Trade in Ozone-Depleting Substances*, Nov. 12, 1998.

[469] *See* Toshio Aritake, *Japanese Police-Customs Agents Arrest Two Men for Smuggling CFC-12*, 25 Int'l Env't Rep. (BNA) 50 (Jan. 2, 2002); *Japanese Customs, Auto Officials Uncover Illegal CFC Trade at Narita*, 24 Int'l Env't Rep. (BNA) 818 (Sept. 26, 2001); *EU Uncovers Illegal Scheme to Import Ozone-Depleting Chlorofluorocarbons*, 20 Int'l Env't Rep. (BNA) 750 (Aug. 6, 1997); *Environmental Investigating Group Finds Widespread Trade of CFCs in Europe*, 20 Int'l Env't Rep. (BNA) 869 (Sept. 17, 1997); *Gummer Says Government to Crack Down on Environmental Crimes Like CFC Smuggling*, 19 Int'l Env't Rep. (BNA) 977 (Oct. 30, 1996) (U.K. Environment Secretary John Gummer's Pronouncement).

[470] Backgrounder, *supra* note 219 at § 8. Earlier, the concern was with new chemicals being substituted for ODSs which also had the potential of depleting the ozone. *See generally U.N. Fears Replacement Chemicals May Delay Recovery of Ozone Layer*, 24 Int'l Env't Rep. (BNA) 817 (Sept. 26, 2001) (UNEP's warning to nations, urging them to immediately assess a range of substitute new chemicals); *Ozone Depletion*, 24 Int'l Env't Rep. (BNA) 907, 908 (concern about new chemicals at the Meeting of the Parties in Colombo Sri Lanka in October 2001 and the meeting's call on UNEP Secretariat to begin work on new procedures for assessing the ozone-depleting potential of these chemicals); *U.S. Government Scientists Say Ozone Hole Has Remained Stable Over Past Three Years*, 24 Int'l Env't Rep. (BNA) 923 (Oct. 24 2001), referring to statement of Joseph Farman, consultant to European Ozone Research Coordinating Unit, one of team of British Antarctic Survey scientists who discovered ozone hole, that several new unlisted bromine compounds that drift up into the stratosphere now thwart recovery.

Finally, developing countries face enormous difficulties with phaseout of HCFCs and methyl bromide, especially as they rely heavily upon funding from the Protocol's Multilateral Fund to support their phaseout efforts.[471]

Despite these difficulties, the ozone regime has successfully brought together industrialized countries and developing countries in appreciating their common interest in phasing out ODSs and finding flexible mechanisms in response to scientific data and in the form of setting targets and revising them through a review process and amendments.[472] The recognition of the needs of developing countries and the tailoring of the control mechanisms to those needs has been a special feature of this regime. The continued focus on implementation of the Protocol while meeting these challenges remains a major part of the unfinished agenda.

10.3   Global Climate Change

10.3.1   Introduction

One of the most alarming trends the world now faces is the rise in global temperatures resulting from increasing concentrations of greenhouse gases (GHGs) in the atmosphere.[473] This human-induced pollution problem[474]

---

[471] *See* Backgrounder, *supra* note 219, at § 8. *See also* Vienna Ozone Convention – Montreal Protocol 2011, *supra* note 161 at § X, XXIII/14, by the 23rd Meeting of the Parties to the Montreal Protocol: Key Challenges Facing Methyl Bromide Phase-out in Parties Operating Under Paragraph 1 of Article 5; Decision XXIII/5: Quarantine and Pre-shipment Uses of Methyl Bromide. This challenge has been ongoing. For earlier reports, *see, e.g., Implementation Issues Top Agenda of Annual Montreal Protocol Ozone Meeting,* 24 Int'l Env't Rep. (BNA) 907–08 (Oct. 24, 2001); *Montreal Meeting Considers Fine-Tuning of Protocol on Ozone-Depleting Chemicals,* 24 Int'l Env't Rep. (BNA) 640 (Aug. 1, 2001) (the European Union's concern about the developing countries' phaseout of HCFCs).

[472] As mentioned earlier, the Montreal Protocol was amended by the London Amendment in 1990, Copenhagen Amendment in 1992, Montreal Amendment in 1997, and Beijing Amendment in 1999. Adjustments to the phaseout schedules were made after periodic assessments. These adjustments were made in 1990 (London Adjustments), 1992 (Copenhagen), 1995 (Vienna), 1997 (Montreal), 1999 (Beijing), and 2007 (Montreal). Backgrounder, *supra* note 219, at § 2.

[473] Initial parts of this section draw on George (Rock) Pring, *The United States Perspective in* KYOTO: FROM PRINCIPLES TO PRACTICE 185 (Peter D. Cameron & Donald Zillman eds. 2001). Refer to that chapter and the authorities footnoted *infra* for in-depth discussion and detailed citation of sources. *See* JOHN FIROR, THE CHANGING ATMOSPHERE: A GLOBAL CHALLENGE (1990) for what is still one of the best, most accessible explanations of the science of climate change and related atmospheric pollution problems, by one of the respected early leaders in the field.

[474] It is the human-caused or "anthropogenic" GHG emissions that the majority of scientists view as substantially increasing GHG concentrations. UN INTERGOVERNMENTAL PANEL

threatens us with global climate change, also called "global warming," on a scale unprecedented in human history. Few issues in international environmental law have been as polarizing as climate change. Because the emission of GHGs is closely linked to materials, products, and processes that are integral to economic growth and development, many countries, including the US, have been unwilling to commit to significant reductions.

International attention was first drawn to climate change in the 1980s, leading to the 1992 United Nations Framework Convention on Climate Change (UNFCCC),[475] which entered into force in 1994. However, as a "framework" convention (some might say "an agreement to agree"), it contained no mandatory limits or enforcement mechanisms. Thus, the convention deferred to subsequent agreements to set actual requirements. The Kyoto Protocol,[476] the intended enforcement agreement, entered into force in 2005. Unfortunately, this treaty has fallen short of controlling climate change because it has not been joined by some of the world's largest emitters – including the US and the "emerging economies" or "mega-developing" countries such as China, Brazil, and India.[477] The failure of the Kyoto Protocol has demonstrated that

---

ON CLIMATE CHANGE (IPCC), CLIMATE CHANGE: THE IPCC SCIENTIFIC ASSESSMENT xxxvi (J. T. Houghton *et al.* eds., 1990); for the latest IPCC Guidelines for National Greenhouse Gas Inventories, *see* http://www.ipcc.ch/.

[475] Consult the UNFCCC Secretariat website for detailed information on and copies of the climate change agreements, http://www.unfccc.int.

[476] *Id.*

[477] More detailed analyses of the history of the climate change problem and the treaty regime include Pring, *supra* note 473; DANIEL PERLMUTTER & ROBERT ROTHSTEIN, THE CHALLENGE OF CLIMATE CHANGE: WHICH WAY NOW? (2011); HUIFANG TIAN & JOHN WHALLEY, CHINA'S PARTICIPATION IN GLOBAL ENVIRONMENTAL NEGOTIATIONS (2008), Daniel Bodansky, *The Copenhagen Climate Change Conference: A Postmortem*, 104 AM. J. INT'L L. 230 (2010); Anita Halvorssen, *Climate Change Treaties – New Developments at the Buenos Aires Conference*, in COLO. J. INT'L ENVTL. L.: 1998 Y.B. 1 (1999); Paul Harris, *Common But Differentiated Responsibility: The Kyoto Protocol and United States Policy*, 7 N.Y. U. ENVTL. L.J. 27 (1999); Ved Nanda, *The Kyoto Protocol on Climate Change and the Challenges to Its Implementation – A Commentary*, 10 COLO. J. INT'L ENVTL. L. & POL'Y 319 (1999); Clare Breidenich *et al.*, *The Kyoto Protocol to the United Nations Framework Convention on Climate Change*, 92 AM. J. INT'L L. 315 (1998); David Driesen, *Free Lunch or Cheap Fix?: The Emissions Trading Idea and the Climate Change Convention*, 26 B.C. ENVTL. AFF. L. REV. 1 (1998); Eduardo M. Peñalver, *Acts of God or Toxic Torts? Applying Tort Principles to the Problem of Climate Change*, 38 NAT. RESOURCES J. 563 (1998); Gaetan Verhoosel, *Beyond the Unsustainable Rhetoric of Sustainable Development: Transferring Environmentally Sound Technologies*, 11 GEO. INT'L ENVTL. L. REV. 49 (1998).

A number of very useful climate change websites exist, including the UN FRAMEWORK CONVENTION ON CLIMATE CHANGE (FCCC) SECRETARIAT, http://www.unfccc.int; US ENVIRONMENTAL PROTECTION AGENCY (EPA), http://www.epa.gov/climatechange/index .html; US DEPARTMENT OF ENERGY, http://www.eia.gov/environment/; US DEPARTMENT OF STATE, http://www.state.gov/e/oes/climate/index.htm; WHITE HOUSE http://www

any action on climate change must secure the cooperation of the major emitting states in order to be successful. This section will begin with a brief explanation of the greenhouse effect and the chemical culprits responsible for it. This will be followed by an outline of preventative strategies and the problems associated with those strategies. A brief account of the history of the UNFCCC and the Kyoto Protocol will come next, followed by an assessment the strengths and weaknesses of the Kyoto Protocol. The section will finish with a description of the actions taken since the ratification of the Kyoto Protocol and predictions about the future of a climate change regime.

10.3.2   *The "Greenhouse" Effect*

Ironically, climate change stems from a very essential and beneficial natural process called "the greenhouse effect," without which life on earth would be impossible. Somewhat like the glass in a greenhouse, gas molecules in the upper atmosphere allow solar energy to pass through to the surface of the earth then trap some of the radiant energy (heat) reflected upward, thus maintaining the narrow range of temperature in which our life forms can thrive. Without this protective shield of GHGs, our Earth would be a frozen, dead planet. However, since the 19th century Industrial Revolution, we have been increasing our GHG emissions, thickening this gas "ceiling" and trapping more radiant heat, thus raising the temperature in our earthly "greenhouse."

Over a decade ago, Robert T. Watson, then Chairman of the UN Intergovernmental Panel on Climate Change (IPCC) reported:

> [T]he overwhelming majority of scientific experts, whilst recognizing that scientific uncertainties exist, nonetheless believe that human-induced climate change is already occurring and that future change is inevitable. It is not a question of whether the Earth's climate will change, but rather by how much, how fast and where. It is undisputed that the two last decades [have been]...the warmest for the last 1,000 years, sea level is rising, precipitation patterns are changing, Arctic sea ice is thinning and the frequency and intensity of El-Nino events appear to be increasing. In addition, many parts of the world have recently suffered major heat-waves, floods, droughts and extreme weather events leading to significant loss of life and economic costs. While individual extreme weather events cannot be directly linked to human-induced climate change, the frequency and magnitude of these types of events are expected to increase in a warmer world.... [I]factions are not taken to reduce the projected increase in greenhouse gas emissions, the Earth's climate is likely to change at a rate unprecedented in the

.whitehouse.gov/energy; and other web sites noted below. For excellent links to most of the major climate change web sites, go to http://www.nrdc.org/reference/topics/global.asp.

last 10,000 years with adverse consequences for society, undermining the very foundation of sustainable development.[478]

Computer-generated climate models project an increase in global mean surface temperature of 1.1 to 6.4 degrees centigrade between 1900 and 2100,[479] a change that will alter every ecosystem on Earth.[480] As the Earth warms, the models project greater water-stress in arid lands in Southern Africa, the Middle East, Southern Europe, Australia, and the western US; decreased agricultural production in many tropical and sub-tropical countries, especially in Africa and Latin America; increased vector-borne diseases like malaria and dengue in tropical nations; sea level rises displacing tens of millions of people in small island states (SISs) and low coastal areas; and damaging change in critical ecological systems like coral reefs and forests.[481]

The chemical culprits are in widespread use and released in tremendous volumes.[482] They include natural substances like carbon dioxide (CO_2), methane (CH_4), and nitrous oxide (N_2O), and human-made substances not found in nature, including halocarbons and other halogenated substances[483] (like CFCs, HFCs, HCFCs, PFCs, and sulphur hexafluoride (SF_6)).[484]

---

[478] Robert T. Watson, Report to the Sixth Conference of the Parties of the United Nations Framework Convention on Climate Change, 1–3 (Nov. 20, 2000), http://www.ipcc.ch/graphics/speeches/robert-watson-november-20-2000.pdf; *Hotting up in the Hague*, Economist (Nov. 16, 2000), http://www.economist.com/node/423384.

[479] Watson, *supra* note 478, at 1. EPA, *Future Temperature Changes*, http://www.epa.gov/climatechange/science/futuretc.html.

[480] Brown et al., *supra* note 1, at 6.

[481] Watson, *supra* note 478, at 1–2.

[482] Detailed background studies exist – from which this chapter's data are drawn – including US Department of Energy (DOE), Energy Information Administration (EIA), Emissions of Greenhouse Gases in the United States 2009 (Mar. 2011), http://205.254.135.24/environment/emissions/ghg_report/pdf/0573%282009%29.pdf (this is an annual report revised and released each year covering the preceding year); EPA, Inventory of US Greenhouse Gas Emissions and Sinks (1990–2009) (Apr. 2011), http://epa.gov/climatechange/emissions/downloads11/US-GHG-Inventory-2011-Complete_Report.pdf (this is also an annual report, covering the preceding complete year). For the international emissions statistics, *see* http://unfccc.int/ghg_data/ghg_data_unfccc/items/4146.php.

[483] A "halogen" is any of the five nonmetallic chemical elements – chlorine, fluorine, bromine, astatine, or iodine. "Halogenated" refers to a substance which has been treated with or combined with a halogen. A "halocarbon" is a halogenated substance comprised of carbon and one or more halogens.

[484] A number of different gases exhibit this "greenhouse" or "radiative forcing" effect. Naturally occurring GHGs include water vapor (H_2O), carbon dioxide CO_2), methane (CH_4), nitrous oxide (N_2O), and ozone (O_3). Human-engineered halogenated substances containing chlorine, bromine, or fluorine are also GHGs, including halocarbons that contain chlorine (such as chlorofluorocarbons (CFCs) and hydrochlorofluorocarbons (HCFCs)),

CO_2 is by far the most prevalent of GHGs. The inevitable by-product of human energy use, CO_2 is primarily caused by the combustion of carbon-based fossil fuels such as coal, oil, gasoline, and natural gas and the burning of wood, including forests. In developed countries, like the US, electricity generation and transportation produce the most CO_2, followed by industrial, residential, and commercial emissions.[485] In developing countries, on the other hand, this break down is usually much different. For example, 33% of China's emissions in 2005 were due to the production of exports rather than the result of their own consumption.[486]

CO_2 concentrations in the atmosphere have been growing steadily with industrialization and the economy, from an estimated level of 280 parts per million (ppm) in 1860 to 390 ppm in 2011, an increase of almost 40%, with accelerating increases of 1%–1.5% percent projected to continue compounding annually in the foreseeable future.[487] Global emissions of CO_2 from fossil fuel burning jumped by the largest amount on record in 2010, a rise of 5.9 percent or 500,000,000 extra tons of carbon released into the atmosphere, the largest jump in any year since the Industrial Revolution began.[488] Put another way, all of the world's volcanoes discharge about 200,000,000 tons of

---

halocarbons that contain bromine (halons), and halogens containing fluorine (such as hydrofluorocarbons (HFCs) and perfluorocarbons (PFCs)) and sulphur hexafluoride (SF_6). In addition, some solvents and other combustion-produced gases appear to have GHG-like effects (*see infra* note 464). New GHGs continue to be discovered, for example in 2000 and 2009 respectively trifluoromethyl sulphur pentafluoride (SF_5CF_3) and sulfuryl fluoride were discovered. *See* Andrew C. Revkin, *Potent New Greenhouse Gas Is Found, but It's Quite Rare (but Expanding)*, N.Y. TIMES (July 28, 2000), at A17. *Sulfuryl Fluoride – Newly Discovered Greenhouse Gas Has 4800 Times The Warming Impact Of CO2*, SCIENCE 2.0 (Mar. 10, 2009), http://www.science20.com/news_releases/sulfuryl_fluoride_newly_discovered_greenhouse_gas_has_4800_times_warming_impact_co2.

The international climate change treaty regime only addresses six of these GHGs – CO_2, methane, N_2O, HFCs, PFCs, and SF_6. The CFCs, HCFCs, and halons, because of their effects on stratospheric ozone depletion, are controlled by the Montreal Protocol on Substances that Deplete the Ozone Layer, Sept. 16, 1987, 26 I.L.M. 1541 (1987), and are not covered by the climate change treaty. Water vapor, the most common GHG, is not covered by either treaty regime, since it is so plentiful that additional anthropogenic emissions are unlikely to affect atmospheric concentrations.

[485] EPA, *Human Related Resources and Sinks of Carbon Dioxide*, http://www.epa.gov/climate change/emissions/co2_human.html.

[486] Christopher Weber *et al.*, *The Contribution of Chinese Exports to Climate Change*, IIOMME, (July 2008) http://www.iioa.org/pdf/Intermediate-2008/Papers/3b2_Weber.pdf.

[487] *See* CO2Now.org, *Home Page*, http://co2now.org.

[488] Justin Gillis, *Carbon Emissions Show Biggest Jump Ever Recorded*, N.Y. TIMES, Dec. 4, 2011, http://www.nytimes.com/2011/12/05/science/earth/record-jump-in-emissions-in-2010-study-finds.html.

CO_2 into the atmosphere each year – an amount that human activities emit *in less than three days.*[489]

Methane (CH_4) is a much smaller proportion of GHGs (less than 10% of the total), but it is 21 times more effective at trapping heat than CO_2 (so one ton of methane has the "radiative forcing effect" of 21 tons of CO_2). Methane occurs both naturally and anthropogenically from biological decomposition (landfills, rice paddies, even livestock flatulence) and fossil fuel emissions (coal mines, pipeline leakage, etc.). While its volume does not appear to be increasing, this could be a function of the rudimentary measuring and estimation methodology currently used.

Nitrous oxide (N_2O) appears to be half the amount of methane quantitatively, but it is a very potent GHG, 310 times more powerful than CO_2 at trapping heat. Like methane, it comes from biological decomposition, fugitive fossil fuel emissions, and various other sources. The agricultural sector is also a major source of N_2O emission due to nitrogen-based fertilizers, as are catalytic converters in motor vehicles, fossil fuel combustion, and production of synthetic fibers. While N_2O is not apparently increasing, the science and estimation methodology here is even more speculative than with methane and significant uncounted sources are suspected to exist.

A very small volume of GHGs consist of human-engineered halogenated substances not found in nature, but these are incredibly potent GHGs, ranging from 140 to 23,900 times more powerful than CO_2 at trapping heat in the atmosphere. These include halocarbons – hydrofluorocarbons (HFCs) and perfluorocarbons (PFCs) – and sulphur hexafluoride (SF6), which do not affect the stratospheric ozone layer. Other GHG halocarbons – like the well-known chlorofluorocarbons (CFCs), hydrochlorofluorocarbons (HCFCs), and halons (brominated halocarbons) – do affect the ozone layer and are regulated exclusively by the Stratospheric Ozone Treaty regime (*see* § 10.2). HFCs, rare until recently, are used as refrigerants (ironically to replace CFCs in automobile air conditioners). PFCs (CF_4, C_2F_6, and C_3F_8) are emitted by the aluminum and semiconductor industries. Sulphur hexafluoride is used as an insulator in utility electrical equipment. The US and other developed country emissions of these gases increased dramatically in the 1990s. While their total emissions are small (a few thousand metric tons), their extreme global warming potency and long lifetimes (hundreds or thousands of years) make them extreme contributors to climate change. Additional pollutants have or are suspected to have global warming impacts, but are not currently included on the Kyoto list of regulated GHGs.[490]

---

[489] *Last Words*, Sierra Magazine, Nov/Dec 2011, at 76, http://www.sierraclub.org/sierra/201111/lastwords.aspx.

[490] Most of these are regulated in the US under the Clean Air Act (CAA). The solvents carbon tetrachloride, methyl chloroform, and methylene chloride have direct radiative forcing

Counteracting these GHGs are the world's "sinks" – forests, croplands, pastures, and the oceans – which absorb CO_2 from the atmosphere and "sequester" or lock it in plant tissues and the oceans' waters, keeping it from adding to concentrations in the upper atmosphere. One study indicates North America may be a huge carbon sink possibly capable of sequestering more than 2 billion metric tons of carbon equivalent (MTCE).[491] Unfortunately, sinks can become saturated, may burn down, be paved over, or otherwise lose their carbon-sequestering abilities. So, they have presented a hugely divisive issue in the current debate, with the US, Russian Federation, and forested developing countries like Brazil and Indonesia arguing that the uptake of carbon of their immense forest sinks should be subtracted from their carbon-reduction requirements, a position that has been heavily opposed by the EU and some environmentalists.

10.3.3   Preventive Strategies and Problems

The solution to global warming is simple – stop emitting carbon – but the simplicity of the solution only underscores the complexity of the problem. Overwhelmingly, anthropogenic GHG emissions are caused by the combustion of fossil fuels such as coal, petroleum, and natural gas (75% of all GHGs worldwide and 98% of all US CO_2 emissions), and so it is our energy usage that is the problem. In 1987 US Senate hearings, then-US Senator Timothy Wirth made this point bluntly:

> Today, these scientists are going to tell us that our use of energy and the destruction of the world's rain forests already have committed the Earth to a significant warming. More important, they are here to warn us that unless the United States government works with other governments around the world to redirect our energy policies and to halt deforestation, global climate change on a scale never before experienced by man could overwhelm our planet –

---

effects. Three combustion-produced gases – carbon monoxide, nitrogen oxides, and non-methane volatile organic compounds (NMVOCs) – are also are thought to play an indirect (but as yet undetermined and unquantified) role in global warming. Lastly, there is a class of gases – including sulphur dioxide – which create small solid articles (aerosols) in the atmosphere and may accordingly contribute to cloud formation and a net cooling effect.

[491] *North America a Major "Sink" for Carbon Dioxide, Researchers Find*, 29 ENV'T REP. (BNA) 1236 (Oct. 23, 1998) (describing a study by scientists from Princeton and Columbia Universities and the National Oceanic and Atmospheric Administration published in the Oct. 16, 1998, issue of SCIENCE).

"MTCE" (metric tons of carbon equivalent or 2,200 pounds of carbon) is the conversion unit used to compare and equivalence the different GHGs and provide a common denominator for describing (equalizing) their warming impacts.

potentially in our lifetimes, certainly within the lifetimes of our children and grandchildren.[492]

Are we prepared to stop being a carbon-based energy culture? Are we even prepared to reduce somewhat the rate of increase in our energy use? There are strong indications to the contrary. The US, with less than 5% of the world's population, consumes over 21% of all energy produced globally, emits over 26% of the entire globe's anthropogenic GHGs, and monopolizes 23% of the global economy.[493] Even more disturbingly, the US's resource-intensive lifestyle is fast becoming the global standard to which people in developing countries aspire. Obviously, current consumption patterns will have to change dramatically to avoid the environmental problems associated with present resource use.

In China, reductions in the rate of energy use seem even less likely. China is in the midst of an economic boom that has produced GHGs at an unprecedented rate, making it the world's biggest carbon emitter since 2006, and its emissions increased another 23% from 2007 through 2009.[494] Currently, China and the other "mega-developers" (namely India, Brazil, Mexico, Indonesia, etc.) are in a race against themselves – trying to establish enough economic growth to alleviate population and political pressures, while at the same time trying to prevent overwhelming environmental destruction – with economics generally winning out over ecology. This trend, however, is beginning to have deadly effects on the populations of these countries (*see* § 10.1.3.4). The question of whether the mega-developing countries will continue to consume resources at the current increasing rate is of vital importance, because this will control our planet's energy and environmental future.

The US and other countries are currently exploring preventive options, such as energy conservation, emissions trading, restructuring of energy prices, revised tax policies and subsidies, improved energy efficiency, voluntary energy reduction programs, research and development (R&D) in

---

[492] Greenhouse Effect and Global Climate Change: Hearings Before the Senate Comm. On Energy and Natural Resources, 105th Cong., 1st Sess. 5 (1987) (statement of Sen. Timothy Wirth).

[493] Christopher Flavin & Seth Dunn, Reinventing the Energy System, in LESTER R. BROWN, ET AL., STATE OF THE WORLD-1999 38 (1999). Thus, on a per capita basis, the US consumes roughly twice as much energy as Japan and 6 times as much as China. World Resource Institute, *Searchable Database*, http://earthtrends.wri.org/text/energy-resources/variable-351.html.

[494] US emissions declined nearly 10% during the same period. Joe Kirkland, *China's Booming Economy May Produce the Majority of World's Coal Emissions by 2035*, N.Y. TIMES, Feb. 4, 2011, http://www.nytimes.com/cwire/2011/02/04/04climatewire-chinas-booming-economy-may-produce-the-major-52705.html.

renewable energy sources, etc.[495] But is putting the world on an "energy diet" realistic – technologically, economically, or culturally? The energy optimists resoundingly conclude "yes," proffering economic analysis models that show acceptable costs per ton of carbon reduction, limited gasoline price hikes, modest employment impacts in energy-intensive sectors, scant international business competitiveness losses, and huge benefits in averting climate change, in human health and environmental benefits from improved air quality, and in an economic renaissance with thousands of new jobs in the energy efficiency and renewable energy industries.[496] On the other hand, the "energy pessimists" estimate energy costs more than an order of magnitude higher, provoking severe unemployment, loss of agricultural productivity, huge hikes in gasoline, natural gas, coal, and electricity prices, etc.[497] The two extremes are supported by technically competent models, skewed by very different assumptions about the effectiveness of carbon reduction technologies and international emissions trading.

Additional factors make the GHG-reduction debate a very difficult issue for policymakers. There still exists (1) scientific uncertainty about the accuracy of the current climate change models,[498] (2) scientific uncertainty about the global and regional patterns of climate change (e.g., Siberia could benefit!), (3) regulatory uncertainty about acting on the "prevention" and "precautionary principles" (*see* §§ 2.2.3, 2.2.4) given the time lag before the impacts are certain, and (4) political division about whether the "common but differentiated responsibilities principle" (*see* § 2.1.12) should relieve developing countries from having to control their carbon-based economic growth.

All of these factors – physical, scientific, technological, economic, political, and cultural – have held up progress toward effective international environmental law on climate change. Like a play, the drama is heightened by the conflicts among the actors. The developed world is split in its approach – with the EU largely pushing for strict controls[499] and the US national

---

[495] For a detailed look at the range of preventive options *see* KYOTO: FROM PRINCIPLES TO PRACTICE, *supra* note 473.

[496] Pring, *supra* note 473.

[497] *Id.*

[498] The uncertainty that exists is in regards to the extent and severity of climate change. The overwhelming majority of scientists now agree that climate change is occurring and will continue. Doyle Rice, *Report: 97 percent of scientists say man-made climate change is real*, USA TODAY (June 22, 2010), http://content.usatoday.com/communities/sciencefair/post/2010/06/scientists-overwhelmingly-believe-in-man-made-climate-change/1.

[499] European Commission, *Climate Action: What We Do*, http://ec.europa.eu/dgs/clima/mission/index_en.htm.

government hamstrung by climate-change skeptics[500] while some state and local governments in the US forge ahead with regulation.[501] The developing world is also split – with the rapidly industrializing developing countries like Brazil, India, and China until recently adamantly opposed to controls on their economies,[502] the fossil-fuel producers like OPEC in denial about oil's role in climate change,[503] and the small island states (SISs) desperately arguing for the strictest reductions possible in what they view as a life or death struggle for their very survival against rising seas.[504]

10.3.4   *The Framework Convention on Climate Change*

The basis for international law to address climate change, as with stratospheric ozone depletion and other global harms, is Principle 21 of the Stockholm Declaration (*see* §§ 2.1.1–2.1.3). State responsibility (*see* § 2.1.14) under the transboundary "no harm" rule, however, has not by itself proved an adequate remedy for such global problems for a number of reasons. First, the sources of climate change are widespread, difficult to measure, trace, and allocate responsibility – in short, climate change is a result of the combined activities of many nations. Second, Principle 21 seeks to balance a state's responsibility to avoid harming other nations with its right to exploit its environment, and many states (developing nations, fossil-fuel-producers, etc.) view the latter concern, which translates into the right of economic development, as more powerful than the former more abstract responsibility to the globe. Third, the time lag between the GHG emissions and their adverse effects makes attribution and allocation of responsibility extremely difficult. Fourth, alternatives to fossil fuel dependence are not always readily available or affordable, particularly for impoverished developing countries, raising the thorny issues of common but differentiated responsibilities (*see* § 2.1.12), intragenerational equity (*see* § 2.1.7), foreign aid, capacity building, and technology transfer. Fifth, the traditional liability remedy of monetary damages is not

---

[500] *See* Pew Center of Global Climate Change, *Climate Debate in Congress* http://www.pew climate.org/federal/congress.

[501] *See* Pew Center of Global Climate Change, *U.S. States & Regions: Climate Change*, http://www.pewclimate.org/states-regions.

[502] Shawn McCarthy, *China, India, Brazil must pull weight in climate change accord, Baird says*, THE GLOBE AND MAIL, Toronto, Ontario, (Dec. 2, 2010), http://www.theglobeand mail.com/news/politics/china-india-brazil-must-pull-weight-in-climate-change-accord-baird-says/article1823097/.

[503] Tom Bergin, *OPEC says oil not to blame for climate change*, REUTERS, Apr. 2, 2009, http://www.reuters.com/article/2009/04/02/opec-environment-idUSL225721020090402.

[504] *See, e.g.*, Press Release, Pacific Islands Forum Secretariat, *SG: Climate change a danger now, not tomorrow* (Sept. 7, 2011), http://forum.forumsec.org/pages.cfm/newsroom/press-statements/2011/sg-climate-change-danger-now-not-tomorrow.html.

adequate – no amount of money will allow a nation to purchase more favorable weather, a cooler climate, or adequate rainfall, after the fact.

The UN International Law Commission (ILC) examined "international liability for injurious consequences arising out of acts which are not prohibited by international law" (*see* § 2.1.14), and found it not well suited to remedy such global issues as climate change. As the Special Rapporteur of the ILC's Draft Articles on Liability remarked, the liability approach is premised on state obligations to take preventive measures, to consult, and to make reparations for harm, and, since

> those obligations presupposed an identifiable State of origin, affected State and identifiable harm... [t]he framework of the topic did not seem to be appropriate for dealing with harm to the human environment as a whole, when there were many States of origin and virtually the whole community of mankind was affected.[505]

Thus, a new approach based on cooperation rather than liability became the new model adopted to respond to the problem of global climate change. In the 1980s, concern about climate change spilled over from the scientific journals to the popular press, intensifying public calls for action and laying the groundwork for international cooperative action in the 1990s.

During the negotiations leading to the 1985 Vienna Convention for the Protection of the Ozone Layer (*see* § 10.2), participants recognized that stratospheric ozone depletion was one part of the broader problem of climate change, but no comparable international consensus had coalesced for action on the latter. In 1988, the UN General Assembly passed a resolution instructing UNEP and the UN World Meteorological Organization (WMO) to create an Intergovernmental Panel on Climate Change (IPCC),[506] to assess the scientific, technical, and socioeconomic information relevant to climate change based on published and peer-reviewed technical literature and to work toward a future international treaty.[507] In 1990, the IPCC produced its First Assessment Report, predicting severe climate changes and calling for large reductions in GHGs under a new treaty regime.[508]

---

[505] Report of the International Law Commission on the Work of Its Fortieth Session, 43 U.N. GAOR, Supp. (No. 10) and U.N. Doc. A/43/10 (1988), at 24. The view was not unanimous; some ILC members disagreed, preferring to include within the scope of the Draft Articles "harm to the common area of the high seas, outer space, ozone layer, etc.," indeed "the whole of the human environment." *Id.* at 23–24. *See also* 53rd Session Report, *supra* note 55.

[506] G.A. Res. 43/53, U.N. GAOR 2d Comm., 43d Sess., Supp No. 49, at 133, U.N. Doc. A/43/49 (1989).

[507] *Organization*, IPCC, http://www.ipcc.ch/organization/organization.shtml.

[508] Intergovernmental Panel on Climate Change, IPCC First Assessment Report: Overview and Summaries (1990). The IPCC has become highly respected (and controversial) in its

UNGA eventually established a multilateral treaty preparation body, the Intergovernmental Negotiating Committee (INC), which began meeting in 1991. After numerous preparatory sessions, the INC produced the Framework Convention on Climate Change (FCCC)[509] in time for signing at the 1992 Rio Earth Summit.

From the outset, the US negotiating position on the FCCC was roundly viewed as negative – characterized by extreme divisions within the US government and a very heavy special-interest-lobbying tug-of-war – despite the fact that public opinion polls showed more than 75 percent of Americans believed global warming was already happening and a solid majority wanted action.[510] The Republican administration of the first President Bush (George H. W. Bush, 1989–93) initially opposed any treaty, but grudgingly agreed to a compromise based on the assurance it would contain no binding commitments or timetables. The US Congress was also a key player in FCCC negotiations because it controls the budget and because a two-thirds concurrence of the US Senate is necessary for a President to ratify a treaty.[511] Congress in the Bush Sr. era was reasonably supportive, making the US the first industrialized country in the world to ratify the new treaty.[512] During the

---

proactive efforts to promote understanding of and action on climate change. The Third Assessment Report, released in early 2001, was even more definitive about the reality and risks of global warming. In its Fourth Assessment Report of 2007, the IPCC stated that it was "unequivocal" that climate change was occurring and that it was very likely that human activities are causing global warming. This report successfully returned the public's attention to the climate change issue at a time when interest was lagging (*see* § 9.3.6). While these reports have, at times, been strongly criticized, by and large most scientists find them an accurate representation of projected trends. The reports can be found at http://www.ipcc.ch/publications_and_data/publications_and_data_reports.shtml.

[509] United Nations Framework Convention on Climate Change, May 9, 1992, 31 I.L.M. 849 (1992), http://unfccc.int/resource/docs/convkp/conveng.pdf.

[510] A July 2000 survey conducted by the Melman Group for the World Wildlife Federation showed 62 percent believe global warming "is happening now" and another 24 percent believed it will happen in the future; 73 percent believed it was a "serious threat," with only 14 percent of conservatives denying the reality of global warming, along with 8 percent of the moderates, and only 1 percent of liberals; and voters express strong support for US government action by a ratio of 8 to 1 (80 percent to 10 percent). *Global Warming Is Serious Threat, 73% of American Voters Say*, a synopsis of this report is available at http://www.worldwildlife.org/who/media/press/2000/WWFPresitem10668.html. A 2011–12 Stanford study of climate change surveys shows 83% of all adults say that global warming has been happening while only 15% say they believe it has not been happening. Stanford University Woods Institute for the Environment, *Survey Research Illuminating American Public Opinion on Climate and Energy*, http://woods.stanford.edu/research/surveys.html.

[511] U.S. CONST. art. II, § 2, cl. 2.

[512] The US signed on June 12, 1992, and formally ratified on Oct. 15, 1992. 194 countries and the EU have ratified the FCCC as of the start of 2012, http://unfccc.int/essential_back ground/convention/status_of_ratification/items/2631.php.

Clinton Administration, however, the US Congress became strongly, bipartisanly negative about US climate change commitments due to the "enormous influence" of the US energy and automobile industries.[513]

Thus, out of the 1991–1992 INC negotiations emerged an FCCC constructed of compromises. However, considering US ambivalence and the vastly different goals of the more than 140 countries involved, any agreement was somewhat remarkable. The 1992 FCCC rather schizophrenically:

- Based itself on the Stockholm Principle 21 principle,[514] but avoided a liability approach in favor of "cooperation";[515]
- Recognized climate change as a serious threat and set an "ultimate objective" of achieving "stabilization of [GHGs]…at a level that would prevent dangerous anthropogenic interference with the climate system,"[516] but without concrete steps for achievement;
- Established a goal of reducing GHG emissions to 1990 levels by the year 2000,[517] but deferred development of any binding state targets and timetables for a later protocol;
- Created a framework for future action through a Conference of the Parties (COP), Secretariat, and other bodies,[518] but without compliance powers;
- Targeted developed ("Annex I") countries as the "largest" source of GHG emissions and conversely recognized that developing countries have "common but differentiated responsibilities" (*see* § 2.1.12),[519] but without resolving their respective share of responsibilities;
- Encouraged national and regional mitigation programs, research, education, information exchange and reporting,[520] but without specific requirements or funding; and
- Promoted cooperation, while failing to resolve whether "market approaches" (so-called "flexible mechanisms") for meeting reductions, such as emissions trading or joint implementation can be used.[521]

---

[513] Ed Smeloff & Fred Branfman, *Kyoto, Global Warming and the 21st Century,* Environmentally Friendly 1, 4 (Pace University School of Law, Spring 1998), copy with authors; *Big U.S. Industries Launch Attack on Warming Treaty,* Wall St. J. (Dec. 12, 1997), at A3. For more details on the US politics of climate change, *see* Pring, *supra* note 473.

[514] FCCC, *supra* note 509, 8th preamble and art. 3.

[515] *Id.* art. 3.

[516] *Id.* art. 2.

[517] *Id.* art. 4(2)(a), (b).

[518] *Id.* arts. 7–11.

[519] *E.g., id.* 3d, 6th, 10th, 18th, 20th, 22d preambles, arts. 3(2), 4.

[520] *Id.* arts. 4–6, 12.

[521] Passing mention only is made to the possibility of states "jointly" reducing GHGs, *id.* art. 4(2)(b).

As the curtain fell on Rio, it was clear that the FCCC was only a first step and would require further negotiation of a more concrete enforcement protocol in order to become effective.

10.3.5 *The Kyoto Protocol*

By the Third Conference of the Parties of the FCCC (COP3), held in Kyoto, Japan, in 1997, the parties were able to sign the Kyoto Protocol,[522] which provided more concrete requirements to implement the vague terms of the FCCC. Most significantly, these requirements included commitments by specified developed countries to reduce GHGs, averaging 5.2 percent below the chosen benchmark of 1990 concentration levels.

The Democratic administration of President William Clinton (1993–2001) was supportive of international climate cooperation, particularly under strong urging by Vice President Al Gore. However, to complicate matters for the US, five months before the Kyoto meeting, the energy/auto coalition lobbied through the US Senate a unanimous resolution admonishing the Administration not to agree to a protocol unless it both (1) required GHG limits on developing countries and (2) would do no substantial harm to the US economy.[523] While a one-house resolution technically has no legal effect, the power of this signal drove – and still continues to drive – US negotiating, forcing it to advocate provisions that minimize the amount of actual domestic US energy reductions required. The resulting US position on the issues provides a prism through which we can see the major current disputes over climate change controls:[524]

- *Emissions Targets.* The US opening position in Kyoto was that the protocol should merely stabilize nations' GHGs at their 1990 level. It failed in

---

[522] Kyoto Protocol to the UN FCCC, FCCC Conference of the Parties, 3d Sess., U.N. Doc. FCCC/CP/1997/7/Add.2 (Dec. 10, 1997) (final version), 37 I.L.M. 22 (1998), http://unfccc .int/kyoto_protocol/items/2830.php. By the start of 2012, 192 countries and the EU had ratified the Kyoto Protocol, http://unfccc.int/kyoto_protocol/status_of_ratification/ items/2613.php.

The US has signed the Kyoto Protocol (Nov. 12, 1998), the last major industrial country to do so, but it has not ratified it. Under international law, signing does not bind a nation to comply with a treaty (only evidencing its willingness to proceed to consider ratification, which is the binding step). However, signing is not legally meaningless; it does create a legal obligation "to refrain from acts which would defeat the object and purpose of a treaty" pending ratification or rejection. *See* Vienna Convention on the Law of Treaties, May 23, 1969, art. 18, 1155 U.N.T.S. 331, http://untreaty.un.org/ilc/texts/instruments/eng lish/conventions/1_1_1969.pdf.

[523] The Byrd-Hagel Resolution, S8113, 143 Cong. Rec. S8113 (daily ed. July 25, 1997).

[524] For further details and sources, *see* Pring, *supra* note 473, particularly pts. III and VII.

this and was pressured into accepting its reduction of 7-percent-below-1990–levels (a 93 percent limit).[525]

- *Differentiated Targets.* Both the US and EU initially demanded the same reduction target for all countries. They failed in this and finally acceded to the Australia-Japan proposal for different quantified emission limitation and reduction commitments (QELRCs) for different countries, in accordance with their circumstances. The range is from a low of 92 percent of 1990 levels (EU, France, Germany, U.K., etc.) to a high of 110 percent (Iceland), with the US's 93-percent limit or target being more demanding than the overall average of 94.8 percent (or 5.2 percent reduction average).[526]

- *Developing Country Commitments.* The US also failed to accomplish the major instruction given it by its Senate – to get developing countries to agree to firm QELRCs as well. The US seeks reduction commitments from developing countries for multiple reasons: (1) it is not mathematically possible to eliminate the threat of global warming through developed country efforts alone, since GHGs from developing countries were then already projected to exceed developed country emissions within a few years (and have today) and constitute the majority of new emissions growth;[527] (2) developed country business interests fear being placed at an economic disadvantage relative to competitors located in developing nations not subject to the same control requirements and costs; (3) developing country requirements are predicted to increase the demand for "technology transfer" from (hence profits for) developed country businesses; and (4) a belief that developing countries actually can limit GHG emissions without slowing their growth.[528] This remains one of the most contentious of these ongoing issues.

- *Multi-Year Deadline.* The US opposed a single-year deadline for meeting emission targets. Here, it succeeded in persuading the parties to adopt

---

[525] Kyoto Protocol, *supra* note 522, art. 3(1), Annex B.

[526] *Id.*

[527] EPA, *Global Greenhouse Gas Data*, http://www.epa.gov/climatechange/emissions/global ghg.html.

[528] This is the conclusion of the highly respected RAN D Corporation think tank, in a study prepared for the Pew Center on Global Climate Change; it is based on changes in planning, privatization, use of renewables and natural gas, and efficiency increases. *Climate Change: Developing World Can Limit Emissions Without Slowing Growth, Study Claims,* Daily Rep. for Executives: Regulation, L. & Econ (BNA), 116 DER A-43, 1999 (June 17, 1999). Another interesting proposal on how this can be done is provided in a Brookings Institution study: Jeffrey Frankel, *Greenhouse Gas Emissions* (Brookings Institution Policy Brief #52, June 1999), http://www.brookings.edu/papers/1999/06energy_frankel.aspx.

a more "flexible" five-year budget period over which emissions "spikes" could be averaged.[529]

- *Decade Delay.* The US also opposed early deadlines (as early as 2003 in one proposal) and succeeded in lobbying for a delay of a "full decade before the start," pushing the five-year compliance period out to 2008–2012.[530]
- *Comprehensive Approach.* The US opposed the EU-Japan plan to cover only three GHGs (CO_2, methane, and nitrous oxide), successfully insisting on including the synthetic HFCs, PFCs, and SF6. Synthetics-producing nations like the US, which wish to avoid domestic CO_2 reductions as much as possible (for fear of reducing energy production), can do so in exchange for reducing any of their (more potent and less politically controversial) synthetic GHGs.[531]
- *Later Base Year.* The US sought successfully to make 1995 the base year for the three synthetics, because this also makes the targets more lenient.[532]
- *Sinks.* Opposed by environmentalists, the EU and many other nations, the US – in a further effort at leniency (to avoid actual GHG domestic reductions) – urged that "land use change and forestry" (LUCF) sinks should be allowed as an offset. The US succeeded in keeping this an open issue,[533] and subsequent negotiations have permitted limited use of sinks.
- *Mandatory Measures.* The US succeeded in staving off requirements that all Annex I parties institute certain specified "mandatory domestic measures," such as energy taxes.
- *Emissions Trading* (ET). The US (opposed by the EU, but supported by other non-EU developed countries) succeeded in keeping free market trading of emissions permits alive. This Article 17 "target-based" ET allows Annex I developed countries to purchase emissions credits from other Annex I parties that reduce their GHGs more than required.[534]
- *"Bubbling."* The EU argued for special treatment as an economic umbrella group to permit its member nations to share their emissions limits collectively, as long as the overall EU reduction was met. Recognizing that this was in effect a regional ET group or multi-nation "bubble," the US successfully lobbied for Article 4, which allows any group of countries to fulfill their target-based commitments jointly.[535] All countries have their eyes on the Russian Federation, where the 1990s collapse of their

---

[529] Kyoto Protocol, *supra* note 522, arts. 3(1), (7).
[530] *Id.*
[531] *Id.* art. 3(1), Annex A; *see* Driesen, *supra* note 477, at 20.
[532] Kyoto Protocol, *supra* note 522, art. 3(8).
[533] *Id.* arts. 3(3)–(4), 3(7).
[534] *Id.* art. 17.
[535] *Id.* art. 4.

very dirty industrial economy has dropped GHGs far below Russia's high (1990-benchmarked) Kyoto allocation, and countries like the US and Japan envision buying up these enormous credits in a "bubble" agreement with Russia. However, the US and EU together "could nearly meet their Kyoto Protocol targets by purchasing offsets from Russia and taking little domestic action," so environmentalists are fighting what they call these "hot air" credits.[536]

- *Joint Implementation* (JI). Furthering its "market-based flexibility" approach, the US pushed successfully (against vehement opposition by China and many of the Group of 77 developing nations) for Annex I developed parties to be able to acquire credits for projects reducing GHG emissions or enhancing sinks in other Annex I developed countries.[537] While in reality just another form of ET, this Article 6 "project-based" JI is distinguished from Article 17 "target-based" (or paper) emissions trading (above) by virtue of the quid pro quo being a tangible project or development rather than simply cash-for-paper-credits.

- *Clean Development Mechanism* (CDM). Another important free-market mechanism successfully advocated by the US and developing countries together is the Article 12 right to engage in joint-implementation-type "projectbased" credits for technology transfer or other projects done in developing countries by governments of or private parties from Annex I developed countries. This too is just another form of ET, distinguished only by being done by projects with and within a developing nation.[538]

- *Domestic Action, "Supplementarity," and "Caps" on Trading.* The US strongly fought for no restrictions or "caps" on the amount or proportion of paper ET, JI, CDM, and bubble credits a country might acquire to avoid actual domestic GHG emissions. The EU strongly opposed this, insisting on language requiring JI and ET to be "supplemental to domestic action"[539] and arguing that such "supplementarity" required a cap of 50 percent on trading (in other words, arguing a minimum of one half of a country's reductions must be actual, domestic limitations on GHGs). This is a crucial issue for the US, because the Clinton Administration's rosy economic analysis – that the US's Kyoto commitments could be met without significant US economic disruption, thus meeting Congress's second condition – was premised on the US being allowed to meet as much as 75 percent of

---

[536] *Climate Change: US Opposes Cap on Amount of Trading Allowed to Meet Domestic Emission Goals*, NAT'L ENV'T DAILY (BNA), 5/27/98 (May 27, 1998).

[537] Kyoto Protocol, *supra* note 522, art. 6.

[538] *Id.* art. 12.

[539] *Id.* arts. 6(1)(d), 17.

its reductions through these trades without domestic reductions in actual energy use (as high as 85 percent in one estimate).[540]

• *Compliance.* US calls for effective implementation and compliance measures were not immediately successful.[541] Nevertheless, the Kyoto Protocol provisions on measurement, reporting, and review of information provided a greater start on a compliance regime than most international treaties have to date and, at the very least, a basis for building a true enforcement regime through later amendment.

The text of the Kyoto Protocol was adopted by consensus at COP3 on December 11, 1997. Some 83 countries plus the EU signed it by the COP's March 16, 1999, deadline.[542] However, the Protocol was met with staunch resistance from many key states – including the US[543] – and President Clinton never submitted the treaty to the US Senate for ratification.[544] This resistance has continued, and it seems unlikely that the US will ever ratify the enforcement protocol, although one is necessary to make the FCCC treaty regime effective. Thus, in recent years, the participating nations have engaged in a string of annual COP meetings to work out the Protocol's troublesome details.

10.3.6   *Negotiating the Implementation of Kyoto 1998–2005*

In the US in 1998, both Congress and industrial interests responded furiously to the Clinton Administration's signing of the Kyoto Protocol.[545] To

---

[540] *Climate Change: US Opposes Cap, supra* note 536.

[541] *But see* Kyoto Protocol, *supra* note 522, art. 18.

[542] *Climate Change: 83 Countries Sign Kyoto Protocol by March 15 Deadline, UN Says,* Daily Env't Rep (BNA), 51 DEN A-1, 1999 (Mar. 17, 1999). Additional countries are still permitted to join by ratification or comparable acts.

[543] As will be discussed in more detail below, the US's refusal to participate in the Kyoto Protocol has undermined the treaty's effectiveness because the US represents such a substantial percentage of emissions.

[544] American Society of International Law, *Reports on International Organizations: The United Nations Framework Convention on Climate Change (UNFCCC),* http://www.asil.org/rio/unfccc.html.

[545] It culminated in a provision in the FY 1999 US EPA Appropriations Act barring EPA from using federal funds to propose or issue rules to implement the Kyoto Protocol. Pub. L. No. 105-276, "Departments of Veterans Affairs and Housing and Urban Development, and Independent Agencies Appropriations Act, 1999" (Oct. 21, 1998). A virtual "gag order" to stop EPA even from doing even "educational outreach" on global warming was defeated on the floor of the House. *Climate Change: Gore Chastises Congress for Bill Provision to Block Action, Discussion on Issue,* Nat'l Env't Daily (BNA), July 15, 1998, BNA-NED database citation 7/15/1998 NED d2; San Loewenberg, *Lobby Talk: Chill Hits Global Warming Pact,* Legal Times (Sept. 21, 1998), at 4 (key lobbyists for the rider were Ford Motor, Mobil Oil, and the National Mining Association). Congressional efforts to block

counter this opposition, the pro-Kyoto forces began fighting back with a truly unusual strategy – "defection" – enlisting high-profile energy and other business leaders to support the Protocol. British Petroleum, Royal Dutch/ Shell, Dupont, General Motors, Monsanto, the giant Southern electric util- ity, several energy company coalitions, and numerous other industries came out in dramatic public statements, jointly with environmentalists, recogniz- ing the seriousness of global climate change, voluntarily cutting their energy use and GHG emissions, and calling for US government action.[546] This pro- Kyoto industry line-crossing continued despite the new Bush Administra- tion opposition to the treaty.[547] While adherence to stricter standards by US entities operating in the US is completely voluntary, US corporations with global operations may be required to comply with the emissions standards adhered to by other countries in which their properties, plants, equipment, or customers are located.[548]

A year after Kyoto, at the 1998 COP4 meeting in Buenos Aires, the par- ties were still unable to reach a legal agreement, so they adopted the "Buenos Aires Plan of Action," which attempted to set out a program of work to accelerate the operational details of the Kyoto Protocol.[549] The plan of action was a staggering list of 140 items that needed to be resolved before countries could ratify the Protocol.[550] The list ranged from working out an enforce- ment regime to establishing the rules for an emissions-trading system.[551] In 1999, at the COP5 in Bonn, the parties made little forward progress on these issues, and at the 2000 COP6 in The Hague, the meeting fell apart completely in a split between the EU and US (and hard line Green Party activists vs.

---

funding for Administration GHG planning continue. *Climate Change: USDA Money Bill in House Would Ban Emissions-Trading Spending*, Daily Rep. for Executives: Regula- tion, L. & Econ (BNA) (May 17, 2000).

[546] Collected in Pring, *supra* note 473, at part IV.

[547] Keith Bradsher & Andrew C. Revkin, *Many Companies Cut Gas Emissions to Head Off Tougher Regulations*, N.Y. Times (May 15, 2001).

[548] "The treaty regulates emissions based on the geography of a facility, rather than the citizen- ship of the facility's owner...[O]ne likely response to Kyoto is that [US] companies with significant overseas holdings will establish company-wide environmental compliance poli- cies...Indeed, at least one international company with large US holdings, Royal Dutch/ Shell, has adopted a company-wide policy[.]" Jennifer Alvey, Onward Kyoto!, 140 Pub. Util. Fort. 46, 46 (2002). For an excellent article on the subject, *see* Stuart Eizenstat & Ruben Kraiem, *In Green Company*, Foreign Policy, Sept. 1, 2005, at 92.

[549] Copy at http://unfccc.int/resource/docs/cop4/16a01.pdf. For an overall view of the negoti- ating process *see* UNFCCC Climate Secretariat, *Guide to the Climate Change Negotiation Process* [hereinafter *Guide*], http://unfccc.int/resource/process/guideprocess-p.pdf.

[550] Press Release, UNFCCC, Climate Change Meeting Adopts Buenos Aires Plan of Action, (Nov. 14, 1998), http://unfccc.int/cop4/infomed/p111498.html.

[551] *Id.*

moderate environmental NGOs) over the US's demand for greater counting of its forest sinks as offsets.[552]

In 2001, the Administration of the newly elected President George W. Bush hardened the US government's position against the Kyoto Protocol, calling the agreement "fatally flawed,"[553] and announced an energy plan based on increased fossil fuel production and use.[554] USEPA Administrator, Christine Todd Whitman, "announced that the Protocol was as good as dead in the Administration's eyes,"[555] opposing the Kyoto Protocol to the shock of environmentalists and EU allies.[556] EU officials were deeply angered at the isolationist-unilateralist stance taken by the US, and, with a great show of political will, the EU spearheaded a continuation of negotiations by convening COP6 Part II, later that year in Bonn, Germany.

At COP6 Part II, the parties adopted the Bonn Agreements, registering political consensus on some key issues under the Buenos Aires Plan of Action. They also completed drafting a series of detailed decisions, which they tentatively agreed to adopt at COP7.[557] The highly politicized nature of COP6 Part II and the EU's sense of urgency in the wake of the pullout by the US, resulted in significant compromise. For instance, the GHG reduction goal

---

[552] Andrew C. Revkin, *News Analysis: Odd Culprits in Collapse of Climate Talks*, N.Y. TIMES (Nov. 28, 2000), http://www.nytimes.com/2000/11/28/science/news-analysis-odd-culprits-in-collapse-of-climate-talks.html; Eric J. Lyman, *Climate Change: U.S. Compromises on Kyoto Protocol Fail to Gain Support of EU, Industry Groups*, 31 Env't Rep. 2458 (BNA) (Nov. 24, 2000).

[553] Miranda A. Schreurs, *Competing Agendas and the Climate Change Negotiations: The United States, the European Union, and Japan*, 31 ENVTL. L. REP. 11218 (2001).

[554] Editorial, *A Misguided Energy Proposal*, N.Y. TIMES (May 18, 2001), http://www.nytimes.com/2001/05/18/opinion/a-misguided-energy-proposal.html; *Environmentalists Blast U.S. Energy Plans*, REUTERS (May 18, 2001), http://www.commondreams.org/headlines.shtml?/headlines01/0518-01.htm; David E. Sanger, *In Energy Plan, Bush Urges New Drilling, Conservation and Nuclear Power Review*, N.Y. TIMES (May 17, 2001), http://www.nytimes.com/2001/05/17/us/in-energy-plan-bush-urges-new-drilling-conservation-and-nuclear-power-review.html?pagewanted=all&src=pm. For two differing viewpoints on the efficacy and integrity of the Bush plan, *see* Paul Krugman, *Ersatz Climate Policy*, N.Y. TIMES (Feb. 15, 2002), http://www.nytimes.com/2002/02/15/opinion/ersatz-climate-policy.html; Glenn Hubbard, *Realism in Cutting Emissions*, N.Y. TIMES (Feb. 15, 2002), http://www.nytimes.com/2002/02/15/opinion/15HUBB.html.

[555] *Id.*

[556] *See e.g., International Issues: U.S. Rejection of Kyoto Pact Jeopardizes Sustainable Development Plan, OECD Says*, DAILY ENV'T REP.: News (BNA), 93 DEN A7, 2001 (May 14, 2001); Andrew C. Revkin, *After Rejecting Climate Treaty, Bush Calls in Tutors to Give Courses and Help Set One*, N.Y. TIMES (Apr. 28, 2001), http://www.nytimes.com/2001/04/28/us/after-rejecting-climate-treaty-bush-calls-tutors-give-courses-help-set-one.html?pagewanted=all&src=pm.

[557] *See Guide*, "Key Landmarks in the Climate Change Process," *supra* note 549.

was diminished (in fact if not on paper) from an average of 5.2 percent to 1.8 percent[558] due to what at least one observer deems "creative accounting" measures.[559]

COP6 Part II was a turning point in the life of the Kyoto Protocol,[560] because the world community decided to proceed with Kyoto even without the participation of the world's largest producer of GHGs – the US.[561] At the break-through 2001 COP7 in Marrakesh, Morocco, the parties resolved the Bonn Agreement issues. The resulting Marrakech Accords settled a number of open issues, including credit provisions to minimize the "hard" emission reductions requirements of Annex I (developed) parties:[562] emissions trading, joint implementation projects, a clean development mechanism (CDM);[563] and development of sinks (LUCFs) both internally and abroad.[564] Thus, the Bonn and Marrakech agreements effectively completed the work began under the Buenos Aires Plan of Action, and provided sufficiently detailed rules so that the industrialized countries could ratify Kyoto. Ironically, the details formulated in Bonn and finalized in Marrakech closely resemble the US position at COP3 in Kyoto (*see* 10.3.5 above), where the Protocol was initially agreed to, but it was too late to bring the new US administration back into the fold.[565]

In 2002, both the EU and Japan ratified the Kyoto Protocol.[566] However, without the US support, the parties had a difficult time achieving ratifications sufficient for the Protocol to enter into force, since that required ratification by at least 55 countries representing at least 55 percent of global GHG

---

[558] Schreurs, *supra* note 553.

[559] Richard Schmalensee, *The Lessons of Kyoto*, 43 MIT SLOAN MGMT. REV. 96 (2002).

[560] *See* Guide, "The Road Ahead," *supra* note 549.

[561] Hossein Esmaeili, *International Law Response to Climate Change in* ROUTELEDGE HANDBOOK ON CLIMATE CHANGE AND SOCIETY 446 (Constance Lever-Tracy ed. 2010).

[562] *See* Schreurs, *supra* note 553; Schmalensee, *supra* note 559.

[563] A 15-member Executive Board of the CDM was elected at COP7 to "ensure a prompt start to the CDM, whose mandate is to promote sustainable development by encouraging investments in projects in developing countries that reduce or avoid emissions; developed countries then receive credit against their Kyoto targets for emissions avoided by these projects. Press Release, UNFCCC, Governments Ready to Ratify Kyoto Protocol (Nov. 10, 2001), http://unfccc.int/files/press/releases/application/pdf/pressrel101101.pdf.

[564] Schreurs, *supra* note 553.

[565] For a detailed discussion of all the issues negotiated and voted on at the COP7 meeting, *see Report of the Conference of the Parties on its Seventh Session, Held at Marrakesh from 29 October to 10 November*, 2001, U.N. Doc. FCCC/2001/13 (Jan. 21, 2002), http://unfccc.int/resource/docs/cop7/13.pdf.

[566] Press Release, Europa, European Union Ratifies Kyoto Protocol, (May 31, 2002) http://europa.eu/rapid/pressReleasesAction.do?reference=IP/02/794&format=HTML&aged=0&language=EN&guiLanguage=en; *Japan Ratifies Kyoto Pact*, BBC NEWS, June 4, 2002, http://news.bbc.co.uk/2/hi/asia-pacific/2024265.stm.

emissions.[567] Then, in 2004, Russia agreed to ratify Kyoto, in a *quid pro quo* return for being admitted to the World Trade Organization (WTO), giving the Protocol sufficient GHG-emitting parties to finally enter into force on February 16, 2005, and set out the rules for the first "commitment period" of controls from 2008–2012.

10.3.7   *An Assessment of the Kyoto Protocol*

The Kyoto Protocol can best be viewed as a flawed "first step" in regulation. While the Protocol creates a base from which GHG regulation can evolve, sufficient GHG reduction will require considerably more negotiation and agreement. This subsection will analyze the strengths and weaknesses of the Kyoto Protocol focusing on what more is needed in future climate agreements.

First among the Protocol's strengths is its inclusion of innovative market-based approaches that may improve the feasibility of a global climate change regime.[568] Specifically, the emissions trading feature of Article 17 may be key for cost-effectiveness, environmental effectiveness, and equity.[569] The EU Emissions Trading Scheme (EU ETS) serves as a model for the potential success of this market-based approach. Launched in 2005, the EU ETS operates on the "cap and trade" principle.[570] First the emissions of factories and power plants within the system are capped at a certain level, and then companies receive proportions of that total as their emissions allowances which they can sell or buy as needed.[571] As of November 2010, the EU ETS operated in 30 countries and covers 40% of the EU's GHG emissions.[572]

---

[567] Kyoto Protocol, *supra* note 522, art. 25.

[568] Cedric Philibert, *Lessons from the Kyoto Protocol: Implications for the Future*, 5 Int'l Rev. for Env. Strategies 1 (2004) http://philibert.cedric.free.fr/Downloads/Transforming%20Kyoto.pdf.

[569] UNFCCC, *Emissions Trading*, http://unfccc.int/kyoto_protocol/mechanisms/emissions_trading/items/2731.php.

[570] European Commission, *Emissions Trading System*, http://ec.europa.eu/clima/policies/ets/index_en.htm.

[571] *Id.*

[572] *Id.* Emissions trading has been the subject of numerous books and articles. *See, e.g.,* Emissions Trading: Institutional Design, Decision Making, and Corporate Strategies (Ralf Antes *et al.* eds., 2008); Francesco Gulli, Markets for Power and Carbon Pricing in Europe: Theoretical Issues and Empirical Analyses (2008); Legal Aspects of Carbon Trading (David Freestone & Charlotte Streck eds., 2009); Denny Ellerman, *The EU Emission Trading Scheme: A Prototype Global System? in* Post-Kyoto International Climate Policy: Implementing Architectures for Agreement 88 (Joseph E. Aldy & Robert N. Stavins eds., 2010); Robert N. Stavins, *A Meaningful U.S. Cap-and-Trade System to Address Climate Change*, 32 Harv. Envtl. L. Rev. 293 (2008).

Another strength of the Kyoto Protocol is that it gives nations the flexibility to meet their national emission targets in a variety of ways, as they individually choose[573] (*see* subsection 10.3.5 above). The compliance mechanisms promote experimentation while Article 2 prompts member countries to share "their experience and exchange information on such policies and measures, including developing ways of improving their comparability, transparency and effectiveness."[574] Thus, the Kyoto Protocol preserves national sovereignty while still endorsing international cooperation and experimentation.

A final strength is that the Protocol has garnered a wide base of support, despite all the political wrangling. It was signed by more than 180 countries, subsequently ratified by a sufficient number of Annex I countries to come into force, and has been ratified by 193 parties as of the beginning of 2012. The Kyoto Protocol merits respect for generating international consensus on the need for concrete emissions reductions, showing that nations have accepted climate change as a serious problem requiring solutions, while still disagreeing over the best way to control it.

Despite these strengths, the Kyoto Protocol has also been marred by weaknesses. First and foremost, the world's largest GHG emitters are not constrained by the Kyoto Protocol. The US and Canada among others have refused to join it, largely because of domestic opposition, principally from the fossil fuel, electrical, and automotive industries.[575] As long as the *status quo* is more agreeable than the ratification of the Kyoto Protocol, these constituencies have little reason to support any climate treaty.[576] China, India, Brazil, Indonesia, Mexico and other large developing nations have thus far also been able to avoid quantitative emission reduction commitments, since they are not on the Annex I list of countries with such requirements. This lack of binding commitment has proved increasingly problematic because these nations represent some of the largest and most rapidly growing economies in the world.[577] The exemption for developing countries has particularly distressed the US and many environmentalists because the developing world

---

[573] Joseph E. Aldy & Robert N. Stavins, *Introduction* to Post-Kyoto International Climate Policy: Implementing Architectures for Agreement 4 (Joseph E. Aldy & Robert N. Stavins eds., 2010).

[574] Kyoto Protocol, *supra* note 522, art. 2.

[575] See Frank Grundig, Hugh Ward, Ethan R. Zorick, *Modeling Global Climate Negotiation, in* International Relations and Global Climate Change 170 (Urs Luterbacher, Detlef F. Sprinz eds. 2001).

[576] *Id.*

[577] China overtook the US as the world's largest emitter in 2006. China is not required to make any emissions reductions until 2012. CBC News, *Kyoto and Beyond: Kyoto Protocol FAQs*, Feb. 14, 2007, http://www.cbc.ca/news/background/kyoto/.

now emits more GHGs than the industrialized world.[578] As noted previously, China has surpassed the US as the largest emitter in the world, and its emissions are projected to continue growing for the foreseeable future.[579]

These issues reflect a more fundamental problem with the Kyoto Protocol: it lacks internal mechanisms to deal with a changing world. The world has changed dramatically since the UNFCCC divided countries into two simplistic categories in 1992. Today, developing nations produce the majority of GHGs, but the Kyoto Protocol has no mechanism to accommodate changes such as these, so it is perceived as putting regulatory burdens unfairly on some nations but not others.[580]

Another weakness of the Kyoto Protocol – a result of asking a relatively small number of countries to make emissions reductions – is that GHG emissions may be outsourced in a process known as "carbon leakage."[581] Carbon leakage occurs when some countries adopt climate controls, only to drive GHG-producing activities to other countries. Even though the emissions are reduced locally, there may be an increase in emissions elsewhere, resulting in no net reduction in greenhouse gases.[582] Thus far, it has proven difficult to measure carbon leakage, but, as the cost of producing carbon intensive goods in Annex I countries rises, developing countries that lack reduction restraints may develop a comparative advantage in producing those goods.

Finally and perhaps most troubling, the Kyoto Protocol takes a short-term approach to a fundamentally long-term problem.[583] Remember that the Kyoto Protocol is inherently limited: it only asks Annex I countries to reduce emissions an average of five per cent against 1990 levels over the five-year period of 2008–2012. When one considers that GHGs can stay in the atmosphere for decades, or even centuries (*see* § 10.3.1), the need for a longer term solution becomes obvious. At best, the Kyoto Protocol was the first step towards controlling international climate change. Further steps are essential to prevent the massive loss in biodiversity, changes in oceanic currents, weather disruptions, population displacement, and other potentially catastrophic effects of climate change.

---

[578] Aldy & Stavins, *supra* note 573, at 4.

[579] Kahn & Yardley, *supra* note 147.

[580] Aldy & Stavins, *supra* note 573, at 4.

[581] *Id.*

[582] Allison Crimmins, *Carbon Leakage: New Report From the MIT Joint Program on the Science and the Policy of Global Change Analyzes the Impact of Border Carbon Adjustments,* MIT News, Mar. 8, 2011, http://web.mit.edu/newsoffice/2011/carbon-leakage.html.

[583] Aldy & Stavins, *supra* note 573, at 7.

10.3.8   *Developing a Post-Kyoto Framework*

The months leading up to the 2007 COP13 in Bali, Indonesia, were filled with unprecedented media coverage of climate change issues.[584] The IPCC published the Fourth Assessment Report in that year, giving dire warnings of the socioeconomic impacts of projected climate change if GHG emissions were to continue at the current rate.[585] The feeling of urgency was heightened by the fact that the first Kyoto Protocol "commitment period" was to begin the following year and end five years after that. With this background, the 2007 Bali conference succeeded in departing from the previous six years of political stalemate.[586] During the negotiations, participants adopted a consensus "Bali Agreement" that "deep cuts in global emissions will be required to reach the ultimate objective of the Convention."[587] The four pillars of the agreement are: (1) mitigation to reduce global warming pollution, (2) adaptation to unavoidable impacts, (3) technology development and transfer to developing countries, and (4) financial investment in mitigation and adaptation in developing countries.[588] With this plan, the parties set their sights on the COP15 conference to be held two years later in Copenhagen, Denmark, hoping that they would be able to negotiate the successor to the Kyoto Protocol at that time.

The goal of the highly anticipated 2009 COP15 in Copenhagen was to complete and adopt the legal framework that would come into effect in 2012 when the first commitment period under the Kyoto Protocol expired. Unfortunately, this goal was not accomplished, and COP15 will be remembered as one of the most tumultuous and unsuccessful multilateral events in history.[589] The Copenhagen meetings generated worldwide publicity. High-level representatives from 192 nations attended, including US President Barack Obama,[590] and thousands of protesters demonstrated outside of the convention center where meetings were being held.[591] Despite this international attention, the

---

[584] Raymond Clemençon, *Rethinking Global Negotiations, in* Routeledge Handbook on Climate Change and Society 454 (Constance Lever-Tracy ed. 2010).

[585] Intergovernmental Panel on Climate Change, IPCC Fourth Assessment Report (2001).

[586] Clemençon, *supra* note 584, at 455.

[587] *Id.*

[588] US House of Representatives, Select Committee on Energy Independence and global Warming, *Quick Guide to the Bali Action Plan,* http://globalwarming.house.gov/media center/pressreleases?id=0147.

[589] Raymond Clemençon, *Preface, supra* note 584.

[590] *Clayton Sandell, Climate Conference Opens in Copenhagen,* ABC News, Dec. 7, 2009, http:// abcnews.go.com/WN/copenhagen-climate-change-conference-begins/story?id=9267280.

[591] *Climate Activists Condemn Copenhagen Police Tactics,* BBC News, Dec. 13, 2009, http:// news.bbc.co.uk/2/hi/europe/8410414.stm.

only document generated during the conference, the "Copenhagen Accord," was a face-saving political gesture, not a legal agreement.[592] The Copenhagen Accord is not legally binding and does not commit countries to reductions even in the way to the Kyoto Protocol did.[593]

The basic terms of the Copenhagen Accord were bargained by the leaders of the United States, China, India, Brazil, and South Africa on the final day of the conference.[594] This last-minute document capped two weeks of extremely confrontational negotiations on substantive and procedural issues that made the prospect of any agreement highly uncertain.[595] In the end, the conference of the parties did not even adopt the agreement, but only "took note" of it, demonstrating that the accord was unable to get the full support of the COP. The UNFCCC Executive Secretary at the time, Yvo de Boer, explained the term "taking note" as "a way of recognizing that something is there, but not going so far as to associate yourself with it."[596]

The Copenhagen Accord contained some good provisions that, if adopted, would make progress. It called for:

- Recognition of "the scientific view that the increase in global temperature should be below 2 degrees Celsius" (35.6 degrees Fahrenheit),[597] the commonly accepted threshold beyond which the planet's climate patterns could be seriously destabilized.
- Developed countries to provide $30 billion in "new and additional" resources in 2010–2012 to help developing countries reduce emissions, mitigate climate damage, and prevent deforestation.[598]
- A review by 2015 to ensure the world is avoiding dangerous climate change and to "include consideration of strengthening the long-term goal," for example to limit temperature rises to 1.5 degrees C (34.7 degrees F).[599]

---

[592] Copenhagen Accord of the UN FCCC, art. 12, Dec. 18, 2009, http://unfccc.int/files/meet ings/cop_15/application/pdf/cop15_cph_auv.pdf.

[593] Gerard Wynn & Jon Hemming, *Factbox: What Was Agreed and Left Unfinished in U.N. Climate Deal*, REUTERS, Dec. 20, 2009, http://in.reuters.com/article/2009/12/20/idINIndia-44872920091220?sp=true.

[594] The Pew Center on Global Climate Change has produced an excellent summary of the COP15 and the Copenhagen Accord, at http://www.pewclimate.org/docUploads/copen hagen-cop15-summary.pdf.

[595] *Id.*

[596] US Climate Action Network, *Understanding the Copenhagen Accord*, http://www.uscli matenetwork.org/policy/understanding-the-copenhagen-accord.

[597] Copenhagen Accord, *supra* note 592, art. 2.

[598] *Id.* art. 8.

[599] *Id.* art. 12.

- Explicit emission pledges by all the major economies – including for the first time China and other major developing countries.[600] This pledge system respects national sovereignty and cultivates flexibility. Annex I countries were to "commit to implement individually or jointly the quantified economy-wide emissions targets for 2020,"[601] with the result that parties had flexibility in the amount of their reduction and in choosing the base year for calculating targets.[602] For example, the US has adopted 2005 as its base year, while the EU has maintained the 1990 base year set in the Kyoto Protocol.[603]
- Non-Annex I parties to have even more flexibility. They would need only to submit "nationally appropriate mitigation plans" detailing their actions to reduce emissions of greenhouse gases.[604] These plans could include, emissions reduction targets relative to business as usual projections, reductions in emissions per unit of gross domestic product (GDP), expansions in forest cover, and investments in energy efficiency and biofuels.[605] China and India have committed to reducing their emissions per unit of gross domestic product (GDP) relative to 2005 by 40 and 20 percent respectively.[606]

While the unusual structure of the Copenhagen Accord may have been necessary to garner political support in an unfavorable negotiating environment, delegating emission reduction targets to the individual countries could undermine the ultimate goals of the UNFCCC. First, the proposed commitments may not be enough to prevent dangerous climate change. Second, allowing countries to adopt widely disparate approaches makes comparisons of likely emissions reductions almost impossible to calculate.[607] Third, a variety of commitments and regulations may make it difficult for multinational companies to adopt internal policies. Markets need rules and predictability, and the heterogeneous approach may hinder the corporate decision making process.[608] Despite these weaknesses, by 2011, 141 countries, including the

---

[600] *Id.* art. 5.

[601] *Id.* art. 4.

[602] *Id.* art. 4.

[603] *Who's on Board with the Climate Accord*, CLIMATE ACTION NETWORK, http://www.uscli matenetwork.org/policy/copenhagen-accord-commitments.

[604] Copenhagen Accord, *supra* note 592, art. 5.

[605] Warwick McKibben *et al. Comparing Climate Commitments: A Model Based Analysis of the Copenhagen Accord*, BROOKINGS INSTITUTE, 2 May 27, 2010.

[606] *Id.*

[607] McKibben *et al. supra* note, 605 at 2.

[608] David Doniger, *The Copenhagen Accord: A Big Step For*ward, SWITCHBOARD: THE NATU-RAL RESOURCES DEFENSE COUNCIL BLOG, (Dec. 21, 2009), http://switchboard.nrdc.org/ blogs/ddoniger/the_copenhagen_accord_a_big_st.html.

27-member EU, had submitted emission reduction pledges or mitigations plans, representing 87.24% of global emissions.[609]

The Copenhagen Accord has met with varied responses. U.N. Secretary General, Ban Ki Moon, took an optimistic outlook, stating: "Bringing all the leaders to the table paid off. The Copenhagen accord may not be everything everyone hoped, but this is an essential beginning. We now have a foundation for the first truly global agreement that will limit and reduce greenhouse gas emissions."[610] President Obama took a similarly favorable position, calling it a "meaningful and unprecedented" deal.[611] Many NGOs were disappointed with the Accord, calling it "an abject failure"[612] and saying that it "effectively signed a death warrant"[613] for the world's most vulnerable populations. While the Accord certainly fell short in numerous respects, it did engage the mega-developer countries of China, India, and Brazil and encouraged them to acknowledge the need for emission controls in developing countries.

A year later, in December 2010, COP16 was held in Cancún, Mexico. While some negotiators left Copenhagen hoping (perhaps naïvely) that a successor agreement to Kyoto would finally be achieved in Cancún, it was not to be.[614] Nevertheless, COP16 was not a complete failure. The parties "agree[d] to put aside for that meeting the issues that had stalemated international climate talks for years,"[615] and negotiated the "Cancún Agreements," which gave the more than 190 countries participating in the conference another year to decide whether to extend the Kyoto Protocol.[616] One positive evaluation of COP16 states:

---

[609] *Who's on Board with the Climate Accord, supra* note 603.

[610] Molly Moore, *COP15 Debrief: U.N. Says World Leaders Rolled Up Their Sleeves*, Environmental Defense Fund Blog (Dec. 19, 2009), http://blogs.edf.org/climatetalks/2009/12/19/cop15-debrief-u-n-says-world-leaders-rolled-up-their-sleeves/.

[611] *Obama Announces Climate Change Deal with China, Other Nations*, CNN Politics, Dec. 18, 2009, http://articles.cnn.com/2009-12-18/politics/obama.copenhagen_1_climate-change-conference-senior-obama-administration-official-key-nations?_s=PM:POLITICS.

[612] *Copenhagen Deal Reaction in Quotes*, BBC News, Dec. 19, 2009, http://news.bbc.co.uk/2/hi/science/nature/8421910.stm#nongovernmental.

[613] *Id.*

[614] Lisa Friedman & ClimateWire, *Future of Kyoto Protocol in Doubt as Cancun Climate Talks Enter Final Day*, Sci. Am., Dec. 10, 2010, http://www.scientificamerican.com/article.cfm?id=future-of-kyoto-protocol-in-doubt.

[615] Pew Center on Global Climate Change, *Summary: Sixteenth Session of the Conference of the Parties to the United Nations Framework Convention on Climate Change*, http://www.pewclimate.org/docUploads/cancun-climate-conference-cop16-summary.pdf.

[616] John M. Broder, *Climate Talks End with Modest Deal on Emissions*, N.Y. Times, Dec. 11, 2010, http://www.nytimes.com/2010/12/12/science/earth/12climate.html?adxnnl=1&ref=unitednationsframeworkconventiononclimatechange&adxnnlx=1313972514-6jdlAiU8DP1/3RCQNxMSMg.

In large measure, the Cancún Agreements import the essential elements of the Copenhagen Accord into the U.N. Framework Convention on Climate Change (UNFCCC). They include the mitigation targets and actions pledged under the Accord – marking the first time all major economies have pledged explicit actions under the UNFCCC since its launch nearly two decades ago. The Agreements also take initial steps to implement the operational element of the Accord, including a new Green Climate Fund for developing countries and a system of "international consultations and analysis" to help verify countries' actions.[617]

Because of the voluntary nature of the commitments, other officials were somewhat less enthusiastic. Yvo de Boer, UNFCCC Executive Secretary at the time, noted: "This process has never been characterized by leaps and bounds. It has been characterized by small steps. And I'd rather see this small step here in Cancún than the international community tripping over itself in an effort to make a large leap."[618]

The pressure was on the delegates again as they convened in December 2011 for COP17 in Durban, South Africa. The Kyoto Protocol's first commitment period for GHG controls (2008–2012) was about to end, with nothing in its place. Given major holdouts by the US, Canada, Russia, and Japan, after 2012 the Kyoto Protocol would only cover some 15 percent of global GHG emissions.[619] Also alarmingly, scientists had just reported the previous year (2010) saw the sharpest rise in CO_2 emissions on record, and a recalculation showed cumulative carbon emissions had risen almost 50 percent since 1990, higher than previously thought.[620]

Despite these incentives, the "Durban Platform for Enhanced Action"[621] that emerged at the end of COP17 was roundly criticized as an insufficient agreement – "[They] kicked the can down the road" editorialized the N.Y. Times.[622] It is a "betrayal of both science and the world's poor" opined New Scientist.[623] True, by itself, the Durban Platform will not achieve the COP's stated goal of preventing global temperatures from rising 2 degrees Celsius above preindustrial levels. However, the Durban Platform "did rewrite the

---

[617] Pew Center, *Summary, supra* note 615.

[618] Broder, *supra* note 616.

[619] Fred Pearce, *Dangerous Decade: What Follows the Durban Climate Deal*, New Scientist, Dec. 13, 2011, http://www.newscientist.com/article/dn21278–dangerous-decade-what-follows-the-durban-climate-deal.html.

[620] *Editorial: Beyond Durban*, N.Y. Times, Dec. 16, 2011, http://www.nytimes.com/2011/12/17/opinion/beyond-the-durban-climate-talks.html.

[621] UNFCCC COP17, *Establishment of an Ad Hoc Working Group on the Durban Platform for Enhanced Action*, Draft Decision -/CP.17 (Dec. 18, 2011), http://unfccc.int/files/meetings/durban_nov_2011/decisions/application/pdf/cop17_durbanplatform.pdf.

[622] *Id.*

[623] Pearce, *supra* note 619.

rule book for fighting climate change,"[624] because it forced major developing nations like China, India, Brazil, and South Africa to accept the principle of future binding targets on their GHGs – for the first time.

The good news is that the world's countries agreed to finalize a new protocol by 2015, to enter into force by 2020 that would have legal force and would impose GHG reduction targets and the same rules on all major emitters, regardless of whether they are developed or developing countries. Overlooked by many critics is that this agreement is only the tip of the iceberg, and Durban actually produced three separate substantive agreements:

1. An extension of the Kyoto Protocol, set to expire in 2012, so that it will continue until 2020,
2. Implementation instruments and revisions of the 2009 Cancún Agreements, especially the new Green Climate Fund for developing nations, and
3. Creation of the new Durban Platform for Enhanced Mitigation, which both kick-starts the process for a new treaty to replace Kyoto "applicable to all nations" and a separate process to meet the goal of stabilizing the global temperature increase at the goal of 2 degrees C.[625]

The bad news is that the Durban agreement will not do anything to address the climate for the next decade. Moreover, it is unclear what the promised binding targets will actually be, and it remains uncertain whether world leaders will be able to comply with their proposed timeline.[626] As a disgruntled UNEP Director Achim Steiner said on leaving Durban:

> I can't see anything in these negotiations that will prevent warming beyond 2° C. To do that will require the world's carbon dioxide emissions to peak by 2020.[627]

At least Durban avoided the disaster of a Copenhagen and kept the international cooperative process alive. However, its substantive achievements are few, and the agreement primarily shifts the work of actually cutting emissions to the voluntary efforts, if any, of the individual nations for the next decade. Voluntary efforts have not been a formula for success to date, as major GHG emitters like the US and China illustrate.

---

[624] *Id.*
[625] Andrew Light, *Six Reasons Why the Durban Decision Matters*, Climate Progress Blog, Dec. 18, 2011, http://thinkprogress.org/romm/2011/12/18/391533/six-reasons-why-the-durban-decision-matters/.
[626] Pearce, *supra* note 619.
[627] *Id.*

Climate change remains perhaps the most threatening and intractable problem in international environmental law because it is so closely associated with economic development. It is also a long-term problem, with effects that are neither entirely clear nor predictable, thus giving politicians and negotiators little incentive to address the issue in the present because they are unlikely held accountable for future climate catastrophes. Under the present legal regime, it is politically more expedient to delay concrete commitments that could hurt economic development. However, many believe that it is already too late to prevent disastrous climate change. The international community must seriously consider whether the current COP "platform" can effectively address climate issues. After many false starts and failed attempts, the world is overdue for a successful climate agreement.

Chapter Eleven

The Marine Environment

11.0   *Introduction*

A decade following the 1972 UN Conference on the Human Environment in Stockholm,[1] the 1982 United Nations Convention on the Law of the Sea (UNCLOS)[2] made a significant contribution to the progressive development of international environmental law. While several noteworthy measures had been taken during the period 1972–1982 to control marine pollution on the regional level,[3] there had been no comprehensive effort for the protection of the marine environment. As noted in the UNEP Nairobi Declaration –

---

[1]   *See* Report of the United Nations Conference on the Human Environment (Stockholm, June 5–16, 1972), U.N. Doc. A/CONF. 48/14/Rev. 1 (1972) [hereinafter Stockholm Rep.].

[2]   UN Convention on the Law of the Sea, opened for signature Dec. 10, 1982, U.N. Doc. A/CONF. 62/122 (1982), 1833 U.N.T.S. 396, 21 I.L.M. 1261 (1982) [hereinafter UNCLOS]. The Convention and other pertinent U.N. documents, including the Agreement Relating to the Implementation of Part XI of the United Nations Convention on the Law of the Sea, U.N. GAOR, 48th Sess., 101st plen. mtg., Annex, U.N. Doc. A/Res./48/2631 (1994), 33 I.L.M. 1309, Annex at 1313 (1994) (modifying the seabed provisions of the Convention) are available at the UN Oceans Office website at Oceans and the Law of the Sea, http://www.un.org/Depts/los/. As of May 2012, 161 states and the European Union had ratified or acceded to the Convention, http://un.org/Depts/los/reference_files_chronological_lists_of_ratifications.htm.

[3]   On regional arrangements to control marine pollution, *see generally* D. Dzidzornu, *Marine Pollution Control in the West and Central African Region*, 26 Queen's L.J. 439 (1995); L. Alexander, *Regional Arrangements in the Oceans*, 71 Am. J. Int'l L. 84 (1977); C. Okidi, *Toward Regional Arrangements for Regulation of Marine Pollution: An Appraisal of Options*, 4 Ocean Dev. & Int'l L.J. 1 (1977); Thacher & Meith, *Approaches to Regional Marine Problems: A Progress Report on UNEP's Regional Seas Program, in* 2 Ocean Yearbook 153 (E. Borgese & N. Ginsburg eds., 1980). For a summary assessment of regional arrangements established to control environmental degradation, *see* V. Nanda & P. Moore, *Global Management of the Environment: Regional and Multilateral Initiatives, in* World Climate Change: The Role of International Law and Institutions 93, 112–16 (V. Nanda ed., 1983).

adopted on May 19, 1982, to commemorate the tenth anniversary of the Stockholm Conference – the Action Plan adopted at the Stockholm Conference

> [had] only been partially implemented, and the results cannot be considered as satisfactory, due mainly to inadequate foresight and understanding of the long-term benefits of environmental protection, to inadequate coordination of approaches and efforts, and to unavailability and inequitable distribution of resources.... Some uncontrolled or unplanned activities of man have increasingly caused environmental deterioration [including] pollution of the seas.[4]

This chapter will focus on the framework of UNCLOS for the protection and preservation of the marine environment, highlighting pertinent environmental provisions of the Convention. Following a discussion of the Convention, selected additional developments regarding the protection of the marine environment will be noted.

11.1 *Framework of the Convention*

The Convention gives expression to the common interest in the protection and preservation of the marine environment and exploitation of living and nonliving resources in the most efficient manner. It defines marine pollution broadly, thus obligating the states parties to take the issue seriously. Under the Convention, "pollution of the marine environment" encompasses:

> the introduction by man, directly or indirectly, of substances or energy into the marine environment, including estuaries, which results or is likely to result in such deleterious effects as harm to living resources and marine life, hazards to human health, hindrance to marine activities, including fishing and other legitimate uses of the sea, impairment of quality for use of sea water and reducing of amenities.[5]

The Convention strikes a delicate balance between environmental protection and resource management on the one hand, and the requirements for navigation on the other. This notion of balancing competing interests is important for two reasons. First, it illustrates the willingness of states to compromise their preexisting rights and accept binding obligations in an effort to establish a global framework with which to govern oceanic uses. Second, this balance demonstrates a realization by states that environmental interests and concerns, and navigational freedom and uses, are not mutually exclusive.[6]

---

[4] UNEP, Nairobi Declaration, UNEP/GC. 10/INF.5, at 1 (May 19, 1982).

[5] UNCLOS, *supra* note 2, art. 1.1(4).

[6] *See, e.g.*, W. L. Schachter, Jr., *The Value of the 1982 UN Convention on the Law of the Sea: Preserving our Freedoms and Protecting the Environment*, 23 Ocean Dev. & Int'l L. 55 (1992).

UNCLOS represented an important step forward by raising to binding treaty obligations the contents of Principle 21 of the Stockholm Declaration on the Human Environment.[7] It may be recalled that Principle 21, while recognizing the sovereign right of states to exploit their own resources pursuant to their own environmental policies, enunciated the correlative responsibility of states "to ensure that activities within their jurisdiction and control do not cause damage to the environment of other states or areas beyond the limits of national jurisdiction."[8]

Under the Convention, states parties are generally obligated "to protect and preserve the marine environment."[9] Although the sovereign right of states to exploit their natural resources pursuant to their environmental policies is acknowledged in the Convention,[10] this right is to be exercised by states "in accordance with their duty to protect and preserve the marine environment."[11] Next, states are obligated to take all necessary measures, individually or jointly, "to prevent, reduce and control pollution of the marine environment from any source, using for this purpose the best practicable means at their disposal and in accordance with their capabilities."[12]

Other obligations include a duty not to transfer "damage or hazards from one area to another or transform one type of pollution into another"[13] and the duty to take all necessary measures "to prevent, reduce and control pollution of the marine environment resulting from the use of technologies under their jurisdiction or control, or the intentional or accidental introduction of species, alien or new, to a particular part of the marine environment, which may cause significant and harmful changes thereto."[14]

States are obligated also to undertake cooperative measures on both global and regional levels for the protection and preservation of the marine environment.[15] Such measures include immediate notification of imminent or actual damage,[16] contingency plans against pollution,[17] and research programs and exchanges of information and data.[18] Provisions are contained for technical

---

[7] *See* Declaration of the United Nations Conference on the Human Environment, in Stockholm Rep., *supra* note 1, at 2, 7.

[8] *Id.*, Principle 21.

[9] UNCLOS, *supra* note 2, art. 192.

[10] *Id.* art. 193.

[11] *Id.*

[12] *Id.* art. 194(1).

[13] *Id.* art. 195.

[14] *Id.* art. 196(1).

[15] *Id.* arts. 197–201.

[16] *Id.* art. 198.

[17] *Id.* art. 199.

[18] *Id.* art. 200.

assistance to developing states by developed states[19] and international organizations.[20] Also, states are obligated to perform monitoring of the risks or effects of pollution[21] and environmental assessment of activities that may cause substantial pollution.[22]

The Convention grants states varying degrees of competence to prescribe and apply laws to prevent, reduce, and control pollution of the marine environment from different sources. Six different sources of pollution are identified: (1) pollution from land-based resources,[23] (2) pollution from seabed activities subject to national jurisdiction,[24] (3) pollution from activities in the area beyond the national jurisdiction of states,[25] (4) pollution from dumping,[26] (5) pollution from ships,[27] and (6) pollution from or through the atmosphere.[28] Safeguards are provided to prevent possible abuses by states on the pretext of undertaking enforcement measures.[29] Special provisions exist for ice-covered areas.[30]

The Convention provides for state responsibility and liability,[31] sovereign immunity for state-owned ships or aircraft used for noncommercial purposes and warships,[32] and state obligations under other conventions on the protection and preservation of the marine environment.[33] On protection of the marine environment, UNCLOS is all-encompassing. Its provisions include those for conservation and protection of living resources and on management standards for their exploitation.[34] In the exclusive economic zone, it grants the coastal state jurisdiction to protect and preserve the marine environment.[35] It obligates states to protect and preserve the marine environment

---

[19] *Id.* art. 202.
[20] *Id.* art. 203.
[21] *Id.* art. 204.
[22] *Id.* art. 206.
[23] *Id.* arts. 207, 213.
[24] *Id.* arts. 268, 214.
[25] *Id.* arts. 209, 215.
[26] *Id.* arts. 210, 216.
[27] *Id.* arts. 211, 217–221.
[28] *Id.* arts. 212, 222.
[29] *Id.* arts. 223–233.
[30] *Id.* art. 234.
[31] *Id.* art. 235.
[32] *Id.* art. 236.
[33] *Id.* art. 237.
[34] *Id.* arts. 61–67, 116–120.
[35] *Id.* art. 56.1(b)(iii). The "territorial sea" is defined as not exceeding 12 nautical miles from a country's marine baselines, and the "exclusive economic zone" is defined as not extending beyond 200 nautical miles from the same baselines. *Id.* arts. 3, 57.

as they develop deep seabed resources[36] by setting forth rules and regulations for the International Seabed Authority (ISA),[37] the body established under the Convention to administer development of the resources in the seabed area beyond national jurisdiction (the "Area"). The Convention also has elaborate provisions on dispute settlement.[38]

Finally, due to the interrelatedness of the issues addressed in UNCLOS and the unique negotiating process by which it came into existence, the Convention became a "package deal," thus precluding severance of provisions from the whole and prohibiting reservations to specific provisions at the time of signing.[39] Several states chose not to sign the Convention because of these limitations. It could be argued that the package deal approach undermines the Convention's strength as customary international law, for states may assent to provisions which they do not support merely to solicit support for other provisions.[40] Following from this premise is a plausible contention that, because of many such compromises, the Convention may not clearly indicate that party states feel bound by each of its provisions, resulting in a lack of *opinio juris*, an essential element of customary international law formation.[41] Ultimately, time and consistent state practice will reveal the extent to which controversial provisions become transformed into customary international law.

11.2   *Contribution of the Convention to International Environmental Law*

The Convention provides a comprehensive framework for the protection and preservation of the marine environment. It made a special contribution toward the development of international environmental law by imposing a legal obligation upon states parties to the Convention to protect and preserve the marine environment and, more specifically, to prevent, reduce, and

---

[36] *Id.* art. 145. The seabed, ocean floor and subsoil beyond the limits of national jurisdiction are termed the "Area" and are to be overseen by the authority as "the common heritage of mankind" and not subject to state sovereignty. *Id.* arts. 1(1), 136–137. Activities pertaining to deep seabed mining are to be carried out "to ensure effective protection for the marine environment from harmful effects which may arise from such activities." Further, damage to the "flora and fauna of the marine environment" is to be prevented. *Id.* art. 145(b).

[37] *Id.* arts. 156, *et seq.*; Annex III, art. 17.

[38] *Id.* arts. 279–285.

[39] *See* H. Caminos & M. R. Moliter, *Progressive Development of International Law and the Package Deal*, 79 Am. J. Int'l. L. 871, 886 (1985).

[40] *See id.* at 883.

[41] *See id.* at 886.

control pollution in the marine environment. An appraisal of the Convention's contributions follows under the following headings: (1) environmental assessment provisions; (2) law-making and law enforcement provisions; (3) recognition of the special status of developing states; (4) provisions regarding conservation, protection, and utilization of living resources; (5) dispute settlement provisions; and (6) the relationship of the Convention and customary international law.

11.2.1 *Environmental Assessment Provisions*

The Convention obligates states to undertake cooperative measures, including notification, consultation, exchange of information and data, and technical assistance.[42] It also provides for monitoring of the risks or effects of pollution.[43] Of particular importance, however, is the obligation of states to assess the potential effects of planned activities under their jurisdiction or control when they have reasonable grounds for believing that such activities may cause "substantial pollution of or significant or harmful changes to the marine environment."[44] The exact meaning of "substantial" pollution or "significant" or "harmful" changes is not delineated in the Convention, but the terms have attracted sufficient attention over the years; consequently their interpretation in a contextual setting should not pose insurmountable difficulties.[45] States are to make public reports upon such assessments.[46]

It should be noted that the Environmental Impact Statement (EIS) procedure, instituted in the US National Environmental Policy Act of 1969,[47] provided an important precedent for the requirement that states file EISs for their major activities in the marine environment. Experience gained under the EIS procedure[48] has been useful in the implementation of this provision (*see* Chapter 6).

11.2.2 *Law-Making and Law Enforcement Provisions*

The Convention codifies the then-existing state practice on pollution from land-based sources. The competence of states parties to prescribe and

---

[42] UNCLOS, *supra* note 2, arts. 197–201.

[43] *Id.* art. 204.

[44] *Id.* art. 206.

[45] *See, e.g.*, V. Nanda, *The Law of the Non-Navigational Uses of International Watercourses: Draft Articles on Protection and Preservation of Ecosystems, Harmful Conditions and Emergency Situations, and Protection of Water Installations*, 3 Colo. J. Int'l Envtl. L. & Pol'y 175 (1992).

[46] UNCLOS, *supra* note 2, art. 205.

[47] National Environmental Policy Act of 1969, 42 U.S.C. § 4321, *et seq.*

[48] *See, e.g.*, T. Schoenbaum, Environmental Policy Law 86–186 (1982).

enforce laws and regulations to prevent, reduce, and control such pollution is acknowledged.[49] Also, states are asked to "endeavour to establish global and regional rules, standards and recommended practices and procedures" for this purpose.[50] In so doing, they are to take into account "characteristic regional features, the economic capacity of developing States and their need for economic development." In addition, states are to implement applicable international rules and standards.

On the subject of pollution from seabed activities within national jurisdiction – internal waters, the territorial sea, and the continental shelf – the Convention recognized states' competence to prescribe and apply laws and regulations. However, states parties are obligated to ensure that such laws and regulations "shall be no less effective than international rules, standards and recommended practices and procedures."[51] This obligation to implement minimum international standards for the safety of such operations concerning the exploration and exploitation of the seabed within national jurisdiction was a new obligation that the Convention imposed upon states parties. Also, seabed activities in the international area beyond the limits of national jurisdiction which cause pollution will be regulated by the International Seabed Authority.[52] As for activities undertaken by ships, installations, structures, and other devices flying the flag or operating under the authority or registry of states parties, the Convention recognizes states' competence to prescribe and apply laws which "shall be no less effective than the international rules, regulations and procedures" pertinent to such activities.[53]

On the question of pollution from dumping, the Law of the Sea Convention builds upon the 1972 London Convention on the Prevention of Marine Pollution by Dumping of Wastes and Other Matters.[54] For enforcement purposes, the existing jurisdiction of the flag state or the state of registry of aircraft is acknowledged.[55] The coastal state's right to permit, regulate, and control such dumping is acknowledged under the Convention, which explicitly provides that the express prior approval of the coastal state is a prerequisite for dumping within its territorial sea, exclusive economic zone, or continental shelf.[56] National laws, regulations and measures are to be "no less effective in preventing, reducing and controlling such pollution than the

---

[49] UNCLOS, *supra* note 2, arts. 207, 213.

[50] *Id.* art. 207(4).

[51] *Id.* art. 208(3).

[52] *Id.* art. 145.

[53] *Id.* art. 209(2).

[54] Done Dec. 29, 1972, 26 U.S.T. 2403, T.I.A.S. No. 8165 [hereinafter London Dumping Convention].

[55] UNCLOS, *supra* note 2, art. 216(1)(b).

[56] *Id.* art. 210(5).

global rules and standards."[57] It should be noted that the provision on the right of coastal states to regulate and control dumping onto their continental shelves or in their exclusive economic zones was an innovation not previously recognized under customary international law.

On the question of pollution from or through the atmosphere, states are recognized as competent to prescribe and apply laws within the airspace covered by their sovereignty or with regard to their registry, "taking into account internationally agreed rules, standards and recommended practices and procedures and the safety of air navigation."[58]

It is, however, in the area of marine pollution by vessels that the Convention made a special contribution to international environmental law. The Convention built on the existing law, borrowing, clarifying, and expanding the law, and the result was a comprehensive and well-balanced framework. During negotiations, coastal states' concern with flag-of-convenience vessels and likely pollution from them resulted in the recognition of coastal states' interest in controlling pollution in coastal waters. Clearly, the preexisting regime did not meet the environmental needs of the coastal states. Consequently, it was felt essential that a balance be sought between the shipping interests of flag states and environmental and fishing interests of coastal states.

It is worth recalling that jurisdictional problems in finding a legal regime to solve vessel-source pollution were emphasized by the first major oil tanker accident causing marine pollution, the Torrey Canyon spill of 1967.[59] The vessel was owned by a Bermuda corporation, controlled by an American company, registered in and flying the flag of Liberia, manned by an Italian crew, chartered by a British oil company partially owned by the British government, insured by companies in the United Kingdom and the United States, and claimed for salvage by a Dutch corporation. Although the ship capsized off the southwest coast of England and sank in international waters, polluting the United Kingdom and French coastal waters, official investigation was done on behalf of Liberia in Italy by Americans.

Among the existing laws and treaties on vessel-source pollution, most of which have been implemented, are the 1954 International Convention for the

---

[57] *Id.* art. 210(6).

[58] *Id.* arts. 212(1) and 222.

[59] *See generally* V. Nanda, *The 'Torrey Canyon' Disaster: Some Legal Aspects*, 44 Denver L.J. 400 (1967). *See also* P. Dempsey & L. Helling, *Oil Pollution by Ocean Vessels—An Environmental Tragedy*, 10 Denv. J. Int'l L. & Pol'y 37 (1980); L. Herman, *Flags of Convenience—New Dimensions to an Old Problem*, 24 McGill L.J. 1 (1978).

Prevention of Pollution of the Sea by Oil[60] and its subsequent amendments;[61] the 1958 Convention on the High Seas,[62] which obligated states to draw up regulations to prevent pollution of the seas "by the discharge of oil by ships"[63] and from the dumping of radioactive waste;[64] and the 1962 Convention on the Liability of Operators of Nuclear Ships.[65] Two important conventions were adopted by a 1969 international conference convened by the International Maritime Consultative Organization:[66] the International Convention on Civil Liability for Oil Pollution,[67] and the International Convention Relating to Intervention on the High Seas in Cases of Oil Pollution Casualties.[68]

Other pertinent conventions include: the 1971 Convention on the Establishment of an International Fund for Compensation for Oil Pollution Damage,[69] the 1972 Convention on the Prevention of Marine Pollution by Dumping of Wastes and Other Matters,[70] the 1973 International Convention for the Prevention of Pollution from Ships (MARPOL Convention) and its 1978 Protocol (which absorbed the Convention, hence the alternative title MARPOL 73/78),[71] the 1974 International Convention for the Safety of Life

---

[60] International Convention for the Prevention of Pollution of the Sea by Oil, entered into force July 26, 1958, 12 U.S.T. 2989, T.I.A.S. No. 4900, 327 U.N.T.S. 3.

[61] Amendments were adopted in 1962, 1969, and 1971. The text of the 1962 amendments, ratified by the United States in 1966, appears at 17 U.S.T. 1523, T.I.A.S. No. 6109, 600 U.N.T.S. 332. For the 1969 amendments, *see* 28 U.S.T. 1205, T.I.A.S. No. 8505, 9 I.L.M. 1 (1970), and for the 1971 amendments, *see* 11 I.L.M. 267 (1972).

[62] 1958 Convention on the High Seas, 13 U.S.T. 2312, T.I.A.S. No. 5200, 450 U.N.T.S. 82.

[63] *Id.* art. 24.

[64] *Id.* art. 25.

[65] *Reprinted in* 57 Am. J. Int'l L. 268 (1963).

[66] *See generally* L. Juda, *IMCO and the Regulation of Ocean Pollution from Ships*, 26 Int'l & Comp. L.Q. 558 (1977); UNEP, "Environmental Law: An In-Depth Review" 128 (1981) [hereinafter cited as "UNEP Rev."].

[67] International Convention on Civil Liability for Oil Pollution, done at Brussels, Nov. 29, 1969, 9 I.L.M. 45 (1970).

[68] International Convention Relating to Intervention on the High Seas in Cases of Oil Pollution Casualties, done at Brussels, Nov. 29, 1969, 26 U.S.T. 765, T.I.A.S. No. 8068, entered into force for the United States, May 6, 1975, 9 I.L.M. 25 (1970).

[69] Convention on the Establishment of an International Fund for Compensation for Oil Pollution Damage, done Nov. 18, 1971, 11 I.L.M. 284 (1972).

[70] Convention on the Prevention of Marine Pollution by Dumping of Wastes and Other Matters, done Dec. 29, 1972, 26 U.S.T. 2403, T.I.A.S. No. 8165.

[71] 1973 International Convention for the Prevention of Pollution from Ships, done Nov. 2, 1973, 23 I.L.M. 1319 (1973). As it had not yet entered into force when the 1978 Protocol was adopted following a number of tanker accidents in 1976–1977, the Protocol absorbed the Convention, and the two combined in one instrument entered into force on October 2, 1983 – hence the alternative title "MARPOL 73/78." Protocol of 1978 Relating to the

at Sea (SOLAS Convention)[72] and the and SOLAS Protocol.[73] Regional agreements include the 1969 Agreement concerning Pollution of the North Sea by Oil (Bonn),[74] the 1972 Convention for the Prevention of Marine Pollution by Dumping from Ships and Aircraft (Oslo),[75] the 1974 Convention on the Protection of the Marine Environment of the Baltic Sea Area (Helsinki),[76] and the UNEP Regional Seas Programme.[77]

The Law of the Sea Convention, building upon these conventions, took many of their provisions verbatim and clarified and expanded upon certain others, providing a comprehensive and balanced approach. Thus, the Convention recognizes the competence of flag states to prescribe laws and regulations and to set standards for vessels flying their flags or of their registry, but in addition obligates flag states to have their laws meet "generally accepted international rules and standards established through the competent international organization or general diplomatic conference."[78] For vessel-source standards, such an organization is the International Maritime Organization (IMO). Since the IMO standards are those contained in the 1978 MARPOL Protocol,[79] and since only a few developing nations had ratified MARPOL,[80] the Law of the Sea Convention made a major contribution by mandating compliance by states that ratified it with the stringent vessel-source pollution standards of the MARPOL Protocol.

The Convention, moreover, went beyond recognizing flag state competence and introduced an innovative concept of "port state jurisdiction" to set and enforce pollution standards for ships voluntarily entering a state's ports.[81] It also authorized coastal states to establish antipollution laws and

International Convention for the Prevention of Pollution from Ships, done October 2, 1978, 1340 U.N.T.S. 61, 17 I.L.M. 546 (1978).

[72] International Convention for the Safety of Life at Sea, done Nov. 1, 1974, 14 I.L.M. 959 (1975).

[73] SOLAS Protocol, 17 I.L.M. 546, 579 (1978).

[74] Agreement concerning Pollution of the North Sea by Oil, done June 9, 1969, 9 I.L.M. 359 (1970).

[75] Convention for the Prevention of Marine Pollution by Dumping from Ships and Aircraft, done Feb. 15, 1972, 11 I.L.M. 262 (1972). Now replaced by the OSPAR Convention.

[76] Convention on the Protection of the Marine Environment of the Baltic Sea Area, done Mar. 22, 1974, 13 I.L.M. 544 (1974).

[77] *See generally* UNEP Rev., *supra* note 66, at 26–27; authorities cited in note 3, *supra*.

[78] UNCLOS, *supra* note 2, art. 211(2).

[79] *See supra* note 71, at 549.

[80] MARPOL entered into force October 2, 1983. As of 1983 it had been ratified by only 15 states, four of which were developing states. U.S. Dept. of State, Treaties in Force (1983). As of May 31, 2012, there are 155 states parties to MARPOL 73/78, http://www.imo.org/About/Conventions/StatusOfConventions/Pages/Default.aspx.

[81] UNCLOS, *supra* note 2, arts. 211(3), 218.

regulations for the territorial sea with a provision that any construction, design, equipment and manning standards established by the coastal state must conform to international standards.[82] It should be noted that under the Convention a coastal state's enforcement competence in its territorial waters is unlimited. This regime of coastal state jurisdiction applies to the territorial waters outside of straits used for international navigation; states bordering such straits may adopt antipollution laws and regulations only by giving effect to international regulations.[83] Ships in transit passage are obligated to comply with international standards regarding environmental pollution[84] as well as safety.[85]

UNCLOS, however, does impose certain limitations on punishment for activities in the territorial waters. Imprisonment may not be imposed under the Convention, for example, "except in the case of a willful and serious act of pollution in the territorial sea."[86] Also, the coastal state has a concomitant duty not to hamper innocent passage through territorial waters by the imposition of any standards or requirements,[87] although it may adopt measures regulating innocent passage where necessary to ensure the "preservation of the environment of the coastal State and the prevention, reduction and control of pollution thereof."[88]

In the exclusive economic zone, the Convention does not authorize the coastal state to set standards that differ from those established by "the competent international organization or general diplomatic conference."[89] It does, however, authorize the coastal state to take enforcement action in this zone, including detention of a vessel for a violation "resulting in a discharge causing major damage or threat of major damage" to the coastline or to the resources of the territorial sea or the exclusive economic zone.[90] Also, under special circumstances, a coastal state may, after consultation with the IMO, promulgate standards in its exclusive economic zone when they are warranted by special oceanographical and ecological conditions, or for the utilization or protection of the state's resources, or because of the particular character of its traffic.[91] In ice-covered areas, which are particularly fragile and susceptible to damage from oil pollution, coastal states are authorized

---

[82] *Id.* art. 21(2).

[83] *Id.* art. 42(1)(b).

[84] *Id.* arts. 39(2)(b) and 43(b).

[85] *Id.* arts. 39(2)(a) and 43(a).

[86] *Id.* art. 230(2).

[87] *Id.* art. 24(1)(a).

[88] *Id.* art. 21(1)(d).

[89] *Id.* art. 211(5).

[90] *Id.* art. 220(6).

[91] *Id.* art. 211(6)(a).

to prescribe and enforce laws and regulations for the prevention, reduction, and control of marine pollution from vessels within their exclusive economic zones.[92]

Port state jurisdiction authorizes a port state to set unilaterally its own entry requirements with respect to ship construction or crew standards.[93] Port state enforcement includes investigation and possible institution of proceedings pertaining to "any discharge from that vessel outside the internal waters, territorial sea or exclusive economic zone of that State in violation of applicable international rules and standards established through the competent international organization or general diplomatic conference."[94] A port state may also inspect vessels in its port,[95] and if the ship is unseaworthy the port state may refuse to release it or have the release made conditional "upon [its] proceeding to the nearest appropriate repair yard."[96]

UNCLOS contains safeguards to ensure that coastal states in their zeal and enthusiasm to control marine pollution (or perhaps for political reasons) do not abuse the power and authority given to them, causing unnecessary delay by investigations and proceedings.[97] Although some commentators have expressed concern that pollution controls may cause interference with navigation, particularly for specialized ships and ships containing specific cargoes – under the guise that they pose a significant pollution risk – the Convention provides a necessary, if delicate, balance between navigational rights and the protection and preservation of the marine environment.[98]

In the Area, the seabed region beyond national jurisdiction, which is designated the "common heritage of mankind,"[99] the ISA governs the exploration and exploitation of minerals. Only a state party to the Convention is authorized to sponsor prospective exploration and exploitation activities, and it must apply for a license from the ISA to do so, submitting two broadly similar areas for consideration. Specific provisions apply to the licensing process.[100]

The Convention provides in part with regard to legal responsibilities and obligations of a state sponsoring such activities:

---

[92] *Id.* art. 234.

[93] *Id.* art. 211(3).

[94] *Id.* art. 218(1).

[95] *Id.* arts. 218 and 220.

[96] *Id.* art. 226(1)(c).

[97] *Id.* arts. 223–233.

[98] *See, e.g.*, N. Wulf, Comment, 46 Law & Contemp. Probs. 155, 166 (1983).

[99] UNCLOS, *supra* note 2, art. 137.

[100] *Id.* Annex III, art. 8.

> States Parties shall have the responsibility to ensure that activities in the Area, whether carried out by States Parties, or state enterprises or natural or juridical persons which possess the nationality of States Parties or are effectively controlled by them or their nationals, shall be carried out in conformity with this Part [Part XI: The Area].[101]

Furthermore, state sponsors have the responsibility to ensure, pursuant to the preceding provision, "within their legal systems, that a contractor so sponsored shall carry out activities in the Area in conformity with the terms of its contract and its obligations under this Convention."[102]

Also, under UNCLOS,

> Without prejudice to the rules of international law and Annex III, article 22, damage caused by the failure of a State Party or international organization to carry out its responsibilities under this Part shall entail liability; States Parties or international organizations acting together shall bear joint and several liability. A State Party shall not however be liable for damage caused by any failure to comply with this Part by a person whom it has sponsored under article 153, paragraph 2(b), if the State Party has taken all necessary and appropriate measures to secure effective compliance under article 153, paragraph 4, and Annex III, article 4, paragraph 4.[103]

Additionally a State Party is required to adopt "laws and regulations and [take administrative measures] which are, within the framework of its legal system, reasonably appropriate for securing compliance by persons under its jurisdiction."[104]

Thus, perhaps the most basic aspect of the enforcement provisions embodied in the Law of the Sea Convention depends upon the relationship between the duties and responsibilities of the coastal states, flag states, and port state authorities. It has been suggested that this relationship is an attempt to strike a balance between the interests of the coastal states in controlling pollution in their waters, and the shipping interests of the flag states. Additionally, the Convention places these states under a duty to promulgate rules, regulations, and standards that meet the minimum accepted standards in the international community. In doing so, the Convention leaves the enforcement of its provisions to the states themselves, while setting a threshold of acceptable conduct.

The net effect of some of these enforcement provisions is a system by which multiple states may have proper jurisdiction over a vessel discharging pollution into the water. By ensuring that flag states and coastal states apply

---

[101] *Id.* art. 139(1).

[102] *Id.*

[103] *Id.* art. 139(2).

[104] *Id.* Annex III, art. 4(4).

rules that meet the minimum requirements set forth by the international community, the Convention recognizes the need to balance the special interests of those states on the one hand and the common interests of the world community on the other. However, the enforcement provisions of the Convention have been criticized as limited due to the fact that several significant states, notably the United States,[105] chose not to become parties.

11.2.3   *Special Status of Developing States*

The Convention recognizes the special interests of developing countries by underscoring the responsibility of industrialized nations to protect and preserve the marine environment. For example, it obligates states to take measures to prevent, reduce, and control pollution of the marine environment but adds that they should take steps "in accordance with their capabilities."[106]

The same term, "in accordance with their capabilities," is used in connection with states' obligations to develop and promote contingency plans against pollution.[107] The term is again used with regard to both the monitoring of the risks or effects of pollution and the assessment of potential effects of activities.[108] This language thus allows for varying standards to be used in assessing whether states have met their obligations under the Convention.

Furthermore, the concept of sustainable development (*see* § 2.4.1) has been addressed in the Convention through a balance between the needs of the environment and the need of developing countries to continue their development. The notion of sustainable development suggests that a threshold level of economic development can be achieved without overextending the Earth's various ecosystems.[109] An example of this balance can be seen in

---

[105] *See* Mark Landler, *Law of the Sea Treaty is Found on Capitol Hill, Again*, N.Y. Times, May 23, 2012, http://www.nytimes.com/2012/05/24/world/americas/law-of-the-sea-treaty-is-found-on-capitol-hill-again.html?_r=1; Ronald Reagan, "Statement on United States Participation in the Third United Nations Conference on the Law of the Sea," January 29, 1982, http://www.reagan.utexas.edu/archives/speeches/1982/12982b.htm. *See also* Jeane J. Kirkpatrick, *Testimony before the Senate Armed Services Committee*, April 8, 2004, http://armed-services.senate.gov/statemnt/2004/April/Kirkpatrick.pdf; Steven Groves, *Why Reagan Would Still Reject the Law of the Sea Treaty*, Webmemo #1676, The Heritage Foundation, http://www.heritage.org/research/reports/2007/10/why-reagan-would-still-reject-the-law-of-the-sea-treaty#_ftn1.

[106] UNCLOS, *supra* note 2, art. 194(1).

[107] *Id.* art. 199.

[108] *Id.* arts. 204, 206.

[109] For a useful discussion of sustainable development and its importance in the modern world, *see, e.g.*, George (Rock) Pring, *Sustainable Development: Historical Perspectives and Challenges for the 21st Century, in* UN Development Programme & UN Revolving Fund for Natural Resources Exploration, Proceedings of the Workshop on the Sustainable Development of Non-Renewable Resources Toward the 21st

the Convention's consideration, in relation to global and regional standard-setting for land-based source pollution, of "the economic capacity of developing states and their need for economic development."[110]

Finally, there exists within the Convention a special relationship between developing and developed nations regarding scientific and technical assistance. This relationship can be seen in Article 202, which calls for states to "promote programmes of scientific, educational, technical, and other assistance to developing states for the protection and preservation of the marine environment and the prevention, reduction, and control of marine pollution." This article goes on to enumerate types of assistance which include, among others, training of scientific and technical personnel,[111] supplying them with equipment and facilities,[112] and assistance in minimizing the effects of major incidents which may cause significant marine pollution.[113] International organizations are also required to give preferential treatment to developing states.[114]

Delegates of industrialized countries initially charged that these provisions set up "double standards." However, the delegate from Mexico, who chaired the informal consultation group on the protection and preservation of the marine environment at the Third United Nations Conference on the Law of the Sea, stated that they "must not be construed as recognizing double standards but merely as emphasizing the obvious limitations of developing countries and the special duties of those who have the technology and the economic means to protect the oceans."[115]

Thus, an important facet of the Convention is the balance it created between the rights, duties, and responsibilities of nations, and their need for continued economic development. This balance is demonstrated in the environmental provisions of the Convention and can be viewed as an attempt to codify the notion of sustainable development.

CENTURY (James Otto & Hyo-Sun Kim eds., 1999); Peter H. Sand & Stephen McCaffrey, TRANSNATIONAL ENVIRONMENTAL LAW: LESSONS IN GLOBAL CHANGE (2000); INTERNATIONAL LAW AND SUSTAINABLE DEVELOPMENT: PAST ACHIEVEMENTS AND FUTURE CHALLENGES (Alan Boyle & David Freestone eds., 2000); Patricia Romano, *Sustainable Development: A Strategy that Reflects the Effects of Globalization on the International Power Structure*, 23 HOUS. J. INT'L L. 91 (2000); R. Houseman & D. Zaelke, *Trade, Environment and Sustainable Development*, 15 HASTINGS INT'L & COMP. L. REV. 535 (1992).

[110] UNCLOS, *supra* note 2, art. 207(4).

[111] *Id.* art. 202(a)(i).

[112] *Id.* art. 202(a)(iii).

[113] *Id.* art. 202(b).

[114] *Id.* art. 203.

[115] J. L. Vallarta, *Protection and Preservation of the Marine Environment and Marine Scientific Research at the Third United Nations Conference on the Law of the Sea*, 46 LAW & CONTEMP. PROBS. 147, 148 (1983).

11.2.4   *Protection of Living Resources*

The Convention imposes a duty on states to take measures to protect and preserve rare or fragile ecosystems and the habitats of depleted, threatened, or endangered species.[116] It also requires states to cooperate "with a view to the conservation of marine mammals" and to work through "the appropriate international organizations for their conservation, management and study."[117] The "appropriate international organization" referred to is the International Whaling Commission (IWC). As for conservation of the living resources, coastal states are required to consider "the effects on species associated with or dependent upon harvested species with a view to maintaining or restoring populations of such associated or dependent species about levels at which their reproduction may become seriously threatened."[118]

11.2.5   *Dispute Settlement Provisions*

The most noteworthy aspect of the dispute settlement provisions in the Convention was the inclusion of compulsory third-party adjudication of disputes related to the violation of standards for the protection of the marine environment.[119] The Convention mechanism contained in part XIV was heralded by some as a model for all future conventional dispute settlement mechanisms.[120] It includes a conciliation procedure[121] and the option of submitting disputes to the International Tribunal for the Law of the Sea,[122] the International Court of Justice,[123] or an arbitral tribunal constituted in accordance with the Convention.[124] However, parties to a dispute are encouraged to exhaust other possible remedies, such as a negotiated settlement[125] and regional or bilateral dispute settlement procedures,[126] before turning to the Conventional dispute settlement provisions.

An important facet of these dispute settlement provisions is that parties to the Convention agreed, by signing it, to follow these provisions for the

---

[116] UNCLOS, *supra* note 2, art. 194(5).

[117] *Id.* arts. 65 and 120.

[118] *Id.* arts. 61(4) and 119(1)(b).

[119] *Id.* art. 297(1)(c).

[120] *See* J. W. Kindt, *Dispute Settlement in International Environmental Issues: The Model Provided by the 1982 Convention on the Law of the Sea*, 22 Vand. J. Transnat'l L. 1097 (1989).

[121] UNCLOS, *supra* note 2, Annex VIII.

[122] *Id.* art. 287(1)(a).

[123] *Id.* art. 287(1)(b).

[124] *Id.* art. 287.

[125] *Id.* art. 280.

[126] *Id.* art. 282.

settlement of all disputes relating to the Law of the Sea, including environmental infractions. This aspect of the enforcement provisions has been described as "remarkable," since there is no general international obligation to accept compulsory third-party adjudication, and states agreeing to be bound face embarrassment and political costs should they fail to comply with their conventional obligations.[127] The reasons attributed to the acceptance of these provisions by the parties to the Convention included the attempt to protect a state's nationals from a biased trial in a foreign jurisdiction,[128] the belief that this system would allow for uniform interpretation of the Convention,[129] and the notion that a tribunal can interpret Convention provisions rather than apply general notions of international law, thereby narrowing the issues presented.[130]

The environmental implications of the dispute settlement provisions of the Convention were far-reaching, for in all disputes involving alleged violations of the marine protection and preservation standards set forth in the Convention, the forum of the past – a biased unilateral Convention interpretation in a domestic court system – was no longer a threat to the parties to a dispute. Additionally, by replacing domestic courts with international tribunals, the integrity of the environmental provisions of the Convention will be solidified through uniformity of interpretation.

11.2.6   *The Relationship of the Convention and Customary Law*

The Convention codified preexisting customary international law. During its negotiations it also established new norms, thus beginning the process of customary international law generation.[131] The articles of the Convention that address land-based pollution sources illustrate the fact that the Convention codified areas of preexisting international law.[132] The provisions of the Convention relating to the exclusive economic zone are examples of customary international law that would be crystallized through the Convention.

On the other hand, the provisions relating to the duties, rights, and responsibilities of port states were new to international law and are likely to serve as the basis for the formation of new customary international law.

---

[127] J. E. Noyes, *Compulsory Third-Party Adjudication and the 1982 United Nations Convention on the Law of the Sea*, 4 Conn. J. Int'l L. 675, 677–78 (1989).

[128] *Id.*

[129] *Id.* at 682.

[130] *Id.* at 681.

[131] *See generally* H. Caminos and M. R. Moliter, *supra* note 39, at 872–73 (1985).

[132] V. Nanda, *Protection of the Internationally Shared Environment and the United Nations Convention on the Law of the Sea*, *in* Consensus and Confrontation: The United States and the Law of the Sea Convention 403, 417 (J. Van Dyke ed., 1985).

For instance, the provision on pollution from land-based sources[133] codified existing norms on the subject, but the state obligation to prescribe and apply international rules and standards "no less effective than" the pertinent international rules and standards concerning the exploration and exploitation of the seabed within national jurisdiction[134] was an innovation introduced by the Convention. The articles on dumping codified the existing competence of flag states or states of registry of aircraft, but also introduced the new element of coastal state competence to control pollution within the exclusive economic zone or continental shelf.[135] It should be noted that, although a coastal state's jurisdiction to control pollution within its national jurisdiction already existed under the prevalent rules of international law, there was no customary international law regarding the scope and extent of its competence beyond its territorial waters.

The regime to control vessel-source pollution[136] in the Convention introduced innovative elements not contained in customary international law, some allowing the coastal state an enlargement of its competence, and others narrowing its competence. In the territorial waters, for instance, the Convention authorizes the coastal state to set standards for discharges but not for construction, design, equipment, and manning of ships unless such standards give effect to generally accepted international rules and standards.[137] Under previous international law, coastal states had suffered no such limitations except that they were not permitted to set standards that hampered innocent passage.[138]

The Convention does not authorize the coastal state to set standards in the exclusive economic zone. Coastal state enforcement in this zone is permissible, however, including detention of a vessel for a violation "resulting in a discharge causing major damage or threat of major damage" to the coastline or the resources of the territorial sea or the exclusive economic zone.[139] On marine casualty, the Convention explicitly recognizes the right of states to take and enforce measures beyond the territorial sea proportionate to the

---

[133] UNCLOS, *supra* note 2, art. 207.

[134] *Id.* arts. 208(3) and 214.

[135] *Id.* arts. 210 and 216.

[136] *Id.* art. 211.

[137] *Id.* art. 211(6)(c).

[138] *See, e.g.*, art. 15(1) of the 1958 Geneva Convention on the Territorial Sea and Contiguous Zones, 15 U.S.T. 1606, 516 U.N.T.S. 205, T.I.A.S. No. 5639, which states: "The coastal State must not hamper innocent passage through the territorial sea." The Law of the Sea Convention likewise states in Article 24(1)(a) that coastal states shall not "impose requirements on foreign ships which have the practical effect of denying or impairing the right of innocent passage."

[139] *Id.* art. 220(6).

actual or threatened damage to protect their coastline or related interests, including fishing, from pollution or threat of pollution following upon a maritime casualty or acts relating to such a casualty, which may reasonably be expected to result in major harmful consequences.[140]

A gradual shift had occurred in the law regarding coastal state competence to deal with marine casualties by the time the Convention was negotiated. Traditionally, coastal states could intervene only in cases of severe marine casualties and then only in their territorial waters or contiguous zones. Anticipatory intervention was authorized in the Convention in certain cases, which was a desirable development.

The provision regarding ice-covered areas permits the coastal state to set standards for such vulnerable areas. The 1970 Canadian Arctic Waters Pollution Prevention Act,[141] which provided for preventive measures against oil pollution in a 100-mile area from Canada's Arctic coast, was the first such major unilateral attempt. The Convention legitimized such unilateral acts. Perhaps the most innovative part of the Convention was the universal port state jurisdiction, which was discussed in Section 10.2.2.[142]

11.2.7   *Appraisal*

An important facet of the Law of the Sea Convention is the balance of rights, duties, and responsibilities of nations with their need for continued economic development emphasized in the environmental provisions of the Convention, which can be viewed as an attempt to codify the notion of sustainable development. Particularly significant contributions of the Convention included the elevation of Principle 21 of the Stockholm Declaration to treaty level and codification in one document of provisions from several prior treaties that had failed to attract a large number of states as parties. Although one could argue that some of the provisions in the Convention might have unduly hampered efforts by coastal states to take preventive action in their territorial waters,[143] the enhanced role of coastal state and port state authority

---

[140]   *Id.* art. 221(1).

[141]   Canadian Arctic Waters Pollution Prevention Act 18–19, Eliz. 2, c. 45 (Can. 1970), 9 I.L.M. 543 (1970). Initial reaction to such a unilateral action was generally unfavorable. For a commentary, *see* R. Bilder, *The Canadian Arctic Waters Pollution Prevention Act: New Stresses on the Law of the Sea*, 69 MICH. L. REV. 1 (1970). *See generally* on the Arctic environment, David VanderZwaag, Rob Huebert, Stacey Ferrara, *The Arctic Environmental Protection Strategy, Arctic Council and Multilateral Environmental Initiatives: Tinkering While the Arctic Marine Environment Totters*, 30 DENV. J. INT'L L. & POL'Y 131 (2002); John E. D. Larkin, *UNCLOS and the Balance of Environmental and Economic Resources in the Arctic*, 22 GEO. INT'L ENVTL. L. REV. 307 (2010).

[142]   *See* text accompanying notes 77, 93–96, *supra*.

[143]   *See, e.g.*, UNCLOS, *supra* note 2, arts. 19(2)(h) and 21(2).

in controlling marine pollution, especially port state enforcement, was a most desirable development.

Several prescriptions in the Convention are vague and fail to set clear obligations for states and precise international standards and implementation measures. For instance, the provision on responsibility and liability basically constitutes a reiteration of Principle 22 of the Stockholm Declaration,[144] and progress has indeed been slow in the development of international environmental law regarding state responsibility and liability. Similarly, the Convention provisions on land-based sources demonstrated no marked progress beyond the existing norms contained in earlier conventions, such as the 1974 Convention for the Prevention of Marine Pollution from Land-Based Sources,[145] the 1974 Convention on the Protection of the Marine Environment of the Baltic Sea,[146] and the Protocol for the Protection of the Mediterranean Sea Against Pollution from Land-Based Sources.[147]

In the enforcement provisions, states are to take the necessary measures to implement "applicable international rules and standards established through competent international organizations or diplomatic conference" to control pollution.[148] Although in many instances the pertinent international organization was clear, such as with the IMO or IWC, these provisions lack certainty. Also, the provision on pollution from activities in the area beyond the national jurisdiction of states lacks specificity.[149]

The Convention represented a major achievement, both as a comprehensive expression of the rights and duties of nations in relation to the marine environment and as an illustration of the type of cooperation attainable in the international community. However, as mentioned in the discussion of the Convention in relation to customary intentional law, time and state practice are essential to the attainment of universal acceptance and mandatory submission to the Convention. Although the Convention codified existing customary law, many of its provisions were innovative and cannot be enforced

---

[144] *Id.*, art. 235(3). Article 22 of the Stockholm Report provides that states shall cooperate in the implementation of existing international law and the further development of international law relating to responsibility and liability for the assessment of and compensation for damage and the settlement of related disputes, as well as, where appropriate, development of criteria and procedures for payment of adequate compensation, such as compulsory insurance or compensation funds. *See supra* note 1 at 7.

[145] Convention for the Prevention of Marine Pollution from Land-Based Sources, opened for signature June 4, 1974, 13 I.L.M. 352 (1974).

[146] Convention on the Protection of the Marine Environment of the Baltic Sea, adopted Mar. 22, 1974, 13 I.L.M. 546 (1974).

[147] Protocol for the Protection of the Mediterranean Sea Against Pollution from Land-Based Sources, opened for signature May 18, 1980.

[148] *See* UNCLOS, *supra* note 2, arts. 213, 214, 216, 217(1), 218(1), 219, 220(1), and 222.

[149] *Id.* art. 209.

against nonparties without the passage of time and the development of state practice – two of the three traditional elements of customary law formation. Also, although the Convention stated in many cases that states are to apply, at the minimum, environmental standards developed by the international community and international organizations, one theoretical result of such a provision is the promulgation of many different and perhaps inconsistent rules and regulations. Finally, although many of the environmental provisions of the Convention are praiseworthy attempts to preserve and protect the marine environment, there may, in fact, be no way of ever knowing with certainty the extent to which Convention parties comport with the Convention, due to the inability of the international community to monitor the activities of states, and the unlikelihood that states will police themselves when it is not in their interests.

Despite its shortcomings, UNCLOS represents a major achievement for both international environmental law and multilateral treaty negotiations. This Convention forms a comprehensive framework for addressing all aspects of oceanic environmental concerns. It prescribes standards of conduct, assigns responsibility for enforcement, takes into account the needs of the developing states and the notion of sustainable development, and provides for the peaceful settlement of disputes.

11.3   *Regional and International Conventions*

UNEP and the IMO have been actively engaged in drafting conventions and taking appropriate measures for the protection of the marine environment. These include measures aimed at strengthening several existing arrangements. A few selected instruments are noted here.

11.3.1   *Regional Conventions*

Several regional conventions and protocols have originated under UNEP's Regional Seas Program.[150] These systems reflect a new emphasis on the importance of considering the entire ecosystem of a region. The first was the Mediterranean Action Plan (MAP),[151] which brought together sixteen of

---

[150] For the various Regional Seas Conventions and Protocols related to the Marine Environment, *see* http://www.unep.ch/regionalseas/legal/conlist.html [hereinafter UNEP Conlist]. *See also* ECOLEX databases operated jointly by the Food and Agriculture Organization, IUCN; and UNEP, www.unep.ch/regionalseas/legal/ecolex.htm.

[151] *See, e.g.*, Medwaves, The magazine of the Mediterranean Action Plan, No. 58, 2010, http://195.97.36.231/acrobatfiles/Medwaves/English/MW58.pdf. UNEP, Mediterranean Action Plan Text, document UNEP/WG.2/5, Annex, http://195.97.36.231/dbases/webdocs/BCP/

the eighteen Mediterranean coastal states in 1975 for negotiations resulting in three legal instruments: the 1976 Convention for the Protection of the Mediterranean Sea Against Pollution (Barcelona Convention),[152] constituting the framework convention; the Protocol for the Prevention and Elimination of Pollution of the Mediterranean Sea by Dumping from Ships and Aircraft (Dumping Protocol);[153] and the Protocol Concerning Cooperation in Combating Pollution of the Mediterranean Sea by Oil and other Harmful Substances in Cases of Emergency (Emergency Protocol).[154]

The remaining protocols constituting the Mediterranean Action Plan are:

- Protocol for the Protection of the Mediterranean Sea against Pollution from Land-Based Sources (LBS Protocol);[155]
- Protocol Concerning Mediterranean Specially Protected Areas (SPA Protocol);[156]

MAPPhaseI_eng.pdf. *See* Barcelona Convention, UNEP, http://www.unepmap .org/index.php?module=content2&catid=001001004. *See generally* Suh-Yong Chung, *Is the Convention-Protocol Approach Appropriate for Addressing Regional Marine Pollution?: The Barcelona Convention System Revisited*, 13 PENN ST. ENVTL. L. REV. 85 (2004), discussing the separate components of the MAP, the status of its implementation, and obstacles to its full effectiveness, and assessing efficacy of the hard-law instrument for achieving full commitment to its standards.

[152] The Convention for the Protection of the Marine Environment and the Coastal Region of the Mediterranean (Barcelona Convention), adopted on 16 February 1976, in force 12 February 1978 revised in Barcelona, Spain, 9–10 June 1995 as the Convention for the Protection of the Marine Environment and the Coastal Region of the Mediterranean (not yet in force).

[153] Protocol for the Prevention and Elimination of Pollution of the Mediterranean Sea by Dumping from Ships and Aircraft (Dumping Protocol), adopted in Barcelona, Spain, on 16 February 1976, in force 12 February 1978, revised in Barcelona, 9–10 June 1995 as the Protocol for the Prevention and Elimination of Pollution of the Mediterranean Sea by Dumping from Ships and Aircraft or Incineration at Sea.

[154] Protocol Concerning Cooperation in Combating Pollution of the Mediterranean Sea by Oil and other Harmful Substances in Cases of Emergency (Emergency Protocol), adopted in Barcelona, Spain, on 16 February 1976, in force 12 February 1978.

[155] Protocol for the Protection of the Mediterranean Sea against Pollution from Land-Based Sources (LBS Protocol), adopted in Athens, Greece, on 17 May 1980, in force 17 June 1983, amended in Syracusa, Italy, 6–7 March 1996 as the Protocol for the Protection of the Mediterranean Sea against Pollution from Land-Based Sources and Activities.

[156] Protocol Concerning Mediterranean Specially Protected Areas (SPA Protocol), adopted in Geneva Switzerland, on 2 April 1982, in force 1986, revised in Barcelona, Spain, on 9–10 June 1995 as the Protocol Concerning Specially Protected Areas and Biological Diversity in the Mediterranean (SPA and Biodiversity Protocol).

- Protocol for the Protection of the Mediterranean Sea against Pollution Resulting from Exploration and Exploitation of the Continental Shelf and the Seabed and its Subsoil (Offshore Protocol);[157] and
- Protocol on the Prevention of Pollution of the Mediterranean Sea by Transboundary Movements of Hazardous Wastes and their Disposal (Hazardous Wastes Protocol).[158]

Since its inception, MAP has extended its focus to an ecosystem-based approach to the health of the Mediterranean region, including a considerably broader set of primary objectives:

- to assess and control marine pollution;
- to ensure sustainable management of natural marine and coastal resources;
- to integrate the environment in social and economic development;
- to protect the marine environment and coastal zones through prevention and reduction of pollution, and as far as possible, elimination of pollution, whether land or sea-based;
- to protect the natural and cultural heritage;
- to strengthen solidarity among Mediterranean coastal States; [and]
- to contribute to improvement of the quality of life.[159]

Additional regional programs include:

Kuwait Region

Kuwait Regional Convention for Co-operation on the Protection of the Marine Environment from Pollution (Kuwait Convention), adopted 1978, entered into force 1979, and its Protocols:

Protocol Concerning Regional Co-operation in Combating Pollution by Oil and Other Harmful Substances in Cases of Emergency, adopted 1978, entered into force 1979;

---

[157] Protocol for the Protection of the Mediterranean Sea against Pollution Resulting from Exploration and Exploitation of the Continental Shelf and the Seabed and its Subsoil (Offshore Protocol), adopted in Madrid, Spain, 13–14 October 1994.

[158] The Protocol on the Prevention of Pollution of the Mediterranean Sea by Transboundary Movements of Hazardous Wastes and their Disposal (Hazardous Wastes Protocol); adopted in Izmir, Turkey, 30 September–1 October 1996, not yet in force.

[159] UNEP, Mediterranean Action Plan for the Barcelona Convention, http://www.unepmap .org/index.php?module=content2&catid=001001004; Annex: Amendments to the Convention for the Protection of the Mediterranean Sea Against Pollution, http://195.97.36.231/ dbases/webdocs/BCP/BC95amendments_Eng.pdf (Convention for the Protection of the Marine Environment and the Coastal Region of the Mediterranean.

Protocol for the Protection of the Marine Environment Against Pollution from Land-Based Sources, adopted 1990, entered into force 1993;

Protocol on the Control of Marine Transboundary Movements and Disposal of Hazardous Wastes, adopted 1998; and

Protocol Concerning Marine Pollution Resulting from Exploration and Exploitation of the Continental Shelf, adopted 1989, entered into force 1990.

West and Central Africa

Convention for Co-operation in the Protection and Development of the Marine and Coastal Environment of the West and Central African Region (Abidjan Convention), adopted 1981, entered into force 1984, and its Protocol:

Protocol Concerning Cooperation in Combating Pollution in Cases of Emergency, adopted in 1981, entered into force 1984.

South-East Pacific

Convention for the Protection of the Marine Environment and Coastal Area of the South-East Pacific (Lima Convention), adopted 1981, entered into force 1986;

Agreement on Regional Cooperation in Combating Pollution of the South-East Pacific by Hydrocarbons or Other Harmful Substances in Case of Emergency, adopted 1981;

Supplementary Protocol to the Agreement on Regional Co-Operation in Combating Pollution of the South-East Pacific by Hydrocarbons or Other Harmful Substances in Cases of Emergency, adopted 1983, entered into force 1987;

Protocol for the Protection of the South-East Pacific against Pollution from Land-based Sources, adopted 1983, entered into force 1986;

Protocol for the Conservation and Management of Protected Marine and Coastal Areas of the South-East Pacific, adopted 1989, entered into force 1994;

Protocol for the Protection of the South-East Pacific Against Radioactive Contamination, adopted 1989, entered into force 1995; and

Protocol on the Programme for the Regional Study on the El Niño Phenomenon (ERFEN) in the South-East Pacific, adopted 1992.

Red Sea and Gulf of Aden

Regional Convention for the Conservation of the Red Sea and Gulf of Aden Environment (Jeddah Convention), adopted 1982, entered into force 1985, and its Protocol:

Protocol Concerning Regional Co-Operation in Combating Pollution by Oil and Other Harmful Substances in Cases of Emergency, adopted 1982; entered into force 1985.

Caribbean

Convention for the Protection and Development of the Marine Environment of the Wider Caribbean Region (Cartagena Convention), adopted 1983, entered into force 1986, and its Protocols:

Protocol Concerning Co-operation in Combating Oil Spills in the Wider Caribbean Region, adopted 1983, entered into force 1986;

Protocol concerning Protected Areas and Wildlife (SPAW), adopted 1990; and

Protocol on the prevention, reduction and control of land-based sources and activities, adopted 1999.

Eastern Africa

The Convention for the Protection, Management and Development of the Marine and Coastal Environment of the Eastern African Region (Nairobi Convention), adopted 1985, entered into force 1996, and its Protocols:

The Protocol Concerning Protected Areas and Wild Fauna and Flora in the Eastern African Region, adopted 1985; and

The Protocol Concerning Co-operation in Combating Marine Pollution in Cases of Emergency in the Eastern African Region, adopted 1985.

South Pacific

Convention for the Protection of Natural Resources and Environment of the South Pacific Region (Noumea Convention), adopted 1986, entered into force 1990, and its Protocols:

Protocol for the Prevention of Pollution of the South Pacific Region by Dumping, adopted 1986, entered into force 1990; and

Protocol Concerning Co-operation in Combating Pollution Emergencies in the South Pacific Region, adopted 1986, entered into force 1990.

Black Sea

> Convention on the Protection of the Black Sea Against Pollution (Bucharest Convention), adopted 1992, entered into force 1994, and its Protocols:

> Protocol on Protection of the Black Sea Marine Environment Against Pollution from Land-based Sources, adopted 1992, entered into force 1994;

> Protocols on Cooperation in Combating Pollution of the Black Sea Marine Environment by Oil and other Harmful Substances in Emergency Situations, adopted 1992, entered into force 1994; and

> Protocol on the Protection of the Black Sea Marine Environment Against Pollution by Dumping, adopted 1992, entered into forc. 1994.

North-East Pacific

> The Convention for Cooperation in the Protection and Sustainable Development of the Marine and Coastal Environment of the Northeast Pacific, adopted 2002.

11.3.2   *International Conventions and Actions*

The IMO's main international convention for preventing pollution of the marine environment by ships from operational or accidental causes is the International Convention for the Prevention of Pollution from Ships (MARPOL), adopted on November 2, 1973,[160] and amended by the 1978 MARPOL Protocol, which absorbed the parent convention (collectively referred to as MARPOL 73/78). MARPOL 73/78 has been updated by amendments through the years. The Protocol's six annexes contain regulations aimed at preventing and minimizing pollution from ships:

> Annex I – Regulations for the Prevention of Pollution by Oil (entered into force October 2, 1983), amended in 1992, making it mandatory for new oil tankers to have double hulls and prescribed a phase-in schedule for existing tankers to fit double hulls.

> Annex II – Regulations for the Control of Pollution by Noxious Liquid Substances in Bulk (entered into force October 2, 1983);

> Annex III, Prevention of Pollution by Harmful Substances Carried by Sea in Packaged Form (entered into force July 1, 1992);

---

[160] MARPOL *supra* notes 71, 80.

Annex IV, Prevention of Pollution by Sewage from Ships (entered into force September 27, 2003), amended in July 2011, which was aimed at introducing the Baltic Sea as a special area and added new discharge requirements for passenger ships in special areas. The amendments are expected to enter into force on January 1, 2013.

Annex V – Prevention of Pollution by Garbage from Ships (entered into force December 31, 1988), which prohibits the discharge of garbage into the sea, and institutes a complete ban on disposal into the sea of all forms of plastics, was amended July 2011; revisions are expected to enter into force on January 1, 2013.

Annex VI – Prevention of Air Pollution from Ships (entered into force May 19, 2005). It sets limits on sulphur oxide and nitrogen oxide emissions from ship exhausts and prohibits deliberate emissions of ozone depleting substances. In 2011 IMO adopted mandatory technical and operational energy efficiency measures in Annex VI, which will significantly reduce the amount of greenhouse gas emissions from ships. These measures were included in Annex VI and are expected to enter into force on January 1, 2013.

The Antarctic Protocol on Environmental Protection to the Atlantic Treaty entered into force on January 14, 1998, and designates the continent as a natural reserve and prohibits mineral resource development there.[161] In March 1998, the 1992 Convention for the Protection of the Marine Environment of the North-East Atlantic (OSPAR) came into force, replacing the Oslo and Paris Conventions, setting a target date of the end of 2020 for reduction of the dumping of radioactive wastes and other hazardous substances, and prohibiting the dumping of steel oil-drilling installations.[162]

Protection of the marine environment from land-based activities has become a priority item on the international agenda. In 1995, the Washington Declaration on this topic recommended preventive and remedial action and international and regional cooperative measures.[163] Two years later, UNEP set up a coordinating office in The Hague for the Global Programme of Action for the Protection of the Marine Environment from Land-Based Activities to accomplish this objective.[164] The UN Commission on Sustainable

---

[161] *See* U.S. Dept. of State, *Statement on Antarctica Protocol on Environmental Protection to the Antarctic Treaty* (Dec. 22, 1997).

[162] *See OSPAR Commission Bans Dumping of Steel Oil-Drilling Installations in Atlantic*, 21 Int'l Env't Rep. (BNA) 761 (Aug. 5, 1998).

[163] For the text, *see* 18 Int'l Env't Rep. (BNA) 891 (Nov. 15, 1995).

[164] *See* 20 Int'l Env't Rep. (BNA) 409 (Apr. 16, 1997).

Development stated in 1999 that land-based sources of pollution and over-fishing are the two most pressing issues facing the oceans.[165]

In May 1996, a conference of the IMO adopted the International Convention on Liability and Compensation for Damage in Connection with the Carriage of Hazardous and Noxious Substances by Sea.[166] The Convention establishes a compensation mechanism for loss or damage which might result from pollution, fire or explosion that is threatened or caused by hazardous and noxious substances carried on ships, such as chemicals, magnesium and iron oxide.[167] It also set up the International Hazardous and Noxious Substances Fund.[168]

The London Dumping Convention has been strengthened. A worldwide prohibition on dumping of low level radioactive waste in the oceans took effect in November 1993.[169] In November 1996, a Protocol to the London Dumping Convention was adopted,[170] embodying the polluter-pays principle and the precautionary principle (appropriate preventive measures are to be taken even when "there is no conclusive evidence to prove a causal connection" between wastes and their effects).[171] The Protocol prohibits the dumping of any wastes or other matter, with some exceptions,[172] prohibits the incineration of wastes at sea,[173] and obligates the parties not to export "wastes or other matter to other countries for dumping or incineration at sea."[174] In May 1995, the 1990 International Convention on Oil Pollution Preparedness, Response and Cooperation came into force.[175]

---

[165] *Sustainable Development*, 22 Int'l Env't Rep. (BNA) 389 (May 12, 1999).

[166] International Convention on Liability and Compensation for Damage in Connection with the Carriage of Hazardous and Noxious Substances by Sea, May 3, 1996, 35 I.L.M. 1415 (1996).

[167] *Id.* art. 1(5).

[168] *Id.* arts. 13–30.

[169] *See London Convention Agrees to Ban Dumping of Radioactive Waste at Sea*, 16 Int'l Env't Rep. (BNA) 839 (Nov. 17, 1993).

[170] 1996 Protocol to the Convention on the Prevention of Marine Pollution by Dumping of Wastes and Other Matter," 1972, adopted Nov. 7, 1996, IMO Doc. LC/SM 1/6, 36 I.L.M. 1 (1997).

[171] *Id.* art. 3(1)–(2).

[172] *Id.* art. 4 and Annex I.

[173] *Id.* art. 5.

[174] *Id.* art. 6.

[175] *See Treaty On Marine Pollution By Oil to Come Into Force in May 1995, IMO Says*, 16 Int'l Env't Rep. (BNA) 595 (July 13, 1994). *See generally* Emeka Duruigbo, *Reforming the International Law and Policy on Marine Oil Pollution*, 31 J. MAR. L. & COM. 65 (2000).

In 1998 the International Year of the Ocean was marked.[176] The Independent World Commission on the Oceans released a report in September 1998,[177] highlighting the various threats to the world's oceans and making recommendations for the preservation of the marine environment and resources. In December 1998, the Organization of Economic Cooperation and Development (OECD) announced a plan designed to eliminate the use of sub-standard ships that pose a threat to the marine environment.[178] Under the Convention on Arrest of Ships,[179] drafted by the IMO and the United Nations Conference on Trade and Development (UNCTAD) in March 1999, national authorities are authorized to arrest ships that present a threat to the environment.

In April 1999 the Commission on Sustainable Development (CSD) devoted a major agenda item of its seventh session to a review of progress made by regions under the "oceans and seas" sector of Agenda 21, especially chapter 17.[180] In November of that year, the UN General Assembly endorsed the CSD's recommendations regarding international coordination and cooperation and established an open-ended working group aimed at coordinating international efforts to protect and preserve the oceans, including the marine environment, to be called the "open-ended informal consultative process on oceans and the law of the sea."[181] The resolution called for annual review by the General Assembly of the Secretary-General's annual report on oceans and the law of the sea.[182]

---

[176] The UN General Assembly declared 1998 the International Year of the Ocean in 1995. *See* G.A. Res. 131, U.N. GAOR, 49th Sess., U.N. Doc. A/Res/49/131 (1995). For a statement by the then-UNEP Director, Elizabeth Dowdeswell, *see* 21 Int'l Env't Rep. (BNA) 48 (Jan. 21, 1998).

[177] INDEPENDENT WORLD COMMISSION ON THE OCEANS, THE OCEAN, OUR FUTURE (1998).

[178] *See Maritime Affairs*, 21 Int'l Env't Rep. (BNA) 1244 (Dec. 9, 1998).

[179] *See Marine Affairs*, 22 Int'l Env't Rep. (BNA) 234 (Mar. 17, 1999).

[180] *Division for Sustainable Development*, UN DEPARTMENT OF ECONOMIC AND SOCIAL AFFAIRS, http://www.un.org/esa/dsd/susdevtopics/sdt_oceaseas.shtml. *See* United Nations Economic and Social Council, Commission on Sustainable Development, Oceans and Seas, Report of the Secretary-General, Addendum, Trends in national implementation, document E/CN.17/1999/4/Add.1, February 1, 1999, http://daccess-dds-ny.un.org/doc/UNDOC/GEN/N99/027/74/PDF/N9902774.pdf?OpenElement.

[181] Results of the review by the Commission on Sustainable Development of the sectoral theme of "Oceans and seas": international coordination and cooperation, U.N. Doc. A/RES/54/33, January 18, 2000 [hereinafter Resolution 54/33]. *See* United Nations, Division for Ocean Affairs and the Law of the Sea, Oceans and Law of the Sea, United Nations Open-ended informal consultative process on oceans and the law of the sea, June 1, 2007, http://www.un.org/depts/los/consultative_process/consultative_process_background.htm. *See also* Environment: New U.N. Group to Oversee World's Oceans, ITER PRESS SERVICE, Dec. 6, 1999.

[182] Resolution 54/33, *supra* note 181, at 2.

In 2005, when the General Assembly agreed to its Resolution 59/24 on Oceans and Law of the Sea, it created another important working group, the Ad Hoc Open-ended Informal Working Group to study issues relating to the conservation and sustainable use of marine biological diversity beyond areas of national jurisdiction.[183]

Among other significant instruments covering specific aspects of the marine environment, we note here the following:

Revised Guidelines for the Identification and Designation of Particularly Sensitive Sea Areas, adopted by the IMO Assembly on December 1, 2005.[184]

Protocol of 2003 (Supplementary Fund Protocol) to the International Convention on the Establishment of an International Fund for Compensation for Oil Pollution Damage, 1992, adopted at London, 2003, entered into force 2005.[185]

Antarctic: Convention on the Conservation of Antarctic Marine Living Resources (CCAMLR), entered into force 1982.

Baltic: Convention on the Protection of the Marine Environment of the Baltic Sea Area (Helsinki Convention), adopted 1974, in force 1980, revised 1992, entered into force 2000.

Caspian: Framework Convention for the Protection of the Marine Environment of the Caspian Sea, adopted 2003.

No regional conventions have yet been developed for East Asian Seas, South Asian Seas, North West Pacific, North-East Pacific, and the Arctic.[186]

---

[183] General Assembly Resolution 59/24, Oceans and the law of the sea, U.N. Doc. A/RES/59/24, February 4, 2005, http://daccess-dds-ny.un.org/doc/UNDOC/GEN/N04/477/64/PDF/N0447764.pdf?OpenElement.

[184] IMO, Revised Guidelines for the Identification and Designation of Particularly Sensitive Sea Areas, December 1, 2005, IMO doc. A.982 (24)(Annex). *See generally* Jon M. Van Dyke & Sherry P. Broder, *Particularly Sensitive Sea Areas – Protecting the Marine Environment in the Territorial Seas and Exclusive Economic Zones*, *in* Perspectives on International Law in an Era of Change 472 (Anjali Nanda & Alissa Mundt eds., 2012).

[185] Protocol of 2003 (Supplementary Fund Protocol to the International Convention on the Establishment of an International Fund for Compensation for Oil Pollution Damage, 1992, adopted at London, May 16, 2003, entered into force March 3, 2005, CM6245, http://www.iopcfund.org/npdf/Conventions%20English.pdf.

[186] Links to the conventions and protocols are available at UNEP Conlist, *supra* note 158.

11.4   *International Tribunal for the Law of the Sea*[187]

The International Tribunal for the Law of the Sea (ITLOS) was established by UNCLOS to settle disputes arising in connection with UNCLOS.[188] The Tribunal formed the Chamber for Marine Environment Disputes as a standing special chamber of the Tribunal.[189] The Seabed Disputes Chamber has jurisdiction over disputes in "the Area" – the seabed and subsoil beyond national jurisdiction – and has the authority to issue advisory opinions arising within the scope of the activities of the International Seabed Authority. The opinions of the Tribunal in selected cases are discussed here.

The MOX Plant Case (Ireland v. UK)[190]

This dispute concerning disclosure of information was initiated by Ireland regarding the United Kingdom's authorization of a government-owned company, British Nuclear Fuels, to start manufacturing mixed oxide fuel (MOX) from spent nuclear material, uranium and plutonium oxides, at a plant in northwest England on the coast of the Irish Sea. Ireland attempted through diplomatic means to obtain environmental and safety information about the plant but, having failed to get the information, it resorted to arbitration under UNCLOS and the OSPAR Convention.[191] It claimed before ITLOS that operation of the MOX Plant would result in an increased level of radioactive discharges into the marine environment, and alleged this would

---

[187] *See generally* Helmut Tuerk, *The Contribution of the International Tribunal for the Law of the Sea to International Law*, 26 Penn St. Int'l L. Rev. 289 (2007); Christoph Schwarte, *Environmental Concerns in the Adjudication of the International Tribunal for the Law of the Sea*, 16 Geo. Int'l Envtl. L. Rev. 421 (2004); Yoona Cho, *Precautionary Principle in the International Tribunal for the Law of the Sea*, 10 Sustainable Dev. L. & Pol'y 64 (2009).

[188] Statute of the International Tribunal for the Law of the Sea, Annex VI to UNCLOS, *supra* note 2, art. 25.

[189] ITLOS, Resolution on the Chamber for Marine Environment Disputes, doc. ITLOS/2011/RES.2, October 6, 2011 (recording the selection of the members of the Tribunal to serve on the Chamber), http://www.itlos.org/fileadmin/itlos/documents/basic_texts/ITLOS_2011_Res_2_E__Marine_Environment_.pdf.

[190] MOX Plant Case (Ir. v. U.K.) (Provisional Measures), ITLOS, December 3, 2001, *reprinted in* 41 I.L.M. 405 (2001), http://www.itlos.org/fileadmin/itlos/documents/cases/case_no_10/Order.03.12.01.E.pdf [hereinafter MOX Plant Case]. *See* M. Bruce Volbeda, *Comment: The MOX Plant Case: The Question of "Supplemental Jurisdiction" for International Environmental Claims Under UNCLOS*, 42 Tex. Int'l L.J. 211 (2006).

[191] OSPAR Arbitral Tribunal, final award July 2, 2003, http://www.pca-cpa.org. *See generally* Ted L. McDorman, edited by David D. Caron, Access to Information under Article 9 of the Ospar Convention (Ireland v. United Kingdom), Final Award, 98 A.J.I.L. 330 (2004), concerning the arbitration and award.

be a violation by the UK of its basic procedural and substantive obligations under UNCLOS, including assessment of environmental impacts. Hence Ireland sought provisional measures under UNCLOS.

Rejecting Ireland's request, ITLOS instead prescribed alternative measures requiring the two countries to cooperate and consult in order to exchange information on risks for the Irish Sea from this operation and to devise appropriate measures to prevent environmental pollution that might result from the plant's operation.[192] It referred to the duty to cooperate as a fundamental principle for the prevention of pollution of the marine environment under UNCLOS, as well as general international law.[193] ITLOS implicitly supported a state's duty to conduct transboundary environmental assessment.

Case Concerning the Conservation and Sustainable Exploitation of Swordfish Stocks in the South-Eastern Pacific Ocean (Chile/European Union)[194]

In this case, initiated by Chile and the European Community, the issues for consideration were: (1) the EC's obligations under UNCLOS to ensure conservation of swordfish in the fishing activities undertaken by vessels flying the flag of any EC Member States on the high seas adjacent to Chile's exclusive economic zone; (2) whether the Chilean decree purporting to apply Chile's relevant conservation measures was in breach of the Convention; and (3) whether the "Galapagos Agreement" of 2000 was negotiated pursuant to the provisions of UNCLOS. ITLOS created a special chamber to address the dispute in December 2000. However, the parties held bilateral consultations and in a joint communication informed the Tribunal's special chamber that they had reached a settlement which committed the parties to cooperate for the long-term conservation and management of the swordfish stocks in the South-Eastern Pacific Ocean. The case was therefore removed from ITLOS' list of cases.[195]

Case Concerning Land Reclamation by Singapore in and Around the Straits of Johor (Malaysia v. Singapore)[196]

This dispute concerned land reclamation activities carried out by Singapore which allegedly impinged upon Malaysia's rights in and around the Straits of

---

[192] MOX Plant case, *supra* note 190, para. 89.1(a)–(c).

[193] *Id.* para. 82.

[194] Case concerning the Conservation and Sustainable Exploitation of Swordfish Stocks in the South-Eastern Pacific Ocean (Chile/European Union), Order 2009/1, December 16, 2009, http://itlos.org/fileadmin/itlos/documents/cases/case_no_7/Ord.2009.1–16.12.09.E.pdf.

[195] *Id.*

[196] ITLOS, Case concerning Land Reclamation by Singapore in and around the Straits of Johor (Malay. v. Sing.), Provisional Measures, Case No. 12, Order of October 8, 2003, http://www.itlos.org/fileadmin/itlos/documents/cases/case_no_12/Order.08.10.03.E.pdf.

Johor, which separate Singapore from Malaysia, and the potentially adverse effects on the marine environment there. Following Malaysia's submission of a request for the prescription of provisional measures by ITLOS, the Tribunal found that in the particular circumstances of the case, the land reclamation works may have adverse effects on the marine environment in the area, and hence considered that prudence and caution required Malaysia and Singapore to establish mechanisms for exchanging information on and assessing the effects of such work. Pending a decision by the Arbitral Tribunal provided for under Annex VII, it unanimously directed Singapore "not to conduct its land reclamation in ways that might cause irreparable prejudice to the rights of Malaysia or serious harm to the marine environment, taking especially into account the reports of the group of independent experts."[197]

Southern Bluefin Tuna Cases (N.Z. v. Japan; Austl. v. Japan)[198]

New Zealand and Australia requested provisional measures against Japan to immediately stop the latter's fishing program. The Tribunal noted that notwithstanding a consensus that the stock of Southern Bluefin was severely depleted, there was no scientific certainty regarding measures to be taken to conserve the stock. The Tribunal considered that under these circumstances the parties should act with caution and prudence to ensure that effective conservation measures are taken so as to prevent serious harm to the stock of Southern Bluefin Tuna. The parties were also ordered to restrict their catches and to negotiate without delay to reach agreement on conservation and management measures.[199]

11.5   Conclusion

As discussed above, the 1982 United Nations Convention on the Law of the Sea, which entered into force on November 16, 1994,[200] provided a comprehensive framework and a set of detailed guidelines for the protection and preservation of the marine environment. As of May 2012, the 30th anniversary of the Convention, 161 states and the European Union had ratified or acceded to it, thus affirming their commitment to the protection and preservation of the marine environment.

---

[197] *Id.* para. 106(2).

[198] ITLOS, Southern Blue Fin Tuna Cases, Order of August 27, 1999, http://www.itlos.org/fileadmin/itlos/documents/cases/case_no_3_4/Order.27.08.99.E.pdf.

[199] *Id.*

[200] "Status of the United Nations Convention on the Law of the Sea, etc.," Division for Ocean Affairs and the Law of the Sea, http://www.un.org/Depts/los/convention_agreements/convention_agreements.htm, accessed Feb. 6, 2002.

In 1992, the then-UN Secretary General had reported to the United Nations Conference on Environment and Development (UNCED) in Rio that UNCLOS

> provides a model for the evolution of international environmental law in its incorporation of several newly developed concepts and principles, such as the prevention of transboundary pollution; the requirement of prior environmental impact assessment, habitat protection and ecosystem considerations; an integrated approach to various sources of pollution; and contingency planning against pollution emergencies.[201]

That statement aptly describes the significant contribution of UNCLOS to international environmental law. UNCED made its own contribution by adopting in Chapter 17 of Agenda 21 a set of recommendations on the marine environment that were based on the environment provisions of the Law of the Sea Convention.[202]

As noted in the preceding section, many developments have occurred since UNCLOS was signed which have strengthened the existing arrangements and established new obligations to protect the marine environment.[203] Coupled with the elaborate provisions under the Law of the Sea Convention, these developments show a clear trend demonstrating a willingness of states to limit their sovereignty and, to some degree, their economic development in pursuit of the common interest in maintaining a healthy marine environment. Of course, the key to success will ultimately be measured by the effectiveness of state practice implementing the obligations they have undertaken to protect and preserve the marine environment.

---

[201] Report of the UN Secretary General to the UN Conference on Environment and Development, U.N. Doc. A/CONF.151/10, para. 12(a) (1992).

[202] "Protection of the Oceans...," Ch. 17, Agenda 21, in I REPORT OF THE UNITED NATIONS CONFERENCE ON ENVIRONMENT AND DEVELOPMENT (1992) (U.N. Sales No. E.93.1.8).

[203] *But see generally* David S. Ardia, *Does the Emperor Have No Clothes? Enforcement of International Laws Protecting the Marine Environment*, 19 MICH. J. INT'L L. 497 (1998).

Chapter Twelve

Hazardous Waste, Chemicals, and Technology

12.0 *Introduction*

The international movement of hazardous wastes, toxic chemicals, and high-risk technology virtually exploded into public attention in the 1980s.[1] A number of sensational cases provoked widespread media coverage and public outrage, particularly "toxic exports" from developed countries to developing

---

[1] Background and historical references for this chapter include Ved Nanda & Bruce Bailey, *Export of Hazardous Waste and Hazardous Technology: Challenge for International Environmental Law*, 17 Den. J. Int'l L. & Pol'y 155 (1988); George (Rock) Pring, *Increasing International Environmental Law Limitations on Trade in Secondary Metals for Recycling*, in Asia Pacific Economic Cooperation Forum (APEC)/Expert Group on Minerals and Energy Exploration and Development (GEMEED), Third Environmental Cooperation Workshop on Sustainable Development of Mining Activities (1999) (copy with author); George (Rock) Pring, James Otto, & Koh Naito, *Trends in International Environmental Law Affecting the Minerals Industry*, 17 J. Energy & Nat. Res. L. 39 (Part I) and 151 (Part II) (1999); United Nations Environment Programme (UNEP), *Guidance Document on Transboundary Movements of Hazardous Wastes Destined for Recovery Operations* (Aug. 28, 1996), http://www.basel.int/meetings/sbc/workdoc/old%20docs/guidelns.pdf; Kofi Asante-Duah, International Trade in Hazardous Waste, (1998); Bill Moyers, Global Dumping Ground: The International Traffic in Hazardous Waste (1990); M. E. Hemstock, The Recycling of NonFerrous Metals (ICME 1996); Jennifer Clapp, Toxic Exports (2001); Jason Gudofsky, *Transboundary Shipments of Hazardous Waste for Recycling and Recovery Operations*, 34 Stan. J. Int'l L. 219 (1998); Rozelia Park, *An Examination of International Environmental Racism Through the Lens of Transboundary Movement of Hazardous Wastes*, 5 Ind. J. Global Legal Stud. 659 (1998); Jonathan Krueger, *Prior Informed Consent and the Basel Convention: The Hazards of What Isn't Known*, 7 J. Env't & Dev. 115 (1998); James Crawford & Phillippe Sands, *Article 11 Agreements and Basel Convention Export Ban*, ICME Newsletter No. 2, at 1 (1997); James O'Reilly & Lorre Cuzze, *Trash or Treasure? Industrial Recycling and International Barriers to the Movement of Hazardous Waste*, J. Corp. L. 507 (1997); Dean Poulakidas, *Waste Trade and Disposal in the Americas: The Need for and Benefits of a Regional Response*, 21 Vt. L. Rev. 873 (1997); Elli Louka, Overcoming National Barriers to International Waste Trade: A New Perspective on the Transnational Movements of Hazardous and Radioactive Waste (1994); Jim Puckett, *The Basel Ban: A Triumph over Business-as-Usual* 8–9 (1997), http://www.ban.org/about_basel_ban/jims_article.html.

ones in Africa, Asia, Latin America, and the Caribbean. Examples of these "North-South" scandals included:

- shipments of waste chemicals, metal scrap, plastics, batteries, computer parts, and other hazardous wastes from US and European sources for "disposal" in developing countries wholly lacking adequate sites, treatment technology, and regulation;
- "garbage barges," ships, trains, and trucks of hazardous wastes turned back by countries only to result in illegal "midnight dumping";
- shipments of wastes disguised as agricultural "fertilizers" or materials for "recycling";
- uncontrolled trade in pesticides and other commercial chemicals (including those outlawed in the US and other developed countries where they are manufactured);
- the siting of dangerous industries in developing countries, resulting in disasters like the tragic 1984 release of methyl isocyanate at the majority-US-owned Union Carbide plant in Bhopal, India, which left thousands dead and thousands more severely injured;
- the shipment in 2006 of oil-products waste and caustic chemicals to the Ivory Coast by a large Netherlands company, where it was illegally dumped, killing 16 people and sickening thousands more, according to the Ivory Coast government.[2]

In large part, these stories elicit public outrage because hazardous waste is such a feared substance, conjuring up images of poisoning, birth defects, sterility, cancer, and multigenerational mutations. Even more frightening is the fact that scientists are only beginning to understand the relationship between hazardous waste and human health. Unfortunately, hazardous waste promises to be a continuing problem in the 21st century. The world produces by some estimates as much as 3.4–4.0 billion metric tonnes annually of wastes (10 million tonnes per day!) of which 250–450 million tones is hazardous or toxic waste,[3] and most of it is generated by the 34 industrialized countries of

---

[2] *See further* Nanda & Bailey, *supra* note 1; Gudofsky, *supra* note 1, at 220 n. 8; Andrea Marcus, *Transboundary Toxic Waste Disposal: Understanding the Gravity of the Problem and Addressing the Issue Through the Human Rights Commission*, 1 INT'L DIMENSIONS 11–13 (1997); Cahal Milmo, Dumped in Africa: Britain's toxic waste, The Independent (London), Feb. 18, 2009, http://www.independent.co.uk/news/world/africa/dumped-in-africa-britain8217s-toxic-waste-1624869.html; Marlise Simons, *The Netherlands: Court Upholds Fine for Dumping Waste in Africa*, N.Y. TIMES, Dec. 29, 2011, http://www.nytimes.com/2011/12/24/world/europe/court-upholds-fine-against-trafigura-over-toxic-waste-dumping-in-africa.html.

[3] The figures for total waste (hazardous plus non-hazardous) come from Philippe Chalmin & Catherine Gaillochet, *From Waste to Resource: An Abstract of World Waste Survey 2009* 10–11 (2009), http://www.uncrd.or.jp/env/spc/docs/plenary3/PS3-F-Veolia_Hierso-Print%20abstract.pdf – and are likely low according to the study. While exact statistics

the Organization of Economic Cooperation and Development (OECD), the majority of whose members – including the US, EU nations, CANZ (Canada, Australia, New Zealand), and Japan – make it synonymous with the developed "North."[4]

Today, Asian countries, particularly Thailand and Malaysia, are heavy importers of metal scrap, lead acid automobile batteries, computer parts, and plastics from Australia and other OECD member countries.[5] India, Pakistan, and Bangladesh virtually monopolize the ship scrapping business (with lowtech, on-the-beach operations that release PCBs, asbestos, waste oil, leaded paints, and other metals and toxic substances into the environment).[6] The Philippines had been a key center for lead acid battery disposal from Australia, New Zealand, and elsewhere, until a national ban closed secondary lead smelters there. India is a major importer of zinc residues for fertilizer, most notably from Australia, leading to a 1996 order by the New Delhi High Court banning many zinc-bearing imports for public health reasons.[7] In 1998, several Cambodians died in riots protesting the alleged dumping of mercurycontaminated industrial wastes from Taiwan in their country. Germany exports metals, mercury wastes, and waste paints to suspect recovery operations in the Ukraine and elsewhere in the emerging economies of Central and Eastern Europe. China imports large amounts of computer waste from Australia and other countries for the copper wire then burns the associated waste plastic, chlorinated compounds, and metal residues producing dioxins and other toxics.[8] In 1992, in a particularly notorious case, a US firm sold dust containing lead and cadmium as "fertilizer" to Bangladesh where it was

---

on the hazardous waste component of this are understandably difficult to assemble, those are the figures in UNEP, Div. of Tech. Indus. and Econ., Cleaning Up: Experience and Knowledge to Finance Investments in Cleaner Production, 2 (2003), http://www.financingcp.org/docs/cleaningup.pdf. The nine major categories of what the UN calls "harmful substances and hazardous waste" (HSHW) are (1) hazardous waste; (2) persistent organic pollutants (POPs); (3) heavy metals; (4) pesticides; (5) electronic waste; (6) persistent, bioaccumulative, and toxic substances (PBTs), (7) healthcare waste; (8) ozone depleting substances; and (9) immediate hazard chemicals. UN Association of the USA, *Global Classrooms – Topic: Harmful Substances and Hazardous Waste* 3 (2012), http://www.unausa.org/Document.Doc?id=1136.

[4] The OECD has been called everything from "a think tank" to "a rich man's club", OECD, *Resource Productivity and Waste,* http://www.oecd.org/department/0,3355,en_2649_34395_1_1_1_1_1,00.html; Krueger, *Prior Informed Consent, supra* note 1, at 5.

[5] Adam Minter, *Malaysia in the Middle,* Scrap Magazine, June 2011, http://www.isri.org/imis15_prod/ISRI/_Program_and_Services/Scrap_Magazine_Features/Scrap_Magazine_Feature_May_June_2011_.aspx.

[6] Maria Sarraf et al., Ship Breaking and Recycling Industry in Bangladesh and Pakistan, World Bank Report 58275-SAS, (Dec. 2010) http://siteresources.worldbank.org/SOUTHASIAEXT/Resources/223546–1296680097256/Shipbreaking.pdf.

[7] UNEP, *Hazardous Waste: Special Reference to Municipal Solid Waste Management, in* India: State of the Environment 2001, 145 http://moef.nic.in/soer/2001/ind_waste.pdf.

[8] *See, e.g.,* Chien Min Chung, *China's Electronic Waste Village,* Time, http://www.time.com/time/photogallery/0,29307,1870162_1822148,00.html.

spread on farms.[9] Brazil's 1995 ban on imports of scrap batteries has resulted in a marked decline in licensed secondary lead smelters but a large increase in black market "backyard" smelters (now estimated at 60 percent of the country's secondary lead production).[10]

The negative impacts of this international transfer of wastes, chemicals, and technology are daunting. They include severe worker-community health impacts and air, surface water, groundwater, and soil contamination. These deleterious effects are aggravated by unsuitable sites, lack of environmentally sound technologies, untrained personnel, inadequate national regulatory laws, limited enforcement capability, lack of spill management and remediation funding, as well as deliberate mislabeling, illegal trade, secret dumping, and sham recycling. Moreover, hazardous waste can remain dangerous for decades, if not centuries, making it a multi-generational problem.

Perhaps the biggest objection to waste transfer – including even its legitimate recycling component – is that allowing it "can reduce the incentive to find and use other cleaner production options."[11] Companies have no incentive to engage in pollution prevention (nongeneration of hazardous wastes at the outset) and waste minimization (reduction at the source of the amount and/or hazardousness of the wastes generated) so long as they have access to cheap and easy waste transfer. Thus, waste transfer should be understood as a form of cost externalization whereby the true cost of production is not transmitted in its price. Rather, communities overseas incur the cost of disposal and the environmental and health damage associated with the product. This has been poignantly expressed by Jim Puckett of the Basel Action Network:

> [W]e must realize that when we sweep things out of our lives and throw them away…they don't ever disappear, as we might like to believe. We must know that "away" is in fact a place. In a world where cost externalization is made all too easy by the pathways of globalization, "away" is likely to be somewhere where people are impoverished, disenfranchised, powerless and too desperate to be able to resist the poison for the realities of their poverty.[12]

The toxic trade persists because of three primarily economic factors: (1) dramatically cheaper disposal costs in developing countries; (2) difficulties creating new disposal facilities in many developed countries – from the "NIMBY" or "Not-In-My-Back-Yard" syndrome, as well as cost and geographic factors;

---

[9] Basel Action Network ("BAN"), *A Chronology of the Basel Ban,* http://www.ban.org/about_basel_ban/chronology.html.

[10] For more details of these and other problems, see the websites of two of the most active environmental NGOs in the hazwaste opposition arena: the Basel Action Network (BAN), http://www.ban.org and Greenpeace, http://www.greenpeace.org; see also authorities, *supra* note 1.

[11] UNEP Guidance, *supra* note 1, at ¶ 2.

[12] Jim Puckett, *A Place Called Away,* http://www.ban.org/library/AwayIsAPlaceEssayFINAL.pdf.

and (3) the potential value of the waste to developing countries as needed secondary raw materials and foreign exchange.[13] Materials recycling, for example, is an enormous global industry employing about 1.6 million people, handling over 600 million tones of materials, with an annual turnover in excess of US$200 billion, a third of which is international trade.[14] Thus, despite the problems associated with materials recycling many developing countries have built their economies around it.

Starting in the 1980s, international environmental lawmakers responded to the crises, media attention, and public outcry over these "toxic exports" with an outpouring of new guidelines and multilateral environmental agreements (MEAs), as well as new national law regimes.

12.1   *The International Environmental Laws Governing Hazardous Waste*

12.1.1   *Developments Leading up to the Basel Convention*

At the start of the 21st century, a heterogeneous mixture of international, regional and national legal authorities dealt with international hazardous waste trade. Until recently, it was "almost impossible to identify any unity of purpose" among the complicated and conflicting multilateral environmental agreements (MEAs).[15] At one extreme, some laws *promote* the transboundary shipment of hazwaste (like the OECD and EU regimes, below); at the other extreme some laws wholly *prohibit* the trade (the Lomé IV/Cotonou and Bamako treaties, below); and in the middle are laws that merely seek to *regulate* the safety of the trade, particularly from developed to developing nations (as the Basel Convention did when first adopted). However, starting with the "Basel Ban" amendment in 1995, the majority of the world's nations seem focused on banning hazardous waste trade (with some notable exceptions like the US, CANZ, and Japan).

To predict what will happen in the coming decades, it is first important to understand how the laws evolved from passiveness to prohibition. Before the advent of the MEAs, few international laws or regulations governed transboundary hazardous waste shipments. There existed the general principles of "good neighborliness" (*see* § 2.1.2) and "no transboundary harms" (*see* § 2.1.3), which in 1972 were incorporated in Principle 21 of the Stockholm Declaration:

---

[13] *See* Krueger, *Prior Informed Consent, supra* note 1, at 2.
[14] Bureau of International Recycling (BIR), *The Industry*, http://www.bir.org/industry/.
[15] O'Neill, *Out of the Backyard, supra* note 1, at 140.

States have…the sovereign right to exploit their own resources pursuant to their own environmental policies, and the responsibility to ensure that activities within their jurisdiction or control do not cause damage to the environment of other States or of areas beyond the limits of national jurisdiction.[16]

In theory, such principles impose a general duty of environmental responsibility extending beyond national boundaries. With regard to hazardous waste, the "no harm" rule posits duties on exporting states to notify, consult, and possibly negotiate with importing and transit states before allowing a shipment of waste that could cause damage (*see* general discussion of these duties in § 2.2.2). However, the generality and lack of regulatory detail in these principles resulted in little effectiveness, and thus parties were forced to turn to more concrete MEAs as a solution.[17]

The first foray into the world of MEAs was taken by the OECD (whose 34 members, as of 2012, generate over 90 percent of all the world's hazardous waste). In 1976, the same year the US adopted its national hazardous waste law,[18] the OECD issued the first multilateral effort on the subject, the OECD Council Decision on a Comprehensive Waste Management Policy.[19] This initial Council Decision was a weak statement geared more to protecting economic growth and energy resources than the environment.[20] Throughout the 1980s and 1990s, however, the OECD adopted increasingly more comprehensive Decisions and Recommendations (*see* § 12.1.3.1) to collectively regulate and promote transboundary trade in hazardous waste. Because of its pioneering status, the OECD remains a very important force in issuing expert guidelines and data on hazardous waste trade today.

In the mid-1980s, UNEP undertook the task of moving nations toward a global agreement on the management of hazardous waste. UNEP's 1987 Cairo Guidelines,[21] a nonbinding but authoritative set of principles and practices for hazardous waste, first articulated many of the modern hazwaste concepts, including: (1) responsibility of export states beyond their borders; (2) necessity of international controls; (3) "preventive measures" to reduce hazardous

---

[16] United Nations Conference on the Human Environment, Stockholm, Swed., June 5–16, 1972, *Stockholm Declaration of the UN Conference on the Human Environment*, Principle 21, U.N. Doc. A/CONF.48/14/Rev 1 at 3 (1973), UN Doc. A/CONF.48/14 at 2–65 and Corr. 1 (1972), 11 I.L.M. 1416 (1972), http://www.unep.org/Documents.Multilingual/Default.asp?documentid=97&articleid=1503.

[17] *See* Gudofsky, *supra* note 1, at 221–22.

[18] The Resources Conservation and Recovery Act (RCRA), 42 USC § 6901 *et seq.*

[19] C(76) 155 Final (1976).

[20] *See* Philippe Sands, Principles of International Environmental Law I: Frameworks Standards and Implementation 493 (1995).

[21] UNEP Governing Council Decision on Cairo Guidelines and Principles for the Environmentally Sound Management of Hazardous Wastes, adopted June 17, 1987, U.N. Doc. UNEP/GC/DEC/14/30, UNEP ELPG No. 8 (1987), http://www.unep.org/Documents.Multilingual/Default.asp?DocumentID=100&ArticleID=1663.

waste at the source; (4) "environmentally sound management" (ESM) as the standard for import and transit states' capacity to handle wastes; (5) "best practicable means" (BPM) as the standard for states' efforts at compliance; and (6) "prior informed consent" (PIC) as the key regulatory concept, which requires export states to make detailed advanced disclosures to import and transit states and secure their permission before shipping.[22] A month after these guidelines were adopted, Greenpeace launched the NGO's campaign to ban the international hazardous waste trade entirely.[23]

12.1.2   *The Basel Convention*

Not satisfied with nonbinding guidelines, UNEP immediately set up an experts working group to begin drafting a formal treaty. Between 1987 and 1989, experts from 96 countries, observed by over 50 international NGOs, participated in five heated negotiation sessions.[24] Feeling they were the targets of "neocolonialist" dumping, many developing nations argued for outright prohibition, and, indeed, during the negotiations, the African nations joined together to adopt a ban.[25] The OECD nations rejected the ban approach however, and, in the compromise, regulation initially won out over prohibition in the rest of the world.

The resulting 1989 Basel Convention on the Control of Transboundary Movements of Hazardous Wastes and Their Disposal (Basel Convention)[26] has three key objectives: (1) minimizing the generation of hazardous wastes at the source;[27] (2) controlling and reducing transboundary movements;[28] and (3) providing "environmentally sound management" (ESM) of wastes in the form of "pollution prevention," and protection of "human health and environment" throughout the process.[29] While developing countries were unable to negotiate an outright ban on the transport of hazardous waste, they did succeed in inserting a number of quite strict provisions. These provisions

---

[22] *Id.*

[23] BAN *Chronology, supra* note 9.

[24] For detailed accounts of the negotiation of the Basel Convention, *see* Gudofsky, *supra* note 1, at 225; authorities cited in Krueger, *supra* note 1, and Puckett, *supra* note 1, at 5.

[25] Resolution on Dumping of Nuclear and Industrial Waste in Africa, May 23, 1988, OAU Doc. CM/RES/1153/(XLVIII), Res. 1153, 28 I.L.M. 567 (1989), http://www.chr.up.ac.za/test/images/files/documents/ahrdd/theme15/environment_resolution_dumping_nuclear_waste_1989.pdf (declaring all dumping of nuclear and industrial waste in Africa by non-Africans to be a crime and demanding that transnational corporations involved in past dumping clean up areas of Africa they had polluted).

[26] Basel Convention on the Control of Transboundary Movements of Hazardous Wastes and Their Disposal, Mar. 22, 1989, UNEP Doc. IG.80/L.12, 28 I.L.M. 649, http://www.basel.int/.

[27] *Id.* art. 4.2(a).

[28] *Id.* art 4.2(d).

[29] *Id.* art. 4.2(b)–(d).

include: (1) PIC requirements;[30] (2) right of a party to prohibit the import of any waste;[31] (3) prohibition on waste trade with (exports to or imports from) any state not a party to the treaty;[32] (4) a limit on exports only to those states lacking technical "self-sufficiency" to dispose of their own wastes with ESM;[33] (5) duty of an export state to "take back" wastes if the disposal cannot be completed with ESM;[34] and (6) detailed information, packaging-labeling, and movement document requirements.[35]

A fundamental problem with Basel is that its definition of "hazardous waste" encompasses many valuable items not traditionally deemed hazardous, making it difficult to remove them from the strict requirements of the treaty. It defines "hazardous wastes" to include (1) any item listed in the extensive Annex I (unless demonstrated not to have any of the 14 toxic, ecotoxic, etc., characteristics of Annex III) and (2) any item defined as "hazardous waste" by the national laws of any party. Thus, for example, while Basel Article 4.9(b) expressly approves of recycling, metal recycling is presumptively "hazardous" until proved otherwise.[36]

The Basel Convention was ratified by enough parties to enter into force in 1992. It is overseen by a Conference of the Parties (COP) that had met ten times by 2011 to debate and adopt amendments and annexes that have greatly changed the 1989 approach. By early 2012, it had been ratified by 179 nations (including all EU member states, the EU itself, CANZ, and Japan),[37] with the US the only industrialized or OECD nation that has not yet ratified it.[38]

12.1.3   *Post-Basel Developments: The "Banners" vs. the "Boosters" of Hazardous Waste Trade*

Despite the high number of countries ratifying Basel, its "middle-of-the-road" approach did not satisfy many (in fact, it is perhaps the most unpopular

---

[30] *Id.* arts. 4.1(c), 4.2(f), and 6.

[31] *Id.* arts. 1.1(b), 4.1(b), and 4.2(e).

[32] *Id.* art. 4.5.

[33] *Id.* art. 4.9(a).

[34] *Id.* art. 8.

[35] *Id.* art. 4.7.

[36] For an elaborate, section-by-section analysis of Basel, *see* Gudofsky, *supra* note 1.

[37] For lists and dates of the 179 Basel Convention ratifiers (as of 2012), *see* http://www.basel .int/Countries/StatusofRatifications/PartiesSignatories/tabid/1290/Default.aspx.

[38] The US has signed the treaty (1990), and the US Senate has given consent to its ratification (1992); however, the US has not taken the last step in the process of becoming a party, by depositing of articles of ratification with the Basel Secretariat. Before the US can take that step, the US Congress must still pass implementing legislation to bring the US law (RCRA) into compliance with the Convention's requirements (the Convention being stricter in some regards than current US law). The legislation is stalled by US concerns over the "Basel Ban" (*see* § 11.1.3.2). US Bureau of Oceans and International Environmental and Scientific Affairs, Department of State, *Basel Convention on Transboundary Movements of Hazardous Wastes* (Sept. 15, 1998), http://www.state.gov/www/global/oes/fs_basel.html.

treaty ever ratified). This dissatisfaction promptly led to the creation of a number of regional treaties and national laws *overriding* Basel with, at one extreme, trade-promoting laws and, at the other extreme, actual bans on such trade.

12.1.3.1   *The Trade-Promoting Approach*

Nations of the industrialized North have generally taken the position, both before and after Basel, that international hazardous waste trade is an economic "good" and deserves to continue, provided it is appropriately regulated to protect human health and the environment.[39] The only context in which the North supports prohibition is on hazwaste shipments from themselves, the developed nations, to developing nations. Some ascribe this to mere "political correctness" while the more cynical ascribe it to a desire to eliminate competition and lock up the recyclable resources. The two most prominent multinational regulatory regimes are those of the OECD and the EU.

The OECD Decisions and Recommendations (*see* § 12.1.1)[40] set up two different regulatory schemes to implement Basel – differentiating materials

---

[39] The USEPA has taken this view on the subject: "There are a number of reasons why US entities export hazardous waste. Often, the nearest waste management facility capable of handling a particular waste stream may be just over the international border from the point of generation. In other cases, there may be a facility in another country that specializes in treating, disposing of, or recycling a particular waste. Such a facility may be the only one of its kind in the world, or it may present more environmentally sound management solution for the waste. In some cases, hazardous wastes constitute 'raw' material inputs into industrial and manufacturing processes. This is the case in many developing countries where natural resources are scarce or non-existent." US EPA, *International Trade in Hazardous Waste: An Overview* (1998) http://www.epa.gov/compliance/resources/policies/civil/rcra/intnltrahazwas-rpt.pdf.

[40] They include: OECD Council Decision and Recommendation on Transfrontier Movements of Hazardous Waste, C(83)180(Final), Feb. 1, 1984, 23 I.L.M. 214 (1984) (recommendations for members' implementation of national control and notification procedures) http://webnet.oecd.org/oecdacts/Instruments/ShowInstrumentView.aspx?InstrumentID=53&InstrumentPID=50&Lang=en&Book=False; OECD Council Decision and Recommendation on Exports of Hazardous Waste from the OECD Area, C(86)64(Final), June 5, 1986, 25 I.L.M. 1010 (controls on hazardous waste transport to non-OECD countries) http://webnet.oecd.org/oecdacts/Instruments/ShowInstrumentView.aspx?InstrumentID=54&InstrumentPID=51&Lang=en&Book=False; OECD Council Decision on Transfrontier Movements of Hazardous Waste, C(88)90(Final), May 27, 1988 (key definitions of terms and the waste classification system) http://webnet.oecd.org/oecdacts/Instruments/ShowInstrumentView.aspx?InstrumentID=64&Lang=en&Book=False; OECD Council Decision and Recommendation, C(90)178(Final), Jan. 31, 1991 (implementing Basel, governing members' hazardous wastes slated for final disposal (not recovery/recycling), and establishing proximity, self-sufficiency, and ESM standards) http://webnet.oecd.org/oecdacts/Instruments/ShowInstrumentView.aspx?InstrumentID=60&InstrumentPID=57&Lang=en&Book=False; OECD Council Decision Concerning the Control of Transfrontier Movements of Wastes Destined for Recovery Operations, C(2001)107(Final), June 14, 2001 (implementing Basel and governing members' wastes destined for recovery/recycling) http://webnet.oecd.org/oecdacts/Instruments/ShowInstrumentView.aspx?InstrumentID=221&InstrumentPID=217&Lang=en&Book=False. OECD Council "Decisions" are immediately binding on all adopting

destined for final disposal from materials destined for recovery/recycling. Transboundary disposal is permitted and relies on principles of self-sufficiency (where feasible), PIC, ESM, and other safeguards.[41] Transboundary recycling is likewise permitted, assigning all wastes/materials to three progressively more strictly managed (but still legal) groups ("green," "amber," or "red") based on their increasing hazard potential.[42] OECD member states, including the US,[43] have formally incorporated into and implemented these rules in their own national laws governing transboundary shipments of hazardous waste.

The EU has its own separate, detailed regulations to implement Basel, the OECD rules, and its other international hazardous waste agreements (like Lomé IV/Cotonou and others below), and these rules govern the EU member states (most of whom are OECD members as well).[44] They establish a Basel-compatible system of controlled hazardous waste shipments, specifically recognizing the distinction between wastes for disposal vs. those for recovery. Accordingly, EU hazwaste importers-exporters face a somewhat bewildering variety of laws, so that the identical hazwaste, if destined for recycling, is governed differently based on which states are involved in the shipment.

In addition to these multilateral regional agreements, there are a number of bilateral agreements facilitating hazardous waste trade for both disposal and recovery. The US, for example, is party to several, including the 1986

---

member nations; "Recommendations" are nonbinding suggestions, the goals of which must be achieved in national legislation.

[41] For more detailed descriptions, *see* Pring, *Increasing International Environmental Law Limitations, supra* note 1, at 19; Gudofsky, *supra* note 1, at 237, 262.

[42] *Id.*

[43] 61 Fed. Reg. 161290–16316 (Apr. 12, 1996). The 1992 OECD Decision predates the entry into force of the Basel Convention, and so clearly qualifies as a valid Basel Article 11 agreement. Thus, it allows the US (a non-Basel party) to trade hazardous wastes for recovery with the other OECD members, all of whom are parties to the Basel Convention and would otherwise be barred from trading with a nonparty like the US under Basel Article 4(5).

[44] The 1975 Waste Framework Directive was the EU's foundational rule governing all wastes, Directive 75/442/EEC (July 15, 1975). Its modern version is Directive 2008/98/EC on Waste (Waste Framework Directive), http://eur-lex.europa.eu/LexUriServ/LexUriServ.do?uri=OJ: L:2008:312:0003:0030:en:PDF. Overviews of EU waste and hazardous waste law include: EU Commission, *European Waste Shipment Legislation: Introduction, Background, Problems & Solutions* (2008), http://www.bipro.de/waste-events/doc/events08/cz_pres_2_bipro_aj.pdf, and BiPRO GmbH, *EU- Legislation Shipment*, http://www.bipro.de/waste-events/ship/eu-lex.htm.

US-Canada Agreement,[45] the 1987 Annex III to the US-Mexico Agreement,[46] the US-Malaysia Agreement,[47] and the US-Costa Rica Agreement.[48] These, with varying degrees of environmental strictness, authorize and control trade between the parties, pursuant to the exception provided in Basel Article 11.

12.1.3.2   *The Trade-Banning Approach and the "Basel Ban"*

At the opposite end of the spectrum, from the start, many developing nations of the South argued for a ban on transboundary hazardous waste shipments, fearing they would become the dumping grounds for the North. Basel Article 4 permits parties to prohibit hazwaste imports, and before the ink was dry on the treaty developing nations began taking advantage of that provision. First, the African, Caribbean, and Pacific (ACP) nations concluded a waste ban treaty with the EU – the 1989 Lomé IV Treaty[49] – which flatly prohibited EU nations from exporting nuclear or hazardous wastes to the ratifying ACP states. Then in 1991, 51 African nations signed the 1991 Bamako Convention,[50]

---

[45] Agreement Between the Government of the United States of America and the Government of Canada Concerning the Transboundary Movement of Hazardous Waste, Oct. 28, 1986, T.I.A.S. 11099, as amended, http://www.epa.gov/osw/hazard/international/canada86and92.pdf. For detailed analysis, *see* Hirschi, *supra* note 1, at 183; Gudofsky, *supra* note 1, at 268.

[46] Agreement of Cooperation Between the United States of America and the United Mexican States Regarding the Transboundary Shipments of Hazardous Wastes and Hazardous Substances (Annex III to the Agreement on Cooperation for the Protection and Improvement of the Environment in the Border Area, US-Mexico), Jan. 29, 1987, T.I.A.S. 11269, 26 I.L.M. 16 (1987) http://www.cpa.gov/osw/hazard/international/mexico86.pdf. For detailed analysis, *see* Hirschi, *supra* note 1, at 187; Gudofsky, *supra* note 1, at 270.

[47] Agreement Between the Government of the USA and the Government of Malaysia Concerning the Transboundary Movement of Hazardous Wastes from Malaysia to the United States, Mar. 10, 1995, T.I.A.S. 12612, http://www.basel.int/Portals/4/Basel%20Convention/docs/article11/malaysia-us.pdf. *See* Cheryl Hogue & Joe Kirwin, *Hazardous Waste: Basel Convention Parties to Discuss Possible Exceptions to Waste Trade Ban*, Int'l Env't Rep. (BNA), Feb. 4, 1998, at 87.

[48] Agreement on the Transboundary Movement of Hazardous Waste from Costa Rica to the United States, http://www.basel.int/Portals/4/Basel%20Convention/docs/article11/eu-costarica.pdf.

[49] Lomé IV Convention, Dec. 15, 1989, art. 39, 29 I.L.M. 809 (1990), description in UNEP Guidance, *supra* note 1, at 8. In 2000, the Cotonou Agreement replaced the four previous Lomé Conventions to structure ACP-EU trade, development, and broader relations. The Cotonou Agreement, June 23, 2000, 41 I.L.M. 767 (2002), the 2010 "second revision" of which is now in force, http://ec.europa.eu/development/icenter/repository/second_revision_cotonou_agreement_20100311.pdf.

[50] Bamako Convention on the Ban of Import into Africa and the Control of Transboundary Movement and Management of Hazardous Waste Within Africa, Jan. 29, 1991, 30 I.L.M. 775 (1991), http://www.au.int/en/sites/default/files/Convention_En_Bamako_Ban_Import_into_Africa_and_Transboundary_Movement_hazardouswastes_Bamako_30January1991.pdf. For a detailed analysis of the Bamako Convention, *see* Gudofsky, *supra* note 1, at 245.

which bans all non-African imports of nuclear and hazardous waste and regulates the intra-African trade.

Since then, multilateral hazwaste bans have been instituted by some Central American[51] and South American nations,[52] and South Pacific states,[53] and have been considered by Mediterranean countries[54] and South East Asian nations.[55] Most do not distinguish between wastes destined for disposal and those destined for recovery/recycling, prohibiting both. In addition, reportedly nearly 90 individual countries have adopted national bans on hazardous waste imports.[56]

Meanwhile, by the mid-1990s the Basel COP became dominated by nations favoring a ban – chiefly developing nations and Nordic and EU states. At COP3 in 1995, the parties approved by consensus the "Basel Ban," an amendment to the treaty which requires "Annex VII" states (Basel parties and other states that are members of OECD, plus the EU and Liechtenstein) to prohibit all hazwaste shipments to non-Annex VII countries (1) immediately as to hazwastes destined for disposal and (2) by the end of 1997 as to hazwastes

---

[51] Acuerdo Regional Sobre Movimiento Transfronterizo de Desechos Peligrosos, Cumbre XIII de Presidentes del Istmo Centroamerico, Dec. 11, 1992, http://www.ecolex.org/ecolex/ ledge/view/RecordDetails?id=TRE-001167&index=treaties; the parties are Costa Rica, El Salvador, Guatemala, Honduras, Nicaragua, and Panama. A description appears in UNEP Guidance, *supra* note 1, at 7.

[52] The Southeast Pacific Countries Protocol, *reported in* UNEP Guidance, *supra* note 1, at 6, 7. This Protocol bans hazardous and radioactive waste imports into its signatories, Chile, Colombia, Ecuador, Panama, and Peru.

[53] Convention to Ban the Importation into Forum Island Countries of Hazardous and Radioactive Wastes and to Control the Transboundary Movement and Management of Hazardous Wastes Within the South Pacific Region (Waigani Convention), Sept. 16, 1995, http:// www.sprep.org/attachments/Waigani_Convention.pdf. Signatories include Australia, Cook Islands, Micronesia, Fiji, Kiribati, Nauru, New Zealand, Niue, Palau, Papua New Guinea, Marshall Islands, Solomon Islands, Tonga, Tuvalu, Vanuatu, and Western Samoa. Since 2001, this treaty bans imports of hazardous wastes into member states and exports from Australia and New Zealand to other member states, but exports to Australia and to New Zealand and between the two are allowed. *See, The Waigani Convention Factsheet*, Aug. 2008, http://www.sprep.org/attachments/waiganiconv.pdf.

[54] Protocol on the Prevention of Pollution of the Mediterranean Sea by Transboundary Movements of Hazardous Wastes and Their Disposal to the Barcelona Convention for the Protection of the Mediterranean Sea Against Pollution (the Izmir Hazardous Waste Protocol), Oct. 1, 1996, UNEP(OCA/MED/IG.9/4) (not yet in force), Protocol on the Prevention of Pollution of the Mediterranean Sea by Transboundary Movements of Hazardous Wastes. It would ban export of hazardous and radioactive wastes to non-OECD countries and imports by convention parties that are not EU members. *See* Pablo Cubel, *Transboundary Movement of Hazardous Wastes in International Law: The Special Case of the Mediterranean Area*, 12 INT'L J. MARINE & COASTAL L. 447 (1997).

[55] In 1993, the Association of South East Asian States (ASEAN) voted in principle on the need to develop a regional convention to ban hazardous waste imports into member states, but so far no treaty has emerged. Hirschi, *supra* note 1, at 181; Puckett, *supra* note 1, at 6.

[56] Puckett, *supra* note 1, at 6.

destined for recovery/recycling.[57] Most, if not all, Annex VII countries have generally abided by the first ban, stopping shipments to non-Annex VII countries for final disposal. However, the ban on shipments of secondary materials for recovery/recycling to non-Annex VII countries has provoked a firestorm of controversy – opposed in particular by leading industrialized nations (Australia, Canada, France, Germany, Japan, the Netherlands, UK, and US, especially with regard to their secondary trade with Asia, Eastern and Central Europe), as well as by some developing nations economically dependent on imports of secondary materials.[58] Despite widespread support, the ban amendment has not yet entered into force, having been "stalled due to uncertainty as to how to interpret the Convention" about the amendment process.[59]

However, a "major breakthrough" occurred at COP10 in October 2011, when 178 parties sliced through the confusion. They voted to allow the Basel Ban Amendment to enter into force when and if it is ratified by 68 of the 90 countries that were parties to the Convention when the amendment was voted on in 1995.[60] As of then, 51 have ratified, leaving just 17 more needed, which optimistic supporters feel can be achieved by 2013 or 2014.[61] Major players still oppose it, so time will tell.

Opponents of the ban claim that it: (1) wastes valuable secondary resources contrary to the principle of "sustainable development;" (2) starves developing nations of secondary materials needed by their industries; (3) unnecessarily encourages environmentally damaging "virgin" materials developments, like mines; (4) constitutes "eco-imperialism," whereby industrialized countries impose their standards on developing countries in violation of the latters' sovereign right to manage their own resources; (5) is just "camouflage" for EU protectionist attempts to monopolize and retain recyclables (particularly metals) for EU recyclers; (6) does nothing to control hazardous waste trade between developing countries; (7) ignores the real need for creating effective controls and technologies at the downstream end, particularly in developing countries; (8) puts unrealistic pressure on waste management in developed countries, many of which have little to no disposal capacity left; (9) is

---

[57] Geneva Amendment to the Basel Convention on the Control of Transboundary Movement of Hazardous Wastes and Their Disposal, Decision III/1, UNEP/CHW.3/35 (Sept. 22, 1995) (not yet in force), http://www2.unitar.org/cwm/publications/cbl/synergy/pdf/cat3/convention_basel/convention_basel/amendment_cop3_III_1.pdf.

[58] Hirschi, *supra* note 1, at 189; Puckett, *supra* note 1, at 10.

[59] The NGO Basel Action Network, which supports the ban, provides a summary explanation of the controversy over the Ban Amendment entering into force at *178 Countries Agree to Allow the Ban on Exports of Toxic Wastes to Developing Countries to Become Law* (Oct. 21, 2011), https://app.e2ma.net/app/view:CampaignPublic/id:1400891.7310563069/rid:0f191f9 2ae3e1290a8e318cc85a7141d.

[60] *Id.*

[61] *Id.*

"an unabashedly discriminatory trade barrier;" and (10) will fail and consequently stimulate illegal trade.[62]

Supporters, on the other hand, argue that the ban: (1) is "the most significant environmental achievement since the Rio Earth Summit in 1992;" (2) removes the "loophole" of recycling "through which more than 90% of exported hazardous waste...flow[s];" (3) recognizes that "toxic wastes can never be recycled safely even in the best of conditions;" (4) will stop recycling from diverting attention from cleaner front-end production (pollution prevention and waste reduction at the source); (5) will cause developed countries to become more self-sufficient in waste management strategies (particularly disposal); (6) recognizes that all recycling operations in developing countries are at best "dirty" and at worst "sham" operations; (7) protects human health and environment in developing nations from the risks of hazardous wastes; (8) faces the fact that rich countries are "using" recycling as an excuse to continue "dumping their toxic wastes in Third World countries;" and (9) admits that the Basel Convention's "control" approach through PIC is a "noble but failed concept."[63]

12.1.3.3   *Recent Basel Issues Affecting Recycling*

Given these polarized views, it is difficult to see a common ground for compromise on other waste issues that are in dispute, but that is what Basel representatives, their governments, environmentalists, and the recycling industry are working on. Five issues showing progress stand out in particular:[64]

First, to free legitimate recycling from being treated as hazardous waste, in 1998 the parties created two lengthy lists – "List A" (now Annex VIII) containing the wastes still deemed hazardous and banned from export from developed to developing countries and "List B" (Annex IX) containing scores of waste categories deemed sufficiently nonhazardous to be exempt from the ban. While there are still some problems, the US and the recycling industry generally view this as an acceptable solution.[65] Second, at COP5 in December 1999, the parties adopted a long-awaited liability protocol, basically creating "Superfund-like" financial responsibility for damage resulting

---

[62] For detailed references for these arguments, *see* Pring, *Increasing International Environmental Law Limitations, supra* note 1 at 23.

[63] *Id.* at 24.

[64] For a detailed analysis of these major issues, *see id.* at 25 *et seq.*

[65] However, the EU may be moving in the opposite direction – actually strengthening and expanding the ban against EU exports to non-OECD nations. In 1997, it adopted the Basel Ban as binding law on all EU members and subsequently has moved to expand its lists of banned (Annex VIII-type) wastes, greatly upsetting the US and the industry. Hazardous Waste: Commission, *Recycling Industry Still up in Arms Over Expanding Basel List,* Int'l Env't Rep. (BNA) (Mar. 18, 1998) at 253.

from transboundary movement of wastes.[66] Third, for the present the parties have decided not to "open" Annex VII to allow additional countries to join it and thereby escape the Basel Ban, but this is a "sleeper" issue which could reemerge in the years ahead as developing nations (like Israel and the emerging economies of the former USSR) seek to join the hazwaste "trading club."[67] Fourth, another unresolved issue sure to cause contention in the future is whether parties may escape the bans on trade with non-Basel parties and non-Annex-VII countries by entering into bilateral or multilateral trade agreements that would override the ban, as is apparently provided in Basel Article 11.1.[68] Finally, perhaps the biggest undecided issue of all is whether Basel and the Basel Ban are "unabashedly discriminatory trade barriers," in violation of the World Trade Organization (WTO) free-trade rules, since they arguably create trade barriers that discriminate against non-Basel parties and non-Annex-VII nations, and the WTO has yet to definitively resolve the extent to which bilateral and multilateral environmental treaties may use economic sanctions as enforcement mechanisms without violating the free-trade laws (*see* Chapter 14).[69]

12.2   *International Controls on Chemicals*

12.2.1   *Introduction*

Regulations concerning hazardous waste are just one example of the growing international movement to bring chemicals under comprehensive control and reduction.[70] Humankind's production, spread of, and dependency on

---

[66] Protocol on Liability and Compensation for Damage Resulting from the Transboundary Movement of Hazardous Wastes and Their Disposal, Dec. 10, 1999, http://treaties .un.org/doc/Treaties/1999/12/19991210%2012-52%20PM/Ch_XXVII_03_bp.pdf. By 2011, however, the Protocol had only 13 signatories and 10 ratifications. A number of issues remain to be resolved with regard to the Liability Protocol's coverage and are expected to be resolved in coming COP sessions.

[67] *See*, Basel Action Network, *Annex VII Expansion – An Ignoble Attempt to Undo the Basel Ban*, Briefing Paper: No. 3, May 1999, http://ban.org/library/briefing3.html.

[68] Basel Convention, *supra* note 26 art. 11.1. The OECD Convention is one recognized "article 11" agreement, which is why Basel parties can trade with the US (which is an OECD member but not a Basel party), but it predates Basel. The current controversy is whether Article 11 agreements can be entered into post-Basel and override it and the Basel Ban, a position supported by the US and CANZ, but opposed by the EU, environmentalists, and other Basel Ban supporters.

[69] *See* WTO, *The Environment: A Specific Concern*, http://www.wto.org/english/thewto_e/ whatis_e/tif_e/bey2_e.htm; Bette Hileman, *WTO and the Environment: Activist Groups Consider Some World Trade Organization Rulings Environmentally Destructive and Demand Reforms*, CHEMICAL AND ENGINEERING NEWS (Nov. 2, 1998), http://ban.org/library/wto .html.

[70] *See* Pring *et al.*, *Trends in International Environmental Law Affecting the Minerals Industry*, *supra* note 1, at 159, and sources there cited.

chemicals and chemical products has increased exponentially since World War II – in a spiral some critics refer to as the "Chemical Feast."[71] Nobody truly knows how many chemicals we currently use. Over 50 million chemicals are known to science, and 75,000 of these in regular use, with new chemical substances being discovered or synthesized ever 2.6 seconds,[72] fueling an over-US $3 trillion/year global industry employing more than 20 million people.[73]

Four sectors dominate production and distribution: (1) the industrial chemical sector produces the basic building blocks for the rest of industry – including the bulk organics or petrochemicals (carbon-based) and the bulk inorganics (like chlorine, ammonia, etc.); (2) the agriculture and fertilizer chemical sector (pesticides, herbicides, plant growth chemicals, etc.); (3) the finished chemicals sector (plastics, synthetic fibers, paints, pharmaceuticals, cleaning products, photographic chemicals, etc.); and (4) the minerals industry (gold, lead, cadmium, zinc, etc.). Modern industry, agriculture, and the consumer economy in general rely heavily on synthetic and other human-produced chemicals. Today, chemicals are ubiquitous in every facet of life – food production and processing, paper, motor vehicles, energy production, medicine, construction, electronic technology, and a endless variety of other products – so that they are at once both an essential part of "sustainable development" and one of its biggest threats.

Pesticides (insecticides, herbicides, fungicides, and other biocides, typically human-synthesized organic compounds) were among the first of these chemicals to come under scrutiny. Today, such biocides are a huge global industry with over 1,400 active ingredients in over 60,000 formulations, sales of over US $39 billion/year, 2.5 million tons/year used, and with developing countries being the fastest growing market for sales.[74] While these chemicals offer significant benefits in terms of controlling human disease and crop damage, they can have immense negative impacts – first warned of in Rachel Carson's seminal 1962 book, *Silent Spring*. These negative impacts include

---

[71] James S. Turner, The Chemical Feast (1970).
[72] UNUSA, *Global Classrooms, supra* note 3; David Hunter, James Salzman & Durwood Zaelke, International Environmental Law and Policy 909 (4th ed. 2011); Peter Lallas & Steve Wolfson, *International Cooperation to Address Risks from Pesticides and Hazardous Chemicals, in* Edith Brown Weiss, Stephen C. McCaffrey, Daniel B. Magraw, Paul C. Szasz & Robert E. Lutz, International Environmental Law and Policy 703 (2007).
[73] International Council of Chemical Associations, *Facts & figures*, http://www.icca-chem.org/en/Home/About-us/.
[74] EPA, Pesticide Industry Sales and Usage (2011), http://www.epa.gov/opp00001/pestsales/07pestsales/market_estimates2007.pdf. For further details on pesticides, *see* Bartlett P. Miller, *The Effect of the GATT and the NAFTA on Pesticide Regulation: Hard Look at Harmonization*, 6 Colo. J. Int'l Envtl. L. & Pol'y 201, 203–05 (1995); Hunter, et al., *supra* note 72 at 928; Lallas & Wolfson, *supra* note 72, at 703.

production and processing releases, millions of worker-handlers in developing countries suffering occupational pesticide poisoning each year, thousands of deaths in a typical year, industrial accidents, inadequate warning labels, on-farm spills, unsafe disposal, poisonous residues left on food (the "Circle of Poison"), export of domestically banned pesticides, and increasing target resistance. The scope of their threats is multiplied by their three characteristics of persistence,[75] bioaccumulation,[76] and biomagnification.[77]

Concern is mounting about the broader group of synthetic organic industrial chemicals, of which pesticides are a part, known as persistent organic pollutants (POPs). The "dirty dozen" leading POPs are the pesticides aldrin, dieldrin, chlordane, toxaphene, DDT, endrin, mirex, and heptachlor, the industrial-process byproducts dioxins, furans, hexachlorobenzene, and toxaphene, to which dozen one can add PCBs and hexachlorobenzene produced as industrial chemical products.[78] POPs can persist in the environment for decades, some lasting more than 100 years.[79] While POPs include other chemicals, the "dirty dozen" are all derived from the manufacture, utilization, and disposal of chlorine compounds (and are therefore called organochlorines). Chlorine is one of the most ubiquitous chemicals in all of our industries, underpinning 40 percent of the US economy (and 45 million jobs) in such diverse industries as pulp and paper, petroleum, plastics, solvents, disinfectants, refrigerants, flame retardants, paints, insulation, food processing, dry cleaning.[80] POPs are persistent, fat-soluble, and bioaccumulative. They are transferred by wind, ocean currents, and migrating wildlife, and are even becoming concentrated in the cold/polar regions far from their sources. Over 170 different POPs have been found in human tissues, and even more in animals.[81] We are just beginning to understand the human and environmental damage of POPs. Many are highly toxic, cause cancer, sterility, deformities, reproductive failures, multigenerational mutations, and – at the cutting edge of our scientific understanding – may cause disruption of human and

---

[75] The ability of a chemical to retain its molecular integrity and hence its physical, chemical, and functional characteristics in the environment through which such a chemical may be transported and distributed for a considerable period of time.

[76] The uptake of organic compounds by biota through respiration, ingestion, or contact in which the chemicals attain concentrations in the organism greater than their ambient concentrations, exceeding the organism's ability to remove the substance from the body, also called bioconcentration.

[77] The increase in concentration of a substance in a food chain, not an organism, also called bioamplification.

[78] For further details on POPs, *see* Elizabeth B. Baldwin, *Reclaiming Our Future: International Efforts to Eliminate the Threat of Persistent Organic Pollutants*, 20 HASTINGS INT'L & COMP. L. REV. 855 (1997); HUNTER ET AL., *supra* note 72, at 928.

[79] HUNTER ET AL., *supra* note 72 at 928.

[80] *Id.*

[81] *Id.* at 923.

animal endocrine systems, the hormone-producing systems that chemically control critical aspects of our development and behavior.[82]

Metals are another group of substances that are just beginning to be understood by environmental scientists and government regulators.[83] In addition to natural releases from erosion, volcanic activity, etc., every stage of the mineral resources industry releases mineral byproducts, from mining, through production and processing, to the end-product stage and disposition thereafter. Metals are vital both to life and our way of life – the industry's favorite aphorism is "If it isn't grown, it's mined." However, metals are also known to be toxic at varying levels and are now widespread in the environment. The toxicity of lead, for example, (in gasoline, paints, and other commercial products) has caused it to be the leading regulated metal of the 1980s and 1990s.

In today's technology dependent world, the mining of so-called "rare earth" metals has become the new 21st-century flashpoint for this issue. The metals found in permanent magnets, phosphors, lasers, capacitors, and superconductors are essential for the production of laptops, cellphones, MP3 players, electric vehicles, compact fluorescent bulbs, and wind turbines.[84] While rare earth metals are actually relatively common in the earth's crust, they are notoriously difficult to extract,[85] and currently they are almost exclusively mined and processed in China. Processing is a dangerous, polluting business because it uses toxic chemicals, acids, sulfates, and ammonia.[86] Additionally, radioactive thorium and uranium almost always contaminate rare earth ore.[87] For many years, China supplied the developed world with rare earth metals at an extremely reduced cost, partly because it was willing to overlook the environmental devastation associated with an unregulated minerals process. In recent years, however, China has been flexing its political muscle and promising to increase regulation, which has led to a jump in the pricing of these metals.[88] This has the US and other countries scrambling to launch

---

[82] Baldwin, *supra* note 78, at 855–62.

[83] "Metals" form the bulk of the periodic table. The term "heavy metals" is often used to describe metals such as lead, mercury, cadmium, etc., which are five or more times denser than water; "trace metals" is used to describe those found in very low concentrations in the environment such as copper, iron, zinc, etc. JOHN HARTE ET AL., TOXICS A TO Z 103 (1991); *see also* US DEPT. OF THE INTERIOR, MINERAL FACTS AND PROBLEMS (Bureau of Mines Bull. 675, 1985 ed.); DUCHIN ET AL., *supra* note 73, at 100.

[84] *See* Willie D. Jones, *The Rare Earth Metal Bottleneck*, IEEE SPECTRUM, Jan. 2010 at 80, http://spectrum.ieee.org/consumer-electronics/gadgets/the-rareearthmetal-bottleneck.

[85] *Id.*

[86] *Newshour: Are Rare Earth Metals Too Costly for the Environment,* (PBS television broadcast Dec. 14, 2009), http://www.pbs.org/newshour/bb/asia/july-dec09/china_12-14.html.

[87] Keith Bradsher, *Challenging China in Rare Earth Mining,* N.Y. TIMES, Apr. 21, 2010, http://www.nytimes.com/2010/04/22/business/energy-environment/22rare.html.

[88] *Times Topics: Rare Earths,* N.Y. TIMES, updated Mar. 13, 2012, http://topics.nytimes.com/top/reference/timestopics/subjects/r/rare_earths/index.html.

their own rare earth mines. Because both the demand and environmental cost of these metals is so high, the mining of rare earth metals promises to be a contentious issue for years to come.

12.2.2   *The Beginnings: Voluntary International Chemical Control Efforts*

Comparing the 1972 Stockholm Declaration[89] with the 1992 Rio Declaration[90] highlights how dramatically the concern has evolved – moving from a simple focus in Stockholm Principle 6 on "the discharge of toxic substances" to a more holistic "prevent the relocation and transfer to other States of any activities and substances that cause severe environmental degradation or are found to be harmful to human health" in Rio Principle 14. The year 1976 stands out as "the year the US discovered toxics" with the passage of both its hazardous waste and toxic substance control laws,[91] and international preoccupation with toxic chemicals soon followed, under the leadership of the UN Food and Agriculture Organization (FAO) and UNEP. Other key modern players are the OECD, UN World Health Organization (WHO), the International Programme on Chemical Safety (IPCS),[92] and the Intergovernmental Forum on Chemical Safety (IFCS).[93]

In 1985, the FAO began adopting guidelines for pesticides, most notably the first International Code of Conduct on the Distribution and Use of Pesticides.[94] The FAO Code provided only voluntary, nonenforceable standards to bridge the gap until binding national and international regulations emerged. Nevertheless, the FAO Code's detailed provisions on pesticide management, testing, health protection, distribution and trade, information exchange, prior

---

[89] Stockholm Declaration, *supra* note 16.

[90] United Nations Conference on Environment and Development, Rio de Janeiro, Braz., June 3–14, 1992, Rio Declaration on Environment and Development, U.N. Doc. A/CONF.151/26 (vol. I) (1992), 31 I.L.M. 874 (1992), http://www.unesco.org/education/information/nfsunesco/pdf/RIO_E.PDF.

[91] Respectively, The Resource Conservation and Recovery Act (RCRA), 42 USC. § 6901 *et seq.*, and the Toxic Substances Control Act (TSCA), 15 U.S.C. § 2601 *et seq.*

[92] The International Programme on Chemical Safety is an IGO "partnership" comprised of the WHO, ILO, and UNEP, coordinated by WHO, http://www.who.int/ipcs/en/.

[93] The Intergovernmental Forum on Chemical Safety is a non-UN experts group of IGO and NGO representatives that provides policy and coordination of efforts on chemicals; *see* http://www.who.int/ifcs/en/.

[94] International Code of Conduct on the Distribution and Use of Pesticides, Nov. 28, 1985, 23 FAO Conf. Res. 10/85, U.N. Doc. M/R8130, E/8/86/1/5000 (1986), as amended to include PIC in art. 9 FAO Conf. 25th sess., FAO Doc. M/U0610E/I9.90 (1989) http://www.fao.org/agriculture/crops/core-themes/theme/pests/pm/code/en/. *See also* Edith Brown Weiss, Paul C. Szasz & Daniel B. Magraw, International Environmental Law: Basic Instruments and References 104–05 (1992).

informed consent (PIC), labeling, packaging, storage, and disposal were a milestone, and form the basis for much of today's regulation.[95]

In tandem with the FAO's guidelines on pesticides, UNEP focused on industrial chemicals and in 1989 produced the London Guidelines for the Exchange of Information on Chemicals in International Trade,[96] also a voluntary, nonbinding set of guidelines. Its detailed provisions, including PIC, are intended to be complementary to and defer to the FAO Code on pesticides but to establish the primary system for controlling the other hazardous chemicals internationally.

12.2.3   *The Recent Development of Binding Chemical Treaties*

Progress was made in the 1990s on developing binding, enforceable treaties for controlling chemicals. Significantly, Agenda 21 specifically addresses the necessity for "The Environmentally Sound Management of Chemicals," with action goals for increasing knowledge of chemicals, building capacity to manage them, eliminating or reducing chemical risks, and preventing traffic in illegal or dangerous chemicals.[97] This has spurred action on numerous fronts.

In 1998, the PIC process for chemicals was formalized in the Rotterdam PIC Convention.[98] Intended to replace and expand the existing voluntary FAO/UNEP code PIC process, this treaty, which entered into force in 2004, provides for the listing of hazardous chemicals and pesticides. It also requires notification to, hazard information exchange with, and approval by an importing country ("prior informed consent") before chemicals banned or restricted in the country of export may be shipped. The chemical and mineral industries' have expressed some concern that products of theirs could be added to the list by the COP in the future (such as Sweden's "sunset chemicals" list) for a variety of reasons – both environmental (e.g., adding lead to support efforts to phase out leaded gasoline) and economic (e.g., adding a

---

[95] *See* Margo Brett Baender, Note, *Pesticides and Precaution: The Bamako Convention as a Model for an International Convention on Pesticides Regulation*, 24 N.Y.U. J. INT'L L. & POL. 557, 579–83 (1991); HUNTER ET AL., *supra* note 72, at 920.

[96] UNEP Governing Council Decision on London Guidelines for the Exchange of Information on Chemicals in International Trade, May 25, 1989, U.N. Doc. UNEP/PIC/WG.2/2, at 9, UNEP ELPG No. 10, UNEP/GC/DEC/15/30 (1987) http://www.chem.unep.ch/ethics/english/longuien.htm.

[97] Agenda 21, June 13, 1992, ch. 13 U.N. Doc. A/CONF.151/26, http://www.un.org/esa/dsd/agenda21/res_agenda21_19.shtml.

[98] Prior Informed Consent Procedure for Certain Hazardous Chemicals and Pesticides in International Trade (PIC or Rotterdam Convention). Sept. 10, 1998, 38 I.L.M. 1 (1999) http://www.pic.int/Portals/5/en/ConventionText/RC%20text_2008_E.pdf. The PIC Convention currently has 147 parties and it entered into force on Feb. 23, 2004.

substance to gain advantage for a competitive product or producer, to discourage sales, force alternatives, etc.).[99]

Also in 1998, the UN Economic Commission for Europe (UNECE) concluded two new protocols under the Convention on Long-Range Transboundary Air Pollution (LRTAP), the Protocol on Heavy Metals and the Protocol on Persistent Organic Pollutants (POPs) (discussed in Chapter 10). These focus specifically on the transboundary air emissions of these chemicals, but are part of the safety net which may lead to a total chemical-control treaty across all media.

In a momentous step in 2001, 151 nations signed the Stockholm Convention on Persistent Organic Pesticides, a treaty promoted by UNEP to reduce and eliminate POP releases to the environment, which entered into force in 2004 and by 2012 has 177 parties.[100] The treaty provides for the elimination of intentionally produced POPs; minimization and, where feasible, elimination of unintentionally produced byproduct POPs; elimination of POPs from stockpiles and wastes; removal of PCBs from use; restriction of uses of DDT; prevention of production and use of new pesticides or chemicals that have POP characteristics; controls on imports and exports of listed chemicals; as well as financing mechanisms, research, and information exchange.

Numerous additional chemical-control initiatives are under way focused on risk management, global standards for classification and labeling, test guidelines, chemical accidents, endocrine disrupting chemicals (EDCs), to name a few.[101] Finally, a comprehensive chemicals convention has been proposed that would combine, integrate, and harmonize the Basel Convention, the Montreal Ozone Protocol, the PIC Treaty, POPs, and all other chemical-control laws into one "mega" framework treaty. While this proposal was sidelined by the IFCS in 1997, pending development of the PIC and POPs Conventions, it could be reactivated in the future.

12.3   International Controls on Hazardous Technologies, Industries, and Activities

The 1984 Bhopal disaster shocked the world into realizing that the developed nations were "exporting" to the developing world (some would say

---

[99] Pring *et al.*, *Trends in International Environmental Law Affecting the Minerals Industry*, *supra* note 1, at 160.

[100] Stockholm Convention on Persistent Organic Pesticides, May 22, 2001, 40 I.L.M. 532 (2001), http://chm.pops.int/default.aspx.

[101] *See, e.g.* UNECE, The Globally Harmonized System of Classification and Labelling of Chemicals (4th ed., 2011) http://www.unece.org/fileadmin/DAM/trans/danger/publi/ghs/ghs_rev04/English/ST-SG-AC10-30-Rev4e.pdf.

"dumping") more than just hazardous waste and toxic chemicals. Whether driven by lower wages and raw materials costs (as industry argues) or by lesser regulation and liability concerns (as critics argue), US and other developed-country companies were locating high-risk industries and activities outside their borders, particularly in developing countries.[102] These include chemical plants like Bhopal, "maquiladora" industries in northern Mexico, new mines, hazardous waste treatment/storage/disposal facilities, metals recovery-recycling plants, pollutive industries, genetically modified organisms, and the like.

To date, no international agreement deals broadly with the transfer of hazardous technologies, industries, and activities from one country to another, although small pieces of the puzzle are beginning to drop into place. An initial "soft law" step was the Draft Code of Conduct on Transnational Corporations adopted by the UN Economic and Social Council (ECOSOC) in 1988,[103] which states:

> Transnational corporations shall carry out their activities in accordance with national laws...relating to the preservation of the environment of the countries in which they operate and with due regard to relevant international standards...take steps to protect the environment and where damaged rehabilitate it and should make efforts to develop and apply adequate technologies for these purposes.[104]

Unfortunately, such national laws often do not exist or are not enforced and such international standards are plainly lacking, as the perceived positive advantages of economic development continue to overshadow concerns about the negatives. In a rather glaring example, the 1972 Stockholm Declaration Principle 9 states:

> Environmental deficiencies...can best be remedied by accelerated development through the transfer of substantial quantities of financial and technological assistance as a supplement to the domestic effort of the developing countries....[105]

Significantly, 20 years later, Rio Declaration Principle 14 takes the reverse approach:

> States should effectively cooperate to discourage or prevent the relocation and transfer to other States of any activities and substances that cause severe environmental degradation or are found to be harmful to human health.[106]

---

[102] *See* Sudhir K. Chopra, *Multinational Corporations in the Aftermath of Bhopal: The Need for a Comprehensive Global Regime for Transnational Corporate Activity*, 29 Val. U. L. Rev. 235 (1994).

[103] UN Draft Code of Conduct on Transnational Corporations, Feb. 1, 1988, U.N. Doc. E/1988/39/Add. 1, 27 I.L.M. 974 (1988).

[104] *Id.* ¶ 43.

[105] Stockholm Declaration, *supra* note 16, Principle 9.

[106] Rio Declaration, *supra* note 90, Principle 14.

Both piously urge states to "develop further international law regarding liability and compensation" for victims of pollution and environmental damage (Stockholm Principle 22, Rio Principle 13), in effect conceding little-to-no progress in that arena.[107]

The 1993 Lugano Civil Liability Convention,[108] which has received no ratifications as of 2012, would be the first binding treaty to create civil liability for damage from environmentally dangerous activities. It covers production of dangerous substances and waste and recycling operations, whether public or private, and creates an international tort cause of action covering damages to persons or property and costs of environmental rehabilitation and preventive measures.[109] Should the world's nations ever ratify and implement it, it would go a long way toward solving the problem, which is perhaps why it languishes without attracting parties.

National environmental impact assessment (EIA) laws (*see* Chapter 6) have proved somewhat beneficial in controlling risk enterprises, but their international counterparts – such as the 1991 Convention on Environmental Impact Assessment in a Transboundary Context (*see* § 6.2) – are not terribly helpful on this front because they focus exclusively on activities located in one nation that have transboundary impacts in another, rather than situations where both the activity and the impacts are transferred from one nation to another. The 1992 UNECE Convention on the Transboundary Effects of Industrial Accidents[110] likewise focuses on accidents in one country that have cross-border effects in another, but, by requiring states to develop emergency preparedness, accident prevention, notification, and public information systems, should be a stimulus to the development of national laws controlling dangerous activities.

Taking a different approach to the problem, Principle 10 of the Rio Declaration states that:

---

[107] While the International Law Commission and other respected international law expert bodies have put out "soft law" or draft principles on state responsibility for wrongful acts (responsibility) and for injurious consequences of legal acts (liability), little applies to the acts of private, non-state actors (corporations, businesses, etc.), and little has made its way into binding international law. *See generally* discussion and sources in LAKSHMAN D. GURUSWAMY, BURNS H. WESTON, GEOFFREY W. R. PALMER & JONATHAN C. CARLSON, INTERNATIONAL ENVIRONMENTAL LAW AND WORLD ORDER: A PROBLEM-ORIENTED COURSEBOOK 335 *et seq.* (2d ed. 1999).

[108] Council of Europe Convention on Civil Liability for Damage Resulting from Activities Dangerous to the Environment, June 21, 1993, E.T.S. No. 150, 32 I.L.M. 1228 (1993) (not yet in force), http://conventions.coe.int/treaty/en/treaties/html/150.htm.

[109] *See* David Wilkinson, *The Council of Europe Convention on Civil Liability for Damage Resulting from Activities Dangerous to the Environment: A Comparative Review*, 2 EUR. ENVTL. L. REV. 130 (1993).

[110] Convention on the Transboundary Effects of Industrial Accidents, Mar. 17, 1992, UN/E/ECE/1268 (1992), U.N. Doc. ENVWA/R.54 and add. 1, 31 I.L.M. 1330 (1992) (entered into force Apr. 19, 2000), http://ec.europa.eu/environment/seveso/pdf/98685ec_conv.pdf; also *see* http://www.unece.org/env/teia/welcome.html.

each individual shall have appropriate access to information concerning the environment that is held by public authorities, including information on hazardous materials and activities in their [sic] communities, and the opportunity to participate in decision-making processes... [and] [e]ffective access to judicial and administrative proceedings....[111]

This promise has been promoted to the status of hard law by the 1998 Aarhus Convention,[112] which entered into force in 2001 and requires parties to make environmental information available to the public on request, provide public participation opportunities in authorizing covered industrial, commercial, and agricultural developments and activities, and establish judicial or administrative procedures for the public to challenge governmental environmental decisions (*see* full discussion in § 2.2.1). Should the convention be implemented by enough states, it could produce a paradigm shift in the transfer of problematic industries and activities to those states, much as the Freedom of Information Act, National Environmental Policy Act, and related transparency/public participation laws have done in the US.

12.4   *Conclusion*

Hazardous waste, chemicals, and technology are the by-products of our modern way of life. Synthetic fertilizers are needed to maintain the large crop returns that sustain the world's growing population. Farmers turn to POP-laden pesticides and biocides to protect those crops and ensure their yields are as large as possible. Industry drives the global economy, but large-scale manufacturing processes – for example, petroleum refining, paper production, and electricity generation – also produces almost all of the world's toxic chemicals. The world's growing dependence on electronic technology poses a host of new problems. The production of computers, cell phones, and other devices requires inputs of rare earth metals and hazardous chemicals. The disposal of these devices jeopardizes the health and the environment of those involved.[113]

---

[111] Rio Declaration, *supra* note 90, Principle 10.

[112] UNECE Aarhus Convention on Access to Information, Public Participation in Decision-Making and Access to Justice in Environmental Matters, June 25,1998, U.N. Doc. ECE/CEP/43 (1998) http://www.unece.org/fileadmin/DAM/env/pp/documents/cep43e.pdf.

[113] The disposal of electronic devices is now being described as "e-waste." The more complex the circuitry, the more complicated the equipment's disposal, since electronics contain both toxic chemicals and metals that pose a hazard to both humans and the environment. Chris Carrol, *High Tech Trash*, NAT'L GEOGRAPHIC Jan. 2008, http://ngm .nationalgeographic.com/2008/01/high-tech-trash/carroll-text. For other resources on the subject, *see* EPA, *Management of Electronic Waste in the United States, Introduction*, http://www.epa.gov/epawaste/conserve/materials/ecycling/index.htm; GREENPEACE, *Where Does E-Waste End Up?* (Feb. 24, 2009), http://www.greenpeace.org/international/

What we throw away reveals a lot about who we are. The developed world has achieved an extremely high standard of living, but the waste associated with that lifestyle is formidable. Even if all production were to halt today, dangerous chemicals and minerals would remain in the environment for generations, interacting in ways that are difficult to predict. At this point, all indicators suggest that the problem of hazardous waste, chemicals, and technology will only continue to grow in the future. As this chapter has indicated, international trade in waste can only be, at best, a placebo. To prevent serious harm to the environment and human health, future efforts must be geared toward pollution prevention and waste minimization.

en/campaigns/toxics/electronics/the-e-waste-problem/where-does-e-waste-end-up/;   CBS NEWS, *Following the Trail of Toxic Waste,* updated Jan, 8, 2010, http://www.cbsnews.com/stories/2008/11/06/60minutes/main4579229.shtml.

Chapter Thirteen

Biotechnology in Food and the Biosafety Protocol

13.0 *Introduction*

The biotech industry has introduced genetically modified (GM) crops and foods derived from them that promise to improve food quality and increase supplies available to meet the needs of the growing world population. But these developments also engender criticism from health, environmental, and consumer groups concerned about the unknowable and unpredictable consequences of interfering with natural processes at the genetic level. The critics urge authorities to regulate the evaluation and introduction of GM agriculture and its products more stringently and to honor the consumer's right to know the contents of foods.

This chapter will use the terms "bioengineering," "biotechnology," and "genetic modification" interchangeably. Biotechnology may be defined as "any technological application that uses biological systems, living organisms, or derivatives thereof, to make or modify products or processes for specific use."[1] A genetically modified organism (GMO) is one "in which the genetic material has been altered in a way that does not occur naturally by mating and/or natural recombination."[2] Modern biotechnology is, in the language of the Biosafety Protocol to the Convention on Biological Diversity, the application of:

a. *In vitro* nucleic acid techniques, including recombinant deoxyribonucleic acid (DNA) and direct injection of nucleic acid into cells or organelles, or

---

[1] United Nations Convention on Biological Diversity, June 5, 1992, art. 2, 31, I.L.M. 818, 823 (1992) available at http://treaties.un.org/doc/Treaties/1992/06/19920605%2008-44%20PM/Ch_XXVII_08p.pdf [hereinafter CBD].

[2] [European Union] Council Directive 90/220/EEC of Apr. 23, 1990, on the deliberate release of GMOs into the environment, art. 2, 1990 O.J. (L 117) 16 [hereinafter Council Directive 90/220/EEC].

b. Fusion of cells beyond the taxonomic family, that overcome natural phys-
iological reproductive or recombination barriers and that are not techniques used in traditional breeding and selection.[3]

GMOs are also known as living modified organisms (LMOs), defined by the
Biosafety Protocol as "any living organism that possesses a novel combination
of genetic material obtained through the use of modern biotechnology."[4]

Application of modern biotechnology in agriculture has spawned strident
controversy that shows little sign of resolution in the near future. While farmers have been genetically modifying their crops for hundreds if not thousands
of years,[5] it is recognized that modern biotechnology innovations represent
a dramatic leap in human capacity to manipulate the natural environment,[6]
and they carry huge risks.

In response to the issues being raised by modern biotechnology, the United
States has acted differently from many industrialized nations for, instead
of instituting a new legal system, it regulates GMOs under the preexisting
regulatory scheme. While many observers feel this is adequate, others feel it
advantages industry and exposes the natural environment to grave risks.[7]

At the international level, the Cartagena Protocol on Biosafety (Biosafety
Protocol) seeks to protect biodiversity from modern biotechnology's potential risks by regulating international trade in GM substances. The Protocol
is limited in its scope[8] but promises some degree of harmonization between

---

[3] UNEP, Convention on Biological Diversity, Report of the Extraordinary Meeting of the
Conference of the Parties for the Adoption of the Protocol on Biosafety to the Convention
on Biological Diversity, Pt. Two, Annex to decision EM-I/3: Cartagena Protocol on Biosafety
to the Convention on Biological Diversity, art. 3(i), U.N. Doc. UNEP/CBD/ExCOP/1/3,
Feb. 20, 2000, http://www.cbd.int/doc/meetings/cop/excop-01/official/excop-01-03-en.pdf
[hereinafter Biosafety Protocol Text].

[4] *Id.* art. 3(g).

[5] This constitutes the basis for a number of the arguments in favor of genetically modified
foods, on the ground that there is nothing especially different between modern methods
and earlier ones in respect of their results. *See, e.g.,* Jonathan Adler, *More Sorry Than Safe:
Assessing the Precautionary Principle and the Proposed International Biosafety Protocol,* 35
Tex. Int'l L.J. 173, 176–82 (2000).

[6] *See generally, e.g.,* Thomas O. McGarity, *Seeds of Distrust: Federal Regulation of Genetically
Modified Foods,* 35 U. Mich. J.L. Ref. 403 (2002).

[7] For a fairly unbiased treatment of the issue, analyzing a number of scientific tests, *see* Debo-
rah Katz, *The Mismatch Between the Biosafety Protocol and the Precautionary Principle,* 13
Geo. Int'l Envtl. L. Rev. 949 (2001).

[8] The Protocol does not apply to pharmaceuticals, Biosafety Protocol Text, *supra* note 3, art.
5; nor does it apply to commodities such as soybeans or maize intended for direct use as
food or feed, or for processing. *Id.* art. 11. These were among the contentious issues primarily responsible for the failure of the Cartagena meeting to reach an accord on the Biosafety
Protocol. The United States, expressing its concerns through its allies in the Miami Group,
was the major opponent of any regulation pertaining to food commodities and pharmaceuticals in the proposed Protocol. *See* Stephen McCaffrey, *Biotechnology: Some Issues of
General International Law,* 14 Transnat'l Law. 91, 94 (2001).

the national regulatory schemes. As the major thrust of the debate over biotechnology is on food issues, this chapter will focus on the basic issue of GM material in food products.[9] We will highlight here the different issues bearing on the subject as they are currently presented in the literature.[10] We do not pretend to have the answers to the perplexing, unanswerable questions, but we will demonstrate them to the best of our ability. As the difference in attitudes seems to manifest so much on a "gut level," compromise may be a long way away – either it is scientifically appropriate to release bioengineered organisms into the environment or it is not.[11] As a keen observer asked in 2002,

> How can we know whether we'll say in ten years, "We were right – this was the solution to end world hunger," or "We were right – these were Frankensteins that have caused major damage to the earth's environment and to our bodies"?[12]

Now, ten years later, we still do not know.

13.1 Background

13.1.1 The Process

The processes by which living organisms[13] are modified demonstrate the novelty of the technology at the heart of the biotechnology debate. A gene is that part of the DNA (deoxyribonucleic acid) in a living cell that holds the

---

[9] On other topics, *see, e.g.*, Jane Kay, *"Frankenfish" Spawn Controversy; Debate Over Genetically Altered Salmon*, San Francisco Chronicle, Apr. 29, 2002 at A4; Clive Cookson, *Advisers Urge New Controls on GM Animals; Biotechnology Commission Concerned at Potential Risk from Genetically Modified Species Escaping and Interbreeding*, Fin. Times (London), Sept. 4, 2002, at 4; Carol K. Yoon, *Special Report, Altered Salmon Leading Way to Dinner Plates, But Rules Lag*, N.Y. Times, May 1, 2000, at A1, col. 4.

[10] Two very interesting analyses of the science involved in the GM issue may be found at Debashis Banerji, *R-DNA debate needs much more seriousness*, The Hindu (India) www.hindu.com/2001/07/10/stories/08100001.htm, July 10, 2001; Steven H. Yoshida, *The Safety of Genetically Modified Soybeans: Evidence and Regulation*, 55 Food Drug L.J. 193 (2000).

[11] *See, e.g.*, Natalie M. Henry, *Debate Over Regulation Heats Up as Crop Acreage Expands*, Land Letter (online), Feb. 14, 2002; Steve Lash, *Americans Evenly Divided Over Biotech Foods, Survey Finds; Genetically Modified Foods Do Not Have Support or Opposition from a Majority of the Population, IAC (SM) Newsletter Database*, Food Chemical News, Feb. 11, 2002, No. 52, Vol. 43, at 7; *Americans Evenly Divided Over Environmental Risks and Benefits of Genetically Modified Food and Biotechnology; Risks Seen As Greater Initially, But Benefits Ranked Higher Once Information Is Given*, PR Newswire, Feb. 4, 2002.

[12] Richard A. Leach, Executive Director, Friends of the UN World Food Program, and President, international consulting firm of Leach & Associates, Washington, D.C., telephone interview July 21, 2002.

[13] The Biosafety Protocol defines a living organism as "any biological entity capable of transferring or replicating genetic material, including sterile organisms, viruses and viroids." *Supra* note 3, art. 3(h).

chemical information required to produce the specified protein that controls or influences inheritable traits. In genetic modification, a human intervenes in the transmission of genetic material from a parent to an offspring. This practice, which has been in application for literally centuries in the form of traditional selective breeding,[14] has been eclipsed by the new methods that permit transfer of genes across species boundaries.

The new techniques available to scientists permit them to work on the level of the cell rather than the whole organism. Once the target genetic material is isolated, it is manipulated by one of several methods.[15] "In the ideal situation, the new gene is incorporated into the recipient cell's DNA and the production of the protein associated with the new gene begins."[16] When the *in vitro* transfer is successful, an offspring individual results with new cellular qualities and a phenotype (the appearance and qualities of the organism) that includes the desired trait. Success is, of course, not guaranteed, and the experimentation process incorporates a high degree of unpredictability. Nevertheless, the process offers results that could never have been achieved through traditional methods, because (1) the natural process is concerned with success of the organism on its own terms and within its own distinct environmental conditions, while human bio-engineering targets a specified goal; (2) the time necessary for generations to demonstrate and express the desired traits may otherwise be prohibitive for experimental work; and (3) above all, traditional genetic selection methods were limited to transfers

---

[14] For insightful descriptions of these practices and their differences from the new methods, *see* Sarah L. Kirby, *Note: Genetically Modified Foods: More Reasons to Label Than Not*, 6 DRAKE J. AGRIC. L. 351, 352–53 (2001); Ellen Messer, *Food Systems and Dietary Perspective: Are Genetically Modified Organisms the Best Way to Ensure Nutritionally Adequate Food?*, 9 IND. J. GLOBAL LEG. STUD. 65, 71–73 (2001); John Charles Kunich, *Mother Frankenstein, Doctor Nature, and the Environmental Law of Genetic Engineering*, 74 S. CAL. L. REV. 807, 808–13 (2001).

[15] The methods include:
1. Recombinant DNA, in which "plasmids and viruses, two biological vectors" that "typically move between cells of different organisms," are used "to carry genetic material into cells [,...taking] the new genes with them as they go.... Plasmids and viruses bring the new genetic material into the recipient cell's nucleus, and sometimes the recipient cell will integrate the new genetic material into its own genes and begin to produce the protein for which the gene codes";
2. Microinjection, in which "the new genetic material is injected directly into the cell;"
3. "[E]lectro and chemical poration, where scientists create pores or holes in the recipient cell membrane that allow the new genes to enter;" and
4. "Bioballistics," which "uses a type of gun to shoot the DNA into the recipient cell. If all goes as planned, the projectiles are shot into the cell with the gene gun, and the foreign DNA is carried into the nucleus."

Sophia Kolehmainen, *Genetically Engineered Agriculture: Precaution Before Profits: An Overview of Issues in Genetically Engineered Food and Crops*, 20 VA. ENVTL. L.J. 267, 270–72 (2001). Another excellent explanation is found in Kunich, *supra* note 14, at 809.

[16] Kolehmainen, *supra* note 15, at 272.

of genetic material between individuals capable of mating and producing offspring, which generally meant within a single species.[17]

Thus, traits from widely varying sources have been used to create novel strains. The oldest example of a GMO in continuous use in the United States is that of "Bt" corn and other crops manufactured to resist the lepidopteran class of insects (those that go through a caterpillar stage). This corn strain was first developed by splicing a gene from the naturally toxic soil bacterium Bacillus thuringensis into the corn genome.[18] Bt plants produce the insecticide internally throughout their life cycle, obviating the need for Bt to be sprayed onto the crop. Bt corn was introduced in 1996; by 1999 it constituted 26 percent of US corn acreage and 65 percent in 2011.[19] Bt cotton is also in wide use, increasing from 37 percent of the US crop in 2001 to 75 percent in 2011.[20]

The bioengineered crops in most widespread use are those made tolerant to herbicides, enabling weed control without damage to the crops. Soybeans developed to tolerate herbicides have been available since 1996 and were used in 68 percent of US crops in 2001 and 94 percent in 2011.[21] While the adoption of herbicide-tolerant corn was initially slow (at a "plateau" of 8 to 9 percent in 1998–2001), in 2011 it had increased to 72 percent. On the other hand, cotton strains with this trait were at 56 percent use in the US in 2001 and 73 percent in 2011.[22] The dominant example is "Round-Up Ready" seeds, developed by the agricultural chemical company Monsanto for resistance to that company's "Round-Up" glyphosate herbicide.[23] Almost all canola oil in the US is made from genetically altered rape seed,[24] and nearly all foods produced in the US have at least some amount of GM ingredients.[25]

---

[17] *See* Kunich, *supra* note 14.

[18] *See, e.g.*, Kolehmainen, *supra* note 15, at 273–74.

[19] Jorge Fernandez-Cornejo, Economic Research Service, US Dept. of Agriculture, *Adoption of Genetically Engineered Crops in the US: Extent of Adoption*, July 1, 2011, http://www.ers .usda.gov/data/biotechcrops/adoption.htm [hereinafter USDA Report].

[20] *Id.*

[21] *Id.*

[22] *Id.*

[23] *See Round-Up Ready Seeds*, MONSANTO, http://www.monsanto.com/weedmanagement/ pages/roundup-ready-system.aspx.

[24] *See* Ruth Walker, *Safety Rules for Genes and Food*, CHRISTIAN SCIENCE MONITOR, Jan. 25, 2000, at 1; Andrew Pollack, *130 Nations Agree on Safety Rules for Biotech Food*, N.Y. TIMES, Jan. 30, 2000, at A1, col. 1 [hereinafter Pollack].

[25] *See, e.g.*, Edward Alden & David Landes, *GM Food Industry Gears Up Campaign Against Labels: An Initiative on Genetically-Engineered Ingredients Could Result in Significant Losses for the Biotechnology Industry*, FIN. TIMES (London), Oct. 31, 2002, at 1.

13.1.2   *The Controversy*

The controversy over GM foods[26] is intense and the issues complex – easily sufficient to fill a book of its own. A central point of contention is the consumer's right to know whether foods s/he buys contain genetically modified components. The principle of "substantial equivalence,"[27] which posits that when the product of a GM operation is unchanged from its conventional counterpart it does not warrant different regulatory treatment than the counterpart, underlies the US approach. Its regulatory system does not scrutinize the agricultural biotech process, but only the product. This concept in fact establishes a presumption against the position that GM foods are "different" and thus require advisory labeling.

Critics argue that the potential long-term risks caused by the release of GMOs into the environment and their use in foods must not be dismissed.[28] Among unanticipated outcomes, they say, the new genes might jump to other crops or species and unexpected toxins or allergens may be introduced into crops, causing unforeseen allergic reactions in humans.[29] Laboratory studies have shown that the pollen of genetically altered corn can harm caterpillars of the monarch butterfly,[30] that the lives of ladybugs are shortened when they are fed aphids living on GM crops, and that lacewings, natural predators of insect pests, are killed when they are fed corn borer worms raised on genetically altered corn plants.[31] Certainly it has been demonstrated that very little can be done to control unintended pollination of crops in the vicinity of – or even at great distances from – transgenic crops.[32] The overarching concern expressed by those opposed to GM agriculture is that, while the proponents

---

[26] Critics express concern over adverse health effects, such as allergic reactions and unknown environmental effects, among others. *See, e.g.,* Henry, *supra* note 11. *See generally* MARK A. POLLACK & GREGORY C. SHAFFER, WHEN COOPERATION FAILS: THE INTERNATIONAL LAW AND POLITICS OF GENETICALLY MODIFIED FOODS (2009); John Vidal, *Report Casts New Doubt on "Miracle" of GM Crops: Plants Have Led to Growth of Superweeds, Says Study: Leading GM Seed Supplier Disputes Claims by NGOs,* THE GUARDIAN (London), October 20, 2011, at 22 (global citizens' Report on the State of GMOs, a report by 20 Indian, Southeast Asian, African and Latin American food and conservation groups claiming the adverse impacts of GM crops, with Monsanto disputing the report).

[27] *See* discussion § 12.2.1.2, *infra.*

[28] *See, e.g.,* Julie Deardorff, *Next Crop of Altered Genes Adds Promise – and Fears,* CHICAGO TRIB., May 23, 2002, at 12.

[29] *See* Peter N. Spotts, *The Brave New World of Biotechnology and Beyond,* CHRISTIAN SCIENCE MONITOR, Oct. 28, 1999, at 17.

[30] *See* Update: *EPA Renews Permits for Bt Crops; PNAS [Proceedings of the National Academy of Sciences] Publishes Monarch Data,* Union of Concerned Scientists, Dec. 13, 2001, http://www.ucsusa.org/index.html [hereinafter PNAS].

[31] *See* Robert C. Cowen, *New Findings Say Genetically Altered Corn Can Poison the Soil,* CHRISTIAN SCIENCE MONITOR, Dec. 2, 1999, at 2; Paul Brown, *From Gung-Ho to Acceptance of Legitimate Concerns,* THE GUARDIAN (London), Feb. 28, 2000, at 6.

[32] *See, e.g., Panel to Look for Banned Corn,* N.Y. TIMES, June 21, 2002, at C14, col. 4 (discussing reports of bioengineered corn contaminating native crops in southern Mexico); *but see*

cite multifarious tests concluding there is no danger in genetically modified foods, no test is yet capable of gauging the long-term effects on the environment and human health.

Clearly the advantages afforded to agriculture by biotechnology present a compelling case. The opportunity exists to revolutionize our ability to produce crops of maximum nutritional value while avoiding many of the customary obstacles of farming, such as pests and weeds. Supporters point to benefits to the environment, such as the reduced necessity for spraying harmful chemicals over crops that have been modified for insect or herbicide resistance.[33] They point to improvements in the color or flavor, resistance to weather, or longer shelf-life of modified produce. And they argue that genetic modification allows greater yield from the Earth's finite arable land and thus will make more food available to the Earth's growing population. This position has received a great deal of attention.[34]

While proponents' claim that food will be increased for the use of the world's hungry through the use of bioengineered crops seems convincing, numerous experts note instead that it is not for lack of ability to produce more food, but for politics, lack of access, distribution, and sustainable agricultural practices that so many remain hungry.[35]

Those who oppose biotech foods counter the other arguments by claiming that spraying has in fact continued because other insects remain in addition to those for which plants are modified and that even more spraying may be done on crops engineered for herbicide resistance.[36] These opponents offer the lessons of the Green Revolution of the 1970s that, while a great degree of additional productivity was purchased by scientific advances, it was at the cost of virtual chemical dependency throughout the world's agricultural

---

Carol Kaesuk Yoon, *Journal Raises Doubts on Biotech Study*, N.Y. Times, Apr. 5, 2002, at A21, col. 4 (on controversy over original study and problems faced by authors).

[33] *See, e.g., Biotech Crop Use Benefits Environment; CAST [The Council for Agricultural Science and Technology] Releases New Scientific Report Showing Environmental Gains*, Business Wire (online), June 26, 2002.

[34] *See* Adler, *supra* note 5, at 199–200; Alan Beattie, *et al.*, *WHO urges use of GM food aid; UN Health body Says Genetically Modified Food is Safe to Eat*, Fin. Times (London), Aug. 31, 2002, at 6; *Win in Hunger War: Rice Genome Mapped*, Indian Express Online Media Ltd., Apr. 9, 2002; Ronald Bailey, *EU Fear-Mongers' Lethal Harvest*, L.A. Times, Aug. 18, 2002, at M3; Damon Franz, *Nobel Prize Winner, Former Greenpeace Head Endorse Conventional [as opposed to organic] Methods*, Greenwire, May 1, 2002 ("Growing more crops and trees per acre leaves more land for nature," said Norman Borlaug, who won a Nobel Prize in 1970 for his work on agricultural techniques that boosted crop production in the so-called Green Revolution. "Most environmental groups are not solution-oriented. They are drama-oriented and scandal-oriented, because that's what helps raise funds").

[35] *See generally* Ellen Messer, *Food Systems and Dietary Perspective: Are Genetically Modified Organisms the Best Way to Ensure Nutritionally Adequate Food?* Symposium Issue, 9 Ind. J. Global Leg. Stud. 65 (2001); *see also* Kolehmainen, *supra* note 15, at 286–87.

[36] *See, e.g.,* Kohlemainen, *supra* note 15; *id.*, at 285–87.

system.[37] A 2002 European Union study of the coexistence of genetically engineered and non-GE crops indicated that commercialization of genetically engineered oilseed rape, maize, and potatoes would cause farming costs to rise between 9 and 41 percent, and that most all seeds, including those on non-GM farms, would become contaminated with genetically engineered traits to one extent or another.[38]

Another concern raised by opponents is the possibility of allergens being present in foods that are not labeled for consumers' knowledge. This issue was dramatically illustrated by the work done in 1996 on Pioneer Hi-Bred soybeans that were modified to contain a protein taken from Brazil nuts in order to increase their protein levels. In analyzing the result, the researchers tested for allergens and found that the modified soybeans indeed contained sufficient genetic material from the Brazil nuts to cause an allergic reaction in humans.[39]

The threat of damage to the environment in general is another major concern. GM opponents find problematic the unpredictability of genetic modification due simply to the behavior of living systems which, ultimately, is beyond the control of scientists, even though genetic material itself can be manipulated just as intended in the laboratory.[40] This is seen in a number of areas.

Because the added genetic elements are generally designed to affect the plant's vulnerability to insects (by the addition of pesticidal factors) and herbicides (by the addition of herbicide resistance), the highly toxic agents are internalized and widespread in the environment. Their effects are only gradually becoming known.

Food security issues present another concern, both as to the natural biodiversity of the ecosystem and as to the exercise of "ownership" over the genetic bases of living organisms.[41] For simple business reasons, the corporations that develop novel plants through genetic engineering may feel compelled to control the use of the products of their research, often through patent protection. This may lead to the necessity of requiring fees to be paid from farmers for the use of the technology and, moreover, the interlocking of technologies that requires a farmer to use several of the corporation's

---

[37] *See id.*

[38] *See Suppressed Study Shows Engineered Crops Raise Costs*, ENVIRONMENT NEWS SERV., May 21, 2002.

[39] *See* Kolehmainen, *supra* note 15, at 278; David Nicholson-Lord, *GM Foods: The Natural Result of Genetic Change*, THE INDEPENDENT (London), Oct. 12, 1999, Features sec.; Andrew Pollack, *We Can Engineer Nature. But Should We?*, N.Y. TIMES, Feb. 6, 2000, Sec. 4, at 16, col. 1.

[40] *See* Kolehmainen, *supra* note 15, at 275–77.

[41] *See generally id.* at 282–84.

products to achieve the intended result, such as a herbicide and the seeds for the resistant plant that accompanies it.

As only a few large corporations presently dominate most of the bio-tech agriculture industry, they have in effect gained control over this ever-growing sector of the food supply. In 1999, it was reported that Empresas La Moderna owned 25 percent of the world seed market.[42] In the biotechnology field, Aventis CropScience, Dow Agro Science, and Monsanto are basically in control. Thirteen companies own 80 percent of the GM crop patents.[43] Those opposed to biotech foods fear that these corporations are in position to influence not only the business but also the policy of agriculture.[44]

There is considerable evidence of environmental harm being caused by transference of genes between intended targets and non-intended plants. In 2002 the London Daily Mail reported a number of such studies or incidents from the EU, France, the US, and Canada that raised fears of "superweeds" and other consequences of contamination of other plants by GM crops. The British government's conservation agency, English Nature, reported findings that pollen from GM oilseed rape in Canada had traveled great distances to create superweeds by breeding with conventional plants.[45] The European Environmental Agency reported similar findings of "gene stacking" and multiple tolerance occurring with oilseed rape and beet crops, in which one variety of GM seed pollinates another.[46] Such superweeds could reverse many of the advantages of GM crops suggested by proponents, including that they would require increasing doses of herbicides beyond those eliminated by the resistant genes in the first place, and they would also result in reducing crop yields.

The phenomenon called horizontal gene transfer (HGT) is another factor of GM production that is causing significant concern.[47] In HGT, genetic material is passed from a GM organism into the environment through a

---

[42] *Id.* at 283, citing MARTIN TEITEL & KIMBERLY WILSON, GENETICALLY ENGINEERED FOOD: CHANGING THE NATURE OF NATURE 42 (1999).

[43] *See 13 Firms Own 80% of GM Crop Patents*, TIMES OF INDIA (online), Jan. 14, 2002.

[44] *See* Kohlemainen, *supra* note 15, at 282–283. *See also* John Humphreys, *The GM crop gamble could mean famine, not feast*, SUNDAY TIMES (London), July 1, 2001 (citing the charity Christian Aid as reporting that "GM crops would create 'classic preconditions for hunger and famine,'...because the multinationals have spent a fortune buying up many of the biggest seed companies and patenting the different seed varieties. Christian Aid says a food supply based on too few varieties of patented crops is the worst option for food security").

[45] *See* Geoffrey Lean, *Frankenstein foods: Blair's great betrayal; As evidence grows of wide-spread GM crop contamination...*, DAILY MAIL (London), Aug. 16, 2002, at 12 [hereinafter Frankenstein foods].

[46] *See Pressure on EU to Ban GM Crops*, MAIL & GUARDIAN REP. (South Africa), Apr. 5, 2002.

[47] *See* Bernie Napp, *Swapping genes without sex*, THE EVENING POST (Wellington, NZ), Mar. 19, 2001, at 5 [hereinafter Swapping Genes].

process of DNA exchange between bacteria. In hearings before the New Zealand Royal Commission on Genetic Modification it was reported that HGT had been seen, for example, in antibiotic resistance being transferred from GM maize plants into the mouth tissues of field workers, or chickens developing antibiotic resistance after eating GM corn feed.[48] In the same hearings an incident in Britain in the 1990s was related, in which farm pigs were fed the antibiotic streptothricin to reduce disease in crowded pens, but antibiotic resistance in the disease bacteria spread first into the intestines of the pigs, then within the next year into the intestines of farm workers, and in the next year resistance was found in the intestines of the general public.[49] A related difficulty is that the antibiotic-resistant bacterial marker genes employed in the modification process will have the effect of increasing the antibiotic resistance that is already causing problems for both humans and animals.[50]

And there is the issue of monocultures in the agricultural ecosystem, a "byproduct" of agricultural biotechnology.[51] As illustrated by the 1845 Irish Potato Famine, care must be taken to preserve the genetic diversity of crops, which is defeated by the production of super-crops impervious to known diseases and pests through the creation of single genetic lines. The replication of exactly similar strains leaves crops unprotected by the natural processes of genetic development that enhances inherent, natural tolerance to shifts in predators, disease, and weather.

Finally, on the economic side, liability theories for the various kinds of damage that could be caused by modified crops, such as contamination of neighboring nonmodified crops, are being developed.[52] A related question is the assessment of liability between nations for transboundary GMO pollution.[53]

The possibilities of the unintended consequences of biotechnology in agriculture are indeed overwhelming. The stakes are almost unacceptably high on both sides of the debate – the well-being of countless poor people and the future viability of the earth's ecosystem – and that is why there has been such a determined effort to establish regimes for regulation of genetic modification that make the prospects as predictable as possible.

---

[48] *Id.*

[49] *Id.; see* Frankenstein foods, *supra* note 45.

[50] *See* Kolehmainen, *supra* note 15, at 277.

[51] *Id.* at 283.

[52] *See generally, e.g.,* Richard A. Repp, *Biotech Pollution: Assessing Liability for Genetically Modified Crop Production and Genetic Drift,* 36 IDAHO. L. REV. 585 (2000) [hereinafter Assessing Liability].

[53] *See* McCaffrey, *supra* note 8, at 99–102; Kanchana Kariyawasam, *Legal Liability, Intellectual Property and Genetically Modified Crops: Their Impact on World Agriculture,* 19 Pac. Rim L. & Pol'y J. 459 (2010); Thomas Connor, *Comment and Casenote: Genetically Modified Torts: Enlisting the Tort System to Regulate Agricultural Contamination by Biotech Crops,* 75 U. CIN. L. REV. 1187 (2007). *See* McCaffrey, *supra* note 8, at 99–102.

13.2   *Regulation of Genetically-Modified Foods – The Key Concepts*

A few concepts that are key to the understanding of the genetically modified foods issue will be discussed here. These are especially important because they are in large part at the core of the principal regulatory systems and therefore attract a great deal of debate.

13.2.1   *The Precautionary Principle*

Application of the precautionary principle (*see* Chapter 2) is central to many international instruments and much national regulation in the field of the environment, where the science involved in a specific area is often incomplete, including two instruments that led to the Biosafety Protocol. Rather than postponing the action necessary to counter a given environmental risk in order to give science time to catch up, the precautionary principle directs that action be taken to avoid the risk.

The 1992 Rio Declaration on Environment and Development states at Principle 15:

> In order to protect the environment, the precautionary approach shall be widely applied by States according to their capabilities. Where there are threats of serious or irreversible damage, lack of full scientific certainty shall not be used as a reason for postponing cost-effective measures to prevent environmental degradation.[54]

The precautionary principle is also written into the Biodiversity Convention: "[W]here there is a threat of significant reduction or loss of biological diversity, lack of full scientific certainty should not be used as a reason for postponing measures to avoid or minimize such a threat."[55] In the Biosafety Protocol, the Principle is stated in Article 10:

> Lack of scientific certainty due to insufficient relevant scientific information and knowledge regarding the extent of the potential adverse effects of a living modified organism on the conservation and sustainable use of biological diversity in the Party of import, taking also into account risks to human health, shall not prevent that Party from taking a decision, as appropriate, with regard to the import of the living modified organism in question... in order to avoid or minimize such potential adverse effects.

This principle is the target of a considerable amount of opposition from those who favor advancing the role of biotechnology in food production.

---

[54] UNCED, Rio Declaration on Environment and Development, U.N. Doc. A/CONF.151/26/ Rev.1 (Vol. I), Annex I, at 3 (1992), reprinted in 31 I.L.M. 874 (1993) [hereinafter Rio Declaration]. On the distinction between the precautionary approach and the precautionary principle, *see* McCaffrey, *supra* note 8, at 97.

[55] CBD, *supra* note 1, 31 I.L.M. at 822.

One commentator described it as an "anti-science regulatory concept that allows regulators to ban new products or technologies on the barest suspicion that they might pose some unknown threat. It is an approach of 'impose a ban first, ask questions later.'"[56]

The precautionary principle is, however, a concept that operates to restrain action that can have devastating consequences in this area where the stakes are unimaginably great. A number of national regulatory schemes contain the principle, requiring solid scientific proof for approval of the release of GMOs, failing which it is not granted.

13.2.2   *Substantial Equivalence*

A major consideration in the regulation of genetically modified foods is whether they are "substantially equivalent" to their unmodified counterparts. The concept of substantial equivalence is the basis for US and some other nations' regulators[57] to treat such food without distinction from conventional food. This approach is based on the similarity between the modified and unmodified products. It is employed by the US Food and Drug Administration (FDA) in testing GM foods, and allows for commercialization of GM crops without a requirement for testing.

Critics argue that a modified food's similarity to a conventional food "is not adequate evidence that it is safe for human consumption."[58] They contend that, while this "approach might seem plausible and attractively simple,... it is misguided, and should be abandoned in favour of one that includes biological, toxicological, and immunological tests rather than merely chemical ones."[59] The reasoning follows:

> The concept of substantial equivalence has never been properly defined; the degree of difference between a natural food and its GM alternative before its "substance" ceases to be acceptably "equivalent" is not defined anywhere, nor has an exact definition been agreed by legislators. It is exactly this vagueness that makes the concept useful to industry but unacceptable to the consumer. Moreover, the reliance by policymakers on the concept of substantial equivalence acts as a barrier to further research into the possible risks of eating GM foods.[60]

Scientists are in disagreement on the subject. At an international conference on genetically modified crops in late February 2000, held in Edinburgh,

---

[56] Bailey, *supra* note 34.

[57] For example, a thorough explanation of the theory as applied in evaluations by Health Canada can be found at the Food Biotechnology Communications Network web site, http://www.foodbiotech.org/index.cfm?app=faq&a=faqitem&questionID=25.

[58] Erik Millstone, Eric Brunner & Sue Mayer, *Beyond 'Substantial Equivalence,'* 401 Nature 525, 525 (Oct. 7, 1999).

[59] *Id.*

[60] *Id.*

Scotland, under sponsorship of the Organization for Economic Cooperation and Development and funded by the British government, there was a clash of views on the presumption of substantial equivalence.[61] An FDA scientist, Dr. Linda Kahl, revealed in a memo that scientists within the agency were not altogether in support of the scientific conclusions behind the concept. She said, "The process[es] of genetic engineering and traditional breeding are different, and according to the technical experts in the [FDA], they lead to different risks."[62]

Substantial equivalence was a focus of a recent recommendation from a Canadian panel of experts exploring ways to improve the Canadian system of evaluating GM foods. That panel found that "the use of 'substantial equivalence' as a decision threshold tool to exempt GM agricultural products from rigorous scientific assessment to be scientifically unjustifiable and inconsistent with precautionary regulation of the technology."[63] It recommended replacing substantial equivalence with "rigorous scientific assessment of [GMOs'] potential for causing harm to the environment or to human health."[64]

13.2.3   *Generally Recognized as Safe (GRAS)*

The regulatory counterpart of the substantial equivalence concept is the idea that a food product is "generally recognized as safe" or GRAS. This is the element in the evaluation process that exempts a genetically novel food from regulation on the basis that it contains the same chemical and protein makeup of the conventional counterpart. It is found, for example, in US law in the 1992 FDA Policy Statement that underlies federal regulation in this area,[65] which states that, for purpose of determination under the US Food, Drug and Cosmetic Act, section 409:[66]

> When the substance present in the food is one that is already present at generally comparable or greater levels in currently consumed foods, there is unlikely to be a safety question sufficient to call into question the presumed GRAS status

---

[61] *See* Michela Wrong, *Differences Widen on Use of Modified Foods*, FIN. TIMES (London), Feb. 29, 2000, at 14.

[62] Quoted in Jack O'Sullivan, *US Covered Up Warnings from Its Scientists on Dangers of GM Foods*, THE INDEPENDENT (London), Feb. 29, 2000, at 2.

[63] Royal Society of Canada, The Canadian Academy of the Sciences and Humanities, Expert Panel on the Future of Food Biotechnology, Aug. 29, 2001, Chapter 7, http://www.rsc.ca/foodbiotechnology/indexEN.html.

[64] *Id.* Recommendation 7.1.

[65] Statement of Policy: Foods Derived from New Plant Varieties, 57 Fed. Reg. 22,984, 22,988 (1992) [hereinafter FDA Policy Statement].

[66] A "food additive" is defined as "any substance the intended use of which results or may reasonably be expected to result, directly or indirectly, in its becoming a component of food or otherwise affecting the characteristics of any food…, if such substance is not generally recognized, among experts qualified by scientific training and experience to evaluate its safety…to be safe under the conditions of its intended use." 21 U.S.C. § 321(s) (1994).

of such naturally occurring substances and thus warrant formal premarket review and approval by FDA.

Thus, under GRAS, genetically modified organisms are seen to pose no greater risk *per se* to human health than unmodified ones, based upon the characteristics of the resulting products, because they are governed by the same physical and biological laws as the nonmodified versions,[67] and, as a result, no products are actually reviewed before being placed on the market.

13.2.4   *The Consumer's Right to Know*

The consumer's right to know the composition of marketed food products is at the center of much of the debate in this area. The presence or absence of labeling of foods is contingent upon the weight that a regulatory scheme places on the consumer's right to know if his/her food purchases contain genetically engineered components. Switzerland has given consumers' concerns preeminence in enacting a mandatory labeling law. In contrast, the United States' presumption that a genetically modified product is the same in all its food aspects as the "regular" one makes it unnecessary to label it as being different.

13.3   *International Standards for Genetically Modified Foods – The Codex Alimentarius Commission*

The Codex Alimentarius Commission (Codex or CAC) is an intergovernmental body established by the UN Food and Agriculture Organization (FAO) and the World Health Organization (WHO), the UN agency whose mission is to set international food standards. The World Trade Organization (WTO) Agreement on the Application of Sanitary and Phytosanitary Measures (SPS Agreement)[68] in 1995 assigned to the Codex the responsibility for setting GM food standards that would be recognized by the WTO, that is, in disputes over trade within the terms of the SPS Agreement and the Agreement on Technical Barriers to Trade (TBT Agreement).[69]

In the drafting meetings, Codex's Committee on General Principles (CCGP) considered both the elements of precaution and general nonscientific matters

---

[67] FDA Policy Statement, *supra* note 65, at 22,990.

[68] Agreement on the Application of Sanitary or Phytosanitary Measures, GATT Doc. M.T.N./ FA II-A1A-4, art. 2.2 (Dec. 15, 1993), *reprinted in* THE RESULTS OF THE URUGUAY ROUND OF MULTILATERAL TRADE NEGOTIATIONS: THE LEGAL TEXTS 69, 70 (1995) [hereinafter SPS Agreement].

[69] Agreement on Technical Barriers to Trade, Apr. 12, 1979, GATT, BISD, 26th Supp. 8 (1980), *reprinted in* H.R. Doc. No. 103–316, vol. I, 103d Cong., 2d Sess. 1427, 33 I.L.M. 81 (1994).

as they relate to food safety. The US objected to incorporation of precaution in food safety analysis and of nonscientific aspects, as well, asserting that they were "not relevant to the protection of consumers' health and the promotion of fair practices of trade were not within the mandate of Codex."[70] In 2003, Codex published three documents, all amended in 2008 and 2011: (1) Principles for the Risk Analysis of Foods Derived from Modern Biotechnology,[71] (2) Guidelines for the Conduct of Food Safety Assessment of Foods Derived from Recombinant-DNA Plants,[72] with annexes adopted in 2008 and 2011, and (3) Guidelines for the Conduct of Food Safety Assessment of Food Produced Using Recombinant-DNA Microorganisms.[73] Subsequently, in 2008 it issued Guideline for the Conduct of Food Safety Assessment of Foods Derived from Recombinant-DNA Animals.[74] In 2007 the Codex issued Working Principles for Risk Analysis for Food Safety for Application by Governments.[75] Codex also issued in 2011 a compilation of texts relevant to labeling of food derived from modern biotechnology.[76]

13.4   *Efforts to Regulate GMOs*

Many governments in the developed world and regional organizations have established regulatory schemes designed to oversee the production and

---

[70] Codex Alimentarius Commission, ALINORM 01/33, Report of the Fifteenth Session of the Codex committee on General Principles 5–7, 11–12 (2000).

[71] Principles for the Risk Analysis of Foods Derived from Modern Biotechnology, document CAC/GL 44–2003 (adopted in 2003, amendments 2008, 2011), ftp://ftp.fao.org/docrep/fao/011/a1554e/a1554e00.pdf. These principles are designed "to provide a framework for undertaking risk analysis on the safety and nutritional aspects of food derived from modern biotechnology." *Id.* ¶ 7. The principles include those relating to risk assessment, risk management, risk communication, and capacity building and information exchange.

[72] Guideline for the Conduct of Food Safety Assessment of Foods Derived from Recombinant-DNA Plants, document CAC/GL 45–2003, http://www.codexalimentarius.org/standards/list-of-standards/en/. Annex I to the document is on "Assessment of Possible Allergenicity, Annex II is on "Food Safety Assessment of Foods Derived from Recombinant-DNA Plants Modified for Nutritional or Health Benefits," and Annex III is on "Food Safety Assessment in Situations of Low-Level Presence of Recombinant-DNA Plant Material in Food."

[73] Guideline for the Conduct of Food Safety Assessment of Foods Produced Using Recombinant-DNA Microorganisms, document CAC/GL 46–2003, http://www.codexalimentarius.org/standards/list-of-standards/en/. Annex I is on "Assessment of Possible Allergenicity."

[74] Guideline for the Conduct of Food Safety Assessment of Foods Produced Using Recombinant-DNA Animals, document CAC/GL 68–2008, http://www.codexalimentarius.org/standards/list-of-standards/en/. It also includes an annex on "Assessment of Possible Allergenicity."

[75] Working Principles for Risk Analysis for Food Safety for Application by Governments, document CAC/GL 62–2007, http://www.codexalimentarius.org/standards/list-of-standards/en/.

[76] Compilation of Codex Texts Relevant to Labeling of Foods Derived from Modern Biotechnology, document CAC/GL 76–2011, http://www.codexalimentarius.org/standards/list-of-standards/en/.

release of genetically modified organisms and foods. The US, on the other hand, operates within a scheme that existed prior to the development of modern biotechnology; and there is little or no regulation in place in most developing countries. They display a patchwork of regulatory attitudes that seems ultimately untenable, given the natural forces militating against segregation of non-GM crops and the expansion of GMO use.

The leading producers of biotech crops are the United States (69 million hectares), Argentina (23.7 million), Brazil (30.3 million), and India (10.6 million), followed by Canada, China, Paraguay, Pakistan, South Africa, and Uruguay, each growing more than one million hectares of biotech crops – altogether 1.25 billion hectares[77] – a dramatic increase in the estimated 90 million hectares that were in biotech crops in 2005.[78]

13.4.1   *The European Union*

Consumer resistance to GM foods in Europe has been intense since US farms first began shipping GM produce to Europe in 1996. Consequently, US exports to Europe of corn and soybeans, both genetically modified and conventional, declined from nearly $3 billion in 1996 to about $1 billion in 1999.[79] European regulators imposed a four-year moratorium on the approval of new GM seed strains,[80] and the New York Times reported on March 14, 2000, that "[p]lanting, importing or selling genetically altered seeds or foods has virtually stopped, because farmers will not plant the seeds, consumers will not buy the foods, and stores decline to stock them."[81]

13.4.1.1   *The EU Measures in the 1990s*
The EU attempted to protect European crops from contact with GM crops and foods from the US by imposing regulations including the following: (1) no approval of new GM releases or products, (2) a ban on imports, and (3) strict scientific evaluation and mandatory labeling. This caused a great

---

[77] Kathryn McConnell, *Biotech Adoption Rates Highest Ever*, February 7, 2012, US Mission Geneva, According to the research group International Service for the Acquisition of Agri-biotech Applications' report, "Global Status of Commercialized Biotech/GM Crops: 2011, http://geneva.usmission.gov/2012/0208/biotech/adoption/rates/highest/ever/.

[78] Kathryn McConnell, *World Trade Agency Upholds Challenge of European Biotech Ban*, September 29, 2006, http://www.usembassy.it/viewer/article.asp?article=file2006_09/alia/a6092905.htm.

[79] *See* David Barboza, *In the Heartland, Genetic Pioneers*, N.Y. TIMES, Mar. 17, 2000, at C1, col. 2, C6, col. 5.

[80] *See, e.g., New GM food rules backed by Parliament; EU Labelling – US "Losing $300M a Year,"* FIN. TIMES (London), July 4, 2002, at 6.

[81] Donald G. McNeil, Jr., *Protests on New Genes and Seeds Grow More Passionate in Europe*, N.Y. TIMES, Mar. 14, 2000, at A1, col. 1, 2.

deal of friction between the EU and the US, which resulted in litigation before the World Trade Organization.[82]

In addition to the EU's extensive measures to regulate GMOs,[83] largely in response to consumers' concern with the potential hazards of GMO foods and crops, many European states unilaterally imposed even more stringent regulations. In 1990 the Council of the European Communities adopted Directive 90/220[84] to harmonize the different laws of the member states with respect to raw materials. The Council provided its rationale for prescribing a legal framework specific to the deliberate release of GMOs: the need to take preventive action; the potential effects of GMO releases on the environment, which may be irreversible; and the need to approximate the laws of the member states to ensure that the likely unequal conditions of competition or barriers to trade because of disparity in member states' regulations do not adversely affect the functioning of the Common Market. The Directive sought to provide "a high level of protection throughout the Community" on health, safety, environmental, and consumer protection and to ensure the safe development of industrial products utilizing GMOs. Additionally, however, the discrepancy between the European and US approaches led inevitably to conflicts. In October 1998 the Commission put in place a *de facto* moratorium on authorizing GM products, which blocked bulk shipments of US corn, as well as two Swedish rapes and one fodder beet, although all these products had been approved as safe by EU scientists.[85]

The primary focus of the Directive was a mandatory approval process before the "deliberate release" of any GMO into the environment within the EU "without provisions for containment."[86] Under this "premarket approval" requirement, each member state must take "appropriate measures" to avoid adverse effects on human health and the environment from the deliberate release or placing into the market for the deliberate release of GMOs.[87] A GM producer must provide detailed information as to the "specific conditions of use and handling and a proposal for labeling and packaging."[88] After a

---

[82] *See, e.g.*, Michael Mann, *US warns EU on modified crops; Food Exports – Washington Again Threatens Legal Action at WTO Over Approval*, FIN. TIMES (London), June 21, 2002.

[83] *See generally* Terrence P. Stewart & David S. Johanson, *Policy In Flux: The European Union's Laws on Agricultural Biotechnology and Their Effects on International Trade*, 4 DRAKE J. AGRIC. L. 243, 248–252 (1999) [hereinafter Stewart & Johanson].

[84] Council Directive 90/220/EEC, *supra* note 2.

[85] *See* USDA Office of Agricultural Affairs, *US Mission to the European Union, Update: Genetically Modified food and Feed – Labeling & Traceability Proposals*, July 17, 2002, at 2 [hereinafter USDA EU Mission Update]; Mike Smith, *EU Defers Modified Products Approval – Genetically Changed Foods De Facto Moratorium Stays*, FIN. TIMES (London), Mar. 10, 2000, at 12.

[86] Council Directive 90/220/EEC, *supra* note 2, art. 2(3).

[87] *Id.* art. 4(1).

[88] *Id.* art. 11(1).

lengthy application review procedure, if the state to which the application for release was directed decided to reject it because the state found the proposed introduction of the GMO into the environment presented too high a risk to human health and the environment, this determination worked to reject the application for use throughout the EU.[89]

If a member state approved the use of the GMO after notification, other states had 60 days to object to the approval. If there was no objection, the original approving state gave written consent to the use throughout the EU.[90] In case of objection, the European Commission would make the determination whether the use would be approved throughout the EU, as it approved the application to market Novartis' genetically altered maize.[91] Once a GMO was approved through this procedure, no member state could restrict its marketing.[92]

The Commission decisions approving GMO products for release pursuant to the procedures prescribed under Directive 90/220 caused considerable concern and controversy in member states and in the European Parliament.[93] Several attempts were made to strengthen prior prescriptions regarding the release of GMOs and to extend the scope of European regulations regarding GMOs. A few important developments will be noted here.

In 1997, the European Union adopted Regulation Number 258/97,[94] the "Novel Foods Regulation," governing food safety assessments and labeling for most genetically modified foods. This regulation applied to GMOs in processed foods likely to be purchased by consumers. It was aimed at providing a uniform law for novel foods all over the European Union[95] and minimizing the possibility that a food or product could enter the member state without its knowledge. The regulation applied to foods "which have not hitherto been used for human consumption to a significant degree within the Community,"[96] including food products containing GMOs, foods produced by but not containing GMOs, and those "with a new or intentionally modified primary molecular structure."[97] Labeling was required to inform the consumer of:

---

[89] *See id.* arts. 12(1), 12(2)(b).

[90] *See id.* arts. 13(3), 21.

[91] *See* Commission Decision 97/98, 1997 O.J. (L 31) 69; Euro. Parl., Briefing: 07-04-97(s), Genetically Modified Maize (Apr. 7, 1997).

[92] The procedure allows for restriction of marketing pending review by the European Commission if a state finds an approved GMO to "[constitute] a risk to human health and/or the environment." Council Directive 90/220/EEC, *supra* note 2, art. 16.

[93] For a discussion of these developments, *see* Stewart & Johanson, *supra* note 83, at 259–68.

[94] Regulation No. 258/97, 1997 O.J. (L 43).

[95] For the legislative process leading to the adoption of this regulation, *see id.* at 275–78.

[96] *Id.* art. 1(2).

[97] *Id.* art. 1, ¶¶ (2)(a)–(c).

any characteristic or food property such as composition, nutritional value or nutribional effects, [or] intended use of food, which renders a novel food or food ingredient no longer equivalent...if scientific assessment, based upon an appropriate analysis of existing data, can demonstrate that the characteristics assessed are different in comparison with a conventional food or food ingredient, having regard to the accepted limits of natural variations for such characteristics.[98]

Scientific assessment was used to determine whether a food was not equivalent to an existing food, and thus novel.[99] The purpose was to ensure that the final consumer was advised through labeling that GMOs were present in the food or that the food "may contain" GMOs.[100] There were detailed provisions regarding the assessment of such food and the role of the Commission to authorize measures proposed by the applicant,[101] and also for provisional restrictions which could be imposed by a member state if the food posed risks to human health or the environment.[102]

The procedure for approval required the producer of the food to specify how the product was to be labeled,[103] indicating whether because of the food's characteristics it was no longer equivalent to an existing food.[104] This regulation incorporated a version of the GRAS threshold employed in the United States, exempting certain novel food products from premarket approval (though not from notification, approval and labeling requirements) if

on the basis of the scientific evidence available and generally recognized or on the basis of an opinion delivered by one of the competent bodies..., [they] are substantially equivalent to existing foods or food ingredients as regards their composition, nutritional value, metabolism, intended use and the level of undesirable substances contained therein.[105]

As the Novel Foods Regulation, which mandated labeling, did not apply retroactively, the Council adopted Regulation 1139/1998[106] to apply to "foods and food ingredients which are to be delivered as such to the final consumer...produced, in whole or in part," from genetically modified soybeans and genetically modified maize,[107] which had been earlier authorized under Directive 90/220/EEC. This regulation covered labeling of food products derived from "Round-Up Ready" soybeans and Novartis Bt-176 corn,

[98] *Id.* art. 8(1)(a).
[99] *See id.*
[100] *See id.* art. 8(1)(d).
[101] *See id.* arts. 6–7, 13.
[102] *See id.* arts. 12–13.
[103] *See id.* art. 6(1).
[104] *See id.* art. 8(1)(a).
[105] Council Regulation 258/97, art. 3(4), 1997 O.J. (L 43) 1.
[106] Council Regulation No. 1139/1998, 1998 O.J. (L 159), May 26, 1998.
[107] *Id.* art. 1(1).

which were commercialized before the effective date of the Novel Foods law, and which it was determined could not be approved as equivalent.[108]

The Council identified as one of the purposes of the new regulation the necessity of adopting uniform EU labeling rules for these products[109] because several member states had unilaterally taken measures on labeling and there was concern that "differences between those measures [could] impede the free movement of those foods and food ingredients and thereby adversely affect the functioning of the internal market."[110] The Council also felt that it was

> necessary to ensure that the final consumer is informed of any characteristics or food property, such as composition, nutritional value or nutritional effects or the intended use of the food, which renders a food or food ingredients no longer equivalent to an existing food or food ingredient; [and] for that purpose, foods and food ingredients produced from genetically modified soybeans or from genetically modified maize which are not equivalent to conventional counterparts should be subject to labeling requirements.[111]

It further said that labeling requirements were to be based on scientific evaluation,[112] and that they should not be "more burdensome than necessary but sufficiently detailed to supply consumers with the information they require."[113]

In June 1999, Europe's environment ministers agreed on even tougher controls on GMOs by introducing new "risk assessment" rules to monitor scientific evidence and to provide for a clear label that read: "This product contains genetically modified organisms," for products containing more than a certain percentage of GM ingredients, and substituting a reapproval process for all new GM plants and seeds approved for sale instead of the currently available permanent consent mechanism.[114]

13.4.1.2 *EU Measures in the New Century*

The EU has been proactive in enacting strict legislation to regulate GMOs so as to control their spread. On July 25, 2001, the European Commission

---

[108] *Id.* preamble, ¶ 16.
[109] *Id.* preamble, ¶ 4.
[110] *Id.*
[111] *Id.* ¶ 9.
[112] *Id.* ¶ 10.
[113] *Id.* ¶ 12. This regulation was amended by Commission Regulation 49/2000, which entered into force on April 10, 2000, and set a threshold for inadvertent contamination, as might occur during cultivation, harvest, transport, storage or processing, to products which cannot be guaranteed to contain less than one percent GMOs, provided that the appropriate steps have been taken to avoid such contamination. *See* USDA EU Mission Update, *supra* note 85, at 3.
[114] *See* Stephen Castle, *EU Agrees on Tougher GM Food Control,* (London), THE INDEPENDENT, June 26, 1999.

adopted new legislation for labeling and traceability of GMOs.[115] The Commission added three main requirements to the existing scheme: mandatory labeling for food and feed products containing or derived from more than one percent biotech materials, regardless of whether they can be detected; event-specific identity markers to accompany shipments; and tolerance levels for "adventitious" presence of unapproved biotech materials (which also must have undergone risk assessment within the EU procedure).[116] Substantial equivalence would no longer be applicable for assessment of genetically modified food or food products in the EU.

A 2001 European Council directive[117] outlines the approval process for the deliberate release of GMOs into the environment. The Directive regulates and restricts the distribution of GMOs and foods that contain GM ingredients. It states measures for assessing human health and environmental risks before releasing any GM product into the environment or marketing it. In addition, no GMOs could be marketed unless Regulation 1829/2003 was given in accordance with which applications from member states ought to be sent to the European Food Safety Authority (EFSA) for scientific assessment of the potential health and environmental risks.[118] Additionally, if a member state requests to cultivate a GMO it must perform an environmental risk assessment.

The US and Canada were concerned that the European Community (EC) regulations on the approval of biotech products had blocked imports of agricultural and food products from their countries into the European Union, and hence on May 13, 2003, they requested consultations with the EC, as a prerequisite to instituting a complaint in the World Trade Organization (WTO), and the next day Argentina joined them with a request for consultations regarding the same concern.[119] The consultations did not result in an agreement and the WTO was requested to establish a panel to review the dispute. The panel initially issued its interim confidential report on

---

[115] *See* USDA EU Mission Update, *supra* note 85.

[116] *See id.* at 1.

[117] European Council Directive 2001/18/EC of the European Parliament and of the Council of March 12, 2001, on the Deliberate Release into the Environment of Genetically Modified Organisms and Repealing Council Directive 90/220/EEC/2001O.J. (L106).

[118] *Id. See* Commission Regulation 1829/2003 of the European Parliament and of the Council of September 22, 2003, on Genetically Modified Food and Feed, 2003 O.J. (L268). For EFSA's Role in the GMO Regulatory Framework, *see* http://www.EFSA.europa.eu/en/gmo-topics/docs/gmoauthorizations.pdf. The British approval of GM food is also performed by EFSA. *See* Advisory Committee on Novel Foods and Processes, http://acnfp.food.gov.uk.

[119] Complaints by the United States (WT/DS291), Canada (WT/DS292), and Argentina (WT/DS293).

February 7, 2006,[120] and its final report to the parties on May 10,[121] circulated to members on September 29.[122] Subsequently, on November 21, 2006, the Dispute Settlement body of the WTO adopted the panel reports.[123]

Although the WTO did not rule on the safety of GM crops, the panel found that by 2003 six EC member states had invoked "safeguard provisions" under EC Directive 90/220, five had banned the marketing of GMOs, and one member state banned the import of GMOs.[124] Additionally, several member countries had prohibited the importation and marketing of specific biotech products.[125] It also found that the EC had applied a "general *de facto* moratorium"[126] on the approval of biotech products, which caused undue delay in approvals of US GM crop imports and that no GMOs were approved on the member state level during 1999 and 2003.[127] Hence it held that the EU was in violation of its trade obligations within the authority of Sanitary and Phytosanitary (SPS) Agreement.

The EC did not appeal the ruling of the panel. After prolonged negotiations the US requested the Dispute Settlement Body in January 2008 to suspend concessions and other obligations with respect to the EC because in the US's view the EC had failed to comply with the DSB's recommendations and rulings.[128] In response, on July 13, 2010, the EU proposed a regulation under which member states would be allowed to decide whether to cultivate GMOs within their borders.[129] Under the Directive, member states cannot

---

[120] WTO Interim Reports of the Panel, European Communities – Measures Affecting the Approval and Marketing of Biotech Products, WT/DS291, WT/DS292, WT/DS293 (February 7, 2006).

[121] WTO, Reports of the Panel, European Communities – Measures Affecting the Approval and Marketing of Biotech Products, WT/DS291, WT/DS292, WT/DS293 (May 10, 2006).

[122] WTO, Reports of the Panel, European Communities – Measures Affecting the Approval and Marketing of Biotech Products, WT/DS291R, WT/DS292R, WT/DS293R (September 29, 2006) [hereinafter Panel Report].

[123] WTO, Panel Reports, Action by the Dispute Settlement Body, European Communities – Measures Affecting the Approval and Marketing of Biotech Products, WT/DS291R, WT/DS292R, WT/DS293R (November 29, 2006).

[124] *Id.* at 31.

[125] *Id. See generally* Margaret Rosso Grossman, *The Coexistence of GM and Other Crops in the European Union*, 16 KAN. J.L. & PUB. POL'Y 324 (2007); Bernd van der Meulen, *The EU Regulatory Approach to GM Foods*, 16 KAN. J.L. & PUB. POL'Y 286 (2007). *Id.*

[126] *See* Panel Report, *supra* note 122, at 612–613.

[127] *Id.* at 613.

[128] Recourse to Article 22.2 of the DSU by the United States, European Communities – Measures Affecting the Approval and Marketing of Biotech Products, WT/DS 291/39 (January 21, 2008).

[129] Proposal for a Regulation of the European Parliament and of the Council Amending Directive 2001/18/EC as Regards the Possibility for the Member States to Restrict or Prohibit the Cultivation of GMOs in Their Territory, at 2, COM (2010) 375 final (July 13, 2010) (noting that "the European Union Authorization System is aimed at avoiding adverse effects of GMOs on human and animal health and the environment, which establishing an internal market for those products").

interrupt the free circulation of products containing GMOs, GMO seeds or related planting materials and the EU retains the right to decide the GMO seeds that may be placed on the market, as it pertains to the cultivation and not to the free circulation of GMOs,[130] and member states are not authorized to affect the cultivation of plants that have "technically unavoidable traces" or an adventitious presence of any GMO that the EU has approved.[131]

The European Parliament adopted the proposal amending the 2001 Directive at its first reading on July 5, 2011.[132] As of May 2012 the Council has not taken action to adopt the amending regulation.[133]

Member states are authorized to impose restrictions or prohibitions on a case-by-case basis regarding the particular GMOs or groups of GMOs,[134] basing them on "scientifically justified grounds relating to environmental impacts which might arise from the deliberate release or the placing on the market of GMOs,"[135] and the amended Directive states several reasons for excluding GMOs:

> The prevention of the development of pesticide resistance amongst weeds and pests; the invasiveness or persistence of a GM variety, or the possibility of inter-breeding with domestic cultivated or wild plants; the prevention of negative impacts on the local environment caused by changes in agricultural practices linked to the cultivation of GMOs; the maintenance and development of agricultural practices which offer a better potential to reconcile production with ecosystem sustainability; the maintenance of local biodiversity, including certain habitats and ecosystems, or certain types of natural and landscape features; the absence of adequate data or the existence of contradictory data or persisting scientific uncertainty concerning the potential negative impacts of the release of GMOs on the environment of a Member State or region, including on biodiversity.... The impracticability or the high costs of coexistence measures or the impossibility of implementing coexistence measures due to specific geographical conditions such as small islands or mountain zones; the need to protect the diversity of agricultural production; the need to ensure seed purity; other

---

[130] *Id.* at 12.

[131] *Id.*

[132] European Parliament, Texts Adopted – European Parliament legislative resolution of 5 July 2011 on the proposal for a regulation of the European Parliament and of the Council amending Directive 2001/18/EC as regards the possibility for the Member States to restrict or prohibit the cultivation of GMOs in their territory (COM(2010)0375-C7-0178/2010-2010/0208 (COD)), http://www.europarl.europa.eu. *See* Report on the Proposal for a Regulation of the European Parliament and of the Council Amending Directive 2001/18/EC as Regards the Possibility for the Member States to Restrict or Prohibit the Cultivation of GMOs in Their Territory, Comm. on the Env't, Pub. Health & Food Safety, at 56 (April 20, 2011), http://ec.europa.eu/food/food/biotechnology/docs/proposal_en.pdf [hereinafter 2011 Regulation Text].

[133] *See* Janusz Wojciechowski (ECR), *Question for written answer to the Council*, 26 March 2012, www.europarl.europa.eu.

[134] 2011 Regulation Text, *supra* note 132, amendment 15.

[135] *Id.* amendment 16.

grounds that may include land use, town and country planning, or other legitimate factors.[136]

It is noteworthy that member states are not authorized to take measures
regarding "the free circulation and import of genetically modified seeds and
plant propagating material, as or in products, and of the products of their
harvest," and can only take measures regarding the cultivation of GMOs.[137]
Also, member states are not authorized to prevent or restrict the cultivation
of authorized GMOs in other member states, so long as those member states
take "effective measures" to prevent cross-border contamination.[138]

13.4.2   *The United States*

Concern in the United States with potential risks of GM foods[139] motivated
some food and beverage companies and several grocery chains not to carry
modified foods. For example, General Mills announced in 2002 it would
introduce a new line of organic cereals – certifiably uncontaminated by
GMOs.[140] Gerber and Heinz announced that they would not use genetically
altered corn or soy ingredients in their baby foods because of public concern
about safety.[141] In January 2000, Frito-Lay, Inc., told the farmers who grow
the corn used in its snack foods not to use genetically engineered seed for
that year's planting.[142] Whole Foods Markets, a chain of 304 natural foods
supermarkets, committed itself to not using GM ingredients in its Whole
Foods brand or private label products.[143] Over 30 farm groups across the
country warned their members that planting GM crops might be risky to
their livelihoods because of the unpopularity of such crops with consumers,
and that the farmers could be vulnerable to "massive liability" from damage

---

[136] *Id.*

[137] *Id.* amendment 7.

[138] *Id.* amendment 9.

[139] *See* David Barboza, *Modified Foods Put Companies In a Quandary*, N.Y. Times, June 4,
2000, sec. 1, at 1, col. 5.

[140] *See Future of Genetically Modified Corn in Question Given Recent Decision by General Mills
to Go Organic*, PR Newswire, June 10, 2002, http://www.prnewswire.com/news-releases/
future-of-genetically-modified-corn-in-question-given-recent-decision-by-general-mills-
to-go-organic-77843432.html.

[141] *See* David Stipp, *Is Monsanto's Biotech Worth Less than a Hill of Beans?*, Fortune, Feb. 21,
2000, at 157, cited in Thomas O. McGarity, *Seeds of Distrust: Federal Regulation of Geneti-
cally Modified Foods*, 35 U. Mich. J.L. Ref. 403, 474 (2002); Alex Salkever, *Are These New
Bio-Crops Safe?*, Christian Science Monitor, Aug. 5, 1999, at 3; Lawrent Belsie, *New
Genes Meet a Wary Market*, Christian Science Monitor, Dec. 8, 1999, at 1; *Eating Well:
What Labels Don't Tell You (Yet)*, N.Y. Times, Feb. 9, 2000, sec. F, at 5, col. 3 [hereinafter
Eating Well]. A leading brand of baby food, Earth's Best, a division of the Hain Food
Group, also announced in January 2000 that it would not use GM ingredients. *See* Florence
Fabricant, *Foodstuff*, N.Y. Times, Jan. 26, 2000, sec. F, at 2, col. 1.

[142] *See Eating Well, supra* note 141.

[143] *Id.*

caused by the spread of biologically modified pollens.[144] A survey by the American Corn Growers Association published in February 2000 showed a 16-percent drop in sowings of GM maize across the US Midwest.[145] And a major grain distribution company, Archer Daniels Midland, in the Fall of 1999 advised farmers to keep GM and non-GM grain separate.[146]

The battle against GM crops at one point even led Monsanto to renounce the use of "terminator" genes, by which subsequent generations of seeds are rendered infertile, thus preventing farmers from saving seeds from year to year.[147] In 2002 Monsanto's pledge not to commercialize terminator was due to business considerations that were no longer applicable and the company announced that it intended to bring it back into production and marketing.[148] And beginning in 2000 shareholders of several corporations called for shareholder votes to halt the development and sale of GM food and crops until they are tested on a long-term basis and are shown to be safe to both humans and the environment.[149]

Unlike many countries that apply process-oriented approaches and thus have developed specialized biotechnology laws to regulate GMO releases, the U.S regulates GMOs under previously existing statutes. For a decade beginning in the mid-1970s, the National Institutes of Health was primarily responsible to ensure genetic engineering safety, and hence it was this agency that established guidelines for research involving recombinant DNA in 1976.[150]

In 1986 the White House Office of Science and Technology (OST) established a "Coordinated Framework for Regulation of Biotechnology,"[151] which addressed the new phenomenon of genetic engineering in foods by prescribing jurisdiction among a number of federal agencies. Under this Framework,

---

[144] *See generally* Assessing Liability, *supra* note 52; *see also* William Claiborne, *Biotech Crops Spur Warning; 30 Farm Groups Say Consumer Backlash Could Cost Markets*, WASH. POST, Nov. 24, 1999, at A11.

[145] *See* Michela Wrong, *Modified Crop-Sowings to Fall*, FIN. TIMES (London), Feb. 23, 2000, at 6.

[146] *See* Stipp, *supra* note 141, at 158.

[147] *See generally* James Erlichman, *GM Foods: Fighting for the Future of our Food*, THE INDEPENDENT (London), Oct. 12, 1999, Features section; *Ending a Genetic Food Fight*, Editorial, CHRISTIAN SCIENCE MONITOR, Sept. 28, 1999, at 20; John Vidal, *The Seeds of Wrath; Thousands Will Demonstrate Today at a Meeting of the Leading Economic Powers*, THE GUARDIAN (London), Weekend Page, June 19, 1999, at 10.

[148] Philip Cohen, *When is GM food not really GM? When it's been Exorcised*, NEW SCIENTIST, July 6, 2002, at 32.

[149] *See* Mary Dejevsky, *Big US Firms Face Investors' Revolt Over GM Foods*, THE INDEPENDENT (London), Feb. 15, 2000, at 13.

[150] For a discussion of NIH's role, *see* Judy J. Kim, *Out of the Lab and Into the Field: Harmonization of Deliberate Release Regulations for Genetically Modified Organisms*, 16 FORDHAM INT'L L.J. 1160, 1178–79 (1993).

[151] Coordinated Framework for Regulation of Biotechnology, 51 Fed. Reg. 23301 (1986).

several general principles apply: (1) foods and pesticides, among other products, are regulated under the preexisting legal scheme – the same as applied to conventional products;[152] (2) the products of biotechnology and not the processes are to be regulated;[153] (3) the safety of biotechnology products is to be determined on a case-by-case basis;[154] and (4) a coordinated effort is to be undertaken between all the agencies involved in regulating biotechnology.[155]

The following discussion will address the roles of the major agencies involved in the process – the USDA, EPA and FDA.

13.4.2.1   *The United States Department of Agriculture (USDA)*
The USDA's regulation of the release of GMOs is carried out through its Animal Plant and Health Inspection Service (APHIS) when the GMOs in question are genetically engineered microorganisms derived from plant pests.[156] As genetically engineered plants are considered plant pests until APHIS determines otherwise,[157] those developing a new GMO plant must submit a petition to APHIS showing that, based upon the company's field trials, the plant is safe and poses no risks as a plant pest.[158] APHIS's task is to conduct an environmental assessment to determine the GMO's possible effects on human health and the environment.[159]

APHIS will issue a "determination of non-regulated status" if it finds that the GMO is not a plant pest.[160] Then, the GMO may be released into the environment, that is, planted. From 1992 to 1998 APHIS provided nonregulated status to 36 genetically modified plants.[161]

In March 2000, the Department of Agriculture proposed strict rules prohibiting the use of GM ingredients in products carrying the organic label. The new rules address concerns about the use of three processes – genetic engineering, sewage sludge, and irradiation – in the production of food products that are labeled "organic."[162] This was a revision of the 1995 USDA

---

[152] *Id.* at 23302 and 23304.
[153] *Id.*
[154] *Id.*
[155] *Id.*
[156] *See* T. Morath, *Office of US Trade Representative, US Regulation of Products Derived from Biotechnology* 1 (1998). APHIS' authority is under Federal Plant Pest Act (7 U.S.C. §§ 150aa–150jj) and the Plant Quarantine Act (7 U.S.C. §§ 151–167).
[157] *See* 7 C.F.R. §§ 340.0(a)(2) n. 1, 340.1, 340.2, 340.6.
[158] *See* Morath, *supra* note 156, at 5.
[159] *See id.* at 4.
[160] *See id.* at 1.
[161] Animal and Plant Health Inspection Service, USDA, Crop Lines No Longer Regulated by USDA, http://www.aphis.usda.dov/biotech/not reg.html, *cited in* Stewart & Johanson, *supra* note 83, at 250 n. 38.
[162] *See* Elizabeth Becker, *Organic Gets an Additive: A U.S.D.A. Seal to Certify It*, N.Y. Times, Oct. 21, 2002, at A10; col. 5; *New Rules on Organic Foods*, N.Y. Times, Mar. 9, 2000, at A28, col. 1.

proposal to establish a nationwide certification program for organic foods. Now in order for raw products to be considered 100 percent organic, "they must be grown or manufactured without added hormones, pesticides or synthetic fertilizers."[163] The USDA also monitors farmers' use of GM technology and its effectiveness.[164]

In *Monsanto v. Geertson Seed Farms*,[165] the US Supreme Court reversed and remanded the decision of the lower federal courts, finding that the district court had abused its discretion in denying APHIS the right to deregulate Monsanto's genetically modified crop Roundup Ready Alfalfa and also in prohibiting the possibility of planting and harvesting of Roundup Ready Alfalfa in the future.[166] The US District Court for the Northern District of California had earlier found that, by not preparing an Environmental Impact Statement (EIS), APHIS had violated the National Environmental Policy Act (NEPA). Hence the court ordered APHIS to prepare an EIS.[167] The court had also vacated APHIS' deregulation of Roundup Ready Alfalfa, entering an injunction preventing future action by APHIS while it prepared an EIS.[168] On appeal, in the ruling later reversed by the US Supreme Court, the Ninth Circuit Court of Appeals upheld the district court's findings.[169] The case has obvious international trade implications.

13.4.2.2   *The Environmental Protection Agency*

The EPA has partial jurisdiction over microbial products of biotechnology and pesticides manufactured with biotechnology under the Toxic Substances Control Act (TSCA)[170] and the Federal Insecticide, Fungicide and Rodenticide Act (FIFRA).[171] The EPA requires manufacturers to register pesticides derived from biotechnology and bioengineered plants, including plants with

---

[163] *Id. See also Strict Rules to Limit Genetic Engineering on Organic Foods*, N.Y. TIMES, Mar. 5, 2000, sec. 1, at 1, col. 5: "The [new rules] indicate an about-face in the agency's attitude on organic farming and represent one of several steps it is taking to help small and medium-sized farmers, who have received comparatively little attention from the agency for decades."

[164] *See, e.g.*, USDA Report, *supra* note 19.

[165] Monsanto v. Geertson Seed Farms, 130 S.C. 2743 (2010). *See generally* Christine K. Lesicko, *Note: Attempting to (De)Regulate Genetically Modified Crops: The Supreme Court Overrules the Injunction denying Deregulation of Roundup Ready Alfalfa: Monsanto v. Geertson Seed Farms*, 18 MO. ENVTL. L. & POL'Y REV. 351 (2011).

[166] 130 S.C. at 2761.

[167] Geertson Seed Farms vs. Johanns, 570 F.3d 1130, 1135 (9th Cir. 2009), reversed 130 S.Ct. 2743 (2010).

[168] 570 F.3d at 1136.

[169] *Id.* at 1141.

[170] Pub. L. No. 75–717, 52 Stat. 1040 (1938) (codified as amended at 21 U.S.C. §§ 301–395 (1994).

[171] 7 U.S.C. §§ 136–136y.

pesticidal qualities, for example, those that contain the Bt toxin,[172] before placing them on the US market.[173] The EPA establishes maximum tolerance levels for pesticide residues in foods and must be notified before new microorganisms, which include intergeneric organisms derived through biotechnology, can be manufactured or imported, in accordance with the Toxic Substances Control Act.[174]

Because of the rising concern over the safety of biotech crops and after the controversial Cornell laboratory study suggesting that GM pollen could harm monarch butterfly caterpillars, the EPA announced new regulations, effective in 2000. These regulations, *inter alia*, ask farmers "to voluntarily protect butterflies by planting traditional corn around the edges of Bt corn fields, creating a buffer to prevent toxic pollen from blowing into butterfly habitats."[175] They also require farmers to plant at least 20 percent of their crops as non-Bt corn, the purpose being to slow the evolution of resistance to the Bt toxin, which is in use as a natural insecticide by some organic farmers.[176]

The issue of EPA oversight in the GM foods area came into sharp focus in November 2000 when the biotech company Aventis CropScience, which holds a registration to produce corn seed bearing the Bt protein Cry9C,[177] marketed as "StarLink Corn," confirmed that traces of the protein had been found in test samples outside its licensed sales. Aventis' registration was limited by the EPA to sales for animal feed or industrial use because of unresolved questions about possible allergens. It was discovered that certain corn products on grocery store shelves were contaminated with the "StarLink" genetic material. After the reports surfaced, Aventis requested voluntary cancellation of its registration for Cry9C.[178] Later, although there was no evidence of the presence of allergens in "StarLink" corn, still it could not be ruled out, as the EPA announced it had decided not to let even trace amounts into human food.[179]

---

[172] *See, e.g.*, Environmental Protection Agency Office of Pesticide Programs, Biopesticide Fact Sheet: Bacillus thuringiensis subspecies tolworthi Cry9C Protein and the Genetic Material Necessary for Its Production in Corn [OPP Chemical Code 006466], Mar. 2001 [hereinafter EPA Biopesticide Fact Sheet]; Novartis Seeds – Approval of a Pesticide Product Registration, 63 Fed. Reg. 43935 (1999). *See* Morath, *supra* note 156, at 1.

[173] *See id.*

[174] 15 U.S.C. § 2603(d).

[175] Carol K. Yoon, *E.P.A. Announces New Rules on Genetically Altered Corn*, N.Y. TIMES, Jan. 17, 2000, at A13, col. 1.

[176] *See id.*

[177] *See* EPA Biopesticide Fact Sheet, *supra* note 172.

[178] *Id.*; News Release: *Aventis CropScience Finds Bioengineered Protein in Non- StarLink Corn Seed*, posted on FDA web site, http://www.fda.gov/oc/po/firmrecalls/aven-tis11_00.html, Nov. 21, 2000.

[179] *See* Andrew Pollack, *E.P.A. Rejects Use of a Gene-Altered Corn in Human Food*, N.Y. TIMES, July 28, 2001, at C4, col. 3. This regulatory approach had been suggested by Aventis in a

13.4.2.3   *The Food and Drug Administration*

The FDA is responsible for ensuring the safety of the public from harmful food products under the Federal Food, Drug and Cosmetic Act of 1938.[180] The statute's general safety clause directs the FDA to "[protect] the public health by ensuring that…foods are safe, wholesome, sanitary, and properly labeled."[181] If it is found that there is a risk – the presence of a "poisonous or deleterious substance which may render [the food] injurious to health"[182] – the agency is to ban the food.[183] If a significant hazard to the public safety is found to exist or there is a "sincere" need for consumers to be made aware of aspects of a food so as to distinguish it from others, the FDA is to balance the risk presented by the food against its benefits, then consider whether the consumer's right to be advised warrants the agency's requiring the substance to be labeled.[184]

Genetically modified foods can also be regulated by the FDA under the FDCA's section 409 Food Additives Amendment,[185] applicable to

> any substance the intended use of which results or may reasonably be expected to result, directly or indirectly, in its becoming a component of food or otherwise affecting the characteristics of any food…, if such substance is not generally recognized, among experts qualified by scientific training and experience to evaluate its safety…to be safe under the conditions of its intended use.

This section permits subjecting of foods to a premarket approval process, since bioengineering is seen as adding foreign genetic material intended to affect the characteristics of a food. It requires that new additives in food be demonstrated safe through standard scientific testing prior to their marketing.[186]

In 1992 the FDA announced its first framework policy tailored to genetically modified foods.[187] Under the policy, the FDA provided a "guidance" procedure allowing manufacturers to assess the safety of their own genetically modified food products as compared to the traditional forms. It stated that it

---

request that the agency establish a tolerance level for the modified product. Subsequently, it was revealed that very little control had been exercised by Aventis over its licensees in the use of its product, also raising questions as to the enforcement of EPA regulations to prevent mishaps. Andrew Pollack, *1999 Survey on Gene-Altered Corn Disclosed Some Improper Uses*, N.Y. Times, Sept. 4, 2001, at C2, col. 1. Some of the information on which the report was based was obtained under a freedom of information request.

[180] Federal Food, Drug, and Cosmetic Act, Pub. L. No. 75–717, 52 Stat. 1040 (1938), codified as amended at 21 U.S.C. §§ 301–395 (1994).

[181] *Id.* § 393.

[182] *Id.* § 342(a)(1).

[183] *See* Kelly A. Leggio, *Limitations on the Consumer's Right to Know: Settling the Debate Over Labeling of Genetically Modified Foods in the United States*, 38 San Diego L. Rev. 893, 912–13 (2001).

[184] *See id.*

[185] Food Additives Amendment of 1958, Pub. L. No. 85–929, 72 Stat. 1784 (1958).

[186] *Id.*

[187] FDA Policy Statement, *supra* note 65.

would apply a presumption that foods produced through recombinant technology were GRAS under the FDCA and therefore not subject to regulation as food additives, because the added genetic material is from sources already found in the food supply. It stated also that modification was not a "material fact" under the FDCA that would cause a food to require labeling.[188]

The FDA policy requested manufacturers voluntarily to consult with the agency establishing the product's GRAS status or, alternatively, to give the agency the grounds to regulate the product as a food additive that would require approval before being marketed. This plan was based on the conclusion that such foods are exempt even from the voluntary approval procedures under FDCA Section 409.

Under the 1992 policy, five areas are to be considered by a company in determining the relative safety and nutrition of GM-derived foods: (1) toxicity characteristics of both the host and genetically modified species; (2) potential for transfer of food allergens from one food source to another through genetic transfer; (3) concentration and bioavailability of nutrients in the original as well as modified plant; (4) safety and nutritional value of the new genetic material; and (5) assessment of identity and nutritional value of modified carbohydrates or fats.[189]

Companies do, in fact, usually consult the FDA before marketing their products, and the FDA has issued guidelines to assist them in this regard.[190] If it is discovered through consultations that a new product raises health concerns, the FDA may require that a premarket review be performed.[191] Those introducing the food product into the market are under a legal obligation to ensure that the food is safe.[192] Thus, the responsibility for ensuring food safety is on the producer, who could be criminally liable for introducing an unsafe food into the marketplace.[193] The FDA may also stop the food's distribution if it is proven unsafe.

The theory of substantial equivalence or GRAS is at the center of the agency's decision to reject mandatory labeling in the bulk of GM food cases. There are exceptions that must be labeled, such as risks in genetic material derived from known allergenic substances being transferred to manufactured substances.[194]

Among several cases challenging the FDA's policy and procedures, the following two cases upheld the FDA's position against mandatory labeling. In *Alliance for Bio-Integrity v. Shalala*,[195] the plaintiff alleged that the FDA

---

[188]   *Id.* at 22991, § 321(n).
[189]   *Id.* at 22992.
[190]   *Id.*
[191]   *Id.* at 22987–22989.
[192]   *Id.* at 22988.
[193]   *Id.*
[194]   *Id.* at 22992.
[195]   116 F. Supp. 2d 166 (D.D.C. 2000).

policy under which GM foods are authorized to be marketed without testing and labels violates the agency's statutory mandate to protect public health and to provide consumers with relevant information about the foods they eat.[196] It claimed that this policy raised issues of environmental safety, statutory construction, and consumers' right to know.[197] All claims were rejected.[198] The court reviewed the FDA's statutory authority to require labeling only where there is a material difference with the conventional counterpart, and where failing to label as to "consequences which may result from the use of the article to which the labeling...relates;"[199] and the agency's policy that GM foods are not "materially" different from non-GM foods.[200] The court accordingly found that the FDA "lacks a basis upon which it can legally mandate labeling, regardless of the level of consumer demand."[201]

International Dairy Foods Association v. Amestoy[202] concerned a Vermont mandatory labeling law for milk products produced with recombinant bovine somatotropin (rbST). The Second Circuit upheld the FDA's position that GM foods are equally safe and not nutritionally different from non rbST milk, and said that requiring such milk to be labeled for inclusion of GMOs violated the dairy's First Amendment rights.[203]

Among other cases, in *Organic Seed Growers and Trade Association v. Monsanto*, the plaintiffs argued that Monsanto's products migrate onto their fields, contaminating the organic produce. A US District Court in New York issued a ruling dismissing the complaint on February 24, 2012, which was appealed on March 28.[204]

Among other developments, the FDA held hearings in February 2010 regarding the requested approval of a genetically modified fish, AquAdvantage

---

[196] *See Landmark Lawsuit Challenges FDA Policy for Genetically Engineered Food, Press Rel.*, ALLIANCE FOR BIO-INTEGRITY, www.biointegrity.org (copy on file with the authors); *See also* ALLIANCE FOR BIO-INTEGRITY, *Statement of Steven M. Druker, Lawsuit Uncovers Disagreement Within FDA Over Safety of Biotech Foods*: www.biointegrity.org, stating that the FDA's records reveal it declared genetically engineered foods to be safe in the face of broad disagreement from its own experts – all the while claiming a broad scientific consensus supported its stance. Internal reports and memoranda disclose: (1) agency scientists repeatedly cautioned that foods produced through recombinant DNA technology entail different risks than do their conventionally produced counterparts and (2) that this input was consistently disregarded by the bureaucrats who crafted the agency's current policy, which treats bioengineered foods the same as natural ones (copy on file with the authors).

[197] 116 F. Supp. at 170.

[198] *Id.* at 181.

[199] 21 U.S.C. § 321(n) (1994).

[200] 116 F. Supp. at 179.

[201] *Id.*

[202] 92 F.3d 67 (2d Cir. 1996).

[203] *Id.* at 73.

[204] Organic Seed Growers and Trade Association, 2012 US Dist. N.Y. LEXIS 25822.

Salmon, for public consumption.[205] The company requesting approval, Aqua Bounty Technologies, Inc., which intends to sell the genetically modified salmon's eggs commercially to farmers, argued that the product poses little environmental risk and is safe for consumption. However, consumer and environmental groups oppose the approval, contending that the current risk assessment methods are not effective with respect to animals.

In November 2012 California voters will decide on a ballot initiative whether labeling of GMO foods will be required. Pursuant to an on-line petition drive of signatures submitted to the FDA, the initiative, entitled "Just Label It," seeks to establish rules similar to those in the European Union, China, India, Australia, and Japan, requiring statement of transgenic food in a package.[206] A few local governments have enacted mandatory prohibitions on GM crops.[207]

13.4.2.4   *Appraisal of the US Approach*

While the EU has continued to adapt its measures to regulate GMOs, the US approach to the regulation of GM foods is based upon a system that was designed for a starkly different genre of foodstuffs. This approach presumes that GMOs are no different from conventional foods. This regulatory system has almost no internal flexibility to adapt to developments in the body of knowledge on the topic. As a result, although the present level of information and data, especially on environmental effects, is advancing rapidly, US regulations would be unable to respond without a comprehensive overhaul.

13.5   *Cartagena Protocol on Biosafety to the Convention on Biological Diversity*

13.5.1   *Events Leading Up to the Biosafety Protocol*

The UN Convention on Biological Diversity[208] (CBD) was concluded during the course of the 1992 UN Conference on Environment and Development – the Earth Summit – at Rio de Janeiro, Brazil. Its objectives are: (1) "the

---

[205] *See generally* Katherine Wilinksa, *Note: AquAdvantage is Not Real Advantage: European Biotechnology Regulations and the United States' September 2010 FDA Review of Genetically Modified Salmon*, 21 Minn. J. Int'l L. 145 (2012).

[206] *See* Julia Moskin, *Modified Crops Tap a Well-Spring of Protest*, N.Y. Times, February 8, 2012, at 3.

[207] *See generally* Charles J. Bissell, *Note: As Montville, Maine Goes, So Goes Wolcott, Vermont? A Primer on the Local Regulation of Genetically Modified Crops*, 43 Suffolk U. L. Rev. 727 (2010).

[208] CBD, *supra* note 1. An International Treaty on Plant Genetic Resources for Food and Agriculture, which aims to ensure global food security through protecting the world's most important agricultural plant species, entered into force June 29, 2004. With respect to GM

conservation of biological diversity," (2) "the sustainable use of its compo-nents," and (3) "the fair and equitable sharing of the benefits arising out of the utilization of genetic resources."[209] President Bill Clinton signed the treaty on June 4, 1993, but the US Senate has not ratified it, and hence the US is not bound by its terms nor able to participate as a party in negotiations coming under it.

Under the Convention, in the effort to conserve biological diversity, states parties are to develop their own "national strategies, plans or programs,"[210] including, *inter alia*, dedication of protected areas such as buffer zones to ensure "conservation and sustainable use;"[211] and also to develop measures to recover and rehabilitate threatened species,[212] measures to "facilitate access to genetic resources for environmentally sound uses,"[213] and the transfer of advanced biotechnologies from developed to developing nations.[214]

The CBD provides for a protocol to be negotiated under Article 19 to regulate "the safe transfer, handling and use of any living modified organ-ism resulting from biotechnology that may have adverse effect on the con-servation and sustainable use of biological diversity."[215] The concern is that new, biotechnologically created species may overtake native species, thereby threatening diversity.[216] The CBD calls specifically for the biosafety proto-col to provide for use of an "advance informed agreement" process in the transfer of genetically modified organisms or derivative products between countries.[217]

Although there are several related articles in the Biodiversity Convention that call for the signatories either to share technologies or provide remunera-tion as reparations to a developing country for genetic materials taken out of such country,[218] the one specifically applicable to safety issues is Article 19.[219]

---

agriculture, the treaty aims to protect nonmodified resources from threat from GM tech-nologies, but not to do away with biotechnology.

[209] CBD, *supra* note 1, art. 1.

[210] *Id.* art. 6.

[211] *Id.* art. 8.

[212] *Id.* art 9.

[213] *Id.* art. 15.

[214] *Id.* art. 16.

[215] *Id.* art. 19.3. The procedures concerning protocols to the CBD are contained in Articles 23, and 29.

[216] *See* McCaffrey, *supra* note 8, at 94.

[217] Biosafety Protocol Text, *supra* note 3, art. 10. *See* McCaffrey, *supra* note 8, at 95–96.

[218] For example, Articles 16, 20, 21 of the CBD, *supra* note 1.

[219] It should also be mentioned that Articles 19, ¶¶ (1) and (2), of the CBD, *id.*, address the participation of the developing countries in biotechnological research and access to such countries "on a fair and equitable basis" to the "benefits arising from biotechnologies based upon genetic resources provided by" them. These, however, will not be discussed here. The issue of intellectual property rights in genetic materials and the equitable sharing of these was a central concern in a UN Food and Agriculture Organization (FARO) online survey as a "factor considered of direct importance for the appropriateness of biotechnologies in

The debate centered on whether biotechnology as a process should be regulated. The US objected to the proposed regulation of biotechnology, contending that as a process it was not a threat to biological diversity. Article 19(4), as a compromise, obligates each party

> directly or by requiring any natural or legal person under its jurisdiction...[to] provide any available information about the use and safety regulations required by that Contracting Party in handling such organisms, as well as any available information on the potential adverse impact of the specific organisms concerned to the Contracting Party into which those organisms are to be introduced.

In addition, Article 19(3) calls upon the parties to consider the need for and modalities of a protocol setting out appropriate procedures, including, in particular, advanced informed agreement, in the field of the safe transfer, handling, and use of any living modified organism resulting from biotechnology that may have adverse effect on the conservation and sustainable use of biological diversity.

Regarding the introduction of living modified organisms, the Convention obligates each party, as far as possible and appropriate, to

> [e]stablish or maintain means to regulate, manage or control the risks associated with the use and release of living modified organisms resulting from biotechnology which are likely to have adverse environmental impacts that could affect the conservation and sustainable use of biological diversity, taking also into account the risks to human health.[220]

The US, however, did not sign the Convention, contending that it was "seriously flawed in a number of important aspects."[221] The US found "particularly unsatisfactory the text's treatment of...technology transfer and biotechnology."[222]

As to Agenda 21, its Chapter 16, entitled "Environmentally Sound Management of Biotechnology," states Agenda 21's goal as to foster international principles for the environmental management of biotechnology and to promote sustainable applications of biotechnology.[223] Among other chapters, Chapter 14 provides for the sharing of research and plant genetic resources

---

developing countries.... The fact that a small number of powerful [multinational corporations] from developed countries had built up extensive patent portfolios meant that there was often a strong socio-political aspect to the discussion." Report of the first six e-mail conferences of the FAO Electronic Forum on Biotechnology in Food and Agriculture, 2.2.1, FAO, Rome 2001, http://www.fao.org/waicent/search/default.asp.

[220] *Id.* art. 8(g).

[221] Declaration of the United States of America, attached to the Nairobi Final Act, *reprinted in* 31 I.L.M. 842, 848, ¶ 3 (1993).

[222] *Id.* ¶ 4.

[223] *See* Agenda 21, U.N. Doc. A/CONF.151/26/Rev.1 (Vol. I), ch. 16, at 218 (1993). The final program areas in biotechnology include establishing enabling mechanisms for the development of and the environmentally sound application of biotechnology. *Id.*

among nations,[224] Chapter 15 aims at improving the conservation of biological diversity and supporting the Biodiversity Treaty,[225] and Chapter 19
addresses the issue of risk management of toxic chemicals and may also apply
to certain biopesticides and other hazardous products of biotechnology.[226]

It was pursuant to the Article 19(3) mandate of the CBD that the discussions on the drafting of a Protocol began as a complementary agreement to
the CBD. Between July 1996 and February 1999 the ad hoc working group
on biosafety held six meetings.[227] The working group was made up of representatives of the parties, broken into five major interest blocs:[228] (1) the EU
was motivated by public outrage over scandals such as "mad cow" disease
to press for strong controls on GM food products and GMOs used in feed,
food, or food processing;[229] (2) the Miami Group, the major GMO exporting countries, led by Canada and made up of Argentina, Australia, Chile,
and Uruguay, with the US participating as a nonparty observer, albeit an
especially powerful one;[230] (3) the Like-Minded Group, a developing country negotiating coalition supporting a strong protocol with comprehensive
regulations;[231] (4) the Compromise Group, a diverse group of countries,
including some with high levels of biodiversity and vulnerability and some
with advanced biotech industries, with Switzerland and Norway at the head,
sought primarily to reach compromises between the competing parties;[232]
and (5) the Central and Eastern Europe (CEE) countries, which negotiated
from a moderate position, frequently in line with the EU or the Like-Minded
Group, and comprising most of the developed countries but for those in the
Miami Group.[233]

The developing countries' Like-Minded Group, the largest coalition, supported strict regulations on the trade of GMOs because of the perception of

---

[224] *Id.* ch. 14.57(d), at 195: "To take appropriate measures for the fair and equitable sharing
of benefits and results of research and development in plant breeding between sources and
users of plant genetic resources."

[225] *Id.* ch. 15, at 210.

[226] *Id.* ch. 19, at 315.

[227] UNEP, Convention on Biological Diversity, Conference of the Parties to the Convention
on Biological Diversity, "Draft Report of the Extraordinary Meeting of the Conference of
the Parties for the Adoption of the Protocol on Biosafety to the Convention on Biological
Diversity," U.N. Doc. UNEP/CBD/ExCOP/1/L.2/Rev. 1, ¶ 28, Feb. 23, 1999 [hereinafter
Cartagena Report].

[228] *See* International Institute for Sustainable Development, Report of the Sixth Session of the
Open-Ended Ad Hoc Working Group on Biosafety and the First Extraordinary Session of
the UN Convention on Biological Diversity of the Parties, February 14–23, 1999 (Earth
Negot. Bull. No. 117 Feb. 26, 1999).

[229] *See id.*

[230] *See id.*

[231] *See id.*

[232] *See id.*

[233] *See id.*

their risk to the environment and human health. The group was concerned that developing countries, as they are unequal in technological capacity, needed the protection of a strong protocol to reflect socioeconomic inequalities and equalization of competition between its members and the industrialized nations. The Miami Group's goal was the least restrictive possible protocol, in order to protect its members' highly profitable biotechnology industries. The group sought free trade of GMO products and thus opposed extensive procedures or bureaucratic requirements, as well as environmental policies that could disguise protectionist trade barriers.[234] The European Union,[235] the Miami Group,[236] and the Like-Minded Group[237] all presented proposals to the meetings, held in Cartagena, Colombia, in February 1999. These meetings, however, did not result in a consensus and were adjourned in an impasse,[238] to be concluded at the next meeting in Montreal.[239]

The period between the Cartagena meeting and the resumed session in Montreal provided members with an opportunity to continue informal discussions. Although there was concern that the Montreal negotiations might also collapse, meeting a fate similar to that of the Cartagena session, the parties did reach an agreement, to the surprise even of many of the negotiators.[240] As The Economist reported, while the Cartagena session had failed because of the opposition of the Miami Group, "the softening-up process that has occurred during the past eleven months – the consumer and producer revolt, and the vacillation about the technology by the purveyors themselves – seems to have made these countries more amenable to a deal."[241]

13.5.2   *Content and Analysis*

The Biosafety Protocol reflects the commitment of the international community to protect biodiversity from the potential risks caused by modern biotechnology in the form of living modified organisms (LMOs), or in common parlance, genetically modified organisms (GMOs). Thus it seeks to provide for safety in biotechnology and is, indeed, an historic attempt to reconcile economic and trade policies with environmental concerns. It incorporates the precautionary principle in the process of decision making

---

[234] *See id.*
[235] *See id.* Annex II.
[236] *See id.* Annex III.
[237] *See id.* Annex IV.
[238] *See id.* ¶ 22.
[239] For the contents of the Draft Protocol on Biosafety, *see id.* Annex V.
[240] *See* Edward Alden, *Greens and Free-Traders Join to Cheer GM Crop Deal*, Fin. Times (London), Jan. 31, 2000, at 11; John Burgess, *Trade Rules Set on Food Genetics; Compromise Gained on Labeling Issue*, Wash. Post, Jan. 30, 2000, at A1.
[241] *A Conventional Argument*, The Economist (London), Jan. 29, 2000.

and underscores the need to enhance capacity building in developing states in biotechnology safety.

The Protocol establishes that strict "Advance Informed Agreement" procedures be applied to GMOs, including seeds, plants, live fish and other organisms, that are to be intentionally introduced into the environment. The exporter in these cases is required to provide detailed information to each importing country in advance of the first shipment, and the importer must then authorize the shipment. This procedure is designed to ensure that recipient countries have both the opportunity and the capacity to assess risks pertaining to GMOs, the products of modern technology, before they agree to their import.[242]

However, this does not apply to the intentional transboundary movement of GMOs if they are in transit or destined for contained use[243] or are "not likely to have adverse effects on the conservation and sustainable use of biological diversity, taking also into account risks to human health."[244] The procedure calls for a party deciding to place on the market a GMO commodity "that may be subject to a transboundary movement for direct use as food or feed, or for processing," to inform the parties through the Biosafety Clearinghouse,[245] established under the Protocol to:

(a) Facilitate the exchange of scientific, technical, environmental and legal information on, and experience with, living modified organisms; and
(b) Assist parties to implement the Protocol, taking into account the special needs of developing country Parties, in particular the least developed and small island developing States among them, and countries with economies in transition as well as countries that are centres of origin and centres of genetic diversity.[246]

Another contentious issue on which a compromise was eventually reached was the labeling of any commodity shipment containing GMOs. The European Union and developing countries sought a clear labeling by exporters of any shipment of commodities containing GMOs. To illustrate, at the Cartagena meeting, the European Union submitted its proposal under which an exporter would be required to clearly indicate as GMOs those commodities "intended for direct use as food, feed or processing."[247] The United States and other exporting countries claimed that such labeling would be impossible

---

[242] *See* Biodiversity Protocol, *supra* note 3, arts. 7–16, 25–26.
[243] *Id.* art. 6.
[244] *Id.* art. 7(4).
[245] *Id.* art. 11(1); Annex II (information required to be given under Article 11).
[246] *Id.* art. 20(1).
[247] Cartagena Report, *supra* note 227, Annex II, ¶ 2(2)(a).

for bulk commodity shipments where grain is mixed from many different sources.[248] As it stands, Article 18, paragraph 2(a) now reads:

> Each Party shall take measures to require that documentation accompanying:
>
> a) Living modified organisms that are intended for direct use for food or feed, or for processing, clearly identifies that they "may contain" living modified organisms and are not intended for intentional introduction into the environment, as well as a contact point for further information. The Conference of the Parties serving as the meeting of the Parties to this Protocol shall take a decision on the detailed requirements for this purpose, including specification of their identity and any unique identification, no later than two years after the date of entry into force of this Protocol.[249]

At the first meeting of the Conference of the Parties of the Biodiversity Convention on Biodiversity serving as the Meeting of the Parties to the Protocol on Biosafety (COP-1), it was decided that labels must state that the shipment carries GMOs and that it must identify the organism, provide handling and storage requirements, and also provide a contact for further information.[250] Subsequently, at the COP-3 in 2006, requirements were imposed for GMOs intended for use as food, feed, or for processing.[251] In October 2010 it was decided to use online means to gather and disseminate information necessary for the control of GMOs.[252]

There is no specific identification required of the type or nature of GMOs, and there is a two-year period following the Protocol's ratification by 50 states when it will enter into force,[253] before any further action can be taken regarding the commodities. The Protocol entered into force on September 11, 2003, after receiving its 50th ratification. As of May 7, 2012, 163 states had ratified it.[254]

---

[248] *See* Alden, *supra* note 238.

[249] Biosafety Protocol Text, *supra* note 3, art. 18(2)(a).

[250] Convention on Biological Diversity, Report of the First Meeting of the Conference of the Parties Serving as the Meeting of the Parties to the Protocol on Biosafety 88–89 (2004) [hereinafter Biosafety COP-1].

[251] Convention on Biological Diversity, Report of the Third Meeting of the Conference of the Parties to the Convention on Biological Diversity Serving as the Meeting of the Parties to the Cartagena Protocol on Biosafety, 60–61 (2006).

[252] Fifth Meeting of the Conference of the Parties to the Convention on Biological Diversity Serving as the Meeting of the Parties to the Cartagena Protocol on Biosafety, BS-V/9 (2010).

[253] *Id.* art. 37.

[254] Convention on Biological Diversity, Parties to the Protocol and signature and ratification of the Supplementary Protocol, http://bch.cbd.int/protocol/parties/.

Article 7 of the Protocol exempts LMOs "intended for direct use as food or feed, or for processing" from the advance informed agreement procedure.[255] States are to develop their own national regimes.[256]

Another contentious issue was inclusion of the precautionary principle, which had been embodied as Principle 15 in the Rio Declaration on Environment and Development[257] at the 1992 Earth Summit. At Cartagena, the Miami Group had taken the position that the Biosafety Protocol should make simple reference to the precautionary approach – rather than stating in its objective that it is in accordance with the precautionary approach[258] – and that any reference to it should be deleted from the decision procedure.[259] The Miami Group was unsuccessful in this attempt. The Biosafety Protocol reaffirms the precautionary approach in its preamble and retains the language, "In accordance with the precautionary approach contained in Principle 15 of the Rio Declaration... the objective of this Protocol is...."[260] Furthermore, the language contained in the decision procedure is unequivocal:

> Lack of scientific certainty due to insufficient relevant scientific information and knowledge regarding the extent of the potential adverse effects of a living modified organism on the conservation and sustainable use of biological diversity in the Party of import, taking also into account risks to human health, shall not prevent that Party from taking a decision, as appropriate, with regard to the import of the living modified organism in question..., in order to avoid or minimize such potential adverse effects.[261]

The same language is also used pertaining to the procedure for GMOs intended for direct use as food or feed, or for processing.[262]

Finally, the question of the relationship between the Biosafety Protocol and the WTO was resolved by noting in the preamble the understanding that the Protocol would not be subordinate "to other international agreements," which meant primarily in this context the WTO. The point of contention was that under WTO trade rules it is not the precautionary approach but certain scientific evidence that determines if an importing country could block the shipment of a GMO. To illustrate the applicable law, the SPS Agreement requires that measures undertaken by an importing country and designed to protect human, animal or plant life must have a scientifically supported

---

[255] Biosafety Protocol Text, *supra* note 3, art. 7(2).
[256] *See id.* arts. 10–16, 25–26.
[257] Rio Declaration, *supra* note 54, Annex I, at 3.
[258] Cartagena Report, *supra* note 227, Annex III, ¶ 4(a).
[259] *Id.* ¶ 4(b).
[260] Biosafety Protocol Text, *supra* note 3, art. 1.
[261] *Id.* art. 10(6). *See also id.* arts. 15 and 26(1).
[262] *Id.* art. 11(8).

and verifiable basis.[263] At the WTO meeting in Seattle in the fall of 1999, no decision could be reached about the regulation of biotechnology under the WTO processes.[264]

The Biosafety Protocol provides for risk assessment[265] and risk management.[266] The Biosafety Clearinghouse is designed to assist parties in implementing the Protocol, with special attention to the needs of developing countries.[267] Special provisions address capacity-building of developing countries, including appropriate scientific and technical training; risk assessment and risk management for biosafety; and the enhancement of technological and institutional capacities in biosafety.[268] The importing country may make its decision by taking into account "socio-economic considerations arising from the impact of living modified organisms on the conservation and sustainable use of biological diversity, especially with regard to the value of biological diversity to indigenous and local communities."[269] As to liability and redress for damage resulting from transboundary movements of LMOs, the Protocol postponed any decision to the first meeting of the Conference of the Parties.[270] At that meeting a binding regime was established.[271] The Protocol does not allow any reservations.[272] In 2010 a supplementary Protocol on Liability and Redress was adopted which authorizes countries to use their domestic laws to seek redress against states for damages.[273]

13.5.3   *Appraisal*

As the first treaty to recognize both the potential and the problems of GMOs, the Biosafety Protocol is a major achievement. However, time is a large factor weighing heavily against the ecological integrity of the planet as GMOs are being released into the environment every day.

---

[263] SPS Agreement, *supra* note 68.
[264] On the Seattle meeting, *see, e.g.,* Ved Nanda, *Battle in Seattle,* DENVER POST, Nov. 30, 1999, at 11B.
[265] Biosafety Protocol Text, *supra* note 3, art. 15, Annex III.
[266] *Id.* art. 16.
[267] *Id.* art. 20(b).
[268] *Id.* art. 22.
[269] *Id.* art. 26.
[270] *Id.* art. 27. The Conference of the Parties is to serve as the meeting of the Parties to the Biosafety Protocol. Art. 29.
[271] Biosafety COP-1, at 104–105.
[272] Biosafety Protocol Text, *supra* note 3, art. 38.
[273] Ngoia-Kuala Lumpur Supplementary Protocol on Liability and Redress (2010), BS-V/11, art. 3.

Chapter Fourteen

International Trade and the Environment

14.0   *Introduction*

Champions of the growth and liberalization of international trade and those equally passionate about the environment have traditionally carved separate paths, finding little in common. For proponents of liberalizing international trade, focus on the environment meant a potential adverse impact on world trade. Environmentalists, on the other hand, generally perceived the liberalization, growth, and integration of world trade as a threat to the environment.[1] The substantive law of the General Agreement on Tariffs and Trade (GATT) always opted for free trade, and GATT panels never considered applying any law or international agreement not contained in GATT or its "covered agreements," thus excluding international environmental law. However, as Klaus Töpfer, former Executive Director of the UN Environment Programme, has aptly stated, "The need today is to ensure that trade and environment policies are mutually supportive."[2]

The argument that increased trade leads to greater wealth, thus allowing a state to undertake environmentally protective measures and resulting in a win-win situation, is attractive.[3] Equally promising are the assertions that,

---

[1] *See generally* T. J. Schoenbaum, *Free International Trade and Protection of the Environment: Irreconcilable Conflict?* 86 Am. J. Int'l L. 700 (1992); G. Feketekuty, *The Link Between Trade and Environmental Policy*, 2 Minn. J. Global Trade 171 (1993); Michael J. Ferrantino, *International Trade, Environmental Quality and Public Policy*, 20 The World Econ., Iss. 1, at 43 (1997); David Vogel, *The Environment and International Trade*, 12 J. Pol. Hist., Iss. 1, at 1 (2000); Jeffrey Frankel, *Global Environmental Policy and Global Trade Policy*, Discussion Paper 2008-14, Cambridge, Mass. Harv. Proj. on Int'l Climate Agreements, October 2008.

[2] United Nations Environment Programme (UNEP) and International Institute for Sustainable Development (IISD), Environment and Trade – A Handbook, at v (2000) [hereinafter Environment & Trade].

[3] *See id.* at 4 (the trade perspective: "Trade can actually be good for the environment, since it creates wealth that can be used for environmental improvement, and the efficiency gains

since trade agreements involve many countries working together for a common interest, these agreements present convenient fora in which to discuss other common interests\such as the environment,[4] and the notion that liberalized trade fosters "common standards for environmental protection,"[5] which all states must meet. On the other hand, the environmental perspective, simply stated, is: "Trade means more goods produced and thus in many cases more environmental damage. The wealth created by trade will not necessarily result in environmental improvements."[6]

On the linkages between trade and the environment, Lester Brown of the Worldwatch Institute has noted, "Little progress has been made in integrating environmental considerations into economic policy. There is a need to reverse traditional roles in policy development, so ecologists design projects before economists decide on their feasibility."[7] In any event, the full benefits that liberalized trade could offer toward increased human well-being cannot be achieved without close integration of trade and environmental policies, for "[i]t is possible, but by no means automatic, that trade and environmental policies should support each other in achieving their objectives."[8]

This chapter will examine the current status of key environmental protection efforts in the context of international trade. The first section discusses the contribution of the 1992 UN Conference on Environment and Development (UNCED), followed in the second section by an examination of environmental efforts under the GATT and World Trade Organization (WTO). A review of the North American Free Trade Agreement (NAFTA) and its Side Agreement on the Environment constitutes the third section, followed by the concluding section.

---

from trade can mean fewer resources used and less waste produced."); S. Charnovitz, *The Environment vs. Trade Rules: Defogging the Debate*, 23 Envtl. L. 475 (1993). A study by the Organization for Economic Cooperation and Development (OECD) released in May 1994 concluded that the effects of trade on the environment are not substantial, although it did add that the positive effects of trade liberalization on the environment "should be 'significant.'" (*Direct Effects of Trade on Environment Generally Small, OECD Report Maintains*, Int'l Env't Daily (BNA), June 8, 1994.) Subsequently, in its 1998 study, "Open Markets Matter: The Benefits of Trade and Investment Liberalization," OECD stated: "But the evidence shows that trade and investment liberalization, by promoting a more efficient use of resources and sustaining growth, can make a vital contribution towards creating the conditions necessary for environmental improvement. There is a positive link between countries' environmental performance and rising per capita income levels, security of property rights and administrative efficiency." OECD Policy Brief No. 6 – 1998.

[4] *See* Charnovitz, *supra* note 3, at 576.

[5] Schoenbaum, *supra* note 1, at 702.

[6] Environment & Trade, *supra* note 2, at 4.

[7] Commission for Environmental Cooperation of North America (Cec), The Environmental Effects of Free Trade 3 (2002).

[8] Environment & Trade, *supra* note 2, at vii.

14.1   *The 1992 United Nations Conference on Environment and Development – Agenda 21*

The purpose of the 1992 UN Conference on Environment and Development (UNCED or Rio)[9] (*see* Chapter 4) was to revisit the environmental issues raised at the 1972 Stockholm Conference and provide a better linkage of environmental and development issues. One commentator observed that UNCED "may mark the eruption of vastly complex issues of environmental management and sustainability into every nook and cranny of international economic relations."[10] The establishment of the Commission on Sustainable Development (CSD) and, ten years later, the convening of the World Summit on Sustainable Development (WSSD or Brundtland Commission) in Johannesburg, South Africa, attest to the validity of the observation (*see* Chapter 4). UNCED did reach its goal, at least in part, by establishing "irrevocably the connection between environmental protection and economic growth."[11] However, critics may argue that it did not focus enough on that nexus.

With respect to international trade, UNCED adopted Agenda 21,[12] which calls for making trade and environment mutually supportive. It states:

> An open, multilateral trading system makes possible a more efficient allocation and use of resources and thereby contributes to an increase in production and incomes and to lessening demands on the environment. It thus provides additional resources needed for economic growth and development and improved environmental protection. A sound environment, on the other hand, provides the ecological and other resources needed to sustain growth and underpin a continuing expansion of trade. An open, multilateral trading system, supported by the adoption of sound environmental policies, would have a positive impact on the environment and contribute to sustainable development.[13]

Agenda 21 cautions that trade restrictions should address the "root causes of environmental degradations so as not to result in unjustified restrictions on trade,"[14] and should be implemented with care. This responds to the concern that a state may utilize an environmental trade restriction as a protectionist measure. The challenge, therefore, is to ensure that trade and environmental

---

[9] *See generally* D. Esty, *Beyond Rio: Trade and the Environment*, 23 ENVTL. L. 3–87 (1993); P. H. Sand, *UNCED and the Development of International Environmental Law*, C795 ALI-ABA 747 (1993).

[10] K. von Moltke, *The Last Round: The General Agreement on Tariffs and Trade in Light of the Earth Summit*, 23 ENVTL. L. 519, 520 (1993).

[11] Un Esty, *supra* note 9, at 388.

[12] *Ágenda 21, Report of the United Nations Conference on Environment and Development*, Vol. 1, Annex II, at 9, U.N. Doc. A/CONF.151/26/Rev.1 (1993).

[13] *Id.* § 2.19.

[14] *Id.* § 2.20.

policies complement each other, so they can advance the goal of sustainable development. Agenda 21 also calls on GATT/WTO to "develop more precision, where necessary, and clarify the relationship between GATT provisions and some of the multilateral measures adopted in the environment area,"[15] and to "ensure that environmental policies provide the appropriate legal and institutional framework to respond to new needs for the protection of the environment that may result from changes in production and trade specialization."[16]

Following the Rio Summit, UNEP has been collaborating with WTO and UNCTAD on trade and environmental issues, with a view to ensuring that trade and environmental policies become mutually supportive.[17]

14.2   *General Agreement on Tariffs and Trade and the World Trade Organization*

This section will first review the trade tools generally used for the protection of the environment by states, and will then examine them in the context of the GATT[18] and its implementing body, the WTO.[19]

---

[15] *Id.* § 2.22(2).

[16] *Id.* § 2.22(8).

[17] UNEP, Report of the Governing Council, 21st Sess. (5–9 Feb. 2001), 56 GAOR Supp. 25, decision 21/14, U.N. Doc. A/56/25 (2001).

[18] General Agreement on Tariffs and Trade, Oct. 30, 1947, T.I.A.S. 170, 55 U.N.T.S. 194 [hereinafter GATT]. *See generally* Charnovitz, *supra* note 3; Schoenbaum, *supra* note 1; S. Spracker & D. Lundsgaard, *Dolphins and Tuna: Renewed Attention on the Future of Free Trade and Protection of the Environment*, 18 Colum. J. Envtl. L. 385 (1993); D. Ross, *Making GATT Dolphin-Safe: Trade and the Environment*, 2 Duke J. Comp. & Int'l L. 345 (1992); F. L. Kirgis, Jr., *Environment and Trade Measures After the Tuna/Dolphin Decision*, 49 Wash. & Lee L. Rev. 1221 (1992); M. Smith, *GATT, Trade, and the Environment*, 23 Envtl. L. 533 (1993); G. K. Beacham, *International Trade and the Environment: Implications of the General Agreement on Tariffs and Trade for the Future of Environmental Protection Efforts*, 3 Colo. J. Int'l Envtl. L. & Pol'y 655 (1992); J. McDonald, *Greening the GATT: Harmonizing Free Trade and Environmental Protection in the New World Order*, 23 Envtl. L. 397 (1993); S. Charnovitz, *Environmentalism Confronts GATT Rules*, 27 J. World Trade 37 (1993); von Moltke, *supra* note 10; U. Kettlewell, *GATT – Will Liberalized Trade Aid Global Environmental Protection?*, 21 Denv. J. Int'l L. & Pol'y 55 (1992); and R. F. Housman & D. J. Zaelke, *Making Trade and Environmental Policies Mutually Reinforcing: Forging Competitive Sustainability*, 23 Envtl. L. 545 (1993).

[19] Final Act Embodying the Results of the Uruguay Round of Multilateral Trade Negotiations, opened for signature Apr. 15, 1994, 33 I.L.M. 1125 (1994) (entered into force Jan. 1, 1995) [hereinafter WTO].

14.2.1   *Environmental Trade Measures*

There are several types of environmental trade measures (ETMs) available to a state, including taxes and tariffs, product and process standards, subsidies, sanctions, and import and export prohibitions.[20] These may be used by states, usually in the form of restricting imports and/or exports, in order to protect domestic resources, the state's environment, and public health and safety. A second purpose that ETMs can serve is to provide "a policy [punishment] tool to enforce environmental standards in international agreements,"[21] as in the Convention on International Trade in Endangered Species (CITES) or the Montreal Protocol to protect the ozone layer. Thirdly, a state might want to impose ETMs in order to address the issues arising out of another state's less restrictive environmental controls.

However, controversy surrounds the potential use of ETMs as protectionist measures. For example, some believe that the European Community's 1989 ban on hormone-treated beef squarely fit that description,[22] as there was debate over whether there was adequate scientific proof that hormone treated beef was a health risk, and its ban favored untreated EU beef. Without scientific data supporting the imposition of an ETM, a state is likely to face considerable international skepticism and scrutiny.

The critical question for a state is whether its ETMs potentially violate GATT. GATT contains three important provisions which usually prohibit ETMs[23] – the Most-Favored-Nation (MFN) principle, the National Treatment principle, and the general ban on quantitative restrictions. To illustrate,

---

[20] *See generally* Charnovitz, *supra* note 3.

[21] *See* Schoenbaum, *supra* note 1, at 703.

[22] *See* Smith, *supra* note 18, at 536–38.

[23] The MFN principle is stated in Article I(1):

> With respect to customs duties and charges of any kind imposed on or in connection with importation or exportation... any advantage, favour, privilege or immunity granted by any contracting party to any product originating in or destined for any other country shall be accorded immediately and unconditionally to the like product originating in or destined for the territories of all other contracting parties....

The National Treatment Principle, contained in Article III(4), provides that:

> The products of the territory of any contracting party imported into the territory of any other contracting party shall be accorded treatment no less favourable than that accorded to like products of national origin in respect of all laws, regulations and requirements affecting their internal sale, offering for sale, purchase, transportation, distribution or use....

The general ban on quantitative restrictions, addressed in Article XI(1), mandates:

> No prohibitions or restrictions other than duties, taxes or other charges, whether made effective through quotas, import or export licenses or other measures, shall be instituted or maintained by any contracting party on the importation of any product of the territory of any other contracting party or on the exportation or sale for export of any product destined for the territory of any other contracting party.

taxes and tariffs imposed by one contracting party against another will violate the MFN. Product standards may also violate the MFN, and may violate the National Treatment principle as well. For a product standard to be in compliance with GATT, it must apply equally to like imported and domestic goods from all contracting parties and its purpose must be other than protectionism. State sanctions against a specific country will usually violate both the MFN and National Treatment principles. Finally, import and export prohibitions will generally violate the Article XI ban on quantitative restrictions. Preceding a discussion of selected decisions under both GATT and WTO, which follows, it is worth noting that the Preamble of the WTO Agreement makes specific reference to environmental protection, reading in pertinent part:

> [R]elations in the field of trade and economic endeavor should be conducted with a view to raising standards of living, ensuring full employment and a large and steadily growing volume of real income and effective demand, and expanding the production of trade in goods and services, while allowing the optimal use of the world's resources in accordance with the objective of sustainable development, seeking both to protect and preserve the environment and to enhance the means for doing so in a manner consistent with the needs and concerns at different levels of economic development....[24]

This is in contrast with the Preamble of the predecessor GATT of 1947, where the focus was on ensuring full employment, growing of real income, and developing the full use of the resources of the world.[25]

14.2.2   *GATT Panel Decisions Before the Establishment of the WTO*

For a better understanding of how GATT applies to ETMs, it is instructive to look at several panel decisions handed down prior to the establishment of the WTO in 1995: the 1983 *Canada – US Tuna* case;[26] the *Canada – Herring and Salmon* case;[27] the *Thailand – Cigarettes* case;[28] and the *US – Tuna-Dolphin* cases.[29] All of these cases involved decisions handed down by a GATT

---

[24] WTO, *supra* note 19, Preamble.

[25] GATT, *supra* note 18, Preamble.

[26] *United States – Prohibition of Imports of Tuna and Tuna Products from Canada*, GATT, BISD, 29th Supp. 91 (1983) [hereinafter *1983 Canada – US Tuna* case].

[27] *Canada – Unprocessed Salmon and Herring*, GATT, BISD, 35th Supp. 98 (1989) [hereinafter *Canada – Herring and Salmon* case].

[28] *Thailand – Restrictions on Importation of and Internal Taxes on Cigarettes*, GATT, BISD, 37th Supp. 200 (1990) [hereinafter *Thailand – Cigarettes* case].

[29] *United States – Restrictions on Imports of Tuna*, Report of the GATT Panel, Aug. 16, 1991, GATT doc. DS 21/R, *reprinted at* 30 I.L.M. 1594 (1991) [hereinafter Tuna-Dolphin I]; United States – Restrictions on Imports of Tuna, June 16, 1994, Report of the GATT Panel, GATT doc. DS 29/R, *reprinted at* 33 I.L.M. 842 (1994) [hereinafter *Tuna-Dolphin II*].

adjudication panel. Under GATT, dispute resolution involves a complaint filed by one contracting party. A panel is then convened and, after it issues its decision, the GATT Council's adoption of the decision makes it official. All of these cases involved an interpretation of GATT Article XX:

> Subject to the requirement that such measures are not applied in a manner which would constitute a means of arbitrary or unjustifiable discrimination between countries where the same conditions prevail, or a disguised restriction in international trade, nothing in this Agreement shall be construed to prevent the adoption or enforcement by any contracting party of measures:
>
> (b) necessary to protect human, animal or plant life or health;
>
> ....
>
> (g) relating to the conservation of exhaustible natural resources if such measures are made effective in conjunction with restrictions on domestic production or consumption.

14.2.2.1   *The 1983* Canada – US Tuna *Case*

The 1983 *Canada – US Tuna* case involved an import prohibition on the part of the US of all tuna and tuna products from Canada. Canada considered the sea within 200 nautical miles of its coast to be under its fisheries jurisdiction, as opposed to the 12 miles recognized by the US. Thus, US fishing vessels were allowed, under US law, to fish outside 12 miles and within 200 miles of Canada's coast. Canada seized 19 US vessels fishing for albacore tuna, and arrested many of the fishermen who were US nationals. Consequently, the US prohibited imports of all tuna and tuna products from Canada, pursuant to the Fishery Conservation and Management Act of 1976.[30] Section 205 of the Act mandates the Secretary of State to determine whether such seizure has occurred and, if so, to certify to the Secretary of the Treasury, who, in turn, must immediately "prohibit the importation into the [US] of all fish and fish products from the fishery involved."[31] Following this procedure, the US banned the import of the Canadian fish and fish products.

After unsuccessful consultations between Canada and the US, as required under GATT, Canada filed a complaint claiming that the US ban violated GATT and impaired benefits accruing to Canada under GATT.[32] Canada argued that the US import prohibition on Canadian tuna and tuna products violated GATT Articles XI:1 (reprinted above), in that the US utilized a prohibition "other than duties, taxes or other charges," Article I (MFN)

---

[30] 16 U.S.C. § 1825.

[31] *Id.* § 205.

[32] *1983 Canada – US Tuna case, supra* note 26, ¶ 1.1. Although the parties reached agreement during the Panel's consideration of the matter, Canada requested the case be fully decided, as prohibitions remained a possibility under similar circumstances in the future.

(reprinted above), and Article XIII,[33] as the prohibition was discriminatory. The US defended its actions under Article XX(g) (above).

The GATT Panel decided that the US import prohibition was, indeed, a "prohibition" under Article XI:1,[34] and held that none of the exceptions to that article[35] applied, since the prohibition included species – such as albacore – whose capture had not been restricted domestically.[36] Furthermore, the import prohibition had been maintained by the US even after it removed domestic restrictions on catching some species of tuna, such as Pacific yellowfin.[37] The GATT Panel also decided that Article X1:2(c) did not apply, since it only applied to "restrictions" instead of "prohibitions or restrictions," as in XI:2(a) and (b).[38]

As for the applicability of Article XX(g), the Panel did agree with the US argument that the import prohibition was not necessarily arbitrarily or unjustifiably discriminatory, citing similar US import prohibitions levied against imports from Costa Rica, Ecuador, Mexico, and Peru.[39] Furthermore, considering the small percentage of US tuna imports comprised by Canadian tuna, the Panel also agreed that the import prohibition was not imposed for protectionist measures.

---

[33] Article XIII:1 provides: No prohibition or restriction shall be applied by any contracting party on the importation of any product of the territory of any other contracting party or on the exportation of any product destined for the territory of any other contracting party, unless the importation of the like product of all third countries or the exportation of the like product to all third countries is similarly prohibited or restricted.

[34] *1983 Canada – US Tuna case, supra* note 26, ¶ 4.4.

[35] GATT, *supra* note 18, art. XI:2, enumerates the exceptions:
The provisions of paragraph I of this Article [XI] shall not extend to the following:
   (a) Export prohibitions or restrictions temporarily applied to prevent or relieve critical shortages of foodstuffs or other products essential to the exporting contracting party;
   (b) Import and export prohibitions or restrictions necessary to the application of standards or regulations for the classification, grading or marketing of commodities in international trade;
   (c) Import restrictions on any agricultural or fisheries product, imported in any form, necessary to the enforcement of governmental measures which operate:
      (i) to restrict the quantities of the like domestic product permitted to be marketed or produced...
      (ii) to remove a temporary surplus of the like domestic product...
      (iii) to restrict the quantities permitted to be produced of any animal product the production of which is directly dependent, wholly or mainly, on the imported commodity....

[36] *1983 Canada – US Tuna case, supra* note 26, ¶ 4.6.

[37] *Id.*

[38] *Id.* n. 2.

[39] *Id.* ¶ 4.8.

However, the Panel noted that, while the import prohibition covered all tuna and tuna products from Canada, the US only had correlating domestic restrictions on the catching of some, but not all, species of tuna. Therefore, the panel decided that, as the US import prohibition was not made effective in conjunction with restrictions on domestic production or consumption, as required under Article XX(g),[40] it violated Article XI, was not justified by any of the exceptions, and thus violated GATT.

14.2.2.2 *The* Canada – Herring and Salmon *Case*

The *Canada – Herring and Salmon* case concerned an export prohibition imposed by Canada on certain types of salmon and herring under the authority of the Canadian Fisheries Act of 1970.[41] On February 20, 1987, the US filed a complaint with the GATT, alleging that Canada's export prohibitions violated GATT Article XI[42] and requesting establishment of a panel to resolve the matter. Canada defended its export prohibitions by arguing that the measures were a longstanding part of Canada's conservation regime for the West Coast, and thus were allowed under Article XX(g).[43] Moreover, Canada's strict quality and marketing regulations were operated subject to the export prohibitions.[44] Therefore, Canada contended that they were also justified by the Article XI:2(b) exception that allowed "export prohibitions or restrictions necessary to the application of standards or regulations for the classification, grading or marketing of commodities in international trade."

The Panel decided that Canada's restrictions did violate GATT Article XI:1, because they served to prohibit export of certain products to other contracting parties.[45] Turning to the Article XI:2(b) exception, the Panel noted that Canada not only prohibited fish that did not meet its quality standards from being exported, but also banned from export the unprocessed herring and unprocessed salmon that did meet its quality standards.[46] Consequently, the Panel found that the export restrictions could not be "necessary" for the application of standards, as required under Article XI:2(b).

---

[40] *Id.* ¶¶ 4.10 and 4.12.

[41] The Fisheries Act, Can. Rev. Stat. 1970, C.F-14, Subsection 34(j) (as amended). For the Pacific Commercial Salmon Fishery Regulations, *see* CRC 1978 ch. 823 Canada Gazette, Part II, November 8/78, p. 3900. For the Pacific Herring Fishery Regulations, *see* Canada Gazette, Part II, May 2/84, p. 1693.

[42] *Canada – Herring and Salmon case, supra* note 27, ¶ 3.1.

[43] *Id.* ¶ 3.3.

[44] *Id.* ¶ 3.4.

[45] *Id.* ¶ 4.3.

[46] *Id.* ¶ 4.6.

The Panel then examined the Article XX(g) exception. Under this exception (reprinted above), the wording of XX(g) only necessitates that actions relate to conservation, as opposed to the requirements under some other subparagraphs (e.g., subparagraphs (a) and (b)) that the measures be "necessary" or "essential" to the attainment of the subparagraph's goal. The Panel therefore concluded that, under XX(g), the measure did not have to be necessary or essential to the conservation of exhaustible natural resources.[47] But, noting the preamble of Article XX, the Panel decided that the purpose of XX(g) was not necessarily to widen the scope of restrictions that a state may impose, but rather to allow states to pursue national policies of conservation of exhaustible resources.[48] Consequently, the Panel decided that a trade measure, in order to "relate to" the conservation of an exhaustible resource, must be "primarily aimed at" that conservation.[49] Furthermore, a trade measure had to be "primarily aimed at" rendering domestic production or consumption restrictions effective in order to be deemed "in conjunction with" them under Article XX(g).[50]

In light of Canada's export restrictions under these guidelines, the Panel noted Canada's own claim that the trade measures were not conservation measures in themselves, but merely had an effect on conservation by providing the statistical foundation for the restrictions. In addition, other species for which Canada collected this statistical data were not banned from export. Therefore, the Panel decided that the export prohibitions were not "primarily aimed at" conservation of an exhaustible resource.[51] Since Canada did not limit the purchases of these unprocessed herring and salmon by domestic processors and consumers, the export prohibitions were also not "primarily aimed at" rendering domestic consumption and production restrictions effective.[52] Thus, the Panel concluded that Canada's export prohibitions violated Article XI:1, were not justified by either the Article XI:2(b) or the Article XX(g) exceptions, and were illegal under GATT.[53]

14.2.2.3   *The* Thailand – Cigarettes *Case*

The *Thailand – Cigarettes* case involved import restrictions and internal taxes placed by the government of Thailand on cigarettes.[54] In 1990 the US claimed

---

[47] *Id.*
[48] *Id.*
[49] *Id.*
[50] *Id.* ¶ 4.7.
[51] *Id.*
[52] *Id.* ¶ 5.1.
[53] *Id.*
[54] For a summary of the facts, *see Thailand – Cigarettes case, supra* note 28, ¶¶ 6–11.

that these restrictions and taxes were in violation of GATT and requested that the contracting parties convene a panel in order to resolve the matter.

The Panel concluded that the import restrictions did violate Article XI:1, noting the fact that no import licenses on cigarettes had been granted in ten years.[55] It then held that the Article XI:2(c)(i) exception did not apply.[56] Considering the meaning of "agriculture" and products "imported in any form," as contained in XI:2(c)(i), the Panel decided the product must be in an early stage of processing in order to qualify. And, while tobacco would qualify under this exception, the Panel concluded that cigarettes, having already undergone substantial processing, are not "agriculture" or agricultural products "imported in any form."

Addressing the Article XX(b) exception, the Panel acknowledged that smoking is a serious risk to human health, and that the exception applies to measures designed to reduce smoking. But, it noted, in order for Article XX(b) to apply to a particular restriction, that restriction must be necessary.[57] The Panel, in defining "necessary," looked to a previous Panel decision that had addressed the issue in relation to Article XX(d), which also contained a requirement that a restriction be "necessary." That Panel had stated:

> [A] contracting party cannot justify a measure inconsistent with other GATT provisions as "necessary" in terms of Article XX(d) if an alternative measure which it could reasonably be expected to employ and which is not inconsistent with other GATT provisions is available to it. By the same token, in cases where a measure consistent with other GATT provisions is not reasonably available, a contracting party is bound to use, among the measures reasonably available to it, that which entails the least degree of inconsistency with other GATT provisions.[58]

Since the term "necessary" was used in the same context in both Articles XX(b) and XX(d), the Panel decided to adopt this definition of "necessary" for the application of Article XX(b).[59] Applying this definition of "necessary" to the facts of the case, the Panel held that the import restrictions were not necessary with respect to the goal of improving the quality of cigarettes sold in Thailand.[60] The Panel determined that the other goal – to reduce the quantity of cigarettes sold in Thailand – could also be achieved by alternative measures consistent with GATT that Thailand could reasonably be expected to employ, and hence the import restriction was not necessary under Article

---

[55] *Id.* ¶ 67.

[56] *Id.* ¶¶ 68–70.

[57] *Id.* ¶ 73.

[58] Report of the panel on United States – *Section 337 of the Tariff Act of 1930* (L/6439, ¶ 5.26, adopted on Nov. 7, 1989).

[59] *Thailand – Cigarettes case, supra* note 28, ¶ 74.

[60] *Id.* ¶ 77.

XX(b) and was a violation of GATT.[61] Regarding the internal taxes on ciga-rettes, the Panel decided that, even though Thailand's Tobacco Act, 1966, permitted taxes that would violate Article III:2 (national treatment principle), such possibility did not in itself violate Article III:2.[62]

14.2.2.4   *The* US – Tuna Ban *Case* (Tuna-Dolphin I)

Tuna-Dolphin I[63] involved US import prohibitions on tuna and tuna prod-ucts from certain states pursuant to the Marine Mammal Protection Act of 1972, as revised (MMPA).[64] The MMPA was designed to reduce the inci-dental killing of marine mammals, notably dolphins. In the Eastern Tropical Pacific Ocean (ETP), dolphins regularly swim above schools of tuna. Thus, fishermen look for dolphins, knowing that there will be a school of tuna underneath, and cast their net around the dolphin. This method nets the school of tuna, but also injures or drowns the air-breathing dolphin. The nets used in this method are purse-seine nets, although there are other nets which, if used, would enable the dolphins to escape unharmed.

Designed to prevent the incidental injuring and killing of dolphins through this method of fishing, the MMPA prohibits the "taking" of marine mam-mals without a permit. "Taking" is defined as the "harassment, hunting, capture, killing, or attempt thereof."[65] Sections 103 and 104 of the MMPA prescribe the criteria for the issuance of a permit. With a permit, the holder can incidentally kill or injure no more than 20,500 dolphins annually in the ETP. Prior to the time of the case, only the American Tuna-Boat Association had been granted a permit. Section 101(a)(2) requires the Secretary of the Treasury to "ban the importation of commercial fish or products from fish which have been caught with commercial fishing technology which results in the incidental kill or incidental serious injury of ocean mammals in excess of United States standards." In order to avoid the import ban, a foreign fishing fleet cannot kill more than 125 percent of the number of dolphins killed by the US in the same period.

---

[61] *Id.* ¶¶ 78–81.

[62] *Id.* ¶¶ 84 and 86. The Panel cited an earlier panel's conclusion, Report of the Panel on EEC-Regulation on Imports of Parts and Components (L/6657, ¶ 5.25, adopted on May 16, 1990).

[63] *Tuna-Dolphin I, supra* note 29. This decision was not adopted by the GATT Council, due to an arrangement between the governments of the US and Mexico.

[64] Pub. L. No. 92–522, 86 Stat. 1027 (1972), as amended by Pub. L. No. 100–711, 102 Stat. 4755 (1988) and Pub. L. No. 101–627, at 104 Stat. 4467 (1990).

[65] *Id.*

Under its applicable statutory regime,[66] the US placed import restrictions on yellowfin tuna and tuna products from Mexico, Venezuela, and Vanuatu. On January 25, 1991, Mexico asked the contracting parties to form a panel in order to resolve this matter.[67]

Mexico argued that the import prohibition violated Article XI, as did the possible extension of the prohibition to include all fishery products, under the Pelly Amendment.[68] Furthermore, Mexico argued that the import prohibitions, which were aimed at intermediary nations, were inconsistent with Article XI, as were the Pelly Amendment provisions for those import prohibitions, which allowed for extension of the embargo in order to include all fishery products.[69]

The US, in defense, claimed that the import prohibitions were internal regulations which affected the "internal sale, offering for sale, purchase, transportation, distribution or use"[70] of tuna and tuna products, and were thus consistent with Article III:4.[71] In the event that the import prohibitions were not consistent with Article III, though, the US claimed that they were allowed under the Article XX(b) and XX(g) exceptions.[72]

The Panel first considered whether the import prohibitions were internal regulations under Article III or quantitative restrictions under Article XI. It concluded that, since the import prohibitions applied to the process by which tuna was harvested, as opposed to the tuna itself, they were not internal regulations covered by the Note Ad Article III.[73] Furthermore, even if the import prohibitions did regulate the sale of tuna as a product, they would not meet the requirements of Article III:4, which mandates that the US could not treat Mexican tuna less favorably than it treated domestic tuna,[74] regardless of how the tuna was harvested.

Having concluded that the import prohibitions were quantitative restrictions under Article XI, the Panel considered the exceptions contained in Article XX(b) and (g), which the US claimed should apply. It reviewed the

---

[66] The statutory regime includes the "Pelly Amendment" to the Fishermen's Protective Act of 1967 (22 U.S.C. § 1978(a)) and § 101(a)(2)(c) of the MMPA applicable to intermediary states.

[67] Tuna-Dolphin I, *supra* note 29, ¶ 3.1.

[68] *Id.* ¶ 3.2.

[69] GATT, *supra* note 18, art. III:4.

[70] *Tuna-Dolphin I, supra* note 29, ¶ 3.6(a).

[71] *Id.* ¶ 3.6(b).

[72] *Id.* ¶ 5.14.

[73] *Id.* On the product/process distinction, *see* generally S. Charnovitz, *The Law of "PPMs" in the WTO: Debunking the Myth of Illegality*, 27 YALE J. INT'L L. 59 (2000); R. Howse & D. Regan, *The Product/Process Distinction – An Illusory Basis for Disciplining Unilateralism*, 11 EUR. J. INT'L L. 249 (2000).

[74] *Tuna-Dolphin I, supra* note 29, ¶ 5.15.

drafting history since the text did not cover the situation, and decided that Article XX(b) does not apply to measures taken to protect human, animal, or plant life outside the jurisdiction of the state taking the measure.[75] However, even if Article XX(b) were to operate extrajurisdictionally, the Panel noted, the US import prohibitions were not "necessary,"[76] as the US had not exhausted all GATT-consistent alternatives, such as seeking international agreement on the subject. Furthermore, since the MMPA prohibited foreign fishing fleets from killing 125 percent of an unpredictable number of dolphins (i.e., the number killed by the US fishing fleet during the same time period), it could not be "necessary" to protect the lives or health of dolphins, as was required by Article XX(b).

In light of Article XX(g), the Panel reiterated its reasons for stating that Article XX(b) did not operate extrajurisdictionally, and then concluded that, for the same reasons, Article XX(g) did not operate extrajurisdictionally.[77] Even if it were to operate extrajurisdictionally, the Panel noted, Article XX(g) still required that measures "relate to the conservation of exhaustible natural resources"[78] and determined that the import prohibitions were not primarily aimed at the conservation of dolphins.[79] Consequently, the Panel concluded that the MMPA import prohibitions imposed by the US violated Article XI and were not justified by the exceptions contained in Article XX. The Panel also stated the rule that "a contracting party may not restrict imports of a product merely because it originates in a country with environmental policies different from its own."[80]

The Panel's decision in this case can be criticized on several grounds.[81] For instance, the MMPA is obviously not exercised extraterritorially, since it only considers which tuna can be imported into the US. It does not prohibit any activity outside the US territorial jurisdiction; it is merely a customs restriction. Therefore, the Panel realized that it could not challenge the MMPA import prohibitions for functioning extraterritorially. Consequently, it decided that these restrictions operated "extrajurisdictionally." However, the Panel failed to define "extrajurisdictionally;" presumably, it means that the prohibitions act in such a way as to influence activity outside the jurisdiction of the US. But many customs laws operate in this fashion, such as laws that prohibit the importation of automobiles that fail to meet certain safety and

---

[75] *Id.* ¶¶ 5.26–27.
[76] *Id.* ¶ 5.28.
[77] *Id.* ¶¶ 5.31 and 5.32.
[78] *Id.* ¶ 5.33.
[79] *Id.*
[80] *Id.* ¶ 6.2.
[81] *See* Charnovitz, *supra* note 3.

environmental standards, for these laws certainly affect the activity of automobile manufacturers outside the US.

14.2.2.5   Tuna-Dolphin II

Three years after the decision of the GATT panel on *Tuna-Dolphin I*, another GATT panel decided on the validity of the US action in prohibiting the import of tuna processed in certain European countries because they had not banned the import of tuna from Mexico or other states subject to the direct US embargo under the MPPA.[82] Under the secondary embargo provision of the MPPA, intermediary states exporting tuna to the US must prove that the tuna had not originated from nations which the US had directly targeted for embargo.[83] The European Economic Community (now the European Union) and the Netherlands had complained to the GATT about this secondary embargo, arguing that it did not fall under GATT Article III, which authorizes internal regulations that treat domestic and foreign products alike, that the embargo violated Article XI's prohibition against quantitative restrictions but for tariffs, and that it was not a valid exception under Article XX.

The Panel rejected the extrajurisdictional interpretation regarding the scope of Article XX given by the GATT Panel on *Tuna-Dolphin I*,[84] saying that it "could see no valid reason for supporting the conclusion that the provisions of Article XX(g) apply only to policies related to the conservation of exhaustible natural resources located within the territory of the contracting party invoking the provision."[85] Referring to jurisdictional principles under general international law, the Panel held that "the policy to conserve dolphins in the eastern tropical Pacific Ocean, which the US pursued within its jurisdiction over its nationals and vessels, fell within the range of policies covered by Article II(g)."[86] However, it stated that the exceptions contained in Article XX apply to a state's policy measures to the extent that they are implemented within its jurisdiction to effect a direct conservation or protective outcome.[87]

The Panel's focus was on whether the embargo was "primarily aimed" at conservation, as that is the meaning it gave to the term "related to" conservation, and inquired into whether it was necessary for domestic requirement to be effective.[88] Observing that the US had prohibited tuna imports regardless

---

[82] *Tuna-Dolphin II, supra* note 29.
[83] *See id.* ¶ 2.12.
[84] *See id.* ¶ 5.20. *See generally id.* ¶¶ 5.14–5.20, 5.32.
[85] *Id.* ¶ 5.10.
[86] *Id.* ¶ 5.20.
[87] *Id.* ¶¶ 5.33, 5.39.
[88] *Id.* ¶¶ 5.24–5.27.

of whether or not the particular tuna was harvested in a manner that harmed or could harm dolphins,[89] the Panel found that both the primary embargo as well as the secondary embargo were taken so as to force other countries to change their policies with respect to persons or things within their own jurisdiction," and hence did not fall within the exception of Article XX(g).[90]

The Panel, however, refused to consider the relevance of multilateral environmental agreements, including the Convention on International Trade in Endangered Species (CITES),[91] in interpreting GATT provisions.[92]

14.2.3   WTO Cases

14.2.3.1   *The* Reformulated Gasoline *Case*

The first major case in which US environmental law and policy was challenged after the WTO was established in 1995 arose as Venezuela and Brazil brought a complaint against the US in the *Reformulated Gasoline* case.[93] The pertinent facts were that the US Congress passed the 1990 Clean Air Amendments (CAA)[94] to reduce air pollution, including ozone, by motor vehicle emissions. Four years later, the US Environmental Protection Agency (EPA), which was required under the CAA to promulgate regulations governing gasoline characteristics (i.e., its reformulation) necessary to meet the objective of vehicle emission reductions, published its final rule as mandated.[95]

The CAA divided the country into two parts for the sale of gasoline – the ozone "non-attainment areas," which are heavily polluted with ground-level ozone and where only reformulated gasoline may be sold, and the rest of the country, in which regular or conventional gasoline may be sold, provided that it "remain[ed] as clean as it was in 1990."[96] Under the regulations,

---

[89] *Id.* ¶ 5.23.

[90] *Id.* ¶ 5.24.

[91] Convention on International Trade in Endangered Species of Wild Fauna and Flora, Mar. 3, 1973, 27 U.S.T. 1087, 993 U.N.T.S. 243, *reprinted at* 12 I.L.M. 1085 (1973).

[92] *See Tuna-Dolphin II, supra* note 29, ¶¶ 5.18–5.20. *See generally* J. L. Nissen, *Achieving a Balance Between Trade and the Environment: The Need to Amend the WTO/GATT to Include Multilateral Environmental Agreements*, 28 L. & Pol'y in Int'l Bus. 901 (1996–97).

[93] Panel Report, *United States – Standards for Reformulated and Conventional Gasoline (Treatment of Imported Gasoline and Like Products of National Origin)*, Jan. 29, 1996, doc. WT/DS 2R, *reprinted at* 35 I.L.M. 274 (1996) [hereinafter *Reformulated Gasoline*]. For a detailed discussion of the case, *see* Martin A McCrory & Eric L. Richards, *Clearing the Air: the Clean Air Act, GATT and the WTO' Reformulated Gasoline Decision*, 17 UCLA J. Envtl. L. & Pol'y (1998/1999); Jennifer Schultz, *The Demise of Green Protections, The WTO Decision on the US Gasoline Rule*, 25 Denv. J. Int'l L. & Pol'y 1 (1996).

[94] Air Pollution Control (Clean Air) Act Amendments of 1992, 42 U.S.C. § 7401, *et seq.*

[95] EPA, Regulation of Fuels and Fuel Additives; Standards for Reformulated and Conventional Gasoline, Final Rule, 59 C.F.R. 7716 (1994).

[96] *Reformulated Gasoline, supra* note 93, ¶ 2.4.

different methods of determining baselines for acceptable quality of gasoline were established for domestic refiners and importers of gasoline.[97] Also, for reformulated gasoline, individual and statutory baselines were established; most importers could not use the 1990 baseline due to very stringent conditions for demonstrating the quality of their product.

Venezuela and Brazil requested the Panel to find that the EPA's gasoline rule violated Articles I (MFN treatment) and III (National Treatment) of GATT, was not covered by Article XX exceptions, and was contrary to Article II of the Agreement on Technical Barriers to Trade.[98] The US responded that the gasoline rule was consistent with its obligations under international trade law.[99] As interested third parties, the European Community[100] and Norway[101] made submissions.

In January 1996, the Panel concluded that the baseline establishment methods contained in US regulations were "not consistent with Article III:4 of the General Agreement, and cannot be justified under paragraphs (b), (d) and (g) of Article XX."[102] Thus, it found it unnecessary to determine whether the measure was "made effective in conjunction with restrictions on domestic production or consumption."[103] It also found it unnecessary to determine whether the measure was inconsistent with the Agreement on Technical Barriers to Trade[104] or Article[105] or Article III.[106]

The US appealed the Panel's decision. The Appellate Body (AB), in its first ever ruling,[107] reversed the Panel's analysis as well as its conclusions on the issue whether the measures taken by the US related to the conservation of exhaustible natural resources. The AB interpreted Article XX(g) in context, in light of prior case law, and in light of the "general rule of interpretation" contained in the Vienna Convention on the Law of Treaties.[108] It said that "if such measures are made effective in conjunction

---

[97] *Id.* ¶¶ 2.5–2.13; 40 C.F.R. 80.59, 80.91; 59 Fed. Reg. 7785–7788.

[98] *Reformulated Gasoline, supra* note 93, ¶ 3.1.

[99] *Id.* ¶¶ 3.17–3.84.

[100] *Id.* ¶¶ 4.1–4.8.

[101] *Id.* ¶¶ 4.9–4.11. *Id.* ¶¶ 4.9–4.11.

[102] *Id.* ¶ 8.1. *See generally id.* ¶¶ 6.16–6.43.

[103] *Id.* ¶ 6.41.

[104] *Id.* ¶ 6.43.

[105] *Id.* ¶ 6.19.

[106] *Id.* ¶ 6.17.

[107] Appellate Body Report, *United States – Standard for Reformulated and Conventional Gasoline*, WT/DS2/AB/R, (May 20, 1996) *reprinted at* 35 I.L.M. 603 (1996) [hereinafter *AB on Gasoline Rule*].

[108] Vienna Convention on the Law of Treaties, *opened for signature* May 23, 1969, U.N. Doc. A/CONF. 39/27, 1155 U.N.T.S. 331, art. 31(1) (entered into force Jan. 27, 1980), *reprinted at* 8 I.L.M. 679 (1969) [hereinafter Vienna Convention].

with restrictions on domestic product or consumption" in Article XX(g), that provision should be "appropriately read as a requirement that the measures concerned imposed restrictions, not just in respect of imported gasoline, but also with respect to domestic gasoline. The clause is a requirement of even-handedness in the imposition of restrictions, in the name of conservation, upon the production or consumption of exhaustible natural resources."[109]

It also found that the Panel had erred in not considering the introductory clauses (*chapeau*) of Article XX. Here, the AB found that the US regulations failed to meet the requirements of the chapeau and hence were not justified under Article XX exceptions. Its reasoning was that the US had not explored adequate means, including cooperative agreements with the governments of Venezuela and Brazil, of mitigating the administrative problems relied on as justification by the US for rejecting individual baselines for foreign refiners.[110] Second, the US had omitted "to count the costs for foreign refiners that would result from the imposition of statutory baselines."[111] It added that the US must have foreseen the resulting discrimination, which "was not merely inadvertent or unavoidable."[112] Thus the Appellate Body concluded that, in their application, the baseline establishment rules "constitute 'unjustifiable discrimination' and a 'disguised restriction on international trade.'"[113] Hence, they were not justifiable under Article XX as a whole, although they fell under the terms of Article XX(g).[114] The US government changed its regulation, allowing foreign refiners to apply for and use an individual baseline in order to comply with the WTO decision.[115]

---

[109] *AB on Gasoline Rule, supra* note 107, at 624–25.

[110] *Id.* at 632.

[111] *Id.*

[112] *Id.*

[113] *Id.* at 633.

[114] *Id.* It should be noted that section V of the Appellate Body Report specifically states that at issue was not "the ability of any WTO Member to take measures to control air pollution or, more generally, to protect the environment," and that there is specific acknowledgment about the importance of co-ordinating policies on trade and environment. WTO members have a large measure to autonomy to determine their own policies on the environment (including its relationship with trade), their environmental objectives and the environmental legislation they enact and they implement. So far as concerns the WTO, that autonomy is circumscribed only by the need to respect the requirement of the *General Agreement* and other covered agreements.

[115] Regulation of Fuels and Fuel Additives; Baseline Requirements for Gasoline Produced by Foreign Refiners, 62 Fed. Reg. 45533 (1997). On a challenge to this ruling, the US court upheld the EPA regulation. Warren Corporation v. EPA, 159 F.3d 616 (D.C.Cir. 1998).

14.2.3.2   *The* US – Shrimp-Turtle *Case*

In the *US – Shrimp-Turtle* case,[116] US regulations aimed at protecting endangered sea turtles pursuant to the 1989 US Endangered Species Act provisions were challenged. The applicable law[117] precluded shrimp imports without certification by the President to Congress that the harvesting nation's practices did not pose a threat to sea turtles, or that the foreign government had adopted an appropriate "regulatory program governing the incidental taking of such sea turtles."[118] Subsequently, the Department of State issued guidelines for the certification process.[119] The guidelines required all foreign shrimp operators to use "trap door" devices in nets called Turtle Excluder Devices (TEDs) wherever they harvested shrimp if they were to qualify for such certification.

India, Malaysia, Pakistan, and Thailand complained that the US regulations imposing the shrimp embargo violated the US obligations under Articles I.1 (MFN principle), XI.1 (elimination of quantitative restrictions), and XIII.1 (differential treatment of like products) of the 1994 GATT, and did not qualify as exceptions to Article XX.[120] The US claimed that the shrimp embargo was justifiable as a measure necessary to protect the sea turtle under the Article XX(b) or XX(g) exceptions. The Panel found the US measure not to be consistent with Article XI.1, and could not be justified under Article XX,[121] since it did not satisfy the requirement of the chapeau conditions, and the exceptions in Article XX could be considered only if those conditions were met.

On appeal, the AB found that the US was not entitled to an exception under Article XX. While the US qualified for provisional justification under Article XX(g), it failed to meet the requirements of the chapeau of Article

---

[116] Panel Report, *United States – Import Prohibition of Certain Shrimp and Shrimp Products,* May 15, 1998, doc. WT/DS58/R, *reprinted at* 37 I.L.M. 832 (1998) [hereinafter Shrimp-Turtle Panel]. Among the many comments discussing the case, *see* Howard F. Chang, *Toward a Greener GATT: Environmental Trade Measures and the Shrimp-Turtle Case,* 74 S. Cal. L. Rev. 31 (2000); Robert Howse, *The Appellate Body Rulings in the Shrimp/Turtle Case: A New Legal Baseline for the Trade and Environment Debate,* 27 Colum. J. Envtl. L. 491 (2002); Petros Mavroidis, *Trade and Environment After the Shrimp-Turtle Litigation,* 34 J. World Trade 73 (2000).

[117] Pub. L. No. 101–162, § 609, 103 Stat. 1037 (1990), codified at 16 U.S.C. § 1537.

[118] *Id.* at § 609(b).

[119] Turtles and Shrimp Trawl Fishing Operations Protection: Guidelines, 56 Fed. Reg. 1051 (1991); Revised Guidelines, 58 Fed. Reg. 1915 (1993); 1996 Guidelines, 61 Fed. Reg. 17342 (Apr. 19, 1996).

[120] *Shrimp-Turtle Panel, supra* note 116, ¶¶ 7.13, 7.22, 7.62, 8.1.

[121] *Id.* ¶ 8.1.

XX.[122] However, it arrived at this conclusion after reversing the Panel's finding that it could not accept nonrequested submissions from nongovernmental organizations,[123] and also reversing the finding that the US shrimp embargo was "not within the scope of measures permitted under the chapeau of Article XX."[124] It should be noted that the Panel did not reject the nonrequested information,[125] but stated that any party could "put forward these documents, or parts of them, as part of their own submissions to the panel,"[126] and the US had annexed two NGO submissions to its own submission to the Panel.

The AB found the Panel's determination that measures which "undermine the WTO multilateral trading system" must be regarded as "not within the scope of measures permitted under the chapeau of Article XX" to be flawed.[127] The analysis, it said, should have been "two-tiered: first, provisional justification by reason of characterization of the measure under XX(g); second, further appraisal of the same measure under the introductory clause of Article XX."[128] It emphasized: "The sequence of steps indicated above in the analysis of a claim of justification under Article XX reflects, not inadvertence or random choice, but rather the fundamental structure and logic of Article XX."[129]

The AB then undertook its own analysis of Article XX(g). It first concluded that the sea turtles constitute "exhaustible natural resources" for purposes of Article XX(g).[130] Second, it found that the US measure in question related to the conservation of sea turtles.[131] Third, it found that the US measures "are made effective in conjunction with restrictions on domestic production or consumption" within the language of XX(g).[132]

The AB, however, found that the US had not satisfied the ordinary meaning of the words of the chapeau, which required that a measure must not be applied in a manner that would constitute a means of "arbitrary or unjustifiable discrimination between countries where the same conditions prevail,"

---

[122] Appellate Body Report, *United States – Import Prohibition of Certain Shrimp and Shrimp Products*, WT/DS58/AB/R (Oct. 12, 1998), *reprinted at* 38 I.L.M. 118 (1999), ¶ 187(c) [hereinafter *AB Shrimp-Turtle*].

[123] *Id.* ¶ 187(a).

[124] *Id.* ¶ 187(b).

[125] Under Article 13.2 of the DSU, a panel is authorized to seek information from any relevant source, but doing so is totally within its discretion.

[126] *Shrimp-Turtle Panel, supra* note 116, ¶ 7.8.

[127] *AB Shrimp-Turtle, supra* note 122, ¶¶ 116–117.

[128] *Id.* ¶ 118, citing United States-Gasoline case.

[129] *Id.* ¶ 119.

[130] *Id.* ¶¶ 126–134.

[131] *Id.* ¶¶ 135–142.

[132] *Id.* ¶¶ 143–145.

or a "disguised restriction on international trade."[133] It found the US application of the measure unacceptable in that it used "an economic embargo to require other Members to adopt essentially the same comprehensive regulatory program, to achieve a certain policy goal," as in force in the US, "without taking into consideration different conditions which may occur in the territories of those other Members."[134] It also found that the US had failed to explore cooperative measures, bilaterally or multilaterally, for the protection and conservation of sea turtles before undertaking the shrimp embargo. It found the US application of the embargo to constitute unjustified and arbitrary discrimination between countries where the same conditions prevail.[135]

The AB emphasized that, although the US measure in dispute "serves an environmental objective that is recognized as legitimate under paragraph (g) of Article XX of the GATT 1994," the manner of its application "constitutes arbitrary and unjustifiable discrimination between Members of the WTO, contrary to the requirements of the chapeau of Article XX," and consequently does not qualify under the Article XX exceptions.[136]

It is worth noting that, in deciding this case, the AB recognized the importance of environmental considerations. Also, the acceptance by the AB of non-requested submissions is a promising response to the criticism that the WTO dispute resolution process lacks transparency and that there is no scope for participation by NGOs.

Three years after its *Shrimp-Turtle* decision, the AB ruled in 2001 on Malaysia's challenge to the US revised measures in response to the AB's earlier

---

[133] *Id.* ¶ 186.

[134] *Id.* ¶ 164.

[135] *Id.* ¶¶ 148–184.

[136] *Id.* ¶ 186. It is noteworthy that the Appellate Body Report stated:

[W]e wish to underscore what we have not decided in this appeal. We have not decided that the protection and the preservation of the environment is of no significance to the Members of the WTO. Clearly it is. We have not decided that the sovereign nations that are Members of the WTO cannot adopt effective measures to protect endangered species, such as the sea turtles. Clearly, they can and should. And we have not decided that sovereign states should not act together, bilaterally, plurilaterally, or multilaterally, either within the WTO or in other international fora, to protect endangered species or to otherwise protect the environment. Clearly they should and do.

What we have decided in this appeal is simply this: although the measure of the United States in dispute in this appeal serves as an environmental objective that is recognized as legitimate under paragraph (g) of Article XX of the GATT 1994, this measure has been applied by the United States in a manner which constitutes an arbitrary and unjustifiable discrimination between Members of the WTO, contrary to the requirements of the chapeau of Article XX.

Id. ¶¶ 185–186.

decision.[137] Rejecting Malaysia's contention, the AB held that the corrective turtle-friendly measures the US had adopted, permitting shipment-by-shipment certification, were in compliance with Article XX,[138] and that the US was not required to conclude a multilateral environmental agreement.[139]

14.2.3.3   *The* Beef Hormone *Case*

In the *Beef Hormone* Case, the first case under the WTO Agreement on the Application of Sanitary and Phytosanitary Measures (SPS Agreement),[140] the US challenged the European Community's (EC) ban on the import of beef treated with growth promoting hormones, claiming that it violated the EC's obligations under the SPS Agreement. A WTO Panel found that the EC prohibition was indeed in violation of the SPS Agreement,[141] since it was not based on existing international standards and was not supported by scientific justification.[142] The EC appealed the Panel's decision and the Appellate Body (AB) also determined that the EC prohibition violated the SPS Agreement,[143] although it modified and reversed the panel report in several respects. Only a few pertinent issues will be noted here.

---

[137] Appellate Body Report: *US – Import Prohibitions of Certain Shrimp and Shrimp Products*; Recourse to Article 21.5 of the DSU by Malaysia, WT/DS58/AB/RW (Oct. 22, 2001) [hereinafter AB *2001 Report*].

[138] *Id.* ¶¶ 93–95. On the issue of trade measures linked to the production process, *see* generally Steve Charnovitz, *Solving the Production and Processing Methods (PPMs) Puzzle* (PSIO Occasional Paper, WTO Series No. 05) (2001).

[139] *AB 2001 Report, supra* note 137, ¶ 123.

[140] Agreement on the Application of Sanitary and Phytosanitary Measures (Marrakesh Agreement Establishing the World Trade Organization, Apr. 15, 1994), Annex IA, in Final Texts of the Gatt Uruguay Round Agreements Including the Agreement Establishing the WTO as Signed on April 15, 1994) [hereinafter SPS Agreement]. The SPS Agreement is aimed at developing rules for the implementation of the Article XX(b) exception, i.e., measures "necessary to protect human, animal, plant life or health" in restraint of trade. Such measures must not be protectionist, creating an unnecessary barrier to international trade.

[141] Panel Report: *EC Measures Concerning Meat and Meat Products (Hormones), Complaint by the United States*, WT/DS 26/R/USA (Aug. 18, 1997). Canada also challenged the EC decision. The same panel ruled on both complaints; the reports are similar. For the Canadian report, *see* Panel Report, *EC Measures Concerning Meat and Meat Products (Hormones), Complaint by Canada*, WT/DS 48/R/CAN (Aug. 18, 1997). Here I will refer only to the US panel report [hereinafter *EC Meat Panel Report*].

[142] These are the requirements of Articles 3 and 5 of the SPS Agreement.

[143] Appellate Body Report, *EC – Measures Concerning Meat and Meat Products (Hormones)*, WT/DS26/AB/R, WT/DS48/AB/R, ¶ 209 (Jan. 16, 1998) [hereinafter *AB Report Meat*]. *See* generally Terence P. Stewart & David S. Johanson, *The WTO Beef Hormone Dispute: An Analysis of the Appellate Body Decision*, 5 U.C. Davis J. Int'l L. & Pol'y 219 (1999); Layla Hughes, *Note: Limiting the Jurisdiction of Dispute Settlement Panels: The WTO Appellate Body Beef Hormone Decision*, 10 Geo. Int'l Envtl. L. Rev. 915 (1998).

The EC had argued that under the precautionary principle, as part of customary international law, it would interpret the SPS Agreement's scientific justification requirement pertaining to the prohibition on the import of beef to allow it to do so in the absence of definitive, specific scientific proof. The Panel ruled that the precautionary principle did not overrule the explicit requirement of risk assessment contained in Articles 5.1 and 5.2 of the SPS Agreement.[144] Article 5.1 requires that SPS measures be based on a risk assessment,[145] while Article 5.2 lists factors that members should take into account as they conduct risk assessment.[146]

The AB provided guidance on risk analysis by indicating that this was not a closed list and modifying the Panel's interpretation of Article 5.1 by ruling that risk assessment is not limited just to risks scientifically verifiable in the laboratory, but also extends to risks in human society as they actually exist, which would include societal values.[147] The AB affirmed the Panel in its findings regarding the requirement of scientific justification so far as the precautionary principle was concerned and agreed that there was not sufficient scientific evidence to support the EC Directive.[148]

The AB interpreted Article 3.3 of the SPS Agreement to conclude that a member must support its higher level of health protection measures by satisfying both a risk assessment and a justification based on scientific evidence.[149] Rejecting the EC argument that, if it could establish a scientific justification for its prohibition, it was not required to meet the Article 5 requirement of risk assessment,[150] the AB concluded that the EC's policies were inconsistent with Article 3.3 as the measures were not based on risk assessment.[151]

---

[144] *See Meat Panel Report, supra* note 141, paras. 8. 157–58.

[145] Article 5.1 requires that members base their SPS measures "on an assessment, as appropriate to the circumstances, of the risks to human, animal or plant life or health, taking into account risk assessment techniques developed by the relevant international organizations." Under the SPS Agreement, a risk assessment is defined as "the evaluation of the potential for adverse effects on human or animal health." SPS Agreement, *supra* note 140, Annex A. The panel determined that this required a member to establish a scientifically identifiable risk. *Meat Panel Report, supra* note 141, ¶¶ 8.124, 8.134–36, 8.151 and 8.161–62.

[146] These factors include "available scientific evidence; relevant processes and production methods; relevant inspection, sampling and testing methods; prevalence of specific diseases or pests; existence of pest- or disease-free areas; relevant ecological and environmental conditions; and quarantine or other treatment."

[147] *AB Report Meat, supra* note 143, ¶ 187.

[148] *Id.* ¶¶ 123–25, 135–42.

[149] *Id.* ¶ 177.

[150] *Id.* ¶ 175. The AB rejected the EC contention by interpreting the language of Article 3.3, including a footnote in the article.

[151] *Id.* ¶ 209.

The AB, however, also determined that a member has an "autonomous right" to set higher levels of protection as it deems appropriate, and this right is not an exception to the harmonization requirement of Article 3.1. In doing so, the AB reversed the Panel's determination that Article 3.1, requiring harmonization on the basis of international standards, states the general rule and Article 3.3, authorizing a state to introduce higher levels of health protection measures, is the exception.[152] It observed that the objective of harmonization contained in Article 3.1 "is projected in the Agreement, as a goal, yet to be realized in the future."[153] It also found the Panel's determination that the European Community's practice of providing different levels of protection for the hormones under dispute resulted in "discrimination or a disguised restriction on international trade"[154] prohibited under Article 5.5 to be legally incorrect.[155] However, it agreed with the Panel that, for reasons of "judicial economy" it was unnecessary to discuss the claims of Canada that the EC had violated Articles 2.2 and 5.6.[156]

14.2.3.4   *The* Salmon Importation *Case*

The *Salmon Importation* case[157] arose out of Australia's prohibition on the import of "fresh, chilled and frozen salmon product destined for human consumption that has not been subject to heat treatment."[158] Following unsuccessful consultations between Canada and Australia, Canada requested the WTO Dispute Settlement Body (DSB) to establish a panel[159] to consider its claim that Australia's measure was inconsistent with Articles 2, 3, and 5 of the SPS Agreement and Articles XI and XIII of GATT 1994.[160] The SPS

---

[152] *Id.* ¶ 104.

[153] *Id.* ¶ 165. The preamble of the SPS Agreement also promotes such harmonization.

[154] *Meat Panel Report, supra* note 141, ¶ 65.

[155] *AB Report Meat, supra* note 143, ¶ 246. On the AB's analysis of Article 5.5, *see id.* ¶¶ 214–246.

[156] *Id.* ¶¶ 250–251. Under Article 2.2, SPS measures based upon international standards, guidelines, or recommendations are presumed to be consistent with the SPS Agreement, while Article 5.6 provides that WTO Members "shall ensure that [their SPS] measures are not more trade-restrictive than required to achieve their appropriate level of sanitary or phytosanitary protection." The rationale on Article 2.2 was that, while Article 2 addresses members' basic rights and obligations, Articles 3 and 5 concern specific rights and obligations. Article 5.6 was not considered, since the measures were already determined to have violated Article 5.5.

[157] Panel Report, *Australia – Measures Affecting Importation of Salmon*, WT/DS 18/R/Corr. 1 (July 13, 1998) [hereinafter *Salmon Panel Report*]; Appellate Body Report, *Australia – Measures Affecting Importation of Salmon*, WT/DS 18/AB/R (Oct. 20, 1998) [hereinafter *Salmon AB Report*].

[158] *Salmon Panel Report, supra* note 157, ¶ 2.1.

[159] *Id.* ¶¶ 1.1–1.3.

[160] *Id.* ¶ 1.3. For the pertinent Australian laws, *see id.* ¶¶ 2.15–2.16.

Agreement refers to international standards, guidelines and recommendations relevant for animal health developed under the International Office
of Epizootics (OIE) and contained in OIEs "International Aquatic Animal
Health Code."[161] Following the consultations, Australia conducted an import
risk analysis and issued two draft reports, the first in May 1995 and the second in May 1996, and the final report in December 1996.[162] In accepting
the recommendation of the final report, the Director of Quarantine decided
not to permit entry of uncooked salmonid products from Canada and the
US, "given the unique circumstances, range of potential disease agents and
potential socio-economic and environmental impacts."[163]

The Panel found that Australia had acted inconsistently with respect
to SPS Articles 5.1, 5.5, and 5.6 and, by implication, Articles 2.2 and 2.3.[164]
Specifically, it said that Australia's import prohibition was not based on a
risk assessment and hence it had acted inconsistently with Article 5.1 and,
consequently, Article 2.2 requirements.[165] Second, "by adopting arbitrary or
unjustifiable distinctions in the levels of sanitary protection it considers to be
appropriate in different situations...which result in discrimination or a disguised restriction on international trade," Australia had acted inconsistently
with Article 5.5 requirements, and hence also those of Article 2.2.[166] Third,
by maintaining the import prohibition "which is more trade-restrictive than
required to achieve its appropriate level of sanitary protection," Australia
had acted inconsistently with Article 5.6 requirements.[167]

On appeal by Australia, the Appellate Body reached the same conclusion
but under its own analysis and after modifying and reversing the Panel in
several instances. First, the AB reversed the Panel's findings that the issue
in this dispute was the heat-treatment requirement, and found instead the
import prohibition on fresh, chilled or frozen salmon to be the product at
issue to which the Australian import prohibition applied.[168] It decided that
"the 1996 final report [was] not a proper risk assessment within the meaning of Article 5.1 and the first definition paragraph 4 of Annex A,"[169] and
that therefore Australia had acted inconsistently with Article 5.1 of the SPS

---

[161] *See id.* ¶ 2.18.
[162] *Id.* ¶ 2.30.
[163] *Id.*
[164] *Id.* ¶ 9.1.
[165] *Id.*
[166] *Id.*
[167] *Id.*
[168] *Salmon AB Report, supra* note 157, ¶¶ 90–104.
[169] *Id.* ¶¶ 135. *See also id.* ¶¶ 121–134. The AB also referred to Article 2.2, which requires that
"Members shall ensure that any sanitary...measure is based on scientific principles and is
not maintained without sufficient scientific evidence. . . ." *Id.* ¶ 130.

Agreement,[170] and has, by implication, acted inconsistently with Article 2.2, as well.[171]

The AB then analyzed Article 5.5, following its *Beef Hormone* Case analysis, and concluded, as the Panel had done earlier, that Australia had acted inconsistently with its obligations under Article 5.5, and, by implication, Article 2.3 of the SPS Agreement, which mandates that SPS measures undertaken by a member "do not arbitrarily or unjustifiably discriminate between Members where identical or similar conditions prevail, including between their own territory and that of other Members...."[172] Next, the AB stated that it could not conclude whether Australia had violated Article 5.6 and possibly 2.2, "due to the insufficiency of the factual findings of the Panel and of facts that are undisputed between the parties."[173]

Finally, in its analysis of Article 2.3 of the SPS Agreement, the AB was unable to determine whether Australia had acted inconsistently within the meaning of that article, because of a lack of factual findings by the Panel or undisputed facts between the parties on the matter.[174] Thus, the AB recommended that the DSB request Australia to bring its measure found inconsistent with the SPS Agreement into conformity with its obligations.[175]

14.2.3.5   *The* European Communities – Measures Affecting Asbestos and Asbestos-Containing Products *Case* (EC Asbestos)[176]

The French government prohibited the manufacture, import, and marketing of asbestos fibers or any product containing asbestos fibers.[177] Canada claimed that the French action was inconsistent with the obligation of the EC under Article II of the Agreement on Technical Barriers to Trade (the TBT Agreement), Articles III and XI of the GATT 1994, and that under Article XXIII:1(b) of the GATT, the French action nullified or impaired advantages accruing to Canada directly or indirectly under the WTO Agreement, or impeded the attainment of an objective of that Agreement.[178]

---

[170]   *Id.* ¶ 136.

[171]   *Id.* ¶ 138.

[172]   *Id.* ¶¶ 139–178.

[173]   *Id.* ¶ 213. *See generally id.* ¶¶ 179–213.

[174]   *Id.* ¶¶ 243–255.

[175]   *Id.* ¶ 280.

[176]   Appellate Body Report, *European Communities – Measures Affecting Asbestos and Asbestos-Containing Products* (EC Asbestos), WT/DS135/AB/R (March 12, 2001), http://www.wto.org/english/tratop_e/dispu_e/135abr_e.pdf.

[177]   *Id.* ¶ 2.

[178]   *Id.* ¶ 3.

Pertinent for our discussion here, the Panel found the prohibition violated Article III:4 of the GATT. However, it also found the prohibition was justified under Article XX(b) of the GATT 1994.[179] Canada and the EC both appealed and the AB determined that the appeal raised issues pertaining to the Panel's interpretation of the terms "technical regulation," "like products," and "necessary to protect human...life or health" and the Panel's interpretation of whether Article XXIII:1(b) applies to measures for health objectives.[180] The discussion here will be confined primarily to the AB's examination of the issue of "like products" and its clarification of the word "necessary" in Article XX(b).

On the issue of "likeness," the AB stated:

> [I]n examining the "likeness" of products, panels must evaluate *all* of the relevant evidence. We are very much of the view that evidence relating to the health risks associated with the product may be pertinent in an examination of "likeness" under Article III:4 of the GATT 1994. We do not, however, consider that the evidence relating to the health risks associated with chrysotile asbestos fibers need be examined under a *separate* criterion, because we believe that this evidence can be evaluated under the existing criteria of physical properties, and of consumers' tastes and habits....[181]

The AB found that the Panel had erred in excluding the health risks related to chrysotile asbestos fibers when it examined the physical properties of that product.[182] It rejected the Panel's bases for reaching the conclusion that chrysotile asbestos and PCG fibers are "like products" under Article III:4 because the Panel had disregarded the quite different "properties, nature and quality" of these fibers and also their different tariff classifications; considered no evidence on consumers' tastes and habits; and failed to consider many of the end-uses for the fibers that are different, and thus, the AB reversed the Panel's conclusion.[183] After conducting its own analysis, the AB concluded:

> As Canada has not demonstrated that chrysotile asbestos fibers are "like" PCG fibers, or that cement-based products containing chrysotile asbestos fibers are "like" cement-based products containing PCG fibers, we conclude that Canada has not succeeded in establishing that the measure at issue is inconsistent with Article III:4 of the GATT 1994.[184]

---

[179] *Id.* ¶ 4.

[180] *Id.* ¶ 58.

[181] *Id.* ¶ 113. The Panel had focused on market access, end-use, and consumers' tastes and habits as the three criteria to determine its conclusion on "likeness" under Article III:4.

[182] *Id.* ¶ 116.

[183] *Id.* ¶¶ 125–126. *See also id.* ¶ 131.

[184] *Id.* at ¶ 148.

As to the nullification of the effect of Article XX(b), the AB did not agree with the Panel that the consideration of evidence relating to the health risks associated with a product under Article III:4 nullifies it. On the contrary, the AB ruled;

> Article XX(b) allows a Member to "adopt and enforce" a measure *inter alia*, necessary to protect human life or health, even though that measure is inconsistent with another provision of the GATT 1994. Article III:4 and Article XX(b) are distinct and independent provisions of the GATT 1994 each to be interpreted on its own.[185]

On the issue of necessity, the AB referred to its earlier decision, *Korea-Measures Affecting Import of Fresh, Chilled and Frozen Beef (Korea Beef)*,[186] where it had indicated that one aspect of the "weighing and balancing process" in determining whether a WTO-consistent alternative measure is "reasonably available" depends upon the extent to which the alternative measure "contributes to the realization of the end pursued."[187] Additionally, it had observed there that the more vital or important the "common interests or values" pursued the easier it would be to accept measures designed to achieve those ends as "necessary."[188] Applying that reasoning, the AB stated:

> In this case, the objective pursued by the measure is the preservation of human life and health through the elimination, or reduction, of the well-known, and life-threatening, health risks posed by asbestos fibers. The value pursued is both vital and important in the highest degree. The remaining question, then, is whether there is an alternative measure that would achieve the same end and that is less restrictive of trade than a prohibition.[189]

It upheld the Panel's finding that the EC had demonstrated a *prima facie* case that there was no "reasonably available alternative" to the French prohibition. The AB also stated that there is no obligation under Article XX(b) to quantify the risk to human life or health, as in its words, "The pathologies which the Panel identified as being associated with chrysotile area of a very serious nature, namely lung cancer and mesothelioma, which is also a form of cancer. Therefore, we do not agree with Canada that the Panel relied on the French authorities' 'hypotheses' of the risk."[190]

---

[185] *Id.* at ¶ 115.

[186] Appellate Body Report, *Korea – Measures Affecting Import of Fresh, Chilled and Frozen Beef (Korea Beef)*, ¶¶ 159, *et seq.*, WT/DS161/AB/R (Jan. 10, 2001) http://www.world tradelaw.net/reports/wtoab/korea-beef(ab).pdf.

[187] *Id.* ¶¶ 163, 166.

[188] *Id.* at ¶ 162.

[189] *Id.* at ¶ 172.

[190] *Id.* at ¶ 167.

14.2.3.6   *The* Brazil – Measures Affecting Imports of Retreaded Tyres (Brazil Tyres)[191]

The European Communities complained that certain measures imposed by Brazil on the importation and marketing of retreaded tires violate Article XI:1 or alternatively Article III:3 of the GATT 1994, and that certain exemptions are inconsistent with Articles I:1 and XIII:1 of the GATT 1994.[192]

Here again, the AB was called upon to analyze the term "necessary" within the meaning of Article XX(b) of the GATT 1994. It first noted that the term, to which Article XX(b) refers as measures "necessary to protect human, animal or plant life or health," is also mentioned in several other articles, including XX(a) and XX(d) of the GATT 1994, as well as in Article XIV(a), (b), and (c) of the General Agreement on Trade in Services.[193] The AB referred to *Korea Beef* as it had referred earlier to that decision in *EC Asbestos*, noting that it had underscored there that "the word 'necessary' is not limited to that which is 'indispensable.'"[194] The AB in *Korea Beef* had also explained that the determination of whether a measure is "necessary" within the meaning of Article XX(d):

> involves in every case a process of weighing and balancing a series of factor which prominently include the contribution made by the compliance measure to the enforcement of the law or regulation at issue, the importance of the common interests or values protected by that law or regulation, and the accompanying impact of the law or regulation on imports or exports.[195]

The AB, however, added in *Brazil Tyres* that

> when a measure produces restrictive effects on international trade as severe as those resulting from an import ban, it appears to us that it would be difficult for a panel to find that measure necessary unless it is satisfied that the measure is apt to make a material contribution to the achievement of its objective. Thus, we disagree with Brazil's suggestion that, because it aims to reduce risk exposure to the maximum extent possible, an import ban that brings a marginal or insignificant contribution can nevertheless be considered necessary.[196]

---

[191] Appellate Body Report, *Brazil – Measures Affecting Imports of Retreaded Tyres (Brazil Tyres)*, WT/DS332/AB/R (Dec. 3, 2007), http://www.worldtradelaw.net/reports/wtoab/ brazil-tyres(ab).pdf [hereinafter Brazil Tyres AB Report]. The Panel's report is at Panel Report, *Brazil Tyres*, WT/DS332/R, June 12, 2007. For a thoughtful analysis, *see* generally Nikolaos Lavranos, *The Brazilian Tyres Case: Trade Supersedes Health*, 1 TRADE L. & DEV. 230 (2009).

[192] *Id.* ¶¶ 1–3.

[193] *Id.* ¶ 141.

[194] *Korea Beef, supra* note 186, at ¶ 161.

[195] *Id.* ¶ 164, *cited in Brazil Tyres, supra* note 191, at ¶ 142.

[196] *Brazil Tyres, supra* note 191, ¶ 150 (fn. omitted).

Thus, the AB focused on "material contribution" to the achievement of the objective of reducing exposure to risk caused by the accumulation of waste tires.[197]

For a measure to be "necessary" within the meaning of Article XX(b) of the GATT 1994, the AB said that a panel

> must consider the relevant factors, particularly the importance of the interests or values at stake, the extent of the contribution to the achievement of the measure's objective, and its trade restrictiveness. If this analysis yields a preliminary conclusion that the measure is necessary, this result must be confirmed by comparing the measure with possible alternatives, which may be less trade restrictive, while providing an equivalent contribution to the achievement of the objective. This comparison should be carried out in the light of the importance of the interests or values at stake. It is through this process that a panel determines whether a measure is necessary.[198]

On the exemption given by Brazil to MERCOSUR countries in compliance with the decision of the MERCOSUR Arbitral Panel, the AB agreed with the Panel's decision that such compliance

> cannot be viewed as "capricious" or "random." Acts implementing a decision of a judicial or quasi-judicial body – such as the MERCOSUR Arbitral Tribunal – can hardly be characterized as a decision that is "capricious" or "random." However, discrimination can result from a rational decision or behavior, and still be "arbitrary" or "unjustifiable," because it is explained by a rationale that bears to relationship to the objective of a measure provisionally justified under one of the paragraphs of Article XX, or goes against that objective.[199]

In clarifying the meaning of the chapeau of Article XX, the AB stated that

> there is arbitrary or unjustifiable discrimination...when a Member seeks to justify the discrimination resulting from the application of its measure by a rationale that bears no relationship to the accomplishment of the objective that falls within the purview of one of the paragraphs of Article XX, or goes against this objective.[200]

---

[197] *See generally* D. Regan, *The Meaning of "Necessary" in GATT Article XX and GATS Article XIV: The Myth of Cost-benefit Balancing*, 6 World Trade Rev. 347 (2007); G. Kapterian, *A Critique of the WTO Jurisprudence in "Necessity,"* 59 Int'l & Comp. L.Q. 89 (2010).

[198] *Brazil Tyres, supra* note 191, at ¶ 178 (footnotes omitted).

[199] *Id.* ¶ 232 (footnote omitted).

[200] *Id.* ¶ 246.

14.2.4 *WTO's Trade and Environment Committee*[201]

At the end of the Uruguay Round in 1994, the eighth round of multilateral trade negotiations under GATT, trade ministers from participating states created the Trade and Environment Committee. Thus, environmental and sustainable development issues have become part of the mainstream of WTO's work. Negotiations on some aspects of the subject began at the 2001 Doha Ministerial Conference.[202] The Trade and Environment Committee's functions encompass all areas of the multilateral trading system – goods, services, and intellectual property – and it studies the relationship between trade and the environment and makes recommendations about changes needed in the trade agreements.

As the WTO website shows, the individual WTO members drive the Committee's agenda by their proposals upon issues they consider important, such as: What is the relationship between the WTO agreements and various international environmental agreements and conventions? How are the WTO trading system and "green" trade measures related to each other?

According to the Committee, the provisions in the WTO agreements on goods, services, and intellectual property allow governments to give priority to their domestic environmental policies. It notes that when trade is a direct cause of the environmental problems, actions taken to protect the environment with an impact on trade can play an important role in some environmental agreements. It observes that alternatives to trade restrictions include helping countries to acquire environmentally-friendly technology and providing them training and financial assistance. The Committee's concern is with what happens when a country invokes an environmental agreement to take action against another state that has not signed the environmental agreement.

As to dispute resolution, when a dispute arises over a trade action taken under an environmental agreement and if both sides to the dispute are signatories to that agreement, then they should try to settle the dispute under the environmental agreement. But if one side is not a signatory to the environmental agreement then the only possible forum for settling the dispute is the WTO.

On eco-labeling, the key point for the WTO is that labeling requirements and practices should not discriminate, as required under the most-favored-nation treatment and national treatment articles. Other issues the Committee

---

[201] *See generally Understanding the WTO – The Environment: A New High Profile*, WTO, http://www.wto.org/english/thewto_e/whatis_e/tif_e/bey2_e.htm; *Trade and Environment*, WTO, http://www.wto.org/english/tratop_e/envir_e/envir_e.htm.

[202] *See generally Environment: Negotiations – The Doha Mandate on Multilateral Agreements*, WTO, http://www.wto.org/english/tratop_e/envir_e/envir_neg_mea_e.htm.

has explored and for which it has given recommendations include transparency, intellectual property rights, services, liberalization and sustainable development, and domestically prohibited goods such as dangerous chemicals. On several of these issues the Committee is continuing further discussions.

It is promising that collaboration is occurring between the WTO and MEA secretariats, which is aimed at ensuring that the trade and environment regimes develop coherently.

14.2.5   *Appraisal*

In the GATT cases decided before the establishment of the WTO, the Panels held that, in order for an ETM to fall under the Article XX(b) exception, the measure must be "necessary." That is, there must be no alternative available to a state that it could reasonably be expected to employ that would either be consistent with, or less inconsistent with, GATT (*Thailand – Cigarettes* case). For an ETM to fall under the Article XX(g) exception, it does not have to be "necessary" but it must be "primarily aimed at" the conservation of the targeted natural resource and must also be "primarily aimed at" making a state's domestic production or consumption restrictions effective (*Canada – Herring and Salmon* and *Tuna-Dolphin* cases). The restrictive interpretation of the word "necessary" in the *Tuna-Dolphin* cases was softened with some flexibility as the AB in *EC Asbestos* broadened it by using the term "reasonably available." Furthermore, "a contracting party may not restrict imports of a product merely because it originates in a country with environmental policies different from its own" (*Tuna-Dolphin I*). Finally, for both Articles XX(b) and (g), while *Tuna-Dolphin I* held that the ETM must not act extra-jurisdictionally, *Tuna-Dolphin II* rejected that interpretation, not considering it a requirement.

These decisions regarding ETMs have implications for a wide range of international agreements and domestic laws currently thought to be legal. The Vienna Convention on the Law of Treaties enunciates the basic rule that the later treaty between states parties to two treaties will prevail in the event of a conflict with the earlier treaty.[203] This may create a problem where

---

[203] Vienna Convention, *supra* note 108. Article 30 states:

[T]he rights and obligations of States Parties to successive treaties relating to the same subject-matter shall be determined in accordance with the following paragraphs....

3. When all the parties to the earlier treaty are parties also to the later treaty but the earlier treaty is not terminated or suspended in operation ... the earlier treaty applies only to the extent that its provisions are compatible with those of the later treaty.

4. When the parties to the later treaty do not include all the parties to the earlier one:
(a) as between States Parties to both treaties the same rule applies as in paragraph

some, but not all, of the parties of GATT have acceded to a treaty, especially if that treaty mandates or permits the imposition of an ETM. To illustrate, CITES[204] and the Montreal Protocol[205] may conflict with the recent GATT construction of Article XX. CITES allows states to protect wildlife by imposing import and export prohibitions and restrictions, and these state-imposed ETMs are applied to all states, even those that are not parties to CITES. Consequently, these ETMs are imperiled by GATT with regard to states that are either members of GATT but not of CITES, or have ratified GATT after having ratified CITES. Under the Montreal Protocol, parties are required to implement import and export prohibitions on several ozone-depleting controlled substances, which may violate GATT Articles I (MFN) and XI. Several pertinent US laws come into conflict with GATT, including the International Dolphin Conservation Act (IDCA) of 1992,[206] the High Seas Driftnet Fisheries Enforcement Act,[207] and the Endangered Species Act.[208]

However, many other states utilize ETMs, as well, such as the EC's import ban on fur from countries that still use a leghold trap. States' defiance of GATT's prohibition on ETMs that do not fulfill the requirements of Article XX, along with public outcry over GATT panel decisions, calls for resolution of this difficult problem. In response to the criticism, GATT revived its long-dormant Group on Environmental Measures and International Trade.[209] Although under WTO's modified dispute settlement procedure, further clarification regarding the scope of the Article XX exceptions has occurred, a satisfactory solution has yet to be found.

The GATT Panel reports in *Tuna-Dolphin I* and *Tuna-Dolphin II* seemed to favor free trade over unilateral trade restrictions by a state to protect the environment and for conservation purposes. However, the AB ruling in the *Shrimp-Turtle* case explicitly rejected that approach and suggested that environmental measures for conservation of exhaustible natural resources resulting in unilateral trade restrictions could be justified as an exception allowed in Article XX. The AB, nonetheless, found that the US had engaged in unjustified discrimination among countries under embargo, for it treated certain Asian countries differently from countries in the western hemisphere.

3; (b) as between a State Party to both treaties and a State Party to only one of the treaties, the treaty to which both States are parties governs their mutual rights and obligations.

[204] CITES, *supra* note 91.

[205] Montreal Protocol on Substances That Deplete the Ozone Layer, Sept. 16, 1987, *reprinted at* 26 I.L.M. 1550 (entered into force Jan. 1, 1989).

[206] Pub. L. No. 102–525, § 302(a), codified at 16.U.S.C. § 1412(a).

[207] Pub. L. No. 101–582, § 101, codified at 16 U.S.C. § 1826(a).

[208] Pub. L. No. 101–162, § 609, 103 Stat. 1037 (1990), codified at 16 U.S.C. § 1537.

[209] *See* Charnovitz, *supra* note 3, at 479–80.

In the *Beef Hormone* decision, the AB did not allow the EC to rely upon the "precautionary principle" to override Articles 5.1 and 5.2. However, its discussion on risk analysis and the role of science was confusing, for while it admitted that Article 3.3 was "not a model of clarity in drafting and communication," it still held that both a risk assessment and a justification based on scientific evidence were prerequisites for a state to support its health protection measures. The AB should have considered the EC's measures by reference to Article 2.2, which, although mandating scientific evidence as a requirement for SPS measures, provides that such measures shall be presumed to be consistent with the SPS Agreement. However, since this is still a work in progress, future WTO decisions will shed more light on how to balance unilateral trade restrictions to protect the environment.

Trade and environment regimes should work in harmony and not at cross-purposes. There appears to be movement in this direction with the recent developments pertaining to the role of the WTO's Trade and Environment Committee and the endeavors undertaken at the Doha Round. These recent initiatives are very encouraging.

14.3   *North American Free Trade Agreement*[210]

14.3.1   *Overview*[211]

A major development which thrust international trade liberalization into a partnership with environmental protection in the 1990s was the passage of

---

[210] North American Free Trade Agreement, Dec. 17, 1992, Can.-Mex.-US, chs. 1–9, 32 I.L.M. 289 (1993); chs. 10–22, 32 I.L.M. 605 (1993), *entered into force* Jan. 1, 1993 [hereinafter NAFTA].

[211] *See generally* Schoenbaum, *supra* note 1; R. Ludwiszewski, *"Green" Language in the NAFTA: Reconciling Free Trade and Environmental Protection*, 27 Int'l Law 691 (1993); A. Jenkins, *Comment, NAFTA: Is The Environmental Cost of Free Trade Too High?*, 19 N.C.J. Int'l L. & Com. Reg. 143 (1993); E. B. Weiss & J. Jackson, *Trade, Environment and NAFTA: Introductory Remarks*, 5 Geo. Int'l Envtl. L. Rev. 515 (1993); S. Gomez, *Environmental Risks Related to the Maquiladora Industry and the Likely Environmental Impact of NAFTA*, 6 Laraza L.J. 174 (1993); J. Bailey, *Free Trade and the Environment – Can NAFTA Reconcile the Irreconcilable?*, 8 Am. U. J. Int'l L. & Pol'y 839 (1993); C. Schwenker, *Protecting the Environment and U.S. Competitiveness in the Era of Free Trade: A Proposal*, 71 Tex. L. Rev. 1355 (1993); A. Holmer & J. Bellow, *U.S. Trade Law and Policy Series No. 22: Trade and the Environment: A Snapshot from Tuna/Dolphins to the NAFTA and Beyond*, 27 Int'l Law 169 (1993); M. Robins, *The North American Free Trade Agreement: The Integration of Free Trade and the Environment*, 7 Temp. Int'l & Comp. L.J. 123 (1993); K. De La Garza, *Linking Trade Growth and the Environment: One Lawmaker's View*, 23 Envtl. L. 701 (1993); M. H. McKeith, *The Environment and Free Trade: Meeting Halfway at the Mexican Border*, 10 UCLA Pac. Basin L.J. 183 (1991); J. Ikegawa, *NAFTA: How*

the North American Free Trade Agreement (NAFTA) and its Side Agreement on the Environment. While proponents of international trade liberalization welcomed the lowering and eradication of trade barriers between Canada, Mexico, and the US, environmentalists worried that NAFTA would substantially hinder environmental protection activities. Already concerned with the environmental problems the maquiladoras had caused,[212] they feared that NAFTA might present similar problems, and perhaps on a much larger scale. However, through extensive negotiations, NAFTA incorporated many environmentally protective provisions. In fact, in its preamble, NAFTA commences with the affirmation that liberalization of trade must be consistent with sustainable development, among other environmental goals. The Side Agreement on the Environment was designed to strengthen the existing NAFTA provisions on the protection of the environment.

14.3.2   *Review of the Pertinent NAFTA Provisions*

On October 7, 1992, the governments of Canada, US, and Mexico initialed NAFTA, and the implementing legislation was signed into law by President Clinton on December 8, 1993,[213] ushering in a new era of trade agreements. Of particular importance is that, as a trade agreement, NAFTA contains several provisions regarding environmental protection, which are discussed below.

14.3.2.1   *Article 104*
The objectives of NAFTA are contained in its first chapter. Article 104 specifically applies to environmental and conservation agreements. With respect to those agreements, NAFTA states that if there are any inconsistent

---

Will it Affect U.S. Environmental Regulations?, 6 Transnat'l Law 225; and S. Spracker, G. Brown & A. Connolly, *Environmental Protection and International Trade: NAFTA as a Means of Eliminating Environmental Contamination as a Competitive Advantage*, 5 Geo. Int'l Envtl. L. Rev. 669 (1993).

[212] "Maquiladora" is a Spanish term for foreign-owned assembly plants also known as "export processing" plants. Situated on the Mexican side of the border, these are American-owned export processing plants that import raw materials and machinery from the US and produce goods primarily for the US market. *See generally Six Years of NAFTA: A View from Inside the Maquiladoras*, Comite Fronterizo de Obreras, Oct. 1999; D. Voigt, *The Maquiladora Problem in the Age of NAFTA: Where Will We Find Solutions?*, 2 Minn. J. Global Trade 323 (1993); *see also* Gomez, *supra* note 211.

[213] The implementation in the US occurred through the adoption of the NAFTA Implementation Act of 1993, 19 U.S.C. §§ 3301–3473.

obligations imposed upon parties, the obligations contained in the environmental and conservation agreements will prevail.[214]

Also, NAFTA allows the parties to continue to incur greater environmental
obligations through amendments to old agreements or through new agreements without violating NAFTA.[215] However, the parties still have an obligation to choose the least inconsistent alternative. The parties' compliance
with current and future environmental obligations, therefore, is an objective
of NAFTA.

14.3.2.2   *Chapter Nine*

Chapter Nine – on standards-related measures – contains the majority of
NAFTA's environmental provisions. Article 904(1) allows each party to prescribe, apply, and enforce any environmental or health standards-related
measure and even to ban the importation of a good or service from another
party "that fails to comply with the applicable requirements of those measures or to complete the Party's approval procedures."[216]

Article 906(2) prevents downward harmonization. While it calls for parties to harmonize their standards-related measures,[217] it creates a ratchet-like
rule by requiring a party to raise its less restrictive measures to meet the level
of the more restrictive measures of another.[218] Thus, this article is intended
to allay any fears that the US might lower its environmental standards so as
to reduce costs to its businesses, thereby making the US more competitive
with Mexico as a location for business.

---

[214] Specifically, NAFTA provides:

> In the event of any inconsistency between this Agreement and the specific trade obli-
> gations set out in [CITES; the Montreal Protocol; the Basel Convention; the Can-
> ada-US Agreement Concerning the Transboundary Movement of Hazardous Waste
> (Ottawa, 1986); and the US Mexican Agreement on Cooperation for the Protection
> and Improvement of the Environment in the Border Area (La Paz, 1983)], such obliga-
> tions shall prevail to the extent of the inconsistency, provided that where a Party has
> a choice among equally effective and reasonably available means of complying with
> such obligations, the Party chooses the alternative that is the least inconsistent with
> the other provisions of this Agreement. NAFTA, *supra* note 183, art. 104(1).

[215] *Id.* art. 104(2) provides: "The Parties may agree in writing to modify [the article] to include
any amendment to an agreement referred to in paragraph 1, and any other environmental
or conservation agreement."

[216] *Id.*

[217] This is allowed under article 904. The parties must do so "[w]ithout reducing the level
of safety or of protection of human, animal or plant life or health, the environment or
consumers."

[218] *See* Ludwiszewski, *supra* note 211, at 694.

Chapter Nine, however, does not allow the parties total freedom in creating such environmental standards-related measures.[219] Excepted are situations in which international standards would be "ineffective or inappropriate" to achieving "legitimate objectives."[220] If a party wants to impose standards-related measures that provide greater environmental protection than do international standards, it is also permissible.[221] Thus, like the ratchet effect of Article 906(2), this article provides a minimum level from which the parties may design their standards-related measures.

The assessment of risk is left to each individual party for its pursuit of objectives (i.e., "the protection of human, animal or plant life, health, the environment, or consumers").[222] Article 907 allows a party, when conducting a risk assessment, to take into account, among other factors relating to a good or service, prevailing environmental conditions.[223] Chapter Nine also addresses the possibility of a party using environmental standards-related measures as illegitimate trade restrictions.[224] Moreover, with respect to its standards-related measures, a party must treat the goods and services of another party the same way that it treats its own goods and services, "in accordance with Article 301 (Market Access) or Article 1202 (Cross-Border

---

[219] Article 905 provides that "[e]ach Party shall use, as a basis for its standards-related measures, relevant international standards or international standards whose completion is imminent." NAFTA, *supra* note 210, art. 905(1).

[220] *Id.*

[221] Article 905(3) provides that: "Nothing in [article 905(I)] shall be construed to prevent a Party, in pursuing its legitimate objectives, from adopting, maintaining or applying any standards-related measure that results in a higher level of protection than would be achieved if the measure were based on the relevant international standard."

[222] *Id.* art. 904(2).

[223] *Id.* art 907(1) and (2). These factors include:
  (a) available scientific evidence or technical information;
  (b) intended end uses;
  (c) processes or production, operating, inspection, sampling or testing methods; or
  (d) environmental conditions.
  ...
  [However, a Party conducting a risk assessment] should avoid arbitrary or unjustifiable distinctions between similar goods or services in the level of protection it considers appropriate, where the distinctions:
  (a) result in arbitrary or unjustifiable discrimination against goods or service providers of another Party;
  (b) constitute a disguised restriction on trade between the Parties; or
  (c) discriminate between similar goods or services for the same use under the same conditions that pose the same level of risk and provide similar benefits.

[224] *Id.* art 904(3)(b) prohibits a party from according, with respect to its standards-related measures, any good or service of another party "treatment…less favorable than it accords to like goods, or in like circumstances to service providers, of any other country."

Trade in Services)."²²⁵ Parties may not "prepare, adopt, maintain or apply any standards related measure with a view to or with the effect of creating an unnecessary obstacle to trade between the Parties."²²⁶

14.3.2.3   *Chapter 11*²²⁷

One of Chapter 11's major goals is environmental protection. Article 1114 provides the environmental measures that relate to investment. It authorizes a state to adopt measures for protecting the environment and preventing a relaxation of health and environmental measures designed to attract foreign investment.²²⁸ The first provision of this article is aimed at allowing parties to take steps necessary to protect the environment "otherwise consistent with this chapter."²²⁹

The term "otherwise consistent with this chapter" assumes special importance, for while parties are not prohibited from creating or maintaining measures to protect the environment, even if they serve to limit investment, they are subject to the requirement that the measures taken be consistent with other provisions of Chapter 11. These other provisions include the requirement of according the investors not simply national treatment,²³⁰ but also what could be a higher threshold, the minimum international standard of treatment.²³¹ It is also worth noting that parties are not allowed to relax their health and environmental measures in an attempt to attract investment.²³² However, if a party does relax its own measures as an encouragement to investment, another Party may "request consultations with the

---

²²⁵ *Id.* art 904(3)(a).

²²⁶ *Id.* art. 904(4). This section explains, however, stating:
>   An unnecessary obstacle to trade shall not be deemed to be created where:
>   (1) the demonstrable purpose of the measure is to achieve a legitimate objective; and
>   (2) the measure does not operate to exclude goods of another Party that meet that legitimate objective.

²²⁷ Chapter 11 of NAFTA provides norms pertaining to investment.

²²⁸ NAFTA, *supra* note 210, art. 1114.

²²⁹ *Id.* art. 1114(1) states: "Nothing in this Chapter shall be construed to prevent a Party from adopting, maintaining or enforcing any measure otherwise consistent with this Chapter that it considers appropriate to ensure that investment activity in its territory is undertaken in a manner sensitive to environmental concerns."

²³⁰ Article 1102 provides the national treatment principle. Art. 1102(1) states: Each Party shall accord to investors of another Party treatment no less favorable than that it accords, in like circumstances, to its own investors with respect to the establishment, acquisition, expansion, management, conduct, operation, and sale or other disposition of investments. *Id.* art. 1102(1).

²³¹ *Id.* art. 1105(1).

²³² *Id.* art. 1114(2) states: The Parties recognize that it is inappropriate to encourage investment by relaxing domestic health, safety or environmental measures. Accordingly, a Party should not waive or otherwise derogate from, or offer to waive or otherwise derogate from,

other party and the two Parties shall consult with a view to avoiding any such encouragement."[233] Thus, although these provisions contain admirable guidelines, they are not easily enforceable.

NAFTA Chapter 11 is, however, aimed at ensuring investors that their investments will be secure and protected from discriminatory treatment, as there have been concerns with potential nationalization, such as Mexico's nationalization of its oil refineries in 1938. Among many new protections is a provision for foreign investors and corporations to directly sue governments and seek damages in special arbitral tribunals under an "investor-state" dispute resolution mechanism,[234] by alleging that the government's regulatory action has injured their investment, causing a loss of profits.

The investor may invoke the Chapter 11 prescriptions, including the government's obligation (1) to treat a foreign investor "in no less favorable" a manner than a domestic investor who is "in like circumstances;"[235] and (2) to accord a foreign investor minimum international standards of treatment, including "fair and equal treatment and full protection and security."[236] Also, the foreign investor may invoke the Chapter 11 prohibitions on performance requirements,[237] or its prohibition from undertaking direct or indirect expropriation of investment,[238] or from taking a measure "tantamount to nationalization or expropriation of such an investment,"[239] unless it is taken for a public purpose, is nondiscriminatory, is in accordance with due process of law,[240] and meets the requirement of "fair and equal treatment and full protection and security."

These phrases – "in no less favorable manner," "in like circumstances," "fair and equal treatment," "full protection and security," and "tantamount to expropriation" – are vague and subject to varying interpretations. Similarly, the meaning of the term "investment" for the purposes of Chapter 11,[241] or as to what amounts to a breach of performance requirement, has become

---

such measures as an encouragement for the establishment, acquisition, expansion or retention in its territory of an investment of an investor.

[233] *Id.*

[234] *Id.* art. 1120. The disputing parties "should first attempt to settle a claim through consultation or negotiation." *Id.* art. 1118.

[235] *Id.* art. 1102(1) on National Treatment and art. 1103(1) on Most-Favored-Nation Treatment.

[236] *Id.* art. 1105(1) on Minimum Standard of Treatment.

[237] *Id.* art. 1106(1) enumerates seven such prohibited requirements.

[238] *Id.* art. 1110.

[239] *Id.*

[240] *Id.*

[241] NAFTA article 1139 provides an expansive definition of investment. *Id.* art 1139.

controversial. Thus, Chapter 11 procedure has become contentious, as later discussion will show.

The US and Canada, involved in many of the investor suits against states under Chapter 11, sought a narrower standard of "customary international law" in deciding whether investors have been afforded "fair and equitable treatment" and, in July 2001, the three Member Countries of NAFTA agreed upon such an interpretation.[242] The US and Canada had argued that Chapter 11 was aimed at preventing unlawful expropriation by governments, and should not be used, as Canada had said, as "a catch-all for every grievance or disappointment that a foreign investor may raise."[243]

14.3.2.3.1   Case Law

The main concern with Chapter 11 in the environmental context is that foreign investors invoking its provisions sue governments and seek damages by challenging regulations promulgated by governments to protect the environment and human health. Six selected cases will be briefly noted here to illustrate the concern.[244] Article 1102 on national treatment was invoked against Canada in three cases – *Ethyl Corp. v. Canada*, *S.D. Myers v. Canada*, and *Pope & Talbot Inc. v. Canada*, and in one case against the US, *Methanex Inc. v. United States*. Article 1105 on minimum international standards was invoked in *S.D. Myers, Pope & Talbot, Methanex*, and *Glamis Gold*, and also in a case against Mexico, *Metalclad Corp. v. Mexico*. Article 1106 on performance requirements was the basis of *Ethyl, S.D. Myers*, and *Pope & Talbot*. Article 1110 on expropriation was invoked in all these cases.

Ethyl Corporation, a US company, manufactured a fuel additive, MMT (methylcyclopentadienyl manganese tricarbonyl), to increase the octane level in unleaded gasoline. MMT contains manganese, a potential human neurotoxin. Ethyl's wholly owned Canadian subsidiary, Ethyl Canada, imported this gasoline additive into Canada and, after processing it, distributed it across the country. In 1997, because of health and environmental considerations, the Canadian parliament prohibited the import of MMT into Canada and

---

[242] *See* Edward Alden, *NAFTA Deal Changed to Curb Companies*, Fin. Times (London), Aug. 1, 2001, at 3.

[243] *Id.* For various interpretations to the phrase "fair and equitable treatment," *see* remarks by Ved P. Nanda, *Fair and Equitable Treatment under NAFTA's Investment Chapter*, 96 Proc. Am. Soc. Int'l L. 19 (2002). *See also* remarks by Charles H. Brower, II, Murray J. Belman, J.C. Thomas & Jack J. Coe, *id.* at 9–19.

[244] The cases discussed here may be found at www.harmonizationalert.org; www.naftalaw .org. For an insightful study on the subject, *see* David A. Gantz, *Potential Conflict Between Investor Rights and Environmental Regulation Under NAFTA's Chapter 11*, 33 Geo. Wash. Int'l L. Rev. 651 (2001). *See also* Howard Mann & Konrad van Moltke, NAFTA's Chapter 11 and the Environment (IISD Working Paper, 1999).

also prohibited inter-provincial trade of the additive within Canada under a federal statute.[245] In the first suit filed under Chapter 11, Ethyl claimed damages in a tribunal established under the rules of the UN Commission on International Trade Law (UNCITRAL).[246] Invoking the "national treatment" article, Article 1102, it alleged that by banning MMT's import in the absence of a ban on internal production and sale, Canada had breached its obligation to treat foreign investors in a "no less favorable manner" than domestic investors, although there had never been any domestic Canadian production of MMT.

Ethyl's claim under Article 1106 was based upon its allegation that the import restriction on MMT was an illegal performance requirement, for it was aimed at forcing Ethyl either to use other Canadian-made products or to produce the MMT in Canada. Its claim on expropriation under Article 1110 was supported by allegations that the import ban on MMT would eliminate profits the company expected to earn through its sale of MMT in Canada, thus amounting to either an expropriation or a measure "tantamount to expropriation," for which Ethyl sought full compensation.

The arbitral tribunal rejected all of Canada's arguments: the Canadian action was not a performance requirement under Chapter 11, but a trade measure beyond the scope of that chapter; since the MMT legislation was not in force when the case was initiated, it could not be considered as a "measure" in law under Chapter 11; and Canada was exercising its regulatory power authorized under Article 1114(1).[247] These major threshold issues having been found against it, Canada settled the case before it could be considered on the merits, by paying Ethyl CA$13 million for lost profits and costs, and withdrew the legislation.

In Metalclad,[248] a US corporation sued Mexico, invoking Article 1105 on minimum international standards of treatment and Article 1110 on expropriation and claiming $90 million in damages. Metalclad Corporation purchased a waste management company in Mexico and sought to build and operate a hazardous waste landfill facility in the municipality of Guadalcazar. The necessary municipal construction permits were denied, although the appropriate federal and state permits had been granted. The main concern

---

[245] Manganese-based Fuel Additives Act, 1997, Ch. 11.
[246] Ethyl Corp. v. Canada, 38 I.L.M. 708 (1999). For a digest of the case, *see* IISD, PRIVATE RIGHTS, PUBLIC PROBLEMS – A GUIDE TO NAFTA'S CONTROVERSIAL CHAPTER ON INVESTOR RIGHTS 71–74 (2001) [hereinafter Private Rights, Public Problems]. *See also* Timothy Ross Wilson, *Trade Rules – Ethyl Corporation v. Canada (NAFTA Chapter 11): Part I: Claim and Award on Jurisdiction,* 6 NAFTA L. & BUS. REV. AM. 52 (2000).
[247] NAFTA, *supra* note 210, art. 1114(1).
[248] For a digest of the case, *see* Private Rights, Public Problems, *supra* note 246, at 74–79.

of grassroots organizations which opposed Metalclad was with the environmental hazards posed by the site.

Metalclad claimed that it had acted upon the federal representations and the arbitral tribunal accepted that contention. In August 2000, a special NAFTA tribunal operating under the Additional Facility Rules of the World Bank International Center for the Settlement of International Disputes (ICSID) awarded $16,685,000 to Metalclad. The tribunal found that, under Mexican law, the municipality had exceeded its jurisdiction by denying Metalclad a construction permit and, by tolerating the actions of the municipality and of the federal and state officials who had failed to clarify the situation for Metalclad, Mexico had failed to provide the transparency and orderly process necessary for business planning and investment. Further, it equated the expanded reach of Article 1105 with expropriation under Article 1110. The bases for the tribunal's award were that there was "covert or incidental interference" with Metalclad's property rights, and, as Mexico had not compensated Metalclad, it had breached Article 1110 on expropriation.

In an unprecedented move, Mexico sought judicial review in British Columbia, the province which was the site of the tribunal, to set aside the award.[249] In May 2001, the Supreme Court of British Columbia accepted Mexico's contention that the arbitral tribunal had made decisions on matters beyond the scope of Chapter 11 when it interpreted Article 1105 to equate Mexico's domestic law violation with violation under the minimum international standards requirement of Article 1105.[250] The court held that the NAFTA tribunal had inaccurately read the transparency provisions of NAFTA Chapter 18 into Chapter 11 and that transparency is not a requirement under customary international law. It also ruled that the tribunal's finding that a violation of Article 1105 constituted a violation of Article 1110 was in error. As to the claim under Article 1110 on expropriation, the court agreed with the tribunal that the governor's action of declaring the area an ecological zone, which precluded the operation of the facility by Metalclad, constituted expropriation,[251] and concluded that under the ICAA there was no ground to set aside the award. However, it reduced the award to $15.6 million by postdating the calculation of damages to the date the governor declared the area an ecological zone.[252]

---

[249] United Mexican States v. Metalclad Corp., 2001 B.C.S.C. 664.

[250] *Id.* It held the governing law to review the award to be the British Columbia statute of the International Commercial Arbitration Act (ICAA), R.S.B.C. 1996, Chapter 233. Metalclad, *supra* note 249, at ¶¶ 66–76.

[251] *Id.* ¶¶ 77–105.

[252] *Id.* ¶¶ 133–137.

Mexico initially intended to appeal this decision, but instead decided to settle the case by paying Metalclad $15.6 million, the amount ordered by the Canadian court.[253] The implications are serious. The tribunal's ruling that the municipal government did not have the authority to deny a construction permit and to characterize it as amounting to expropriation, raises serious questions. Why should the NAFTA tribunal and not a Mexican domestic court have the competence to provide an authoritative interpretation of Mexican domestic law? Also, the tribunal paid little attention to the applicable NAFTA provisions on environmental protection – its Preamble and Article 1114.

In *S.D. Myers v. Canada*,[254] S.D. Myers, a US hazardous waste disposal company, which operated a PCB waste treatment service in Ohio, had a Canadian affiliate, S.D. Myers Canada. The affiliate was seeking Canadian customers for its parent company's treatment and recycling services in Ohio. The USEPA authorized such imports through an "enforcement discretion," although it had determined them to be harmful both to humans and the environment and had banned them under its Toxic Substances Control Act for 15 years prior to that time. Canada banned exports of PCB wastes under its Environmental Protection Act. Subsequently, two pertinent events occurred. The EPA action permitting imports of this type was overturned by a US court of appeals decision, and then Canada replaced its "interim order" banning the export of PCBs from Canada with a regulation under which PCB waste exports were permitted within carefully prescribed conditions.[255]

S.D. Myers alleged violations of Article 1102 on national treatment, Article 1105 on minimum international standards of treatment, Article 1106 on performance requirements, and Article 1110 on expropriation.[256] The Article 1102 claim was based on the ground that Canada favored Canada PCB waste disposers by closing its border to its exports. It is worth noting that no Canadian companies were permitted to export PCB waste. S.D. Myers was in fact claiming damages concerning a Canadian measure for its activities in the US. As to the violation of minimum international standards of treatment, S.D. Myers' argument was that the Canadian treatment amounted to a denial of justice, as not fair or equitable.

---

[253] *See* David Hechler, *U.S. Firm Gets $16M Settlement*, NAT'L L.J., Nov. 12, 2001, at A17.

[254] In a NAFTA arbitration under the UNCITRAL Arbitral Rules, S.D. Myers, Inc. (Claimant) and Government of Canada (Respondent), Partial Award, Nov. 13, 2000, 40 I.L.M. 1408 (2001), http://italaw.com/documents/SDMeyers-1stPartialAward.pdf [hereinafter Myers Partial Award]. For a digest of the case, *see* Private Rights, Public Problems, *supra* note 246, at 84–91.

[255] For a summary of these events, *see* Myers Partial Award, *supra* note 253, ¶¶ 123–28, 161–95.

[256] *Id.* ¶¶ 130–43.

As to the claim that Canada's ban constituted an illegal performance requirement, S.D. Myers argued that by banning exports, Canada was implicitly requiring the investor to dispose of PCBs in Canada. Regarding the invocation of Article 1110 on expropriation, S.D. Myers' contention was that the Canadian ban deprived it of business opportunities to export PCB waste from Canada to its US facilities, which was "tantamount to expropriation," requiring full compensation.

A NAFTA UNCITRAL tribunal ruled in favor of S.D. Myers. The tribunal construed the terms "investor" and "investment" broadly, implicitly including within their ambit S.D. Myers' market share in Canada.[257] It said that a violation of Article 1102 on national treatment could constitute a violation of Article 1105, and also read into Article 1102 other NAFTA provisions, such as those on least trade restrictiveness. Similarly, in defining "in like circumstances" among the factors to be considered, the tribunal included Canada's need to avoid trade distortions by adopting "least trade restrictive" measures, thus going beyond Chapter 11 to read other provisions from NAFTA and WTO. It, however, rejected the company's claims on the performance requirement and expropriation allegations.[258]

Canada sought judicial review to set aside the award in the Federal Court of Canada, invoking its Commercial Arbitration Act,[259] which allows such review. Canada's claim was based on the grounds that the tribunal misconstrued the term "in like circumstances," as it included the operations of the investor in the US and that, as Canada would be in breach of its international obligations under the Basel Convention by allowing exports of PCB wastes, the award conflicted with Canada's public policy.

Subsequently, the tribunal gave a partial award on damages[260] and a final award on costs.[261] After it issued its final award, the Canadian court scheduled hearings in December 2003 and issued its judgment in January 2004.[262] The court rejected the arguments that the tribunal had lacked jurisdiction over a dispute in which the claimant had no Canadian investment and where the claimant had acted only as a provider of cross-border services. It also rejected arguments that the tribunal had erred in concluding that S.D. Myers, Inc. and its Canadian competitors were in "like circumstances" for purposes

---

[257] *Id.* ¶¶ 222–31.

[258] For the tribunal's review of the claims under NAFTA, *see id.* ¶¶ 237–88.

[259] Commercial Arbitration Act, R.S.C. 1985, ch. 17 (2nd Supp.).

[260] S.D. Myers, Inc. v. Canada, Second Partial Award (Damages), October 21, 2002, http:// italaw.com/documents/SecondPartialAward_Myers.pdf.

[261] S.D. Myers, Inc. v. Canada, Final Award, December 30, 2002, http://www.biicl.org/ files/3921_2002_sd_myers_v_canada.pdf.

[262] *See* Attorney Gen. of Can. v. S.D. Myres, Inc. [2004].

of national treatment under Article 1102, and that the tribunal's awards violated Canada's public policy.

Again, the implications are far reaching, for the tribunal construed the terms "investor" and "investment" broadly. It also ignored Canada's obligations under a multilateral environmental agreement, the Basel Convention to which Canada is a party. On the other hand, it determined that Canada was obligated to undertake "least trade restrictive" measures that are not provided for in Chapter 11.

In *Pope & Talbot Inc. v. Canada*, Pope & Talbot, a US company, sued under UNCITRAL rules, claiming that its duty-free export quota of Canadian softwood to the US under the Canada-US Softwood Lumber Agreement had been reduced by Canada disproportionately to other exporters, thus damaging the company's profits.[263] Its allegations, based on the quota system established under the Agreement, involved violations of Articles 1102, 1105, 1106, and 1110. In an interim award on June 26, 2000, the arbitration tribunal ruled in favor of Canada on the performance requirement and expropriation obligations. However, it construed investment subject to protection under Article 1110 on expropriation to include access to the US market, thus giving it an expansive definition.

Canada, however, lost in the final ruling on the merits. The tribunal concluded that Canada had acted unreasonably when verifying Pope & Talbot's compliance with the requirements of the Agreement, and thus had acted in violation of the "fair and equal treatment" required under NAFTA. It held the term to be independent of and not to be subsumed by international law.[264] In doing so, it rejected Canada's argument that to find a violation of minimum standard of treatment, the tribunal must find the conduct amounting to a "willful neglect of duty or an insufficiency of governmental action so far short of international standards that every reasonable and impartial person would recognize its insufficiency."[265]

In *Methanex Inc. v. United States*,[266] Methanex, a Canadian company, sought approximately $1 billion in damages from the US The allegation is that California banned a fuel additive, MTBE, in all gasolines sold in that state by December 31, 2002, and required MTBE to be labeled at gasoline

---

[263] For a digest of the case, *see* Private Rights, Public Problems, *supra* note 246, at 92–95. The Canada-US Softwood Lumber Agreement is a trade agreement that was corporate managed and not renewed after it expired in March 2001.

[264] In the Matter of an Arbitration Under Chapter Eleven of the North American Free Trade Agreement Between Pope and Talbot, Inc. and Government of Canada, Award in Respect of Damages by Arbitral Tribunal, ¶ 9, May 31, 2002, http://italaw.com/documents/Pope-InterimAward.pdf.

[265] *Id.* n. 42.

[266] For a digest of the case, *see* Private Rights, Public Problems, *supra* note 219, at 96–97.

pumps. MTBE is known to be hazardous to human health and California found that the additive had contaminated drinking water wells in the state.

Since Methanex manufactures methanol, which is one of the constituent components of MTBE, it invoked Articles 1102, 1105, and 1110, alleging that the US measures lacked substantive fairness, were discriminatory, and injured its profits, for nearly 40 percent of Methanex's US sales are for making MTBE. It argued that, since California had not used the "least trade restrictive" method to solve the water contamination problem, it was in violation of Article 1105's fair treatment standard. By giving preferential treatment to ethanol, a US-produced fuel additive, it argued, California violated Article 1102's national treatment provisions. Regarding the violation of Article 1110, Methanex claimed that California's measure in effect constitutes a substantial taking of the company's business, amounting to expropriation, since the state prevented the company from maintaining its market share and the outcome was California's transferring that share to US ethanol producers. California disputed these claims.[267]

The arbitration tribunal established under UNCITRAL held on January 15, 2001, that it had jurisdiction to accept petitions from third persons to intervene with written amicus briefs. Meanwhile, Methanex asked the Secretariat of the Commission for Environmental Cooperation to develop a factual record as to whether California is effectively enforcing its environmental laws against leaking underground gasoline tanks, which it contended were the real problem. It also argued that, under WTO rules, governmental measures must meet the "least trade restrictive" standard and must not be a disguised restriction on international trade.

Methanex submitted an amended statement of claim on February 12, 2001, adding a new claim of discrimination on the basis of nationality.[268] The tribunal considered US challenges on jurisdiction and admissibility.[269] The tribunal said that it had "no view at all" on the merits of the facts alleged by Methanex and disputed by the US, calling them "only assumed facts."[270] Based on the assumed facts, however, the tribunal dismissed the US challenges to the admissibility of Methanex' claims.[271] It also held that Methanex' original statement of claim did not meet jurisdictional requirements

---

[267] *See Methanex v. USA*, IISD, http://www.iisd.org/investment/dispute/methanex.asp for a time line of the case.

[268] *See* 1st Partial Award (Aug. 7, 2002), http://www.state.gov/documents/organization/12613 .pdf [hereinafter First Partial Award] at ¶¶ 12, 72–75.

[269] *See id.* ¶¶ 82–169, 172.

[270] *Id.* ¶¶ 44–71.

[271] *Id.* ¶ 172(1).

of Article 1101(1).[272] However, regarding Methanex' amended statement of claim, the tribunal held that the claim "as a whole" failed to meet the jurisdictional requirements of Article 1101(1) as well,[273] but it allowed Methanex 90 days to submit a fresh pleading and evidentiary material.[274]

In late 2002, Methanex filed such a pleading and the tribunal then held evidentiary hearings in June 2004 and issued a final award on August 3, 2005,[275] finding that Methanex had not provided credible evidence to support its claim of impermissible intent of Governor Davis, and hence its claims under NAFTA Articles 1102, 1105, and 1110 failed.[276] Because the tribunal found that there was "no illicit pretext" on the part of the US, nor was there an intent "to harm foreign methanol producers...or benefit domestic ethanol producers," it confirmed its earlier interim award that it lacked jurisdiction under NAFTA Chapter 11[277] and awarded all costs to the US.[278]

In *Glamis Gold, Ltd. v. United States*,[279] a Canadian mining company brought a claim against the US, invoking NAFTA Articles 1105 (fair and equitable treatment) and 1110 (expropriation), and alleging a breach on the part of the US. The company alleged wrongful delay by the US in approving its open-pit gold-mining project in southeastern California, the "Imperial Project." Finally, when it appeared likely that there would be federal approval, the State of California introduced a mandatory backfilling requirement aimed at protecting Native American sacred sites located in the area, thus rendering the project economically unfeasible. The tribunal rejected the expropriation claim on the ground that mining at a profit had not been made impossible. It also found that there was no breach of NAFTA Article 1105, citing the 1926 *Neer* case decision of the Mexican-US General Claims Commission for the proposition that no violation of the customary international law minimum standard had occurred.[280]

The issue in this case was the tribunal's act of balancing property rights as an investment interest with a non-investment interest – the protection of Native American sacred sites against possible harm caused by open-pit

---

[272] *Id.* ¶ 172(2).

[273] *Id.* ¶¶ 83–84.

[274] *Id.* ¶¶ 172(4), (9).

[275] Methanex Corp. v. United States, Final Award, NAFTA Ch. 11 Arb. Trib., August 3, 2005, http://www.state.gov/documents/organization/51052.pdf [hereinafter Methanex Final Award].

[276] *Id.* pt. IV.B, ¶ 38; pt. IV.C, ¶ 27; pt. IV.D, ¶ 18.

[277] *Id.* pt. IV.E, ¶ 22.

[278] *Id.* pt. V, ¶¶ 5–12.

[279] Glamis Gold, Ltd. v. United States, NAFTA Ch. 11 Arbitral Tribunal Award, June 8, 2009, http://ita.law.uvic.ca/documents/Glamis_Award_001.pdf [hereinafter Glamis Award].

[280] Neer (United States) v. Mexico, Opinion, October 15, 1926, 4 U.N.R.I.A.A. 61–62.

mining operations. The tribunal's observation on Article 1105 is instructive, as it stated that

> a violation of the customary international law minimum standard of treatment, as codified in Article 1105 of the NAFTA, requires an act that is sufficiently egregious and shocking – a gross denial of justice, manifest arbitrariness, blatant unfairness, a complete lack of due process, evident discrimination, or a manifest lack of reasons – so as to fall below accepted international standards and constitute a breach of Article 1105.[281]

Environmental and civil society activists have been critical that investors are able to successfully attack governmental regulations aimed at health and environmental protection. Also, WTO rules have been invoked that go beyond the reach of NAFTA Chapter 11's already expansive grant of rights to investors. However, both *Methanex* and *Glamis Gold* provide assurances that the tribunals are showing sensitivity and understanding of regulatory autonomy and balancing it carefully with investor interests.

14.3.2.3.2   Official Interpretations of Chapter 11

In response to the concern expressed primarily by Canada and the US about the vague provisions of Chapter 11, the trade ministers from the three NAFTA countries, sitting as the Free Trade Commission, gave an official interpretation of some of the provisions.[282]

The Commission responded to the concerns that the arbitral process is not open and transparent, since tribunals have held hearings in camera and documents have been kept confidential, thus not allowing the public timely information. The Commission adopted an interpretation in order to open the process and make it more transparent. It said that, apart from the limited exceptions contained in the relevant arbitral rules, parties agree "to make available to the public in a timely manner all documents submitted to, or issued by, a Chapter Eleven tribunal, subject to redaction" of confidential or privileged material or "information which the Party must withhold pursuant to the relevant arbitral rules, as applied."[283] Thus, tribunals still have the final say as to what documents to release and when to do so. The Commission also said that the member governments "may share with officials of their respective federal, state or provincial governments all relevant documents in

---

[281] Glamis Award, *supra* note 279, at ¶ 627.

[282] This is in accordance with NAFTA Article 1131(2), which states that an "interpretation by the Commission of a provision of this Agreement shall be binding on a Tribunal established under this Section."

[283] Article 24(4) of the UNCITRAL Rules states that "hearings shall be held in camera unless the parties agree otherwise."

the course of dispute settlement under Chapter Eleven of NAFTA, including confidential information."[284]

The Commission clarified Article 1105 on minimum standards of treatment to investors by limiting its terms to their rights and protections under customary international law.[285] It could, however, be argued that the standard remains rather vague, for what is included in customary international law could be subject to varying interpretations. Thus, this clarification fails to provide precision regarding the criteria to judge the validity of a corporation's challenge to a member state's rules and regulations aimed at protecting health and the environment.

As mentioned earlier, in interpreting Article 1105 the tribunal in Pope & Talbot had explicitly referred to the fairness elements as being in addition to the minimum requirements under international law. It had thus held that for NAFTA investors the standard for meeting the "fairness" requirement is without any threshold limitation. On its face, this interpretation would seem to be incompatible with the Commission's interpretation. However, on May 31, 2002, the tribunal found that it was not necessarily so. First, the tribunal said that it would determine the Commission's action in clarifying the meaning of Article 1105 as constituting an amendment and not an interpretation of that provision.[286] It nonetheless said that since this determination was not required, it would treat the clarification as an interpretation instead.

Next, the tribunal held that the phrase "shall be binding" in Article 1131(2) "is better regarded as mandatory than prospective."[287] It then examined the meaning behind the "fairness" element under customary international law, concluding that it had evolved beyond the standard of "international

---

[284] Notes of Interpretation of Certain Chapter 11 Provisions (NAFTA Free Trade Commission, July 31, 2001), A.2(d), http://www.international.gc.ca/trade-agreements-accords-commerciaux/disp-diff/nafta-interpr.aspx?lang=en&view=d.

[285] In the Commission's words,
   1. Article 1105(1) prescribes the customary international law minimum standard of treatment of aliens as the minimum standard of treatment to be afforded to investments of investors of another Party.
   2. The concepts of "fair and equitable treatment" and "full protection and security" do not require treatment in addition to or beyond that which is required by the customary international law minimum standard of treatment of aliens.
   3. A determination that there has been a breach of another provision of the NAFTA, or of a separate international agreement, does not establish that there has been a breach of Article 1105(1). *Id.* at B.

[286] Award, In re Arbitration under Chapter Eleven of the North American Free Trade Agreement between Pope & Talbot Inc. and Government of Canada, http://www.dfait_maeci .gc.ca/tna_nac/damage_award_pdf; First Partial Award, *supra* note 238, ¶¶ 17–47.

[287] *Id.* ¶ 51.

delinquency" and the meaning given to it in the 1920s as in the 1926 *Neer* case on which Canada had relied.[288] The tribunal referred to the 1967 OECD Draft Convention on the Protection of Foreign Property, the standard used in Bilateral Investment Treaties negotiated since 1967, and the International Court of Justice's formulation in a 1989 case by reference to the concept of "due process" to support its contention.[289] However, it concluded that even applying Canada's proposed standard of "egregious" conduct as the proper standard under customary international law to find a violation of Article 1105, Canada indeed had violated that article, for its conduct as a result of the "Verification Review Episode" that followed after the investors sought arbitration had shocked and outraged the tribunal.[290] It thus awarded the investor $407,646 plus interest.[291]

14.3.2.3.3   Appraisal

A major concern noted above is that investors can directly enforce rights against the state, through the investor-state private enforcement mechanism. Why should corporations have special rights to enforce treaties to which they are not parties? Critics note a related issue, that these are public interest disputes which should not be submitted to special arbitration bodies that have expertise in resolving commercial disputes, but have shown little interest in understanding and appreciating health and environmental concerns. Governmental rules and regulations enacted after public debate and designed to protect the health and environment are frequently ignored.

As tribunals have given expansive definition to the terms "investor" and "investment," the Chapter 11 rights of foreign investors or corporations are seen as going beyond those available to domestic corporations: why should they enjoy preferential treatment relative to local investors? Also, the interpretation has failed to provide guidance on other substantive issues. The meaning of the term "tantamount to expropriation" is far from clear. Prior NAFTA tribunals' rulings have not acknowledged the traditional doctrine under which states have the authority to promulgate regulations under their

---

[288] *Id.* ¶¶ 57–66.

[289] *Id.* ¶ 30 n. 55.

[290] In the tribunal's words,

> Figuring in this new attitude were assertions of non-existent policy reasons for forcing them to comply with very burdensome demands for documents, refusals to provide them with promised information, threats of reductions and even termination of the Investment's export quotas, serious misrepresentations of fact in memoranda to the Minister concerning the Investor's and the Investment's actions and even suggestions of criminal investigation of the Investment's conduct. *Id.* ¶ 68.

[291] *Id.* ¶ 87.

"police power," provided such regulations are for a public purpose and are not discriminatory.

Through case law, the tribunals have in effect imposed a regulatory takings doctrine that nullifies members' attempts to undertake measures to protect public health and the environment.[292] Thus, there is a chilling effect on governments' regulatory functions since they are required to provide compensation to foreign corporations even when these businesses are minimally affected by the regulations. Another criticism is that these special arbitral tribunals decide issues in secrecy; the lack of transparency is an affront to democracy.

14.3.3   Criticisms of NAFTA

In addition to the criticism of Chapter 11 of NAFTA, another major criticism of NAFTA on environmental grounds is that it does not provide a sufficiently effective enforcement regime.[293] To illustrate, Chapter 20 provides the dispute settlement procedure of NAFTA. If a dispute arises, the parties are to enter into consultations.[294] If the matter is not resolved within the appropriate time limit,[295] any of the involved parties may refer the dispute to the Free Trade Commission (the Commission), NAFTA's principal governing body, comprising "cabinet-level representatives of the Parties or their designees."[296]

Once a matter is referred to the Commission, the Commission is required to meet promptly (normally within ten days) to consider the dispute.[297] It has a wide range of options available to resolve the dispute, although within a limited amount of time.[298] If it fails to achieve such resolution within the time limit, any party involved may request that the matter be heard by an arbitral panel, established by the Commission,[299] which must issue a final report, normally within 120 days of its establishment.[300]

The dispute settlement procedure, therefore, does contain promising, and in some situations novel, provisions. First, the procedure is designed to be as expeditious as possible. Normally, the entire procedure should take no

---

[292] For a comment suggesting that US regulatory takings jurisprudence should be used to determine this issue under Chapter 11, *see* Terri L. Lilley, *Note: Keeping NAFTA 'Green' for Investors and the Environment*, 75 S. CALIF. L. REV. 727 (2002).

[293] *See* Ludwiszewski, *supra* note 211.

[294] NAFTA, *supra* note 210, art. 2006(1).

[295] *Id.* art. 2007(1).

[296] *Id.* art. 2001(1).

[297] NAFTA, *supra* note 210, art. 2007(4).

[298] *Id.* arts. 2007(5), 2008(1).

[299] *Id.* art. 2008(2).

[300] *Id.* arts. 2017(1), 2008(2).

longer than 165 to 195 days to complete.[301] Moreover, the arbitral panel is given the opportunity to "seek information and technical advice from any person or body that it deems appropriate,"[302] with the agreement of the parties. It may also "request a written report of a scientific review board on any factual issue concerning environmental…matters raised by a disputing Party."[303] As one commentator has explained: "This provision creates, for the first time in a trade agreement, a formal mechanism that provides trade experts facing an environmental issue with the scientific and environmental expertise that they require to make a fully informed decision."[304]

Another unique provision of Chapter 20 regarding GATT dispute settlement is contained in Article 2005.[305] Normally, a complaining party is allowed to pursue dispute settlement through either the NAFTA procedure or the GATT procedure, at the discretion of that party. However, if the dispute involves an environmental or conservation agreement, a sanitary or phytosanitary measure, or a standards-related measure, the responding party is authorized to invoke the more environmentally sensitive NAFTA dispute settlement procedures.

However, while the NAFTA dispute resolution regime contains these beneficial provisions, it contains only weak provisions to enforce any decision rendered by the arbitral panel. After receiving the final report of a panel, the disputing parties are to agree on the resolution of the dispute, which will normally reflect the decision of the panel. However, if a party does not

---

[301] Fifteen to 45 days for consultation (*id.* art. 2007(1)), 30 days for the Commission to attempt resolution (art. 2008(1)), and 120 days for the arbitral panel to issue its final report (*id.* arts. 2016(2) and 2017(1)), not including the time spent in actually forming the arbitral panel.

[302] *Id.* art. 2014.

[303] *Id.* art. 2015(1).

[304] Ludwiszewski, *supra* note 211, at 698.

[305] Specifically, article 2005 states:

> 3. In any dispute [regarding a matter that arises under both NAFTA and GATT] where the responding Party claims that its action is subject to Article 104 (Relation to Environmental and Conservation Agreements) and requests in writing that the matter be considered under this Agreement, the complaining Party may, in respect of that matter, thereafter have recourse to dispute settlement procedures solely under this Agreement.
> 4. In any [such] dispute…that arises under Section B of Chapter Seven (Sanitary and Phytosanitary Measures) or Chapter Nine (Standards-Related Measures):
>   (a) concerning a measure adopted or maintained by a Party to protect its human, animal or plant life or health, or to protect its environment, and that raises factual issues concerning the environment, health, safety or conservation, including directly related scientific matters,
> …the complaining Party may, in respect of that matter thereafter have recourse to dispute settlement procedures solely under this Agreement. NAFTA, *supra* note 183, art. 2005(3) and (4).

comply with that provision, the other Party "may suspend the application to the Party complained against of benefits of equivalent effect until such time as they have reached agreement on a resolution of the dispute."[306] This provision appears to be particularly ineffective when addressing environmental concerns. For example, if one party relaxes its environmental standards-related measures in order to attract investment, the complaining party will not likely lower its measures in retaliation, and if it did, it certainly would be counterproductive toward the goal of environmental protection.

Another weakness regarding the enforcement regime in NAFTA is contained in Article 2021: "No Party may provide for a right of action under its domestic law against any other Party on the ground that a measure of another Party is inconsistent with this Agreement." Thus, individuals who are affected by any violations of NAFTA that result in environmental degradation may only rely on their state to protect them, rather than the ability to take action themselves. As mentioned earlier, NAFTA Chapter 11 on Investment has raised special environmental concerns.

14.3.4   *North American Agreement on Environmental Cooperation*

William Reilly, while EPA Administrator, urged Congress to support NAFTA's ratification:

> NAFTA will help improve the quality of the environment throughout North America. This is the most environmentally sensitive, the greenest free trade agreement ever negotiated anywhere. It marks a watershed in the history of environmental protection. NAFTA sets the environmental standard against which future trade agreements will be measured.... If Congress does not ratify NAFTA, it will be the environmental mistake of the decade.[307]

Despite this enthusiastic endorsement, environmental concerns regarding NAFTA were sufficient to force the Canadian, US, and Mexican governments to formulate a side agreement that would provide extra protection for the environment. The North American Agreement on Environmental Cooperation between the governments of the USA, Canada, and Mexico (NAAEC or Side Agreement) was passed,[308] concurrently with NAFTA, by Congress in November 1993 and signed into law by President Clinton in December

---

[306] *Id.* art. 2019(1).

[307] News Conference with William Reilly, EPA Administrator: North American Free Trade Agreement, Fed. News Service, Aug. 13, 1992, at 2–3, Lexis Fedcom Library, FEDNEW file.

[308] North American Agreement on Environmental Cooperation Between the Government of the United States of America, the Government of Canada and the Government of the United Mexican States, 32 I.L.M. 1480 (1993) Dec. 17, 1993 [hereinafter Side Agreement].

1993.[309] The Side Agreement is comprised of five parts: objectives, obligations, the North American Commission on Environmental Cooperation, cooperation and provision of information, and consultation and resolution of disputes.

14.3.4.1   *Objectives*

The Side Agreement proclaims ten objectives, nine of which relate to the environment, while the remaining objective, which falls in the middle of the list, concerns trade.[310] This demonstrates the primary intent of this agreement – to allay environmental protection concerns. However, since NAFTA is a trade agreement, to which this is a side agreement, any "new trade barriers," or "trade distortions," even to protect the environment, are to be discouraged.

14.3.4.2   *Obligations*

This part of the Side Agreement imposes many new mandatory duties upon the parties. For example, each party is obligated to prepare and release to the public reports on the state of its environment,[311] prepare measures to deal with environmental emergencies,[312] promote environmental education,[313] promote "scientific research and technology development" regarding the environment,[314] and conduct environmental impact assessments.[315] Furthermore, the Side

---

[309] *See supra* note 23; *see also* M. Sandalow, *House Approves NAFTA*, SAN FRANCISCO CHRONICLE, Nov. 18, 1993, at A1.

[310] Side Agreement, *supra* note 271, art. 1. The objectives are to:
  - (a) foster the protection and improvement of the environment in the territories of the Parties for the well-being of present and future generations;
  - (b) promote sustainable development based on cooperation and mutually supportive environmental and economic policies;
  - (c) increase cooperation between the Parties to better conserve, protect, and enhance the environment, including wild flora and fauna;
  - (d) support the environmental goals and objectives of the NAFTA;
  - (e) avoid creating trade distortions or new trade barriers;
  - (f) strengthen cooperation on the development and improvement of environmental laws, regulations, procedures, policies and practices;
  - (g) enhance compliance with, and enforcement of, environmental laws and regulations;
  - (h) promote transparency and public participation in the development of environmental laws, regulations and policies;
  - (i) promote economically efficient and effective environmental measures; and
  - (j) promote pollution prevention policies and practices.

[311] *Id.* art. 2(1)(a).

[312] *Id.* art. 2(1)(b).

[313] *Id.* art. 2(1)(c).

[314] *Id.* art. 2(1)(d).

[315] *Id.* art. 2(1)(e).

Agreement adds to NAFTA's prohibition on downward harmonization of environmental standards by obligating each party to "ensure that its laws and regulations provide for high levels of environmental protection and [to] strive to continue to improve those laws and regulations."[316] The Side Agreement also addresses the problem of governments that maintain high environmental standards but do not enforce them. Article 5(1) requires each party to "effectively enforce its environmental laws and regulations through appropriate governmental action...."[317]

It is a promising development that, unlike NAFTA, the Side Agreement enables private citizens to seek enforcement. Article 6 requires each party to "ensure that interested persons may request the Party's competent authorities to investigate alleged violations of its environmental laws and regulations and shall give such requests due consideration." Under an innovative procedure, the use of courts or agencies to enforce environmental measures is also sanctioned.[318]

The requirement for a private citizen to begin such a proceeding is that s/he have "a legally recognized interest under [his or her Party country's] law in a particular matter."[319] Thus, for example, a private citizen in any Party country may file suit in order to force a nearby factory to cease dumping

---

[316] *Id.* art. 3.

[317] The article then provides several examples of such enforcement, such as "monitoring compliance and investigating suspected violations, including through on-site inspections" (art. 5(1)(b)); "promoting environmental audits" (art. 5(1)(f)); and even "providing for search, seizure or detention" (art. 5(1)(k)).

[318] *Id.* art. 5(2) and (3). Article 5 reads in part:

  2. Each Party shall ensure that judicial, quasi-judicial or administrative enforcement proceedings are available under its law to sanction or remedy violations of its environmental laws and regulations.

  3. Sanctions and remedies provided for a violation of a Party's environmental laws and regulations shall, as appropriate:

     ...

     (b) include compliance agreements, fines, imprisonment, injunctions, the closure of facilities, and the cost of containing or cleaning up pollution.

[319] *Id.* art. 6(2). The redress includes the right:

  (a) to sue another person under that Party's jurisdiction for damages;

  (b) to seek sanctions or remedies such as monetary penalties, emergency closures or orders to mitigate the consequences of violations of its environmental laws and regulations;

  (c) to request the competent authorities to take appropriate action to enforce that Party's environmental laws and regulations in order to protect the environment or to avoid environmental harm; or to seek injunctions where a person suffers, or may suffer, loss, damage or injury as a result of conduct by another person under that Party's jurisdiction contrary to that Party's environmental laws and regulations or from tortious conduct. *Id.* art. 6(3).

hazardous waste into the local water supply and also receive monetary damages from the factory.

14.3.4.3   *North American Commission on Environmental Cooperation*
The Side Agreement established a new institution, the North American Commission on Environmental Cooperation (CEC), to build cooperation among the NAFTA members in implementing the Side Agreement. The CEC consists of a Council, a Secretariat, and a Joint Public Advisory Committee.[320]

14.3.4.3.1   The Council
The Council, the governing body of CEC,[321] comprises cabinet-level parties' representatives.[322] Its supervisory responsibilities include overseeing the implementation of the Side Agreement,[323] as well as considering data on the environment and trade, assessing transboundary environmental impacts, and addressing questions of interpretation of the Side Agreement.[324] Transparency seems to be an important goal of the Council, for all decisions and recommendations of the Council are to be made by consensus and made public, "except as the Council may otherwise decide."[325]

Among the tasks that the Council is required to undertake is to "strengthen cooperation on the development and continuing improvement of environmental laws and regulations."[326] In doing so, the Council must attempt to make environmental regulations, improve compatibility of standards and regulations among parties, and encourage effective enforcement of domestic environmental laws.[327]

14.3.4.3.2   The Secretariat
The Side Agreement creates a Secretariat of the CEC, which is headquartered in Montreal, Quebec, Canada.[328] The Secretariat is intended to be a truly independent body[329] that provides technical and administrative support. In addition, its main functions include hearing allegations of nonenforcement of environmental laws[330] and reporting on the general state of the environment

---

[320] *Id.* art. 8(2); COMMISSION ON ENVIRONMENTAL COOPERATION, http://www.cec.org.
[321] *Id.* art. 10(1).
[322] *Id.* art. 9(1).
[323] *Id.* art. 10(1).
[324] *Id.*
[325] *Id.* art. 9(6). and (7).
[326] *Id.* art. 10(3).
[327] *Id.* art. 10(4).
[328] Int'l Env't Daily (BNA), Mar. 29, 1994.
[329] Side Agreement, *supra* note 308, art. 11(4).
[330] *Id.* art. 14.

in North America and on the environmental activities of each party.[331] Since the reports are made public, private citizens are enabled to hold their governments accountable for environmental conditions.

The Side Agreement provides two distinct enforcement procedures to ensure compliance with substantive environmental obligations under the Agreement – the private enforcement procedure and the governmental enforcement procedure. Under the private enforcement procedure of Article 14, known as the "Citizen Submissions Process," the Secretariat is empowered to "consider a submission from any nongovernmental organization or person asserting that a Party is failing to effectively enforce its environmental law."[332] The identity of the submitting entity must be revealed, the submitting person or organization must reside "in the territory of a Party,"[333] the Secretariat must find that the submission "appears to be aimed at promoting enforcement rather than at harassing industry,"[334] and the submission must include "sufficient information."[335] Additionally, NGOs may file under the private enforcement mechanism of Article 13 as they seek a factual report from the Secretariat pertaining to any matter of environmental concern, for under this Article, the Secretariat is authorized to prepare a report on any environmental issues, except those "related to whether a Party has failed to enforce its environmental laws and regulations" under Articles 14–15.

While the private enforcement procedure does allow transboundary supervision by private citizens, its value is, however, limited by the weak enforcement powers given to the Secretariat. It cannot hold parties accountable for lax environmental enforcement, but can only publish a factual record, this, too, only with the Council's permission.[336]

Under the governmental enforcement procedure, the Side Agreement provides for a dispute resolution regime similar in design to that contained in Chapter 20 of NAFTA. Parties may turn to this regime when "there has been a persistent pattern of failure by [another] Party to effectively enforce its environmental laws."[337] The regime consists of consultations between

---

[331] *Id.* art. 12.

[332] *Id.* art. 14(1).

[333] *Id.* art. 14(1)(f).

[334] *Id.* art. 14(1)(d).

[335] *Id.* art. 14(1)(b) and (c).

[336] *Id.* arts. 14(3); 15(2); 15(7). The Secretariat must seek the Council's permission to prepare a factual record and then again after preparing the record to make it publicly available. This last provision, which requires the Council to authorize the publication of factual records, was a source of concern for several environmental groups in the three member countries that had urged the Council to operate openly. Int'l Env't Daily (BNA), Feb. 25, 1994.

[337] Side Agreement, *supra* note 308, art. 22(1).

disputing parties,[338] the Council's intervention,[339] and finally the arbitration mechanism.[340] The regime displays its potency through the enforcement of the final report. If, in its final report, the arbitral panel concludes that there has been a "persistent pattern of failure by the Party complained against to effectively enforce its environmental law,"[341] a party may ask that the panel be reconvened. The reconvened panel may impose a monetary enforcement assessment,[342] and its decision is final.[343] Ultimately, trade retaliation remains the last resort. However, none of the parties has thus far ever resorted to this procedure.

14.3.4.3.3 The Joint Public Advisory Committee

The Joint Public Advisory Committee (JPAC) comprises 15 independent volunteer members, five from each party.[344] The only real powers of the JPAC, however, are to "provide advice to the Council on any matter within the scope of [the Side Agreement]"[345] and to "provide relevant technical, scientific or other information to the Secretariat."[346]

14.3.4.3.4 Cooperation and Provision of Information

Under this part of the Side Agreement, a party is obligated to notify the other parties of any changes in its environmental measures that it "considers might materially affect the operation of [the Side Agreement]."[347] Also, each party is allowed to inform the other parties of possible violations of their environmental laws, but is not required to do so.[348] Finally, the parties are to provide information to the Council or the Secretariat at their request, but again, they are not required to do so.[349] The monetary enforcement assessment, however, has a ceiling,[350] and the proceeds are to be spent on the improvement of the environment or on the enforcement of environmental law in the offending party.[351] Canada has a different enforcement procedure.[352]

---

[338] *Id.* art. 22(4).
[339] *Id.* art. 23.
[340] *Id.* arts. 24, 31–32, 34.
[341] *Id.* art. 34(1).
[342] *Id.* art. 34(5)(a).
[343] *Id.* art. 34(6).
[344] *Id.* art. 16(1).
[345] *Id.* art. 16(4).
[346] *Id.* art. 16(5).
[347] *Id.* art. 20(2).
[348] *Id.* art. 20(4).
[349] *Id.* art. 21.
[350] *Id.* Annex 34(1).
[351] *Id.* Annex 34(3).
[352] *Id.* Annex 36(A).

14.3.4.3.5   The Border Environment Cooperation Commission and the
North American Development Bank
NAFTA's failure and that of the Side Agreement to address environmental
issues in the US-Mexico border area led to the establishment of two new
institutions – another commission, the Border Environment Cooperation
Commission (BECC), and a development bank, the North American Development Bank (NADB) to "help develop and finance solid waste, water supply, and wastewater infrastructure" in this area.[353] Several new projects have
been undertaken under this initiative.[354]

In 1996, the Border XXI Program was established to build on prior binational environmental efforts. The goal of the program is to "promote sustainable development in the border region by seeking a balance among social
and economic factors and the protection of the environment in border communities and natural areas...."[355] The program has also worked in partnership with the BECC and the NADB, especially in activities pertaining to
water, wastewater, and solid waste infrastructure.[356] The program's strategies include ensuring public involvement, building capacity and decentral-
izing environmental management, and ensuring interagency cooperation.[357]
UNEP and the Mexican Secretariat of Environment, Natural Resources, and
Fisheries, the coordinators of the program, reported in 2001 that it had made
great strides in preventing further environmental deterioration through projects that have fostered improvements in environmental stewardship. This
binational cooperation has enabled significant improvements to be made in
both the continuity and the uniformity of natural ecosystem and biodiversity
preservation.[358] Nine work groups, including those on air, water, environmental health, hazardous and solid waste, natural resources, and pollution
prevention are primarily responsible for initiating and conducting binational
program activities.[359]

---

[353] US-Mexico Border XXI Program: Progress Report 1996–2000, at 2 (2001) [hereinafter
Border XXI]. The US and Mexico signed the Agreement Concerning the Establishment
of a Border Environment Cooperation Commission and a North American Development
Bank, Nov. 16, 18, 1993, US-Mex., 32 I.L.M. 1545 (1993). *See generally* F. Guerrero,
U.S. General Accounting Office, International Environment – Environmental
Infrastructure Needs in the U.S.-Mexico Border Region Remain Unmet (GAO
Report GAO/RCED-96-179, 1996), LEXIS, Legis Library, GAORPT file.

[354] *See* Kori Westbrook, *The North American Free Trade Agreement's Effects on Mexico's Environment*, 10 Currents: Int'l Trade L.J. 86, 88 (2001).

[355] Border XXI, *supra* note 353, at 4, 15.

[356] *Id.* at 3.

[357] For a summary of these strategies and activities, *see id.* at 5–9.

[358] *Id.* at 9.

[359] For a brief overview, *see id.* at 9–15. The work groups comprise elected officials from
both countries, tribal nations and NGO representatives. *See also* I. S. Moreno, *et al.*, *Free*

14.3.4.3.6   Assessment

At its beginning, the Side Agreement, as with NAFTA, had both supporters and critics. The supporters generally noted the revolutionary nature of the agreement, as it focused primarily on the environment – considering that it is a trade agreement.[360] Some critics, however, argued that the agreement failed to fully protect domestic environmental measures from the accusation that they were illegal trade barriers.[361] Also, some argued that the agreement did not take enough steps in order to make parties enforce their own environmental laws.[362] And, while the agreement provides for funds, through trade sanctions and fines, to remedy future environmental damage, it does not provide funding to clean up the already damaged US-Mexican border.[363] Still, many environmental groups at the outset decided to support the Side Agreement and help it to protect the environment successfully rather than ignore its existence.[364]

The concern about the Side Agreement was initially caused by the uncertainty as to whether the regime created under it will be as effective functionally as it seemed theoretically.[365] For instance, one critic called the procedure to compel enforcement (viz. trade sanctions or fines) "absurd," claiming that trade sanctions would really only be enforced "[s]ome day, (in) some bizarre set of circumstances where the planets are aligned."[366] Others questioned the effectiveness of the Citizen Submissions Process and CEC's ability to compel enforcement of domestic environmental standards. The following discussion addresses some of these questions, with a primary focus on the Citizen Submissions Process.

14.3.4.3.7   The Side Agreement in Action

A few specific developments related to the implementation of the Side Agreement will be highlighted here. These include two Secretariat Reports

---

Trade and the Environment: The NAFTA, the NAAEC, and Implications for the Future, 12 Tulane Int'l L.J. 405, 410 (1999).

[360] *See* Int'l Env't Daily (BNA), Sept. 14, 1993.

[361] *See id.*

[362] *See id.*

[363] *See id.*

[364] *See NAFTA: Environmentalists Seek Openness in North American Environment Commission*, Int'l Env't Daily (BNA), Feb. 25, 1994. The US environmental groups sharing this view included: the Center for International Environmental Law; Defenders of Wildlife; the Environmental Defense Fund; Friends of the Earth; the National Wildlife Federation; the National Audubon Society; the Natural Resources Defense Council; and the Sierra Club.

[365] *See* Int'l Env't Daily (BNA), *supra* note 360.

[366] *Id.* The statement was made by Robert Housman, an attorney for the Center for International Environmental Law.

authorized under Article 13 and three factual records prepared by the Secretariat under the Articles 14–15 Citizen Submissions Procedure.[367]

The Secretariat Report on the Silva Reservoir,[368] located 200 miles northwest of Mexico City in the State of Guanajuato, identified the probable causes of the death of thousands of migratory water fowl in the winter of 1994–95. In June 1995 three NGOs requested the CEC to prepare an Article 13 report. The CEC prepared a detailed study after a preliminary report by a group of experts. The outcome was the undertaking of an integrated program for the cleanup of the Silva Reservoir, effective remediation activities, and a management plan for the pertinent watershed and the reservoir. The report stated: "The work undertaken in the wake of this waterfowl die-off shows that, through international cooperation, public participation, the commitment of business, and the vision of local government and the CEC joining forces, it is possible to transform an environmental problem into an opportunity for local development."[369]

In June 1999 the CEC published an Article 13 report prepared by the Secretariat entitled "Ribbon of Life – An Agenda for Preserving Transboundary Migratory Bird Habitat on the Upper San Pedro River."[370] The CEC Secretariat had launched the Upper San Pedro Initiative[371] in May 1997 following an Article 13 submission in November 1996 by Earthlaw, an environmental organization that ran at that time the Environmental Law Clinic at the University of Denver College of Law,[372] requesting the Secretariat to prepare a report examining the effects of all human activities on the San Pedro ecosystem and suggesting measures to promote "national or multilateral

---

[367] The CEC has published a guide to Articles 14–15 submissions, Bringing The Facts To Light – Submissions on Enforcement Matters (2000).

[368] An example of regional environmental cooperation in North America, CEC: Silva Reservoir, http://www.cec.org/pubs_docs/documents/index.cfm?var-lan=english&ID=282.

[369] *Id.*

[370] *Ribbon of Life, An Agenda for Preserving Transboundary Migratory Bird Habitat on the Upper San Pedro River*, CEC Report, http://www.cec.org/Storage/31/2263_Ribbon-engl_EN.pdf.

[371] *Id.* at 2. The initiative was aimed at advancing three concrete objectives:
- To initiate a process where diverse stakeholders from the region can develop and implement economically and environmentally sustainable strategies for enhancing and preserving the riverine ecosystem of the upper San Pedro watershed;
- To develop a model of cooperation that could have relevance to other transboundary basins; and
- To inform the broader public about the regional importance of preserving migratory bird habitat and the challenges and opportunities in conserving and protecting valued transboundary resources.

[372] Submission Pursuant to Article 13 of the NAAEC, Nov. 1996 (on file with the authors). Earthlaw has now merged with Earthjustice Legal Defense Fund.

conservation strategies" for protection of the ecosystem.[373] It is noteworthy that millions of songbirds migrate from Mexico and Central America to Canada and the Northern US, traveling along the rivers, including the San Pedro River, to their summer breeding habitats. The Secretariat prepared a comprehensive report with the assistance of experts, public review, and an advisory panel's recommendations, which warns: "Should the human demand for water continue to exceed supply, the outstanding riparian habitat of the upper San Pedro Valley, one of the most biologically diverse regions in all of North America, could be irreversibly compromised."[374]

As of June 2012, the CEC had 12 active citizen submissions under Article 14.[375] Six of those submissions alleged the nonenforcement of Mexican environmental laws, four were about Canada and one was about the US.[376] The submissions are often rich in detail regarding what the submitters expect from the environmental law enforcement, and why the submitters feel that those expectations are not being met.[377] By June 2012, the CEC had also publicly released sixteen factual records. The first three factual records released by the CEC will be briefly discussed here. These cases set the stage for future decisions by the CEC, and show how the organization has grappled with Art. 14.

In the first released case, the *Cozumel Reef* case (Sem-96-001),[378] NGOs alleged in their submission that during the evaluation process of the project, "Construction and Operation of a Public Harbor Terminal for Tourist Cruises on the Island of Cozumel, State of Quintana Roo," Mexico had failed to effectively enforce its environmental laws – the project was initiated without a comprehensive environmental impact assessment (EIA) for the entire port, rather than only for the proposed pier, and, located within the limits

---

[373] *Id.* at 5–8.

[374] Ribbon of Life, *supra* note 333, at 1. *See generally id.* at 2–31.

[375] For the current status of filed submissions, *see* http://www.cec.org/Page.asp?PageID=751& ContentID=&SiteNodeID=250&BL_ExpandID=156.

[376] *Id.*

[377] Opalka Katia, *Enforcement Indicators and Citizen Submissions on Enforcement Matters Under the North American Agreement on Environmental Cooperation*, INECE, http://www .inece.org/conference/7/vol1/23_Opalka.pdf.

[378] For submission documents, *see Citizen Submissions on Enforcement Matters: Registry and Public Files of Submissions*, CEC, http://www.cec.org/Page.asp?PageID=2001&ContentID= 2346&SiteNodeID=543&BL_ExpandID=;. For an extensive discussion on the case, *see* Paul S. Kibel, *The Paper Tiger Awakens: North American Environmental Law after the Cozumel Reef Case*, 39 Colum. J. Transnat'l L. 395, 447–70 (2001). For a summary, *see* CEC, *Lessons Learned – Citizen Submissions Under Articles 14 and 15 of the North American Agreement on Environmental Cooperation* (Final Report to the Council of the CEC Submitted by the Joint Public Advisory Committee, June 6, 2001, at 8–9 [hereinafter *Lessons Learned*]. The following description is drawn from the official documents.

of a protected natural area, the project represented an immediate danger for the survival and development of the Paradise Reef and the Caribbean Barrier Reef.

The Secretariat prepared the factual record, which included the findings of three technical experts on the possible ecological risks of construction and operation of the pier, who held varying interpretations on the issue. It provided a summary of the Parties' contentions and the respective claims and analysis on both sides of the dispute. However, the Secretariat reached no conclusion as to the effective enforcement of applicable environmental laws of Mexico and made no recommendations.

The Secretariat released the *BC Hydro* record (Sem-97-001) on June 11, 2000.[379] In April 1997, the Sierra Legal Defense Fund (a Canadian NGO) and the Sierra Club Legal Defense Fund (a US NGO) had filed an Article 14 submission alleging that Canada had failed to effectively enforce its Fisheries Act[380] against BC Hydro, a corporation wholly owned by the Province of British Columbia, "to ensure the protection of fish and fish habitat in British Columbia's rivers from ongoing and repeated environmental damage caused by hydroelectric dams."[381] The groups also alleged that the Canadian government had failed to utilize its powers pursuant to the National Energy Board Act.[382]

The CEC Secretariat recommended to the Council that the factual record was appropriate only in respect to the alleged failure to effectively enforce the Fisheries Act. Following the Council's approval, the Secretariat began collecting information involving public participation, as well. It established an expert panel to assist it in the process and also requested information from the Joint Public Advisory Committee (JPAC).

The factual record included the history of hydroelectric projects in British Columbia, their operational methods, their usefulness in providing electricity and their impact upon fish and habitat. It also contained information on Canada's, British Columbia's, and the expert panel's interpretation of "failure to enforce environmental laws effectively." The factual record summarizes

---

[379] *Citizen Submissions on Enforcement Matters, Registry and Public Files of Submissions, BC Hydro*, CEC, http://www.cec.org/Page.asp?PageID=2001&ContentID=2358&SiteNodeID= 543&BL_ExpandID= [hereinafter BC Hydro].

[380] Section 35 of the Fisheries Act (R.S.C. 1985, c. F-14, Sec. 35(1)) provides: "No person shall carry on any work or undertaking that results in the harmful alteration, disruption or destruction of fish habitat." Sec. 35(2) provides an exception if authorized by the Minister of Fisheries and Oceans or by a regulation made under the Act.

[381] BC Hydro, *supra* note 379, at 1; for a summary record, *see* Lessons Learned, *supra* note 341, at 5–8.

[382] National Energy Board Act, R.S.C. 1985, c. N-7 § 119.06.

the contentions of the parties without a determination of what constituted "effective enforcement."

The third citizen submission regarding which the Secretariat released a factual record was *Metales y Derivados* (Sem-98-007),[383] released February 11, 2002. In October 1998 NGOs filed the submission alleging that Mexico had failed to effectively enforce its environmental law in connection with an abandoned lead smelter in Tijuana, Mexico, that posed serious threats to the environment and to the health of the neighboring community.[384] They asserted that a San Diego-based company did not return the hazardous waste generated by Metales y Derivados, its Mexican subsidiary, to the United States as required by Mexican law, and that Mexico failed to take the necessary measures to contain or neutralize the abandoned hazardous waste.[385] Mexico responded by contending that it had attempted to find a solution to the problem but had not been able to remedy it. The environmental situation existing at the site, it said, was not because of a failure to effectively enforce the environmental law, but due to causes "that surpass its scope of authority."[386]

In preparing the factual record, the Secretariat collected information from various sources and from independent experts, and also gathered technical information. The Secretariat noted that, regarding the maquilladores, and especially the situation in this case, "the scarcity of resources and the opportunity for the offenders to use the border as a shield against legal action are obstacles to the effective enforcement of environmental law."[387]

As in the prior two factual records, the Secretariat here, again, did not reach conclusions of law on whether Mexico had failed to enforce its environmental law effectively. However, it stated that "the information presented by the Secretariat in this factual record...reveals that, as a matter of fact, no actions have been taken to restore the soil to a condition in which it can be used in the industrial activities corresponding to the zoning of the area...in order to enforce effectively [the pertinent environmental law]."[388] It should be noted that the Secretariat altered the language in this statement from "in order to enforce effectively [the pertinent environmental law]" to "which

---

[383] *Metales y Derivados*, CEC, http://www.cec.org/Page.asp?PageID=2001&ContentID=2372& SiteNodeID=543&BL_ExpandID=.

[384] For a summary of the submission *see id.* at 13–14.

[385] *Id.* at 13–14.

[386] *Id.* at 16 (citation omitted). *See also id.* at 15–16.

[387] *Id.* at 42 (citation omitted).

[388] *Id.* at 59–60.

relates to the issue of whether it is effectively enforcing [the pertinent environmental law]," in response to a comment by the US.[389]

Other Article 13 Reports include *Electricity and the Environment*,[390] *Continental Pollutant Pathways*,[391] *Green Building*,[392] *Maize and Biodiversity*,[393] *Sustainable Freight Transportation*,[394] and *Environmental Hazards of the Transborder Movement and Recycling of Spent Lead-Acid Batteries.*[395]

The CEC also created a North American Fund for Environmental Cooperation in October 1995 to award grants to NGOs in the three member countries. As of July 2002, the Fund had made 176 grants totaling $6.22 million to support community-based projects that promote the goals and objectives of the CEC.[396] The program is on-going – for example, the CEC announced on February 16, 2012 a $1.3 million award to support communities in their efforts to address environmental problems locally across the Americas.[397]

Pursuant to Article 16(4) of the NAAEC, which states that the Joint Public Advisory Committee "may provide advice to the Council on any matter within the scope of this agreement," the JPAC submitted a report to the Council in June 2001, "Lessons Learned – Citizen Submissions Under Articles 14 and 15 of the North American Agreement on Environmental Cooperation,"[398] suggesting reforms.[399] The Council accepted the advice on

---

[389] *See* comment by Judith E. Ayres, Assistant Administrator, US EPA, to the Executive Director of the CEC Secretariat, Nov. 16, 2001, *id.* at 153–4.

[390] CEC, Independent Secretariat Reports: Electricity and the Environment, June 2002, http://www.cec.org/Storage/31/2244_CEC_Art13electricity_Eng.pdf.

[391] CEC, Independent Secretariat Reports: Continental Pollutant Pathways, 1997, http://www.cec.org/Storage/31/2264_polluten_EN.pdf.

[392] *See Green Building,* CEC, http://www.cec.org/Page.asp?PageID=1293&SiteNodeID=341.

[393] *See Maize and Biodiversity,* CEC, http://www.cec.org/Storage/56/4837_Maize-and-Biodiversity_en.pdf.

[394] *See Sustainable Freight Transfer,* CEC, http://www.cec.org/Page.asp?PageID=1293&SiteNodeID=539&BL_ExpandID=364.

[395] The CEC Secretariat is developing this report, aimed at promoting sound management of spent lead-acid batteries to ensure that human health and the environment are protected in all three countries. *See Environmental Hazards of the Transboundary Movement and Recycling of Spent Lead-Acid Batteries,* CEC http://www.cec.org/Page.asp?PageID=751&SiteNodeID=1075.

[396] *Community-based Energy Grants Announced by North American Environmental Commission,* http://www.cec.org/news/details/index.cfm?varlan=english&ID=2491. See also, *General Information on Grants for Environmental Cooperation,* CEC, http://www.cec.org/grants.

[397] *CEC, Canada, Mexico, and the United States Announce Grants to Address North American Environmental Challenges,* February 16, 2012, http://www.cec.org/Page.asp?PageID=122&ContentID=25167&SiteNodeID=655&BL_ExpandID=.

[398] Lessons Learned, *supra* note 378.

[399] *Id.* at 14–17.

the timeliness of the review and as to providing public statements of its reasons when it declines preparation of a factual record.[400] The JPAC has continued its efforts to reform the process as, for example, it has again sought citizen participation in the revision of citizen submissions on Enforcement Matters Guidelines.[401] Subsequently, in March 2002 and again in July 2002, the JPAC expressed its "serious concern about potential negative effects of NAFTA Chapter 11 provisions on government's ability to act in the public interest," repeating the earlier recommendation on monitoring and follow-up to factual records, and again emphasized transparency, due process, openness, and accountability.[402]

The CEC established an advisory group on assessing the environmental effects of trade and held a symposium, the North American Symposium on Assessing the Linkages Between Trade and Environment in October 2000.[403] The Commission decided to hold the second such program in March 2003.[404] It had earlier conducted several workshops on the subject.[405] The activities undertaken by the CEC during 2011–2012 show that the Commission continues to pursue a very active agenda.[406]

14.3.4.3.8   Appraisal

As shown in § 14.3.4.3.7, NGOs have contributed to protecting the environment in Canada, the US, and Mexico by initiating the process and assisting in the preparation of the Secretariat's Article 13 Reports and Articles 14 and 15 Citizen Submissions Process factual records. However, whether voluntary compliance can ensure protection of the environment remains an

---

[400] Council Resolution 01–06, Response to the Joint Public Advisory Committee (JPAC) Report on Lessons Learned regarding the Articles 14 and 15 Process, C/01–00/RES/06/Rev.4, Jun. 29, 2001.

[401] *See, e.g., JPAC Invites the Public to Participate in the Process of Revising the Citizen Submissions on Enforcement Matters Guidelines*, CEC, April 17, 2012, http://www.cec.org/Page.asp?PageID=122&ContentID=25196&SiteNodeID=655&BL_ExpandID=.

[402] Advice to Council: No. 01–09, Re: The Commission for Environmental Cooperation (CEC) of North America and the North American Free Trade Agreement (NAFTA) Ch. 11, J/02-02/ADV/02-04 and 02-09/Final, July 16, 2002.

[403] For the publication of selected papers presented at the workshop, *see* CEC, The Environmental Effects of Free Trade (2002).

[404] CEC, *Public Call for Papers: The Second North American Symposium on Assessing the Environmental Effects of Trade*, http://www.cec.org/Page.asp?PageID=122&ContentID=1948&SiteNodeID=361.

[405] *See, e.g.,* CEC Assessing Environmental Effects of the North American Free Trade Agreement (NAFTA) (1999).

[406] *See, e.g.,* CEC Events, http://www.cec.org/Page.asp?PageID=924&SiteNodeID=215; CEC News 2012, http://www.cec.org/Page.asp?PageID=924&SiteNodeID=655.

unanswered question at present.[407] Nevertheless, the JPAC's recommendations noted above need to be seriously considered and acted upon favorably by the Council.

The CEC has undertaken a large number of projects toward the accomplishment of its goals and objectives. Its cooperative work program in the context of economic, social, and environmental linkages has centered around four core program areas: (1) environment, economy and trade; (2) conservation of biodiversity; (3) pollutants and health; and (4) law and policy. The CEC has identified a number of roles for itself, including that of a convenor (a forum for exploring trends, bringing key players to exchange views and develop solutions on important issues of environmental protection, conservation and sustainability); catalyst ("to spur on worthwhile existing initiatives, undertaken largely by others"); research and policy analyst on important environmental matters of regional concern; and as an information hub ("as an important repository of regional data and information on the North American environment").[408] It is essential that the Council and the NAFTA Free Trade Commission cooperate to achieve the environmental goals and objectives of NAFTA as envisioned under NAAEC Article 10(6).

14.4   Conclusion

Only recently have the realms of international trade and international environmental protection come closer. That there is a necessary link between the two is being increasingly recognized and appreciated. The Rio Summit, the adoption of NAFTA and its Environmental Side Agreement, and UNEP's collaboration with the WTO and UNCTAD are clear indications of the importance of this link. Progress under NAFTA's Side Agreement and the WTO case law shows some promise that this link will be further recognized and implemented to meet the goal of sustainable development.

---

[407] *See, e.g.*, Chris Dove, *Comment: Can Voluntary Compliance Protect the Environment?: The North American Agreement on Environmental Cooperation*, 50 Kan. L. Rev. 867 (2002) (noting the need for a more sophisticated treaty that defines compliance more sharply and has broad support from the parties). As the parties are obligated under the Side Agreement to report annually on how they carried out their enforcement obligations, CEC has published the reports of the North American Working Group on Environmental Enforcement and Compliance Cooperation composed of senior-level environmental officials appointed by the parties. *See, e.g.*, CEC, Special Report on Enforcement Activities – Report Prepared by the North American Working Group on Enforcement and Compliance Cooperation (June 2001).

[408] CEC, North American Agenda for Action 2002–2004, at 2 (2002), http://www.cec.org/files/PDF//3yr-plan_02-04.pdf.

Chapter Fifteen

The Environment and Human Rights

15.0 Introduction

This chapter examines the interrelationship between the environment and human rights, especially addressing the desirability and feasibility of adding to the corpus of human rights a human right to the environment. Unquestionably, it is essential that we protect and preserve the environment as well as promote and protect human rights. In 1968, the UN General Assembly adopted a resolution acknowledging the close relationship between the two.[1] Based upon current trends, it seems safe to predict that the issues of a healthy environment, the protection of human rights, and the interaction between them will continue to figure prominently on the international law agenda.

15.1 The Challenge of Environmental Degradation

As mentioned in Chapter 1, during the last two decades of the 20th century, the global environment increasingly became a major concern for the international community. During the 1980s, several environmental disasters fostered the perception that environmental degradation had reached crisis proportions. These include the 1984 Union Carbide disaster in Bhopal, India;[2] the Chernobyl meltdown in Russia in 1986;[3] the toxic chemical spill

---

[1] Problems of the Human Environment, G.A. Res. 2398 (XXII), U.N. Doc. A/L 553/Add. 1–4 (December 3, 1968).

[2] In 1984, release of poison gas by a Union Carbide chemical plant in Bhopal, India killed over 2,000 people and injured over 150,000 more. *See* P. M. Boffey, *Few Lasting Effects Found Among India Gas-Leak Survivors*, N.Y. TIMES, Dec. 20, 1984, at 1. *See generally* Ved Nanda & Bruce Bailey, *Export of Hazardous Wastes and Hazardous Technology: Challenge for International Environmental Law*, 17 DENV. J INT'L L. & POL'Y 155 (1988).

[3] In 1986, the meltdown of a nuclear reactor at Chernobyl contaminated soil and water and threatened food supplies in the former Soviet Union, Eastern Europe, and the Scandinavian countries. *See The Nuclear Disaster*, N.Y. TIMES, Apr. 30, 1986, at A1. The number of those

from the Basel chemical plant, also in 1986;[4] and the Exxon Valdez oil spill in 1989 in Prince William Sound, Alaska.[5] Tremendous environmental damage was caused in the 1991 Gulf War.[6] All of these man-made disasters in turn caused severe physical and economic damage to the human environment. Furthermore, the global environmental crisis, including the phenomenon of overpopulation, exacerbates existing social and cultural tensions and worsens the threat of global conflict.[7]

Growing environmental awareness and activism have spurred the international community to consider the adverse impact of human activities on the environment, and to address the resulting challenges. World leaders have convened conferences such as the 1992 UN Conference on Environment and Develop ment (UNCED) in Rio de Janeiro, the 2002 UN World Summit on Sustainable Development in Johannesburg, South Africa, and the 2012 UN Conference on Sustainable Development in Rio de Janeiro,[8] agreed on action plans, and accepted some binding environmental protection obligations as state parties to multilateral and regional conventions.

Among the suggested responses to address the problems caused by deterioration of the environment is the recognitions of a human right to a "decent," "healthy," and "safe" environment as an emerging "third-generation" or "solidarity" right.[9] It may be recalled that in broad terms, "first-generation"

---

actually killed or injured by the disaster cannot be calculated because of the potential long-term effects of the accident.

[4] In 1986, a fire at a chemical plant in Basel, Switzerland, resulted in the release of toxic chemicals into the Rhine River. *See* T. W. Netter, *Mercury a Key Concerning Rhine Spill*, N.Y. Times, Nov. 15, 1986, at 3.

[5] The oil tanker Exxon Valdez ran aground in the Prince William Sound off the coast of Alaska, dumping hundreds of thousands of gallons of crude oil into rich seabeds. *See* P. Shabecoff, *Largest U.S. Tanker Spill Spews 270,000 Barrels of Oil Off Alaska*, N.Y. Times, Nov. 15, 1989, at A1.

[6] *See generally* Modern Warfare and the Environment: A Case Study of the Gulf War (W. A. Arkin ed., 1991).

[7] *See, e.g.*, R. D. Kaplan, *The Coming Anarchy*, Atlantic Monthly, Feb. 1994, at 44, 54–60 (arguing that environmental problems will "inflame existing hatreds and affect power relationships" in the international arena).

[8] For a thorough discussion, *see supra* Ch. 4.

[9] *See, e.g.*, Alexandre Kiss & Dinah Shelton, International Environmental Law 21–31 (1991); W. P. Gormley, Human Rights and Environment: The Need for International Cooperation 48–55 (1976); The Right to Environment in Human Rights in the Twenty-First Century 517–614 (K. Mahoney & P. Mahoney eds., 1993) [hereinafter Human Rights in the Twenty-First Century], especially essays by F. Roots, *id.* at 551, and C. Trinidade, *id.* at 561; W. P. Gormley, *The Right to a Safe and Decent Environment*, 28 Indian J. Int'l L. 1 (1988); Caroline Dommen, *Claiming Environmental Rights: Some Possibilities Offered by the United Nations' Human Rights Mechanisms*, 11 Geo. Int'l Envtl. L. Rev. 1 (1998); Neil A. F. Popovic, *In Pursuit of Environmental Human Rights: Commentary on the Draft Declaration of Principles on Human Rights and the Environment*, 27 Colum. Hum. Rts. L. Rev. 487 (1996); M. Thorme, *Establishing Environment as a Human Right*, 19 Denv. J. Int'l L. & Pol'y 301 (1991); J. T. McClymonds, *Note: The Human Right to a Healthy Environment: An International Legal Perspective*, 37 N.Y.L. Sch. L. Rev. 583

rights are civil and political rights which define personal liberties that governments have assumed the obligation to respect, while "second-generation" rights are economic and social rights that require affirmative action by governments. "Third-generation" rights combine elements of both and may be "invoked against the State and demanded of it,"[10] and include the right to environment, development, and peace.[11] These rights add a temporal element to human rights, thus bringing the concepts of intergenerational and intragenerational equity into sharper focus.[12]

The proposed "third generation" or "solidarity" rights, as newly emerging rights, are neither dependent upon, nor do they replace, the human rights already recognized by the international community.[13] Rather, one of the responses of the international community to changing circumstances and needs has been the recognition of new rights.[14] The gravity of the situation created by continuing environmental degradation is a major factor in the claim for an acknowledgement of a new human right to a healthy environment.

Because a healthy environment requires action by and cooperation between both private and governmental actors, as well as between the governments of states, the framework necessary to implement the right will have to be established on the international level.[15]

15.2 Historical Progression

Early recognition of the link between human rights and environmental protection begun with the 1968 UN General Assembly resolution mentioned

---

(1992); Dinah Shelton, *Human Rights, Environmental Rights, and the Right to Environment*, 28 Stan. J. Int'l L. 103 (1991); Environmental Change and International Law 199–315 (E. B. Weiss ed., 1992) [hereinafter Weiss, Environmental Change], especially R. S. Pathak, *The Human Rights System as a Conceptual Framework for Environmental Law*, in *id.* at 216.

[10] S. P. Marks, Emerging Human Rights: A New Generation for the 1980s?, 33 Rutgers L. Rev. 435, 441 (1981), *citing* K. Vasak (emphasis in original).

[11] *See id.* at 442.

[12] *See generally* Edith Brown Weiss, in Fairness to Future Generations, (1989) [hereinafter Weiss, Future Generations].

[13] *See* Jack Donnelly, Universal Human Rights in Theory and Practice 144 (1989), where he criticizes this characterization as "fly[ing] in the face of" the interdependence of human rights.

[14] *See generally* J. Downs, *A Healthy and Ecologically Balanced Environment: An Argument for a Third Generation Right*, 3 Duke J. Comp. & Int'l L. 351, 352, 357 (1993).

[15] *See* Experts Group on Environmental Law of the World Commission on Environment and Development (WCED), Environmental Protection and Sustainable Development: Legal Principles and Recommendations 40 (1986) [hereinafter Legal Principles].

above[16] and was advanced through the 1969 Declaration on Progress and Development in the Social Arena.[17] At last, in 1972, the UN Stockholm Conference on the Human Environment formally promulgated the right to environment as an aspect of human rights in the Stockholm Declaration.[18] The Stockholm Declaration stated that "Man has the fundamental right to freedom, equality, and adequate conditions of life, in an environment of a quality that permits a life of dignity and well-being, and he bears a solemn responsibility to protect and improve the environment for present and future generations."[19]

Although it was not binding, this proclamation initiated the formal debate over the relationship between the environment and human rights. Also, while it was adopted virtually unanimously, in the absence of state practice and *opinio juris* – the prerequisites for the establishment of customary international law – the right to environment has not yet entered the corpus of customary international law. In fact, participants at the Stockholm Conference expressed reservations about the ideological balance and emphasis on the environment contained in the Declaration.[20]

Nevertheless, many international organizations and national governments have recognized the environment as a human right. As early as the 1970s, the European Parliamentary Conference on Human Rights and the Council of Europe each considered whether the right to a healthy environment should be raised to the level of a recognized human right.[21] The proposal before the Council of Europe was in the form of a Draft Additional Protocol to the 1950 European Convention on Human Rights and Fundamental Freedoms, which linked the protection of life to human rights and declared the protection of life to virtually require "the existence of a natural environment favorable to human health."[22] However, while this proposal was not adopted, the deliberations gave impetus to the issue on the international agenda.

Further positive developments occurred in the 1980s. A UNESCO Symposium on new human rights in 1980 identified the right to a healthy and

---

[16] *Supra* note 1.

[17] G.A. Res. 2542, U.N. Doc. A/7833, A/L 583 (1969) (adopted with only two abstentions and no negative vote).

[18] Declaration of the United Nations Conference on the Human Environment, U.N. Doc. A/CONF. 48/14/Rev. 1 (1972), reprinted in 11 I.L.M. 1416 (1972) [hereinafter Stockholm Declaration].

[19] *Id.* Principle 1.

[20] *See* L. B. Sohn, *The Stockholm Declaration on the Human Environment*, 14 Harv. Int'l L.J. 423, 426–27 (1973).

[21] *See* M. Thorme, *supra* note 9, at 304.

[22] *See* Working Group for Environmental Law, *The Right to a Humane Environment: Proposal for an Additional Protocol to the European Human Rights Convention* (1973), *reprinted in* Human Rights in a Changing East-West Perspective 229 (A. Rosas *et al.* eds., 1990).

ecologically balanced environment as one of the "solidarity rights."[23] The following year, the African Charter on Human and Peoples' Rights was adopted in Kenya by the Organization of African Unity Conference of Heads of State and Government, which incorporated the right of all people to "a general satisfactory environment favourable to their development."[24] In 1982, a UN General Assembly resolution, entitled "World Charter for Nature,"[25] called upon member states, *inter alia*, to respect nature and avoid impairing its essential processes. In Indonesia in 1983, the first General Assembly of the Regional Council on Human Rights in Asia adopted the Declaration on the Basic Duties of Asian Peoples and Governments, which imposes a duty on governments and peoples to preserve natural resources for future generations and prevent environmental degradation.[26]

In 1986, the World Commission on Environment and Development (WCED) Experts Group on Environmental Law adopted a principle stating that "All human beings have the fundamental right to an environment adequate to their health and well-being."[27] Also in 1986, the Inter-American Commission on Human Rights proposed a Draft Additional Protocol to the American Convention on Human Rights in the Area of Economic, Social, and Cultural Rights, which was eventually adopted in 1988 and included a right "to live in a healthy environment," obligating the states parties to promote the "protection, preservation and improvement of the environment."[28] The protocol required ratification or accession by 11 member states before entering into force, which occurred on November 16, 1999, and, as of September 2011, 16 countries had ratified or acceded to the Protocol.[29] In 1996, the OAS Hemisphere Summit on Sustainable Development adopted a declaration, the Declaration of Santa Cruz, reaffirming that "human beings are entitled to a healthy and productive life in harmony with nature and, as such,

---

[23] *See* UNESCO Doc. 55.81/CONF. 806/4, at 3 (1981). *See* also Louis Sohn, The New International Law: Protection of the Rights of Individuals Rather than States, 32 AM. U. L. REV. 1, 59 (1982).

[24] African Charter on Human and Peoples' Rights, June 26, 1981, OAU Doc. CAB/LTG/67/3/ Res. 5, art. 24, *reprinted in* 21 I.L.M. 59 (1982) (entered into force Oct. 21, 1986).

[25] G.A. Res. 37/7, 37 U.N. GAOR Supp. (No. 51) at 17, U.N. Doc. A/37/51 (1982).

[26] *See* J. Symonides, *The Human Right to a Clean, Balanced and Protected Environment*, 20 INT'L J.L. INF. 24, 26 (1992).

[27] LEGAL PRINCIPLES, *supra* note 15, at 25 (Principle 1).

[28] Additional Protocol to the American Convention on Human Rights in the Area of Economic, Social, and Cultural Rights of 14 Nov. 1988 (Protocol of San Salvador), art. 11, *reprinted in* 28 I.L.M. 161, 165 (1989).

[29] Department of International Law, Organization of American States, Argentina, Bolivia, Brazil, Columbia, Costa Rica, Ecuador, El Salvador, Guatemala, Honduras, Mexico, Nicaragua, Panama, Paraguay, Peru, Suriname and Uruguay have all deposited ratifications, available at http://www.oas.org/juridico/english/sigs/a-52.html. *See also* John Lee, *The Underlying Legal Theory to Support a Well-Defined Human Right to a Healthy Environment as a Principle of Customary International Law*, 25 COLUM. J. ENVTL. L. 283, 305 (2000).

are the focus of sustainable development concerns. Development strategies need to include sustainability as an essential requirement for the balanced, interdependent, and integral attainment of economic, social, and environmental goals."[30]

In 1989, the Sierra Club Legal Defense Fund brought before the UN Sub-Commission on Prevention of Discrimination and Protection of Minorities two cases over a threat to the environment and human populations.[31] The cases concerned fumigation programs in Guatemala and a US oil company's proposal to build a road in Ecuador in order to service drilling sites and transport oil in that country. The Sub-Commission found that the information justified consideration of a study to determine the relationship of the environment to human rights and initiated such a study.[32] After reviewing the developments pertaining to the linkage between human rights and the environment and the recognition of an environmental right as a human right, the Sub-Commission issued its final report in 1994,[33] in which it acknowledged that, although a direct link between the environment and human rights is established by "only a few instruments of a binding legal character," a practice is being developed by the regional and international human rights bodies under which "the procedural bases for enforcing the right to a satisfactory environment are becoming more firmly established and the validity of complaints of human rights violations based on ecological considerations is being recognized."[34] The report called for the adoption of a set of norms by the UN under which the right to a satisfactory environment would be recognized as a human right.[35]

In September of 1990, the Council of Europe's Parliamentary Assembly adopted a recommendation providing for a human right to an environment "conducive to... good health, well-being and full development of the human

---

[30] Declaration of Santa Cruz de la Sierra, OAS GT/CCDS-51/96 rev. 2, at ¶ 2 (Nov. 26, 1996), http://www.summit-americas.org/boliviadec.htm.

[31] For a discussion of these cases, *see* Thorme, *supra* note 9, at 305.

[32] *See Human Rights and Scientific and Technological Developments: Proposals for a Study of the Problem of the Environment and its Relation to Human Rights*, Comm. on Human Rights, Sub-Comm. on Prevention of Discrimination and Protection of Minorities, 42 U.N. ESCOR, U.N. Doc. E/CN.4/Sub.2/-1990/12 (1990); Human Rights and the Environment: Preliminary Report Prepared by Mrs. Fatma Zohra Ksentini, Special Rapporteur, pursuant to Sub-Commission resolutions 1990/7/ and 1990/27, Comm. on Human Rights, Sub-Comm. on Prevention of Discrimination and Protection of Minorities, U.N. Doc. E/CN.4/Sub.2/1991/8, Aug. 2, 1991.

[33] Final Report Prepared by Mrs. Fatma Zohra Ksentini, Special Rapporteur, UN ESCOR Commission on Human Rights, Sub-Commission on Prevention of Discrimination and Protection of Minorities, U.N. Doc. E/CN.4/Sub.2/1994/9 [hereinafter Ksentini Final Report]. *See also* Draft Declaration of Principles on Human Rights and the Environment, *id.*, Annex I.

[34] *Id.* ¶ 261.

[35] *Id.* at 42–57, 62–64.

personality."[36] In October 1991, the ECE Experts Meeting in Oslo, Norway, adopted a Draft Charter on Environmental Rights and Obligations, which proclaimed as a fundamental principle everyone's "right to an environment adequate for his general health and well-being"[37] In the same year, the Associations of Environmental Law adopted the "Declaration of Limoges," which recommended recognition of a "human right to the environment."[38] However, in Europe, the Treaty of Amsterdam, which revised the earlier Maastricht Treaty of the European Union and entered into force in May 1999, does not include a right to healthy environment.[39]

At the UN, the right to a healthy environment has been recognized in several resolutions and declarations adopted in the General Assembly and at various conferences held under the UN auspices since the 1972 Stockholm Declaration enunciated the right to environment.[40]

In 1990, at its 45th session, the UN General Assembly adopted a resolution recognizing the "[n]eed to ensure a healthy environment for the well-being of individuals," recalling the Universal Declaration of Human Rights and the International Covenant on Economic, Social and Cultural Rights, and stating:

> [E]veryone has the right to an adequate standard of living for his or her own health and well-being and that of his or her family and to the continuous improvement of living conditions, recognizing the need to promote the universal respect for, and observance of, human rights and fundamental freedoms in all their aspects, considering that a better and healthier environment can help contribute to the full enjoyment of rights by all, reaffirming that in accordance with the Declaration of the United Nations Conference on the Human Environment, men and women have the fundamental right to freedom, equality, and adequate conditions of life in an environment of a quality that permits a life of dignity and well-being, and that they bear a solemn responsibility to protect and improve the environment for present and future generations....The General Assembly recognizes that all individuals are entitled to live in an environment adequate for their health and well-being; calls upon member states and intergovernmental and non-governmental organizations dealing with

---

[36] Parliamentary Assembly of the Council of Europe Recommendation 1130 (1990)(1) on the formulation of European Charter and European Convention on Environmental Protection and Sustainable Development, adopted September 28, 1990 (art. 1 in the European Charter and the Convention on the Environment and Sustainable Development), reprinted in *1 Y.B. Int'l Env't L.* 484 (1990).

[37] *See* Draft Charter on Environmental Rights and Obligations, reprinted in 21 ENV'T. POL'Y & L. 81 (1991).

[38] Reprinted in *id.* at 39, cited in G. Handl, *Human Rights and Protection of the Environment: A Mildly "Revisionist" View, in* HUMAN RIGHTS, SUSTAINABLE DEVELOPMENT AND THE ENVIRONMENT 117, 118 (Seminario de Brasilia de 1992, C. Trinidade ed., 1994) [hereinafter Handl].

[39] *See* Draft Treaty of Amsterdam, European Commission Document CONF/ 4001/97 (1997).

[40] *Supra* note 18.

environmental questions to enhance efforts ensuring a better and healthier environment;…believes that appropriate organs of the United Nations, within their respective competencies, should pursue active efforts in seeking to promote a better and healthier environment.[41]

As the preparatory committee for the 1992 UN Conference on Environment and Development (UNCED or Rio Conference) met, it reviewed proposals to include recognition of the right to a healthy environment in the final document, the Rio Declaration.[42] However, such recognition did not materialize. Rather, the Declaration, while reaffirming the Stockholm Declaration, states in Principle 1: "Human beings are at the center of concerns for sustainable development. They are entitled to a healthy and productive life in harmony with nature."[43] Although this language, when compared with the clear language expressed in the Stockholm Declaration twenty years prior to UNCED, does not explicitly reflect a recognition of the right to a healthy environment; it does in essence capture the concept that such a right exists.

It is noteworthy that several subsequent UN conferences accepted verbatim the language of the Principle in the Rio Declaration noted above. It was reproduced and accepted without reservation by 179 nations at the 1994 UN Conference on Population and Development;[44] by 186 nations at the 1995 World Summit for Social Development;[45] by 175 nations at the 1996 Second Conference on Human Settlements;[46] and by 17 nations at the 1997 Hemispheric Summit on Sustainable Development sponsored by the OAS.[47]

---

[41] G.A. Res. 45/94, adopted on Dec. 14, 1990. The International Seminar of Experts on the Right to the Environment, organized by the United Nations High Commissioner for Human Rights and UNESCO, issued the Bizkaia Declaration on the Right to the Environment, stating that "Everyone has the right, individually or in connection with others, to enjoy a healthy and ecologically balanced environment,… [which] may be exercised before public bodies and private entities, whatever their legal status under national and international law." This right is for everyone "without any discrimination based on race, colour, sex, language, religion, political opinion or of any other nature." International Seminar on the Right of the Environment, Feb. 10–13, 1999, *Declaration of Bizkaia on the Right to the Environment*, U.N. Doc. 30C/INF.11 (Sept. 24, 1999), http://unesdoc.unesco.org/images/0011/001173/117321E.pdf.

[42] *See* UN Prep. Com. for UNCED, Working Group III., Informal Consolidated Draft No. 2, U.N. Doc. A/CONF. 151/PC/No. 9, Principle 3, reprinted in Agenda 21 and the UNCED Proceedings cxv, cxix–cxx (N. A. Robinson ed., 1991).

[43] Rio Declaration on Environment and Development, Principle 1, in I Report of the United Nations Conference on Environment and Development, Rio de Janeiro, June 3–14, 1992, at 3, U.N. Doc. A/CONF. 151/26/Rev. 1 (1993).

[44] Programme of Action, U.N. Doc. A/CONF. 171/13 (1994), at Principle 2. *See* Lee, *supra* note 29, at 308.

[45] Copenhagen Declaration, U.N. Doc. A/CONF.166/7/Annex (1995), Principle 6. None of the many reservations placed by a number of parties concerned Principle 6, *see* Lee, *supra* note 29, at 308.

[46] (Habitat II) UN Conference on Human Settlements, U.N. Doc. A/CONF.165/PC.3/L.3 ch. I, preamble ¶ 2 (1996), *see* Lee, *supra* note 29, at 308.

[47] Declaration of Santa Cruz, *supra* note 30. *See* Lee, *supra* note 29, at 308–309.

Although none of these instruments are binding, a commentator has concluded that since nearly every nation reaffirmed this language in all these instruments without reservation, this demonstrates "evidence of a widespread and consistent state practice [, which] can contribute to the creation of a right to a healthy environment as a principle of customary international law."[48]

Many states, including both developing and developed countries from all regions, have recognized the right to a healthy environment in their constitutions or specially enacted legislation.[49] By the end of the 20th century, the number of states either explicitly recognizing such a right in their constitutions or recognizing a duty to defend or protect the environment in their constitutions had exceeded 80.[50] For instance, the Portuguese Constitution recognizes such a right by declaring that "[a]ll have the right to a healthy and ecologically balanced human environment and the duty to protect it," and the Peruvian Constitution declares that "[e]veryone has the right to live in a healthy environment, ecologically balanced and adequate for the development of life and the preservation of the countryside and nature. Everyone has the duty to conserve the said environment."[51]

15.3   Developments in the United States

Debate in the US over the environment as a human right began in 1960.[52] Eight years later, then-US Senator Gaylord Nelson proposed an amendment to the US Constitution recognizing for every individual "the inalienable right to a decent environment. The United States and every State shall guarantee this right."[53] This proposal did not succeed. Nor did a similar attempt made in 1970 by US Representative Richard Otinger, who proposed a legislative resoulution under which "[t]he right of the people to clean air, pure water, freedom from excessive noise, and the natural, scenic, historic and aesthetic

---

[48] *Id.* at 308.

[49] *See, e.g.,* WEISS, FUTURE GENERATIONS, *supra* note 12, at 297, 327; Symonides, *supra* note 26, at 27–28. *See also* Benjamin W. Kramer, *The Human Right to Information, the Environment and Information about the Environment: From the Universal Declaration to the Aarhus Convention,* 14 COMM. LAW & POL'y 73, 86–88 (2009) (referring to the constitutional and statutory rights to environmental protection in several countries); Barry E. Hill, Steve Wolfson & Nicholas Targ, *Human Rights and the Environment, A Synopsis and Some Predictions,* 16 GEO. INT'L ENVTL. L. REV. 359, 381–389, 401 (App. A) (2004) (referring to national constitutions containing environmental provisions – more than 90 recognizing the duty owed by the national government to its citizens to prevent harm to the environment, and over 50 recognizing the importance of healthy environment, either as a duty of the state or as a right.

[50] *See* Lee, *supra* note 29, at 340 app. A.

[51] Cited in Symonides, *supra* note 26, at 27.

[52] *See id.* at 27–28.

[53] H.R.J. Res. 1321, 90th Cong., 2d Sess. (1968).

qualities of their environment shall not be abridged."[54] That Resolution went on to state:

> The Congress shall, within three years after the enactment of this article, and within very subsequent term of ten years or lesser term as the Congress may determine, and in such a manner as they shall by law direct, cause to be made an inventory of the natural, scenic, aesthetic and historic resources of the United States with their state of preservation, and to provide for their protection as a matter of national purpose.[55]
>
> No federal or state agency, body, or authority shall be authorized to exercise the power of condemnation, or undertake any public work, issue any permit, license, or concession, make any rule, execute any management policy or other official act which adversely affects the people's heritage of natural resources and natural beauty.[56]

It is noteworthy that, while the US does not grant constitutional recognition to such a right, the US National Environmental Policy Act of 1969 (NEPA) states as its purpose to assure "for all Americans safe, healthful, productive, and aesthetically and culturally pleasing surroundings."[57]

Regardless of continuous efforts by several environmental groups, federal courts have consistently refused to grant constitutional recognition of the right to a healthful environment without pertinent federal legislation or recognition of such a right by the US Supreme Court.[58] However, in contrast to the lack of recognition of a human right to the environment in the federal setting, many states have recognized such a right through constitutional amendments of their own.[59]

For instance, the Hawaii Constitution provides, in article 11, section 9:

> Each person has the right to a clean and healthful environment, as defined by the laws relating to environmental quality, including control of pollution and conservation, protection and enhancement of natural resources. Any person may enforce this right against any party, public or private, through appropriate legal proceedings, subject to reasonable limitations and regulation as provided by law.

---

[54] H.R.J. Res. 1205, 91st Cong., 2d Sess., § 1 (1970).

[55] *Id.* § 2.

[56] *Id.* § 3.

[57] National Environmental Policy Act of 1969, Pub. L. No. 91–90, § 101(b)(2), 83 Stat. 852 (1970); likewise, *see id.* § 101(c). For a proposal that the right be created at the state level in the United States, *see* R. O. Brooks, *A Constitutional Right to a Healthful Environment,* 16 Vt. L. Rev. 1063 (1992).

[58] For a discussion of these cases, see *Comment: Judicial Interpretation of State Constitutional Rights to a Healthful Environment,* 20 B.C. Envtl. Aff. L. Rev. 173 (1993).

[59] For a discussion of state constitutional amendments granting such rights and their interpretation, *see* generally *id.* at 179–200. *See* also generally, R. A. McLaren, *Environmental Protection Based on State Constitutional Law: A Call for Reinterpretation,* 12 U. Haw. L. Rev. 123 (1990).

The Massachusetts Constitution provides, in Article 49:

> The People shall have the right to clean air and water, freedom from excessive noise, and the natural, scenic, historic, and aesthetic qualities of their environment; and the protection of the people in their right to conservation, development and utilization of the agricultural, mineral, forest, water, air and other natural resources is hereby declared to be a public purpose.

Similarly, the Pennsylvania Constitution provides, in Article 1, Section 27:

> The People have the right to clean air, pure water, and to the preservation of the natural, scenic, historic and aesthetic values of the environment. Pennsylvania's public natural resources are the common property of all the people, including generations yet to come. As trustee of these resources, the Commonwealth shall conserve and maintain them for the benefit of all the people.

And the Montana Constitution provides, in Article II, Section 3:

> All persons are born free and have certain inalienable rights. They include the right to a clean and healthful environment and the rights of pursuing life's basic necessities, enjoying and defending their lives and liberties, acquiring, possessing and protecting property, and seeking their safety, health and happiness in all lawful ways. In enjoying these rights, all persons recognize corresponding responsibilities.

In Article IX, Section 1, the Montana Constitution provides further:

> (1) The state and each person shall maintain and improve a clean and healthful environment in Montana for present and future generations.
> (2) The legislature shall provide for the administration and enforcement of this duty.
> (3) The legislature shall provide adequate remedies for the protection of the environmental life support system from degradation and provide adequate remedies to prevent unreasonable depletion and degradation of natural resources.

Judicial interpretation of such provisions varies according to the court's determination of several factors, including: the meaning of a "clean" or "healthful" environment; whether the provision in question needs further implementing legislation before a plaintiff can invoke it; who is able to assert the claim; the nature of the available remedies; and the kind of evidence and proof that would suffice to show harm or injury.[60] In a 2003 case, *Cape-France*

---

[60] For a discussion of these and other such issues, *see* R. O. Brooks, *supra* note 57; *Comment*, *supra* note 58; McLaren, *supra* note 59.

Enterprise v. Estate of Peed,[61] the Montana Supreme Court applied the right to clean and healthful environment to a private action which involved a contract for sale of real property.[62] However, subsequently, in a 2007 case, *Shammel v. Canyon Resources Corp.*,[63] the Montana Supreme Court was called upon to determine whether the state's constitutional right to a clean and healthful environment provides for the recovery of money damages in a constitutional tort action between private parties. The court answered the question in the negative, holding that this right does not authorize a distinct cause of action in tort for money damages between two private parties where adequate remedies exist under the common law or statute.[64]

Indigenous peoples and others, too, have sought remedies for environmental harm in American courts through the Alien Tort Claims Act,[65] under which the federal court has jurisdiction over a lawsuit filed by a non-US citizen for a tort committed in violation of the law of nations (*see* § 14.7). For instance, *Aguinda v. Texaco, Inc.*,[66] dealt with allegations that Texaco had polluted the rainforests and rivers in Ecuador and Peru when it was involved in oil exploitation activities in those countries between 1964 and 1992. Indigenous tribes alleged that (1) Texaco improperly dumped toxic by-products of the drilling process in large quantities into the local rivers and had used other improper means of disposing of toxic substances; (2) the Trans-Ecuadoran Pipeline, constructed by Texaco, had leaked large quantities of petroleum into the environment; and (3) that these activities had caused poisoning and the development of precancerous growths within their populations.[67]

An earlier case, *Amlon Metals, Inc. v. FMC Corp.*,[68] concerned a shipment of hazardous copper residue sent to a purchaser in the United Kingdom for reclamation purposes, which had allegedly caused a tortious violation under the Alien Tort Claims Act. The plaintiff relied on the Stockholm Principles to support its claim. Having accepted the complaint, the court nonetheless

---

[61] Cape-France Enterprises v. Estate of Peed, 2001 MT 139, 305 Mont. 513, 29 P.3d 1011 (2001).

[62] *See* Chase Naber, *Note: Murky Waters: Private Action and the Right to a Clean and Healthful Environment – An Examination of Cape-France Enterprises v. Estate of Peed*, 64 MONT. L. REV. 357 (2003).

[63] Shammel v. Canyon Resources Corp., 2007 MT 206, 238 Mont. 541, 167 P.3d 886 (2007).

[64] *Id.*, 238 Mont. 544–45, 167 P.3d 888.

[65] 28 U.S.C. § 1350. The section reads: "The district courts shall have original jurisdiction of any civil action by an alien for a tort only, committed in violation of the law of nations or a treaty of the United States."

[66] 2000 U.S. Dist. LEXIS 745 (S.D.N.Y. 2000), dismissed sub nom. Aguinda v. Texaco, Inc., 142 F. Supp. 2d 534 (S.D.N.Y. 2001).

[67] This case is considered at length in § 14.7, infra. For the original cases regarding Ecuador and Peru, respectively, *see* Aguinda v. Texaco, Inc., 1994 S.D.N.Y. Dkt. No. 93 Civ. 7527; Ashanga v. Texaco, Inc., S.D.N.Y. Dkt. No. 94 Civ. 9266, cited in Jota v. Texaco, Inc., 157 F.3d 153, 155 (2d Cir. 1998).

[68] 775 F. Supp. 668 (S.D.N.Y. 1991).

concluded that the plaintiff had not proven a cause of action since the Stockholm Principles "do not set forth any specific proscriptions, but rather refer only in a general sense to the responsibility of nations to insure that activities within their jurisdiction do not cause damage to the environment beyond their borders."[69]

In *Beneal v. Freeport-McMoran, Inc.,*[70] the plaintiff, the tribal council leader of the Amungme Tribe in Irian Jaya, Indonesia, invoked the Act to bring environmental claims alleging cultural genocide of the tribe and violation of certain human rights. The court found that the plaintiff Beneal had standing to bring the claims on behalf of himself and the tribe but determined that he failed to articulate a violation of international law. He had relied upon three international environmental law principles to support his cause of action: (1) the polluter-pays principle; (2) the precautionary principle; and (3) the proximity principle.

Citing Professor Phillipe Sands's work on environmental law,[71] the court concluded that these principles, "standing alone, do not constitute international torts for which there is universal consensus in the international community as to their binding status and their content."[72] Moreover, the court said, these principles apply to "members of the international community" rather than nonstate corporations.[73] Although the court concluded that Beneal had failed to allege an environmental tort, the important point is that it accepted and adjudicated the complaint under the Alien Tort Claims Act. However, the whether corporations can be sued under the Act is subject to the US Supreme Court's determination in forthcoming cases.

15.4   *The Right to Environmental Protection*

15.4.1   *The Nexus Between Environmental Protection and Internationally Recognized Human Rights*

Despite wide-ranging interest in and awareness and recognition of the right to a healthy environment in many states, debate continues as to whether the language of human rights is the appropriate vehicle for expressing environmental norms and values. Professor James Nickel proposes a middle ground

---

[69] *Id.* at 671.

[70] 969 F. Supp. 362 (E.D. La. 1997).

[71] Principles of International Environmental Law I: Frameworks, Standards and Implementation (Philippe Sands ed., 1995).

[72] Beneal, 969 F. Supp. at 384, *citing* Xuncax v. Gramajo, 886 F. Supp. 162, 186 (D. Mass. 1995).

[73] Beneal, 969 F. Supp. at 384.

between those who enthusiastically support the rights language and those who would avoid it completely:

> Rights should not be the dominant normative concept of environmentalism. It is better to phrase most environmental discourse in terms of environmental goods, of respect for and responsibilities towards nature, and of obligations to future generations. However, speaking of rights is plausible and useful for dealing with some of the most serious human consequences of environmental degradation. In particular, the right to a safe environment can play a useful and justifiable role in protecting human interests in a safe environment and in providing a link between the environmental and human rights movements.[74]

The question remains whether environmental protection falls within the body of human rights or whether environmental protection and preservation of the global ecosystem is a distinct goal. At its heart, this question considers whether human rights and environmental protection are based upon values that are so fundamentally different that they cannot be implemented simultaneously without conflict, or complementary and serving to further each other's goals.[75]

The proposition that laws protecting human rights alleviate threats to human dignity and existence by promoting fundamental rights to achieve freedom, justice, and peace in the world is a sound one.[76] But the objectives of environmental law are more difficult to define. Many commentators follow the Stockholm Declaration in suggesting that the primary purpose of environmental protection is to benefit mankind.[77] Some environmentalists, on the other hand, fear that a purely human-centered notion of environmental law reduces consideration of the ecosystem to its economic value, resulting in insensitivity to excessive exploitation of resources and, thus, environmental deterioration.[78] They argue that the environment is a separate entity, requiring protection for its own sake and not adequately served by the human rights paradigm.

The objectives of human rights law and environmental law may indeed be incompatible. Human survival requires consideration of present needs as well as those of future generations;[79] preservation of resources for the future

---

[74] J. W. Nickel, *The Human Right to a Safe Environment: Philosophical Perspectives on Its Scope and Justification*, 18 YALE J. INT'L L. 281, 282 (1993) (emphasis in original).

[75] *See* Shelton, *supra* note 9, at 104.

[76] *Id.* at 106.

[77] *See, e.g.*, W. P. Gormley, *The Legal Obligation of the International Community to Guarantee a Pure and Decent Environment: The Expansion of Human Rights*, 3 GEO. INT'L ENVTL. L. REV. 85, 86 (1990).

[78] *See* Shelton, *supra* note 9, at 109. *See generally* C. D. Stone, *Should Trees Have Standing? Toward Legal Rights for Natural Objects*, 45 S. CAL. L. REV. 451 (1972); C.D. STONE, EARTH AND OTHER ETHICS: THE CASE FOR MORAL PLURALISM (1987); P. W. TAYLOR, RESPECT FOR NATURE (1986).

[79] *See* WEISS, FUTURE GENERATIONS, *supra* note 12.

requires that their present use be curtailed. And preservation of the natural environment for the future may, at times, conflict with present-day economic development.[80] Developing states especially face a dilemma, as their overriding priority is the alleviation of poverty through economic growth and short-term survival threatens long-term sustainability. Moreover, the depletion of resources in one area forces the movement of populations into more habitable areas, increasing the competition over decreasing resources.[81] Another clear result of such movements is the clash of cultures, increasing the potential for violent conflict.[82]

There is no denying that humankind and the environment and their mutual interests are inseparable. Humans require air, water, and food in order to survive; contamination, pollution, or destruction of these elements poses a direct threat to the health, shelter, food, and well-being of humans and indeed to human life itself. Thus, both human rights law and environmental law are aspects of the common interest of humankind.[83]

Numerous well-recognized human rights are actually threatened by the degradation of the environment. In a fundamental sense, no life is possible without being sustained by a basically healthy environment. Therefore, the right to the healthy environment is arguably a condition precedent to all other human rights – for enjoyment of established human rights presupposes that humankind enjoy at least minimum standards of health and well-being.[84] Thus, the basis for a right to a healthful environment may be found in the most fundamental right recognized in the UN Charter: the right to life.[85] Although the Stockholm Declaration does not explicitly proclaim a distinct right to environment, it implies that basic environmental health is fundamental to the enjoyment of the other human rights.[86]

There is also a good deal of validity in the proposition that several recognized human rights subsume the right to a healthful environment and thus environmental rights may be said to be derived from the internationally recognized human rights. To illustrate, the right to health and well-being,

---

[80] *See* Shelton, *supra* note 9, at 109, 111.

[81] *See* Kaplan, *supra* note 7, at 54–60.

[82] *Id.*

[83] *See* Alexandre Kiss, *An Introductory Note on a Human Right to Environment, in* WEISS, ENVIRONMENTAL CHANGE, *supra* note 9, at 199; Pathak, *supra* note 9.

[84] *See* Kiss, *supra* note 83, at 200–201; Alexandre Kiss, *Concept and Possible Implications of the Right to Environment, in* HUMAN RIGHTS IN THE TWENTY-FIRST CENTURY, *supra* note 9, at 551, 553.

[85] *See* Thorme, *supra* note 9, at 319. The right to life is also contained in the International Covenant on Civil and Political Rights, Dec. 16, 1966, 1999 U.N.T.S. 171 (arts. 6 and 7), reprinted in 6 I.L.M. 368 (entered into force Mar. 23, 1976), and Article 3 of the Universal Declaration on Human Rights, G.A. Res. 217A (III), art. 3, U.N. Doc. A/810.

[86] *See* Stockholm Declaration, *supra* note 18, Annex, at 1 (1972); *See* also Shelton, *supra* note 9, at 112.

recognized especially in the International Covenant on Economic, Social and Cultural Rights,[87] calls for protection from environmental hazards that may produce long-term threats to health. The various rights to a high standard of physical and mental health,[88] to liberty and security,[89] to an adequate standard of living,[90] to suitable working conditions,[91] to home and enjoyment of property, to food, and to culture and indigenous rights[92] are all absolutely dependent on the presence of an environment that sustains productive human life.

The concept of "sustainable development"[93] (*see* § 2.1.4) has gained considerable authority among governments and international institutions. It is especially noteworthy that the International Court of Justice in the 1997 case, Gabcikovo-Nagymaros Project[94] defined the sustainability concept as the "need to reconcile economic development with protection of the environment.[95] Writing a separate opinion, then-Vice President of the Court, Judge Christopher Weeramantry observed that protection of the environment under international law "is a *sine qua non* for numerous human rights, such as the right to health and the right to life itself."[96] He discussed in detail the concept of sustainable development as a principle of international law, stating that "development can only be prosecuted in harmony with the reasonable demands of environmental protection."[97] At the heart of this effort is the critical need for public participation (*see* § 2.2.1) and environmental impact assessment (*see* Chapter 6) in planning for economic and public improvement projects that impact the environment. Sustainability embodies yet another set of links with procedural human rights norms, namely the right to information and the ability to participate in the decision-making process.[98] Participation, particularly for development projects, is undertaken

---

[87] International Covenant on Economic, Social and Cultural Rights, Dec. 16, 1966, G.A. Res. 2200A, U.N. Doc. A/6546, art. 12 (1966), reprinted in 6 I.L.M. 360 (entered into force Jan. 3, 1976).

[88] *Id. See* Melissa Fung, *The Right to a Healthy Environment: Core Obligations under the International Covenant of Economic, Social and Cultural Rights*, 14 WILLAMETTE J. INT'L L. & DISPUTE RES. 97 (2006).

[89] *See* Universal Declaration, *supra* note 81, at 71, 72.

[90] *Id.*, arts 17, 25.

[91] *See* Thorme, *supra* note 9, at 319–331; Shelton, *supra* note 9, at 112.

[92] *Id. See generally* Dinah Shelton, *Human Rights and the Environment: What Specific Environmental Rights have been Recognized?*, 35 DENV. J. INT'L L. & POL'Y 129 (2006).

[93] *See generally* Ved Nanda, *International Environmental Challenges: Sustainable Development and Environmental Challenges*, 3 TOURO J. INT'L L. 1, 5–20 (1992).

[94] Gabcikovo-Nagymaros Project (Hung. v. Slovk.), 1997 I.C.J. 6 (September 25).

[95] *Id.* at 78.

[96] *Id.* at 91.

[97] *Id.* at 92.

[98] *See, e.g.*, Kiss, *supra* note 79, at 201–202. Benjamin W. Kramer, *supra* note 49, at 73.

in developing countries to ensure as well the goal of protection of the rights of indigenous peoples.[99]

On the relationship between human rights and the environment the UN High Commissioner for Human Rights issued an important report on December 16, 2011.[100] The study, entitled "Analytical study on the relationship between human rights and the environment," was in response to a request from the Human Rights Council.[101] The report raised two central theoretical issues: (1) the nature of the relationship between human rights and the environment, and (2) the recognition by the international community of a new human right to a healthy environment.

On the first issue, the report identified three major approaches to explain the nature of this relationship. According to the first approach, the environment is a precondition to the enjoyment of human rights.[102] Under the second approach, "human rights are tools to address environmental issues, both procedurally and substantively."[103] And the third approach "proposes the integration of human rights and the environment under the concept of sustainable development."[104]

On the second issue, which has practical implications, the report raised difficult questions, such as the benefit of formulating a new human right to a healthy environment, since some consider its content difficult to define with clarity, while others find that national courts have provided meaningful content to the right to a healthy environment in their domestic constitutions and that international tribunals have articulated state responsibilities related to the environmental dimension of protected rights.[105]

The report also raised the question whether international law already recognizes such a right and that for some the pertinent question is that of implementation and monitoring, rather than of recognition, since certain international instruments already recognize such a right.[106] Yet another question raised in the report is the legal implications of the recognition of such a right, i.e., the identification of the right-holders and duty-bearers, especially

---

[99] *See, e.g.,* Pathak, *supra* note 9, at 228–35; E. E. Yates, *Public Participation in Economic and Environmental Planning: A Case Study of the Philippines,* 22 Denv. J. Int'l L. & Pol'y 107 (1993).

[100] U.N. General Assembly, Human Rights Council: Report of the United Nations High Commissioner for Human Rights, *Analytical Study on the Relationship Between Human Rights and the Environment,* U.N. Doc. A/HRC/19/34, December 16, 2011.

[101] U.N. General Assembly, Human Rights Council: Resolution 16/11, Human rights and the environment, adopted by the Human Rights Council on March 24, 2011, U.N. Doc. A/HRC/RES/16/11, April 12, 2011.

[102] *Id.* ¶ 7.

[103] *Id.* ¶ 8.

[104] *Id.* ¶ 9.

[105] *Id.* ¶ 11.

[106] *Id.* ¶ 12.

in situations involving environmental degradation from the activities of private actors, such as transnational corporations and legal entities.[107]

Next, the report identified key environmental threats and their impact on human rights and noted that a large number of international human rights and environmental instruments show that environmental protection contributes to the enjoyment of human rights.[108] After further studying the incorporation of environmental rights and responsibilities in national constitutions, the jurisprudence of regional human rights systems and the work of charter-based UN human rights bodies in addressing the intersection of human rights and environmental protection, and similarly the work of the human rights treaty bodies related to the environment, and extraterritorial dimensions of human rights and the environment,[109] the report's conclusion is worth citing in detail:

> While much progress has been made in elucidating the complex and multifaceted relationship between human rights and the environment, the dialogue between the two fields of law and policy has left a number of questions open. The theoretical discussions on the relationship between human rights and environment raise salient questions concerning, inter alia, the need for and the potential content of a right to a healthy environment; the role and duties of private actors with respect to human rights and the environment; and the extraterritorial reach of human rights and environment. Similarly, such questions arise regarding the operationalization of international human rights obligations as to how to implement a rights-based approach to the negotiation and implementation of multilateral environmental agreements; and how to monitor the implementation of human rights treaties that recognize the right to a healthy environment or interconnected rights.[110]

The report recommended that the Human Rights Council consider the use of appropriate mechanisms to study this relationship.[111] Pursuant to this recommendation, the Council decided to appoint "an independent expert to study the issue of "the human rights obligations, including non-discrimination obligations, relating to the enjoyment of a safe, clean, healthy and sustainable environment."[112]

---

[107] *Id.* ¶ 13.
[108] *Id.* ¶¶ 15–28.
[109] *Id.* ¶¶ 29–73.
[110] *Id.* ¶ 78.
[111] *Id.* ¶ 79.
[112] U.N. General Assembly, Human Rights Council, Resolution 19/10 Human Rights and the Environment adopted by the Human Rights Council on March 22, 2012, operative para. 2(a), U.N. Doc. A/HRC/RES/19/10, April 19, 2012.

15.4.2   *International and National Tribunals and the Right to a Healthy Environment*

The international legal community has been reluctant to formally recognize the necessity of a healthy environment as being found within rights already existing and acknowledged. However, as the following discussion shows, there are positive trends in the direction of tribunals' recognizing a human right to the environment. For instance, the European Commission on Human Rights and the European Court on Human Rights have considered cases in which environmental threats have been linked to human rights. In three cases regarding airport noise pollution,[113] the Commission and the Court found that excessive noise pollution resulted in intolerable stress and violated the petitioners' right to privacy, home, and property under Article 8 of the European Convention for the Protection of Human Rights and Fundamental Freedoms (European Convention).[114] But weighing such violations against the interests of the community as a whole and the importance of the airports to international trade and the British economy, the conclusion was that the noise did not violate the European Convention. Nevertheless, the significance of these cases is that the Commission and the Court allowed individuals to bring claims for violation of environmental rights under the Convention, which is silent regarding the relationship between human rights and the environment.[115]

A 1991 case before the European Court of Human Rights, *Fredin v. Sweden*,[116] resulted from Sweden's having revoked the petitioner's permit to extract gravel from his land. The Swedish government had based its decision on environmental protection laws, but when the Court again balanced the community's interests against those of the individual petitioner, it found that Sweden had not honored the petitioner's right to judicial review of an administrative decision, noting that "in today's society the protection of the environment is an increasingly important consideration."[117]

---

[113] Arrondelle v. United Kingdom, App. No. 7889/77, 26 Eur. Comm'n H.R. Dec. & Rep. 5 (1982); Powell & Rayner v. United Kingdom, 172 Eur. Ct. H.R. (Ser. A), at 5 (1990); Baggs v. United Kingdom, App. No. D 9310/81, 44 Eur. Comm'n H.R. Dec. & Rep. 13 (1985) (each addressing petitions based on noise coming from Gatwick and Heathrow Airports). *See also* Shelton, *supra* note 9, at 115–16.

[114] European Convention for the Protection of Human Rights and Fundamental Freedoms, Nov. 4, 1950, 213 U.N.T.S. 222. Article 8 reads in part: "1. Everyone has the right to respect for his private and family life, his home and his correspondence." For a study on the nexus between the environment and human rights in the context of the Convention, *see* Richard Desgagne, *Integrating Environmental Values into the European Convention on Human Rights*, 89 AM. J. INT'L L. 263 (1995).

[115] The point is effectively articulated in Philippe Sands, *Human Rights, Environment and the Lopez-Ostra Case: Context and Consequences*, 6 EUR. HUM. RTS. L. REV. 597, 598 (1996).

[116] Fredin v. Sweden, (No. 1), 192 Eur. Ct. H.R. (Ser.A), at 25–26 (1991).

[117] 192 Eur. Ct. H.R. (Ser.A), at 6 (1991).

In a 1993 case, *Lopez-Ostra v. Spain*,[118] the European Court again referred to Article 8 of the European Convention for the Protection of Human Rights and Fundamental Freedoms[119] and held that environmental degradation may result in affecting an individual's well-being so as to deprive the individual of enjoyment of private and family life. The Court found that Spain had breached its affirmative duty to ensure respect for home and private life under Article 8(1) and awarded the applicant compensatory damages.

Five years later, a similar link was again recognized between Article 8 and the environment in *Balmer-Schafroth & Others v. Switzerland*,[120] in which the applicants challenged the extension of the operating license of a Swiss nuclear power plant, alleging that a cognizable danger existed to the population and the environment under the European Convention on Human Rights. The applicants argued that they did not have an effective national remedy for the protection of their rights under Articles 2 and 8 of the Convention. The Court found that no direct link had been established by the applicants between the operating conditions of the power plant and their right to the protection of their physical integrity, as they had not demonstrated that the operation of the power plant exposed them to a danger that was specific and imminent.

In a 1998 case, *Guerra & Others v. Italy*,[121] the European Court of Human Rights applied Article 8 of the European Convention to hold that Italy had breached its obligation to respect the applicants' right to privacy and family life since it had not provided essential information to enable them to assess the environmental risks of living close to a chemical factory.[122] The applicants lived one kilometer from the factory that produced chemicals and fertilizers. A committee of technical experts determined, even though it was prevented from carrying out an inspection, that "the emission treatment equipment was inadequate, and the environmental-impact assessment incomplete."[123] The Commission found a violation. On Italy's appeal, the Court found that Italy had failed to provide the applicants with access to environmental information and had thus violated its Convention obligation even to take affirmative action in ensuring respect for their family life.[124]

---

[118] 20 Eur. H.R. Rep. 277; 303-C Eur. Ct. H.R. (Ser. A) (1994).
[119] *Supra* note 94.
[120] Application No. 22110/93, 25 Eur. H.R. Rep. 598 (1998).
[121] App. No. 14967/89, 26 Eur. H.R. Rep. 357 (1998) (European Court of Human Rights).
[122] *Id.* at 383.
[123] *Id.* at 362–63.
[124] For a detailed analysis, *see* Mariana T. Acevedo, *The Intersection of Human Rights and Environmental Protection in the European Court of Human Rights*, 8 N.Y.U. Envtl. L.J. 437 (2000).

A few months after *Guerra*, the Court decided *McGinley & Egan v. United Kingdom*.[125] The applicants alleged that the U.K. government had violated Article 8 of the European Convention by not providing them with the necessary information about the impact of nuclear tests on Christmas Island in 1954, for they were members of the armed forces stationed there when those tests occurred.[126] The applicants alleged that this lack of critical information was the reason they could not assess the environmental risks to their health from exposure to the nuclear testing.[127] The Court denied the applicants relief under Article 8 because it found the government had fulfilled its obligation by disclosing what information was available.[128] It stated that the applicants were requesting information the existence of which was a matter of speculation, and distinguished Guerra, stating that in that case, "it was not disputed that the inhabitants of Manfredonia were at risk from the factory in question and that the State authorities had in their possession information which would enable the inhabitants to assess this risk and take steps to avert it."[129] However, the Court concluded, "Where a Government engages in hazardous activities, respect for private and family life under Article 8 requires that an effective and accessible procedure be established which enables such persons to seek all relevant and appropriate information."[130]

It should be noted that, under Protocol No. 11 to the European Convention,[131] the European Commission is no longer in existence and hence the European Court will hereafter directly hear individuals' petitions.[132] Also, there is now an appellate procedure from the Court's decisions to a Grand Chamber, and the Court may also issue advisory opinions.[133] It does not appear that these changes should adversely affect an applicant's environmental claims under the Convention.

In a 1985 case before the Inter-American Commission on Human Rights,[134] the Yanomani Indians alleged that Brazil had violated their right to life, liberty and personal security since it did not take adequate measures to prevent certain environmental damage that resulted in the loss of life and cultural identity of the Yanomani. The Inter-American Commission found

---

[125] 27 Eur. Hum. Rts. Rep. 1 (1998).

[126] *Id.* at 5–12.

[127] *Id.* at 36.

[128] *Id.* at 44–45.

[129] *Id.*

[130] *Id.* at 45.

[131] Protocol 11 to the European Convention for the Protection of Human Rights and Fundamental Freedoms, E.T.S. No. 155, reprinted in 33 I.L.M. 943 (entered into force Nov. 1, 1998).

[132] Under Article 1 of Protocol 11, *id.*

[133] *Id.*

[134] Yanomani Indians v. Brazil, Inter-Am. C. H.R. 7615 OEA/Ser. L. V/II/66 Doc. 10, rev. 1 (1985).

that Brazil had violated the right as claimed. Now that the Protocol of San Salvador has entered into force as noted above, under which the right to a healthy environment is explicitly recognized, the Inter-American Commission on Human Rights will have a sound basis for affirming such a right in the future.

Two more cases from national courts will be briefly noted here, one from India and one from the Philippines. In a case decided by the Supreme Court of India, *Subhash Kumar v. State of Bihar*,[135] the right to a wholesome environment was found to be an integral part of the right to life enshrined in Article 21 of the Indian Constitution. A 1993 Philippines case, *Minors Oposa v. Secretary of the Department of Environment and Natural Resources (DENR)*,[136] was a class suit brought by minors with environmental damage claims. The named petitioners were children representing themselves and generations yet unborn invoking the right to a balanced and healthful ecology. They associated this right with the twin concepts of intergenerational responsibility and intergenerational justice,[137] and called for the cancellation of all existing timber license agreements in the country and for an order that DENR cease and desist "from receiving, accepting, processing, renewing or approving new timber license agreements."[138] It was their claim that excessive deforestation had "resulted in a host of environmental tragedies," such as drought, flooding, water shortages, massive erosion, salinization of the water table, and the disappearance of indigenous Filipino cultures.[139] The petitioners contended that the defendant's action in granting timber license agreements (TLAs) to various corporations was responsible for the alleged environmental tragedies. They invoked the Constitution of the Philippines, which embodies that nation's policies to protect its natural environment as well as, *inter alia*, to "protect and advance the right of the people to a balanced and healthful ecology in accord with the rhythm and harmony of nature."[140]

The lower court initially dismissed the suit on the ground of failure to state a cause of action and that granting the relief sought would amount to impairment of contracts,[141] but the Philippines Supreme Court reversed, concluding that the petitioners did indeed have standing. It stated that "the right of the

---

[135] Noted in a report of the UN Special Rapporteur: Second Progress Report Prepared by Mrs. Fatma Zohra Ksentini, Special Rapporteur, U.N. ESCOR Commission on Human Rights, Sub-Commission on Prevention of Discrimination and Protection of Minorities, U.N. Doc. E/CN.4/Sub. 2/1993/7 1993, at C, pt. 3 (1993).

[136] Reprinted in 33 I.L.M. 173 (1994).

[137] *Id.* at 176.

[138] *Id.* at 177.

[139] *See id.* at 177–78.

[140] *Id.* at 181, quoting Constitution of the Philippines, Section 16, Article II.

[141] *Id.* at 186.

petitioners (and all those they represent) to a balanced and healthful ecology is as clear as the DENR's duty – under its mandate and by virtue of its powers and functions [under statute] – to protect and advance the said right."[142]

Thus, even though international courts and tribunals and some national courts have expressly recognized the importance of environmental protection, the ability of governments to protect the environment has been limited because environmental degradation is generally not considered a separate cause of action in itself. Rather, it generally must be linked to violations of other existing human rights. As environmental degradation is a problem that transcends national and even regional boundaries, the development of a separate right to environment recognized on an international level must be further explored.[143]

15.5   Operationalizing the Right to Environment

Among many hurdles in establishing a recognized right to a healthful environment, perhaps the most essential is the difficulty of defining terms with precision. As suggested earlier, the term "environmental rights" may be interpreted as referring to rights of the elements of the environment (*e.g.*, the trees), independent of humans. On the other hand, the term may refer to rights of humans in the health-sustaining quality of the environment. What sort of quality in the environment would be included in such a right? When would an environmental violation be considered a human rights violation?

Several different characterizations of the right are suggested, depending on various qualities, such as "decent," "healthful," and "safe."[144] Proposals include the right of mankind to be protected from man-made contaminants which are injurious to health as well as from life-shortening influences.[145] A natural ecosystem including wild flora and fauna must also be included. Because the environment encompassing modern human life cannot realistically be expected to revert to its prehuman pure and clean state, a possible standard of environmental health might be one reflecting a minimum level considered essential to the preservation of healthy human existence.[146] The ultimate purpose of the right to the environment must be to protect human

---

[142] *Id.* at 191.
[143] For example, the release of radioactive material from the Chernobyl nuclear plant, discussed *supra* note 1, and the problem of acid rain in Sweden caused by factories in Germany and Poland.
[144] *See* Thorme, *supra* note 9, at 309–10; Nickel, *supra* note 74, at 282, 284–85; Pathak, *supra* note 9, at 209–10.
[145] *See* Thorme, *supra* note 9, at 309.
[146] *Id.*

life and health, preserve the natural environment, and impose an enforceable duty on present and future generations to protect the ecosystem.[147]

One commentator has proposed that "an environmental violation becomes significant enough to become a human rights violation when, as a result of a specific course of state action, a degraded environment occurs with either serious health consequences for a specific group of people or a disruption of a people's way of life."[148]

What kinds of risks are acceptable? In order that a meaningful right to environment exist, an individual right of action must be established.[149] Such a procedural guarantee requires the right to participate in decision-making regarding environmental impact, the right to adequate and timely information, the right of recourse to administrative and judicial fora, and effective means of enforcement.

The necessity for involvement of citizens and the duty of governments to inform citizens regarding decisions about the environment are already recognized in many international documents. For instance, the World Charter for Nature, the EEC Directive on Environmental Assessment, the ASEAN Agreement on the Conservation of Nature and Natural Resources, the UN Convention on Environmental Impact Assessment in a Transboundary Context, and the European Convention on Human Rights all elaborate duties of governments to disseminate information.[150] The 1998 Convention on Access to Information, Public Participation in Decision-making and Access to Justice in Environmental Matters ("Aarhus Convention") was the first multilateral agreement to protect citizens' rights to investigate how their governments' activities affect the environment.[151] However, these rights also generate concerns regarding the scope of the duties of the decision-makers. In particular, in order to be effective, the right to information must extend to individuals outside the boundaries of the acting state, and the final decision and action must be limited substantively. As a result, substantive international regulation is necessary in order to guarantee the extension of information and political participation to all affected people.[152] Such regulation would be facilitated by the establishment of a recognized right to environment.

However, as discussed above, the addition of new human rights is problematic, and some argue that the addition of further claims to rights may

---

[147] *See, e.g., id.* at 310.

[148] Lee, *supra* note 29, at 285.

[149] *See, e.g.,* Shelton, *supra* note 9, at 117.

[150] *See id.* at 117–19.

[151] Convention on Access to Information, Public Participation in Decision-Making and Access to Justice in Environmental Matters, June 25, 1998, United Nations Economic Commission for Europe, 38 I.L.M. 517, 1998, http://www.unece.org/fileadmin/DAM/env/pp/documents/cep43e.pdf.

[152] *See* Shelton, *supra* note 9, at 120–21.

devalue existing rights.[153] Regarding substantive criteria for the development of new human rights, Professor Alston suggests that they must be vital to the protection of human life and to the preservation and enhancement of its quality and conditions; and they must be universal, applying to all human beings across regions and cultures.[154] Professor Pathak suggests that they must be inalienable and indispensable to human existence.[155] He adds that they must be essential and enduring – unvarying in identity within the context of time or circumstances – and they must be grounded in reality.[156]

In 1986, the UN General Assembly adopted Guidelines in Developing International Instruments in the Field of Human Rights, under which newly conceived international human rights instruments should be consistent with the existing body of international human rights law; be of fundamental character; be sufficiently precise so as to give rise to identifiable and practicable rights and obligations; provide realistic and effective implementation machinery; and attract broad international support, among others.[157]

Among skeptics who challenge the desirability of recognizing the right to environment Professor Handl argues that conceptualizing it as a human right "diverts attention and efforts from other more pressing and promising environmental and human rights objectives,"[158] and it cannot be conceptualized as an inalienable right if it means that no derogations are permissible.[159] He further argues that state practice does not support this conceptualization,[160] it is too vague and general and difficult to operationalize.[161] Professor Handl contends that conceptualizing environmental rights as human rights would impose an anthropogenic bias on the environment and thus offer no guarantees against global environmental degradation.[162] Instead, he calls for coordination between global human rights and environmental regimes.[163]

Many of Professor Handl's arguments are valid. However, the same criticism conceivably could apply to many human rights that are currently established and accepted under international instruments, and even more so to

---

[153] *Id.* at 121.

[154] *See, e.g.,* P. Alston, *Conjuring Up New Human Rights: A Proposal for Quality Control,* 78 Am. J. Int'l L. 607 (1984).

[155] *See, e.g.,* Pathak, *supra* note 9, at 210–13.

[156] *Id.* at 214.

[157] G.A. Res. 41/120, at 179, U.N. GAOR, 41st Sess., Supp. (No. 53), U.N. Doc. A/41/53, Dec. 4, 1986.

[158] Handl, *supra* note 38, at 119. For similar criticism, *see* Alan Boyle, *The Role of International Human Rights Law in the Protection of the Environment, in* I Human Rights Approaches to Environmental Protection, 43, 49–57 (Alan Boyle & Michael Anderson eds., 1996).

[159] Handl, *supra* note 38, at 121–22.

[160] *Id.* at 124–29.

[161] *Id.* at 129–32.

[162] *Id.* at 129–38 & 142.

[163] *Id.*

such rights at the time when they are first emerging. It is submitted, as previously discussed, that the right to environment qualifies as a new human right, especially in the context of progress toward sustainable development.[164] To illustrate, the UN Commission on Human Rights passed two resolutions, one in 2003[165] and the other in 2005, on human rights and the environment as part of sustainable development.[166] Thus, as a solidarity right it may be invoked against or demanded of a government.[167]

In addition, the right to environment generates duties beyond those required of the government. The right would also result in imposition on individuals, organizations, and corporations of a duty to refrain from activities that harm the environment.[168] International organizations would also be obligated to avoid environmental risks in their operations. For example, international financial institutions, such as the World Bank, would be obligated to refrain from funding projects that might generate environmental harm; perhaps environmental impact assessments would be required in project proposals.[169] Finally, in addition to a discussion of substantive rights and duties, it is necessary to strengthen existing procedural rights as well as fashion new ones.

15.6   *Appraisal and Recommendations*

The preceding discussion shows how formidable the theoretical and practical hurdles are in developing the right to a healthy environment. To make it happen, requires a broad international effort to coordinate the actions of governments, international organizations, multinational corporations, and individuals.

First and foremost, the international human right to a safe and healthy environment must be clearly and narrowly defined. This requires action by the United Nations. The study conducted by the UN Sub-Commission on Prevention of Discrimination and Protection of Minorities, noted above, is

---

[164] Since the Rio Summit, sustainable development has emerged as a goal for all international organizations and governments to achieve (*see* Chapter 4). *See generally* Lee, *supra* note 29.

[165] Office of the High Commissioner for Human Rights, Commission on Human Rights Resolution 2003/71, Human rights and the environment as part of sustainable development, Resolution 2003/71, April 25, 2003 (adopted without a vote), U.N. Doc. E/CN.4/2003/L.11/Add.7.

[166] Office of the High Commissioner for Human Rights, Human rights and the environment as part of sustainable development, Human Rights Resolution 2005/60, April 20, 2005 (adopted without a vote), U.N. Doc. E/CN.4/2005/L.10/Add.17.

[167] *See* Pathak, *supra* note 9, at 218.

[168] *See, e.g.*, Nickel, *supra* note 74, at 286.

[169] *See id.* at 287.

a useful study, aptly supplemented by the 2011 analytical study on the relationship between human rights and the environment by the UN High Commissioner for Human Rights.[170] Next, the independent expert's report to the Human Rights Council should provide further guidance.

The UN is the appropriate body for action to create a generally recognized right to a safe and healthy environment, which would allow threats to the environment to be justiciable in human rights fora, and provide for the dissemination of information and capability for participation in assessment projects that are prerequisites for preventing environmental damage.

15.7   Rights of Indigenous Peoples

15.7.1   Introduction: A Case Study

Typical of the plight of so many indigenous peoples today, the lives and culture of the Huaorani are threatened by modern development.[171] A small tribe of a few hundred nomadic hunter-gatherers, the Huaorani live a subsistence lifestyle in a rainforest region in the upper Amazon Basin of Ecuador. In the 1970s, petroleum deposits were discovered in the Huaoranis' area, and oil development began. Facing spiraling international debt in the 1990s, the Ecuadorian government intensified oil leasing in the region. Decades of oil exploration, drilling, and development, population in-migration, boom-towns, road and pipeline construction, forest clearcutting and burning, and wildlife meat hunting have resulted in displacement of many of the Huaorani people, destruction of their environment, food base, villages, and culture; in oil spills in rivers in which they fish, drink, and bathe; and in the deaths and "disappearances" of Huarorani opposing oil development. The Ecuadorian government failed to address their concerns or protect them.

Frustrated, in 1993 Ecuadorian citizens representing indigenous peoples filed a class action suit in federal court in New York against Texaco, one

---

[170] *Analytical Study on the Relationship Between Human Rights and the Environment, supra* note 100.

[171] This case study draws from Adriana Fabra, *Indigenous Peoples, Environmental Degradation, and Human Rights: A Case Study, in* Human Rights Approaches to Environmental Protection 245 (Alan Boyle & Michael Anderson eds., 1996); Victoria C. Arthaud, *Environmental Destruction in the Amazon: Can U.S. Courts Provide a Forum for the Claims of Indigenous Peoples?* 7 Geo. Int'l Envtl L. Rev. 195, 197 (1994); Judith Kimerling, *Disregarding Environmental Law: Petroleum Development In Protected Natural Areas and Indigenous Homelands in the Ecuadorian Amazon,* 14 Hastings Int'l & Comp. L. Rev. 849 (1991); William A. Shutkin, *International Human Rights Law and the Earth: The Protection of Indigenous Peoples and the Environment,* 31 Va. J. Int'l L. 479, 493 (1991).

of the multinational oil producers.[172] The complaint alleged numerous environmental and human health injuries in the period 1972–1992 and that the Huarorani were unable to obtain relief from the government or courts of Ecuador. The federal trial court dismissed the suit in 1997 on grounds of *forum non conveniens*.[173] A US appeals court vacated that ruling on procedural grounds and remanded the case back to the trial court for reconsideration,[174] only to have the trial court three years later dismiss the case again on the grounds that an "adequate forum" existed in Ecuador.[175] Texaco merged with Chevron in 2001, and the case continued against both parties.[176] In 2003, the plaintiffs filed lawsuits before the Superior Courts of Nueva Loja and Tena in Ecuador.[177] After a lengthy investigation and trial in Ecuador, the plaintiffs won an $18.2 billion verdict in February 2011.[178] However, this ruling was tainted by accusations of corruption – including the allegation that the presiding judge accepted bribes.[179] Chevron called the ruling "illegitimate" and vowed to get the verdict nullified.[180]

In February 2011, Chevron brought a lawsuit in federal court in New York under the Racketeer Influenced and Corrupt Organizations Act (RICO), alleging that the case against itself in Ecuador was a conspiracy to commit extortion.[181] The Judge presiding over the RICO case preliminarily enjoined Ecuadorian lawyers from enforcing the Lago Agrio judgment anywhere

---

[172] Aguinda v. Texaco, Inc., 945 F. Supp. 625 (S.D.N.Y. 1996). For details, pleadings, and court documents *see* the plaintiffs' web site, http://www.texacorainforest.org/. For Texaco's view of the case, *see* http://www.texaco.com/sitelets/ecuador/en/default.aspx. Other such lawsuits were also filed in the US. See *id.*

[173] Aguinda v. Texaco, Inc., 945 F. Supp. 625 (S.D.N.Y. 1996); motion for reconsideration denied, 175 F.R.D. 50 (S.D.N.Y. 1997). *Forum non conveniens* is a legal doctrine allowing courts to refuse to take jurisdiction over a lawsuit when there is judged to be a more appropriate court available, for example in a foreign plaintiff's home country. *See* Andrew C. Revkin, *Lawyers for Ecuador Indians See U.S. Judge Linked to Texaco*, N.Y. TIMES (Sept. 3, 2000), http://www.nytimes.com/2000/09/03/world/lawyers-for-ecuador-indians-see-us-judge-linked-to-texaco.html.

[174] Jota v. Texaco, 157 F.3d 153 (2d Cir. 1998) (holding that a dismissal on the basis of forum non conveniens was erroneous in absence of a condition requiring oil company to submit to jurisdiction in Ecuador).

[175] 142 F. Supp. 2d 534 (S.D.N.Y. 2001).

[176] HISTORY OF TEXACO AND CHEVRON IN ECUADOR, *Timeline of Events*, http://www.texaco.com/sitelets/ecuador/en/history/chronologyofevents.aspx.

[177] *Id.*

[178] Paul Barrett, *Chevron Looks to Its Home Court for a Comeback Win*, BLOOMBERG BUSINESSWEEK, Jul. 14, 2011, http://www.businessweek.com/magazine/chevron-looks-to-its-home-court-for-a-comeback-win-07142011.html.

[179] *See*, Clifford Krauss, *Revelation Undermines Chevron Case in Ecuador*, N.Y. TIMES, Oct. 29, 2009, http://www.nytimes.com/2009/10/30/world/americas/30ecuador.html?_r=1.

[180] CHEVRON, *Ecuador Lawsuit*, http://www.chevron.com/ecuador/.

[181] Lawrence Hurley, *Chevron's RICO Lawsuit in Pollution Case Part of Wider Legal Strategy*, N.Y. TIMES, Feb. 2, 2011, http://www.nytimes.com/gwire/2011/02/02/02greenwire-chevrons-rico-lawsuit-in-pollution-case-part-o-68778.html.

outside of Ecuador in March 2011.[182] In August 2011, a tribunal, administered by the Permanent Court of Arbitration in The Hague, found that Ecuador's courts violated international law through their significant delays in ruling on certain commercial disputes between Texaco Petroleum and the Ecuadorian government.[183] These developments have electrified corporate lawyers and their clients because they suggest it may be possible to use US courts to extinguish hostile verdicts from foreign courts.[184]

The plight of the Huaorani reflects how difficult it can be for indigenous people to receive justice or even control change in their communities. In response to these systemic problems indigenous people face, a unique body of international human rights law is evolving.[185] This body of law recognizes that, throughout world history, native populations have typically been displaced, robbed of their lands, environments, and lives, and absorbed or destroyed by "invading" cultures, typically seeking resources. Historical patterns of colonialism that suppressed indigenous peoples' political institutions and cultural patterns have led to current inequities in treatment.[186] In the words of James Anaya, the UN Special Rapporteur on the Rights of Indigenous People, "Historical phenomena grounded in racially discriminatory attitudes are not just blemishes of the past but rather translate into current inequities."[187] The reality of indigenous peoples' situations often runs counter

---

[182] Roger Parloff, *Have You Got a Piece of this Lawsuit,* FORTUNE, June 28, 2011, http://features.blogs.fortune.cnn.com/2011/06/28/have-you-got-a-piece-of-this-lawsuit-2/.

[183] *Chevron Awarded $96 Million in Arbitration Claim Against the Government of Ecuador,* WALL ST. J., Aug. 31, 2011, http://online.wsj.com/article/PR-CO-20110831-910130.html.

[184] Barrett, *supra* note 178.

[185] This section is drawn in part from George (Rock) Pring & Susan Y. Noé, *The Emerging Law of Public Participation Affecting Mining, Energy, and Resources Development, in* HUMAN RIGHTS IN NATURAL RESOURCE DEVELOPMENT: PUBLIC PARTICIPATION IN THE SUSTAINABLE DEVELOPMENT OF MINING AND ENERGY RESOURCES 11 (Donald Zillman, Alastair Lucas & George (Rock) Pring eds., 2002). Excellent in-depth references on indigenous peoples include Benedict Kingsbury, *"Indigenous Peoples" in International Law: A Constructivist Approach to the Asian Controversy,* 92 AM. J. INT'L L. 414 (1998); S. K. Date-Bah, *Rights of Indigenous People in Relation to Natural Resources Development: An African's Perspective,* 16 J. ENERGY & NAT. RESOURCES L. 389, 389 n.4 (1998); THE WORLD BANK, THE WORLD BANK PARTICIPATION SOURCEBOOK (1996), http://www-wds.worldbank .org/external/default/WDSContentServer/WDSP/IB/1996/02/01/000009265_39612141755 37/Rendered/PDF/multi_page.pdf; Benedict Kingsbury, *'Indigenous Peoples' as an International Legal Concept, in* INDIGENOUS PEOPLES OF ASIA 33 (R. H. Barnes *et al.* eds., 1995); Robert K. Hitchcock, *International Human Rights, The Environment, and Indigenous Peoples,* 5 COLO. J. INT'L ENVTL. L. & POL'Y 1 (1994); Mary Ellen Turpel, *Indigenous Peoples' Rights of Political Participation and Self-Determination: Recent International Legal Developments and the Continuing Struggle for Recognition,* 25 CORNELL INT'L L.J. 579, 595 (1992); Charles Scheiner, *Indigenous People, Environment and Development* (Nov. 24, 1992); Lee Swepston, *A New Step in the International Law on Indigenous and Tribal Peoples: ILO Convention No. 169 of 1989,* 15 OKLA. CITY U. L. REV. 677 (1990).

[186] S. JAMES ANAYA, INTERNATIONAL HUMAN RIGHTS AND INDIGENOUS PEOPLES 1 (2009).

[187] *Id.* at 4.

to the modern theory of their human rights, succinctly expressed in Rio Declaration Principle 22:

> Indigenous people and their communities and other local communities have a vital role in environmental management and development because of their knowledge and traditional practices. States should recognize and duly support their identity, culture and interests and enable their effective participation in the achievement of sustainable development.[188]

Today, at the intersection of human rights and environmental law, a growing body of international law strives to meet the challenge of preserving and protecting indigenous peoples' rights and cultures. This movement seeks to balance modern considerations of "sustainable development" with indigenous identities that link communities to both the land and the ancestral past.[189]

The most prominent modern manifestation of international concern for indigenous peoples is the 2007 UN Declaration on the Rights of Indigenous Peoples.[190] This section will analyze the meaning of "indigenousness," outline early legal protections, and examine the developments that led to the creation of this landmark declaration.

15.7.2   What Is "Indigenous"?

Defining the term "indigenous peoples" – and the spectrum of related but distinguishable terms like "aborigines," "natives," "tribes," "first nations," "ethnic minorities," "traditionals," "scheduled groups," "local communities," etc. – can be difficult because movements, invasions, and minglings have characterized human settlement patterns. "Indigenousness" is a term with no single agreed definition in international practice,[191] and the prevailing view today is that no formal definition is necessary for the recognition and protection of their rights, substituting instead a "factor analysis."[192] According to the authoritative World Bank definition, "indigenous" factors include: (1) self-identification and identification by others as members of a distinct cultural group; (2) collective attachment to geographically distinct habitats or

---

[188] United Nations Conference on Environment and Development, Rio de Janeiro, Braz., June 3–14, 1992, Rio Declaration on Environment and Development, U.N. Doc. A/CONF.151/26 (vol. I) (1992), 31 I.L.M. 874 (1992), http://www.unep.org/Documents.Multilingual/Default.asp?documentid=78&articleid=1163.

[189] ANAYA, *supra* note 186, at 1.

[190] *Id.* United Nations Declaration on the Rights of Indigenous Peoples, G.A. Res. 61/295, U.N. Doc. A/RES/61/295 (Oct. 2, 2007), http://daccess-dds-ny.un.org/doc/UNDOC/GEN/N06/512/07/PDF/N0651207.pdf?OpenElement (hereafter UNDRIP).

[191] Kingsbury, *A Constructivist Approach*, *supra* note 185, at 414; Hitchcock, *supra* note 185, at 2.

[192] OFFICE OF THE UN HIGH COMMISSIONER FOR HUMAN RIGHTS, GUIDELINES ON INDIGENOUS PEOPLES' ISSUES 8 (2009) http://www2.ohchr.org/english/issues/indigenous/docs/guidelines.pdf.

ancestral territories in the area and to the natural resources in these habitats and territories; (3) customary cultural, economic, social, or political institutions that are separate from those of the dominant society and culture; and (4) possession of an indigenous language, which is often distinct from a national language.[193] At a simpler level, the Bank defines them as "groups with a social and cultural identity distinct from the dominant society that makes them vulnerable to being disadvantaged...."[194] Self-identification as indigenous or tribal is also considered a fundamental criterion, and represents the practice followed in the UN.[195] Specifically, article 33 of the Declaration on the Rights of Indigenous Peoples codifies the right of indigenous peoples to determine their own identity or membership in accordance with their customs and traditions.[196]

However defined, indigenousness has become "a concept with considerable power as a basis for group mobilization, international standard setting, transnational networking, and programmatic activity of intergovernmental and nongovernmental organizations."[197] Part of its power is that it can be applied to more than one quarter billion people in some 70 or more countries,[198] many located in the path of the development desires of the dominant (some prefer "ambient") culture. Given their interdependence on the natural environment, indigenous peoples have some of the strongest stakeholder interests imaginable, because their personal, societal, and cultural *survival* depends on the environment.

"Indigenous" is a disputatious term as well. Like so much of human rights, the concept challenges national sovereignty, causing a number of countries – China, India, Bangladesh, Myanmar, Indonesia, for example – strongly to oppose its being applied to groups within their countries.[199] On the other extreme, some countries – Australia, Philippines, Malaysia, Japan, Taiwan, and the US, for example – attempt actively to support indigenousness with national legislation and action programs. In between are still other countries –

---

[193] THE WORLD BANK, WORLD BANK OPERATIONAL MANUAL, OP 4.10 ¶ 3–4 (2005), http://web.worldbank.org/WBSITE/EXTERNAL/PROJECTS/EXTPOLICIES/EXTOPMANUAL/0,,contentMDK:20553653~menuPK:64701637~pagePK:64709096~piPK:64709108~theSitePK:502184,00.html.

[194] *Id.* ¶ 2.

[195] GUIDELINES ON INDIGENOUS PEOPLES' ISSUES, *supra* note 192, at 9.

[196] UNDRIP, *supra* note 190, art. 33.

[197] Kingsbury, *A Constructivist Approach, supra* note 185, at 414 (footnote omitted).

[198] WORLD BANK PARTICIPATION SOURCEBOOK, *supra* note 185, at 251. For substantially higher numbers, *see* Hitchcock, *supra* note 185, at 2. Taking another measure, of the approximately 5,000–7,000 spoken languages in the world today, 4,000–5,000 are classified as indigenous, and over half of these languages are threatened with extinction. *Globalization: A Threat to Cultural, Linguistic and Biological Diversity*, BUS. WORLD, Feb. 15, 2001, at 19.

[199] Kingsbury, *A Constructivist Approach, supra* note 185, at 426 *et seq.*

Cambodia, Laos, Papua New Guinea, for example – which, while generally rejecting the term "indigenous," nevertheless recognize and provide special treatment for such groups using other, to them less-loaded terms, such as "tribal" or "local communities or populations."

The World Bank notes that indigenous peoples "have often been on the losing end of the development process."[200] Frequently, their lives, homes, environments, and cultures have been devastated, while the financial benefits have gone to others. Even in programs and developments designed to improve their situation, the paternalistic approach typically used – seeking the cultural assimilation of indigenous peoples and ignoring their knowledge and interests – has often served to worsen, rather than improve, their economic, social and cultural wellbeing, according to the Bank.[201] The next section describes how the law is evolving to change the unfortunate treatment that indigenous people have faced for so long.

15.7.3   *Early International Legal Protection*

The attention given to indigenous peoples by international institutions has increased dramatically over the course of the last 50 years. The foundation is, of course, the basic international human rights principles of right to life and environment (as discussed in §§ 2.1.6 and 3.2–3.5). Interestingly, the International Labor Organization (ILO), while created to improve working conditions around the world, was one of the original leaders in developing human rights legal authorities for indigenous peoples.[202] Its 1953 book on Indigenous Peoples[203] and 1957 Indigenous Peoples Convention No. 107[204] were among the first IGO documents to draw attention to the issue. Convention No. 107 was criticized by indigenous peoples advocates for hinting at integration and assimilation[205] and was never widely ratified. Nevertheless, it stands out as one of the pioneering international legal instruments on the rights of indigenous peoples in the 20th century.

This early period was marked by intermittent developments and unorganized attempts at the codification of indigenous peoples' rights. For example,

---

[200] WORLD BANK PARTICIPATION SOURCEBOOK, *supra* note 185, at 251.
[201] *Id.*
[202] Currently, indigenous people's rights only make up a small portion of the work in which the ILO engages. See ILO, *Indigenous and Tribal Peoples,* http://www.ilo.org/indigenous/ lang – en/index.htm.
[203] INTERNATIONAL LABOR ORGANIZATION, INDIGENOUS PEOPLES (1953).
[204] ILO Convention No. 107 on Protection and Integration of Indigenous and Other Tribal and Semi-Tribal Populations in Independent Countries, June 26, 1957, 328 U.N.T.S. 247, http://www.ilo.org/ilolex/cgi-lex/convde.pl?C107. Convention No. 107 is in force in only 18 countries and is no longer open for ratification.
[205] *See* Dean B. Suagee, *Recent Developments: Human Rights of Indigenous Peoples: Will the United States Rise to the Occasion?,* 21 AM. INDIAN L. REV. 365 (1997).

the widely ratified 1966 UN Covenant on Civil and Political Rights recognizes indigenous rights in article 27:

> In those States in which ethnic, religious or linguistic minorities exist, persons belonging to such minorities shall not be denied the right, in community with the other members of their group, to enjoy their own culture, to profess and practice their own religion, or to use their own language.[206]

In 1971, the UN Sub-Commission on Prevention of Discrimination and Protection of Minorities appointed a Special Rapporteur to examine discrimination against indigenous peoples.[207] This move reflected the growing concern for indigenous peoples' rights and recognition of their particular plight. Still, however, the 1972 Stockholm Declaration[208] was silent on the subject. The next major step forward occurred when indigenous peoples held their first international meeting at the 1977 International Nongovernmental Organization Conference on Discrimination Against Indigenous Populations in the Americas.[209] This was followed by the establishment of the UN Working Group on Indigenous Populations (WGIP) in 1982.[210] The WGIP was tasked with reviewing current developments affecting the rights of indigenous populations and charged with creating standards, a project that would take no less than 25 years (*see* section 14.7.4).[211]

In 1989, the ILO proposed a much stronger treaty, ILO Convention No. 169,[212] acknowledging that the state of indigenous populations had significantly changed since 1957. Convention No. 169 emphasizes the importance of public participation by indigenous peoples (*see* § 2.2.1),[213] and, true to that

---

[206] International Covenant on Civil and Political Rights, Dec. 16, 1966, art. 27, 999 U.N.T.S. 171, http://www2.ohchr.org/english/law/ccpr.htm. For an excellent resources on the applicability of UN treaty regimes to indigenous issues, *see* ANAYA, *supra* note 186, at 185–250.

[207] UN Office of the High Comm'n of Human Rights, The Rights of Indigenous Peoples, Fact Sheet No. 9, at 5–6, http://www.ohchr.org/Documents/Publications/FactSheet9rev.1en.pdf.

[208] United Nations Conference on the Human Environment, Stockholm, Swed., June 5–16, Stockholm Declaration of the UN Conference on the Human Environment, Principle 21, U.N. Doc. A/CONF.48/14/Rev. 1 at 3 (1973), U.N. Doc. A/Conf.48/14 at 2–65 and Corr. 1 (1972), 11 I.L.M. 1416 (1972), http://www.unep.org/Documents.Multilingual/Default.asp?documentid=97&articleid=1503.

[209] *See* Suagee, *supra* note 205, at 369.

[210] *See* Sarah Pritchard, *Working Group on Indigenous Populations: Mandate, Standard-setting Activities and Future Perspectives in* INDIGENOUS PEOPLES, THE UNITED NATIONS AND HUMAN RIGHTS 40 (Sarah Pritchard ed., 1998).

[211] Erica-Irene Daes, *The UN Declaration on the Rights of Indigenous Peoples: Background and Appraisal in* REFLECTIONS ON THE UN DECLARATION ON THE RIGHTS OF INDIGENOUS PEOPLES 12 (Stephen Allen & Alexandra Xanathaki eds., 2011).

[212] ILO Convention No. 169, Convention Concerning Indigenous and Tribal Peoples in Independent Countries, June 27, 1989, 28 I.L.M. 1382 (1989) http://www.ilo.org/ilolex/cgi-lex/convde.pl?C169, reprinted in S. JAMES ANAYA, INDIGENOUS PEOPLES IN INTERNATIONAL LAW 193 (1996).

[213] *Id.* arts. 6(1), 7(1), 7(3), 12, 15(1)-(2).

principle, the ILO allowed many indigenous groups and individuals to participate in its formulation. Article 2 states that, "[g]overnments shall have the responsibility for developing, with the participation of the peoples concerned, co-ordinated and systematic action to protect the rights of these peoples and to guarantee respect for their integrity." Articles 13–19 set out provisions concerning land and resources, stressing the importance of protecting them as a means to preserve cultural integrity. Where the state has ownership rights to the land and/or resources, Article 15 requires the government to "consult these peoples, with a view to ascertaining whether and to what degree their interests would be prejudiced, before undertaking or permitting any programmes for the exploration or exploitation of such resources pertaining to their lands." Article 16 states that, with some exceptions,[214] indigenous peoples "shall not" be removed from the land which they occupy.

Convention No. 169 is extremely protective of indigenous peoples.[215] In fact, one of its problems is that it appears to go so far as to subordinate sustainable development and environmental protection principles to the right of self-determination.[216] While Convention No. 169 was meant to supersede Convention No. 107, the older convention is still in force in 18 states,[217] and Convention No. 169 had only 20 state parties as of the start of 2012.[218]

IGOs began to delving into indigenous rights law in the 1990s. In 1989, the Organization of American States (OAS) requested the Inter-American Commission on Human Rights (IACHR) to draft an instrument on the rights of indigenous peoples.[219] This instrument was completed in 1997 as the American Declaration on the Rights of Indigenous Peoples.[220] Similarly, the World Bank began reforming its policies in 1991 to require "participation by indigenous people in decision making throughout project planning, implementation, and evaluation," for Bank-financed projects affecting them.[221] The 1992 Rio Declaration further crystallized these concepts in Principle 22, quoted above.[222] Additionally, Agenda 21 contains an entire chapter on

---

[214] For example, if relocation is "necessary as an exceptional measure," it must be approved by the peoples affected based upon informed consent. *Id.* art. 16(2).

[215] JAMES (SA'KE'J) YOUNGBLOOD HENDERSON, INDIGENOUS DIPLOMACY AND THE RIGHTS OF PEOPLES: ACHIEVING UN RECOGNITION, 59–60 (2008).

[216] George (Rock) Pring, James Otto & Koh Naito, *Trends in International Environmental Law Affecting the Minerals Industry,* 17 J. ENERGY & NAT. RESOURCES L. 39, 176 (1999).

[217] Swepston, *supra* note 185.

[218] Lila K. Barrera-Hernández, *The Legal Framework for Indigenous Peoples' and Other Public's Participation in Latin America: The Cases of Argentina, Columbia, and Peru, in* HUMAN RIGHTS IN NATURAL RESOURCE DEVELOPMENT, *supra* note 185, at 589, 591.

[219] *See* Annual Report of the Inter-American Commission on Human Rights 1988–89, 245–50, OEA/ser.L/V/II.76, doc. 10 (1989).

[220] *See* OAS G.A. Res. OEA/ser.P, AG/doc.3573/97 (1997).

[221] WORLD BANK PARTICIPATION SOURCEBOOK OD 4.10, *supra* note 185.

[222] Rio Declaration, *supra* at note 188.

"Recognizing and Strengthening the Role of Indigenous Peoples and Their Communities," that recommends numerous rights and strengthened consultation procedures.[223] The nonbinding 1992 Forestry Principles also include provisions concerning indigenous peoples and forestry resources.[224] The UN General Assembly proclaimed 1993 as the International Year for the World's Indigenous People.[225] The aim of this proclamation was to strengthen "international co-operation for the solution of problems faced by indigenous communities in areas such as human rights, the environment, development, education and health...."[226] Also that year, the General Assembly proclaimed the International Decade for the World's Indigenous People.[227] These documents and developments demonstrated a general realization of the "unique value and role that indigenous people have 'in environmental management and development because of their knowledge and traditional practices.'"[228]

15.7.4 *The Universal Declaration on the Rights of Indigenous Peoples*

The Universal Declaration on the Rights of Indigenous Peoples was 25 years in the making. The UN Working Group on Indigenous Populations, the organization charged in 1982 with creating standards, completed the final text of its Draft Declaration in 1993.[229] The draft was adopted by the Sub-Commission on Prevention and Discrimination and Protection of Minorities in 1994, and was then referred to the Commission on Human Rights, which established another Working Group to examine its terms.[230] Following extensive discussions, the Working Group submitted the draft to the Human Rights Council, which adopted the draft and submitted the declaration to the 61st session of the General Assembly.[231] The General Assembly at last voted

---

[223] Agenda 21, ch. 26 (1992), June, 13, 1992, U.N. Doc. A/CONF. 151/26 (vols. I–III) (1992), http://www.un.org/esa/dsd/agenda21/; reprinted in 4 AGENDA 21 & THE UNCED PROCEEDINGS at 492 (Nicholas A. Robinson *et al.* eds., 1993). *See also*, INDIGENOUS PEOPLES, THE ENVIRONMENT AND LAW 24 (Lawrence Watters ed., 2004).

[224] Nonlegally Binding Authoritative Statement of Principles for a Global Consensus on the Management, Conservation and Sustainable Development of All Types of Forests, June 13, 1992, U.N. Doc. A/Conf. 151/26 (Vol. III) (1992), 31 I.L.M. 881 (1992), http://www.un.org/documents/ga/conf151/aconf15126–3annex3.htm.

[225] G.A. Res. 45/164, Dec. 18, 1990, http://www.un.org/documents/ga/res/45/a45r164.htm.

[226] *Id.*

[227] G.A. Res. 48/163, Dec. 21, 1993, http://www.un.org/documents/ga/res/48/a48r163.htm.

[228] HENDERSON, *supra* note 215, at 60.

[229] Draft Declaration on the Rights of Indigenous Peoples, Report of the Working Group on Indigenous Populations, 11th Sess., U.N. DOC. E/CN.4/Sub.2/1994/56, 105–115, 34 I.L.M. 541 (Oct. 28, 1994), http://www1.umn.edu/humanrts/demo/1994min.html. For a discussion of the Draft Declaration, *see* Dr. Erica-Irene A. Daes, *Equality of Indigenous Peoples Under the Auspices of the United Nations Draft Declaration on the Rights of Indigenous Peoples*, 7 ST. THOMAS L. REV. 493 (1995).

[230] Julian Burger, *Indigenous Peoples and the United Nations in* HUMAN RIGHTS OF INDIGENOUS PEOPLES 6 (Cynthia Price Cohen ed., 1998); Daes, *supra* note 229 at 34.

[231] Daes, *supra* note 229 at 34.

to adopt the Declaration on September 13, 2007, with 144 countries voting in favor, 4 against (Australia, Canada, New Zealand, and the US), and 11 abstaining.[232]

The Declaration addresses such issues as rights to self-determination, land and territory, environmental integrity, and intangible heritage. Many indigenous people feel that the right to self-determination is primary among these rights because self-determination is vital for the continuing existence of indigenous populations as distinct populations.[233] The Declaration calls on states to consult with indigenous peoples to obtain their free and informed consent prior to approval of any project affecting their lands and resources.[234] Articles 25–32 further deal with land and resources, and the Declaration specifically provides that "Indigenous peoples have the right to the lands, territories and resources which they have traditionally owned, occupied or otherwise used or acquired."[235]

Respect for indigenous land occupation grows out of a recognition that traditional lifestyles, such as hunting and gathering, have co-evolved in balance with specific ecosystems.[236] Thus, environmental degradation not only impoverishes indigenous communities, it may threaten their continued survival.[237] Indigenous people have contributed the least to the emission of greenhouse gases, yet they are often the populations most adversely affected by climate change.[238] The direct and indirect impacts of climate change may threaten the very existence of the people of the Arctic, small islands, high altitude areas, and other vulnerable environments.[239]

The Declaration also takes the novel, and controversial, step of protecting intangible heritage in article 31:

> Indigenous peoples have the right to maintain, control, protect and develop their cultural heritage, traditional knowledge and traditional cultural expressions, as well as the manifestations of their sciences, technologies and cultures, including human and genetic resources, seeds, medicines, knowledge of the properties of fauna and flora, oral traditions, literatures, designs, sports and traditional games and visual and performing arts. They also have the right to maintain, control, protect and develop their intellectual property over such cultural heritage, traditional knowledge, and traditional cultural expressions.

---

[232] *Universal Declaration on the Rights of Indigenous Peoples,* UNPFII http://www.un.org/esa/socdev/unpfii/en/declaration.html.

[233] GUIDELINES ON INDIGENOUS PEOPLES' ISSUES, *supra* note 192, at 17.

[234] UNDRIP, *supra* note 190, art. 3, 4, 18, 19, 23, & 32.

[235] *Id.* art. 26

[236] GUIDELINES ON INDIGENOUS PEOPLES' ISSUES, *supra* note 192, at 18.

[237] *Id.*

[238] *Id.*

[239] *Id.* This relationship is documented in article 29 of the Declaration, which states that: "Indigenous peoples have the right to the conservation and protection of the environment and the productive capacity of their lands or territories and resources."

This article acknowledges that indigenous communities have developed deep wells of cultural knowledge, but recognizes that this knowledge is often exploited without consent or equitable sharing of the benefits.[240] While the Declaration grants indigenous people the right to control this knowledge, in practice this will be difficult to implement.

Unfortunately, many fear that the Declaration as a whole will be difficult to implement. First of all, the Declaration has ambiguous legal effect. It is not obligatory like a treaty, therefore, the individual components will only be considered binding if they can be categorized as customary international law. To be categorized as customary international law, the practice must be representative of widespread state practice and also be recognized as a legal obligation (*opinio juris*). The negative vote by four governments, who have significant populations of indigenous peoples, significantly undermines, but does not necessarily invalidate, any claim that this document represents customary international law.[241]

Second, many of the structural inequalities that have historically led to the dispossession of indigenous communities still remain and continue to negatively impact this group of people.[242] State-centered notions of sovereignty, right to development, and "improving the lot of the uncivilized" continue to cause many national governments to overlook the rights of indigenous inhabitants and see them as "interfering with progress." There are exceptions – IGOs, national governments, private companies, NGOs, and indigenous tribes and nations which are working to create and implement national laws, guidelines, and programs that will ensure indigenous peoples' rights and cultures as provided in the Declaration.[243] The world community now faces the challenge of making the Declaration work on a broader scale to live up to its lofty goals.[244] Given the close linkage between environment and culture, many indigenous peoples are faced with "virtual extinction" by development in their areas,[245] and effective protections cannot come too soon.

---

[240] *Id.* at 19.

[241] ANAYA, *supra* note 186.

[242] Rodolfo Stavenhagen, The Rights of Indigenous Peoples Work: The Challenge Ahead, in REFLECTIONS ON THE UN DECLARATION ON THE RIGHTS OF INDIGENOUS PEOPLES 147 (Stephen Allen & Alexandra Xanathaki eds., 2011).

[243] Pring & Noé, *supra* note 185.

[244] For an informative guide on the subject, see MAKING THE DECLARATION WORK: THE UNITED NATIONS DECLARATION ON THE RIGHTS OF INDIGENOUS PEOPLES (Claire Charters and Rodolfo Stavenhagen eds., 2009).

[245] WORLD COMMISSION ON ENVIRONMENT AND DEVELOPMENT, OUR COMMON FUTURE 12 (1987), http://www.un-documents.net/wced-ocf.htm.

15.8   *Population, Human Rights, and the Environment*

15.8.1   *Introduction*

In a world of over 7 billion people, the numbers keep rising.[246] In many developing countries population growth has been outpacing economic growth, adding to further hardship for the poor and disadvantaged. Coupled with rising standards of living in many countries, rapid rise in population puts strain on resources and adversely impacts the environment. However, there is a lack of universal consensus on what kind of legal regime should be devised to ensure population stabilization. The 1994 International Conference on Population and Development (ICPD) in Cairo led to a landmark 10-year Program of Action which continues to guide national, regional, and international action. Here we examine the nature of the challenge and its various dimensions, especially the population-human rights nexus, and the role of the ICPD Program of Action and subsequent international efforts in addressing the problem.

15.8.2   *The Nature and Scope of the Problem*

The world's population some 2,000 years ago was about 300 million, and it doubled to 600 million in the next 1,600 years. The following numbers tell the story of its recent rapid growth: from a population of one billion in 1804 it took 123 years to reach two billion; 32 years to add another billion; adding each successive billion at 15 years, then 13, then 12, and another 12, to finally reach seven billion in October 2011.[247] The population more than doubled from 1968 to 2012, and from five billion in 1987 it grew by 40 percent, to seven billion in 2011.[248] The Population Division of the UN Department of Economic and Social Affairs in its *World Population Prospects (WPP): The*

---

[246] The population was estimated at more than 7 billion 46 million on June 4, 2012. Current World Population can be found at 7 BILLION ACTIONS, http://www.7billionactions.org. 7 Billion Actions Campaign is a collaborative effort involving several UN and private sector entities and civil society organizations. The campaign calls upon all individuals, organizations, and communities to participate in a variety of ways. As the Executive Director General of UNFPA, Babatunde Osotimehin, said, "Working together, increment actions will create exponential results. UNFPA's slogan is that everyone counts, and now, with nearly 7 billion people sharing our planet, we need to count on each other as never before." UNFPA, Press Release: Challenges, Opportunities and Action in a World of 7 Billion, July 11, 2011, http://www.unfpa.org/public/home/news/pid/7999 [hereinafter Challenges & Opportunities].

[247] United Nations Population Fund (UNFPA), *The State of World Population 2011 – People and Possibilities in a World of 7 Billion*, 2011, at 2, http://www.foweb.unfpa.org/SWP2011/reports/EN-SWOP2011-FINAL.pdf [hereinafter World Population 2011].

[248] Challenges & Opportunities, *supra* note 246.

2010 Revision projects a global population of 9.3 billion in 2050, and more than 10 billion by the end of this century.[249]

It is especially noteworthy that almost all of this population growth – 97 of every hundred people – has occurred in less developed countries, a number of which struggle to meet the needs of their people.[250] Much of the increase in this century is projected to come from 39 countries in Africa, nine in Asia, six in Oceania, and four in Latin America, all high-fertility and less developed countries.[251] To illustrate, under the median variant projection, the population of the high-fertility countries (more than 1.5 surviving daughters average for each woman) would almost triple between 2011 and 2100 – from 1.2 billion to 4.2 billion.[252] During this period the population of the intermediate-fertility countries (between one and 1.5 daughters on average for each woman) would increase from 2.8 billion to 3.5 billion, while the low-fertility countries (women do not have enough children to ensure that each woman is replaced by a daughter) would find their population declining from 2.9 billion to 2.4 billion.[253]

Two other WPP findings are equally important: (1) while the populations of the low-fertility countries and the intermediate-fertility countries are projected to reach a maximum before the end of the century – around 2030 and 2065, respectively – the population of the low-fertility countries will continue to increase throughout the century and would still be increasing by the turn of the century;[254] and (2) while life expectancy is projected to increase in all three groups of countries, population aging is fastest in low-fertility countries, slower among the intermediate fertility countries, and slowest among the high fertility countries.[255]

There is wide divergence in what it takes to sustain the lives of people around the world. To illustrate, it takes 9.5 hectares of the earth's space to sustain the life of the average American, compared to only about 1 hectare for the average person in India or most of Africa, and 2.7 hectares for the average person worldwide.[256] As the UN Population Fund (UNFPA) states:

---

[249] UN Department of Economic and Social Affairs, Population Division, *World Population Prospects: The 2010 Revision (Frequently Asked Questions* – "best approximations," based on "estimates obtained by interpolating the results of the *2010 Revision*"), http://esa.un.org/unpd/wpp/Other-Information/faq.htm. For an abbreviated version of the 2010 Revision, see United Nations, Press Release, World Population to reach 10 billion by 2100 if Fertility in all Countries Converges to Replacement Level, May 3, 2011, http://esa.un.org/wpp/Other-Information/Press_Release_WPP2010.pdf [hereinafter WPP 2010 Rev.].

[250] Challenges & Opportunities, *supra* note 246.

[251] WPP 2010 Rev., *supra* note 247, at 1.

[252] *Id.*

[253] *Id.*

[254] *Id.* at 3.

[255] *Id.* at 6–7.

[256] World Population 2011, *supra* note 247, at 94.

Gaps between rich and poor are growing. Urbanization and migration continue. Climate change is of increasing concern and more people than ever are vulnerable to food insecurity, water shortages and weather-related disasters. Meanwhile, many rich and middle income countries are concerned about low fertility and ageing.[257]

In its October 2011 study, *Keeping Track of Our Changing Environment – From Rio to Rio + 20 (1992–2012),*[258] the UN Environment Program (UNEP) reports that the absolute number of people living in slums (a slum household comprises a group of individuals living under the same roof, lacking one or more of the following conditions: access to improved water, access to improved sanitation, sufficient living-area and durability of housing) has increased by 26 percent between 1990 and 2010, numbering 171 million additional people with total numbers increasing from 656 million in 1990 to 827 million in 2010.[259] Also, the UNEP 2012 report on the global environment, entitled "GEO: Global Environment Outlook," which provides a comprehensive up-to-date assessment of the state of the global environment and the emerging trends to support decisionmaking,[260] noted that the burgeoning population was one of the drivers that "intensify pressure on land by raising demands for food, livestock feed, energy, and raw materials.[261]

The report added:

> [G]rowth in demand is causing land-use conversion, land degradation, soil erosion, and pressure on protected areas. The need to increase agriculture productivity, due, for instance, to population growth, and to compensate for the loss of arable land due to urbanization, infrastructure building and desertification, has to be weighed against potential environmental costs.[262]

In the same vein, the 2012 UNEP Yearbook[263] states,

> Climate change exacerbates pressures to meet a growing and wealthier population's need for food. Global agricultural production may have to increase 70 percent by 2050 to cope with this demand....A recent analysis of historical data shows that observed climate trends have had negative impacts on wheat and maize yields in the past 30 years....Resource consumption could triple by 2050, while current consumption trends differ greatly between developed and developing countries....For many agricultural systems there is the danger of a

---

[257] Challenges & Opportunities, *supra* note 246.

[258] UNEP, *Keeping Track of Our Changing Environment – From Rio to Rio + 20 (1992–2012)*, UNEP/gcss.XII/inf/2, October 2011, http://www.unep.org/geo/pdfs/Keeping_Track.pdf.

[259] *Id.* at 7.

[260] 2012 GEO-5 Report distilled in the *Summary for Policy Makers,* UNEP/gcss.XII/inf/9, http://www.unep.org/geo/pdfs/GEO5_SPM_English.pdf.

[261] *Id.* at 9.

[262] *Id.*

[263] UNEP, UNEP *Year Book 2012 – Emerging Issues in Our Global Environment* (2012), http://www.unep.org/yearbook/2012.

progressive breakdown of productive capacity under a combination of excessive population pressure and unsustainable agricultural use and practices....[264]

Vulnerable societies are hit especially hard, as the Food and Agriculture Organization of the UN (FAO) states:

> With rapid population growth, reduced arable land by subsistence farmers and migration to marginal lands, the deepening effects of climate change and continued economic marginalization of Horn of Africa economies in the global economy, pressure is being sustained on the Horn's relatively scarce resources.[265]

The Program of Action of the 1994 International Conference on Population and Development (ICPD) aptly captured the connection between population growth, environmental degradation, and sustainable development:

> Meeting the basic human needs of growing populations is dependent on a healthy environment.... Demographic factors, combined with poverty and lack of access to resources in some areas, and excessive consumption and wasteful production patterns in others, cause or exacerbate problems of environmental degradation and resource depletion and thus inhibit sustainable development.....Pressure on the environment may result from rapid population growth, distribution and migration, especially in ecologically vulnerable ecosystems.[266]

15.8.3   *The Population – Human Rights Nexus*

The rapid rate of population increase in many developing countries is not sustainable as it puts a strain on their available and likely scarce resources. Thus, it hampers their ability to sustain economic and social development, to reduce poverty, and to halt environmental degradation. It seems obvious that humankind needs to stabilize population growth, achieve an equilibrium between population and the earth's carrying capacity, and sustain ecological balance. This means that the growth rate must be halted or reversed by achieving balance between fertility rates and mortality rates. However, several initiatives undertaken to lower the fertility rate do have human rights implications, especially for women's rights, which will be examined later.

Some assert that population growth is simply not a problem, while others contend that the real problem is unsustainable consumption practices of rich countries or poverty and underdevelopment. However, let us assume that a consensus could be reached on the goal of stabilizing population growth[267] – even

---

[264] *Id.* at 5.

[265] World Population 2011, *supra* note 247, at 98.

[266] United Nations, *Programme of Action of the International Conference on Population and Development* (Cairo, September 5–13, 1994), U.N. Doc. A/CONF.171/13, Annex, October 18, 1994, § 3.24–3.26, http://www.un.org/popin/icpd/conference/offeng/poa.html [hereinafter Programme of Action].

[267] *See, e.g.*, Julian L. Simon, *The Population Debate: The Case for More People in* ENVIRONMENTAL SCIENCE: ACTION FOR A SUSTAINABLE FUTURE 110 (D. Chira ed., 3d ed. 1991),

then, no agreement seems possible on an international legal regime to control population growth and hence achieve that objective, because of several factors. These include the differing perspectives on population, insistence by states on their sovereign right to devise their own population policies and implementation measures, and religion- or culture-based opposition. That is why international action on population issues has been limited to declarations and principles, instead of binding agreements or treaties.

As population policies are set by states, national approaches to reach the objective are likely to vary. Coercive control measures such as those undertaken by India and China to reduce fertility, and by Romania as part of pro-natal policy, are extreme examples. Incentives to influence population preferences of individuals and couples are also widely used and so have psychological pressures become commonplace. On the other hand, as the 1994 ICPD Program of Action focused on "the broad issues of and interrelationships between population, sustained economic growth and sustainable development, and advances in the education, economic status, and empowerment of women,"[268] the alternative approach to achieve the goal of reducing the fertility rate is to pay special attention to economic and social issues, to empower women, and provide them reproductive rights and reproductive health in devising population policies.

15.8.3.1   *Physical Coercive Measures*[269]

15.8.3.1.1   India

After its independence in 1947, India began implementing an official family planning program in the 1950s to curb population growth.[270] Nevertheless, its population more than doubled from 1960 to 2000, and it could overtake China as the world's most populous country by the middle of this century.[271]

Concerned with the specter of overpopulation, the Indian government took drastic measures to curb population growth in the mid-1970s. Then-Prime Minister Indira Gandhi, declared a state of emergency in 1976, suspending democracy, imposing press censorship, and imprisoning dissidents. The

---

[ ]   *cited in* Jonathan C. Carlson, Sir Geoffrey Palmer & Burns H. Weston International Environmental Law and World Order – A Problem-Oriented Coursebook, 1291 (3d ed. 2012).

[268]   *Id.* chapter 1.5.

[269]   *See generally* Reed Boland, *Symposium on Population Law: The Environment, Population, and Women's Human Rights,* 27 Envtl. L. 1137, 1140–1146 (1997).

[270]   *See, e.g., id.* at 1142–1143; GPO for the Library of Congress, *Population, Population Projections, and Population and Family Planning Policy, in* India: A Country Study (James Heitzman & Robert L. Worden eds., 1995).

[271]   *See generally India: Population Control,* Colby University, http://www.colby.edu/personal/t/thtieten/Famplan.htm.

campaign also coerced men with two or more children to have vasectomies and implemented forced sterilization, often under poor medical supervision and in unhygienic conditions. Poor people who were sterilized reported receiving small loans and priorities for houses.

There was such outrage over the forced sterilization program that Mrs. Gandhi's government was defeated in the next election. The succeeding government instituted an inquiry into such activities in the most populous state in India, Uttar Pradesh, which found among other things that government officials had sterilization quotas to fill and workers were often rewarded if they convinced enough people to be sterilized.[272] The government had established mass camps for sterilizations, and many people were forcibly taken there, sometimes even with the help of the police.[273]

Although that particular coercive plan was halted, even after India set up a public health system and embarked on an education campaign, the prior practice created a precedent for coercive action which still continues. To illustrate, *The Guardian* newspaper reported in 2004 that officials in part of the state of Uttar Pradesh instituted a program under which a single-barrel shotgun would be given for the sterilization of two people and for five people being sterilized, a revolver license would be given.[274] The Chief Medical Officer of one of the districts in the state said: "We have to meet our [sterilization] goals. The target in this area alone is 18,000, and so far we only have 3,000 sterilisations. [Guns for sterilization] is a healthy incentive scheme no different to when we offer extra bags of sugar or cash to people to have operations."[275]

In Rajasthan, another state of India, a medical officer told *Agence France Press* (AFP): "Everyone who gets sterilized between today and 30 September will be entered into a lottery to win prizes. We felt we were falling behind on our sterilization targets of 21,000 per year, so the district collector came up with this idea. We hope at least 6,000 people will come forward the next 3 months."[276]

According to a report in *The Observer* (UK) on April 30, 2012, forced sterilization programs in India continue.[277] The report states:

[272] Shah Commission of Inquiry, Ministry of Home Affairs, Third and Final Report (1978).
[273] *Id.* at 195.
[274] Randeep Ramesh, *Outrage at Guns for Sterilisation Policy – Indian Farmers Given Firearms Licenses as an Incentive to Curb Population Growth*, THE GUARDIAN, November 1, 2004, http://www.guardian.co.uk/world/2004/nov/01/india.randeepramesh/print.
[275] *Id.*
[276] *India's "Sex Drive" Solution to Population Explosion*, GLOBAL POST, July 2, 2011, http://www.globalpost.com/dispatches/globalpost-blogs/weird-wide-web/indias-sex-drive-solution-population-explosion.
[277] Gethin Chamberlain, *UK Climate Policy Helps Fund Forced Sterilisation of India's Poor*, THE OBSERVER, April 30, 2012, http://www.guardian.co.uk/world/2012/apr/15/uk-aid-forced-sterilisation-india.

Tens of millions of pounds of UK aid money have been spent on a programme that has forcibly sterilised Indian women and men, the Observer has learned. Many have died as a result of botched operations, while others have been left bleeding and in agony. A number of pregnant women selected for sterilisation suffered miscarriages and lost their babies.[278]

15.8.3.1.2   China

After Communist forces defeated the Chiang-Kai-Shek government and took over China in 1949, the new government urged more births aimed at increasing the rate of socio-economic development. Mao Tse Tung promoted the slogan: "The more babies the more glorious are their mothers."[279] However, by the early-1970s the Chinese government began promoting the "later, longer, fewer" program to urge later marriages, longer wait between children, and a two-children per family limitation. Then, by the late 1970s it decided that the country's arable land could no longer sustain its growing population and thus decided to control the burgeoning population by imposing a one-child family rule. The rationale for this policy included declining health and living standards and especially a lack of adequate food, housing, and jobs for the people.[280]

The government also instituted stringent means for enforcement, including economic pressure and even coerced abortions. This policy met resistance from the rural population and the government relaxed the policy for rural China. The US Congress has held hearings on alleged abuses of China's one-child policy, including forced abortion and sterilizations, fines and other penalties.[281]

---

[278] *Id.*

[279] *Cited in* Xiaorong Li, *License to Coerce: Violence Against Women, State Responsibility, and Legal Failures in China's Family-Planning Program*, 8 YALE J.L. & FEMINISM 145, 148 (1996).

[280] *See generally* Lisa V. Gregory, *Examining the Economic Component of China's One-Child Policy under International Law: Your Money or Your Life*, 6 J. CHINESE L. 45 (1992).

[281] Congressional-Executive Commission (CEC) Report on China, 2005 Annual Report 77, http://www.cecc.gov; CEC Report on China, 2009 Annual Report 151, Patrick Goodenough, *U.S. Lawmakers See Gruesome Reality of China's One-Child Policy*, CNS NEWS, September 22, 2011, http://cnsnews.com/news/article/US-lawmakers-see-gruesome-reality-china-s-one-child-policy. *See also* Nicole M. Skalla, *Note: China's One-Child Policy: Illegal Children and the Family Planning Law*, 30 BROOKLYN J. INT'L L. 329 (2004); Mary H. Hansel, *Note: China's One-Child Policy's Effects on Women and the Paradox of Persecution and Trafficking*, 11 S. CAL. REV. L. & WOMEN'S STUD. 369 (2002); Xizhe Peng, *Population Policy and Program in China: Challenge and Prospective*, 35 TEX. INT'L L.J. 51 (2000); David Barboza, *China Suspends Family Planning Workers after Forced Abortion*, N.Y. TIMES, June 16, 2012, at A6: "China suspended three local family planning officials in northwest China this week following a public outcry over reports that they had forced a young woman to undergo an abortion seven months into her pregnancy, according to Xinhua, the official Chinese news agency," http://www.nytimes.com/2012/06/16/world/asia/china-suspends-family-planning-workers-after-forced-abortion.html?_r=1.

In an appraisal of this policy 30 years later, co-authors Feng Wang of the Brookings-Tsinghua Center and Cai Yong of the University of North Carolina Population Center stated:

> Many of the feared consequences of the one child policy have now become apparent. China's recorded sex ratio at birth has been on a rise since the inception of the policy, escalating from 108 in 1980 to over 120 boys for every 100 girls today, resulting in an estimated 20 to 30 million surplus men.... China's only children [sic] generation will assume the role of sole caretakers of their aging parents and will be the ones to shoulder rising government expenditure obligations for future pension, health care, and social welfare benefits associated with an increasingly aging population.[282]

15.8.3.1.3 Romania

Contrasted with the above, the pro-natal policy introduced in 1966 by President Ceausescu to increase the fertility rate was a reversal of an earlier policy legalizing abortion that was established in 1957. Ceausescu planned to increase Romania's population from 23 million to 30 million by 2000, promoting pregnancy by a state decree as he proclaimed, "The fetus is the property of the entire society. Anyone who avoids having children is a deserter who abandons the law of national continuity."[283]

The measures under the Council of State Decree No. 770 of September 29, 1966, restricted abortion and access to contraception and provided increased allowances for large families.[284] Abortion was allowed in only limited circumstances, such as danger to the woman's life; serious physical, mental, or sensory disorder; rape or incest; age over 45 years (subsequently lowered to 40 in 1972 and raised to 42 in 1984); or that the woman had previously given birth to at least four children who were under her care. Those obtaining illegal abortions, as well as those performing them, were subject to fine and imprisonment.[285]

Although these draconian measures resulted initially in a crude birthrate increase and sharp decline in the number of abortions from 973,000 in 1966 to 206,000 in 1967, the birthrate again began to decrease and by 1983 reached the 1966 level. And the abortion rate also began to increase in 1967 because

---

[282] Feng Wang and Cai Yong, *China's One Child Policy at 30*, BROOKINGS, September 24, 2010, http://www.brookings.edu/research/opinions/2010/09/24-china-one-child-policy-wang.

[283] *See generally* Karen Breslau, *Overplanned Parenthood: Ceausescu's Cruel Law,* NEWSWEEK, Jan. 22, 1990, at 35, http://www.ceausescu.org/ceausescu_texts/overplanned_parenthood .htm.

[284] *See generally* Boland, *supra* note 269, at 1140–1141; United Nations, *Romania,* 52–54, http://www.un.org/esa/population/publications/abortion/doc/romania.doc [hereinafter UN Romania]; Nicki Negrau, *Symposium: The Status of Women in New Market Economies: Listening to Women's Voices: Living in Post-Communist Romania,* 12 CONN. J. INT'L L. 117, 122–126 (1996); Breslau, *supra* note 283.

[285] UN Romania, *supra* note 284, at 53.

of underground illegal abortions, all of which led to a March 1984 directive from the Central Committee of the Romanian Communist Party imposing stringent measures to control the birthrate. Women had to undergo regular gynecological examinations at their place of employment, doctors had to report pregnancies, pregnant women were monitored until delivery, and gynecological wards were under continuous surveillance.[286] Even more severe measures were introduced in 1985, further restricting access to abortion only to a woman who had given birth to a minimum of five children who were currently under her care.

The outcome was that the maternal mortality ratio rose from 85 deaths per 100,000 live births in 1965 to 170 in 1973,[287] with unwanted survivors often ending up in orphanages.[288] Subsequently, women who did not have children, even if they were unable to, had to pay a "celibacy tax" of up to ten percent of their monthly salaries.[289] Also, one in ten babies was born underweight.[290]

15.8.3.1.4   Non-Physical Coercive Measures

Instead of forcing sterilization or abortion or motherhood as coercive population control measures, some governments use incentives or disincentives to accomplish their goal.[291] In all three countries discussed above, governments have used such non-physical coercive measures to influence behavior of individuals as well as that of health and population workers so that they influence others. As already mentioned, Romania provided privileges to mothers with large families and taxed those with no children. Similarly, India and China gave monetary and other rewards to individuals and families to induce them to comply with the government's population policies and penalized couples, denying promotion at work and other benefits and imposing fines on those who did not. Other countries, as well, have similarly offered incentives or imposed penalties to individuals and couples as well as to officials to ensure compliance and achieve the desired result.

15.8.3.1.5   Human Rights Implications of Coercive Policies

Adverse consequences of such coercive population control policies include preference for male children, selective abortion and infanticide, and disproportionate numbers of males to females in several Asian countries, including China, India, Taiwan, and the Republic of Korea. In countries such as India

---

[286] *Id.*
[287] UN Romania, *supra* note 284, at 54.
[288] Breslau, *supra* note 283.
[289] *Id.*
[290] *Id.*
[291] Boland, *supra* note 269, at 1144–1146.

and China, the government has tried to combat this practice by banning most prenatal tests to determine the sex of fetuses, although with mixed results.

These coercive policies obviously result in violation of women's rights under the existing international human rights instruments that most countries have signed or ratified. These include the Universal Declaration of Human Rights,[292] the International Covenant on Civil and Political Rights,[293] and the International Covenant on Economic, Social and Cultural Rights,[294] which provide specific rights being violated – for example, the guaranteed right to life, the right not to be subjected to inhumane or degrading treatment, the right not to be subjected to arbitrary or unlawful interference with life or the family, the right not to be subjected to medical or scientific experimentation without consent, the right to marry and found a family, and the right not to be discriminated on the basis of sex. Other applicable instruments include the Convention on the Elimination of All Forms of Discrimination against Women,[295] which guarantees women reproduction rights, the right of access to health care, the right to information and advice on family planning, the right to freely and responsibly decide on the number and spacing of children, and the right to have access to education and the means to exercise this right; and the Convention on the Rights of the Child,[296] which guarantees the Convention right to every child without discrimination of any kind and obligates states parties to ensure that the child is protected against all forms of discrimination.

There can be no doubt that forced sterilization or abortion or childbirth, as mandated by the countries mentioned above, constitutes violation of the human rights of women. However, whether psychological pressure by the government to accomplish the same objectives constitutes a violation is not so clear. For example, what standards are to be applied to determine whether the incentives or disincentives constitute a violation? And many of these population policies raise the question of balancing individual versus collective rights. How, for example, is one to balance the validity of a government policy aimed at improving the economic wellbeing of society, halting or reversing environmental degradation, conserving resources against the individual's right to privacy and reproductive freedom? A comparison of

---

[292] Universal Declaration of Human Rights, G.A. Res. 217A, U.N. Doc. A/810 (1948), http://www.un.org/en/documents/udhr/.

[293] International Covenant on Civil and Political Rights, December 16, 1966, 999 U.N.T.S. 171, http://www2.ohchr.org/english/law/ccpr.htm.

[294] International Covenant on Economic, Social and Cultural Rights, December 16, 1966, 993 U.N.T.S. 3, http://www2.ohchr.org/english/law/cescr.htm.

[295] Convention on the Elimination of All forms of Discrimination against Women, December 18, 1979, 1249 U.N.T.S. 13, http://www2.ohchr.org/english/law/cedaw.htm.

[296] Convention on the Rights of the Child, November 20, 1989, 1577 U.N.T.S. 3, http://www2.ohchr.org/english/law/crc.htm.

articles 16 and 29 in the Universal Declaration of Human Rights aptly frames this dilemma.

Article 16 states:

> Men and women of full age, without any limitation due to race, nationality, or religion, have the right to marry and found a family.... The family is the natural and fundamental group of society and is entitled to protection by society and the State.[297]

Article 29 states:

1) Everyone has duties to the community in which alone the free and full development 3of personality is possible.
2) In the exercise of his rights and freedoms, everyone shall be subject only to such limitations as are determined by law solely for the purpose of securing due recognition of and respect for the rights and freedoms of others and of meeting the just requirements of morality, public order and the general welfare in a democratic society.

15.8.4   *The ICPD Program of Action and Subsequent Developments*

Building on the prior 1974 Population Conference at Bucharest and the 1984 Conference in Mexico City, the 1994 ICPD Program of Action emphasized interrelationships between population, sustained economic growth, sustainable development, and advances in empowerment of women.[298] The comprehensive program, comprising sixteen chapters, emphasized several issues, including population and environment; gender equality and empowerment of women; reproductive rights and reproductive health; population and sustainable development; fertility, mortality, and population growth rates; and population, sustained economic growth, and poverty.

Among the several Principles the Program of Action highlighted are the following:

- the right to development must be fulfilled "so as to equitably meet the population, development and environment needs of present and future generations,"[299]
- "Everyone has the right to the enjoyment of the highest attainable standard of physical and mental health.... States should take all appropriate measures to ensure... universal access to health-care services, including those related to reproductive health care, which includes family planning and

---

[297] *Id.* article 16(1) and (3).
[298] *Programme of Action, supra* note 266, ¶ 1.5.
[299] *Id.* chapter 2, Principle 3.

sexual health. Reproductive health-care programmes should provide the widest range of services without any form of coercion. All couples and individuals have the basic right to decide freely and responsibly the number and spacing of their children and to have the information, education and means to do so";[300] and

- "Everyone has the right to education,... with particular attention to women and the girl child."[301]

In emphasizing the commitment to reproductive rights and reproductive health, the Program of Action stresses that reproductive rights

> rest on the recognition of the basic right of all couples and individuals to decide freely and responsibly the number, spacing and timing of their children and to have the information and means to do so, and the right to attain the highest standard of sexual and reproductive health. It also includes their right to make decisions concerning reproduction free of discrimination, coercion and violence....[302]

The Program defines reproductive health as

> a state of complete physical, mental and social well-being....[It] therefore implies that people...have the capability to reproduce and the freedom to decide if, when and how often to do so. Implicit in this last condition are the right of men and women to be informed and to have access to safe, effective, affordable and acceptable methods of family planning of their choice, as well as other methods of their choice for regulation of fertility...., and the right of access to appropriate health-care services that will enable women to go safely through pregnancy and childbirth and provide couples with the best chance of having a healthy infant.[303]

At the 1994 Conference, the Vatican opposed the Program's reference to birth control and abortion, and several Latin American countries joined several Muslim countries in blocking consensus in the outcome document.[304]

Subsequently, in 2000, when the UN Millennium Summit adopted by consensus the Millennium Development Goals, the key provisions of the Program of Action – reproductive right and universal access to reproductive health – were not included.[305] However, the heads of state and government

---

[300] *Id.* Principle 8.
[301] *Id.* Principle 10.
[302] *Id.* chapter 7.3.
[303] *Id.* chapter 7.2.
[304] *See* Report of the International Conference on Population and Development, U.N. Doc. A/CONF/171/1/13, at 149–150 (1994). *See also* Gregory M. Saylin, *The United Nations International Conference on Population and Development: Religion, Tradition, and Law in Latin America*, 28 VAND. J. TRANSNAT'L L. 1245, 1255–1256 (1995).
[305] *See* Stephen W. Sindling, *Population, Poverty and Economic Development*, 364 PHILOSOPHICAL TRANSACTIONS OF THE ROYAL SOCIETY 3023, 3026 (2009).

gathered at the September 14–16, 2005 World Summit, which met at UN Headquarters in New York, resolved to promote gender equality, empowerment of women, and elimination of "pervasive gender discrimination," by "[e]nsuring equal access to reproductive health."[306]

The 45th Session of the UN Commission on Population and Development held at the UN Headquarters in April 2012 reaffirmed the Program of Action of the ICPD and the key actions for further implementation of the Program.[307] It called upon

> Governments, in formulating and implementing national development plans, budgets and poverty eradication strategies, to prioritize actions to address challenges relating to the impact of population dynamics on poverty, and sustainable development, keeping in mind that universal reproductive health-care services, commodities and supplies, as well as information, education, skill development, national capacity-building for population and development, and transfer of appropriate technology and know-how to developing countries are essential for achieving the Programme of Action of the International Conference on Population and Development, the Beijing Platform for Action and the Millennium Development Goals.[308]

With the 20th anniversary of the ICPD approaching in 2014, and as the Program of Action expires in that year, plans are underway to ensure that there is a broad recommitment from countries and communities to the goals set in the ICPD and to continue efforts to ensure that the unfinished business of the ICPD is completed. A global review of challenges, achievements, and gaps in realizing the promise of the Program of Action is in process by the UNFPA and ICPD Beyond 2014, and the website www.ICPDBeyond2014.org is online.[309]

One example of the efforts underway is the fifth annual Parliamentarians' Conference on Implementation of the ICPD, at which 300 parliamentarians from 110 countries around the world gathered, in Istanbul, Turkey, in May 2012, and pledged in the Istanbul Statement of Commitment – Keeping Promises – Measuring Results[310] to continue working in the coming years

---

[306] 2005 World Summit Outcome, G.A. RES. 60/1, ¶¶ 58(e), October 24, 2005, http://daccess-dds-ny.un.org/doc/UNDOC/GEN/N05/487/60/PDF/N0548760.pdf?OpenElement. *See generally id.,* ¶¶ 58–59.

[307] U.N. Commission on Population and Development, Report on the forty-fifth session, 15 April 2012 and 23–27 April 2012, ESC Off. Rec. 2012, Supp. (No. 5), U.N. Doc. E (2012) 25; E/CN.9/2012/8 (2012) (advance unedited version), op. para. 1 at 15.

[308] *Id.* op. para. 4 at 16.

[309] "ICPD Beyond 2014 is the official website for the UNFPA-led global review process of the International Conference on Population and Development Programme of Action," ICPD BEYOND 2014, http://icpdbeyond2014.org.

[310] *Istanbul Statement of Commitment: Keeping Promises – Measuring Results,* Istanbul, Turkey, May 25, 2012, http://icpdbeyond2014.org/2012/05/parliamentarians-stand-committed-to-icpd-in-istanbul/.

for implementation of the ICPD Program of Action by 2014 and beyond. They noted that challenges still remain to take concrete measures to fully implement the ICPD agenda, including "systematically integrating population dynamics in national and international development strategies and policies, addressing ageing and lowering fertility, climate change,... reversing the HIV pandemic and comprehensively addressing international migration in the context of the ICPD." To meet those challenges they reaffirmed their commitment to the ICPD Program of Action,

> recognizing that its implementation is essential for countries to reduce poverty, and social and economic inequality, improve the lives of all their peoples, safeguard the health and rights of women, men, girls and boys, including sexual and reproductive health and rights, promote gender equality and women's health,... protect the environment and ensure sustainable development.[311]

15.8.5   *Conclusion*

The ICPD Program of Action identified the following objectives of the population and environment relationship:

(a) To ensure that population, environmental and poverty eradication factors are integrated in sustainable development policies, and programmes;
(b) To reduce both unsustainable consumption and production patterns as well as negative impacts of demographic factors on the environment in order to meet the needs of current generations without compromising the ability of future generations to meet their own needs.[312]

Coercive population control measures violate human rights and are not conducive to bringing about population stabilization, as the previous discussion has shown. And population stabilization is essential to reach the goal of sustainable development. Instead, as the ICPD Program of Action stressed, attention needs to be focused on key issues, including the following: gender equality and women's empowerment; reproductive rights and sexual and reproductive health services, including access to family planning services; equal access to education for all girls; and environmental issues associated with population changes. The success will necessarily and ultimately depend upon international cooperation.

---

[311] *Id.*
[312] Programme of Action, *supra* note 266, chapter 3.28.

Part Four: Conclusion

Chapter Sixteen

The Unfinished Agenda

16.0   *The Challenge*

We have stressed throughout this book that the global environment is under severe pressure and, notwithstanding the ongoing international, regional, and national efforts since the 1972 UN Stockholm Conference, there has been only partial success in protecting it. The Johannesburg Declaration, adopted at the World Summit on Sustainable Development (WSSD), held in September 2002, aptly described the environmental challenges faced by the world community:

> The global environment continues to suffer. Loss of biodiversity continues, fish stocks continue to be depleted, desertification claims more and more fertile land, the adverse effects of climate change are already evident, natural disasters are more frequent and more devastating and developing countries more vulnerable, and air, water and marine pollution continue to rob millions of a decent life.[1]

Ten years after the WSSD, the United Nations scheduled a Conference on Sustainable Development (UNCSD) for June 20–22, 2012, in Rio de Janeiro (Rio+20), to mark the 20th anniversary of the UN Conference on Environment and Development in Rio, and aimed at renewing political commitment for sustainable development, assessing progress and remaining implementation gaps since the 1992 Earth Summit and reflecting on new and emerging challenges.[2] UNCSD's focus is on two selected themes: (1) "Green Economy in the Context of Sustainable Development and Poverty

---

[1] World Summit on Sustainable Development, Johannesburg S. Afr., Aug. 26–Sept. 4, *The Johannesburg Declaration on Sustainable Development*, ¶ 13, UN Doc. A/CONF.1999/L.6/Rev.3 http://www.johannesburgsummit.org/html/documents/summit_docs/1009wssd_pol/declaration.doc.

[2] *See* UN General Assembly, Report of the Secretary-General, Objective and Themes of the United Nations Conference on Sustainable Development, UN Doc. A/CONF.216/7, at 4, December 20, 2010, http://www.uncsd2012.org/files/prepcom/SG-report-on-objective-and-themes-of-the-UNCSD.pdf.

Eradication" (GESDPE), and (2) "Institutional Framework for Sustainable Development" (IFSD).[3]

Notwithstanding the global attention and priority on attaining sustainable development, the goal remains elusive, as the United Nations Environment Programme's (UNEP) periodic reports on the global environment, entitled *GEO: Global Environment Outlook*, attest. These reports provide comprehensive up-to-date assessments of the state of the global environment and the emerging trends to support decision-making, the latest being GEO-5, *Environment for the future we want*, released in 2012.[4] In an earlier report in 2002, after reviewing economic and social factors that result in environmental deterioration related to land, forests, biodiversity, freshwater, coastal and marine areas, atmosphere, and urban areas, GEO-3 reached a sobering conclusion: "In many areas, the state of the environment is much more fragile and degraded than it was in 1972."[5] The report categorized the challenges to sustainable development in four major "divides":

1. *The environmental divide*, characterized by a stable or improved environment in Europe and North America and a degraded environment in most of the developing countries;
2. *The policy divide*, characterized by some regions being engaged in appropriate policy development and implementation, while others are lacking in both;
3. *The vulnerability gap*, "widening within society, between countries and across regions with the disadvantaged more at risk to environmental challenge and disasters;" and
4. *The lifestyle divide*, characterized by one fifth of the world's population accounting for 90 percent of total personal consumption while 1.2 billion people live on less than US $1 per day.[6]

The report warned that among the three pillars of sustainable development – social, economic, and environmental – which are mutually supportive and essential, the environmental pillar is too frequently neglected and its disintegration "will lead to the inevitable collapse of the other, more charismatic pillars of sustainable development to which policy makers everywhere pay particular attention."[7]

---

[3] *Id.*
[4] UNEP, Global Environment Outlook 5 (2012), http://www.unep.org/geo/pdfs/geo5/GEO5_report_full_en.pdf [hereinafter GEO-5].
[5] UNEP, Global Environment Outlook 3, at 297 (2002), http://www.unep.org/geo/geo3 [hereinafter GEO 3].
[6] *Id.*
[7] *Id.* at 402.

On the other hand, the report noted some successes on the environmental front, such as development of a legal framework, proliferation of environmental institutions, and active participation of civil society, along with specific promising developments such as controlling stratospheric ozone depletion, exploring more holistic approaches to land management, wider acceptance of integrated water resource management, reduction of common air pollutants in many countries, an emerging natural "cluster of biodiversity policies," and strengthening of early warning systems.[8]

Two years before the 2002 report, environmental ministers attending a special session of the UNEP Governing Council in Malmö, Sweden in 2000, adopted the Malmö Declaration,[9] which also identified the greatest environmental challenges of the 21st century. Noting the discrepancy between the international community's commitment to halt environmental degradation and action that has been undertaken toward that end, the Declaration concluded that "the root causes of environmental degradation are embedded in social and economic problems such as pervasive poverty, unsustainable production and consumption patterns, inequity and distribution of wealth, and the debt burden."[10] The UN Secretary-General in his Millennium Report of the same year[11] and the UN Millennium Declaration[12] adopted by the General Assembly in 2000 also reached similar conclusions about the critical environmental problems the world faces, their causes and solutions.

Since then, other important assessments of the environment include UNEP's 2007 GEO-4 Report (*Global Environment Outlook – Environment for Development*),[13] the 2012 GEO-5 Report (*Global Environment Outlook – Environment for the future we want*), UNEP's annual reports[14] and annual yearbooks,[15] and reports by the US Environmental Protection Agency (EPA).[16] The GEO-4 report was released in 2007, 20 years after the publication of the World Commission for Environment and Development's book, *Our Common Future*,[17] and five years after the adoption of the Johannesburg Plan

---

[8] *See id.* at 297–298.
[9] UNEP Governing Council decision SS.VI/1, annex. (2000), http://www.unep.org/malmo/malmo_ministerial.htm.
[10] *Id.*
[11] Kofi Annan, We the Peoples: The Role of the United Nations in the 21st Century, UN Doc. A/54/2000 (2000), http://www.un.org/millennium/sg/report/full.htm.
[12] United Nations Millennium Declaration, G.A. Res. 55/2, (Sept. 18, 2000), http://un.org/millennium/declaration/ares552e.pdf.
[13] UNEP, GLOBAL ENVIRONMENT OUTLOOK 4 (2007) http://www.unep.org/geo/GEO4/report/GEO-4_Report_Full-en.pdf, [hereinafter GEO-4].
[14] Annual Reports, UNEP, http://unep.org/publications/contents/Annual_Reports.asp.
[15] Yearbook Series, UNEP, http://www.unep.org/yearbook/2012/uyb_series.asp.
[16] Homepage at http://www.epa.gov.
[17] Report of the World Commission on Environment and Development: Our Common Future, Transmitted to the General Assembly as an Annex to UN Doc. A/42/427, Development and International Co-Operation: Environment, http://www.un-documents.net/wced-ocf.htm.

of Implementation at the World Summit on Sustainable Development.[18] It highlighted the important role of the environment in development and especially for human well-being. It studied environmental and socio-economic trends between 1987 and 2007 and assessed progress in addressing key environment and development issues with reference to "our common future."

The GEO-4 "Summary for Decision Makers" identified environmental changes including climate change, unsustainable land and water use, contaminated water, loss of fisheries, biodiversity decline, and loss of ecosystem services.[19] It called these changes unprecedented and said they were "due to human activities in an increasingly globalized, industrialized and interconnected world, driven by expanding flow of goods, services, capital, people, technologies, information, ideas and labour, even affecting isolated populations."[20] It also reviewed regional perspectives[21] and concluded that

> [t]he intertwined environmental and developmental challenges that *Our Common Future* warned about in 1987 still exist, as do the associated policy challenges. Knowledge of the interlinkages between environment and development, and the impacts on human well-being, gained in the past two decades, can be used effectively for the transition towards sustainable development. Concerns about the global environment may have reached a tipping point of their own, with the growing realization that for many problems, the benefits of early action outweigh the costs.[22]

The GEO-4 report in its overview noted that while some progress toward sustainable development had occurred since 1987, "action has been limited on some issues, for example, climate change, persistent organic pollutants, fisheries management, invasive alien species and species extinction,"[23] and especially highlighted the urgency of the climate change issue, calling for action.

The 2012 GEO-5 report, in its "Summary for Policy Makers,"[24] reiterated the earlier findings that unprecedented Earth System changes are occurring

---

[18] World Summit on Sustainable Development Plan of Implementation (revised, Sept. 23, 2002), http://www.johannesburgsummit.org/html/documents/summit_docs/2309/planfinal.htm.

[19] GEO-4, Summary for Decision Makers, at 8–13 (2007), http://www.unep.org/geo/GEO4/media/GEO4%20SDM_launch.pdf [hereinafter GEO-4 Summary for Decision Makers].

[20] *Id.* at 8.

[21] *Id.* at 13–20.

[22] *Id.* at 30.

[23] GEO-4, Section A, Overview, Ch. 1, Environment for Development, at 5, http://www.unep.org/geo/GEO4/report/GEO-4_Report_Full.en.pdf.

[24] The GEO-5 Summary for Policy Makers, reproduced in document UNEP/gcss.XII/INF/9, was negotiated and endorsed at an Intergovernmental meeting from January 29–31, 2012, in the City of Gwanju, Republic of Korea, and launched at UNEP Governing Council Special Session on February 20, 2012 [hereinafter GEO-5 Summary for Policy Makers]. *See also* Statement by the Global Intergovernmental and Multi-stakeholder Consultation on the Fifth Global Environment Outlook held in Nairobi from 29–31 March 2010, document

as human pressures accelerate and, as a result, "several critical global, regional and local thresholds are close or have been exceeded."[25] With the passing of these thresholds, the report warns, the life-support functions of the planet are likely to face "abrupt and possibly irreversible changes... with significant adverse implications for human well-being."[26] It gives as examples of such changes the accelerated melting of the arctic ice sheet, as well as glaciers, because of global warming; and on a regional scale "the collapse of fresh-water lake and estuary ecosystems due to eutrophication."[27] The report also notes droughts and floods, increased incidences of malaria, the collapse of a number of fisheries, and substantial biodiversity loss, among other changes that have had adverse impacts on human security, food security, health, and the provision of ecosystem services.[28]

After describing advances on the environmental front such as protection of the stratospheric ozone, the report notes that serious challenges remain that threaten development goals. These include climate change and increased pressure on land resources caused by economic growth, population growth, consumption patterns, and global markets, and result in deforestation, land degradation and land conversion, and urbanization.[29] The report paints a bleak picture for sustainability of water resources as 80 percent of the world's population lives in areas with high levels of threat to water security.[30] Among other challenges are continued degradation to the oceans, including marine litter, serious eutrophication of coastal areas and acidification from increased concentrations of CO_2,[31] and biodiversity losses.[32] Ecosystem deterioration continues because of the losses of species. In addition, chemicals pose risks to the environment and human health, and greater urbanization generating more waste, including hazardous waste.[33]

Another publication, a complementary report to GEO-5, entitled *Keeping Track of Our Changing Environment: From Rio to Rio+20 (1992–2012)*,[34] highlights the global environmental changes over the past 20 years on several

---

UNEP/IGMC.2 Rev.2, suggesting the objectives, scope and process of GEO-5, http://www.unep.org/PDF/geo5/GEO-5_Final Statement.pdf. The full 550-page GEO-5 report, Environment for the future we want, was released on June 6, 2012. GEO-5, *supra* note 4.

[25] GEO-5 Summary for Policy Makers, *supra* note 24, at 6.
[26] *Id.*
[27] *Id.*
[28] *Id.* at 6–7.
[29] *Id.* at 7–9.
[30] *Id.* at 10–11.
[31] *Id.* at 11.
[32] *Id.* at 11–12.
[33] *Id.* at 12–13.
[34] UNEP, Keeping Track of Our Changing Environment: From Rio to Rio+20, reproduced in UNEP/GCSS.XII/INF/2, http://www.unep.org/geo/pdfs/Keeping_Track.pdf.

key issues through data, graphics, and satellite images. The report provides a sobering conclusion:

> With limited progress on environmental issues achieved, and few real "success stories" to be told, all components of the environment – land, water, biodiversity, oceans and atmosphere – continue to degrade. And notwithstanding great advances in information and communication technologies, we have not made such breakthroughs when it comes to assessing the state of our environment. Until we apply the same dedication to this issue as we have to other areas, data gaps and inadequate monitoring will continue to hinder sound "evidence-based policy-making."[35]

Each UNEP Year Book features a review of environmental developments during the preceding year, in addition to examining the emerging environmental issues. To illustrate, the 2012 Year Book highlighted two emerging issues: (1) the critical role of soil carbon in regulating climate, water supplies, and biodiversity, and the need to maintain and enhance it by the management of soil so that its economic, societal, and environmental benefits can be sustained; and (2) implications of the increase in the decommissioning of nuclear reactors in the next ten years, with an emerging lesson being applied that future power plants should be designed for safe and efficient decommissioning and operation.[36]

The 2011 Year Book focused on three emerging issues – (1) the need to review current practices in and impact of phosphorus use in food production and to enhance the resource efficiency of this nutrient; (2) growing scientific concern over the chemical and material impact of marine litter on wildlife, human health and the environment; and (3) the critical role of biodiversity in maintaining healthy forests.[37] And the 2010 UNEP Year Book addressed six thematic priorities which reflect the organization's assessment of its agenda to meet major challenges to the environment – (1) impacts of climate change; (2) environmental governance; (3) the effects of continuing degradation and loss of the world's ecosystems; (4) effect of harmful substances and hazardous wastes on human health and the environment; (5) environmentally related disasters and conflicts; and (6) resource efficiency –

---

[35] *Id.* at 90. *See also* Ved P. Nanda, *Introduction, in* Climate Change and Environmental Ethics 1–13 (Ved P. Nanda ed., 2011) (highlighting the international environmental issues caused by climate change).

[36] UNPEG, UNPEG Year Book 2012 – Emerging Issues in Our Global Environment (2012), http://www.unep.org/yearbook/2012.

[37] UNEP, UNEP Year Book 2011 – Emerging Issues in Our Global Environment (2011), http://www.unep.org/yearbook/2011.

sustainable consumption and production.[38] These are the six cross-cutting priorities selected as UNEP's Medium-term Strategy for 2010–2013.[39]

The vision of UNEP for the medium-term future was set out in the Nairobi Declaration on the Role and Mandate of UNEP.[40] It is to focus on being:

> the leading global environmental authority that sets the global environmental agenda, that promotes the coherent implementation of the environmental dimension of sustainable development within the United Nations system and that serves as an authoritative advocate for the global environment.

While UNEP highlights in its annual reports the organization's performance during the year, it also recounts environmental challenges in special reports, such as *Keeping Track of Our Changing Environment.*[41] The 2011 Annual Report discussed the full range of UNEP's work for environment and development, and highlighted six selected cross-cutting thematic priorities: (1) climate change; (2) disasters and conflicts; (3) environmental governance; (4) ecosystem management; (5) harmful substances and hazardous waste; and (6) resource efficiency.[42] The 2010 Annual Report highlighted ecosystems as that year was the UN-declared International Year of Biodiversity.[43] It underscored the threats to the environment.

UNEP's 2009 Annual Report focused on the green economy – green growth, green spaces, green policy, and green lifestyles, publishing several studies on the topic.[44] The US EPA has also published several studies on environmental challenges, such as Coastal Zones and Sea Level Rise: climate change – health and environmental effects;[45] ecosystems and biodiversity;[46] and Polar Regions / Climate Change – health and environmental effects.[47]

On a more positive note, in his policy statement at the opening of a special session of the UNEP Governing Council in Nairobi on February 20, 2012,

---

[38] UNEP, UNEP Year Book 2010 – New Science and Developments in Our Changing Environment (2010), http://www.unep.org/yearbook/2010.

[39] *See* UNEP Medium-Term Strategy 2010–2013 – Environment for Development, http://www.unep.org/pdf/finalmtsgcss-x-8.pdf.

[40] UN General Assembly Official Records, 50th Sess., Supp. No. 25, UN Doc. A/50/25, ch. IV, annex (1995), adopting UNEP Governing Council decision 19/1, annex, http://www.unep.org/roa/Amcen/Amcen_Events/3rd_ss/Docs/nairobi-Decration-2009.pdf.

[41] *Supra* note 34.

[42] UNEP, UNEP Annual Report 2011, http://www.unep.org/annualreport/2011/.

[43] UNEP 2010 Annual Report, http://www.unep.org/annualreport/2010/.

[44] UNEP 2009 Annual Report, http://www.unep.org/publications/ebooks/annual-report09/index/aspx.

[45] *Coastal Zones and Sea Level Rise*, EPA, http://epa.gov/climatechange/effects/coastal/index.html.

[46] *Ecosystems and Biodiversity*, EPA, http://epa.gov/climatechange/effects/eco_animals.html#birds.

[47] *Polar Regions*, EPA http://epa.gov/climatechange/effects/polarregions.html.

UNEP Executive Director Achim Steiner noted that during the 40 years since the Stockholm Conference,

> [T]here is much to celebrate. These years have witnessed the birth and the transformation of the institutions required for environmental policy-making, at the national, regional and international levels – from the establishment of ministries dedicated to environmental protection, to inter-ministerial committees to address climate change or sustainable development, and their equivalents in regional institutions.[48]

Granted that there have been tremendous efforts toward preventing environmental degradation, addressing environmental challenges, and building an institutional and legal framework for international environmental cooperation, the problems continue to mount. As the Zero Draft of the proposed declaration to be adopted at the Rio+20 UNCSD acknowledged, there were setbacks due to financial and economic crises and volatile energy and food prices.[49] The Draft added

> New scientific evidence points to the gravity of the threats we face. New and emerging challenges include the further intensification of earlier problems calling for more urgent responses.... [A]round 1.4 billion people still live in extreme poverty and one sixth of the world's population is under nourished, pandemics and epidemics are omnipresent threats. Unsustainable development has increased the stress on the earth's limited natural resources and on the carrying capacity of ecosystems. Our planet supports seven billion people expected to reach nine billion by 2050.
>
> ....
>
> ...[D]espite efforts by Governments and non-State actors in all countries, sustainable development remains a distant goal and there remain major barriers and systemic gaps in the implementation of internationally agreed commitments.[50]

---

[48] UNEP, Executive Director's Policy Statement by Achim Steiner, Nairobi, Feb. 20, 2012, at 6, http://www.unep.org/gc/gcss-xii/docs/ED_POLICY_STATEMENT_2012_Lores_fa.pdf.

[49] United Nations Conference on Sustainable Development (UNCSD), The Future We Want – The Zero Draft of the Rio+20 Outcome Document, Jan. 10, 2012, http://www.uncsd2012.org/rio20/content/documents/370The%20Future%20We%20Want%2010Jan%20clean%20_no%20brackets.pdf. [hereinafter The Future We Want]. The Document was submitted by the co-chairs on behalf of the Bureau that steers the preparatory committees, in accordance with the decision in Prepcom 2 to present the Zero-Draft of the Outcome Document for consideration by Member States and other stakeholders. *Id.* note 1. The Outcome Document of the Conference states: "We acknowledge that since 1992 there have been areas of insufficient progress and setbacks in the integration of the three dimentions of sustainable development, aggravated by multiple financial, economic, food and energy crises, which have threatened the ability of all countries, in particular developing countries, to achieve sustainable development." Rio+20, Outcome of the Conference – The Future We Want, Rio de Janeiro, Brazil, June 20–22, 2012, ¶ 20, UN Doc. A/CONF.216/L.1, June 19, 2012, https://rio20.un.org/sites/rio20.un.org/files/a-conf.216l-1_english.pdf.pdf. [hereinafter The Future We Want, Final Outcome Document].

[50] The Future We Want, *supra* note 49, ¶ 13. The Final Outcome Document states: "We are deeply concerned that one in five people on this planet, or over 1 billion people, still live in

Summarizing the discussions by ministers and heads of delegation at the twelfth special session of UNEP's Governing Council/Global Ministerial Environment Forum on March 8, 2012, the Council president noted:

> The way in which sustainable development has been addressed since the United Nations Conference on Environment and Development in 1992 has been inadequate. Many multilateral environmental agreements have been adopted and programmes established, but there is a lack of financial resources, adequate monitoring and review mechanisms to support implementation.[51]

As the preceding discussion shows, there is precious little to celebrate as environmental degradation persists. Thus, given the nature and severity of the environmental challenge, a priority item on the agenda for the future has to be concrete action to effectively meet it.

16.1   *Addressing the Challenge*

In the discussion of key issues in this book we have focused on the applicable norms, policies, and programs adopted multilaterally as well as regionally and nationally to take effective action to protect the environment. However, environmental degradation persists, notwithstanding the various efforts at all levels, especially since the 1972 Stockholm Conference on the Human Environment. The lack of effective implementation continues to be a major stumbling block in reaching the goal of sustainable development.

To recapitulate, the Plan of Implementation adopted at the 2002 Johannesburg World Summit on Sustainable Development (WSSD)[52] was designed to expedite the full implementation of Agenda 21 (*see* Chapter 4) and realize the remaining goals of the 1992 Rio UN Conference on Environment and Development (UNCED, *see* Chapter 4), which it acknowledged had at best been only partially met. The governments participating in the Summit committed themselves to undertaking concrete actions and measures at all levels and to enhancing international cooperation, taking into account the Rio Principles, including, *inter alia*, the principle of common but differentiated

---

extreme poverty, and that one in seven – or 14 per cent – is under nourished, while public health challenges, including pandemics and epidemics, remain omnipresent threats." The Future We Want, Final Outcome Document, *supra* note 49, ¶ 21.

[51] UNEP, President's Summary of the Discussions by Ministers and Heads of Delegation at the Twelfth Special Session of the Governing Council/Global Ministerial Environment Forum of the UNEP, held in Nairobi from Feb. 20–22, 2012, at para. 36, Mar. 8, 2012, http://www.unep.org/gc/gcss-xii/docs/Decisions_summary_advance.pdf [hereinafter President's Summary].

[52] World Summit on Sustainable Development, Plan of Implementation, Sept. 5, 2002, http://www.johannesburgsummit.org/html/documents/summit_docs/2309_planfinal.doc [hereinafter Johannesburg Plan of Implementation].

responsibilities as set out in principle 7 of the Rio Declaration on Environment and Development. These efforts were aimed at promoting the integration of the three components of sustainable development – economic development, social development and environmental protection – as interdependent and mutually reinforcing pillars. The overarching objectives of, and essential requirements for, sustainable development were stated as poverty eradication, changing unsustainable patterns of production and consumption, and protecting and managing the natural resource base of economic and social development.[53]

The Plan detailed the strategies to reach these objectives. The means of implementation included a focus on an effective institutional framework on the international, regional, and national levels, and on recommendations for strengthening this framework.[54] Ten years later, the focus of the 2012 Rio+20 UN Conference on Sustainable Development (UNCSD), remained on sustainable development. The conference themes – a green economy in the context of sustainable development and poverty eradication and the institutional framework for sustainable development – reflected this focus.

The UNCSD draft Outcome Document, *The Future We Want*, identified the proposed Sustainable Development Goals to include "sustainable consumption and production patterns as well as priority areas such as oceans, food security and sustainable agriculture, sustainable energy for all, water access and efficiency, sustainable cities, green jobs, decent work and social inclusion, and disaster risk reduction and resilience."[55]

Among the proposed means of implementation, the document focused on finance, science and technology, capacity building, and trade.[56] Under finance there was a call for the fulfillment of all official development assistance commitments and increased aid effectiveness, prioritization of sustainable development in the allocation of resources, affirmation of the key role of the private sector in promoting sustainable development, and the

---

[53] *Id.* at ¶ 2.
[54] *Id.* at 120–53.
[55] The Future We Want, *supra* note 49, ¶ 107. Negotiators at Rio+20 were unable to agree on the themes for sustainable development goals and hence to an "open working group" of 30 nations to develop global sustainable development goals, while ensuring the "full involvement of relevant stakeholders and expertise from civil society, the scientific community and the United Nations system in its work, in order to provide a diversity of perspectives and experience." The group will submit a report to the UN General Assembly for consideration and appropriate action. The Future We Want, Final Outcome Document, *supra* note 49, ¶ 248.
[56] The Future We Want, *supra* note 49, ¶¶ 112–127. The Conference's Final Outcome Document similarly focused on finance, technology, capacity-building, and trade as means of implementation, parallelling the earlier draft. The Future We Want, Final Outcome Document, *supra* note 49, ¶¶ 252–282.

strengthening of the Global Environment Facility.[57] Highlighted under the science and technology rubric was the importance of strengthening both (1) the scientific, technological and innovation capacity of countries to promote sustainable development; and (2) the international cooperation needed for investment, technology transfer, and development.[58]

The capacity building category included regional and subregional structures and mechanisms in developing countries to facilitate cooperation and the exchange of information, as well as the immediate implementation of the Bali Strategic Plan for Technology Support and Capacity Building.[59] And under trade the document called for realization of commitments made in the World Trade Organization in favor of the least developed countries, an early outcome of the Doha Development Round of Multilateral Trade Negotiations, and the eventual phase-out of market distorting and environmentally harmful subsidies, including those on fossil fuels, agriculture and fisheries.[60]

Recitation of sustainable development goals and the means of implementation does not ensure implementation, for what impedes effective implementation has to be addressed. The UNEP Governing Council on March 8, 2012, endeavored to do so. First, it recognized that "there are gaps in our knowledge of the state of the environment resulting from a lack of data and regular monitoring, particularly in areas such as freshwater quality and quantity, groundwater depletion, ecosystem services, loss of natural habitat, land degradation and chemicals and wastes,"[61] and called upon governments and the multilateral system to take action to bridge the data gaps by designing and implementing programs including "building national and regional capacities and establishing regular processes for data-based environmental monitoring and early warning at the national and local levels."[62]

Next, the Council also highlighted the need for "science-based information to support parties and other relevant stakeholders in their transition to sustainable development,"[63] and called upon

> Governments, United Nations bodies, international organizations, the private sector, civil society and the public at large to work with the United Nations Environment Programme and other environmental institutions to integrate science-based environmental information, including from global, regional, and

---

[57] The Future We Want, *supra* note 49, ¶¶ 112–117.

[58] *Id.* ¶¶ 118–120.

[59] *Id.* ¶¶ 121–123.

[60] *Id.* ¶¶ 124–127.

[61] UNEP, Decisions Adopted by the Governing Council/Global Ministerial Environment Forum at its twelfth special session, held in Nairobi from February 20–22, 2011, Decision SS.XII/6: World Environmental Situation, ¶ 10, Mar. 8, 2012, http://www.unep.org/gc/gcss-ii/docs/Decisions_summary_advance.pdf.

[62] *Id.* ¶ 11.

[63] *Id.* ¶ 6.

national assessments, into the preparatory process for the United Nations Conference on Sustainable Development.[64]

The need to build capacity and to support technology transfer for developing countries and countries with economies in transition is also a prerequisite for effective implementation, and hence the Council asked the UNEP Executive Director to make this a priority for the UNEP program.[65] The Council had previously, in 2005, adopted this goal under the Bali Strategic Plan for Technology Support and Capacity-building.[66]

In addition, UNEP has prepared several sets of guidelines to assist countries in their implementation process. These guidelines are non-binding and advisory. They do not alter the nation's or government's obligations under the agreements. The guidelines cover compliance with and enforcement of multilateral environmental agreements (MEAs),[67] strengthening implementation of MEAs and enforcement of national policies, laws, and regulations, and the development of national legislation on the 3 "Aarhus pillars" of access to information, public participation, and access to justice in environmental matters.[68] Additional UNEP guidelines – on the development of domestic legislation on liability, response action, and compensation for damage caused by activities dangerous to the environment[69] – were adopted almost 40 years after Stockholm Declaration Principle 22 stated that "States shall co-operate to develop further the international law regarding liability and compensation for the victims of pollution and other environmental damage caused by activities within the jurisdiction or control of such states to areas beyond their jurisdiction."[70]

Among other measures to enhance implementation, adequate resources and effective international environmental governance are essential. Indeed, the need for adequate resources to address environmental challenges, especially for developing countries, cannot be overstated. The Global Environment

---

[64] *Id.* ¶ 8.

[65] *Id.* ¶¶ 12–13.

[66] Bali Strategic Plan for Technology Support and Capacity-building, document UNEP/GC.23/6/Add.1, December 23, 2004, http://www.unep.org/GC/GC23/documents/GC23-6-add-1.pdf.

[67] UNEP, Guidelines on Compliance With and Enforcement of Multilateral Environmental Agreements, adopted in Decision GCSS.VII/4, Feb. 13–15, 2002, http://www.unep.org/GC/GCSS-VII/Documents/K0100451.e.PDF. The purpose is to provide assistance to all relevant stakeholders in enhancing and supporting compliance with multilateral environmental agreements.

[68] UNEP, Guidelines for the Development of National Legislation on Access to Information, Public Participation and Access to Justice in Environmental Matters, UNEP/GCSS/XI/11, Annex I, Decision GCSS XI/5 A, Annex, February 24–26, 2010.

[69] UNEP, Guidelines for the Development of Domestic Legislation on Liability, Response Action and Compensation for Damage Caused by Activities Dangerous to the environment, UNEP/GCSS/XI/11, Annex I, Decision GCSS XI/5 B, Annex, Feb. 24–26, 2010.

[70] *See* Chapter 4.1.1.

Facility (GEF) has been the primary source of funds for developing countries' environmental protection efforts in several critical areas – biodiversity, international waters, ozone layer depletion, land degradation, and persistent organic pollutants – and since February 2011 the organization will also serve as a financial mechanism for the United Nations Convention to Combat Desertification.[71] Formed in 1991, the GEF has provided grants amounting to more than $ 8.5 billion up to March 2010.[72]

Effective international environmental governance is also a prerequisite for effective compliance and implementation, and the current environmental organization structure is not conducive to accomplishing it. The ministers and heads of delegation at the UNEP Governing Council's Special Session on March 8, 2012, reflected this reality in their discussions and the UNEP Council President expressed their view that "urgent change is needed in the current system of international environmental governance. Incremental reform has been too slow and has not addressed the nature or the severity of environmental issues facing the world, but there remain questions as to the exact architecture of a reformed environmental governance system."[73] A UN system-wide synergy for the environment, improving the effectiveness of and cooperation among multilateral environmental agreements clusters, and strengthening the cooperation between UNEP and other UN bodies, are among several possible reforms being considered.

16.2   A Final Word

It is imperative that wider ratification and implementation of the existing MEAs be secured and that the existing environmental organizational structure be further reformed and strengthened to ensure effective international environmental governance. Among other measures considered critical for global environmental protection are the availability of adequate financial resources, transfer of appropriate technology, and assistance in capacity building to developing countries. It is also essential that, along with governments and intergovernmental organizations, civil society actively participate in the decisionmaking process, without which effective implementation is well-nigh impossible.

---

[71] UNEP Governing Council, Report of the Executive Director, Amendment to the Instrument for the Establishment of the Restructured Global Environment Facility, UNEP/GC.26/12, December 7, 2010, http://www.unep.org/gc/gc26/cow_details-docs.asp?DocID=UNEP/GC.26/12&CatID=15.

[72] Fourth Overall Performance Study of the GEF – Executive Version, March 2010, http://www.thegef.org/gef/sites/thegef.org/files/documents/OPS4-Executive%20Version_ENGLISH.pdf. For the GEF Database for Project Information, *see* http://www.thegef.org.

[73] President's Summary, *supra* note 51, ¶ 35.

UN Secretary-General Ban Ki Moon's warning in his message for UNEP's 2011 Annual Report aptly states the need of the day:

> The global population has reached 7 billion people. In just five years, we will add another half billion people – all needing food, jobs, security and opportunity. Environmental, economic and social indicators tell us that our current model of progress is unsustainable. Ecosystems are under stress. Economies are faltering. We need to chart a course that strengthens equality and economic growth while protecting our planet.[74]

In this light, it seems appropriate to recall the words of then-Secretary-General Kofi Annan in the 2000 Annual Report:

> There is no shortage of ideas on what should be done.... What we need is a better understanding of how to translate our values into practice and how to make new instruments and institutions work more effectively.... We must...ensure that all parties concerned contribute, and that they all benefit from the efficient and environmentally sound use of resources.... And we must build global public awareness so that individuals and groups all round the world can understand what is at stake and join in the effort.[75]

The question remains: Will the international community heed these calls? Rio+20 left the question unanswered, for there were plenty of promises but the action was deferred to another day.[76]

---

[74] *Supra* note 42, at 2.

[75] UNEP Governing Council/Global Ministerial Environment Forum, Seventh Special Session, Cartagena, Colombia, Feb. 13–15, 2002, International Environmental Governance, Report of the Executive Director, UNEP/GCSS.VII/2, ¶ 141, December 27, 2001, cited in Executive Director Report, *supra* note 14, at ¶ 141, http://www.unep.org/gc/GCSS-VII/Documents/k0200009.pdf.

[76] *See, e.g.*, Jonathan Watts & Liz Ford, Rio+20 Earth Summit: Campaigners Decry Final Document, The Guardian, June 22, 2012, http://www.guardian.co.uk/environment/2012/jun/23/rio-20-earth-summit-document/print.

Index